GRATITUDE FOR SHOES

Gerald and Karol:

I hope you enjoy this book and always have a good pair of shoes.

Cleo H. Williams

GRATITUDE FOR SHOES

✦

Growing Up Poor In The Smokies

Cleo Hicks Williams

iUniverse, Inc.
New York Lincoln Shanghai

GRATITUDE FOR SHOES
Growing Up Poor In The Smokies

iUniverse books may be ordered through booksellers or by contacting:

iUniverse
2021 Pine Lake Road, Suite 100
Lincoln, NE 68512
www.iuniverse.com
1-800-Authors (1-800-288-4677)

ISBN-13: 978-0-595-35682-9 (pbk)
ISBN-13: 978-0-595-80159-6 (ebk)
ISBN-10: 0-595-35682-6 (pbk)
ISBN-10: 0-595-80159-5 (ebk)

Printed in the United States of America

Contents

LIVING SIMPLY—SIMPLY LIVING

PLAY

SCHOOL DAYS

INTRODUCTION: UNDERSTANDING MOUNTAIN WAYS AND MOUNTAIN TALK

You may not see much evidence as you read my writing, but I really did pass High School English. I learned about diagramming sentences, correct punctuation, grammar, and all that stuff. I could even undangle a participle if I wanted to. (But I'd also get an A+ in Memory Loss 101 now). But nevermind the grammar and dangling participles—I'm simply going to write for the most part as I'd talk among my mountain family and friends,

When I first started writing about us mountain folks, I knew that many things had changed from my childhood to the present time, but hadn't fully realized the extent of the change in the spoken language. If I wrote the way we spoke, very few people would understand what I had written, so I thought I'd simply enclose a word in parenthesis to follow the word or phrase that needed an explanation, or to show the pronunciation. As I wrote, I came to realize the vast difference in the oral and written language and found myself facing a dilemma. The manuscript was barely readable due to the many parenthetical insertions. On the other hand, if I used only grammatically correct words and sentences, my entire motive for writing was lost.

After much consideration, I decided to insert an explanation or translation at intervals throughout the manuscript in order to help the reader understand as they read. Some words in parenthesis explain how the preceding word would have been pronounced by the native; at other times, it is the generally accepted pronunciation, or an explanation. Sometimes, the meaning is obvious. The first time I use it, Italics are used to spell a word as it was pronounced then, also to identify mountain expressions and *old sayin's*.

In addition, I have compiled a glossary, Mountain Talk, to which you may refer as you read. I worked on this section for years, adding a word now and then as one came to mind, or when I heard someone say it, but I'm sure I still left out many words. You may find it helpful to browse through it before reading the book. I've had many a laugh as I remembered people and events from long ago while working on this section and trying to define words. I put the Mountain Talk word, or "Mountainese," as I call it—as the word to define, and have attempted to explain words, phrases, and add some of the sayin's by using them in a sentence.

I have purposely tried to avoid using profanity, offensive words and content. The reader must remember however, that this is an attempt to describe the old mountain way of life and describe their speech as closely as possible to the way it was. Anyone who was raised in these backwoods knows that life was rough, even harsh, and sometimes so was the language. The very worst will be left out, but many times, you can read between the lines.

People love to travel through the Smokies and drink in the awesome majesty and splendor of the mountains while viewing the changes of time and season. But enjoying their beauty at a distance while passing through, and actually living in them with little more than what you can glean from them, are two very different things. The word *harsh* is defined in the dictionary as, "rough and not pleasing to one's hearing, sight, taste, or touch." And *home* is defined as, "the place where one is born or brought up; is at ease and comfortable." These mountains are "pleasing to one's hearing, sight, taste, and touch," yet can still be rough and harsh. But it is home. We learned to survive and even overcome some of the harshness, and perhaps appreciate home all the more because of it.

One very important tool of our survival is a sense of humor, which I try to maintain. The older generation of mountain folks loved riddles, word play and jokes, and liked to *joke with, tease, or devil one another.* They liked people they could *have fun with*—folks that didn't get mad or insulted if you *deviled 'em*, because they "knowed you was jist a-jokin'."

Many times they jokingly said just the opposite of what they really meant. Dad was the world's worst for that. I've heard him say to people who came to visit: "Make yourself at home, where you ort to be," and everyone had a big laugh as they settled in to stay awhile.

Men, especially, looked for a chance to "stretch the truth" about something another man had done, or even tell *biguns* (outright lies) so outrageous that everyone knew they were lying—all in the name of fun, or *devil-ment*.

This is not intended to be strictly an autobiography—but to tell things as they happened to me gives me the opportunity to show how words were used and the way they were said. Hopefully, you will gain some insight into the people and the times—the way they thought and why they acted as they did. I have not gone into great detail about how things were done, as an instruction manual might, or given a history of the language, as there are many wonderful books already written on these subjects. I simply want to tell enough for the reader to catch the gist of what's being told, and to know what living in these mountains was like—from the perspective of a li'l 'ol scrawny, barefooted youngun who knew very little of a world beyond the horizon of the surrounding mountain tops.

I have carefully thought through, chosen, edited and re-edited each word in each sentence to try to give a sense of the attitude, or mind-set of the mountain folks, as well as describe the speech and way of life. I'm going to try to ease in the Mountainese a little at a time, so you'll understand more each time you finish a chapter. I'll try to make it easy to understand, yet write it as closely as possible to the way it would have been spoken at the time. As they said *in my neck of the woods—"Plain talk is easy understood."*

With all my effort, I realize that there is no way to infuse the full flavor of the speech as it was once spoken, but here's enough explanation to get started:

First of all, forget about the correct use of past, present and future tense of words, also singular and plural.

Especially in the older generations, an extra syllable was sometimes added, as in "ho-wurse" (horse), "yay-uw" (yeah), "be-uhl" (bill), or "hah-yut" (hat)." At times you can still hear that.

Many sentences end in a preposition. As: Where'd you find them berries at? Where'd you get that dress from?

In speaking, we said "they" for *there*, "was" for *were*, and "them" for *those*. No matter how many things were being discussed, it was said as *"They* was." If there were three apples, for example, it was said, *"They was* three apples." If it was one, *"They was* one of them apples." Only it was spoken as, *"They'uz* one." The word *was* was pronounced as "uz," or "wuz," or indicated by adding *uz* onto the end of a word.

"Done" didn't just mean that the *grub* (food) had cooked long enough. It also meant that when somebody finished using the *outhouse* (toilet)—they was *done*. The word "done" was also said instead of *did*. If somebody admitted that they did something, they'd say, "I *done* it." Or, "done" could mean *already*. If they'd already finished a task, they'd say, "I *done and done* it, pronounced "done-en." If somebody had already left, they were *"done'n gone."*

A *d* is sometimes converted to a *t. Didn't, couldn't, hadn't and wouldn't* were pronounced "ditn', coutn', hatn' and woutn'." The *t* on the end is left off or silent.

Sometimes, a *t* takes the place of *ed* at the end of words in the past tense. *Turned, burned,* and *wished,* for example, would be "turnt, burnt," and "wisht". *Found* is "fount." *Ruined* is "rurnt." *Skinned* is the same as "skint" or "skunt."

Sometimes, the *s* is converted to a *d* or a *t,* and an *a* sounds like a *u.* For example, the word *wasn't* would be pronounced "wudn't," or "wutn't," leaving off the *t* sounnd at the end.

The word *that* was usually pronounced "at," as in "*at's awright (*all right*)."* If the whole word was said, it was usually for emphasis. "*That* done it," meant that was the last straw, or that's enough. "*That* ol' heifer!" would be said when the cow got out and they were mad at her (or some woman they ditn' much like).

An *a* was added before a verb, showing action: a-goin', a-comin', a-lyin', a-cussin', and a-fightin'.

An "a" used alone means *of* (as the Irish use *o*). At times, it means *the.* This is heard a lot in mountain talk. Example: Two rows *a* corn. *That's the way* would be said as, "At's a way," as in *"At's a way it's allus* (always) *been."*

A *y* is inserted in some words, which makes them sound similar to a Scottish or Irish brogue. For instance, my grandpaw had a *gyarden,* and *seed* (saw) a *gyarter* snake in it. I *hyerd* my grandmaw talk about *cyardin'* wool to make yarn, and she learnt (or *teached*) me how to use the *cyards.*

Some words that rhyme with heard, pronounced *"hyerd"* (adding in the *y* sound) are: beard/*byerd,* cared/*cyerd,* smeared/*smyered,* feared/*fyerd.*

The pronunciation of *your, ear,* and *year* is the same—"yer." Example: "Ye ort to a-seed *yer* Mammy a-scrubbin' behind his *yers,* and him ten *yer* old." Think of these words as rhyming with *yer* (including the *y* sound) when you read: here, hear, fear, care, beer, appear, chair, dear, deer, gear, steer, spear, tears (and probably others). *Where* is pronounced "whirr," and *clear* is "cler."

Ought is said as "ort," *ought not* as "ortn't."

Or is pronounced as either "er," or "are."

Both *for* and *far* is "fer." But *fire* is pronounced "far."

Confused yet? Don't worry, you'll soon *git it down pat.*

Derivatives of the word *you* is explained in the glossary. *Your* is pronounced "yer," as in: "It was *yer* own fault," But sometimes, *your* is pronounced "yore," as when saying: "It was *yore* fault." And *you* is usually said as "ye." *Don't ye see?*

An *n* may be added to show the possessive form of words, as in *his'n, her'n, our'n, their'n* (his, her, our, their *own*). *Your'n* is pronounced as "yorn," (your own)

Somewhere is usually pronounced as "sumerce," but is also pronounced as "summers."

Please don't ask me to explain about *"sump'm"* (something). I dist know 'at's a way I allus hyerd it said.

The word *just* has several pronunciations: "jist, jis', dist, dis', or 'ist," changing the *u* to an *i*.

An *e* is changed to an *i* in *yet* and *get*, and pronounced as "yit" and "git."

The word *took* is pronounced "tuck," and *shook* as "shuck," but a *crook* is still a "crook."

When I started going to town school, I heard a person say, "idn't" for *isn't*, and thought that sounded real educated. *Idn't* it nice when you learn how to talk proper?

I reckin that trying to get pupils not to say *ain't* is a schoolteacher's nightmare. Well, a-sayin' *ain't* was a step up on the education ladder for us. We said "hain't," and not just when we'uz a-talkin' about ghostes.(And of course, *roasts* and *posts* would be said as "roast-es" and "post-es"). Hain't that logical?

We mostly said *ain't* in the middle of a sentence. A sentence was started with *hain't* for emphasis, asin *"Hain't* you done yit?" when a-body'd be a-crossin' their legs and dancin' next in line at the door to the outhouse.

"Hit" was said to emphasize the word *it*. *"Hit's* about time!" would be said when you fin'ly hyeard the *button* turn inside th' outhouse door.

"Go it," was the answer if we asked and got permission to go. Another answer might have been, *"I don't care."* I've had people who aren't from around here (flatlanders) tell me the phrase "I don't care" confused them. To them, it means just the opposite of what it means to us. If we are asked to do something, or have somebody offer us something, and we say, "I don't care," we mean "Okay, I'll do it," or "I'll take some, thanks." *("Don't mind if I do.")*

"I don't care" means *yes*, to us—or "Whatever pleases you, pleases me. It don't make one dab a differ'nce to me." But *flatlanders* think we mean, "I don't want to do that," or "just keep whatever you've got; I don't want none."

As in *rag'ler* (regular) English, sometimes the same word or phrase has a differ-ent meaning, according to the way it is pronouned or used. The word *awful* has the usual definition, but in addition, we mean *very* or *extremely*, as when we say something is "awful purty," or "awful good."

The extreme description of something really awful, or really good, is *terrible*, pronounced as "ter'ble" or "tar'ble." When the *old woman* (wife) cooked up some *extry good rations* (food), they were said to be *"ter'ble good."*

Now, don't get *ter'ble* mixed up with *tol'able*. *Tol'able* or *tollible* means so-so, *fair-to-middlin'*; nothing to brag about, but bearable—mountain talk for *tolera-*

ble. It was a frequent anwer to the question, "How ye doin'?" When they ditn't feel too good, nor too bad, neither, they'd say, "Jis' tol'able."

If they said "Ter'ble" and nuthin' else, somebody'd go to breakin' out th' cold remedy, or sump'm to *pyearten 'em up with—like corn likker with ginseng, red pepper, various herbs, or rock candy in it.*

I think the biggest problem in writing mountain speech as it is spoken is caused by our tendency to abbreviate words and condense phrases into the least number of syllables possible. We run words together instead of pronouncing each one separately, and sometimes leave out parts of them. We want a smooth, uninterrupted flow of words, with as little mouth movement as possible. I diagnose this as "lazy tongue" or "lazy mouth." If you said you "swept out from under the bed," we'd say we *"swep' ou'fenunder th'bed."*

(If you don't understand when you read a sentence I've written, try saying it aloud.)

Now, you try this one: "A bird'n a han's worth two'n a bush."

Our *sangin' leader* (choir director) was allus a-fussin' and *gittin' onto us* for "chawin'" on the words in a song. I thought that description was funny, but it really is a good way to describe how we talk. Take the word *Boston*, for example. We say, "Baw-ston," real slow. Them Yankees say "Bah-ston," real fast, like they're afraid they'll get their mouth dirty if they don't spit it out real quick. We dist take the time to *waller* a word around (or chaw on it) real good before we *turn aloose of it.* For example, the letter "L" is *a-yul,* "M" is *e-yum,* "N" is *e-yun,* and horse is *hoe-worse.*

Another characteristic is to pronounce a word ending in *a, o,* or *ow* as "er," and many times the *"L"* sound is left out. My older sisters were named Alma and Thelma, and my grandmother's name was Emma. They were called "Am-er, The'm-er," and "Emer." My grandmother even spelled her name E-m-e-r, and said it that way. My other sister is named Juanita, and her name is wallered around and said as "Woineeder."

Then, after I got on up in high school, that same edgycated person I heard a-sayin' "idn't," said "yellow" fer *yeller,* 'stid a *yaller.* Then I heard somebody say, "yella" a few times. Things was already a-changin'.

A pillow is a "piller." A pe-anner is kindly like a organ, only differ'nt.

Some words ending in *a* were changed to "ie" or a "y." My mother's name was Basha, but she was called "Bashie." My aunt Cora was "Corrie," and Culla was "Cullie." We lived up on "Jun'luskie Creek." They put bakin' sodie in their flour (flair) when they made up cathead biscuits.

We called a sodie pop a dope, whether it was a co-colie, big arnj draink (orange drink), or whatever kind it was—which brangs up the substitution of an *a* or *ai* for an *e* or *i* in a lot of words, or just plain leavin' out the sound of 'em. *Singing, drinking,* or *thinking,* would be "sangin', drankin', or thankin'."

A finger is a "fainger," a branch is a "brainch," a bench is a "bainch," and a handkerchief is a "haincher," sometimes pronounced as "hain'-ke-cher."

As shore as *sprang* comes a'ter *win'er* (winter), beg, egg, leg, edge, okra, and watermelon would be pronounced "bag, aig, laig, aidge, okry and wadermillen."

An *e* is changed to *i* in some words. We allus said "git" for *get* and "yit" for *yet*. We said, "Inny, minny, miney, mo" in the old count-down rhyme to see who would be "it" in a game.

At times, an *a* was pronounced as an *e*, as in *any* (enny) and *many* (menny).

Hour is pronounced "air," and at times, so is *are*. Air ye ketchin' on *atall?*

In some words, *b* was substituted for *v*, and *m* for *n*. For example: oven/ub'm, seven/seb'm, eleven/'leb'm, heaven/heb'm, open/op'm. This is as close as I get to explaining "*sump'm.*"

A couch is called a"sofie," a "settee," a "sofer," or a "deb'mport," only we didn't have nary'n (one, not a one) to call it nuthin'. (When I was a child, it was called a davenport.)

A "bainch" (bench) is sump'm you set on 'stid of a sofie, when you ain't got nary'n

I *'spect* (suspect) by now that you've noticed the leavin' off the *g* on the end a words, so I'll dist let it go at that.

The word, *dreckly* (directly) means a little later on, or *a'ter whahl* (after awhile). "Di-reckly" means exact placement, as *di-reckly* on my big toe.

Somebody might try to "*git above their raisin'*" by *actin' biggety* (actin' like a big shot—or gittin' the big-head) and com-mence to talkin' and actin' *hifalutin'* (like you was high soci'ty), and say, "Isn't it almost time for dinner?"

We'd say, "Lesseat supper." (Dinner's done been eat sev'al hours ago.)

Wellsir, them hifalutin' ways dis' *never did go over much* big up hyere on th' creek. They's three meals a day around hyere: They's breakfast—along about daylight. And dinner's eat about twelve noon. An'en they's supper—dist afore it gits dark. Y'unnerstan?

Old means aged, of course, but it's also used before an object or a name, and becomes part of the name. A dog, horse, cow, pet or person was called Ol' Rover, Ol' Bessie, or whatever his or her name was. It also indicated somebody as a buddy, close friend, or something dear, as "this ol' house," or "my *ol' woman*" (wife)…or somebody they *wutn't too crazy about (Ol' Devil)*. Sometimes it was added when someone, in a joking manner, was telling a funny story about about the person (Ol' John, or whoever). And sometimes, it was just put there.

"Un" or "'n" added to the end of a word, means *one*. Choosing a *fried pie* would be said as "I want a peachun. If you ain't got nary peachun, I'll take that cherry-un. That'n looks awful good."

A child, son or daughter, is a "youngen" or a "youngun" (young one). He may be forty year old, but he's still my *youngun*.

As in most English speech, the *e* was left off the end of the word *the*, and said as "th'." I only heard it said as "the" when somebody was *readin' out loud* from a book or letter.

Now, remember, I'm a ol' mountain gal, myself—and *mighty proud* of it. I *don't hold with* (tolerate, agree, take sides with) nobody *a-makin' fun of us* mountain people. In the funny places, we're laughing together *with*—not *at*—mountain folks. They's a mighty big differ'nce, y'know.

GRATITUDE FOR SHOES

This morning I awoke, and sleepily sat on the side of my bed. As I slipped my feet into my old comfortable, much-loved shoes, my mind suddenly seemed to zoom backward in time. I remembered, and for a moment, felt again the embarrassment I once experienced on a cold frosty morning in late fall when I was about eleven years old.

My older sister, Juanita, and her husband, Ralph, had only been married a few weeks. She was fifteen and he was nineteen. They lived with his parents at Topton, a small community in the high mountains several miles east of Andrews. I had spent the night with them and was going to catch the Topton school bus to Andrews school, then go home on my regular bus in the afternoon.

After an early breakfast, I had to walk about half a mile down the mountain to a neighbor's house, where I would catch the school bus. It was just getting daylight, and the frost was so heavy on every blade of grass, leaf and twig that it looked like a light snow had fallen. All along the roadside, the frosty outline of intricate, lacy spider webs shimmered and swayed between glittering fenceposts, barren bushes and dry weeds. The towering hemlocks and pines looked like huge Christmas trees. The gravel on the road sparkled and glistened, and was cold as ice. My breath came out in small puffs, making trails of silvery fog as I made my way down the mountain, walking in the crunchy grass on the roadside to avoid the sharp cold gravel imbedded in ice crystals on the road.

The friendly neighbor invited me inside to wait by the wood heater and watch with their daughter til the bus came by. It felt good to get in out of the cold, and enjoy the lingering aroma of wood smoke, boiled coffee, cathead biscuits and fried meat from an early breakfast in the cozy kitchen.

When the bus came and I got on, I found that I didn't know most of the children. I wished I could be invisible, as I felt like everyone was looking at me and noticing that not only was I not wearing a coat or sweater, but also wore no shoes. I felt that I was an embarrassment to my sister. What would folks think about her having a crazy sister who wore a thin, short-sleeved cotton dress and went barefooted in this cold weather?

Hoping nobody would pay any attention, I tried to avoid the cold bus floor and warm my feet some as I held the bottom of one foot over the top of the other until it felt a little warmer, then switched places.

We only got one pair of shoes a year, and that was in the fall. Cold weather had come early this year, and there was so many of us that Dad hadn't yet got around to buying winter shoes for everybody. One of us might get a pair next payday, or we might not—depending on what all he had to pay out. He didn't buy stuff on the credit; he didn't want to owe nobody nothing (be beholden).

Then, as I sat there on my bedside, I thought about how Dad would repair our old shoes by half-soling them, if they didn't look too bad. It was a lot cheaper to half-sole a pair of shoes than to buy new ones. He would place a shoe upside down over the iron shoe last and cut off the old worn-out shoe sole at the instep. Using a hammer and small short tacks, or "sprigs," as he called them, he attached the new half sole by driving the sharp sprigs through the new shoe sole into the shoe bottom in a neat row all around the edge. He worked fast. He'd pick up a few sprigs at a time, line them up in his mouth with the sharp side in between his lips, to hold them ready. Then he'd reach up and grab the next one as soon as he drove one in.

When he drove a sprig in, the sharp end hit against the metal shoe last on the inside of the shoe, causing it to curl under, or "clench" tightly to hold them together. Then he used his pocket knife to neatly trim the edges of the half-sole flush with the shoe bottom.

Sometimes, the sprig didn't bend over tightly enough, leaving it long enough to stick into your foot as you walked. Then you had to find a piece of *pasteboard* (cardboard) or something to put in your shoe to cover up the sprig so it wouldn't gouge into your foot. As long as the sharp end was bent down, we usually didn't pay too much attention to it, as the skin on the bottom of our feet was pretty thick and tough from runnin' around barefooted all spring and summer. We started going barefooted just as soon as it started warming up in the spring, and didn't wear shoes from Mayday (May 1) til after it frosted in the late fall. Sometimes it snowed before we got new shoes.

It's been a long time since I've seen a shoe sole come loose on someone's shoe. Maybe they make them better now—or it could be that we don't have to wear the same pair of shoes every day for as long as we can.

It was common to see one of us kids with the side of our shoe sole tore loose, maybe just on one side, or maybe the whole toe. I remember seeing my skinny brother Lawerence run and play, with a shoe sole going flap, flap, flap, as he ran. We laughed about it ourselves, but it wasn't so funny when you had to wear them to school and the other kids laughed and made fun of you. Sometimes one of the older kids would try to tack it back down, or maybe Mom could find time to fix it. She could fix 'em just as good as Dad. I learnt how to tack one down good enough to keep it from flapping til Dad could fix it.

A Mr. Gibson had a shoe repair shop on the back street corner in the middle of town. People called it "the shoe shop," and called him "the shoe-shop man." Folks took their shoes and boots there to get them fixed. He sewed up where they came loose, half-soled them, put new heels on them, or did whatever was needed to get some more wear out of them.

There were rows of tagged shoes and boots on shelves all the way up to the ceiling along one side of the shop and on two tables. These were either waiting to be repaired or to be picked up by the customer. It was easy to tell which ones were repaired because they were polished with paste wax and buffed to a high sheen.

I was maybe ten or eleven the first time I remember going to the shoe shop by myself, after walking downtown from the schoolhouse during lunch time. Dad was working away from home during the week then, and didn't have time to fix our shoes, like he always had for my older brothers and sisters.

I can still feel the fascination I had for Mr. Gibson and that shoe shop. He was a kind, friendly man who took great pride in his work. As he worked, the expression on his face showed that he enjoyed what he was doing. It was a grand experience for me to see and hear his machines run, and watch him work at the sewing machine or the brushes and buffers on wheels, and smell the pungent leather and wax. I couldn't imagine how the machine could sew through all those thicknesses of leather and not break the needle, or how he could get a perfect row of stitching inside a shoe. I just stood in awe and watched him.

Sometimes a customer came in and waited while he sewed up a tear or half-soled a pair of shoes for them. I've done that, and now realize that, like me, they may not have had another pair of shoes to wear while those were being repaired.

No matter how small a repair was made, the shoeshop man always buffed the shoes to a high shine before handing them back to the customer. We never polished our shoes at home, and it was amazing how much better they looked, all cleaned up and polished. Shucks, they looked jist about *brown new* (brand new) when he got done with 'em! When a-body put 'em on, you couldn't tell they'd been half-soled jist by lookin' at 'em. Sometimes, one of the businessmen would come in just a-purpose to get their shoes polished.

You could buy new rubber or leather half soles or heels at the shop, in whatever size you needed, and put them on your shoes yourself at home. It was cheaper that way. Also, back then you could buy big flat pieces of thick cowhide, all tanned and smooth, ready to cut to the size you needed for shoe soles. When Dad put that kind of soles on a pair of shoes, he said they was "*as slick as owl manure,*" only that wasn't his exact word.

The cowhide leather come in handy for other things too, like fixin' harness, making boot strings, leather washers, or *hainges* (hinges) for the garden gate or chicken house door. Over near the edges, the leather thinned out some and was softer, and that made good slingshot pouches or leather lacin'.

In the summertime, the shoeshop man made sandals from the raw materials, and sold them at his shoe shop. Some of my school friends wore sandals that he made, and I was so amazed that he could do that. I envied them and wished I could have a pair, but Dad and Mom said they wouldn't last no time atall, it'd be like throwing money away. I tried to make myself a pair, but couldn't get them to stay together.

Some of the kids at school took tap dancing lessons, and went to the shoe shop to have metal toe and heel taps put on their shoes. I loved that clicking noise they made when they walked. One time they danced up on the stage during a program, and I sat spellbound as I listened to the rhythm they tapped out. And I thought them shiny black patent leather shoes the girls wore was the prettiest things anybody could ever hope to wear.

In the fall, when Dad could scrounge the money together, he'd go to town and buy some shoes for whichever one of us needed 'em the worst. He didn't take us with him, but would look at our feet, or take a stick and measure how long our foot was, and put that in his pocket to take with him.

He always got sturdy, heavy, lace-up shoes—made to last a long time. He brought home a pair he thought would fit, but still be a little big, so there'd be room to grow. And then you'd have big old blisters where they'd slip up and down on your heels. He only bought one pair of socks with the shoes, and they soon wore holes in them. Sometimes the shoes were almost too little, and before long, they were so tight they hurt your feet. That didn't make one dab of difference. If he could cram your foot into 'em, you had to wear 'em. We was scared to say anything, for he just might take 'em away from you, and then you wouldn't have no shoes atall. He didn't like to have to take 'em back and swap 'em. My toes have straightened out some through the years, and I've had corrective surgery on one of my feet, but I still have crooked toes from wearing shoes that were too small.

Back then, everybody bought their shoes a little tight and said you had to "break 'em in." I remember grown folks a-limpin' around, sayin' they was breakin' in their new shoes. They used groundhog oil on 'em to soften 'em up, and that made 'em shed water, too.

Looking back, I've come to realize that children, like most of us, have a tendency to see only their side of the story. In all fairness to Dad, I need to back up and view things from his perspective. It's so easy now just to hop in the car and run to town or the shopping center to buy a pair of shoes, and be back home in an hour or so. Easier still, just pick up the phone, call in your order, charge it to your account or credit card, and they'll be delivered right to your door.

It was an all day job for Dad. He didn't have a car or truck and had to walk seven miles just to get to town unless somebody happened to come along and pick him up. If he had a-took one of us with him, that was an awful long way for a barefooted little youngen to have to walk, especially on a gravel road. Passing vehicles were so few that I remember us a-runnin' out to look when we heard one comin' up the road. We also run out when we heard an airplane, and watched it til it went plumb out of sight. That was a big event! The grown folks said it was a mail plane a-goin' over. It flew over about the same time every day.

When I was about thirteen, and very self-conscious, Dad must've figured I was about grown, for much to my horror, he bought me a pair of those old-timey black shoes with the high instep and clunky heels, just like the ones his mother wore. And got me a pair of them tan colored, fine-knit long stockin's like old women wore. He acted like he was so proud of hisself. But girls my age wore white socks with tops that you turned down a couple of turns, and I thought I would just die from shame. He never asked what we wanted—we took what he got us and kep' our mouth shut. It was either wear 'em or go barefooted. I knowed better than to say one word about it.

That year, the First Baptist Church of Andrews sent a young woman missionary to teach Bible school at our newly established church on upper Junaluska Creek. Of course, folks back then wore their Sunday best when they went to church. The other girls had on their purty dresses and sandals, or shiny patent leather shoes with a strap acrost the instep, one, and there I was—stickin' out like a sore thumb with them old-timey black "grandmaw" shoes and them ol' ugly long stockin's that kep' a-scootin' down and baggin' up on my skinny legs, right in the middle of summertime. I felt like crawlin' off somewhere and hidin'.

One day, the bible School teacher and I were having a conversation. I was so ashamed of my shoes, but what was even worse, thought she might think I didn't know no better than to wear shoes like that. Trying to let her know I wasn't that ignorant, I told her Dad had bought them, and I wished he'd let me pick out my shoes my own self. Bless her heart, I know she meant well, and was just trying to make me feel better when she said they looked nice. But here she was, supposed to be a-learnin' us to tell the truth, when I knowed she was really a-stretchin' it when she said that.

Well, that was one pair of shoes that I was glad to see wore out, and I done my best to help 'em along. I'd about as soon a-went barefooted as to wear them shoes. I *brogued* right through ever' mud hole I come to, rode 'em over to the side, and walked in the gravelliest part of the road I could find. I sure was tickled when Dad said he wasn't a-wastin' his money a-buyin' no more of that kind of shoes, if they didn't last no longer'n that.

When I was in high school, it was the fashion for girls to wear blue jeans with one leg rolled up a turn shorter'n the other'n, white socks with long tops that rolled down three turns, and black and white saddle shoes. In our family, it was considered a sin for women to wear pants; the Bible said that women wudn't s'posed to wear men's clothing. I knowed they wutn't no use to ask for no blue jeans, but I did get up the nerve to ask for some saddle shoes. Mom and Dad said they wutn't a-buyin' me no white shoes; you coutn't never keep 'em clean. But I finally did get a pair when I was in the eleventh grade, and even got a bottle each of white and black shoe polish. I want you to know, I kept them shoes polished spotless, and was so proud of 'em I could've slept with 'em.

Today, I can look inside my closet and see rows of shoes on a rack on the floor, more shoes beside the shoe rack, boxes of shoes all up the sides of the closet, shoebags full behind two bedroom doors, shoes beside the bed, under the bed, all over the house and on the porch, here and there.

There are all kinds and colors, from satin to suede; sandals, flip-flops, bedroom shoes, walking shoes, aerobic shoes, flats, heels, and several pair of nurse's shoes. I have shoes for any occasion, and still buy more.

I love shoes!

I am so grateful......

And wonder if other people ever thank God for their shoes.

THEN AND NOW—A COMPARISON

I've tried to imagine my grandmother's reaction if she could suddenly be transported from her last day on earth into the present time. She was born in 1879 and died in 1949, and saw many great changes in her lifetime. When I compare the changes she saw, however, to the ones I have seen, from 1934 to the present time, I am convinced that I have lived not only during the time period of the most changes, but in the most world-changing period of time in all history. It was only sixty years from the time when the Wright brothers did their experimental flight until a man walked on the moon. It's almost like living in a different world today, compared to when I was a child growing up in the mountains.

The only paved road anywhere in these mountains was the main highway that ran through this area. I try to imagine my grandmother riding along with me in a modern car on the paved road to the town of Andrews, and seeing all the changes from her last time there. The narrow, winding gravelled road from her home, the old mill and other landmarks familiar to her have disappeared. Paved streets, highways, modern homes, trailer parks, fast food restaurants, and motels occupy the land where there once was woodlands and fields. She might be fearful of all the traffic, and of going so fast, even in a 45 mph zone—a drastic change of pace from horse-drawn carriages or wagons, or even the cars of the 1940's. Imagine her terror on an expressway in Atlanta!

I wonder what she'd say about people she saw hurrying along the sidewalks—how they dress, wear their hair, and pass right by each other without speaking. Back then, when folks went into town, they knew everyone, and spoke to—or stopped and talked to everyone.

She'd probably think the end of time had come if she heard a jet boom and saw their trails across the sky—or wonder what kind of tom-tom and smoke signals them Indians had come up with.

If she walked into my home, I wonder if she could ever guess what the things I use every day are for, especially in the kitchen, as she never had electricity, gas, telephone or even running water. She never heard of automatic heat and air conditioning.

I'd like to help you visualize what living conditions were like when I was a child growing up in these mountains in the late 1930's and 40's. The following illustration might help you get a better mental image.

Just about everybody loves a cup of steaming hot coffee in the morning. Many people today have an automatic coffee maker, and wake up in the morning to the wonderful aroma of freshly brewed coffee wafting through the house. After enjoying their first cup, if they want another, they simply pick up the pot and pour another—it's automatically kept hot. Or you might pop a cup of tap water into the microwave for three minutes and enjoy instant coffee—with instant creamer if you like. You can pour it into a plastic insulated mug and take it along with you and it will stay hot for hours.

When I was growing up, it took close to an hour to get the coffee made. Then, if anyone wanted more hot coffee, they'd better get it while the stove was still hot. If you *took a notion* for some at any other time and there was no fire in the stove or fireplace, the only way you could have it was to build a fire to heat the water to make it.

First, you must carry in some *kin'lin'* (kindling) to start the fire—if you have any. If not, you have to *split some up* with the axe. Hopefully, you have some stovewood stacked against the kitchen wall, to add on top of the kin'lin' to keep the fire going. Then, while the stove heats, you *go'en dip up* and carry a bucket of water from the spring (through rain, snow, sleet or mud), and pour some in the coffeepot to *bile* (boil)—several minutes more. When the water comes to a bile, the ground coffee is added. Then there is a five to ten minute wait for the coffee to brew and the grounds to settle (we ditn' have no percolator) before you can pour *yeself* a cup. If you have cream to put in it, somebody had gone out to the barn real early in the mornin' and milked the cow.

Like I said, if you wanted a cup of hot coffee, you'd best get it while the stove's hot.

To my grandmother, a gas or electric range would seem like a miracle. Imagine her amazement to see a microwave in action.

When I think of how much the people of her generation did with so little, I'm at a loss for words to express my admiration and respect for the people who settled, lived, and raised their families here. They certainly had to be creative, highly intelligent, and resilient people to survive in these rugged mountains under such harsh conditions and circumstances.

I've seen cartoons depicting a "hillbilly" as a lazy good-for-nothing, lying under a shade tree with a raggedy old straw hat pulled down over his eyes. Maybe there's a jug and a hound dog by his side. This is just one of many misconceptions about mountain people. Mention the word "Appalachian," and many people draw similar mental pictures of what they call those "ignorant hillbillies." This really upsets me. It shows immense disrespect and ignorance about the real mountaineer.

I honestly don't see how my parents raised ten healthy children in that particular time and place, using only the resources they had. It's impossible for someone who has never experienced it to even imagine living in a house like the one we lived in, and have no more than we had. Actually, the house was no more than a shelter to get in out of the weather.

If you will, please take a minute to play an imaginary game. Look around your home, and mentally discard anything in it that is not essential to life itself, and imagine the result. Discard the nice thermal windows and storm doors, everything on the walls, floors and ceiling—the panelling, sheetrock, insulation, drapery and carpeting—and replace them with rough sawmill planks of only one layer, with cracks in between them. The upholstered furniture is replaced with plain wood chairs, nail kegs or homemade seats.

You must give up the dishes, dinnerware, silverware, and cooking utensils except for the barest mis-matched essentials. Away goes the built-in cabinets, along with the shiny countertops, stovetop, wall oven, sink, refrigerator and other appliances, the washer, dryer, stereo, TV, VCR, and computer.

You have no closet, so out goes all your clothing except for perhaps three complete changes of everyday work clothes and one outfit of Sunday clothes hanging on a nail; one pair of shoes, or boots if you're a man, and one all-purpose coat or jacket. Your accessories—hats, scarves, gloves, belts, pantyhose—anything plastic or synthetic is gone, along with most of your make-up, toiletries and bath accessories, as they've not yet been manufactured.

Your nice innerspring mattress or waterbed is now a straw tick over some bare bed springs. The nice color-coordinated sheets, pillowcases, bedspreads, plush fitted mattress covers, electric and acrylic blankets are replaced with feedsack sheets. Homemade quilts cover the strawtick bed.

Your food is basic—flour, cornmeal, lard, salt, black pepper, baking soda, sugar, coffee, dry beans, and maybe a box of oatmeal or bag of rice. The rest is what you've canned at home, grown in your garden and field, gathered from the wild, or pork that you've salted down to preserve. If you have milk and butter, you must feed and take care of a cow; if you have eggs, you must have chickens.

Take away all but three small rooms in your house. Then take away the electricity, gas, oil, telephones, water and plumbing. Oops, there goes the lights, heat, power, outlets, sinks, bathroom, phone and outside communication. Your only link to the outside world is a battery radio.

Let your car, van, truck, or other vehicle(s) disappear. You don't have one. Not even a bicycle. Neither does any of your neighbors.

Throw away your credit cards and checkbook. You have no bank account, so you've nothing in the bank. All the money you have is right in your pocket. No job is available.

Then imagine how you would go about your life with what you have left. What will you do tonight when it's getting cold and dark, and your family is hungry?

There was no Social Security, ADC, WIC, medical or fuel assistance, ESC, or other programs to help people survive. If a family should happen to *be on Welfare* (Medicaid), it was eight dollars a month in 1945. And it was mighty few that was on it, for most of them were too proud to take it. Them that did tried not to let other people know about it, for they were ashamed for people to know they were taking something they hadn't worked for or earned (*takin' handouts, or being beholden to somebody*).

This might give you a better understanding of how we lived.

I hope it will also cause you to respect those *old-timey*, so-called "ignorant hillbillies" for what they truly were. They worked so hard for so little.

I'll tell you one thing *fer shore*—I ain't never one time seen a one of 'em a-layin' around in the shade all day, a—twiddlin' their thumbs.

MY FAMILY

My father was Joel Lawton Hicks, born August 25, 1900, who died of fungal meningitis on August 23, 1957. My mother was Basha Adeline Taylor Hicks, born May 15, 1909, who died of a heart attack at age 95 on August 2, 1998.

They were married September 21, 1919, and had ten children: six boys and four girls. These are our names in order of birth. I think it is interesting to note Mom and Dad's age at the time each child was born. This is listed to the right of each name and birth date.

	Age at time of marriage—	Mom 16	Dad 19
James Alexander (Bud)	June 29, 1920	17	19
Ivane Memory Hicks (Sweetie)	September 3, 1921	18	21
Lewis Billy Jack	July 8, 1923	20	22
Ivy Alma	January 3, 1926	22	25
Lily Thelma	May 1, 1927	24	26
Mary Juanita (Coonie)	May 14, 1929	26	28
Lloyd Lawerence	January 30, 1932	28	31
Cleo Magaline	September 7, 1934	31	34
Oval Akle (Johnny)	August 26, 1937	34	37
Vernon B.	February 5, 1941	37	40

We were born at home and delivered by a *granny doctor* (midwife) except for the last three, who were delivered by a doctor who came to our house.

I was the eighth of ten children. At the time of this writing, only four of us survive: Bud, Juanita, Oval and myself. Our mother outlived her other six children.

I asked Mom, "Where in the world did you get some of our names?" She told me that Bud was named after our grandfather, James (Jim) Hicks.

Ivane was a name she saw in the newspaper, and Memory is her father's name. "Sweetie" is what Bud called him when he was a baby, and it stuck as a lifelong nickname in our family.

The next five names are good. Thelma's first name is Lily, after Aunt Lily Tatham, Ma Hicks' sister. Juanita got the nickname, "Coonie" from Paw Taylor, for her bright eyes—like a 'coon, and to us, she is Coonie. We pronounced Lawerence's name as "Larnce." Mom said she got my name from the "funny papers" (comic strip), and Magaline is Ma Hicks' name. Mom just liked the name "Oval," and must have made up "Akle."

This is what Bud told me about paying the doctor when Oval was born:

Paw Taylor and him had made some apple cider brandy *on the halvers*. Paw bought the sugar and Bud made the brandy. They sold it for 5 dollars a gallon and divided up the money. Bud was savin' up his money to buy him a A-model Ford, and Paw was a-keepin' it fer him. Oval come two months early, and they didn't have no money to pay Doc Herbert with, so Bud went and got his money off of Paw and paid the doctor with it. I asked him how much it was, but he don't exactly remember—said it wutn' much—maybe 25 dollars. And he never did get enough money saved up to buy his A-model.

Oval and I hated our names and still think we got *the short end of the stick* when it comes to names, but I guess they were running short of names by the time we came along. Oval nicknamed himself "Johnny" when he was almost grown, and his wife and family call him by that name. I suspect he called himself "Johnny" because he always admired Johnny Cash so much, and he plays the guitar, too.

Vernon was given the initial "B." instead of a middle name. I remember when he started school, and came home as *mad as a wet hen* because the teacher had argued with him about his middle name. After questioning him, we found out that he thought his middle name was Beatrice. He said our Aunt Bea's name was Beatrice, so his name was Vernon Beatrice. Since he hadn't yet learned the alphabet, it was hard to convince him that there was a difference in the word "Bea" and the letter "B."

Mom was named Basha after her mother's sister, Aunt Basha Kilpatrick.

Dad always signed his name L.L. Hicks. I once asked him why he signed it that way, when his name was Joel Lawton. He said, "It stands for Lyin' Lawton," and laughed real big. And he never gave any other explanation.

Mom's parents were Memory Allen and Emer Lavada Stephens Taylor, known to other folks as "Uncle Mem and Aunt Emer." We called them "Paw and Mammy."

Dad's parents were James Henry and Hannah Magaline Hoyle Hicks, known as "Uncle Jim and Aunt Mag." Back then, it was a sign of respect to call older folks "Aunt" and "Uncle," when they were friends too close to be called "Mister" and "Missus."

They were *well thought of* people. I've written very little about Pa and Ma Hicks because I was never around them very much when I was growing up, although they lived less than a mile from us. After I was grown, they were always friendly and kind to me whenever I saw them.

Ma Hicks lived to be almost 91, and Pa Hicks lived to be 92. Whenever I think of Pa Hicks, I always see him dressed as usual for him—in a white shirt buttoned all the way up, walking *straight as a ramrod* and *stiff as a poker,* and carrying a cane, usually hooked over his arm, bent at the elbow.

What I remember the best about Ma Hicks was watching her pedal her pump organ while she played it, and for the tea cakes she made. I thought that organ was the grandest thing I ever saw, and would've give anything to touch one of the keys, but I never was allowed to. All the grandchildren and everybody loved her tea cakes, and I was no exception. After she baked them and they cooled, she put them down inside a white flour poke and tied a knot in the top of it, then hung it up by the knot on a nail in the kitchen wall.

Once when I was at her house, she gave me a pink cut glass bowl. It was the one she always put canned blackberries in to set on the table, and it held exactly a quart can of them. I still treasure that bowl, and can shut my eyes and just see how pretty it was, a-settin' there on her oilcloth covered table, full of jewel-like deep garnet colored blackberries set against the pink glass.

Until I started to write them, I didn't realize how hard it is to try to put events from memory into the correct time sequence. I may not write in exact sequence, but will simply tell events as I, and others in my family remember them. I've especially relied on Bud for information, for bein' the oldest, he "knows all the dirt."

At times, I've asked Bud, Coonie, or Oval what each one remembers about a certain event, and it's been interesting to compare their memories with mine. While thinking about a particular event, I often found myself wondering where another family member was, what they were doing at the time, and how they remember it. Many times, I couldn't even place them in the picture. I was surprised at the difference in what they remembered, when compared to what I remembered about the same event. I came to realize that children mostly remember things as they relate to them personally. Each child lives in his or her own little world, and each has his or her own memory of an event as it related to them.

These are mostly mine, from my own perception at that point in time.

MAKIN' A LIVIN'

The year I was born in 1934 was at a time when just about everybody was having a hard time making ends meet. It was along toward the end of the Great Depression, and right before World War II changed not only the economy, but many other aspects of living. In 1938, wages were twenty-five cents an hour. In 1943, they'd gone up to forty cents.

Back then, people still thought a whole lot like their ancestors did, from not many generations back when they first come to this country to find freedom from oppression. And they wasn't about to just lay down and give it up. They said, and believed, *"What you do on your own land and in your own house is your own business."* They had the right to make liquor, wine, home brew, or do whatever else they wanted to, and the Federal Gover'ment or nobody else wutn't a-going to come around *a-meddlin'* in their affairs, a-telling 'em what they could or coutn't do. And it wutn't real safe fer nobody to try.

Like just about every other man that lived on Junaluska Creek at the time, for a few years Dad made most of his livin' by makin' and sellin' corn *likker* (liquor, whisky). It was a family tradition that he just *natcherly* follered. That's what his Dad done before him, and his brothers, too. He said, "When you've got a house full of youngens to feed, you do what you got to do to keep 'em from goin' hungry." They wutn't no jobs of no kind, and they had to do sump'm to bring in a little money.

Little as you might think about it, makin' likker wutn't no easy way of makin' a livin'. It was awful hard work, not to mention the *chancet* of gettin' caught. And if that *hapm'd*, then your family'd shore 'nuff be in trouble, 'thout nuthin' atall a-comin' in. They dist had to *root hawg or die pore* for ever how long a man's jail term was. The Federal *gover-ment'* shore wutn't a-goin' to come in and feed a man's family. That's another reason hit wutn't real healthy fer no revenuers or nobody to git caught a-nosin' around a man's stillhouse.

Them rocky mountain sides was awful rough, and *steep as a horse's face*—and plumb kivvered up with laurel thickets and rattlesnakes. They had to have water to run the still, so they usually hunted for a place for their *stillhouse* clost to the head of a branch. When they found a good place, they had to figger out a good trail to git to it to work it.

A-body had t'be awful careful where they went'n stepped. They's rock *clifts* back in there so steep and high that if a man was to fall over the *adge* (edge), he'd hafta take his dinner bucket with him to keep from starvin' to death afore he hit the bottom. Them laurel thickets is so thick you could be right on the adge of a clift afore you knowed it. If you was to trip and fall or lose your balance and slip on them slick leaves and pine needles, next thing you knowed you'd be *a-ballhoo- tin'* down the mountain, and might not ever be seen no more.

When a boy got to be purty good size, he *went'n* helped out at the stillhouse. Bud a-bein' the oldest caused him to have the hardest time. He'd just started in the sixth grade when he stayed out of school two weeks to help Dad make a run of likker, and never went back no more. He's stooped in his upper back, and says it was from *rawhidin'* (carrying) all them sacks a corn and them *hunnert* pound sacks a sugar acrost his shoulder up them mountainsides to the stillhouse when he was so young. Besides all the stuff they needed to make likker, they had to raw- hide in their tools, pots and pans for cookin', and their rations. An'en they had to chop up a *sled load* of wood to keep the fire a-goin'. Bud was allus the shortest, skinniest and toughest one in our family. He still amazes me at all the hard work he can do.

We was learnt to be *close-mouthed* if anybody come around *a-astin'* (asking) questions. We knowed to keep our mouth shet if anybody besides Dad or Mom *asted* us any questions about any thing. People was expected to tend to their own business and was told to *"Keep yer nose out a my business"* when a person asted one too many questions. I've heard somebody *ast* what sump'm was, and the answer'd be, *"Hit's a layover to ketch meddlers."* If Dad had a bruise or skint place and somebody mentioned it, he'd say *"My wife and my stove wood,"* dist a-bein' funny, but they knowed what he meant. That's about as clost as you can get to *p'litely* tell somebody to mind their own business. Mom never would let us ast her questions about nuthin', neither. She'd git aggervated and say, "Git on out a here and quit pesterin' me with *dang fool questions."*

Hit's the worst kind a bad manners to *ast questions about thangs that don't concern ye.* That's a-gittin' *purty clost akin* to accusin' somebody of hidin' sump'm they ain't s'post to have, or has *stoled*, or is a-kivverin' up sump'm they wutn't s'post to be a-doin'. An important thing that most outsiders don't know, that gits 'em off to a bad start with mountain folks a lot a times, is when they ast too many questions. That's 'spacially true when you're talkin' about money or what they've got. Most of 'em is proud people *(as independent as a hawg on ice)*, and eb'm if they was to be *on the verge of starvation*, they woutn't let on to nobody else that they ditn't have no money or rations, or tell how *bad off* they really was.

Older native people won't come to your house and ast you no questions about nuthin'. And they don't 'preciate nobody comin' 'round to their house a-bein' so *nosey, a-prowlin' around* and astin' questions, neither. Their motto is: *You 'tend to yore bus'ness and I'll 'tend to mine.* Their business is kep' strickly to theirself. Now, that never meant we ditn't notice what went on—we was dist raised to *keep our eyes op'm and our mouth shet.*

Us youngens ditn't hardly ever go nowhere, but when we did, we knowed to *set where we was put*: set still, keep our mouth shet, and not git out a Mom or Dad's sight. And we wutn't told but oncet. Eb'm a-settin' there, we better not ast nothin' or look too inter-es'-ted in nuthin' we *seed*, or seed a-goin' on there. We better not tetch nuthin', neither. Hit dist scares the livin' water out a me to think what'd a-hap'med to one of us if we'd a-done what some youngens does nowa-days and gits away with. We knowed better than to be *a-snatchin' and a-grabbin'.*

In them days, we had to be *close-mouthed* to kivver up what Dad done for a livin'. He'd show me or one of the other youngens where he hid a bottle, fruit jar or gallon jug a likker out in the woods. He kep' it scattered out—a pint here, a quart (*cort*) over *yander*—allus out away from the house, and he could allus tell if any thang or anybody'd been *a-messin' around* where he'd hid it. He knowed where ever leaf was s'post to be, and learnt us to fix the place back dist like we found it when we went and got sump'm fer 'im.

Sometimes when he got a customer, he'd call me off to one side and tell me what to go brang back. Then he'd talk and distract the person so they wouldn't notice *which-a-way* I went to go get it. When I brung it back, he'd hold it up to the light and have 'em look at how *"purty and cler"* it was. They was sump'm about the way it *beaded up* on the surface that showed how much alkyhaul it had in it, for he'd give it a little shake and say "Looky there how it beads up. Now that's good likker. This ain't none a them ol' *backin's* like some people sells fer likker."

Funny thang about it was, the Cherokee County Sherff and Chief a Police (po-leece) of Andrews was some a Dad's best customers. They knowed they wutn't a-goin' to get no lead pois'nin' from drankin' his whiskey. He was so proud of it that I've said *a many a time*, "You might git away with *throwin' off on* his dog, his house, or kinfolks, but you better not make the serious mistake of throwin' off on his likker." His'n was the best that could be made.

Down in the woods b'low the house, he'd dug out a deep hole in the ground, squared off like a *shaller* grave. That's where he put tow sacks full a big ol' grains a white corn to sprout. After he put 'em down in there, he laid boards over the top, an'en *ruck* (raked) leafs and scattered out twigs, moss and rocks and stuff over 'em, to make it look like the ground around it. An'en they'd leave it buried in there a few days. Anybody that ditn't know no better could walk right over it and not know nary thang about it. When the corn sprouted out jist right, him, one a my brothers, or his helper, one, would git down in there and pull out them sacks a corn. An'en they'd load 'em up acrost their shoulder and head off into the mountains to *make another run* a likker.

If it hapm'ed to be in th' sprangtime, they'd brang home a big sack full a ramps when they come back. Dad loved them thangs. Folks eat 'em fried in taters or scrambled eggs, but he liked to eat 'em raw and pickled 'em to use for *chasers*. You ort to a-smelt his breath. Now that'd flat out op'm up yer sinuses.

One time, me and Lawerence went'n found a pint bottle a likker down in the swamp where Dad or somebody'd hid it. I was maybe five year old. We took it over acrost the creek and up the bank to the railroad tracks at the side of the road, out of sight from the house. We set down and swapped the bottle from one of us to the other'n til we drunk that whole pint. I remember us a-drankin' it. Lawerence'd show me where to hold my fainger on the side of the bottle to mark where I was s'post to drank it to, and I'd hold my fainger right there and drank til the likker was level with it. An'en he'd git the bottle and do the same thing—or so I thought. I done whatever he said do. Knowin' him, he prob'ly wanted me to drank more'n him, jist to git me drunk. As I got older, I *learnt the hard way* that he was a *devious scutter*, and not to b'lieve ever'thang he said.

Ennyhaow, next thing I knowed, somebody was a-holdin' me up, a-tryin' to get me to stand up by myself, but I coutn't git my legs to work right. They was *limber as a wet dishrag*. They told me I better *straighten up and fly right*, or the Sher'ff'd put me in jail for bein' drunk. It *scared the snot out of me*, but I still coutn't stand up. An'en I remember 'em a-carryin' me to the house and layin' me down on the bed, an'en me a-gittin' sick and thowin' up all over the purty new dark green quilt my sisters had made. I hated I done that. It was so purty that they was a-usin' it fer a *"countypin"* (counterpane; bedspread) and here I had gone and *gommed it up*, and it'd have to be washed.

I don't remember 'em a-giving me *a lickin'* fer that little trick. Maybe they thought I'd learnt my lesson good enough without one. Or maybe they ditn't see no use in whuppin' a youngen that was so sick it might die ennyhow. Or maybe they did whup me and I was too drunk to remember it. Either way, I never stoled or drunk no more likker.

Dad did git ketched with likker one time, and got put in jail. I was too young to remember it much, but I remember us a-goin' to Bryson City to see him while he was in jail there. How come me to remember that, was that I was so amazed at that big long bridge before you git to town. And I remember Mom a-gittin' letters from him while he was there. One time he sent a picture he'd cut out of a newspaper or magazine. It was a picture of a little girl that looked to be about five, and she was squatted down a-playin' with some little fuzzy *diddles* (baby chicks). He wrote on the edge that "this looks like Cleo." I kept that little cut-out piece for sev'al year.

I asked Bud how come Dad was in jail, and he told me about it. Mom's sister, Lizzie had died a few years back, an' Hardie White, her *old man* (husband) had got married again to a widder woman named Tib Hoagens (Hogan), and they had a baby boy named Arlen. They lived right up the road from us. Sometimes when Dad run out of his own likker, he went acrost the mountain down Tuni Gap road in Macon County over to Tusquittee in Clay County to git a load. He bought it for a dollar and a half to two dollars a gallon, an'en resold it for fifty cents a pint. He done the same for them over there when they run out, so they could keep their customers supplied. This time, he got Hardie to drive his car and take him over there to get a load. It was a little ol' one seated Shivalay car with what was called a "grandmaw seat" on the back. Tib, the baby and Mom went with 'em.

They'd bought the likker and headed back home. Dad and Mom and six gallon a likker was in the grandmaw seat. Some Revenuers ketched 'em and arrested Dad and Hardie. They brung Tib and Mom on home, and took Dad and Hardie to the *calaboose* (jail), and dist left the car a-settin' over there by the road, clost to the top of the mountain.

Now, that Tib and Mom was *rounders*. They come home *jist a-dyin' a-laughin'* about it. What them Revenuers didn't know was that Tib had hid a pint bottle a likker in the blanket with the baby. Bud said she fished it out and give him and her step-son, Walt, *a snort a likker* out of it when they got home.

Dad and Hardie had to go to Federal Court, and got a two month sentence that they had to serve in Bryson City jail. That old car set over there on the road for a long time, then it got pushed over the edge of the road down the mountainside, and dist laid there and rusted away.

Lots a people said Dad was as *mean as a suck-egg dog (or meaner'n a striped snake)*. Among the many stories I've heard about Dad is one I've heard ever since

I got old enough to remember. A long time ago Devereaux Birchfield use'ta be the Sher'ff of Cherokee County. One time, a Federal Marshal come in the Sher'ff's office, and told Devereaux he'd been informed that the meanest man in the *Newnited States* was headed this-a-way. He'd jist stopped by to warn him to be on the look—out.

They said Ol' Devereaux dist leaned back in his chair real slow, propped his feet up on his *dest* (desk), looked up at the Marshal, and drawled, "Heck, I didn't know Ol' Lawton'd been gone."

Another'n that was told was about the time Dad and the Mosteller boys had a moonshine still—way back up on the brainch behind the Mosteller place. Well-sir, they was all there, dist *a-cuttin' up*, a-laughin' and *a-carryin' on*, and takin' a little snort a likker ever now and then, and had their still all fired up and a-run-nin' off good. An'en they got to laughin' about how they'd shore *pulled one over* on Ol' Devereaux this time. They said they had this still hid so good that the Sher'ff couldn't find it, eb'm if somebody reported 'em and told him dist e'zackly where it was.

Well, Bass got to laughin' and said he'd jist call Ol' Devereaux up and report it to him *hisownself.* Now, Bass was a good-hearted feller, but was *right comical*, and liked to *cut-up* and joke around. He was *bald-headed as a turnip*, about six feet tall, and *was so pore and bony that he had to stand twicet in th' same place to make a shadder.* He run over and grabbed a-holt of the end of a grapevine a-hangin' down out of a tree there, helt it up to his ear like a phone receiver, and com-menced to *makin' out like* he was turnin' the crank, a-ringin' up the tellyphone operator. He told the operator he wanted to talk to the Sher'ff, give her a little time t'make a connection, an'en said, "Hello Devereaux. I dist wanted t'report Lawton Hicks and them Mosteller boys is a-makin' a run a likker up on Jun'lusky Creek."

He hung up, then, and they'us all a-laughin' and slappin' their leg, when all of a sudden, Ol' Devereaux stepped out fum behind a big tree right acrost the holler from 'em, his shotgun pointed straight at 'em, and said real quiet and slow, "I got ye call, boys."

How come Bass t'be a makin' out like he was a-callin' on the tellyphone was that he knowed what one was and how it worked. They wutn't but a mighty few people had one of 'em, but them Mostellers did. Hit was the only one between Andrews and sumerce away over on *Ninetyhaley* (Nantahala). They wutn't nary nother phone line back then, jist a Forest Service line run acrost the mountains. If a fire broke out, the ranger had to climb a telephone pole or tree and connect into the phone line to make a call.

Trouble with Dad was, he was his own best customer. When he had sev'al dranks, you could tell it dist as fur away as you could see him. He'd be a-staggerin' along with a big lop-sided grin on his face, snuff a-tricklin' down out a one side of his mouth, with his index fainger pointed up *torge* (toward) the sky, a-sangin' "The Sweet Bye And Bye." His words was slurred and it come out as: "There's a land...that is faa-ther......than day," an'en would start hummin' the rest of the song. He allus got the words of the first line of the song, and the last line of the chorus, endin' with, "In the sweet......bye and bye...we shall meet...on that beau—ti—ful......shore............"

When he'd just had a "snort" or two, he got mean and wanted to fight. My aunt Cullie Mathis and her husband, Jess lived across the road from us. Jess'd come over to the house and him and Dad would set out in the yard on the chop block or a log, one, and start passin' a bottle back and forth, a-drankin'. After a few snorts, they'd get in a fight. Jess was a little ol' short man, and Dad was six foot two and a whole lot bigger'n him, and Dad'd just beat the tar out of him. Next time you'd look out, you'd see 'em a-settin' side-by-side, each one with their arm around the other'n, a-holdin' on to that bottle and sangin' gospel songs. Next thing you knowed, they'd be a-tryin' to fight some more, but by then'd be *so drunk they coutn't a hit the ground with their hat.*

They got a set a boxin' gloves one time, and had boxin' matches of a Saturdy evenin'. They'd be other men come, and they'd have their big *prize fights* to see whichun could whup the most men. They'd rang up around whoever was a-boxin' and *agg* (egg) 'em on, dist *a-turnin' the air blue a-cussin',* and a-hollerin' and a-drankin' likker *like they had so much to do and a short time to do it in.* Most a the time, they'd be so *dogg-ed* drunk that one of 'em'd fall over when he throwed a punch at the other'n, or dist stand there a huggin' around the other'n t'keep from fallin', one. Sometimes one'd hit the othern' on the nose (or sump'm) and he'd git mad and jerk off his gloves and go at him with his fistes. An'en everbody else'd start takin' sides and they'd be a-cussin' and fightin' all over the place. I dist stayed away fum there. Hit made me sick t'see ary bit a blood.

They was allus some man or other a-comin' around to drank with Dad, and they'd git into fights, too. One time Dad and some Curtis men was somewhere off away from the house and got in a fight. I don't know all the details, but when somebody brung Dad home, his whole head was so swelled up and bruised I ditn't know who he was. Hit like to a-scared me to death when I seen him. Both of his eyes was dark purple and black, and so swelled up that he jist barely could op'm one of 'em enough to see with, and the whites of his eyes was all bloody lookin' around the blue.

Blood jist oozed out from everwhere on his head and face, and it was so swelled up it looked to be about as big as a bushel baisket. He laid down in the yard under the cherry tree and had me or one of the others to carry a bucket a cold sprang water ever few minutes and pour it over his head.

Then there was the time when him and his brother, Elden, got into a fight and he came home beat up. His lower jaw was broke, and they had to take him to Murphy to git his jaw set and wired into place.His jaw stayed crooked for the rest of his life after that, and from then on, I was allus scared of Elden and anybody with the last name of Curtis.

Dad was an intelligent man who could do almost any kind of work and was a hard worker, but they wutn't no *studdy* (steady) work to be found nowhere. He only went through the third grade, but was good at *figgers* (arithmetic) and readin'. He worked at sev'al different jobs—whatever come along.

The WPA started up a rock *quorry* (quarry) on Junaluska to git gravel to put on state roads, and that made some jobs for local men. The rock crusher was just around the curve above Wib Mosteller's place. I remember Dad a-workin' there so well because I seen him through the school bus *wender* (window) one mornin' as we passed by there. I ditn't have no *idy* (idea) what he done, and never give no thought to it, dist knowed he'd gone to work. They'd *dannymited* off the whole side of the mountain, leaving a sheer rock clift. That mornin', when I seen Dad a-danglin' from a rope a-way up there on that clift, hit jist *skeered me witless*. All at the same time, I was *scared to death* he'd fall but was amazed at seein' him a-doin' that. He wutn't afeared a nuthin'.

Bud told me that Dad used to be a conductor on the railroad that branched off the Southern Railroad in Andrews and run up Junaluska to Aquone and on in to Rainbow Springs. A man named "Back" McClain was the foreman. He lived with us, off and on, for sev'al year. His real name was Bascomb, but we called him "Ol' Back." I wondered why, and it didn't seem very nice, since we allus referred to a dog as Ol' whatever name he was, but Ol' Back seemed to like us a-callin' him that. He was allus good to us youngens, made hisself at home at our house, and fell in and helped *do whatever needed done*. He was Dad's helper at the stillhouse, too. He had sev'al childern, but was separated from his wife. I remember him a-takin' spells of settin' around at the side of the house and cryin', a-talkin' about Omie, his wife, and his younguns. He set me on his lap one time and told me about his little girl and said that he'd like to see her.

Wellsir, that must a-been some train ride a-comin' down offa Jun'lusky, with them steep grades and switchbacks. They called one of them trains a "Black Satchel," and had to change gears on it. Another kind was "an old Shea engine" that was run with steam. The train passed by over next to the road from our house, where the railroad tracks was. You could hear that whistle a way off, an'en the clack-a-lack-a-lack of the wheels, and it seemed to me like the whole world *shuck* (shook) when the train got closter. They was a big stream of black smoke a-spewin' way up in the air above it, and steam a-hissin' and spreadin' out into white clouds down next to the tracks 'nunder it as it went on by. I was bad afeared of it. It ditn't never stop, dist kep' on a-goin'. I remember Dad a-standin' there by the tracks a-waitin' fer it to come by. When it got to where he wanted to get on, he *retched out* (reached) and grabbed aholt of some kind of a bar or ladder-like thing that stuck out on the side of a railroad car, and *clumb* on up onto the train as it went by. *Hit scared the water out of me* to see him do that. I'm still a-scared of trains.

We used to walk along the side of the tracks and pick up little pieces a coal to take and feed the pigs. Every oncet in awhile, one of us'd lay our ear agin' the *arn* (iron) rail to listen and see if we could hear the train a-comin', so we could get outa the way and not git run over by it. They told us if you got too clost, hit'd suck you up inunder it, and that worried me bad. After we listened, we'd go on pickin' up pieces a coal for a little ways, before we'd stop and listen agin. When we got our coal picked up, we lit a shuck fer the hog pen. When we throwed th' coal in th' hog pen, them hogs'd grab up that coal and scrunch it like they was eatin' peanuts, black slobbers dist a-foamin', and smack their mouth like that was th' best stuff they ever eat. I liked to watch 'em eat it.

One time Mom told me about watchin' the train wreck down acrost from the Tatham Mill above Andrews, right clost by to where they lived then. Daddy was on the train and she'us a-watchin' as it went by, a-goin' downhill torge Andrews. As it started roundin' the curve there by the side of the creek, the engine over-turned. The other cars started overturnin', one by one, right into the creek. Dad had got up on top of the train and was runnin' down them cars jist ahead of 'em as they turnt over, then jumped offa the last car jist as it started to turnin' over. He was skint up some, but wutn't hurt bad. I think she said that the engineer got kilt, though.

Bud laughed at hisself when he told me about a train wreck that hapm'd right down the road dist before you git to Elden's house. He was dist a big ol' boy, and was a-standin' around there a-listenin' to them railroad men a-tryin' to figger out how to git the train back up on the track. He heard 'em a-talkin' about puttin' in a "dead man" to pull the train up over the bank. He remembers a-wonderin' how on earth a dead man was a-goin' t'help any, but finally figgered out that they was a-goin' t'anchor sump'm into the ground and use it as a fulcrum or pivet to pull the cars out, and called it a "dead man."

They was a railroad in Hayesville called the "Pea Vine," with a *nar* (narrow) gauge railroad that branched off and went up Farses' (Fires') Creek. They was goin' in there to git out the "*sawg* (sog) *trees,*" which was dead *ches'nit* (chestnut) trees kilt off by the blight that had fell down. Arnold West run the loggin' operation. The trees was loaded onto railroad cars, then took and sold to Teas Extract Company in Andrews to be ground up and boiled to make tannin' acid or extract used for tannin' leather. They also bought hemlock and chestnut oak bark to make a dye for the leather.

Dad worked with the maintenance crew for the railroad over there. It was while he was working up on Fires' Creek that he met a man named Jess Pipes, who worked for the Champion Paper and Fibre Company. They got to be friends, and Dad got a job with Champion and worked there til he died.

The extract plant and a tannery was located between what is now the town of Andrews and the hospital. I remember when Sweetie and Lewis was a-workin' at the Extract. They was grown men then, and I don't know what years they worked there, but it was about the only place around where a man could git a job. They thought it was a good job. It sure beat gittin' out in the weather and peelin' hemlock bark and cuttin' pulpwood. Or makin' likker and risk being sent to prison. Bud had got caught a-carryin' four gallon of likker for Pa Taylor and got sent to prison in Alabama.

Cuttin' pulpwood was about as hard a work as a man could do, but you could make a little money at it—maybe enough to buy a new pair a shoes and keep you in smokin' t'backer for awhile. Bud told me about him and Lewis and Sweetie a-goin' down the road about two mile to the Jake Abernathy place to work up pulpwood. They had to take the crosscut saw and a axe to cut down the trees. Then they had to chop off all the limbs and trim 'em up, an'en take a spud and peel off the bark. They took a mule or steer and skidded the poles down to where they could work 'em up. You needed to work it up purty clost to where it could be loaded on a cordwood truck to be hauled. Lewis done th' skiddin' and Bud and Sweetie sawed it up. It costed 'em a dollar a cord to git it hauled.

Sweetie and Lewis went off to the CCC camps when they was old enough to go. Sweetie had some of his money sent to Mom to keep for him, and Lewis had some of his money sent to Paw Taylor to make payments on some land he was buying from him. They brung back some *'luneum* (aluminum) plates, cups, forks, spoons, and cuttin' knifes that they got at the CC camp. We used 'em for years.

In 1942, Lewis, Sweetie, Dad's brother Shelley, and their wives went over to Fontana, where the men had got a job helping to build the dam. They bought some lumber and built each one of them an 8 x 16 foot "shack," as they called them. I guess that's what's been described as "tarpaper shacks." They was built out of plain ol' rough lumber and didn't have no plumbin' or nuthin' in 'em, but had tarpaper tacked up on the outside to cover the cracks. They lived there side by side, along with sev'al other families, til the dam was finished. They got paid fifty cents a hour, and that was considered awful good wages back then.

A man could keep up a family purty good with that kind a wages.

OUR HOUSE AND THE SPRINGHOUSE

My family has told me the history of the land they built our house on before I was born. Pa Hicks and Paw Taylor owned just about all the land on Upper Junaluska at one time. The lower side of Paw Taylor's land joined Pa Hicks' upper side. One day, Pa Hicks went to see Paw Taylor and made the proposal that if he would deed some of his land to Dad and Mom, he'd deed them some of his next to it, and Dad and Mom would have their own land there in between them. So Paw Taylor made a deed to Mom and her heirs for about thirty-six acres. Then Dad and Mom decided to build a house, and they picked out their house place on the land that Pa Hicks was suppost to give them.

They tore down my uncle Shelley's old house, about a quarter of a mile down the road, to git the lumber to build our house. Bud told me they moved the lumber up to the houseplace on a thang they made, called a *lizard*. They made some *struddy* (sturdy) sled runners, and nailed some thick boards acrost the top, and put a stout crosspiece on the front to hitch a horse to. Then they stacked one end of the lumber up on the lizard and tied it down, a-leaving the other end to drag on the ground. Henry White let 'em borry his big ol' mare, and they hooked her up to the lizard to *snake* (pull) the lumber up to the house place, one load at a time. When they got it up the road to where you turn to go over to the house place, they still had to go down a long, steep bank and cross the creek to git it there. Then Daddy and the boys built the house where my family lived when us three youngest'uns was borned.

As they tore the old house down, they pulled out the nails and saved 'em, an'en straightened 'em out and used 'em again. Nails costed money, and was hard to come by back then. I can remember a-straightenin' out nails myself, where they'd pull 'em out a lumber when they tore sump'm down. I helt it on a piece a railroad arn and used a clawhammer to peck out the bent places. I liked to do that, 'ceptin' when I missed. D'je ever notice how fast you sock yer fainger in yer mouth when ye mash it? Wellsir, I sucked on my faingers *a whole lot* when I straightened out nails.

The big long pieces a lumber was called planks, and the lesser'uns was boards. The way the house was built was called a boxed house. They wutn't no stud space; they put up the framin', then jist nailed one thickness a lumber on all the sides, floor, and top a the house. They was some purty wide cracks left in places in betwixt the planks, because the lumber wudn't planed and square, or the same thickness. After the widest boards was used for the walls, *narr'er* (narrower) strips was nailed over the cracks on the outside to keep out the cold air. It still left places to where, when the wind blowed, you could hear it jist a-whisslin' through 'em. So they used the *adge* of a knife to poke *narr'* (narrow) strips of rags betwixt the planks to stop 'em up and help keep the wind out.

A-body had to be awful careful when ye run around barefooted, too, and not scoot acrost the floor, or ye'd get a big ol' splinter in your foot or yer *hin'end*, one. One a t'other of us was allus a-havin' to git a splinter picked out, from *somerce* or other. Lord-y mercy, I dreaded it when Dad had to take the point of his knife to slip inunder the end a one to git it out. I've still got a inch long splinter in the back of my shoulder where I lost my balance and fell, a-scrubbin' down sideways *agin* a door facin'. It went in so deep they coutn't pick it out 'thout cuttin' too big a hole, so they left it and thought hit'd fester up an'en come on out itself. But it never did.

We ditn't have many *wenders* (windows), and what we did have wutn't much size. The doors was home made, and ditn't have no doorknobs on 'em. They whittled out a *doorlatch* and put it on the inside of the doors to hold 'em shet, but you cout'nt lock 'em from the outside. They nailed a wooden *button* on the door frame to fasten it.

We just had three rooms—a front room and back room on the front side, with a porch all the way acrost the front, and a long narr' kitchen and a porch on the back side. Dad hung *a lookin' glass* (mirror) up on a porch post where he done his shavin,' and a *shorts sack* towel (feed sack) hung on a nail under it. A wide plank was laid flat and nailed up betwixt two porch *postes* to make a *bainch* (bench) where they set the waterbucket, dipper, washpan, and a bar a soap in a saucer.

Paw Taylor subscribed to the Asheville Citizen, and Mom papered the walls with the newspapers, using flour mixed with enough water to make a paste. I liked to look at the colored *funny papers* on the wall. I looked at ever' one of 'em, but never did find my name.

Dad was awful proud of the *chimbly* (chimney) he built out a creek rock. He got 'em out of the creek, piled 'em up on the creek bank, an'en took the horse and sledded 'em to the house. He laid the rocks and chinked 'em with clay mud.

He said it *drawed air so good, hit'd suck a cat up th' chimbly.* He put a iron rod acrost the top inside the fireplace to hang pots on to cook in. The *dogarns* was pieces a railroad track.

The *top a the house* was kivvered in tarpaper. It come on big rolls, and they had to unroll it, lay it in long strips acrost the top a th' house, and tack it down with tarpaper tacks. Hit was allus a-leakin', and we'd set lard buckets and cookin' pots and pans all over the place to catch the leaks.

I remember a-layin' in th' bed at night a-listenin' to the musical sound of the rainwater a-ploppin' and a-pingin' in them buckets. The pitch was differ'nt in ever one of 'em, dependin' on the size of the bucket and how full it was. The more water in the bucket, the higher the pitch, and the harder it rained, the faster the pings got, dist a-playin' up a storm. When the bucket was pyert near full, the musical sound stopped and you heard a *sawgy* "plop" when it splattered, 'stid of a "ping", and knowed somebody *ort* to empty it before it run over. Not that nobody much cared, though, fer the water'd dist run through the cracks in the floor, *ennyhow*, 'less it hapm'd to start leakin' over a bed. Then the leaks dist about had to be patched, fer it hain't no fun a-tryin' to sleep on a sawgy *straw tick*, or wake up with yer piller wet, 'spacially when it's cold weather. They'd take a paddle a some kind, a bucket a tar and some sand up the ladder to *smyere* over the holes in the tarpaper. The sand was to keep the tar from runnin' off of the patched places. Hit'd stop the leaks for a while, but sooner or later, they'd be another'n start, either that'n or some other place.

When it rained on a hot summer day, you could really smell that tar in the steam that *riz* (rose) up offa the top of the house. We used to go out behind the house and take a bath in the rainwater where it run off the overhang on the house. Now, we never *stripped off necked* ner nuthin', dist got 'nunder there and let the rainwater sloosh over us—*guts, feathers and all.* We thought that was a whole lot a fun. When you lent your head back and let the water run in your mouth, you could taste the tar in it, too.

Then we dist run around and drip-dried, and never paid nary bit a 'tention to bein' wet.

They was a cave-like place dist natch'ally hollered out in the mountainside about twenty foot over from the kitchen porch. It was about as high as the house, and half as wide. The cold *cler* (clear) water come up in a stream as big around as Dad's arm, jist a-bilin' up out of that clay bank back in there. Where it come out was kindly up on a rock *lage* (ledge) about three foot higher'n the ground out in front of it. It made a big ol' wide *sprang* (spring) that had purty dark green *ferrins* (ferns) and moss and stuff a-growin' all around it.

Dad took some rock and dammed up the front of it to make the water deep enough to kivver up a iron pipe he stuck back through there in to the spring to make a spout. Bud said it was a piece of flue pipe off of a old Shay steam engine. The water run through the iron pipe to where it come out and made a spout about three foot off of the ground. They lay a big flat rock 'nunder the spout to set the waterbucket on, an'en we could dist stand there and watch 'er fill up. Hit come out so fast, it ditn't take but dist a minute to run it over. When you picked the waterbucket up and moved it, though, the water'd hit that rock and 'ist splatter you good with that cold water. You better grab it up and run if you ditn't want splattered. Usually, they left a big washtub a-settin' under the spout to catch water, an'en it ditn't splatter you none. Then they lay big flat grey rocks on the ground all around the spout and in front of the spranghouse. Thataway, they wutn't never no mudholes t'haf to walk through.

Us youngens jist stuck our mouth over to the runnin' water when we wanted a drank. If a-body wutn't careful, or somebody bumped you, one, hit'd go up yer nose. We was real careful not to put our mouth on the spout, though. That was a-bein' nasty about it.

We thought we was real lucky to have a spout that handy to th' house. Most folks had to dip their drankin' water up out of a sprang or a branch, one, an'en carry it *a pretty good piece* to the house. They dipped their wash water up out a th' creek.

Great big ol' hemlock trees growed right on the side of the mountain above the sprang bank and around one side of it. You could see their big ol' roots back in the sprang bank. Their long wide limbs drooped way down and spread out over the sprang and the *spranghouse* like big ol' fans, dist coverin' ever'thang like a umbreller. When you walked 'nunder there, hit was like goin' in a cool green shady room. On a overcast day, it was dist about dark 'nunder there. The sweet damp-earth smell of mosses, ferrins, mountain ivy, laurels, tetch-me-nots and wild fergit-me-nots all mingleded together with the piney smell of the hemlock trees. An'at runnin' water sounded so soothin', hit made a-body dist want to lay down in them ferrins and go to sleep.

The spranghouse set a few feet over from the sprang. It was built out of small logs with boards nailed over the cracks betwixt them on the inside. It was a purty little ol'spranghouse, with moss a-growin' on the outside walls on the shady places. The floor of it had flat rocks laid *kindly* (kind of) level-like down on the damp dirt. The icy cold sprangwater run 'nunder the bottom log on one side and out the t'other side.

They was a wooden *trawft* (trough) acrost the back end where the water run through, with flat rocks a-linin' the bottom of it. The deep end was where we kep' lard buckets or jugs full a milk, buttermilk, or whatever else we wanted kep' cold. An' it wutn't nuthin' odd atall to see a jug a likker or *home brew* a-settin' in amongst it. Down on t'other end, some flat rocks was stacked up in the water to make it more shaller, accordin to how deep the bowl was that you wanted to set in there. We set butter and stuff in bowls on top of them rocks. It felt so good to go in there on a hot day, but them rocks was so cold it made your necked feet feel numb, and was so cool and damp in there a-body coutn't stand it long.

The inside walls had shelfs where Mom kep' her empty fruit jars. Big ol' 55 gallon wooden barrels and sev'al sizes a churn jars was *rowed up* along the sides, with differ'nt kinds a thangs in differ'nt ones of 'em—like pickled cucumbers, corn, green beans, green tomater pickles, chow-chow, and kraut. Ever'thang was separate in its own barrel or churn. They tied a clean rag over the top of 'em, an'en put a wooden *led* (lid) over that, with a clean rock laid on top of it to hold it down. That kep' rats and thangs from gittin' in 'em. A board'd float if it wutn't weighted down, so sometimes they put a clean rock on a short board or plate on top a the food down inside of a churn jar to hold it down 'nunder th' salt water or vinegar so it woutn't *rurn* (ruin). An'en they tied a rag over the top and laid a board over that t'kivver it up good. The stuff'd keep good all winter, that is, if it lasted long enough.

I *recolleck* the pickle barrel the best, 'cause Dad would send me to go git him one to use for a "chaser" after he *tuck* (took) a drank a likker. Coonie said she remembers a-fishin' down through mush ice with her hand to get *sump'm 'r other* out of a barrel. When a-body says *"As cold as kraut,"* you ain't tellin' no lie, fer they ain't many thangs gits colder'n that. I reckin it had too much salt in it to freeze, but hit shore got cold. And *Nantyhaley kraut* is even colder.

That big ol' washtub we had a-settin' 'nunder the spout at the sprang made a dandy place t'cool thangs, too. Sometimes Dad brung in a *wadermillen* or some *mushmillens*, one, and put 'em out there in that tub a runnin' water to git good 'n cold.

People a-passin' up and down th' road would stop and come over to our house, dist to get a drank out a our sprang. They talked about how good that water was, and said, "That's the coldest sprangwater I ever drunk." It was so cold it hurt your teeth.

Dad brung a cokernut home one time, and that was the firstun I ever seen. After he made holes in the eyes and sucked out all the milk, he sawed it in two and *prized* the cokernut meat out with his knife and we eat it. Then he made a drankin' cup out a the half that ditn't have no holes. He *turnt* it upside down on the wash *bainch* out next to the spout so he could offer people a drank a water out of it. He was so proud a that cokernut shell drankin' cup. He'd ast people if they'd ever seen *ary'n* like that before. Most people said they never had seen *nary'n*. We never got *nary nother* cokernut til Christmas, and Mom made a coker-nut cake.

We kep' a bucket a water a-settin' on the shelf on the back porch. Everybody drunk out of the same dipper. Now, they was certain rules of *cleanness* to foller about drankin' out of a dipper. If the dipper had a hole in the handle, it was kep' hung up on a nail in the porch post next to the water bucket. When you dipped some water out a the bucket to git a drank, you jist dipped out about however much you wanted to drank. You dist barely tetched your mouth to th' edge of the dipper, a-bein' careful not to let none of the water run back in it out of your mouth, and ditn't never put your hands on nothin' but the end a th' handle. If they was any water left in the dipper after you took a drank, you throwed it out, you ditn't pour it back in the bucket fer somebody else t'hafta drank yore *slobbers*. If you ditn't hang the dipper up, and put the dipper back in the waterbucket, you set it down easy-like on top of th' water so's it'd float, and left the handle a-stickin' out over the rim of the bucket. Thataway, the place where you had your hand never touched the water, and the next'un could jist reach and pick it up.

Some woman come to our house one time, and she give her youngen a drank a water out a th' dipper. That youngen put both a hits hands around the dipper part and helt it while it drunk. Then, to make matters worse, 'stid a throwin' out what the youngen hatn't drunk, the woman *soused* that dipper plumb to th' bottom a that waterbucket. Now, igner't as we was, ever last one of us youngens knowed better'n to pull any *sichy* (such a) trick as that. Mom would a beat th' livin' snot out of us. It made Mommy so mad *she like to a-died*. After they left, she jist snorted, "What about anybody a-bein' that dang naisty!" She grabbed that waterbucket, slung ever bit a th' water out acrost th' yard, and give that bucket and dipper a good *skairin'* (scourin') out before she used it again.

"The Lizard Man" use to come around in the summer time a-wantin' to buy sprang lizards. I reckin he sold 'em fer fish bait—I don't know—but he give us a penny apiece fer 'em. We knowed what day he come by, and we'd git out and ketch some and have 'em ready fer him. He was the first feller I ever seen wear laced-up boots that come plumb up to his knees, with his britches legs down in 'em. Somebody said he ketched snakes, too, and they was to keep him from git-tin' snake bit.

We had the most fun a-goin' down the sprang branch a-huntin' lizards. They was enough water run out a th' sprang to make a good size little sprang branch, two or three foot wide, that run down through the swamp a good little ways *torge* (toward) the creek. They was sprang lizards all up and down through there. The lizard man ditn't want no little bitty 'uns; they had t'be a certain size. We ketched 'em and kep 'em in some damp moss in a bucket with some holes punched in the *led* (lid) so they could git some air.

We'd ease up a rock real slow-like, and peep inunder it to see if they was ary'n under there. If they was, we'd grab it up quick and throw it in the bucket. You had t'be quick, or they'd scoot in a hole so fast hit'd make ye head swim. I was kindly skittish about them lizards, a-feared they'd bite me, eb'm if people did say they woutn't. If it wutn't too big a one, I grabbed that thang and slung it in the bucket like a streak a lightnin'. But if it was a big'un, I'd let Lawrence git it. I'd hold the bucket and be ready to raise the led up fer him, an'en clap it back on real fast. We had to watch and not leave the led off long, or they'd git out.

He kep' up with how ever' many he caught, and made dang shore he got th' money fer 'em, too. I never got no credit fer findin' one. He acted like he'us a-doin' me a big favor, anyhow, jist to let me go a-lizard huntin' with him, and git to hold the bucket and take the led on and off for him.

Sometimes we fount a redun. They had little black speckles on 'em, and was purty thangs to look at. Some people called 'em "red dogs." Somehow 'r other, though, they dis' looked kindly pizenous to me. Lawrence told me they'd bite if you ditn't ketch 'em jist right—a certain way by th' back a th' neck, so I mostly let him ketch th' reduns too, spacially if they was much big. Some a them thangs was eight inches long, and I wutn't about to grab one up, eb'm if we did get paid more for one a them than a blackun or a brownun.

Hain't it funny how a boy can make a little sister b'lieve he's actin' in her best inter'st, when all th' time, he's *a-lyin' like a yaller dog*? But sooner or later, she fin'ly *smartens up* to what's a-goin' on.

One time I eased up a fair sized rock, and they was a dang big water snake all *quiled* (coiled) up 'nunder there. Now, hit never took me long t'git done lookin' 'nunder that'n. If hit scared him any worser'n hit scared me, that snake's still a-travellin'.

On the other hand, when I let loost a that big ol' rock an' it slammed down on 'im, I betchey he got *squshed flatter'n a flitter*.

I wutn't us'lly that scared of a snake, but that'n—he kindly s'prised me.

DOIN' THE WASHIN' AND ARNIN'

Some folks said "warshin'" for washin', and called a rub board a "warsh board," but we pernounced it as "woishin." Women allus fixed 'em a place clost to the water to *do the woishin'*, so they woutn' have such a long ways to carry it. Mom made her *woishplace* out there under the hemlocks at the spranghouse, to where the water'd be handy. The spranghouse had a *slainted* overhang built out onto the front of it—kindly like a little porch-shed, and that way, she could git in there out of the sun and weather. Up ag'in the wall, they'd built a table big enough to set two woishtubs on, and they was a wide *bainch* set cornerways over to the side of it. Hit was a dandy woishplace.

The washtubs was allus hung up on big nails *drove up* on the side of the spranghouse, when they wudn't a-bein' used for nuthin'. They had a raised-up number 1, 2, or 3 on the bottom of 'em, accordin' to how much water they helt. A number 3 was the biggest'un. Now, we took care a them tubs. We used 'em fer lots a other thangs besides washin'. We never left nary'n a-settin' out nowhere, or the wind might blow it around and bang it up and make it leak—or blow it away, one. An'en, too, they was kep' clean a-hangin' up.

They was a big ol' round *caist arn* (cast iron) washpot that set over to the side of the washplace, an'at's where we heated up our wash water and biled the clothes. It had three *laigs* spaced out on the bottom of it, an'at's what made it set up, hit a-bein' round *and all.* You could jist build your fire around the pot if you ditn't hang it up, but our'n was hung up and the fire was built inunder it. They was heavy postes set in the ground on each side of it, far enough away so they woutn't get set afire. They was made out of big forked tree limbs that was cut to where they'd be a "Y" at th' top to hold the end of a stout piece of arn rod that was run acrost from one "Y" to the other'n. The arn rod had to be stout enough to hold a washpot full a water and not bend. They put one end of the rod in the "Y" of one post, run it through the bail of the washpot, an'en laid the other end on the other post to hang the pot up over the fire.

They stacked up good-size rocks around the sides and back of the washpot, kindly like a outdoor fireplace. Them rocks kep' the fire together, an'en too, they *th'owed* the heat back torge the washpot to make it heat up good. The pot was plumb kivered up on the outside with a thick crust a black *smut* (soot) from all a th' fires that'd been built 'nunder it, a-heatin' water to wash with, scald a hog, or whatever else we needed hot water for.

My older sisters helped do the washin' and I did too, when I got big enough. Oncet in awhile, though, they had to be a-doin' sump'm else—an'en one of us allus had to watch the baby—so Mom done the biggest part of it.

On wash day, a big pile a wood was stacked up and some kindlin' split up to build a fire with. She had to start early to git done. The first thang, the washpot was filled up with buckets a water dipped up out a the big ol' wash tub that set under the spout. An'en a fire was built inunder the washpot to start heatin' it. Now, you don't never want to build a fire 'nunder a dry washpot and let it git real hot, or hit might crack it when you pour cold water in it. And another thang—you allus want to leave the washpot turnt upside-down in the winter time. It'll ketch water in it and freeze and bust.

She set two washtubs by the side of one another on the washbench. The washin' was done in the left'un, and the rub-board was put in it. When the water got good'n hot, they took a bucket and dipped out some hot water and poured it in that tub. The other'n was for *ranchin'* (rinsing) and they put cold water in it. The washpot was filled back up then, so that more water could be a-heatin' while the first tubfull a clothes was a-bein' washed.

Mom sorted 'em out into differ'nt piles accordin' to what they was. The white pieces, then the light pieces—like shirts and dresses—was washed and ranched first, an'en the dark'uns, dirtiest'uns and the men's work clothes was washed and biled. With ten youngens and two grown people to wash fer, they made good size piles.

Mom put a few *washin' powders* in th' tub where she was a-goin' to be a-*rubbin' 'em out*. Then she put a few pieces a clothes in the soapy water to let them be a-soakin' while she *rubbed out* one piece at a time—up and down over them metal ridges on the rub-board. She took and rubbed a big ol' bar of brown Octagon™ soap on the dirty spots to help get out the worstest dirt and stains. Then she wrung that piece out and either put it in the ranchin' water or in the washpot to bile (boil). She had a *"punchin' stick"* that she'd made out of a old broom handle, and used that to *punch down the clothes* and stir 'em around with, ever' oncet in awhile. As the pieces was dropped in, they got air pockets caught inunder 'em that made 'em stick up out a th' water here and yander. If she ditn't keep the clothes punched down 'nunder the water, hit'd make dirty *raings* (rings) on 'em around the edge of the air pockets. When she used it, she allus laid he punchin' stick up to where it woutn't git dirty, and we knowed to *let it alone*.

When th' pot started to gittin' *scrouged* (crowded), and them clothes had b'iled long enough, she lifted 'em out on the end of th' punchin' stick and dropped 'em in the tub full a ranchin' water. If a piece hatn't come out good 'n clean and needed some more rubbin', she put it back in the first water and scrubbed it some more on the rub board.

After they was *ranched out*, she'd wring 'em out with her hands as good as she could, and laid 'em over in a empty tub. But the water'd still run and drip out of 'em when they was hung up. Them wet clothes was heavy, but Mom was purty stout. She'd carry a whole tub full a wet clothes by her own self.

When she had some, she poured some stuff called bluin' into the ranchin' water to make the white clothes look purty and white. Hit turned that water the purtiest blue color. When she wanted to starch sump'm—like dresser scarfs with *embroidery* on 'em, but ditn't have no starch, she mixed flour and water together and cooked it til the flour turned cler, thinned it down with cold water, and used that for starch. She never starched many pieces, though. They had to be arned jist right, and was a lot of trouble.

Bud said they never had no bleach til he was a great big old boy. He remembers it so well because Mom sent him to the *store truck* (rolling store) one day to get a jug of bleach, and he'd fergot the name of it. He told the *store truck man* that he wanted a jug of "oxen, or oxy-sump'm-or-other," and the store truck man figgered out it was Clorox™. He got a good laugh out a that.

Somebody had to use the punchin' stick ever' oncet in awhile, an'en too, a-body had to keep the fire *chunked up* to keep it a-goin' good. I shore did like t'do that. Now, Mom let me keep the clothes punched down, and stir around in 'em, but when the fire was a-goin' good, she made me let it alone so it wouldn't git to smokin'. And I knowed I better not *mess with it* unless she told me to do sump'm or other to it.

If the smoke got to blowin' over to where she was at, hit'd choke 'er up, make 'er cough, and her eyes burn til the tears dist poured out a her eyes. She'd have to move away til either the smoke settled, or the wind changed, one.

Whenever womenfolks'd be a-standin' around a fire, and the smoke blowed over torge one of 'em, somebody'd allus say, *"Smoke follers beauty."* So, when Mom said, "I shore to heck must be the purtiest woman in the world," I knowed dist e-zackly what she'us a-talkin' about.

Overalls was called "overhalls," denim pants was "overhall pants" or "overhall britches," and any kind of pants was called "britches." Boys wore overhalls til they got grown enough to go *a-sparkin'*

(courtin'), and then they wore overhall pants. If they wanted to look real sharp, or it was a-Sunday, they wore a white shirt with the cuffs turnt back a couple a turns. They still wore overhalls when they worked around the place, though—except for Dad. I never knowed of him a-wearin' overhalls, but he did wear coveralls ever oncet in a while.

The overhalls and britches was washed last because they faded all over ever'thing that was in the washin' with 'em. An'en too, they was the dirtiest. Them ol' overhalls and overhall pants was *stiff as a board* and *rough as a cob*. Them seams was thick, and they was hard to rub on the rub board. Your hands got soft and pruney in the hot soapy water and it hurt bad when you scrubbed your knuckles acrost a seam, buckle on a overhall gallus, a heavy zipper or metal button, one. Hit'd tear th' hide off a yer knuckles, and there you'd be, *a-bleedin' like a stuck hog* on the clothes. They was awful heavy when they was wet too, and was the aggervatin'est thangs in the world t'try t'wring out. Yer wristes got awful sore fum all that twistin' and wringin' out.

Now, washin' clothes was hard work, and *gen'ly* took all day. When she got done, the whole front a Mom's dress'd be soppin' wet, on account a all that wash water a-sloshin' out over top a the rub board as she scrubbed them clothes up and down on it. She had a skin condition or sump'm on her hands that she called "eczemer." Her pore old hands'd be all *chafted* and red, with busted blisters on 'em, and her knuckles so cracked and dry that they bled, from havin' her hands in them ol' strong washin' powders and soap, a-rubbin' on them clothes. She allus used Palmolive™ hand soap, and ordered some Ovelmo™ salve by mail to use on her hands. That salve was the *onliest* thing she ever tried that helped 'em ary bit atall. But they woutn't no sooner start to get better than she'd have to do the washin' agin.

In the wintertime we done the washin' in the kitchen. They set two tubs on the cookstove, and we had to take time about a-carryin' in water to pour in the washtubs. It took sev'al trips with the water bucket to fill up a tub, but the biguns could carry two bucketfulls at a time. I carried wash water when I was so little I had to lean *backerds* to hold the bucket up offa the ground to keep the bottom from hittin' it. If I let it hit the ground or bumped it agin my knee, one, hit'd slosh that cold water out and dist wet my dresstail all over, and git in my shoes, and my feet'd be soakin' wet. Seem like I never could git 'em warm agin all day, with my shoes a-bein' wet, an'all. And *like as not*, I wutn't a-wearin' no socks.

When the water got hot enough, they set the tubs off on the back of two over-turned straight back *chers* (chairs) with a *dannymite* box set 'nunder 'em in the middle t'hold th' backs up level.

Before I got much size, Mom let me wash some of the lightweight clothes. She turnt a straight back chair around with the back to the table so it woutn't turn over, and I *clim* (climbed) up there and *retch't* (reached) over the back a the chair to git to the rub board. I liked to wash, but I *hated like the devil* to hafta wash them ol' slimy *hainchers* (handkerchiefs). Eyuk!

After we got the clothes washed, the soapy water was poured it out on the floor and we give it a good scourin' with the broom. Then we poured the ranchin' water out on it and ranched it off good. We ditn't need no mop, for the water dist run right through the cracks in the floor. We better be awful careful about runnin' around barefooted for a few days, then, for that wash water made splinters come out and stick up all over the place.

Sometimes it took two—three days for the clothes to dry when the weather was cold. They'd freeze *as stiff as a board* a-hangin' out there on the line. If we had to have sump'm, we brung it in and hung it up on the back of a chair in front of the fire to git dry.

Mom done a lot of patchin', 'spacially on britches and shirt sleeves. Knees and elbows wore thin places, and clothes was allus a-gittin' snagged and tore when they was a-gittin' wood. She allus had a pile a patchin' a-waitin' when she got time to set down.

Sometimes her or one of the gals *embroadered* (embroidered) some awful purty little *flares* (flowers) and thangs on dresser scarfs and *piller slips* (pillowcases), but she never had time t'git much a that done. I learnt to patch a-watchin' her.

She'd had a stiff thumb ever since she was five year old. She told me about how she'd hold tree limbs on the chop block while her sister, Lizzie, chopped sticks a wood off of 'em with a axe. When Lizzie'd chop off a stick, Mom'd scoot it up on the chop block so she could chop off another'n. This time, though, Lizzie missed the stick a wood, or it bounced, one, and hit Mom's thumb and chopped it plumb off.

Her daddy rolled the thumb up in a clean rag and took it with her to the doctor, and he sewed that thumb back on. Hit dist *flabbergaist-es* me no end, to think that a doctor could do that back in them days. It had t'be about 1908. Hit healed up jist fine, and growed as she growed, but from then on her thumb was stiff. Hit never hindered her none atall about anything she ever wanted to do, though, except you noticed it when she done any hand sewin'.

Talkin' about washin' made me remember how I used to think Thelma was so lucky to get to go down and help my Aunt Bea—my uncle Elden's wife—to do her washin'. Bea allus give her a *koiter* (quarter) fer helpin' her. I wutn't much size then, and thought, "Boy, I wisht I could go help Bea wash, and make me a koiter." That sounded like a whole lot a money to me.

Well, after Thelma married, they let me go down and help Bea wash a few times when she ditn't feel good, or sump'm. She was allus good to me, and I liked her. She was kind, laughed a lot, and was purty.

I liked to wash them clothes. They was nicer than our'n, and Bea was more pa'tic'ler than Mom was with her washin'—I guess 'cause she didn't have so many to wash fer. She ranched out her clothes at least twicet, and I had to dip the water up out of the creek with a bucket. If the water started lookin' ary bit soapy, hit got poured out, and I had to dip up another tub full. You coutn't dip up but about half of a bucketful at a time 'thout gittin' sand in the bucket with the water.

I tell ye right now, hit takes *a right smart* a-dippin' t'fill a washtub full a water. And I shore did earn m'koiter.

Them clothes got awful *wrankled* up from bein' twisted 'n wrung out no matter how much you *shuck* 'em out when you hung 'em up. Ever'thang was *one hunnert* per cent cotton. They wutn't no *sichy* (such a) thang as permanent press back then. We *sprankled* water on the clothes to *damp'm 'em down* to make 'em easier to *arn* an'en rolled 'em up and *poked* 'em down in a piller slip to keep 'em damp. Then we sprankled water on the table where we was goin' to lay down the old *arnin' quilt*, so hit woutn't scoot around while we arned on it. We never knowed what a arnin' board was.

We set the black cast iron "smoothin' arn" on top of the cookstove to git it *het up* (heated) enough to arn with. Smoke come up around the adges of the stove eyes and got the bottom of the arn all *sutty*, so we laid a *doubled-up* (folded) damp rag on the adge of the table and rubbed the sole plate of the arn acrost it to clean off the *sut* ever time we took it off of the stove to use it. It was hard to get that ol' black sut out of clothes if you ever oncet got it on 'em. And if sump'm got scorched, they wutn't no way in the world to git it out.

We used two arns—one to be a-gittin' hot while the other'n was a-bein' used. Ye'd jist git to arnin' good when you had to swap arns. The iron had to be good 'n hot to git out them wrinkles. But the handle got hot too. You had to double up a purty thick cloth to hold around the handle to keep from burnin' your hand.

Your hand got awful *tard* because that iron was heavy, and you had to grip the cloth purty tight or hit'd slip, and ye'd burn yer hand on the handle. I got a bright *idy* (idea) one time and tried

dampnin' down the rag to keep it from slippin'. I don't *reckin* I need t'tell the end a that story. Ever'body in the world but me knowed that water plus heat makes what? Steam!

I hated arnin', but *I druther shovel manure* than to arn sump'm dipped in that ol' *flair* (flour) starch. You had to watch awful clost about scorchin' it, if the iron was ary bit too hot. But then, if it wutn't hot enough, that starch dist glued the iron to the cloth and *stuck like you-know-what on a baby blanket*, an'en you had to grab it and jerk it loose from it. Hit'd come off in a great big flake, dist growed to yer iron. If it ditn't come off with rubbin' it over some salt, you had to take it down to the branch and scrub it off with fine sand. You had to get it ever bit off, or hit woutn't slide over your clothes—dist pucker 'em up in front of it. We never had no S.O.S. pads® or Teflon™ scrubbers back then. When you fin'ly got the iron clean and het up again, you rubbed the bottom of it acrost a piece of wax paper or *parafeen* (paraffin) wax to git it to where hit'd slide over the clothes easy.

Sometimes it took two—three days to do the ironin', because we had to iron when they was a fire in the kitchen stove. It was all right in winter, but hit shore got hot in there in the summer time. We never ironed a lot a thangs; dist doubled 'em up, or *give 'em a lick and a promise*, one.

We never had no clothes hangers, or no closet to a-hung 'em up in if we'd a-had some. We had a *clothes pack*, or clothes shelf, in there on the wall next to the quilt pack. They was planks nailed up to make shelfs that we put our clothes on after we got 'em ironed and doubled up. Ever'body had their own place and knowed where their clothes went in the clothes pack.

I'd hyerd tell that some folks had a wardrobe, or chifferobe to hang up their clothes in, but we ditn't have nary'n, and never had no place to a-put it if we'd a-had ary'n. We was purty scrouged up like it was. What we did have was a row a big ol' nails *driv* up in the wall where you could hang up your coat, hat or cap, one. That is, if you had ary'n.

Another thing a iron was good for was to git it good and warm and wrap it up in a cloth an'en hold it on yer ear for the earache, or put it next to your feet, if you was sick in the bed and your feet was cold. Some people done that on a cold winter night anyhow, but they was too many of us to do that—they wudn't enough irons to go around. I guess we could a-used rocks, but then they woutn't a-been enough room in the bed fer us and all a them rocks too.

HOLEY SOCKS

Back before socks come into common use, women and girls wore long stockin's. They was light brown combed cotton knit, *sorter* (sort of) like tee shirt stuff. Mammy thought a woman simply wutn't dressed proper til she put her stockin's on; hit jist wutn't nice to go around with your necked laigs a-showin'. And dist as soon as she pulled 'em off, they got a good lookin' over, and if she found ary little hole, hit got sewed up right then, so's it woutn't make a run. An'en she ranched 'em out real careful and hung 'em up. She took care a them stockin's.

You could buy *gyarters* to hold 'em up, but she never had to wear none. She pulled a stockin' on to jist above her knee, took aholt of the top adge and sorter twisted it, turnt it inunder, an'en *kindly* (kind of, sort of) rolled it down a little bit to make 'em stay up.

I had me some stockin's when I was little, too, but I never could git mine to stay up like her'n did. 'Course, she never got out and run chickens and *clim* trees like me, neither. But Mom took and cut narr strips a black rubber off of a old inner tube and made some garters out a them, and that done better. A piece a 'lastic was *skyerce* (scarce) *as hen's teeth.* Leastways, we never had none to spare.

Some old men wore garters, too. I reckin they bought 'em somerce or other. They went around their leg kindly *slaunchways* jist b'low the knee, and had a gallus-like fastener that *ketched aholt* on one side of their sock to hold it up, an'at kep' it from workin' down. And a few times I seen a man a-wearin' sump'm like a garter on their shirt sleeves, up above their elbow. I thought that looked kindly funny. An'en somebody said they was to hold his shirt sleeves up out of the way to keep from gittin' 'em dirty or wet when he unbuttoned his cuffs and pushed up his sleeves to wash his hands or sump'm.

When I got on up a little bigger, though, girls started wearin' socks *'stid* of stockin's. Most a the time, though, I never had neither one, and thought I was lucky to have shoes. Socks was a real luxury. The heels and toes got holes wore in 'em purty quick. Now, let me tell ye, a-gittin' yer toe run through a hole can pain ye some, *a'ter whahl* (after awhile). The more you walk, the tighter it binds. To keep my toes out of a hole, I'd pull my sock way out apast my toes and double it back up inunder 'em, an'en put my shoe back on.

But when the hole in the heel got so big it come up above your shoe in the back, your ol' necked rusty heels'd be *dist a-shinin' like new money*. The only way to fix it was to take off your shoe and pull the sock down over yer foot far enough for the hole to be 'nunder your heel, an'en double the toe part back inunder your foot to hold it. That hid it in yer shoe. Now, a sock jist ain't made to fit thataway. Next thing you knowed, that sock had crawled right back up out a your shoe, and you woutn't eb'm know it. Some of the other kids would laugh and make fun of me and I'd sneak off to myself so I could pull off my shoes and double my socks back up. I'd be so ashamed I dist wanted to crawl off in a hole somerce and hide. Younguns don't know how cruel they're a bein', or how bad they hurt another'n when they make fun a one like that. And you don't hardly ever git over it, neither.

In the summertime, men wore thin socks, or else kep' a pair for Sundy and went without through the week. In the winter time, they wore them big ol' thick boot socks. The kind I remember was them grey'uns with a red heel and stripe around the top edge, or them greenish colored un's that they called "army socks," one. They must a-been wool, fer they *stunk like cyarn* (carrion) when a man come in with his feet wet and hung them wet socks up before the fire to dry. 'Course, they never ranched 'em out before they hung 'em up, neither.

And their boots didn't smell like no rose, neither. They'd be wet and squishy inside, and full a *toe jam*. When the steam riz off of 'em, where they'd set 'em on the hearth, hit'd jist about *gag a maggit*.

Mammy knit wool socks to where the toe and heel could be unravelled when they was wore out, an'en knit back in without havin' to knit a whole sock. I learnt how to do that, but prob'ly coutn't do it now *for the life of me*. She knit with some metal knittin' needles that Pa made from umbreller ribs out of a old umbreller that had b'longed to his daddy.

She must a come from a purty *well-off* family, she acted so lady-like and all. She told me that her fam'ly raised sheep and *shurred* (sheared) the wool in the sprang, and she knowed how to do ever thing they was to know about it—from *shurrin'* the sheep, to spinnin' wool into yarn and dyein' it, to knittin'. She could knit ever'thang from socks and mittens to *coverlids*, and teached me some about it.

Mom could knit too, and could knit socks good enough fer Mr. Anybody, but eb'm if we'd a-had the wool, hit'd a took one person a-knittin' full time to keep enough socks knit for ten youngens and two grown people. I don't see how she done half of what she done as good as she done it.

I wouldn't a-knowed what a sheep was if I'd a-run *slap dab* into one. And we ditn't have no place to raise sheeps, nohow. Our pasture dist barely did have enough grazin' fer our ol' hoss and the cow, as it was, let alone try to raise sheeps. Besides, hit was all we could do to take care a what we had to. We done good to raise enough corn and beans, taters and punkins in that ol' steep rocky field over on the side a the hill, and take keer of a garden too.

And do ever thang else we had to do, besides that.

SNAKIN' IN WOOD AND KEEPIN' WARM

Ain't it funny when you get grown and think back about how things looked to you when you was little? It's amazin' how differ'nt we saw things from what they really was. I know I've gone to a house I hadn't been to since I was grown, and jist coutn' get over how little the place was to what I remembered it a-bein'.

But I really do b'lieve we had more snows—and lots deeper snows—than we do now. I tell ye what's a fact—we had some snows up on the head of Jun'lusky Creek. They was *days on end* that they wutn't no traffic on the road, in or out. The mail man never even run.

One time, when I was about eight year old, 1942, I think it was, the snow was sev'al inches above the level of the front porch, and it was high enough off the ground til I could stand up straight and walk up inunder it. We had to sweep the snow off a the porch up on to the snow out in the yard. Us younguns made us a tunnel from the front steps out into the yard and clered us a little room 'nunder there. We played in it and called it our "eagloo," like Eskimos has. Shucks, hit was warmer in there than it was outside.

I remember watchin' Mom get ready to go out to the barn to milk and feed when they'd be a big snow on the ground. In them days, women ditn't wear britches, at least not in my family they never. That was a sin. Hit plainly says right there in the Bible, that women ain't s'post to wear men's clothes. But Mom did put on a heavy shirt over her dress, an'en she pulled on a big ol' pair of bib overhalls and stuffed her dresstail down in 'em. She didn't have no g'loshers or boots, neither one, so she put on her shoes an'en wrapped strips of tow sack around and around her feet and on up the overhall legs to keep snow out of her shoes and keep her legs warm and dry. She pushed long keen nails through the tow sackin'—like pinnin' straight pins in it—to faisten the ends down so they woutn't work loose.

She picked up the kittle and poured some hot water in the milk bucket to take and wash off the cow's bag (udder) before she milked her. Then she put on Dad's old wool coat and went on out to the barn through the snow. When she come

43

back, her feet and legs would be plumb white where snow stuck and froze to the tow sackin'. She'd unroll the strips off of her legs and shake the snow off an'en hang 'em acrost a straight-back chair by the fire to dry out.

Then too, they was times when she brung back either some cottonseed meal out of the cow feed, or shorts from the hog feed to mix in with the cornmeal or flour one, to stretch it so she could make enough bread for all of us. I still remember how them cottonseed meal biscuits tasted. They was purty and yaller, and was good. We allus kept a cow, usually two, so at least we allus had milk and bread and butter, and eggs for breakfast when the hens was layin'. If the eggs got froze and busted, they was usually still good, if we got 'em before they started to thawin' out and got runny. If it got bad cold, though, the hens'd about quit layin'.

The older youngens used that tow sackin' on their feet and legs when they had to go *snake in* wood. It was hard to keep enough wood cut to keep the house warm and do the cookin', too. I've seen the time when we'd have to go out and git wood when it was too cold t'snow, just little blue snow or ice crystals a-swirlin' around in the air. It shore was purty to look at when the light hit it, but hit ditn't feel none too good on your nose and hands. You could hear your breath a-cracklin' when you breathed out, where it hit the air and made a big *fawg* (fog). They never had no gloves, but they shore did pull them 'boggins a way down over their *yeres* (ears). They'd stop ever few minutes and hold their hands up 'nunder their arms on both sides, to warm 'em up some. Your nose'd git so cold hit'd dist ache, an'en when you went in and started to gittin' warm, it hurt worser for a few minutes.

When we all got around the fireplace, nobody got to stand right up in front of the fire, because it blocked the heat off of ever'body else. We had to either set or stand side by side. At night, Dad set in a straight back chair, us littluns set on th' floor, and the rest of 'em set on dannymite boxes or nail *kaigs* (kegs) one. Mom gen'ly set in the middle and *nussed* the baby (held it on her lap) to keep it warm.

It was awful hard to stay warm, spacially if the wind got up and the weather was much cold. Cold air blowed in through all them cracks in the walls and up through the floor, around the wenders and inunder the door. Seemed like you was in a draift no matter where you got. If you stood a-facin' the fireplace, yer back got cold, and when you turnt around to warm your back, yer front got cold. The bottom a your feet dist stayed cold. Sometimes, the smoke blowed back down the chimbly, and we'd haf'ta op'm the door to let it cler out. And if somebody opm'd the door a-goin' in or out, a big blaist a cold air hit through it, and in jist a thought, the whole house was cold. Somebody'd holler, "Shet the door! *You wutn't raised in no barn.*"

Hit'd a-helped a sight if we'd dist a-had winter clothes like people has now, but we wore purty much the same thing all year round and never thought a thing in the world about it. We dist got use to it. That's all we'd ever knowed. Us girls had on a thin cotton dress over a little ol' thin petticoat, with our laigs plumb *bare neck-ed* when we ditn't have no stockin's to put on. Our legs was purplish-blotchedy all over from standin' up so clost to the fire, and they dist about stayed thataway all winter long. They called that *"pietted laigs."*

I don't reckin we got good and warm all over at one time, all winter long. But *hit's a thousand wonders* we ditn' freeze to death.

Sometimes it got so cold you could hear trees a-bustin' from where they'd froze. Sounded like a rifle shot. You could lay in the bed at night and hear 'em a-bustin' over on the side a the mountain. Then, ag'in, you could hear that wind dist *a-screamin' like a lost soul,* right on and on down through the hollers and through the tree tops up on the mountains. It had the lonesomest sound to it. And hit'd come jist a-whisslin' through the cracks in the house, and seemed like the whole house shuck and shivered when a big blaist hit it. Your nose and ears got so cold it made you *scrooch* down inunder the quilts and kivver up your head. It shore was good to know they was a big rick a wood stacked up on the front porch.

But back to the wood-gittin'. Most a th' time, they jist carried a double-bitted axe to chop down a tree and trim off the limbs. After they cut it down and trimmed it up, they fastened one end of a piece of chain or rope around the ends of the poles or log, one, an'en tied the other end around the middle of a stick of wood about three foot long, to make a bar or handle to hold on to, to pull it by. If it was a good size tree, they called it a *lawg* (log), and if it wutn't too big a one, it was a pole. Then they snaked in the wood theirself. If it was much heavy, two people could pull by one a-gittin' aholt on one side of the stick, and one on t'other side. When you went downhill, though, you had to watch out about them poles a-slidin', or they'd run right over top of you.

If they was a-aimin' to cut down a good size tree, or sev'al trees—enough to go to the trouble a *gyearin' up* (harnessing) the hoss, they'd use him to snake the lawgs down to the yard. This could be a right risky business, 'spacially if they was much snow or the ground was slick. It's been knowed for a load of wood to pull a hoss right down the mountain when it got away from him and went to slidin'. But they had a metal thang called a *jaybar* (or J-bar) that they fastened on up next to the log, and if the hoss was a-pullin' and the log started to slidin' and gittin' ahead of 'im, the jaybar'd turn the log aloost to keep it from pullin' the hoss down the mountain.

Bud said one time up on the mountain, they started pullin' a big ol' poplar log, and hit commenced to slidin'—and then jist ballhooted straight down the mountain *di-reckly* torge the house. Might nigh scared him to death. He jist knowed he thang was a-goin' t' go right through the house, but it jist barely missed it. He said that thang would a tore the whole house down if it'd a-hit it. And *it's a good thang* they wutn't no youngens a-playin' out'n the yard along about then.

They had sev'al *lawgin'* (logging) tools they used when they worked up the wood. I 'spect the most common was the double-bitted axe. This is a axe with a cuttin' edge on both sides. They usually tried t'keep one adge real sharp, and dit'n use hit to grub out roots and stuff like that, to dull the adge on it. Ever'body knowed how t'sharp'm a axe. I can still sharp'm one so fine you could *split a frawg (frog) hair down the middle* with it.

Then they was a crosscut saw, that had a handle on each end, and hit needed two people to use it. They'd *git into it* (argue), and one of 'em would accuse the other'n of *ridin' the saw, or ridin' the handle.* That meant that if the one on t'other end ditn't hold his handle up, but *sorter* (sort of) pushed down on it, hit made the saw harder to pull back torge you. It was awful easy to do that when you was tard and just kindly rested on the handle when you wutn't a-pullin'.

A buck saw was about two thirds as long as a crosscut saw, but dist had one handle, and one person sawed with it. We ditn't have nary one a them, but they's been times when I had to git wood by myself, that I dist took one of the handles off of the crosscut saw to make it balance better, and used hit like a buck saw.

A *peavey* was a tool they used to turn a log over with. It had a long stout handle, and th' business end was metal, and kindly pointed on the end. Up from the end a little ways was a struddy, flat, curved iron bar, kindly like a hinged arm with a turned-in spur on the end, that would snag into the log and hold it. You set the peavey down next to a log with that arm acrost it, an'en used th' handle like a *leever* to flip the log over.

A *spud* was used to peel the bark off of poles. *Grabs* was a short piece of heavy chain with a iron spike on each end. They driv them grabs down in the end of a log with a *grow devil* (go devil, a big old heavy hammer), an'en snaked the log by the chain. Lots a times, though, when they was just a-snakin' in a few poles, they dist put the log chain around the bundle and fastened it around 'em, back a little ways from the end, and pulled 'em thataway.

After they got the wood snaked in, they had to *work it up*. It was hard to cut wood with the pole a-layin' on the ground, so they'd use a *jifflin' rod* (small pole) to poke inunder a pole and prize it up acrost another'n or two to get it up to where they could git to it easy. That way, hit ditn't break your back a-bendin' over so far to saw.

They used a crosscut saw to saw the biggest wood to ever how long they needed it cut. The sticks had to be cut shorter for the cookstove than for the fireplace. They had to either *bust up* the big wood into smaller sticks for stovewood, or leave 'em bigger to use in the fireplace. I used to like to bust wood, m'self. They took the grow devil and driv a steel wedge in the end of a big stick to split it up in halfs or quarters, then used the axe and put the wood on th' *chop block* to finish bustin' it on up. You needed a few sticks busted up a little more for kindlin', but if you busted it all up too fine, hit'd burn up too fast. Besides, you got enough of bustin' up wood without doin' it when you ditn' haf' to. We usually jist busted up some kindlin' ever' day as we needed it. Ever' night, it was somebody's job t'git the kindlin' and carry in wood for the next mornin'.

They chopped up the smaller limbs with the axe. A *broadax* was a axe with a cuttin' adge on one side and a thick flat side that could be used for a hammer, but wutn't good fer nothin' much except splittin' up kindlin', or light work.

Them wood chips and sawdust smelt so good where they'd dist frash *worked up* the wood. The sticks of wood would be a-layin' all over th' ground, and had to be gethered up, toted in, and *ricked up* (stacked). You needed to know how to rick it up right to keep the whole rick from rollin' down or fallin' over on you. Firewood was ricked up on the front porch, part of the stovewood was toted in and ricked up behind the cookstove and the rest put on the kitchen porch. If the ground wutn't plumb froze solid, they was usually slick mud all over where they'd been a-workin', and the wood'd be muddy and kivvered up with sawdust and little pieces of moss and bark and trash like that. Ever' one of us was *as naisty as hawgs* by the time we got done, and usually had mashed faingers, skint knuckles, and splinters in us somerce or other. But hit was dist about as bad when we had to git wood with snow on the ground.

They left a few of the biggest sticks unsplit to use as a *backstick*. It served two purposes—it th'owed the heat *fards* into the room, then when it got hot and caught afire, would keep a fire in the fireplace all night. They made sure they toted in a big backstick and had it a-burnin' good before bedtime. Dad or one of the older boys *toted* it in, for it was too heavy for one of us younguns t'tote. Then Dad would *bank the fire* with ashes so it woutn't burn fast and would keep red coals til mornin'. Next mornin', him or one of the older younguns took the *pokin' arn* (poker) and raked the live coals out torge th' front, laid some kindlin' on 'em, then some bigger wood, and purty soon the fire was ketched up and a-burnin' good.

They was allus wood to be got. You might wonder why they never cut up enough wood durin' the summer t'do through th' winter. Well, for one thang, they was allus a lot of other stuff a-needin' to be done in the summer; and hit'd a took all summer to a cut enough wood t'last us all winter. An'en, too, if you cut up a whole lot of wood and let it dry out, hit'd burn up too fast. They did cut a big rick of wood to season out, but you needed some green wood t'burn in with it to slow it down so th' fire'd last longer on less wood.

On t'other hand if you tried t'use all green wood, you'd *dang nigh* freeze to death. Some of it ditn't th'ow out much heat atall; jist lay in there and smoke and spew sap out a the ends. You could hear steam a-fizzlin' out of the end of the sticks. I loved to smell birch or *sassafack* when it done that. Maple, hickory, bass-wood, and ever kind smelt differ'nt. But oak wood, eb'm a-layin' on the porch, smelt like where sump'm's bowels had moved.

They knowed all kind a sign about predictin' weather—like what it meant when the smoke jist laid over the ground like a blanket, when fog started risin' up out of the hollers after rain, or when the livestock laid down on the ground. Sometimes, when they was chunkin' up the fire, sparks'd come a-shootin' out like the Fourth a July. They said that meant colder weather a-comin'. A smoky-lookin' ring around the moon meant it was goin' to snow. Cloudin' up on a heavy frost meant snow. When yaller jackets and hornets built their nestes under the ground or *wooly worms had* a wide black band, it was sign of a bad winter a-comin' on.

If spiders come inside, soot fell down the chimbly, or the old folks had achin' j'ints and their corns hurt, it was a-goin' to rain. Same thang if you *drap* yer bread with the butter side next to the floor, or if the salt sticks in the *salt shake*.

Some people cut their wood on the dark or the light of the moon, one, sayin' hit made a big differ'nce in the way it helt the sap in it, or rotted 'stid a dryin' out, and made it burn good or not. Now, I know for a fact that it sure made a dif-ference in where the signs was and the phase the moon was in when you cut and split board shingles, put in fence postes, and differ'nt thangs, but I'd have to *study on it some* to tell about it.

What I do know *'thout a doubt* is how purty it was at night when you went outside. It was like steppin' out into a dream world, with a great big ol' silvery moon a-shinin' so bright ever' thang dist stood out from the shadders and looked like they was glowin'. You could look up and see the outline of the barren trees and tall pines a-standin' out ag'in the night sky. They was a million trillion stars of all differ'nt sizes a-twinklin' in a sky so deep it dist went on forever, with maybe a few wispy clouds a-trailin' through 'em. Seemed like you was on top of the whole world, and could dist reach right out and tetch that moon, hit'd be so clost. Maybe they'd be a *little skiff of snow* on the ground, and the air smelt so frash—and it was so quiet that you coutn't hear a thing, jist absolute total silence. It was the peacefulest feelin', and I felt strange, sometimes—like I was the only person in the whole world, a way off up here on the very tip top of ever'thing. And I'd dist marvel and wonder about how God made it all, and where Heaven was at, and what it'd be like to be able to see all that God sees from where He is.

These days, they ain't hardly no place you can go to hear total silence. Most people in this country has never knowed what that's like. The only time I hear it now is when the power goes off, when all of a sudden, they ain't no refrigerator a-runnin', or heater fan, or all them other rackets we're use to hearin' all the time. Eb'm then, if you go outside, you can still hear the four-lane off over yander, or jets a-goin' over, one.

OLD TIMEY MEDICINE AND DOCTORIN' YOUNGUNS

Now, a baby was allus kept warm. A many a time I've heard older women warn, "Now, you keep that baby warm and out of a draift. You got to be awful careful about a littl'un a-gittin' chilled. Hit'll give it *th' croup*." Even in the summertime, a new baby was kep' wrapped up in a blanket. If it was took outside, the blanket was pulled over its face.

I remember a-watchin' mothers take care of a baby. Mom allus chunked up the fire to get the room good and warm, and set up clost to the fireplace or cook-stove, one, when she *bath'd* (bath with a *d*) her'n. The best place to git was to let the ub'm (oven) door down and get up next to the cookstove, where they wutn't no draift. She set the metal washpan on the ub'm door to where she could reach it good, and it kep' the water warm, and the heat from the ub'm helped keep a baby warm.

She was awful careful about strippin' the baby off all at once. It was dressed in a knitted undershirt, belly band, diaper, long *outin'* (flannel) gown, knit or cro-cheted (*cro-she-ated*) cap, socks and booties (*boo'-tees*). At least one receivin' blan-ket was wrapped around it good and snug over top a that. Before she got started, she warmed the baby thangs and rolled 'em up in a blanket to stay warm, or else had one of us to hold a piece of it's clothes next to the fire and have it warm when she got ready for it. When she laid the baby down on her lap to bath it, she unwrapped its head and chest and left its diaper, socks, bootees and blanket over its bottom end while she took its gown and shirt off and bath'd the top part. Then she powdered it and put a clean shirt and gown back on it before she took its clothes off of the lower part.

Diapers was called *hippin's*. Mom had some that she called "birdseye diapers." They was called that on account of the way they was wove—the threads made a little diamond-shaped pattern called a *bird's eye* in the cloth. She doubled 'em up cornerways twicet to pin 'em on. She allus powdered their bottom good when she changed their diaper. She was careful about them big *latch pins*. As she took 'em out of the diaper, she'd pin one through her dress and latch it, an'en pin the other'ns through that'n, so she woutn't lose nary'n or job the baby. She allus used baby soap and baby oil on it, an'en powdered it up good. Hit smelt so good right after it got bath'd.

When they got done bathin' the baby, they *give it its titty* (breast fed it) and it went to sleep. They eased it down on the bed and laid pillers all around it so hit woutn't roll over and fall off the bed. Back then, people ditn't have no screen doors or screen wire over their wenders, and the flies dist come inside in droves. They'd aggervate a-body to death a-lightin' on you and bitin' you, and would swarm all over a baby's face, and hit a-layin' there a-tryin' to sleep. When you was nussin' a baby, you had to keep the flies minded off of it's face, or they'd dis' gang up about it's mouth and nose, where they could smell milk on 'em. What they done was take a thin, gauze wender curtain and faisten it up over the head of the bed, an'en spread it out down over the pillers where the baby was a-layin', and *scotch* the ends down 'nunder the pillers. Them thin curtains let plenty of air in, and fixin' it thataway kep' it up off a baby's face and the flies coutn't git to it.

An'en, too, ever'body knowed to watch about the cat a-gittin' up on the bed with the baby—hit'd put its mouth over the baby's and take its breath.

They never had no baby food in them days, jist mashed up whatever they had to eat real good and fed it to the baby. Hit's mammy would chaw up its meat fer it, an'en put it in its mouth.

Good Friday was a good time to wean a baby. They usually let a youngun nurse til it got on up to three or four year old, or till another'n come along and rooted it off the titty, one. One woman I knowed let her youngest'un suck til she was a big ol' youngun and already a-chawin' tobacker. She'd come in from playin' and tell her mammy she wanted some titty. She'd spit her chaw of tobacker out in her hand and hold it, then stand beside her mammy's chair and nurse til she got done, an'en th'ow the tobacker back in her jaw and take off.

I don't remember much about when Oval was borned, but he was a *seb'm month baby*. The ol' cow kicked Mom in the belly and caused him to come early. He was awful little, and they thought he was dead at first. But somebody seen him wiggle his toes, and they got to workin' with him and got him warmed up, and he come around. Mom said he sounded like a little kitten a-mewin' when he cried.

Hit's a good thang he was borned in August, so they could keep him warm. Mom said she had a time with him for awhile there, but he took his titty good and started in to growin.' They was awful pa'tic'lar with him til he was about two year old, though. I reckin that's why I allus wanted to *pertect* him. I dist coutn't stand the thoughts of him a-dyin'.

People said a baby that was real smart was too wise to live.

I do remember about my youngest brother Vernon, though. Mom loved takin' care of him, and talked baby talk and played with him the whole time she was a-bathin' him. He was *a big ol' fat butterball.* Mom'd put her mouth agin' his belly and blow to make a racket, and he'd jist bust out to laughin' ever time, a-kickin' them fat legs. He laughed a lot, but when he did cry, that youngun could beller louder'n a bawlin'calf.

Ever'body was real pa'tic'lar about that cord, now. They was careful not to get nary drop a water on it, for that might make it go to rottenin', and they was real careful not to pull on it no way atall. They kept a belly band on a baby to cover up the cord til it come off, an'en kept one on it til hit was sev'al months old, to keep it from *gittin' ruptured.* A *belly band* was a strip of white knit cloth about four inches wide that they pinned good and tight around it's belly. I've heard tell of women a-sewin' up a silver dollar in the belly band and puttin' it right over the belly button to keep it from poochin' out. Belly bands were still used, even in hospitals, when my children were born in 1957 and 1958, but I've not seen or heard tell of one in a long time now.

Ever few days, they helt a baby straight up by its feet and laid it down on its other side, turning it completely over. This was to keep its liver from growin' to it and gittin' *liver-bound.* Ain't seen that done or heard tell of it *in many a moon.*

Another thing you don't see no more is little boys a-wearin' dresses. They wore them smocked dresses and ditn't get a haircut til they was three or four year old. And all the littluns wore high top, hard sole shoes to support their ankles and make 'em grow straight. They wutn't allowed to walk, or even bear their weight on their feet without havin' their shoes on.

I remember watchin' women a-doctorin' their babies, too. I don't recolleck what all they done, but do remember some of it. The thing that stands out in my mind the most was that *fittidy* (asafoetida) *bag* ever baby wore. Fittidy was some sorter tan waxy stuff that come in little bars about a quarter of a inch thick, and about a inch square. They took and sewed a piece of it up in a scrap a white cloth and made a little bag. An'en they hung it around a baby's neck on a real stout short cord and tied it real good to where it woutn't come loose or the baby might git choked on it, if it got it in its mouth. That was the stinkin'est thang that ever was—*hit'd puke a buzzard off of a gut wagon*—and got to lookin' plumb naisty after a few days. Hit was spost to help 'em cut their teeth good, and keep 'em from ketchin' diseases.

An'en, too, they put fittidy in some corn likker and let it dissolve, and give it to babies for the colic. I remember a-bein' give a *doast* (dose) or two, myself. Hit tasted purty bad, but I've tasted worser.

They give a baby catnip tea to make it sleep good when it was fussy.

Or give 'em a doast of their old stand-by, Paregoric (Tincture of Opium). Ever'body kep' some a that. You had to sign fer it at the drug store to git it. It come in a little two or four ounce bottle. You dist give it a drop, and hit'd make a baby go right to sleep. Grown people used it, too. Hit'd stop colic, belly cramps and the *bowel complaint* when nuthin' else woutn't.

Babies had "hives," when they'd be whiny and break out in little bitty red pimples. (Recon it could of been heat rash?) They'd give it ground ivy tea for that.

I've seen 'em put dist a little drop a *turp'mtine* on sugar in a teaspoon and give it to a little'un that was big enough not to git choked on it. I think that was for the croup—maybe worms, too. They rubbed groundhog oil or bear oil on it's chest and upper back for a chest cold and croup, too.

When Mom wanted to weaken down medicine she thought was too strong, she put it in a spoon and squirted some breast milk in it. Another thing I seen her do was put some white likker in a spoon and *strack a match* to it and let it burn off some. She called that "chartered" whisky. I think she give that when it's *bowels was a-runnin' off.*

If she needed to warm up some medicine, she put it in a spoon and helt it over the top of the lamp globe, then would touch the spoon to her mouth to see that it wutn't too hot. That's how she warmed sweet oil to put in our ears for the ear-ache, too.

If a baby needed a laxative, they give it Fletcher's Castoria ™. If one of the older youngens needed one, they got a doast of castor *(kyaister)* oil. If a younger jist acted kindly puny, they give 'em a big doast of castor oil to give 'em a good cleanin' out.

The big youngens and grown people got Black Draught ™ *(Drawft)* when they was *bunged up.* That was some kind of ground-up black lookin' herb leafs that come in a yaller box with black letterin' on it. Now hit'd flat-out put a-body on the trail to the toilet.

Another thang babies got was the *thrash* (thrush). That's a fungal infection where a white coatin' forms in patches on the inside of the mouth and back of the throat. This seems to be right painful to the baby, for they get real cranky and fuss a lot, and get so they won't *take their titty.* That could be real serious. They's certain *spacial* persons with a gift to cure the thrash, and a mother'd send word to them to come and cure *(cyore)* their baby, or have somebody take their baby to them, one. How they done it was kep' secret, and they had to be left by theirself with the baby for it to work. Whatever it was that they done, hit worked, and they's still a few people like that around here that can cure the thrash.

I had an interesting experience a few years ago. I had a few very painful white patches in my mouth and the back of my throat, and was diagnosed by both a family doctor and an ENT specialist as having a yeast infection in my mouth and throat. I got the very expensive prescriptions filled, but when I read all the frightening side effects, I decided to wait a day or two and try some *yaller root tea* first. I remembered that people used to use it for sore mouth and stomach problems. My son, David knows what it looks like growing in the wild, and went out and got some for me. I made some tea, used it as a gargle and sipped on it all along.

I felt better before long, and in about three days, the infection was completely gone, and I've not had it since. The only "side effect" was the awful bitter taste. Next time, I'll just save myself time and money on doctors and prescriptions, and dig me some yaller root.

A-body had to be real *bad off* to get a doctor. Somebody'd either have to ride a horse to go get him, or go find somebody with a car to come and take 'em to one. Then, if somebody was bad off enough to be in a hospital, the next thing you expected to hear was that they'd died.

Most of the time, they never went to the doctor unless it was a *haf-to* (have-to) *case*, because they didn't have the money to pay a doctor with. People had their own remedies that they depended on for differ'nt ailments. I think they used lamp oil, turpentine, liquor and Castor oil for just about everything. They tied wounds up in a rag and poured turpentine or lamp oil over cuts, *puncher* (puncture) wounds, and other places where you was hurt at.

Sometimes, they put sugar and turp'mtine on a cut. If it was a-bleedin' bad, they put *spider wibs* (webs) on it, or got soot out of the lamp globe or chimbly to put on it. If it wutn't too bad a cut, they stuck a dry cig'ret paper on it, and the blood *clodded* on that. They's a Bible verse they said would stop blood, too. It's the one where Jesus healed the woman with a issue of blood.

They made Jerusalem Oak candy to give a youngun for worms. They dissolved rock candy in whiskey to make cough syrup. Grown people drunk burnt likker for *the piles* (hemorrhoids). *That's the Gospel truth! I woutn't fruit ye* (lie to you)!

Corn whiskey was used a lot for makin' up medicine and was the base of about all their *"teas"* and concoctions. I guess it either made 'em drunk enough to go to sleep, or *not give a dang* what was a-botherin' 'em, one. Seriously, it was a way to preserve medicine so it woutn't *spile* (spoil).

Ginger tea—corn likker and ginger in hot water, was sweetened and drunk for colds or *female trouble*. Hit'll shore *git yer blood to circalatin'* and warm you up on a cold day. Lots a women took Cardui™ or Lydia Pinkham's Compound ™ for their "*monthly's*" and *female trouble*. We got a calendar from 'em ever year.

Bud said he drunk some Iodine when he was a little youngen. That one time, Dad hapm'ed to be out a likker (prob'ly drunk it all up), and had to go up the creek to git some from somebody else. When he brought some back, he made Bud drink it til it made him sick enough to throw up. Bud said he wisht it had turnt him agin' likker then, but it never.

Bud said Pa Hicks drunk black pepper tea for a cold—or he'd parch red pepper on a shovel over the fire, powder it up and put it in likker. He kep' a pint bottle of it a-settin' on his *farboard* (mantel). Bud and my uncle Aston slipped around and took *a swig* of it ever oncet in a while. All I can say is, they must've wanted *a snort a likker* awful bad.

They put a mustard poultice on the chest for a chest cold. You could buy mustard plasters and a strong salve called Musterole™at the drugstore, and they used that, too. They greased up their chest with it and put a hot flannel cloth over it to loosen up chest congestion.

But one thang they allus used on ever'body for the croup, chest or *head cold*, from a baby on up to grown folks, was *Pneumonie salve* (Vicks Vaporub™). That was one thing no house was ever without. Hit was rubbed on the chest, back or throat under hot flannel cloths, put up the nose, or a small dob put in the mouth to melt—or put it in boilin' water and breathe the steam to *op'm you up*. Now, *you better stay bundled up real good after you rub pneumonie salve on ye, or hit'll make ye worser.*

Salesmans, or drummers, used to come by ever few months and sell all differ'nt kinds a *linny-mint* (liniment). I remember one was White Horse Liniment™. Just to take the cap off and smell it would jist about lift the top offa yer head. Dad put some on his knees one time before he started home from Canton. Comin' acrost Soco mountain, it got to burnin' so bad he pulled his truck over on the side a the road, got out his pocket knife and cut the laigs off of his long-handled underwear.

Of course, rubbin' alkyhol was the usual standby for rubbin' on sore muscles and stuff, as well as put on cuts. And camphor was used as a rub, too, but they kep' some around to put a dab on a haincher for people to smell of and *brang 'em around* when they felt *faintyfied*.

Some folks had little *tee-nincey* bottles a smellin' salts they helt inunder their nose fer *faintin'-away spells*, too. Some women carried one around with 'em in their bosom or apern pocket, one.

For scrapes and *chafted* skin and lips, they used Rosebud salve™ or Cloverine™ salve, one. Hit come in little round flat tin boxes. They use to order it out of a magazine, or the paper, one, an'en sell it fer a little profit or a prize. I think hit costed a quarter a box.

Dad use to make *Bam-a-Gillian* (Balm of Gilead) *salve.* He gethered buds from Bam a Gillian trees and fried 'em in mutton *taller,* and made it like that. It was put on sores and places to make them heal up. He mixed *pine rosum* with taller to make a salve, too.

Lettin' a dog lick yer sores was s'post to help 'em heal up.

But when somebody got the *eatch (itch),* they got sulfur and lard rubbed on 'em.

When somebody got the pink eye, they sent to the drugstore and got some Argyrol™ eye drops (a silver nitrate preparation), and that cured it right up. Now then, they give you a *perscription* for a antibiotic eye oint-ment, and some-times, a run of antibiotic pills on top a that. Don't work *one speck* better, and you'd better have a fat pocketbook when you go to git 'em filled.

When Mom needed herbs to doctor with, she allus sent Bud to go git 'em. He'd go off. an' come back with whatever it was she needed. *I'd give anything if I knowed dist half a what he knows* about plants—where they grow, what they look like, and what they're used for.

Boneset tea, elderberry juice or wine was good for a *bad cold.* (We allus said "bad cold.")

For poison oak and stings, we rubbed wild *tetch-me-not* (Jewel Weed) on it. We used white shoe polish to dry up poison oak. (We allus said "poison oak," too, not poison ivy.)

They was all differ'nt kinds a tonics and blood purifiers—like *sassyfack* tea (sassafras), poke sallet, and sulfur and molasses, that was usually took in sprangtime, jist to *pyearten you up.* They chawed on *sang* (ginseng) *root* or put it in likker to get the medicine out of it. Bud said hit'd *put lead in your pencil,* whatever that means. But mostly, he went a-*sang huntin'* ever day or two and dug it, dried it, and sold it. It sold by weight and it was so light after it dried that it took sev'al bunches to make a pound, but it *fetched a purty penny.*

I used to try to take care of Mom, and took her to the doctor ever once in awhile. He'd write perscriptions (or *subscriptions*) for one thing and another, and I'd get 'em filled and be sure she knowed how to take 'em. Like as not, when I'd go back to see about her, she'd be a-brewin' up a batch of herb tonic out of com-frey, boneset, and stuff she put in a big pot and boilt all together. It worried me, not knowin' what it'd do, all mixed up together with her prescriptions. *Didn't make no nevermind* to her, she was goin' to do dist ezackly what she was goin' to do, and they wutn't no use in nobody a-tryin' to tell 'er no different. Well, she was a-gittin' on up in years, was strong as a horse, and done about anything she wanted to, so I dist kep' my mouth shet. I figgered she hadn't lived that long and done as well as she had by bein' a dang fool, and *I'll tell ye right now*, I don't know of no modern medicine that could do any better. She lived by herself, run off and got married at the age of 93, and died at 95 of a sudden *heart attackt*. Her body was still strong and her mind was still *cler as a bell*, so maybe I ort to of got her recipe.

They used spignet tea or Carter's Little Liver Pills® for liver trouble, and red alder tea or queen-of-the-meader for kidney trouble. They chawed on *camel root* (calomel) for stomach trouble.

Blackberry juice, blackberry wine, birch bark tea, or mountain birch (teaberry, or wintergreen plant) is good to stop the bowels from runnin' off. I jist like to chaw on mountain birch leafs, and eat them purty red berries on it—tastes (tase-tes) like Teaberry chewin' gum.

Black "drawin' salve" was used on a *risin'* (a boil), or they scraped a raw *Arsch* (Irish) tater and made a poultice, or tied a piece of salty fat back on it to *draw it to a head*. You had to wait til it *come to a head* to laince it, or it *might set up blood poisonin'* and kill you.

For any kind of injury, Epsom salts was used as a soak to draw out the sore-ness.

About ever kind of cut or injury was cleaned with salt water, Lysol,™ or Life-boy™ soap, an'en either Iodine or Mercurochrome painted on it. Besides alky-hol, Lysol™ was the only disinfectant I knowed of people a-havin' back then. I associated that smell with a woman a-havin' a baby at home, or cleanin' wounds. It smelt like Lifebuoy™ soap and smells different now to what it did then.

We used butter and salt on chiggers. *Lamp oil* (kerosene) kept the ticks off of you.

Quinine is good for leg cramps. Or *for foot cramps, turn your shoes upside down under your bed at night.*

Back then, hit was common fer jist about all young'uns to have warts on their faingers. They allus said that *playin' with a toad frog causes warts*, from where they peed on you. Different people had different advice on how to get rid of 'em: Rub 'em with a chicken gizzard and hide it under a rock; count the warts, put the same number of little white rocks in a little cloth poke and throw it down where a road forks, and so on, to make warts go away. An'en they was people that conjured or charmed the warts off of you, or bought 'em off of you, one.

Elm bark was used for burns and bedsores. They scraped a Arsch tater and made a poultice to *draw the fire out* of a frash burn. Then they put butter or lard, or some kind a salve on it. They was people that could draw the fire out of a burn. They'd git down clost and blow their breath on it, and done it like that.

I know one thing I'm awful proud they don't do now. If you got burnt, they made you hold the burnt place up clost to the fire or a hot iron, one, to draw the fire out. I remember them a-holdin' me and stickin' my burnt hand out in front of the fireplace, and me a-screamin' bloody murder. *Lordy mercy,* that was awful.

An'en, *to make bad matters worse,* they rubbed lard on it.

GOIN' OUTDOORS

Nowadays, when somebody says they need to go outdoors, everybody thinks they just want some frash air. If they say "I'm goin' to the John," everybody knows they're headed for the bathroom. Well, we woutn't a-knowed what "going to the John" meant, but if somebody said, *"I need to go outdoors,"* we knowed to clear out a trail. That was the polite way to say "I need to use the toilet." When we went to school, we learnt to say "May I be excused, please?"

In our neck of the woods, having a bowel movement (or, *doin' your business)* was called *"takin' a dump"* or to *"dookey, or hockey."* If a baby *messed in its diaper,* they dookied, or hockied in it. If it was wet, they'd "wet," or "peed." We'd better not be caught a-sayin' the four letter "S" or "P" word, for that was considered gittin' a little too clost to cussin'.

You've prob'ly heard about the mailman making his appointed rounds in rain, snow, sleet or hail. Wellsir, that's the way it was when we had to *do our business.* We had to hit the trail to the toilet no matter what the weather was. They better not find it, if anybody done their business in the yard or anywhere clost to the house, neither, so you better not wait too long to git gone.

Our definition of "toilet water" then, to what it means now, wutn't nowhere near clost to the same thing. Mom didn't allow no *stinkin' pee buckets* in our house, to be a-gittin' kicked over. Before we went to bed, we went down to the branch or out behind the house, one, to pee.

After dark, you had to light the lantern and take it to the toilet with you, so you woutn't step on a snake, *stob your toe* on a rock or sump'm. I was afeared of the dark, and allus *bagged* (begged) somebody to go with me. I could dist feel great big ol' hands, or some kind of a *booger*, one, a-reachin' out of the dark to snatch me, or maybe *a snake a-strackin'* and *peckin' me* on the ankle. I learnt that you better go do your business before dark come.

Mom didn't like fer us to wet off of the porch in the summertime, because it got to *smellin' purty rank*, and made bees and yaller jackets swarm around it. But us girls slipped around and seen who could wet through a crack on the porch without gittin' none on the planks. The boys liked to *show out*, and lined up on the edge of the porch and *rared* a wa-a-y back to see who could pee the fudderest out in the yard. They'd pick out sump'm to aim it at, and see whichun could splatter it. Even now, if you're around an old country boy along about bedtime, jist watch him. Shore as the world, he'll slip off outside to *shake the dew off his lily.*

One night one of 'em was out there in the dark, dist a-lettin' it fly, when our big ol' hound dog up and licked him right where his water come out. He jumped like he'd been shot. Now, *that scared his mule!* He thought fer dist a minute there, that he'd done'n lost his *fam'ly jewels.*

Nearly everybody on Jun'lusky had a outdoor toilet, but they was ever' one differ'nt. Most people dist built their toilet out of rough planks, and some was like a lean-to, maybe never eb'm had no door, dist hung tow sacks up. Dist so you got out of sight. Our'n was up on the side of the hill, and was a two holer on account of our big family. They was some man that made his livin' a-goin' around a-buildin' toilets, and Dad *harred* (hired) him to build our'n. He set it on about a six foot square slab of concrete. He said he made all his toilet floors out a ce-ment—they lasted longer, they wutn't no cracks, smelt better, and was cleaner and all. I ditn't know what to think about that cold hard ce-ment floor. You ditn't see much of that back then.

We tore pages out of a catalog or used newspapers, one, to wipe on. We use to like to set in there and read the paper or a Grit© magazine, or look at the Sears and Roebuck™ catalog. We called it our "wish book." But you'd dang near freeze your hin'end off in cold weather if you set in there long.

A-body could latch the door and set in there and read til somebody else come along a-beatin' on the door, a-wantin' in. And if a-body wanted to *git a racket started*, jist let 'em git ketched a-peepin' through a crack at somebody a-doin' their business.

When people built a toilet, they dug a deep pit so hit'd last a long time, and they woutn't have to dig another'n as soon. You'd better not drop nothin' in there that you ditn't want in there, for hit was long gone when you did. And watch about losiin' little stuff through cracks in the floor. But if you wanted *to get shed of* sump'm, like a letter from your sweetheart, and you ditn't want nobody to find it, that was the dandiest place in the world to put it. Fer shore, they wutn't nobody goin' to be a-diggin' nuthin' out of that stinkin' mess.

Some people built their toilet out over the creek bank, or a brainch if they was one clost enough. Them was cleaner and smelt better'n a pit toilet, but hit was kindly scary when the creek got up, with all that muddy water a-roilin' around down under you. If the water got up much high, they dist hit the woods to do their business. Lawerence used to call the dog and go out behind the barn, and that dang dog'd gobble that up like it was the best stuff he ever eat.

Whichever kind a toilet you had, though, you better poke your head through the hole far enough to see whuther any *waspers* or yaller jackets had built their nest 'nunder there before you pulled down yer britches and set down. You was *liable to* come out faster'n you went in.

Some people ditn't eb'm have no toilet. They dist pulled 'em off some green leafs to wipe on, stepped out on to a flat rock in the branch, hunkered down to do their business, and it floated off. People thought it was a awful sorry man that woutn' eb'm build his family a toilet.

We had a door on our'n, and faistened it with a button. The old sayin', "*As handy as a button on a outhouse"* would mystify most folks. They wouldn't know what you was talkin' about. A "button" was a piece of wood about a inch thick, two inches wide, and four or five inches long. A big nail was drove through the middle of it into the door facin', so when you turnt the button *slaunchways*, the end of it stuck out over the edge of the door and helt it shet. Lots a times, the toilet ditn't set *exackly* level, and the door wouldn't stay shet unless you buttoned it.

An'en too, if you wanted to set in there and not be bothered—maybe look at a catalog or sump'm, you needed a way to keep everybody out. They was one button on the outside to hold the door shet when you come out, but they was another'n on the inside to fasten everybody out when you went in. An'en you could go ahead and do your business, and nobody'd *ketch you with your drawers down*.

Another way to fasten the door was to make a *string latch*. You need one piece of board about ten inches long, two inches wide and about a half an inch thick for a bar. Hold it on the inside of the door so it sticks out past the door edge about three inches, then drive one nail through the far end into the door, loose-like, so the bar can swivel up and down.

Take another piece to make the latch so the bar can come down and fit in behind it. You nail this piece up and down on the inside of the door frame, with the notch up, so the end of the bar can come down in the notch to latch the door.

Then bore a hole over a little ways from the edge of the door, about five inches above the bar, jist big enough so your string will work through it easy, and poke the end of *a leather strang* through the hole from the outside. Then fasten the inside end to the bar. When the leather string is pulled from the outside, it pulls the bar up and unlatches the door. When you go in, you can latch the door and pull the strang inside if you don't want nobody to git in.

People had latches on their house doors, too. They wuddent no way to lock 'em. We never eb'm had no door knobs on our'n. But in them days, nobody never locked nuthin' up. I don't know if people was more honest back then, or if it was because we ditn't have nuthin' worth stealin' nohow.

CLEANIN' OURSELF UP

I guess they's folks that'll *snerl up their nose* like they smelt a *polecat* when they hear what I'm a-fixin' to tell now. You've prob'ly heard the old sayin', *"Don't go around a-judgin' nobody til ye've walked a mile in their shoes."* Well, I'll try t'tell it like it was, an'en you can judge for yeself.

Now, you need to stop a minute and think jist *ezackly* how things was back then. By the time one of us was five year old, they was another youngen and a littl'un for Mom to have to take care of, besides all the other stuff she had to 'tend to. So when it come t'keepin' yerself clean, a youngen was dist about on its own when it got about five or six year old. And keepin' ourself clean wutn't exactly at the top of our list of *druthers*.

It wutn' atall uncommon to see rusty heels and dirty feet, and dirt crusted up behind the ears. We changed clothes when Mom handed us a change a clothes and told us to clean ourself up but we usually *ditn't go to no pains to do it*.

What we usually done was *take turn about* and go off to th' kitchen at differ'nt times on differ'nt nights, about oncet a week after the supper dishes was washed. We'd pour some warm water out of the kittle into the washpan, set it on the washstand, and rub off with a washrag. Mom did learn us to wash our face first, and save the bottom part til last.

Washin' our head in th' middle a the winter was sump'm we never done. W'y, *hit'd give a body pneumonie to run around in the cold air with a wet head.*

You've prob'ly seen movies where somebody's a-settin' in a big ol' washtub a-takin' a bath, a-scrubbin' their back with a long handled brush, with rainbow bubbles a-floatin' out in the air and over the side, in front of a big ol' roarin' fire, dist a-sangin' and havin' a high ol' time. Whoooeee!

You might think we could a-took a bath in a washtub, at least ever oncet in a while. Well, dist stop and *think on it a spell*. They was twelve of us altogether. How many buckets a water do you reckin we'd a-had to carry in and heat up?

And what about privacy? Now, one thing we was awful careful about, was *showin' ourself* to anybody. We was raised to *keep yer neckedness kivvered up*. Bud was 14 when I was born, then Sweetie and Lewis after him. They wutn't no way them big ol' boys was a-goin' to *strip off buck neck-ed* in the sight of all us young-ens and Mom and Dad, bath or no bath.

They wutn't enough room nowhere to eb'm hang up a sheet t'git behind. We dist had the kitchen, backroom, and front room, and it was too cold to stay in th' back room unless we was in the bed. It was awful cold, way back up on the head of Jun'lusky Creek, and the only heat we had was that ol' draifty fireplace after th' fire went out in the cookstove

And where would the rest of us a-gone while one of us was a-takin' a bath? Wutn't nowhere to go but outside. And how long do you reckin we'd a-had to a-stayed out there while ever'body got a bath? We shore wutn' a-goin' out in no yard to hang around, a-freezin' ourself t'death. We'd a-*been a-shakin' like a dog spittin' a peach seed.* And the one a-gittin' out of th' tub would a-had t'git out in th' cold air when the nextun got in.

Then, too, we woutn't a-had enough towels and washrags to a gone around for us all to have a cleanun. Eb'm if we'd a had 'em, pore old Mom'd a-wore her-self out a-tryin' to wash 'em all. It was a big enough job dis' t'wash us all a change a clothes.

Mom got off in the kitchen to clean up, when ever'body else was gone off out of the house. I remember her a-havin' one a-tother of us gals to give her back a good scrubbin'. She liked to have that done.

Now, in the summertime, hit was a differ'nt story. Dist about ever evenin', us gals, and usually Mom, took a rag and some soap down to th' spring branch and washed off down there. Sometimes, them gnats'd dist about carry us off. We usu-ally had some black Lava™ soap with pumice in it, and that soap'd shore clean you up good. We was careful t'be *savin' with it,* and not leave it a-layin' in the water, or nothin'. We'd set down on a rock by the side of the branch and scrub our feet with some fine sand or a dried okry pod, one. The sprang branch was warmer'n th' creek, and closter to th' house. We ditn' dry ourself off. Them *shorts* (hog feed) *sacks* we used fer towels didn't dry you off much good, nohow.

I remember a-settin' there on that big flat rock, still warm from the sun, a-watchin' dark come, and seein' the stars come out. We jist set quiet, a-lookin' up at the evenin' sky and watched the bats fly around a-catchin' insects, or the swallers a-swoopin' and divin' here and there. They looked so happy and free when they done that, I wisht I had *wangs* to fly and could sail around up there amongst 'em.

I think back sometimes about how it was back then and how different things is now. Ever' time I take a shower or bath, I think about how things was back then, and am so grateful for what I have. It still seems unreal to me when I come in from the freezin' cold outside, go into my nice warm bathroom, get in the shower, let the water spray me from the top of my head to my toes, and still be cozy and warm. And come out thirty minutes later *a-smellin' like a rose* with my hair all clean and dry and fixed up nice.

Or get in a hot tub with some nice bath salts and just lay back and soak to my heart's content. No havin' to carry in water and heat it up, neither.

And they hain't nary a shorts sack in the house!

My big ol' thick washcloths and soft, fluffy towels are such a joy to use. I still marvel at their velvety texture and beautiful colors. Sometimes when I look around the bathroom at my bath accessories, wonderful scented soaps, shampoo, bath powder, jars and bottles of lotions, creams, hair and nail conditioners, toothbrush, hairbrush, nailbrush and other toiletries, I think how amazed we'd have been just to see these things. We didn't know such things existed.

We ditn't even have no *faingernail file.* (We allus said the two words together: "faingernail file.") They cut their faingernails and toenails and cleaned *ou'fenunder*'em with a pocket knife, an'en scraped the adge of the blade back and forth acrost the ends to smooth 'em off. But people never cut their faingernails or hair on a-Sunday—hit was bad luck. Us youngens jist chawed our'n off *enny-haow.*

But we never knowed we was pore. It was the onliest way we knowed, at the time. Woutn't we a-been *tickled* to a-had a roll a toilet paper or a box a Kleen-exes? I've gone to the toilet with Mom, and when she got done, she'd tear a page out of the catalog, or tear off about a foot square of newspaper. She'd wad it up in her hand real tight, then straighten it out some, and rub it back and forth between her knuckles, t'soften it up, t'use.

I remember Mom a-havin' some Pond's™ cold cream or vanishin' cream at times, but she used it on her own face, and was savin' with it. Mostly, we used Vaseline.™ We woutn't a-knowed what you was talkin' about if you'd a-said "petroleum jelly." Ever once in awhile, somebody come around a-sellin' Clover-ine™ or Rosebud salve™ in little round tin boxes and Mom'd get a box. It was good for chafted hands, raw baby bottoms, or to rub on your nose when you had a bad cold and your nose and lips got chafted. It was kindly like fancy vaseline that smelt good.

That Rosebud™ salve smelt dist like roses, and me and Coonie'd git some out on our finger and smell it and lick it off real slow. It tasted good, too. Ever oncet in a while, we'd get a bar a Ivory™ soap. Coonie liked to eat that too. She'd rake her faingernails acrost a bar of it to get it packed up 'nunder 'em, an'en gnaw on 'em to eat it ou'fenunder 'em. *Boy, howdy*, Mom'd *wear her out* when she saw faingernail marks on the soap. She knowed who done it without havin' to ast.

If we'd a-had an aromatherapy candle, we'd a prob'ly stood around it and sniffed ourself blue in' th' face a-smellin' of it. We never had no candles atall. We didn't waste no money on nothin' like that. We done good t'keep lamp oil in th' lamp, and hit wutn't lit til it got dist nearly plumb dark, so we woutn' waste lamp oil.

Talkin' about havin' a cold made me remember seein' women pull their petti-coat tail ou'fenunder their dress, and either blow their nose or a youngen's nose on it.

Dad liked to *pull jokes* and *go on at* other people. Mountain folks is bad to do that, jist to see how much of it somebody'll *take to heart. It don't make no never-mind* to them if you b'lieve it or don't. One time a Welfare woman come to our house a-*actin uppity*, and Dad dist put on a big show, a-makin' out like he was plumb *ignert*. The littlest younguns was a-runnin around the house, and the baby come runnin' through there where they was a-settin'. Dad hollered out to the kitchen at Mom and said, "Maw, brang the dishrag here and blow this youngen's nose." Then turnin' back to the woman, said, "If they's anything I can't stand, it's dang *naistness*." That ol' Welfare woman turnt right green and coutn't git outta there quick enough to suit 'er. Dad *like to a busted a gut* a-laughin and tellin' about that.

Mom and Mammy both wore their hair pulled back in a bun. They had thick hairpins and combs made out of celluloid (pronounced *settaloy,* or *celloid*). It looked like plastic, only plastic, as we know it, hadn't been invented then. They were usually a mottled, reddish-brown color that looked like tortoise shell. They *took care of* them combs and hairpins, and laid 'em up in a certain place ever time they took 'em out of their hair. *They was hard to come by.*

We never had no hairbrush. Men carried a little pocket comb, but we just had one comb for all of us to use. It was purty good size, and usually had some teeth broke out. The broke-off teeth was put up to use for *gittar* (guitar) picks. That's the only kind a gittar pick I knowed they was, back then. Mammy had a fine tooth comb she used ever night after she got done combin' out her hair with a *rag'ler* (regular) comb. After she got it combed out good, she'd plait it up kindly loose in a long plait that come way down b'low her shoulders. Mommy just let her'n bush out and hang loose when she took th' hairpins out. Her hair was so thick she'd a broke a fine tooth comb all to pieces a-tryin' to run it through her'n. It was natural curly, and her head was *as big as a bushel baisket* when she didn't wad it up in a bun.

For hair curlers, some gals took a Prince Albert™ tobacker can apart. then they took tin snips and cut it up in strips about a quarter of a inch wide. Then they'd wrap strips of brown paper poke around 'em for paddin' so the metal adge wouldn't cut their hair, then bent the ends over and crimped 'em down good with the wire pliers (*wahr plars*) to hold the paper on. They'd part off a section of hair and roll it up on the middle of the roller, then bend the ends over to hold the curled up hair in place. It shore did make it *kainky.*

I 'member one time, somebody told me to damp'm my hair with sugar water when I rolled it, and hit'd hold a curl after you let it dry and took out the curlers. Wellsir, it helt a curl, all right, but you talk about a sticky mess in drizzly weather, now that was. Honey bees and yaller jackets liked it, too, and sounded like a *buzz saw* a-whizzin' around my head.

Dad and the boys shaved with a straight razor. Dad had a wide razor strop that he oiled and stroked the edge of the razor back and forth on to sharp'm it. That was what they used to whup us youngens with, too.

He had some round shavin' soap that fit down in his shavin'mug, and had a shavin' brush. He wet his shavin' brush in hot water, stuck it down in th' shavin' mug and stirred it around on th' soap to make up some lather. An'en he lathered up his face good with the brush before he started shavin'. I 'member watchin' him a-makin' faces and lookin' whopper-jawed when he looked in th' metal framed lookin' glass while he shaved. The lookin' glass hung on a nail by the kitchen door in the winter time, and in the summer, it hung on a nail in a porch post out on the kitchen porch. It was about eight by ten inches and was the only one we had. They was awful careful with it, for *it meant seb'm years a bad luck if you broke one.*

He used rubbin' alkyhaul for aftershave, an'en slapped his own face to keep it from burnin'.

Women didn't shave their laigs or under their arms back then, and I never knowed what deodorant was til I was *purtnear* grown.

I was *mightnear* grown before I knowed what mouthwash was, too, other than yaller root to cure the thrash, and ever'body called mouthwash "Listerine."™ An'en they was was some green liquid in a *little bitty* bottle, called Tips,™ that they used to make their breath smell frash. It was real strong mint. They'd take off the *led* and turn the bottle up and stick their tongue to the tip to get a drop on it. Boys carried it in their pocket whenever they went *a-sparkin'*.

They was some other stuff they used, called Sen-Sen,™ that was solid little black te-nincey flat pieces, about a eighth of a inch square. Hit come in a little flat *en-velop* about one and a fourth inches wide by two inches long. They'd tear a little bit off a one corner of the packet and shake out a piece and put it in their mouth and hold it. An'en double the top back over good, to keep 'em from spillin' out in their shirt pocket. It tasted *kindly* like peppermint with a *liquish whang* (slight licorice flavor) to it. Ever'body that sung carried that when they went to a sangin'. When they all *cut loost* to sangin', you could smell their breath on the back row.

When I got in school, about oncet a year the school nurse give ever'body in school a toothbrush, a little tube of toothpaste or tooth powders, one, and learnt us how to brush our teeth. That never lasted long. We went around a-brushin' our teeth all the time til we got out all the toothpaste we could a-mashin' the tube, an'en we tore it op'm and licked ever last bit out of it. Outside a that, we never had no toothbrush or toothpaste, neither one.

People went out and hunted a birch or black gum tree and broke off a little limb, then broke that up into pieces about four or five inches long, t'make their toothbrushes. They chawed up the very end of it, so it'd get sorter bristly, to make a *brash*. They dipped it down in some bakin' sodie or snuff and used that for tooth powders to brash their teeth with.

I don't recall nobody a-havin' false teeth when I was a youngen. When they lost all their teeth, they jist gummed their rations. I did see a few men with gold teeth set in betwixt their natural teeth. Them gold teeth'd *shine like new money* when they grinned. Jake Abernathy had some of 'em. I thought he must be awful rich t'have gold teeth.

The only time anybody ever went to the dentist was when their jaw got *all swelled up* with th' toothache and they had to have a tooth pulled. Dad pulled one a his'n with th' wire pliers one time. I *ain't never seed* nobody before or since that seemed like pain never bothered 'em atall.

Men used *hair oil* to make their hair lay down. I've watched my brothers a-gettin' ready to go a-sparkin' or *sumerce*. They'd pour out some hair oil in the palm of their hand, rub it agin' the other'n, an'en slick their hands back acrost their hair, a-puttin' on th' hair oil. Then they'd part it and comb it backerds, and push up a little wave on top, on th' side that had th' most hair. Back then, men parted their hair on one side, and women parted their'n on the other'n, but I fergit whichun was which. Sometimes they used some thick stuff called Brilliantine™ that come in a tube or jar. Hit made their hair *so slick a fly coutn't a lit on it 'thout slidin up and bustin' their butt.* The piller slip'd have a big ol' greezy circle on it where they'd laid their head.

All the haircuttin' was done at home. Dad had some haircuttin' scissors, clippers, a dustin'-off brush and a *spacial* barberin' comb. He put a cloth around 'em to keep hair from going down their neck and fastened it with a big ol' *latchpin*. When he got done, he rolled them tools up in the cloth and put 'em up. And nobody'd better not tetch them haircuttin' thangs.

Men was allus a-comin' to the house to git Dad or Mom, one, to cut their hair. They'd take 'em out in th' yard and set 'em down in a straightback chair. If them clippers got dull and commenced t'pullin', hit musta hurt purty bad, fer they shore jumped and hollered when they done that. Dad done more'n holler, but he ditn't allow the boys to cuss. Then they'd haf' to sharp'm up them clippers.

Little boys never got their hair cut and still wore dresses til they was about three or four year old. Us'ally, when they got their hair cut, they started puttin' *britches* on 'em. They thought they was a *"Big Pete"* when they got a haircut and got to wear a pair a britches.

They never let me wear my hair no way except long and parted in th' middle. They said nobody but *huzzies* had "*bobbed*" hair. When Mom cut our hair, she damp'm it down, combed it straight down and cut the ends straight around. I'd ask her to cut me some bangs like other girls had, but she said she wutn't a-cuttin' no bangs, and that was the end a that. When Mom or Dad told you sump'm, you never made the mistake of astin' why but oncet. And you better not ast no more. That was considered *sassin' back* or *argeyin'*.

When I got on up in high school, it was fashionable to have a permanent wave put in at the beauty shop. Most of my friends had one put in. They cut their hair off real short and used a machine to put in a permanent. Hit made it so kainky they coutn't eb'm comb it.

Of course I wanted one too, but I didn't get one a them, neither. Hit costed money to have a permanent wave put in, and it *wutn't necessary*.

We never got nothin' that wutn't necessary.

GNAT SMOKES, FEED SACKS, FLOUR POKES AND BLOOMERS

We never throwed away nary scrap of cloth til it got so wore out it coutn't even be used for a dishrag. Old wore-out rags was used to make *gnat smokes* to smoke away gnats and '*skeeters* in the evenin'. We rolled 'em up in a roll about two inches acrost, and tied it loose so hit'd keep afire, but not blaze and burn it up. Sometimes we put gnat smokes in a ol' rusty surp bucket, so we could move it, 'stid of us a-havin' to move when the wind changed and blowed the smoke torge us.

Dad allus kep' a gnat smoke handy on the porch. He liked to set in a straight back *cher* out on the porch in the evenin'. He'd lean backerds til the top of his chair was *scotched* back agin the wall with the front legs *r'ared up* off the porch and his whole weight on the two back chair legs. Then he'd put his feet on the bottom rung. I 'spect you might call that a hillbilly recliner.

I *come in a bean a gittin' my killin'* when I tried it. I must've been too fer away from the wall, and *r'ared back* too fer, for the back laigs slid fards on the floor, the top of the chair hit the wall, raked down and slammed it down on the porch, with me on the inside of it, there. Wellsir—there I laid, *flat a my back like a mud turkel* (turtle) *on its back*, with my laigs 'n arms a-stickin' up 'n flappin' the air, a-tryin' to git up.

Fool like, though, I kep' at it til I got so I could set like that, too. I never was one to give up easy. *Stubbern as a flop-eared mule*, I was.

The grown folks set out on the porch or in the yard a'ter supper in the evenin', along torge dark when it sorter cooled down some. Us younguns would run around and play in the yard, then, til bedtime. Sometimes them dogged gnats and skeeters'd *dang nigh* eat us alive. We lit our gnat smokes and put 'em to where the smoke'd blow around us to help keep 'em off of us. We called gnats "*no see 'ums*," because the ones that bit the worstest was them little ol' bitty'uns that you coutn't hardly see. I don't know if it was gnats or skeeters, but *one a t'other* of 'em shore liked my flavor. They made round red *whelks* on me about the size of a dime, with a little blister in the center. They *eatched* (itched) *like the devil*. An'en them little blisters made a sore.

We never said "fabric." We called it "cloth," unless it was *"outin"* (outing, or flannel). Back then, clothes and ever'thing *drawed up* (shrunk) when they was washed, because they was cotton. They had to allow for that when they used *bought cloth* to make clothes, too. They made ever'thing about two sizes too big, and when you washed 'em, they drawed up enough to jist about fit.

Another thing we said was feed or shorts *"sacks,"* and flour or sugar *"pokes."* A bag was what we called a mean ol' woman, or else called 'er an ol' bat, witch, or a huzzy, one.

Except for overhalls and overhall pants, or britches, most of our clothes was homemade out of cotton cloth from sev'ral differ'nt sources. One of these was shorts sacks. Shorts is hog feed made from ground whole wheat, I think. It tasted somewhat like graham flour. The shorts was bought in hunderd pound sacks, which was the color and texture of natural muslin, and probably was. It had red letters and some kind of picture stamped on it. They soaked and washed the sacks sev'al times to get the red out and draw 'em up. Sometimes the red didn't all come out, or faded on the rest of the sack, and made it pink. That's what our sheets, pillerslips, towels, wash rags, and quilt linin's was made out of. Some hippin's was made out of shorts sacks or flour pokes.

Cow feed was bought in hunderd pound sacks, too. It was fairly coarse-wove cloth, but soft, and was used to make the *boyses'* shirts and *girlses'* dresses. It usually come in *flairdy* prints. I guess they was a little over a yard in one. They tried to get another sack like one they already had, to get enough cloth to make a dress for one of the girls or Mom. When Dad got back fum town, they coutn't wait to see what kind of sack he'd bought the feed in. Then they decided which one would get the dress. If she ditn't git matchin' sacks, Mom made the top of a dress out of one print, stripe or solid color, and the skirt out of another'n.

I never got hand-me-downs from my sisters. Me being the fourth and youngest girl, with a brother stuck in there betwixt us, their clothes was long gone before they ever got to me. My older sisters had married by the time I was much size, so I got a dress made out of bought cloth ever oncet in a while.

I remember one dress Mom made me out of cloth she got off of the *store truck* (rolling store). It was bright yaller with *little bitty* red and white flairs and green leaves printed on it, and was a little thicker than flour sacks was. She made a curved yoke on the front of it. I thought it was s'purty.

Back then, they had a graduation ceremony when you graduated from the eighth grade into high school. The girls all wore white dresses and the boys wore white shirts. It surprised *the dickens* out of me when Mom ordered some white shantung fabric from the Sears & Roebuck catalog to make me a white dress. She never told me, but she must have been right proud that I'd made it that far in school, for her to do that. That was a big milestone for me. Four more years of school! Now, if I could dist hold out that long, I could graduate and maybe make sump'm out a myself. I coutn't hardly wait.

Mom was so pa'ticular with her sewin' machine that she woutn't let me touch it, afeard I'd tear it up. And I prob'ly would of. She done her sewin' on her old Brunswick foot treadle sewin' machine. She ditn't buy patterns; just cut pieces out and sewed 'em together. She used buttons that was saved off of ever'thang that was wore out. She made the buttonholes *with her faingers* (by hand).

I learnt how to sew in the ninth grade in Home Ec class. Miss Whitaker taught us how to use a 'lectric sewin' machine. We hemmed a haincher, made a apern and a dress. I thought that was great, but that 'lectric iron was the grandest thing I'd ever seen *in all my borned days*. It was light as a feather *to the side of* them old cast iron ones at home. I was *dumbstruck* that it just kep' a-stayin' hot on the bottom, but the handle stayed cool. And it was so slick and shiny—no worryin' 'bout gittin' soot on your clothes!

Mom kept her some *aperns* (aprons) made up. All women wore aperns, and kep' a stack a cleanuns. They was so proud of a purty apern, and was allus a-tradin apern patterns. When a woman seen comp'ny a-comin', she run and grabbed a clean apern and put it on. They was made either with a bib or without, but they all had two big pockets. Mom ditn't dip snuff, but the women that did kept 'em a haincher, a little tin snuffbox, and a birch toothbrush in their apern pocket. The kind of aperns Mammy wore covered up her whole dress front and dresstail, too. They was what we'd call a pinafore today.

Now, aperns was the handiest things in the world. You could pull up your apern tail, double it up and use it to pick up a hot pan, gether it up at the corners to carry *a settin' of eggs*, a mess a green beans or poke sallet, wipe a littlun's nose, and do all kinds a stuff like that. They could throw one over their head to keep it dry when a rain blowed up quick.

They bought flour in twenty-five pound pokes. Sometimes they was white, or was differ'nt kinds of print, but flour poke cloth was the very nicest kind. It was smoother and finer wove than feed sacks. Mom made our *petticoats* (slips) and *bloomers* (underpants) out of white flour pokes Unless you was a little girl, the flour pokes wutn't long enough to make the front or back in one piece…She'd cut one front piece and one back piece with a shaller "U" in the middle for the petticoat neckline, and cut armholes in from the sides. Then she made the bottom and sewed it to the top. One time, she never got the printin' washed out of one flour sack, and made her a petticoat that had "Kansas Best"™ wrote right acrost her hin'end. She jist laughed about it.

Us gals slept in our *petticoat tail* and bloomers. In the winter, we had outin' (flannel) petticoats and bloomers made out a storebought cloth. The petticoat neck was cut so high that we barely could skin it on over our head, and it usually showed above the front neckline of our dress, kind of like a dickey. I used to be so ashamed of that blamed petticoat a-stickin' up there and showin' under my dress that I could dist a-died. I'd try to pull it down, but they wutn't no use a-tryin'…

At school, I ditn't hardly know what to think when I seen other girlses' purty white or pink slips with little narr' straps, and lace on the top and bottom of 'em, and seen their rayon panties with shiny stripes wove in 'em, when they set down to pee. I never even knowed you could buy sich purty things as that.

Boys never wore no underwear atall in the summer. They wore drop-seated union suits in the winter time and jist shucked off their britches and slep' in 'em. If they ditn't have none, they had to sleep with their hin'end necked and dist their shirt tail over it. Mom never let 'em sleep in their dirty britches, a-dirtyin' up the bed. Bud told me that when the weather was real cold, him and Sweetie and Lewis wore two pair of overhalls and shirts of a day to keep warm.

I remember them bloomers. They was like long wide legged panties that come down to your knees. The legs had elastic, or inner tube rubber, one, in the hem of 'em, and when they was pushed up a inch or so above the knee like they was s'posed to be wore, would sort of b'loon out. I usually played with the boys, and it was aggervatin' as the dickens to try to crawl around on the ground a-playin marble or to climb trees with them bloomer legs a-pullin' down over my knees and gittin' in the way. They shore did git grungy on me.

Two of my cousins, *Dephinea* (Daphne) and *Greechen* (Gretchen) had some red bloomers, and you could see them bloomer legs a-peepin' ou'fen'under their dress. I thought them red bloomers was s'purty, the way they bloused out above their knee like that. Made me think of a purty *red leggern* (leghorn) chicken, where it's leg is so fluffed up with red feathers, an'en it tapers off all of a sudden onto the skinny part of their lower leg.

They was allus *all dolled up* real nice. Their dresses was gathered full enough to stand a way out when they was starched and ironed, and had real wide sashes tied in a big ol' purty bow, all fluffed up at their back. Their mammy made their clothes too. Of course, the differ'nce was that my uncle had a good job, and money to buy cloth with. An'en, too they dist had two gals and a boy, and she had more time to sew and iron them purty dresses than Mom did. She ditn't have no babies or little littluns to have to tend to.

Mom never wasted no cloth a-makin' full skirts and wide sashes; dist barely enough gethers so you had room enough to walk around in a dress and set down in without it a-pullin' so tight around your hin'end that it busted loose at the seams. They was more like dist puckered than gethered, and she made the belts about a inch wide and dist barely long enough to tie 'em. Them purty sashes woutn't a-lasted me half a day, nohow. Out a-runnin' and playin', somebody'd grab you by the belt to ketch you and pull it right out by the roots, so I jist let mine go untied most a the time. Thataway, hit'd jist pull right through their hand if they grabbed it…

The only *ready made dress* I remember havin' til I was in high school was a dress my brother Lewis bought me when I was about nine, to wear when he took me to Sunday School at Valleytown church. We ditn't have no coat hangers back then, but I remember that that dress was on a hanger, and was hung up on a nail over the bed. I just stood and looked at it—and looked at it at night when I went to bed, til it got too dark to see it. I can still see it in my mind, and never have had a dress since then that I thought was any purtier. It was short sleeved, with a solid colored, soft heather green top, and had a green plaid collar, cuffs and skirt. But then, when I wore it, there'd be that blasted flour poke petticoat a-stickin' ou'fen'under my dress, and that jist *rurnt* (ruined) it all.

Til I was in the tenth grade, the only coat I remember a-havin' was a little black coat that a kind neighbor, Henry White, bought for me when I was about six. And I remember a-havin' to wear a boy's sweater that I was ashamed of. My tenth grade English teacher took me aside one day and asked me if I would like to have a coat she could no longer wear. It fit me perfectly, was a nice warm coat, and I got a lot of good wear out of it for years. She will never know what that one act of kindness meant to me. Lots of times after that, I wore that coat all day long to cover up and hide my clothes because I was so ashamed of them.

Sugar was usually bought in 25 pound pokes, except when Dad bought hunderd pound sacks to take to his still. They was fine wove cloth. Salt come in cloth pokes, and they was washed and saved, too. Dad and the boys carried their dinner in them *littler* pokes, and tied a knot in the top to carry it by—or put it in a lard bucket, one.

My aunt Cullie rolled her own cig'rets (*sea-grets*) and used Country Gentleman™ smokin' t'backer. It come in little thin muslin *'backer pokes* with a yaller drawstring. They was ravelled apart and saved for quilt scraps. A-body got a purty good little piece a string out a one, too. I thought they was dandy little pokes to keep stuff in, and she give me one of 'em a time or two.

She'd let me roll a cig'ret and smoke it, too—if they wutn't nobody around but me and her. But I never could roll one like she did. She'd hold the cig'ret paper betwixt her left thumb and middle fainger, with her index fainger a-layin' down on top to make a groove, tap just the right amount a 'backer out of the poke, jerk that drawstrang shet with her teeth, roll the cig'ret with one hand, give it a quick lick, twist the ends, give the match a rake with her thumbnail, light 'er up, and she was in business. She'd have one rolled and lit quicker'n anybody else could take a pack of *tailor-mades* out a their pocket and shake one out.

She done lots a inter-estin' things. She eb'm helped Uncle Jess make likker. I'd a-shore liked to of gone and helped 'em. Now, we'd a had some fun, fer I shore liked that Cullie and Jess.

Sometimes Bud smoked that kind of t'backer, 'cause it was cheaper, but he liked Prince Albert™ in a can the best. He carried a book of OCB™ cig'ret papers, and rolled his own too. If he run out a papers, he tore little squares off of a brown paper poke and used that to roll his cig'rets with. Ever' oncet in awhile, somebody come along that had a pack of tailor made cig'rets, usually Lucky Strike or Camels, and it was considered good manners to offer one to whatever other man was there. Bud'd take one, but said them old tailor mades wudn't near as good as Prince Albert™ was. Men said you might dist as well quit as to smoke them ol' Kools™ (menthols). That's the kind boys bought when they first started in a-smokin'. They wutn't as strong.

I think I was born a-likin' cig'rets. If one of the boys laid down their cig'ret papers, I'd slip out two or three at a time so they wouldn't know I'd got nary'n. Then I'd foller Bud, Sweetie or Lewis around, a-waitin' for one of 'em to throw down their *duck* (cigarette butt) so I could get it. I'd jump on one *like a hen on a June bug.* You jist about had to have tweezers to hold it after Bud got done with his'n, it was so short. If they was too short to smoke, I picked 'em up, put out the fire, and saved up ducks til I got enough 'backer to put in a cig'ret paper and roll one. Now, you talk about strong! Hit made my head spin *like a fairrus (ferris) wheel.*

Sometimes I went out and picked me some rabbit t'backer and mixed it with 'backer out of a duck or two to make it taste more like a real cig'ret. One time me and Lawerence was out behind the house a-smokin' rabbit t'backer cig'rets, a-usin' little squares tore off of a brown paper poke fer papers. I must not a-got mine licked and stuck down good, for when I lit it, the paper flared up and burnt a big ol' blister at the corner of my lower lip. I've still a scar from that. It must a got infected, for hit like to a-never healed up.

You'd a-thought I'd learnt my lesson and not a-smoked no more cig'rets—but I never. I jist ditn't use stiff brown paper no more to roll one.

STRAW TICKS AND CHINCHES

What we call a living room now was called the "front room" back then. Ever'body I knowed allus had a bed set up in the front room where the man and his wife slep'. They could keep a eye on the fireplace, and the baby slep' with them and was kep' warm. At our house, they was a dannymite box a-settin' by the bed to use for a table to set the lamp on, so a-body could set on the side of the bed and blow out the lamp, or set up and light it without fum'lin' around in the dark.

The only other thangs in the room was a straight back chair for Dad, Mom's rockin' chair, two or three dannymite boxes for the bigger kids to set on, and a couple a *nail kaigs* (kegs). When comp'ny come, they brung some more chairs, nail kaigs or dannymite boxes out of the kitchen. The littl'uns set in the floor.

One time Mom cut some used inner tubes into strips about a inch wide and wove new bottoms in some straight back chairs. Everybody bragged on them soft chair bottoms when they set down.

I was at some old folkses' house down the creek one time, and they had a *debm'port* in their front room. I hatn't never seen one before. It was upholsteried in a tapestry-like wove stuff. She had the purtiest snow white *cro-she-a-ted* (crocheted) piece across the back of it, and some littler'uns over the arms. Hit was too purty to set on. But it seemed kindly *quare* (queer) to me that they never had no bed in their front room.

When a new baby come, the old baby was rooted out and put in the "back room" to sleep with the other youngens. We had two beds set up in the back room. They was so many of us that two or three of the older youngens slept at the head of the bed and the littluns slept with their heads at the foot, their legs all in a row in the middle. It was a familiar sound to hear a whispered voice tellin' somebody to "get your cold feet offa my back," or "quit hawgin' the kivver." Sometimes somebody hogged the bed, too, and the one on the edge got rooted out into the floor along in the night. Now, that wutn't no fun—dist layin' there

77

a-sleepin' away, and the next thang you knowed, a-hittin' the cold floor, ke-thump.

If one of the biguns pulled the kivver up over their head, it was pulled down off a you. It was *pyore* (pure) misery to try to sleep with somebody that kep' a-jerkin' the kivver off of you, dist about the time you got warm enough to go to sleep. Lawerence thought it was so funny to do that. It'd make me so mad, I'd dist *kick the puddin' out of him*. An'en sometimes somebody'd grab aholt of my ankle and tickle my foot. Lord, I hated that! Even now I can't relax and go to sleep unless my feet are covered up and the sheet's tucked in.

The bedsprangs was made out of rows of heavy wire all *quiled up* (coils) and fastened together on the edges where they *j'ined* one another, and the *dadjim* thangs *screaked* ever time you moved. If you kicked at the smart-aleck that was a-devilin' you, or eb'm turnt over, them *dadblamed* bedsprangs'd *screak like a sled load a rusty hainges*. We knowed not to make no *racket*, or Mom'd come in there and give us all a whuppin', no matter whichun started it.

Nowadays, people say they "spend the night" at someone's home. We called it *"stayin' all night."* If somebody *stayed all night*, some of us youngens had to sleep on a *pallet* on the floor.

One thing about my mother—she was a *stickler* about a clean bed! I never in my life went to bed in a dirty bed. The sheets might be made out a feed sacks, but they was clean. Them beds was *made up* the first thing in the mornin' and we wutn't allowed to go back and even set down on the side of one, much less lay on it. No body laid down on that bed in daylight unless they was really, I mean not able t'set up, *bad-off* sick. You kept strickly away from that bed—don't tetch it *in no shape, form or fashion*, not eb'm to lay nothin' down on it.

We wutn't never allowed to sleep late of a mornin'. When I was a little girl, I remember hearin' women a-talkin' about some other woman they thought was lazy and a sorry housekeeper. One comment I heard was, "Why, I's at their house after nine o'clock t'other day, and she ditn't eb'm have her beds made up." And it was *a cryin' shame* if somebody *laid in the bed* til eight o'clock in the mornin'. It was *pyore laz'ness* if they was still *a-wallerin' in th' bed* apast daylight.

In the summertime we went barefooted, and had to wash our feet ever' night right before goin' to bed. We was *savin'* with soap, and we either set on the branch bank to wash 'em, or washed 'em in a washpan usin' a dry okry pod to scrub 'em. It made a great scrubber and even felt slippery like soap. Dad loved okry and growed big ol' long pods. The ones that got too dry and tough was used for foot scrubbers. *I done'n' tow-je* (already told ye) we never wasted nothin'.

The *matterses* (mattresses) was heavy *tickin'* stuffed with straw, and was called *straw ticks*. Ones stuffed with feathers was called *feather ticks,* but we never had nary one of them. Straw ticks wutn't too bad when the straw was fairly frash, but after a while, it got all broke up and matted down, and them biggest sharp stems would work out through the tickin' and *job* (stick) you good.

When the straw tick got wore out, Mom ordered some new tickin' out a the Sears and Roebuck™ catalog. Back then, nobody on the creek had a checkin' account at the bank. She'd make out her order and figger up the postage and all, an'en put it with the money in the unsealed *en-velop*, addin' in enough to buy a money order and stamp. After the mailman picked up the mail, he got a money order at the post office, put it in with the order, sealed it up and mailed it. If they was any change, he left it and the receipt in the mailbox the next time he stopped. A stamp costed three cents and a postcard was a penny.

The tickin' was heavy stuff, so the straw wouldn't work through it easy, and was blue and white striped. Then after she emptied it, she used the good parts of the old straw tick to make piller ticks.

Them strawticks was cold in the winter, and seems like you could dist feel the cold air a-suckin' right up through the cracks in the floor inunder the bed. We needed to put a quilt inunder the straw tick and 'nunder the bottom sheet in the winter time to help us keep warm, *an'at* kep' the straw from stickin' us, too. Some folks used corn shucks to stuff their mattresses, but we fed all of our'n to the livestock.

The discomfort of the straw a-workin up through the mattress wutn't nuthin' to the side of them devilish chinches (bedbugs), though. When they got to gittin' *so* bad, we'd haf to try to do sump'm about it. No matter how hard my poor ol' mother tried, or what she done to *git shed of* them, them *daggonded* thangs would allus come back to *plague* us. The straw ticks and pillers was took outside and sunned, turnt over and sunned some more, and ever piece a th' beddin' washed and b'iled in the wash pot. Then them ol' iron *bed-stids* (bedsteads, or frames) was took apart, and them and the sprangs was toted outside for a *genu-wine* scrubbin', and lamp oil was rubbed on th' bed legs so them chinches woutn't climb up 'em.

While ever'thang was out a the room, she stripped off all the old newspapers and scrubbed down the walls with hot soapy Red Devil™ lye water—or whatever she thought might kill chinches. She *scoured out* the cracks, where them thangs'd be packed up solid, got up on a chair and as fur up as she could reach, poured b'ilin' water out a th' kittle into th' cracks. Then poured soapy lye water on th' floor and scrubbed it with th' broom. Usin' flour paste, she re-papered th' walls with frash newspapers. We picked pennyrile (penny royal) and put it in and under the beds as a repellent. I loved that frash, minty smell.

It'd be better a few nights, but sooner ot later, they was back in full force—mean as ever, and we'd git up in the mornin' dist plumb speckledy with bite marks. Them *cuss-ed* pestes was the size of a small tick, and only come out in the dark. They'd be all over you, but the instant any light hit 'em, they *hit bush river* (vanished).

I heard a man tell about still a-havin' scars on his legs from where he got burnt when he was dist a little feller. He said his mammy got up and lit the kerosene lantern one night, and took it to his bed to try to catch them dang chinches a-bitin' him. The lantern turnt over agin' his leg, and burnt great big ol' places on it. Sixty year later, he still had them scars.

I've not seen nor hyeard tell of no chinches since I was a youngun. Dist lately, I learnt that them little devils lays their eggs on STRAW! Some time in the early 1940's, I think, a place opened up in town where you could go and make your own mattresses—stuffed with cotton and *turfed* (tufted). We got some a them, and I guess that explains why we never seen no more chinches.

MAKIN' A QUILT

All the feed and flour sacks, and sugar and salt pokes was chainstitched acrost the top with strong, heavy cotton thread which we unravelled and wound it into a ball to save. Quilt tops was *pieced* (sewn together) out of saved-up scraps, and shorts sacks was sewed together to make the linin'. They was hand-quilted with thread saved from the sacks and pokes.

Back then, ever' house had quiltin' frames. They was made out of four long narr' slats of wood with holes bored ever few inches of *lainth* (length). Two of 'em was for the sides, and two of 'em was about a foot shorter—for the top and bottom. They was used to stretch the quilt out on and hold it together while it was a-bein' quilted. First, you fastened four long narr' strips of cloth to the ceilin' or rafters, one, and left 'em a-hangin' down far enough apart to be about where the corners of a quilt would be. Then the ends of the frame was lapped over one another and fastened with a nail through the holes at the corners, and the ends of the long strips tied around the corners to hang it up. To say it simple, you had a suspended rectangle of wood slats.

When the frame was put together and hung up, the quilt linin' was laid out on it, and the edges sewed to it all the way around. The tan cotton quilt battin' come in a good size roll, and was unrolled on top of the linin'. After smoothin' this out, the quilt top was spread over the battin', makin' sure all the adges was eb'm. The frame was took loose one end at a time, and the top and bottom edges was tucked in and rolled inunder, torge the center. When it was rolled up to whatever size you wanted to work on, the frames was fastened in place with the nails. Then you was ready to start quiltin' on it.

The quiltin' was started at the middle of the quilt so the layers would shift to the outside edges and the quilt would lay smooth and flat. Hit could be quilted in any pattern you wanted—straight lines, blocks, etc., but Mom allus quilted her'n in a pattern she called a fan. She took a piece of string with a loop in the end to hold a piece of chalk, helt the string down with her finger on the edge where she wanted to start and swung the chalk around to draw a small quarter circle arc. Then she let the string out about a inch and a half and made another arc, and so on. She repeated this til she made ever how many she wanted. When these was quilted all acrost the middle of the quilt, the frame corners was took loose and the quilted part rolled up, and a unquilted part unrolled, ready to work on.

When she got ready to quit for that time, she wound the cloth strips around the frames at the corners to take up slack til the quilt was up in the air and out of the way. They wutn't room enough to leave it a-hangin' down and still walk around it in the room. I remember a-goin' inunder the quilt to git to the kitchen.

The quiltin' was done in the front room where it was warm. The girls, and sometimes the boys helped Mom quilt, but it had to be to her satisfaction. I learnt to quilt when I got old enough, and I do a good job, but my stitches is differ'nt from her'n. Her quilts is so soft and fluffy, I can feel one in the dark and tell if she quilted it.

I keep a-sayin'—at our house, nothin' got wasted or throwed away. We found a use for ever'thing. 'Stid a throwin' 'em away, Mom made what she called "overhall" quilts out of the good parts of old overhalls and britches, and other heavy scraps she put up and saved. She sewed 'em together on the sewin' machine in no pa'ticlar design, dist sewed 'em together any whichaway. Sometimes she used a old blanket 'stid of battin', and quilted 'em on the machine because they was too stiff and boardy to hand quilt. They might be heavy and stiff, but they was warm. We put them on top of the other quilts and they helt the kivver down on you good. They made real good windbreakers when that cold wind come a-whisslin' in through the cracks, maybe mixed in with little blue snow.

GRANNIES AND SEX EDUCATION

Talkin' about sugar and flour and salt pokes made me remember what women called *"granny rags."* They wudn't no sich a thing as tampons, then. And up on the creek, women never had no Kotex™ or sanitary belts, neither. Now, they was sold at the drugstore, all right, but they never had the money to buy none. And lots of 'em would a-been too bashful to go the drugstore and ast for 'em, or even to ast somebody else to git 'em for 'em, even if they'd a-had the money. A man'd a-died before he'd be seen a-carryin' a box of Kotex. Back then, things was up on shelfs back behind the counter. You never went in any store and picked up stuff—you stood at the counter til the clerk come and asted you what you wanted. And at the drugstore, you had to tell the druggist what you wanted, and he got it for you.

When a woman or girl had her menstrual period, they said, "*I've got my grannies on,*" or "*I'm havin' my granny,*" one. Mom had her own rules for cleanness and naistness, and that was just exactly what she meant for ever' body to foller. Some of the littler pokes, or pieces of flour sacks was specifically set aside for granny rags, and ever'body took care of their own. The cleanuns was doubled up and hid down in the bottom of the clothes pack, and one was got out and used when needed. When one got used, it got washed, and was kept separate from any other clothes, and she better not find nary'n throwed away, neither, a-wastin' cloth like that.

They ditn't have no elastic for sanitary belts, neither. Granny rags was held in place by tyin' a strip of cloth around the waist, looping a short piece over it in the front and back, and the granny rag was pinned to the short ends with a latch pin. They had to fit pretty clost or they woutn't be of no use, but the strips didn't have no "give" to 'em and sometimes pulled purty tight when a woman bent over. Now, if you wanted to see somebody *take a fit*, just let one of them big latch pins come unlatched and *job* 'er good. Because of the strain put on it, hit wutn't hard atall for the business end to bend and slip out of the head of the latch pin.

All this business with the granny rags was kept *strickly* private. Anything concerning the physiological functions of women or sex was whispered about as if it were shameful. When I was a little girl, if Mom would be talkin' to another woman in a hushed voice or whisper, and saw me comin', she'd glance in my direction and give a slight sideways nod to the other person, and they'd stop talkin'. She'd tell me, "Git outta here, this ain't none a your business." I felt like I'd done something wrong, and didn't know what, but I knowed to *make myself scarce*.

I was dumb as a rock when it come to sex. What I learnt, I learnt mostly from other girls at school, and even they didn't talk about it openly. Sayin' *"praignet"* (pregnant) was about worser'n cussin'. They called it *"expectin',"* or *"knocked up."* I overheard conversations at times which left more questions than answers. If I got to be good friends with another girl, we'd sneak around and talk about things, but most of the time she didn't know no more'n I did.

I was still fairly igner't when I started having my period, and was ashamed for Mom to find out. I felt guilty and dirty, somehow. She didn't find out for several months, then one day she told me she'd seen a spot of blood on my bloomers in the washin'. I was mortified! Then she said I'd better not be *"a-foolin' around"* with an ol' boy, or I'd get knocked up. Everybody knowed you was a whore if you "done *that*."

I didn't really know what foolin' around, or *messin' around* with boys meant, but I was careful not to have any close contact with one. Gettin' knocked up was one thing for certain that I didn't want to happen to me. When I was just a little girl, a few times I remember some woman in a house "havin' a baby." I don't remember who it was, but remember the screams, and it scared me to death. And I saw all them bloody sheets in a tub out at the branch a-bein' washed after the baby was borned, too. The whole branch looked like blood a-runnin'. The sight of all that blood made me *as sick as a dog*, and scared me even worse. I ditn't want nothin' atall to do with havin' no baby.

Back then, most babies was born at home with a midwife, or *"granny doctor,"* in attendance, but a Doc Herbert from town come to our house and delivered me and my two younger brothers. When a woman "went to havin' pains," somebody went to get the granny doctor, Mrs. Shields, and she come and stayed til after the baby was born. One time she come to Cullie's and they run me and some of her younguns out of the yard and made us go over in "the pines" to play. They said we ditn't have no business around the house.

One of the biggest fits I ever saw Mom take was one time when I was about thirteen. We lived on up the creek from where I was born, at our new house, and the toilet was down at the creek bank below the house. She had her wash place all set up down there at the side of the toilet, so she could dip her wash water up out of the creek.

I was settin' out on the end of the front porch one day, a-strangin' beans or sump'm, and she was down there a-doin' the washin'. All of a sudden, here she come, a-tearin' up the trail to the house, and stomped on up the porch steps and got right in my face a-shakin' her fistes. Her face was as red as fire, and she busted out to cryin' and started in on me, a-hollerin' something about how she thought she'd raised me better'n that, and was *mad as an ol' settin' hen.* "You nee'n't to set there and look innocent, like you don't know what I'm a-talkin' about. I know better. You know what I'm a-talkin' about."

Come to find out, after berating me awhile, and threatenin' to beat the livin' tar out of me several times, she finally got around to telling me she'd found a used rubber (condom) in the creek. She accused me of foolin' around with a boy somewhere on up the road and throwing the rubber in the creek. I had no idea at the time how they were even used. I guess I was twelve years old before I even knew what they were. When I saw discarded condoms on the school ground sometimes, I thought they were busted balloons til somebody at school told me they were not balloons, and not to pick one up or play with it. "They're nasty." I got the general idea, but that was all.

We weren't allowed to say a word in our defense, as they thought that was *sassin'* our parents, or *talkin' back.* They told us what was what, the way they saw it, and wouldn't listen to any version we had. I couldn't say much, but tried to tell her I hadn't been doing anything like that. I felt as guilty as if I had, though. I still don't know if she believed me. I couldn't then, and don't understand now, how she could even think that about me. I slept right where they could see me, and never went nowhere at night. I was so hurt. And after that, every time I saw that boy, I just cringed with shame.

A few times, a girl would suddenly quit school, and I'd hear that she had to quit because she was going to have a baby. That was the biggest disgrace a girl could have. I sure didn't want that to happen to me. I knew Dad would literally kill me. I'd heard some of the things Dad and Mom said to my older sisters, then to me. They made it clear that if one of us got knocked up, you're on your own; they wutn't a-raisin' no bastards. The same was true when you got married. They said, "*You made your bed, and now you can lay in it.* Don't look to me for nothin'." And, "You *nee'nt* to brang no little snotty-nosed youngens around here for me to feed." When my sisters married and left home, Mom and Dad never went to see them, and didn't make them welcome if they came back to visit, so I didn't see them much after they left home, or my brothers, either.

Back then, here in the mountains, girls didn't have much value. All they were fit for was to *wait on a man*, have youngens and raise 'em. It was a waste of time for them to go to school, for they "don't need no education for what they'll be a-doin'." The man was the boss, and she was expected to do what he told her without asking any questions. I heard men laugh and say, *"The only way for a man to git along with a woman is to keep her barefooted and pragnet."*

Since there was no method of birth control and girls married young, a baby usually came along every ten months to three years, and they had big families. I know one woman who had twelve younguns, and she didn't stop giving milk from the time the first one was born til she weaned the last one. A man up the road had eighteen *childern*. He had a bunch from his first wife, then she died, and he remarried and had a bunch by his second wife.

Mom's sister, Lizzie, two years older than her, married when she was fifteen, had eight babies, and died at the age of thirty-two. I saw her nearly grown son crying about his mother, saying she'd starved to death. When I asked Mom about it, she said Lizzie died of "playgree" (pellagra, a disease caused by a lack of B vitamins in the diet). *It's a thousand wonders* she lived that long, even if she'd had a good diet.

Dad said a girl *"wudn't worth a plug nickel"* to him. He went to the trouble of raisin' her and then she'd run off to wait on some other man, and wudn't no benefit to him. Strangely, Mom also treated the boys better than she did us girls. I always felt inferior, just because I was a girl.

Early on, I learned about discrimination against girls and women. I had to saw and chop wood, and work like a boy at whatever they did, but they didn't have to do things called *"women's work."* They didn't do nothin' in the house—like cleanin' up the house, make up their bed, wash, iron, take care of youngens, or cook. They went to the table and eat their supper, then *trotted off like a big yard dog* while us girls had to clean up the kitchen, wash the dishes, sweep, and carry in water before it got dark.

They let Lawerence go wherever he wanted to go, but I wasn't allowed to go off of the place. They didn't even ask him where he was going, or where he'd been. By the time he was fourteen, he was *goin' a-courtin'* them gals over at Kyle, and *laid out* all night. And guess who ironed his shirt and britches for him when he went.

Around here, there wasn't any restaurants or hotels for girls or women to get a waitress or cleaning job. The only jobs a girl could get was to do people's washin' or some other menial one-day-at-a-time job. It was common for well-off folks to want a girl to stay with them to help out around the house, or take care of their youngens or an elderly parent. Room and board was considered part of their pay, and they'd get maybe five dollars a week. She couldn't make enough to keep her own self up, much less save enough to go off to school.

Even if a girl's people was well off enough to send her to school, about the only thing she could do was either be a teacher or a nurse. Either way, you had to leave here. There was just one little hospital at Murphy in the area, and most of the nursing was done by the Catholic Sisters, but they didn't teach nursing. You had to have tuition money and go off somewhere to college to be a teacher.

I feel as if I owe a debt of gratitude to my older sisters. I saw what happened to them, and made up my mind at an early age, that with God's help, somehow, I was going to do something with my life besides get married at fifteen. Each of them had the intelligence to become anything they might have chosen to be, but they got married at a young age just to escape from the abuse at home. Then they started having babies, one after the other. They had to work so hard to raise their families on a very limited income. Once you have the babies, where can you go or what else can you do?

There's no more important or rewarding work a woman can do than be a good homemaker and mother, and they were certainly that. But it shouldn't be because they had no other choice.

I had very little respect for men, and wanted no part of men or getting married. I figured that getting an education was my only way out, and every day I asked God to help me endure what I had to endure, and find a way to get the education I needed.

DANCES AND DUMPLIN'S

Dad used to do all kind of *dainces* . He could tap daince, do the Charleston, buck daince, and daince all kind of jigs. He had a pair of shoes with toe and heel taps that he dainced in. I've watched Irish dancers on TV before, and several times vaguely wondered why the Irish jigs seemed so familiar to me. Then I saw a program called "Riverdance"© on PBS a few years back, and suddenly realized they were doing the very same dances I'd seen Dad do all those years ago. I was dumbfounded!

Then I remembered something else. When I studied early American History in school, and read about people coming to America from other countries, I became curious about my ancestors and asked Dad about it. He said they were Dutch and Irish, and maybe some Scotch. I wish I'd asked him more.

Sometimes, when we had comp'ny, he made me dance for 'em, jist like he'd done with the older kids. I *ditn't have no more idy* (idea) *than a goose* what I's a-doin', just knowed I better dance if he said dance, so I done like I'd seen him and the other'ns do. Us kids wutn't asked if we wanted to do sump'm, we was told to do it, and knowed we better do as we was told.

Lots of times, on Saturday night, they had square dances at our house. They took down the bed in the front room and stacked the straw ticks and kivvers up on top of each other on a bed in the back room, so they'd have room to dance. They'd be a whole house full of people, and of course the whiskey was enjoyed by most, if not all. Us youngens just tried to stay out of sight and out of the way. Mom and Dad believed that childern ort not to be seen *or* heard.

They played their dance music on a *talkin' machine*, or hand cranked "*graphone*," they called it, that played them big ol' heavy 78 rpm records. It stumped me, how music come out of sump'm like a flattened-out plate with grooves in it. I thought the *pitchure* of that little dog on there was the sweetest thang—dist a-settin' there with his little spotted head cocked over to one side, a-listenin' to his master's voice. I'd shore like to a-had that dog.

Somebody had to crank the Victrolie (Victrola©) back up when the music commenced to slowin' down and soundin' funny. One a t'other of the grown folks or big younguns cranked it, and sometimes had to put in a new needle. I liked t'watch them records spin around, and loved that music. I'd a-liked to a-cranked it, too, but was afeared I might tear it up, an'en I'd be in big trouble. I'd been told not to tetch it. If ye tetched the playin' arm with the needle in it, the needle would take off sideways on them grooves and scratch the record up. Then ever time it was played, you could hear the clickin' racket when it hit the scratched place.

If a record got broke, us youngens would break off a little piece and scrape a corner of it crossways on the grooves on a bigger piece. Hit'd make a racket like a turkey call. Real loud, too.

Mom liked to dance and laughed a lot when she was a-dancin'. They drunk and danced and *hoorawed* and hollered, and *tore up Jack* 'til a way up in the mornin'. You could feel that whole floor a-bouncin'. Us little'uns would get sleepy and want to go to bed, but it was too high for us to get up there on it. I remember a-gittin' some grown person or other to set me up on top of the stacked-up beds so I could lay down and go to sleep. When somebody got a little too drunk, they'd come in and pile up on the other bed and commence snorin'.

Mom and Dad got stuff ready for their "midnight supper." They allus kilt some chickens, either our'n or some they'd *cabbaged* (stoled) sumerce. I remember men a-laughin' while they was pickin' off the feathers and cleanin' 'em, and tellin' about who they'd *swiped* (stoled) a chicken off of and how they'd done it. They cooked 'em in a big black iron pot a-hangin' in the fireplace, an'en Mom made dumplin's on 'em. Ever'body bragged on her dumplin's.

Other people brung stuff t'eat, too. They allus had pickles, raw turnips and thangs for chasers. That chicken shore smelt good, but we knowed to stay out a sight and leave stuff alone. Youngens had to wait til grown people and comp'ny got done eatin' before they got to eat. When they had a dance, we jist eat whatever we could slip and snatch and grab here and yander without nobody a-ketchin' us at it. But we hardly ever got any chicken, hit a-bein' in the pot 'n all, til they'd done'n already eat. And we was asleep long before they got done eatin'.

We had a big old batt'ry radio that set on the floor, and about everbody in the settle-ment come to listen to it a-Saturdy night when they ditn' have a dance. They ditn't listen to it much through the week in order to save the batt'ry so they could listen to the Grand Ol' Opry on Saturdy night. I liked to hear Minnie Pearl, Dave Macon and them other'ns. Sometimes Dad and them listened to the "prize fights," WCKY Cincinnatti, Ohio, or a station in Del Rio, Texas.

Sometimes the sound faded in and out, and they'd be a whisslin' noise in th' background. You could tell by the static when it was a-stormin' somewhere in betwixt here and where it was a-comin' in from. A ground wire in the back of the radio was run out the wender to a metal ground post drove up in the ground in the chimbly corner. When the whistlin' got too bad, or the sound faded out, Dad had one of us to go get some water and take around there to pour on the ground post. Or, sometimes one of the boys peed on it. In dist a minute, the whisslin' stopped, and the sound come in loud and cler.

Nobody but Dad or Mom was allowed to tetch that radio. We wudn't allowed to tetch nothin', much. When they put sump'm down, we knowed not to bother it. One time, when I was about five year old, somebody left a box of 22 shells a-layin' on the dannymite box that set by the front room bed. I wudn't more'n six inches taller'n the box, because I can remember seein' that box a shells a-settin' there right in my face, and wondering what it was. It was open and I could see the ends of the *carterges* a-shinin' like gold.

Ever'body was in the kitchen and they wutn't nobody around, so I eased it up to look at it. It was heavier than I expected, and it slipped right out of my hand. Ever bless-ed one a them shells spilt out. Hit was a full box and I coutn't get 'em put back in like they was; I was scared so bad my hands was dist a-shakin'. Mom caught me a-tryin' to put 'em back in.

She grabbed her hick'ry and went to thrashin' me good. I was a-pullin' back, and my hand come loose from her'n and I fell down and scooted up inunder th' bed. She got down on her knees and was a-hittin' at me up 'nunder there. I was *a-screamin' like a painter*, dist scared to death. Alma n' Thelma 'nCoonie knowed what'd happen to 'em for doin' it, but they all started in *a-cryin' and a-baggin'* Mommy not to kill me. She jumped up from there and give ever last one of 'em a whuppin'. An'en she *retch* (reached) inunder the bed, got me by the ankle, drug me out and *thrashed* me good, an'en give me another'n for crawlin' 'nunder the bed.

I learnt that she'd whup you harder for tryin' to git away from 'er than for what you'd done.

THE STORE TRUCK AND LAMP OIL

Up on Jun'lusky, we called it a *store truck*, but some people called it a rollin' store. The one that come up on the creek was made out of a old remodeled school bus. It had shelfs and a dope cooler in it instid of seats. It run on a certain day, maybe a-Wensdy or a-Thursdy, and it had to be purty bad weather if it ditn't run. People depended on it for what they needed. Back then, they wutn't but very few people had a car, and people never went to town unless they had to, like for shoes, or sump'm the store truck man ditn't have. They mostly bought the stuff they needed off of the store truck, though.

Mom usually dist bought what was necessary. When I say necessary, I mean basics. I remember her a-readin' off the same old list: flour, meal, lard, coffee, sugar, salt, bakin' sodie and lamp oil (kerosene). The store truck man carried all of these, along with other stuff on the shelfs. He had *oats*, corn flakes (which we called *Post Toasties*), puffed wheat, hand and laundry soap, washin' powder, *asperns* (aspirin), BC and Stanback powders, Black Draught,™ and a few other medicines. They was also cloth on bolts, cig'rets, chawin' tobacker and snuff. Mammy used Dental Sweet snuff,™ and it come in a glass, and that's where we got our drankin' glasses from. Dad used that strong Bruton Scotch snuff.™

We got differ'nt kinds a dishes, like plates, cups and saucers, bowls and things out a oats and washin' powder boxes. An'en he had scrap bundles, which was odd pieces of cloth tied up in a bundle. Hit'd have at least three pieces a cloth in it, with anywhere from one to three yard in one of 'em. Coonie told me that Paw and Mammy used to buy one for them ever oncet in a while, and that'd dist tickle them girls to death. That meant they'd git a new dress. The bundle costed thirty five cents.

He had brooms, mops, *fly flaps* (swats), and fly paper. Fly paper was sticky paper that come rolled up in a little roll inside of a pasteboard tube about the size of a shotgun shell. When you pulled on the *led* (lid), the paper unrolled out into a real sticky strip about three foot long. Flies, gnats, waspers and thangs stuck to it if they landed on it. The led had a loop on top to hang it up by, and the pasteboard tube weighted down the strip at the bottom, so it'd hang straight. People hung 'em up, 'spacially around the kitchen, to help keep flies off a stuff. Back then, nobody but rich people in town had screenin' over their doors and wenders.

He had Flit fly spray,™ too, and a metal sprayer to spray it with. The sprayer was a cylinder about ten inches long with a handle that you worked like a bicycle pump to make it spray. They was a little round tank about the size of a snuff glass connected to it, down under the front end, where you poured the fly spray in.

Flies got real bad in the summertime, and would dist come in the house in droves, and aggervate the dickens out of you. We'd break off limbs with green leafs on 'em and wave one over the table ever little bit to keep the flies scared off while we eat. I remember a-mindin the flies off of the table while Mom finished settin' supper on it.

They'd git so bad that people had to use fly spray ever oncet in a while to get shed of 'em. They'd put a bed sheet over the table and kivver up stuff they ditn't want to git fly spray on. They'd shet up the wenders, spray ever'where good, an'en go out and shet the door and stay outside a while til it kindly settled down, so you wouldn't be a breathin' it when you went back in.

A Daisy Fly Killer™ was another thing they used to kill flies, ants, and thangs with. It was a hollow round metal disc, about half a inch thick and six inches acrost. The poison was inside. They was pitchures of daisies side-by-side all around the top adge, and one in the middle. They was a cut-out circle in the middle of ever daisy that had yaller nappy cloth pooched up in it an'at soaked up the poison stuff. It kilt flies, ants and things that got on it and sucked the stuff off. They was real purty thangs, but you had to put 'em to where youngens coutn't reach 'em, or hit'd pison them too.

We'd watch for th' store truck, and when we seen it a-comin', we'd make tracks and holler, "Mo-omm, storetruck's a-comin'!" What us youngens was inter-ested in was the candy. He had Butterfinger,™ Baby Ruth,™ Milky Way,™ Three Musketeers,™ three-colored cokernut planks, peanut planks, and dist all kinds a candy bars. Back then, they costed a nickel apiece.

We usually didn't have enough money to buy a candy bar, though, unless we'd sold some lizards. When we had money, it was a maybe a penny—hardly ever more'n three, from sellin' sprang lizards, or somebody'd give us a penny or two for hoein' corn or sump'm. Mammy give me a penny for emptyin' her spit can or washin' out her chamber sometimes. But a penny was money back then. We took care a that penny.

They was sev'al jars of "penny candy," and some of it was two or three pieces for a penny. You got more candy fer yer money when you bought penny candy.

They was stick candy, jaw breakers, Kits,™ BB Bats,™ Mary Janes,™ suckers, Bit o' Honey,™ Walnetto,™ cokernut haystacks, some little brown striped peanut butter bars, and some other'ns I can't think a the name of right now. The stick candy was striped and was differ'nt colors and flavors.

They was Juicy Fruit,™ Spearmint™ (Spyermint) and Teaberry™ chawin' gum, and Dubble Bubble bubble gum. Mom said that ol' blubber gum was nasty, and growled about us a-gittin' it. She liked Teaberry™ chawin' gum the best. Hit tasted like wild mountain birch.

What I liked better'n anything was to git one a them pinkish-arnj colored wax whistles, or flutes, that had about seb'm whistles lined up together in a bar, kindly. The end of it tapered down from one side to the other'n with short compartments on one end to long'uns on the other'n. It played differ'nt notes when you blowed it like a Franch harp. Hit was the best tastin' thang you ever put in your mouth, and it was awful hard not to eat it. You was spost to dist chew it like chewin' gum, though. It was like bein' *betwixt a rock and a hard place* to decide whuther to chaw off the littlun first, or the bigun. I'd a-like to a-kep' it to jist blow on, but it was so good I'd keep a-nibblin' a little more and a little more, til I'd git down to dist one whistle. Before I knowed it, I had it chawed up too.

Now, Mom didn't dist turn us loose to go a-clamberin' up in the store truck and start *grabbin' and snatchin'* at stuff. She got on first, and we better behaive ourself so she could talk to the man. When we did get to go in, we better keep our hands to ourself and not bother nary thang.

Ever'body was allus glad to see the storetruck come. We never seen nobody, much, and the storetruck man allus had news about other people up and down th' creek, and knowed what all was a-goin' on around the country. I remember different storetruck men. One come along when the other'n quit comin'. One a their names was a Mr. Sneed, one was Dee Kephart, and a Mr. Dockery.

He'd tell her howdy and all that stuff, an'en ast her what he could git fer her today. He done jis' like they did at Arthur Watkins' store in town. She'd tell him one thang, and he'd git it, an'en ast her what next, and she'd tell him one thang at a time, til she got ever'thing she wanted. When he got it all set out there, he'd ast her if that was all, and when she said it was, he'd pick up his tablet, lick off his pencil point and tote it all up. She give him her money and he give her back some change, then.

After she conducted her business, then we could point out what we wanted and let him git it for us. I bet us younguns got more enjoy-ment out a gittin' on the store truck with three pennies then than a youngen now would git out a goin' t'Wal-Mart with *a hunnerd* dollar bill.

He had wooden chicken coops outside acrost the back of the store truck. They was cages made out a wood *dals* (dowels) about a inch apart so you could see inside of 'em. He kept live chickens and *diddles* (baby chicks) in 'em. He'd take a live chicken or eggs as trade on what you wanted, an'en sell 'em to other people.

They was a big metal tank of kerosene oil back there, too. Our gallon oil can had a screw-off cap on the spout so the oil woutn't slosh up or spill out if it got kicked over, and a bigger led on top of the can that screwed off to fill it up. It had a bail with a wood handle on it to carry it by. Mom'd hand him the oil can and he'd pump the oil out to fill it up. I think it was a nickel a gallon then.

Ever'body had a oil can a-settin' in their kitchen. We used lamp oil (kerosene) to start a fire in the stove (Mom said "fart a star," jist a-bein' funny). They used it real sparin', a-pourin' dist a little dab on the kindlin'. If you poured much, hit'd run down in the ashes in th' firebox, anyhow. That didn't do no good; dist a-wastin' lamp oil. Paw Taylor soaked corn cobs in kerosene oil (we allus said both words, "kerosene oil" or "lamp oil"), or whittled shavin's to use for fire starters.

You could make do without kerosene oil to start a fire, but you had to have it to burn in the lamp. You've seen TV shows like The Waltons, where it's so romantic and cozy. Ever'body's scattered out all over the house a—readin', or a-knittin' and a-doin' different things by candle light or lamp light, one, with purty *Franch harp* music a-playin' in the background. Well, you might as well git that pitchure out a yer head. Hit wutn't like that atall. Fact is, you can't hardly see to do nothin'. It ain't so much fun when it comes down to livin' like that, day in and day out. We never made candles, neither. They wutn't no taller because nobody raised sheep or had beef up on the creek. And we ditn't have money to buy no candles, neither. Or flashlight batt'ries. And the only music you was liable to hear, was somebody a-squallin' out when they run into sump'm and *barked* their shin, or *stobbed* their toe agin' a chair or table *laig* in th'dark.

We never set up late and wasted no lamp oil. We had to do our work up before dark, so we'd have daylight to see by. Dark come early in the winter time, spacially down in the hollers. The cow had to be milked, the chickens, horse and other stuff took care of, kindlin' split up, wood brung in, and a bucket a water carried in before dark set in. The whole house got *dark as the inside of a black cat*, and we dist had one lamp. If somebody had to go to the kitchen t'do sump'm, they had to take the lamp with 'em. Anybody in that room had to set in the dark til they come back, or go in there with 'em, one. We usually ditn't light no lantern unless we had to go outdoors. And youngens ditn't pick up and carry no lamp around. We didn't mess with that lamp no way atall. One fallin' down, or droppin' the lamp and the house was burnt down.

Another thing you had to see about while you still had daylight was to see if the lamp had enough oil in it and wipe the *sut* (soot) out of the globe so it'd give good light. A piece a newspaper was good to do that with. If the flame wutn't a-burnin' straight, and was higher on one side than the other'n, hit'd cause soot to gether in a big spot in the globe. Mom'd have to take the scissors and trim off the wick. And if you left the wick rolled up too far, hit'd black the whole top a the globe. You had to watch a lamp. I've seen one of 'em with the flame a-runnin' plumb out the top a the globe, and I tell ye right now, that was scary to look at. Dangerous!

In the late '40's, Dad bought an Aladdin™ lamp. People said the light off a one a them lamps was so bright hit'd put your eyes out. Dad *thought he was dumpin' in the tall cotton* a-havin' that lamp, and was so proud of it. That lamp globe looked as long as your arm *to the side of* the rag'ler globes.

You better not blow out that kind a lamp, though, or you'd blow that mantle into fizzle dust. After it's once lit, hit's as flimsy as ashes dist barely stuck together. You haf'ta turn th' wick down to smother out th' flame. And keep a snuff glass lid over the top a the globe to keep millers and bugs from flyin' in there and tearin' up the mantle.

And them mantles costed.

LIVING SIMPLY—SIMPLY LIVING

APPRECIATION

Politicians and presidents have made good and bad laws and decisions that have affected this country and its people. But it was ordinary people doing what needed to to be done through wars and hard times, that kept this country going and progressing to make the USA the best place in the world in which to live. Regardless of where and when they were born and grew up, people had their own unique challenges to face.

We are better off without some of the things they had to endure in earlier times, but some of the old values are worth holding onto, imitating, and teaching to our children and grandchildren.

My dual purpose in writing some of the earliest events and memories of my life is: (1) to try to help people know what life was really like back then, and (2) to cause us to be more appreciative of what we have now, by seeing how far we've come in such a short time. I look around me and do not know anyone who doesn't have more now than they ever had before in their life. I wonder if they truly appreciate what they have.

I don't think many people today can even imagine life as they lived it here in the mountains in the early days before about 1945. They've grown up with or become accustomed to a world of fast foods, disposables, plastics, telephones, TV, and instant gratification. Just as my grandmother wouldn't know how to use what I have, most people wouldn't know how to survive using only the things my parents and grandparents had. They probably wouldn't know what they are, or how to use the tools and things they used every day.

When I hear people talk about the "good old days," I think of something my husband once said: "It's remembering how good the butter tasted and forgetting what it was like to have to get up at five o'clock every morning, feed and milk the cow, and churn the butter."

In those days, there was no such thing as the work being caught up. Work never ended. There was always something that needed to be done. And you learned from an early age that it took everyone doing their share, even small children. Survival depended on it.

We couldn't run down to the convenience store and buy milk, a loaf of bread and a dozen eggs. Or call 9-1-1 if we got in trouble. We had no car or telephone and had to live on what we canned, dried or otherwise produced ourselves from what we raised or what grew wild in the mountains. We learned to look ahead and be prepared as best we could, and learned to make do with what we had. If you've ever experienced living the way we did, you never get over it. When autumn comes, I want to see a big pile of wood close to the house, have my wood-burning fireplace insert inspected and cleaned, with wood laid ready to strike a match to start a fire—just in case I wake up some morning with the power off and the house cold. If snow makes the road impossible, my pantry is stocked, the freezer full, and I have gravity water. I even know how to open a can without an electric can opener—I can survive.

During the Y2K doomsday forecast, I found myself feeling so sorry for people who were trapped in cities or in circumstances where they are totally dependent on modern technology and conveniences. I felt secure in the knowledge that I had lived without them before and I can do so again if necessary, because of where I live and the way I was raised. Older native mountain people know how to survive because we learned it as children. I must say, though, it wouldn't be easy. I like it much better with my paper towels, microwave, electric blanket and indoor plumbing.

And I just can't navigate the trail up the hillside any more with a kerosene lantern.

SPREADIN' MANURE AND
RAISIN' A GARDEN

Back then, people ditn't say "food," they called it *rations. I'll tell you right now*—hit takes a whole lot a rations to feed a fam'ly of ten growin' youngens and two grown people. We had a purty good size *gyarden* clost to the house, one rocky *patch* up on th' side of th' hill apast the toilet, and another'n over there acrost the creek behind the barn. We raised all kind of stuff: corn, beans, sugar snap peas, *maters, sqush, Arsch* (Irish) *taters*, cabbage, *okry, ungens* (onions), parsnips, *redishes*, lettuce, sweet taters, *carrits*, turnips, beets, *gyarlick, rhuberb* (rhubarb) and *punkins*.

Everything was planted accordin' to *"the signs"* (phase of the moon, or Zodiac signs) in the almanac. Most plantin' was done when the moon was waxin'. Beans was allus planted on Good Friday, but runner beans was planted on the wane of the moon.

The corn, beans, and punkins was planted up in the field. I guess corn was the most important crop we had, as it was used to feed us, the horse, cow, pigs, chickens, and make Daddy's likker, too. I guess taters and beans was the next important.

Our barn had a op'm shed on the upper side where the chickens roosted. They was a pole ladder that went up into th' barn loft. The crib and one stall was in the middle, and two more stalls was on the lower side. They was big ol' wooden barrels in the crib where shelled corn, hog shorts and cottonseed meal was kept, and the floor was piled up with ears of unshucked corn and nubbins. We kept fodder for the cows and horse up in the barn loft. They was a op'm space in the floor of the loft next to the stalls, so the fodder could be throwed down in there to 'em. The barn was not only shelter for the animals and chickens, it was where we got *fertilize* for our crops. I'm talkin' organic gardening here.

They's a big differ'nce in what we called a garden then and what's called a garden now. When we said gyarden, we meant a place to grow sump'm to eat. Where we growed *flares* (flowers) was called *"flarebeds."* I'm mostly givin' Bud's description for the crop raisin' and stuff, as I wudn't big enough to remember all the de-tails of how it was done. I dist remember us a-doin' it, and done whatever I was told t'do.

In the sprangtime, Dad and the boys'd start gettin' the garden ready to plant. They *geared up* (harnessed) Ol' Jim, the hoss, hitched him to the plow and *turned* (plowed) the garden. You could hear 'em a-callin' out "Gee, haw, whoa, or back" to the hoss. *Gee* means go to the right, *haw* means go left, *whoa* means to stop, and *back* means to back up a little bit.

These commands let them control the horse without having to use the plow lines or reins so they could keep both hands on the plow handles. That helped *a sight*, for it was *pyert near* all a man could do to hold the plow up and keep the point down in the dirt, with it a-hittin' rocks, ol' tough grass roots and stuff. If it was new ground, they'd allus hit tree roots. Hit shore *broke a sweat* on a man, and the hoss, too. It was awful hard for him to stay on his feet, a-steppin' on loose rocks or dirt clods, one, a-slidin' off and turnin' his foot over sideways. An' his shoes'd dip up dirt and pack it down inside of 'em.

After it got plowed good, they run the *harr'* (harrow) over it to level it off and bust up any big old dirt clods. Folks that ditn't have no harrow would drag a pair of old bedspraings over the ground. Somebody'd ride on top of 'em to weight it down good.

While they'us a-gittin' the ground ready, the biggest rocks that got turned up was toted over to the side and throwed down next to th' fence. We dist left the ones that wudn't no bigger'n yer fist, or we'd still be out there a-pickin' up rocks.

Ever'body used to made sleds their ownself. They was big old heavy thangs. They'd git out and hunt two sourwood trees the right size to make sled runners out of. They needed to be purt' nigh the same size, with a natural bend or crook in 'em so they'd turn up on the end, When they found two, they cut 'em down and sawed 'em off to the right length and used the axe to flatten off the bottom some. They nailed crosspieces and planks on top of the runners to make a bed, an'en put a big stout crosspiece on the front of it to hitch the hoss to, to pull it by.

Then they took a auger (or brace and bit), and bored holes on each corner to put the ends of the *standards* (posts) in. They cut the standards however long they wanted 'em, trimmed the ends down to fit the holes, and drove 'em in on all four corners. They set some more standards over to the inside a little bit, jist a-leavin' enough room so boards could be slid down betwixt 'em longways to make sides. These sideboards was to keep whatever you was a-sleddin' from fallin' off a the sides. When you got ready to unload, the boards could be pulled out, and the stuff'd be easy to rake off of the sled, then.

We liked to play on the sled. One time me and Oval took one of the planks off a one side and laid it acrost the other side and was usin' it for a see-saw. Somehow or other, his side dist ker-thunked down real hard, and throwed me, and I went a-sailin' up through the air, flipped over and landed belly down with my face down torge his end. Slick as a button, that board scooted over torge his side, whopped down on to the ground with a big jerk, and dist stood up in the air there, with me on it. Hit hapm'd so fast I ditn't know what hit me.

They'd been a good size nail drove through the end of the plank, and it was bradded over torge the end of it. Hit caught me in the top a the foot right at the base of my fourth toe, went through the skin and just hung me upside down there, on that plank. And there I hung, a-screamin' like a wild *painter*. Oval had to run and git somebody to come and lift me up to unhang my foot off a that cuss-ed nail. I want ye to know, I was *a-tellin' the tale!* I've still got a little round scar there. They jist wiped the blood off, poured a little lamp oil on it, and I went on about my business.

After the garden was ready, they needed to put manure to it. They hitched up the hoss to the sled and drug it around the barn clost to the door of one of the stalls to get a load. They put the sideboards on to load it, so it'd stay on the sled. Everybody, girls and all, shoveled manure. We dist waded in there barefooted, up above our ankles in that wet stinkin' stuff. And slick! I found out what it meant when they said, *"As slick as manure."* We used long handled pitchforks for the driest stuff, and shovels for the sawgy stuff, and loaded it on the sled. An'en they drug the sled load out to the garden. We *broadcyasted* load after load of manure all over the garden before any plantin' was done, and unloaded a big pile over to one side to put to the rows later when the seeds was dropped.

After they laid off rows in the garden with a single-foot plow, they put manure in the rows where the seed would be planted. That manure made *vi'grous* (vigorous) plants. They needed to tote the manure up and down the rows, so they split op'm a tow sack and made a sling type apern or pouch that fit around their neck or waist, one, to tote it in. The pouch was carried in front, and was op'm, so they could get to the manure with their hands and put it down where they needed it.

Now maybe you hain't never seen nor felt of a tow sack. Well, hit's a type of feed sack wove out of hemp strang, and is so coarse and rough that it'll *take the hide off* of ye, if you rub it ag'in your skin much. Hit shore made their necks and waistes raw, 'spacially if they broke a sweat. On top a that, there was that stinkin' manure right 'nunder their face.

Bud said *he ditn't care* about handlin' the horse manure so much, as it was sorter dry and crumbly. But that cow manure......hit was soft and sticky where the cow'd peed in it, and you talk about stinkin'! Now, that stuff was *rank*! Hit'd flat out *knock your hat in the creek*! And took you two—three days to get that stink off your hands so you coutn't smell it. Talk about sump'm that'll *snerl up your nose*—now, that'd roll it up some.

Bein' dist a little youngen, a tow sack apern'd a-drug the ground on me. I toted manure too, but done it in bucketfulls as big as I could tote. I had to take both hands to pick up the bucket, and sorter swung it along to tote it. Boy, howdy, hit hurt like the dickens when the rim of that bucket *barked* my shin bone when I stepped fards at the wrong time. Hit'd make a blue knot on me, and I'd wind up with sev'al before I got done.

It took lots of manure and they was many a blister on our hands before we got done, for we took a hoe and kivvered up the rows with dirt after we dropped the seed. When we quit workin' in the garden for the day, we had to set on the branch or creek bank a good long while, a-scrubbin' manure off of our feet and hands.

I was allus glad when the plowin' and sleddin' was done and they ditn' need the horse no more. Dad usually had a few dranks, and was dist a-gettin' mean by the time we started workin', then got him another snort all along through the day. He cussed ever' sentence he said in his ever'day talk, anyhow, but he cussed and beat that horse the whole time he was workin' it. It'd look wild and blare its eyes, toss its head and sling slobbers, prance around and look like it was plum' scared to death. It allus scared me, too, and I felt so sorry for that pore old horse. I wisht I could dist turn it aloose and let it run away. Sometimes I'd go in behind the house so I couldn't see it, or hear the thuds as he beat on it.

Us kids got our share of the cussin' and bein' beat on, too, 'spacially Bud and the older youngens. I jist tried to stay out a sight, for I knowed my time was a-comin' sooner or later. But I also knowed I'd better be right there when he hollered. I'd get a lickin' fer shore if he caught me a-hidin', or not a-workin'. Anyhow, most days, one or the other, sev'al, or all of us got a lickin' before the day was over.

Until I was about twelve years old, I can remember only one day, when I was about seven, when Dad was sober. One day he come out in the yard where I was standing, reached down and took hold of my hand, and told me to come on. I remember looking up at him and being kind of scared and puzzled, and wondered what I'd done—if he was fixin' to whup me, or what.

One thing him and Mom both done, ever oncet in awhile, was to start off talkin' nice and quiet and friendly-like, to get me to talkin' to 'em, you know. After a little bit, I'd get to thinkin' that they really was talkin' to me just to be a-talkin', and it'd make me so happy to have one of 'em a-talkin' to me, like they just wanted to, maybe. Then they'd start sneakin' in questions in a roundabout way, and before I knowed how they done it, they'd trapped me in with my own words, and found a good excuse to give me a whuppin'. They could allus find something.

I never knowed what to do when they done that. If I didn't talk none, they'd get mad and either accuse me of bein' a smart aleck for not answering 'em, or want to know what I was a-keepin' hid. Either way, I was in trouble. I learnt to be *juberous* (dubious) of anybody that started in a-bein' too friendly to me, and astin' me questions about myself.

This one day, though, Dad led me out to the garden and we looked at the snowball bush, his *dallys* (dahlias) and *gladolias* he liked to grow by the garden fence. We walked all around, and he told me all about plantin', and what it took to make things grow. He showed me how to tell one plant or weed from the other'n by its leaves, and we pulled a few weeds. We hunted ground cherries, and eat some of 'em, and he kept on a-talkin' so good to me.

After awhile, I finally figured out that he hadn't been drinkin', and thought "What a nice man he is!" I wisht he'd be like that all the time. He was like a totally differ'nt person. I still treasure that day.

After that, when he was mean to us, I'd try to remember the man I glimpsed that day. I prayed to God that my Daddy would stop drankin', but it was many a year before he did.

TATERS, MATERS AND LEATHER BRITCHES

We saved some seed from from year to year. In the spring when we got ready to plant, Dad bought cabbage plants, onion buttons, mater plants, and sweet tater slips to set out. Sometimes we kept seed of some kinds of maters that he liked, and planted them. They had to be transplanted, or they made "tommy-toes" 'stid of maters. After we set 'em out, we had to carry lots of water to pour around 'em or they'd die. But any woman who had *her grannies on* (her period) couldn't tetch the mater plants. The maters'd rot if she did.

Tomatoes back then had a lot better flavor, and we never had to peel 'em. The skin wutn't tough like the ones you buy now. We raised big ol' red and yaller 'maters both, and tommytoes dist *come up volunteer* all over the garden. Boy them fried green 'maters was good! Mom made green 'mater gravy on 'em sometimes. She rolled 'em in cornmeal and flour, salt and pepper and fried 'em brown, then made gravy on 'em. That was good eatin'!

We made a tater patch off separate from the rest of the garden They allus said to plant taters when it's a dark night in March for new taters in mid-May. Seems to me like Dad bought Green Mountain or Cobbler seed taters to plant, and sometimes we dist planted what taters we had left over, if we had any. When we got ready to plant taters, we'd set down and cut the seed taters in chunks and let 'em cyore out a while, or dry overnight, one. Ever' chunk had to have a eye, or bumpy place where a sprout would grow out of it to make a plant. When the plants got about eight inches high, we had to take the hoe and rake dirt up over the plants to make a tater ridge.

We coutn't hardly wait for the new taters to grow big enough to *grabble*. Mom or Dad picked out which row to grabble for new taters, but we better not do it before they said to. We had a big old fork we used for a grabblin' fork, and just *ruck* out the biggest'uns to eat, and left the littl'uns to grow.

They's many a way to fix taters, and we liked 'em any which a-way they was fixed. Sometimes Mom'd bile 'em with the *jacket* on, or we'd take 'em out to the spout, scrape the jacket off, and cook 'em in salty water and put some milk, butter and black pepper in when they got about done. This'd make a nice thick gravy, and was spacially good when sugar snap peas was cooked in with 'em. Another way was to put 'em in a big bread pan and sprinkle a little flour, salt and black pepper on 'em, an'en pour some meat grease over 'em and brown 'em in the ub'm. They shore was good eatin'.

In the winter time, when we had a fire in the cookstove, we'd scoot the kittle over and use the stove eye to cook taters on. We'd cut the taters in thin slices and lay 'em on the stove eye and let one side brown, an'en flip 'em over to brown t'other side. Big old browned blisters would come up on 'em, and they'd git crispy. We didn't use no grease or salt on 'em—hit'd a-smoked us out a the house, and salt would a-rusted the stove eyes. We sprainkled the salt on 'em when we took 'em off of the eye. I guess you could call that Jun'lusky brand tater chips.

Another thing that was good was taters baked in the fireplace. Remember, we never had no *luneum* (aluminum) foil back then. You had to watch and not put 'em in the red hot coals or they'd burn up. We'd rake some hot ashes over to one side and put the taters on them, an'en kivver 'em up with hot ashes and firecoals. When we raked 'em out, them *pillin's* (peelings) would be scorchedas *black as the ace of spades*. When we fixed taters like that, we'd have black all around our mouth from where we'd pulled the pillin's off with our teeth. But under the pillin' was a thick brown crusty layer all around the tater, and that was the best part. Sometimes, we sopped our tater in meat grease and eat 'em like that.

When we fixed taters in a pot, we *pilled* 'em (peeled) and *kortered* (quartered) 'em up an'en biled 'em in salted water with a little meat grease or butter for seasoning. If they was any left over, Mom made tater biscuits. She made the best tater biscuits—she'd mash up the leftover taters with a fork, put in a little flour, black pepper, chopped onion, and a egg if the hens was a-layin'. She'd leave it thick enough to shape with her hands, dip out enough on her fingers to make a patty, or biscuit, roll it in flour, an'en fry it good and brown. It's one of my favorite foods.

We made a sweet tater patch over there on the other hill, out past the barn. Most of the time, we raised them long skinny white meated kind. We biled 'em or baked 'em in the ub'm, one. They sure was good with a slab a butter and a biscuit. And I liked 'em raw, too. We hardly ever fried 'em, unless they was real big, 'cause they wouldn't a-been much left after you peeled 'em.

Daddy loved okry and the kind he planted growed seb'm or eight foot tall and had great big ol' pods on it. Sometimes Mom rolled the sliced okry in a mixture of flour, cornmeal, salt and pepper and fried it in meat grease or lard, and that was purty good, but Dad and Bud liked it boiled sometimes. Bud liked to do things to aggervate us, and he plumb turned me ag'in okry. He'd hold a pod up in the air between his thumb and fainger, with th' thick, slimy water a-strangin' down from it and holler "look at this good ol' snot," and slurp it into his mouth. He'd wait and catch me not payin' no attention, and holler out, and of course, when he hollered, I looked. Just in time to see him slurp it in and smack his mouth big. He'd *bust a gut* a-laughin'.

Even now as I write about it, my stomach churns. For years, I wouldn't even put it in my home canned soup, but the rest of the family likes it. Fried okra is one of my son's favorite foods. He can eat it like popcorn. I used to say I like it rolled in ce-ment, fried and throwed in the creek.

We used a lot of onions too, and set out sev'al long rows a buttons. We started eatin' green ungens as soon as they got big enough. Dad and the grown folks poured out a little pile a salt on the table by their plate and pecked the end of their ungen down into the salt. Then they'd take a bite and dip it again for the next bite. We eat some of the green top, too.

Onions and taters was two things you ditn't leave out in the sun when you got 'em out of th' ground. It made taters turn green where the sun hit 'em, and they allus said that *that green on a tater will poison you.* When onions growed to full size and the tops died down, we'd pull 'em up and spread 'em out in the shade to dry some. After they'd dried a day or two, the dirt fell off and we tied 'em up by the tops in bunches with strips tore off of old britches legs, an'en hung 'em up on the porch rafters in the shade.

We hardly ever eat plain ol' raw lettuce. We growed leaf lettuce and eat *wilted lettuce.* To make this, you fry some fatback or streak-ed meat to get the grease. You cut up some lettuce and green onions and onion tops in a bowl and pour the sizzlin' hot grease over it while you stir it, a-wiltin' it down. Put some salt and pepper on it and it's made. We also went out and picked wild branch lettuce and turkey mustard and fixed it like that.

When we dug taters in the fall and the dirt dried and fell off of 'em, we'd make tater holes to keep our taters in. We shoveled out a round place in the dirt about one or two foot deep and five foot across, and kivvered the hole with straw. Then we took buckets and toted the taters to the tater hole and mounded 'em up on top of the straw.

We put leaves over 'em, or tow sacks if we had any extry, an'en a thick layer of straw all over the top of the taters to kivver 'em up good. Then we shoveled six or eight inches of dirt over that, an'en put a piece of tin or tarpaper, one, over the top of it to keep it dry.

When we wanted taters, we'd op'm up one side a the tater hole and reach in and pull out ever how many we wanted. We was careful to kivver the hole back up real good, so's they wouldn't freeze and *rurn* (ruin). We done the same thing with cabbage. They'd keep all winter long if we ditn't eat 'em all. (Cabbage was always said as if it was plural.)

We raised some bush beans in the garden, but mostly we raised what we called *cornfield beans*. They was planted next to the corn so they could climb up the corn stalk. One kind was McCaslan beans. And then they was striped creasey back and October beans. What green beans we didn't eat or can, we made *leather britches* out of. If we made leather britches out of 'em, Mom ditn't have to can so many. It saved us a whole lot of work, they never took up much space, woutn't freeze and bust, and they ditn't need to buy *can rubbers*. So we allus made a *right smart* of leather britches.

This is how you make leather britches:

O'course, you allus wash the beans good, look (inspect) 'em, and let 'em dry off some. You break the tip ends off of th' beans to strang 'em. When you get a pile of beans ready, thread a big eyed needle with about a six foot piece a stout thread. Poke the needle right through the middle of the bean and push it down on the thread, and keep on doin' that til you get a strang of beans about five foot long. Then you take the needle off and put it so you don't lose it, and tie the thread ends together to make a loop.

You hang the strung beans up on a nail sumerce in a dry place to where flies and bugs can't get to 'em and let 'em dry til they turn brown and rattley. Then they can be hung up in a flour poke to keep the dust and flies out of 'em til you're ready to cook 'em. They'll keep right on and on, just so you keep 'em in the dry.

When you're ready to cook 'em, you cut the thread and slide off ever how many you want to cook, wash 'em good in warm water, pour that off, and soak 'em in water a few hours to soften up some. Then put enough water in th' pot to kivver 'em up good, add some salt, throw in a chunk a streaked meat, and let 'em simmer till they're done. You may need to add water all along as they cook and swell up, but you need to let most of it jis' bile off when they're about ready to eat.

We left some a the beans on the vine to grow full and dry up 'til the pods rattled, an'en we'd go pick 'em and take 'em to the house to hull out. We'd have big washtubs full a beans to fix. We had to keep the chickens run off of the porch so they wouldn't be a-peckin' in 'em.

Ever'body'd set around the tub and the women got out some beans in their apern-tail to make it easier to work on 'em, and not haf'ta set bent over the tub.

Us younguns set on the floor next to the tub and hulled 'em out. Whichever way we done it, we'd allus put the bean hulls, culls and strings on the floor an'en sweep 'em up to take and feed to the hog or cow. I liked to shell them dry beans, and thought they was so purty. I'd set and play with 'em—dip up big handfuls out of the tub and let 'em slide off a my hands real slow, so I could look at 'em. They was so cool and smooth to touch, was spotted and speckled and all colors, and some of 'em was the purtiest purple color you ever seen.

And them big ol' butter beans we raised then ain't nuthin' like what you get at the store now, that they call butter beans.

ROAS'IN' EARS, NUBBINS, FODDER AND COBS

Before I get to talkin' about raisin corn, I need to tell ye a thang or two about corn. We used ever'thang on the corn plant, except the root. The plant's got a stalk, blades (leaves), *yers* (ears) of corn, and the *tossel* (tassel) at the top. The full grown ears are called *"roas'in' yers"* (roasting ears) while the kernels are still soft. The little ears that didn't get full grown are *nubbins.* We never eb'm fooled with shuckin' them, jist left 'em whole. The dried blades and tassel are *fodder.* Nubbins and fodder is used for horse, cow and hog feed.

Now then, as to how we raised corn. They's differ'nt kind a plows. They used a hillsideside turner, a #6 or #8, that had a button on it so you could flip it over to make the dirt turn torge one side or the other, to break up the ground. A double foot plow had two plow points, one a-settin' behind the other'n, that plowed two rows at a time. A single foot plow made rows to plant in, and they sometimes put a *wang* (wing), or bull's tongue on it. They laid off the corn rows with a single foot, trying to keep 'em straight, then the corn was dropped in the rows, about a foot and a half to two foot apart, and kivvered with a hoe.

Sometimes crows or some other varmint got in the cornfield and dug up some of the seed corn. The first time we hoed the corn, we *replanted* where none hatn't come up. The second time, and sometimes, the third time, we planted beans and punkins in the corn rows. When they come up, the beans climbed up the cornstalks, and we ditn't have to stake 'em…When we finished the third hoein', it was called *"laid by,"* and we didn't have to hoe it no more that year.

Now, you broke a sweat when you hoed corn. We got big old blisters on our hands, and they burnt like the dickens, 'spacially if they got busted, and they usually did before the day was over.

You need to start hoeing corn at the bottom row, or lower edge of the field, because as you hoe, you'll be a-digging up weeds, grass, dirt clods and rocks, called trash, and pullin' it acrost the corn row you're hoein' in, and slingin' it back behind you into the lower row. Somebody was allus a-growlin' about another'n "a-trashing" 'em. One person'd start at the first row, and another'n at the second row, and so on. The one a-hoein' the first row needed a little head start before the one in the second row started. If the second row person got in front, it made it harder for the one in the first row to chop down weeds and hoe too, with all a that trash in their row. But it made the one in the first row work faster to keep in front so they wouldn't get trashed. He knowed he better not piddle around or he'd git kivvered up in trash.

We took a file with a corncob handle on it to the field with us, for we had to sharpen the hoe ever' little bit. Them rocks dulled the edge pretty quick. One thing that hurt bad was when the hoe hit a rock and glanced off and bounced into your toes. A course, we was barefooted. I've lost a few toenails that way. It hurt a right smart if the toenail got tore loose. I've hoed corn right on with dirt a-stickin' to the blood on my toes. I knowed it wouldn't do no good to say nothin' about it. That night, I'd just wash it off in the branch, put a little lamp oil on it and *tie it up* in a strip of rag.

After the corn was laid by, the weeds still come up and got purt near as high as the corn. We went and pulled big armloads of weeds ever' evenin' to take and feed to the hogs, an'en had to give the cow a armload. If you give a cow ragweeds, though, you can taste it in her milk.

One thing I remember about going into the cornfield was watchin' out for packsaddles. A packsaddle is a big bristly, caterpillar-like worm that gets on the blades of corn. They'll sting you good and it hurts sump'm fierce *(fyerss)*. Feels like a coal a fire wherever hit tetches yer skin.

I'd allus thought them corn rows up on the creek was long, but one year Dad rented a field down at the Wilhide place on the river bottom near Andrews. He was working away from home then, and was only home during the week ends, so it was left to Bud to see the crop was made. Bud took us down there to hoe it, and we rode down there on the back of a old pick-up truck. I was a good sized gal by then, and my older sisters had married and gone, but I done whatever work my brothers done. Dad had hired (harred) our cousin Buddy to help hoe it, too.

If I live to be a *hunnerd*, I won't never forgit how I felt when I looked at that field. Hit looked to me like them corn rows was a mile and a haif long. Or more. I'd *never in all my borned days* seen a field that big and that flat. It was easier to hoe because the ground wudn't so rocky, but it was a whole lot hotter down there than it was up on the creek. I thought I never would get to the end of one a them rows. Why, I betchey they was more corn in two rows of that field than they was in a whole patch up on the creek.

But Bud was a kinder taskmaster than Dad would a-been. When we finished up for the day, he let us go play in the river awhile to wash up and cool off. I hadn't never got to play in no river before. That water was ever so much warmer than the creek water on Jun'lusky was. And big ol' deep holes! Deeper'n we could ever a-ponded up in the creek. We jist went on in with our clothes on, and let 'em dry on us when we got out and rode home on the back of that pick-up. Hit shore felt good to cool off.

I ditn't care if I did have to hoe corn down on that big bottom after I knowed Bud'd let us play in the river when we got done.

Shucks, I've took a bath in colder water than that.

We shore liked a-eatin' that corn and them roas'in'yers when corn come in, too. One thing about it, though, that frash corn'd shore clean you out, if you eat much of it all at one time. We eat it til it got too hard, canned some of it, pickled some of it, and Mom made hominy out of the dried shelled corn later on. But we still had aplenty left to take to the mill to have ground up for cornmeal.

At home, we gethered the corn in the fall and sledded it out of the field and put it in the crib til we could shuck it. My sister Juanita (Coonie) wrote down in a notebook about some things we done when we was dist youngens, and I copied this portion from it:

"Fodder is what you call the blades (leaves) on corn. In the fall just when the blades began to dry up, the tops were cut off above the top ear of corn. They were put together til you got a good armload then tied around the tassels with some blades of corn (making bundles). Then they was stood up with the ends jobbed on the ground so they would finish drying. The blades on the lower part of the cornstalk below the ear were stripped off and tied together into small bundles with two or three blades of the corn. They were hung up on the top of a strong stalk to finish drying."

"When they all dried good, all the bundles were gathered up and carried, or hauled with a horse or mule and sled, to one place where a fodderstack pole was put in the ground. It would be from ten to twenty feet high. The tops were placed around the pole in an upright position and snugged close all around the pole. It was stacked around and around the pole til the base of the fodder stack was as big around as you thought it had to be to accommodate all the bundles of fodder blades. It was placed on top of the corn tops, but in an up and down position snugged up to the pole in the center. Layer after layer of the fodder was placed around the pole and was stomped down hard at the center where the pole was."

"Someone had to be on the ground to throw the little bundles up, so the one up on the stack could place it. It would fan out over the tops and kept climbing higher up the pole. The closer you got to the top of the pole, the more narrow it became. When the fodder got up to the top of the pole, the fodder stack was finished, and the person up on the stack would sit down and slide off."

When they was a-makin' a fodder stack, they called it *"shockin' the corn"*, and when it was done, they called it a *shock* of corn or fodder.

"Finally the fodder stack was a work of art and looked kinda like a cone shaped, thatch roofed hut. Then a person could start making a tunnel in the base of the stack, pushing the fodder aside and making a kind of burrow back toward the center pole. That's where pumpkins were placed sometimes, to keep in the winter. Then the outside hole would be plugged up with fodder or dried grass and leaves."

"I've heard it told about people getting lost in snowstorms in cold weather and finding a fodder stack to crawl in, and was kept from freezing to death."

We used to carry in big tubs of shucked dry corn to shell off of the cobs. We brung it in the front room to where we'd be warm while we worked. We had another tub that we all sat around to shell the corn into. We got a ear out of the first tub and held it over the second tub to shell it. Some of it was hard to shell, and rough on your hands. Lord, hit'd brang the hide off. The best way to do it was to get the first ear shelled, then use that cob to rub and push against the kernels of the next ear to get them loose from the cob. We sorter graded it as we shelled. The best, purtiest grains on the middle and big end was what we saved to take to the mill to grind for cornmeal and to make liquor out of. We broke off the end with the little grains and put 'em in a bucket for chicken, cow, horse or hog feed. We left the small ears, called *nubbins*, for feed, too. Mom give the cow a few to eat on so she'd stand still for milkin'. We had to keep it in covered barrels to keep the rats, mice and polecats out of it.

When we got done, we had a great big pile a corncobs. Now, don't think for a minute, that we throwed 'em away. No Siree! Cobs was dandy for startin' a fire, and we used 'em for knife and file handles, scrubbers for crusty feet and pots and pans, and fed 'em to the livestock. They're one of the best *play purties* you could have. We spent a-many a hour on a cold, rainy day out in the crib, a-playin' with corncobs, or brung some in the house to play with when it was too cold to stay out there. We built what we called a chimbly by stacking 'em up log cabin-like, to see who could build one the highest before it fell over. And made out like they was logs to build cabins, forts and buildin's, and for fences around our farm pastures and along the roadsides we laid out on the ground.

Sometimes we had cob fights out in the yard. We made up two sides, usually two people on each side, and each side made theirself a barricade a-facin' one another. Then we'd take a certain number of cobs out there and pile 'em up behind our barricade. We tried to see whichun could hit the other'n the most times with the number of cobs we had. We'd run out from behind the barricade to grab up a cob that was throwed at us, so we could throw it back at them. If we run out of cobs, we had to surrender, so we needed to git and keep as many as we could.

Some people said they used 'em in the toilet, but we was allus lucky enough to have newspapers or pages out of a Sears & Roebuck catalog, one. We shore was lucky not to haf'ta find out first hand what was meant by the sayin', *"as rough as a cob."*

PICKIN' BERRIES AND POKE SALLET

We had to watch for snakes when we picked berries and poke sallet. In the spring, we went all along the garden fence, around the barn, the edge of the field, and up the the roadside to pick poke sallet. And that's where you find copperheads.

We had sev'al messes and canned some of the poke sallet before it got too big. Now, you had to fix poke sallet right or you'd get pizened. It's got to be washed good, boiled, and the water poured off three times, an'en let it *drene* (drain) off. You need to fry it in a pan of meat grease, and that's s'posed to kill any poison left in it. Sometimes, right before puttin' it on the table, we'd scramble up some eggs in it.

If somebody got poisoned on poke root, they give 'em huckleberry wine. Oval got pizened on poke root when he was just a little bitty feller, and like to a-died. I got to thinking about that the other day and asked Bud why that poke root'd been left a-layin' around to where Oval could get aholt of it. He said they used poke root tea to cure the *eatch* (itch). They boiled it, strained off the water and rubbed it on the skin. He said Bass Mosteller made some one time and got it too strong. Hit blistered him good—like to a-took the hide off.

After sarvices, strawberries was the first berries we got in the spring. They ain't no comparing the flavor of a wild strawberry with a tame one. The wild ones has got a lot better flavor to 'em. Trouble is, they're so little that it takes so many to do anything with 'em. *I tell you rat* (right) *now*, they'll give you the awfulest belly ache, if you eat too many of 'em all at once. Coonie liked strawberries better'n anything, I think, and she could pick (and eat) 'em faster'n anybody. She allus was quick with her hands. They was hard to pick, too, as they was scattered out in little patches here and there on the ground. We usually got a gallon or two, though, and Mom made us a strawberry pie. What we called "pie" was actually cobbler, but we allus called it pie.

You had to watch for copperheads when you picked blackberries, too. Blackberry *brars* growed all along the roadside and edges of the fields. They was one of our main foods. Mom canned half a gallon cans of berries and juice by the dozen, and made blackberry jam and jelly. It was hard to make enough jam and jelly to do us through the winter. When Dad made blackberry jelly, he put wild cherry bark in the juice as it boiled, then strained it out. That really changed the flavor, and it was *larpin'* (delicious). I still make some like that ever oncet in awhile.

Blackberry juice and blackberry wine is good medicine, too. Hit's good for upset stomach, and cures the *bowel complaint* (diarrhea).

We'd have our hands all stained up from pickin' berries. You jist had to wear it off—hit woutn' never wash off, or come out of your clothes, neither. Our arms and legs would be plumb kivvered up in brar scratches, and we'd have our faingers stuck full a brars. Sometimes the scratches *festered up* (became infected) and they called it *dew poisonin'*. You had to watch about that, for that could turn into blood poisonin', and that was bad business. You could shore die from that!

Lord, we picked all kinds of berries, I reckin. We went to the woods to pick buckberries, huckleberries, and gooseberries as they got ripe. Like as not, if you seen a snake out in the woods, hit was a rattlesnake. We loved to go pick berries, as that give us a good excuse to get out away from the house and roam around the mountains. We seen all differ'nt kinds of wild flowers. My favorite was the wild tiger lily. They had the sweetest scent! We knowed which berry growed where, and when they got ripe. Buckberry jelly was one of my favorites, but wild goose-berry jam is the best stuff. Mom canned 'em all, and made jam and jelly. But we allus got a pie from the frash un's we picked. I like to lay a big wad a butter on top of mine when it's hot and let it melt. Mmm-mm—*better'n snuff and not half as dusty!*

In the winter time when we went to eat, a big bowl of berries was set in the middle of the table. We crumbled up bread on our plate an'en poured the juice and berries over it, and eat 'em thataway. When rations was scarce, blackberry mush was another thing we eat. Mom called it "blackberry do-ish." She got the berries good and hot an'en stirred some cornmeal and sugar in to thicken 'em up. A many a time, that's all we had for supper, along with a glass of milk.

Sometimes, though, we had mush without the berries—just plain ol' cornmeal mush. It's sump'm like grits, only the corn is more fine-ground. When it gits cold, it sets up solid. For the next meal, if they was any left, she cut the cold mush into slabs and browned it in a iron skillet in lard or meat grease, and we eat that with surp poured over it, if we had any.

We had a few tame grapes, but we mostly went out and picked wild-uns. They had a better flavor, anyhow. They was fox grapes, fall grapes, and possum grapes a-growin' wild all over them mountains. Possum grapes is small, dark purple grapes that grow in big clusters, and ain't real good til after they've been frosted on in the fall. They've got a real concentrated flavor, will stain your mouth purple inside, and won't wash out a clothes.

We liked to gether grapes, as that give us a good excuse t'climb trees t'git 'em. We prob'ly had more canned grape juice and jelly than any other kind. They was real easy to fix. Mom made grape hull jam out of some of 'em. It was a *tee'jous* (tedious) job to squirt the grape out and save the hull, to get enough of 'em to do anything with, but it was sure worth it. You add enough of the grape juice back in the hulls to cook 'em good. She ditn't use storebought pectin to make jams and jellies, just used sugar. Once in a while, she'd get it biled down so thick that you could wind it up on a spoon and it was dist like lickin' on a sucker. She made grape juice pie, too.

They made wine out of grapes, too. Man, that stuff tasted good, but I'd already learnt my lesson about stuff that makes you drunk that time me'n Lawerence stoled that pint a likker and drunk it. I ain't never been so sick—thought my time had come! Makes me think about a tale I heard about a man that drunk so much he got sick. He asked his wife to pray for him, so she got down on her knees and started, "Lord, please have mercy on my pore ol' drunk man." The man broke in and said (expletive deleted), "Don't tell Him I'm drunk—tell 'im I'm sick!"

We had some cherry trees in our yard, and had to watch and keep the birds scared off, or they'd eat ever last one of 'em. Lots of times, when they'us ripe, they put me to climbin' up to the tip-top of the tree where the limbs was too little to hold up a grown person. I took a little surp bucket with me to pick cherries in. I was little and skinny, and could climb trees better'n anybody.

And I'd *druther* climb trees *than to eat when I was hungry*.

WINE AND HOME BREW

I don't reckin they's many things you can't make wine out of, and I liked the taste of all of it. If hit was a fruit or a berry, some wine got made out of it, if they could get a-holt of enough sugar. Blackberry wine is s'post to be good for upset stomach and elderberry wine makes awful good cold medicine. They let us take a little swig (less than half a snuff glass full) about any time we wanted to, jist as long as we ditn't "*mess and gom*" in it. That means we was real clean in how we dipped out jist ever how much we wanted, never took a drink out of it and poured the rest back in, and allus put the kivver back on good to keep out the gnats and flies.

Dad even made wine out of rhuberb. And peach peelin's we saved when they canned peaches. We had more grapes than anything, so they allus made lots of grape wine.

It's easy to make. Just wash your grapes, mash 'em up good, an'en put the *pummies* (pulp) in a churn jar, tie a clean cloth over the top, keep 'em in a warm place and let 'em *work off* (ferment). Then put some sugar in it and let it work off again. That's what gives it a kick. Then strain it out through a flour poke and you've got yer wine. That's gen'ly how you make any homemade wine.

If you want some stuff that'll flat out *sun your moccasins*, let it get about done workin' off and add a little more sugar. It'll work again, and have about the same kick as drankin' pure corn likker. We call that a cordial. It tastes so smooth and sweet, you're fooled into thinkin' it won't do nothin' to you. But take my word for it, like Brilliantine™ hair dressin'—a little dab'll do ye.

One thing you need to know about makin' wine. You don't want to use a crock that you've made pickles in before or it won't make wine. You have to keep your wine jars or churns separate from the ones you make pickles in.

I made some wine one time by mixing leftover juice together from whatever can of fruit was opened over several weeks' time. It was already sweetened, so whatever I put in it was like adding more sugar every time I put more in. I'd always give it a little stir with a tablespoon to mix it in. I was keepin' it in a big mouth glass gallon jar, and it was about half full.

One day I added some more juice and give it the usual little stir, but must've pecked the side of the jar, for it sounded like a gunshot went off. BLAM! It blowed a hole in the side of the jar about as big around as a quarter. *I'm here t'tell ye*, that stuff just exploded through that hole with a big fizzzz and shot all the way acrost the kitchen table, hit ag'in the fur wall and run down it, jist a-blubberin' and foamin'. There I stood with my mouth hung open, a-holdin' that jar, with the wine dist a-streamin' off a my elbows. Hit dang nigh scared me to death! I guess it's a good thing nobody took a swaller a that, or they'd a-had to give some-body else a swig to *a-ketched* 'em. That stuff'd a shore 'nuff *laid ye in th' shade* after you come outta orbit.

Home brew was a kind of beer (*byerr*) they made. It had a right smart of a kick to it. Bud told me how it was done. Mix malted syrup and baker's *east* (yeast) up together in some warm water, then put about four pound of sugar to the gallon and let it work off. If they didn't use malted syrup, they bought barley malt at Frank Bristol's grocery store to use a-makin' it.

They made something called stillhouse beer, too. They made it there at the house, as well as at Dad's stillhouse. They made what they called "malt" by sproutin' corn til the sprouts was about two inches long, an'en ground it up in a sausage grinder. Then they stirred some cornmeal in some water and cooked it. This was all mixed up together, kept warm and let set for a day or two. Then some warm water was stirred in til it was about as thick as buttermilk.

I even liked that stuff, too. I guess it's in my genes. If I went by taste, I'd drink like a fish, but I don't like the feelin' of bein' the least bit drunk, and it don't take much to do it. My husband once told me, "I could hit you in the butt with a rot-ten apple and make you drunk."

And that's a fact! Aside from not liking the feeling, I've seen the results of alco-holism in my family, and there's no way I would start drinking. I love my family too much to ever do that to 'em.

PICKLIN' AND CANNIN'

I reckin you can pickle just about anything, too. Sometimes Dad even pickled eggs. We had pickled corn, beans, beets, okry, green tomaters, and cucumber pickles. They even pickled the cabbage stalks. Sometimes they used salt brine, and sometimes a vinegar and sugar mixture. They made kraut and chow-chow in churn jars. Chow-chow was a mixture they made from chopped cabbage, cucumbers, green tomatoes, corn, and other vegetables—jist whatever they had or wanted to put in it. Dad liked to lay a few pods of hot red pepper in dist about everything. The big barrels and churn jars full of pickles was kept out in the springhouse or on the front porch. I think they canned some of them later, for I remember seeing cans of them.

I wutn't too big a fool over the rest of the pickles, but I liked pickled beets. The beets was cooked a little first, and then the vinegar, water and sugar mixture was poured over 'em and heated together til they boiled. Then they were packed into fruit jars and sealed. I thought they was so pretty.

When you needed to do some cannin', hit took some work to git ready. They was a job for ever'body but the baby, and somebody had to tend to him. Besides fixin' the food, you had to have enough wood cut and ready to keep a fire in the cookstove all day. You had to carry in water and pour it in the canner or the washtub to heat on the stove. Us littl'uns carried in water, too, but the biguns done the pourin' because we couldn't reach up high enough.

Then you had to go get the empty cans and can *leds* (lids) out of the springhouse. They was usually kivvered up with dust and *spider wibs*. Mom inspected the rims of the jars, the lids, and the old rubber rings to see if they was still good enough to use again.

They usually set a washtub down on the kitchen porch to wash the the cans and lids in hot soapy water. That was my job lots a times, because my hands was little and skinny enough to get down inside the jars. I just set down on the porch floor beside the washtub, and laid 'em in another tub as I washed 'em. Then they carried the tub full of clean cans out to the spout and let the water run over 'em awhile to rinse the soap off. Then they was stood upside down in a clean tub to *drene* (drain).

121

Modern Home Economists and County Extension agents would prob'ly faint dead away to see how we canned stuff. We never heard tell of no pressure canner or water bath, but I remember Mom put *cannin' acid* (salicylic acid) in the green beans to help preserve them. None of us ever got sick or died from *food poisonin'*.

Gettin' the stuff ready was the biggest job. We'd go out and pick washtubs full of beans, and they had to be strung and broke and washed. The ones that was full had to be shelled out of the hull. I liked green beans when they had a lot of them shelled-out ones in 'em. We called 'em *shelly beans*.

You had to can corn when it got ready, before it got too hard. It could get too hard in just a day or two, and *buddyrow*, we worked. We had to go out to the cornfield and pull the corn, then carried it to the edge of the pasture so we could shuck it, break off the tip of the ears, and throw the shucks and wormy ears over the fence to the horse and cow.

Then we had to carry it to the house and wash it off inunder the spout. I *druther shovel manure* than silk that corn, though. We never had brushes like we do now, to help get 'em off. My hands'd be about froze off from that icy-cold water from the spout, a-tryin' to pick them *cuss-ed* silks off and get 'em to wash loose.

Mom allus cut off the kernels. I liked to watch her. She slid that knife down under the corn kernels *as slick as a button* and they'd be big long rows of kernels that didn't even come apart. They was so purty a-layin' there in the dishpan. Then she scraped the cob to get all the milky juice off.

Cannin' sure got that kitchen hot. It took a long time to cook stuff in the big pots til it was done, and somebody had to stand and keep stuff stirred to keep it from stickin'. Corn was real bad to stick.

Maters was about the easiest thing to can. Most of the fixin' of them was done out in front of the springhouse so we woutn't have to carry in so much water. It was shady and cool out there.

A man used to go all over the county a-sellin' peaches off of the back of his truck, and we'd allus buy some. We washed the spray off good before we *worked 'em up*. We peeled 'em like peelin' a apple, and saved the peelin's to make wine. We never throwed away nothin' but th' pit. I was glad when they bought the freestone kind that come off the seed good. I thought them with the red around the seed was the purtiest thangs in a can. Them othern's was *awful hateful* about gittin' loose. You had to cut the peach off in pieces, and they wudn't nigh as purty in the can.

The food was cooked in a canner or big pot and kep' boilin' hot. The canner we had was glazed with porcelain enamel that chipped off in places if it got knocked about much. Them fragments would cut like glass. Our'n was a-plenty chipped up, and we was real careful not to scrape hard agin' the bottom to loosen up them bits of glaze and git 'em in whatever we was a-cookin'. The frash washed cans was stood up in some boilin' hot water in a dishpan or washtub right beside the canner. Most of the stuff was canned in half a gallon cannin' jars.

The zinc lids was boiled, and the rubber rings was put in a pot of simmerin' water to soften and sterilize. Them lids was a lot different from the ones we use now. They was a heavy zinc one piece screw-on lid, with a porcelain disc made inside the top to keep the food from coming in contact with the metal. Where the bottom edge of the lid touched the rubber ring was where the can sealed. When the big boys or Dad was around the house, they screwed the lids on, because they had a strong grip in their hands. It took a strong grip to get the can lids off, too. We had about a six inch square of rubber cut off of a inner tube that was used to grip the can lid. I've seen the top of the can break off with somebody a-tryin' to twist off the lid. You could get cut bad thataway.

Mom had a cannin' funnel that she moved from jar to jar as she filled them. She dipped the food out and poured it into the jars with a long—handled dipper. The cans of food was then lifted out of the hot water, and the tops wiped clean and dry. The rubber ring was put over the top of the can and pushed down over the threads of the glass jar to rest on a lip down below the threads. Then the zinc lid was put on and screwed down on the rubber ring as tight as you could get it.

Even after folks started using the new two piece lids, they'd screw that lid down so tight that you'd have to use a pry-up bottle opener to *prize* the ring loose enough to turn it.

After filling the jars, they was set out of the way in the floor over to one side of the kitchen to be sure they'd sealed before they was put away. Nobody touched 'em for a few days. They was checked every day, though, to see if *ary* can looked like it was gittin' *spiled*. If it was a fruit or juice that ditn't seal, they just let it work off and strained it out into wine.

Us kids was tickled when one of the zinc lids got damaged, because we got to take the porcelain disc out and use it for a little saucer in our play house. I thought they was purty, and looked like milk glass, but it was hard to prize one of 'em out without breakin' it.

You had to be careful about lettin' them filled cans freeze and bust in the winter time. Mom put newspapers under 'em and old quilts over 'em to keep 'em from freezing.

I've seen it so cold that the dipper froze solid in the waterbucket, a-settin' right next to the cookstove in the kitchen. After they built a fire, they'd have to set it on the stove to thaw it out. When it got that cold, they brung the punkins in and put them inunder the front room bed so they woutn't freeze.

COOKIN' ON A WOOD STOVE

You've probably heard the phrase, "They's good news, an'en they's bad news—which do you want to hear first?" Wellsir, when it comes to cookin' on a wood cookstove, they's plenty a both. It sure feels good on a cold winter day to come in out of the cold and feel the heat and smell the coffee, a big old pot a pinto beans or homemade soup a-cookin', and slide in there next to th' side of the stove and set on the woodpile to get warm. And maybe split open a big hot cathead biscuit and fill it up with butter or streak-ed meat to eat while you're in there.

Now, the bad news is that somebody's got to cut and carry in all that wood and rick it up by the side of the stove, to keep the fire *(far)* a-burnin'. Somebody's got to pull out the ash pan, or bin, when it gets full, and rake the ashes out of the bottom where they spilt over the edge, and take the ashes outside to dump 'em out. And clean up th' mess. And we ditn' have no vac'um cleaner.

You have to know which wood makes the hottest fire, and which'll last th' longest. If you use all dry wood, it burns up pretty fast, so you have to mix in a little green wood t'keep th' fire a-goin' longer. You've got to watch about lettin' all the wood burn up in the stove or it'll get too cold and the bread'll get *sobby*. That was my biggest trouble: I'd get so busy a-cookin', I'd fergit to put more wood in the stove til I noticed that things wutn't a-cookin' no more. That's why you need wood handy by the stove when you need to put more in.

Idoggeys, it sure is hard to cook when you've got sorry stovewood. Sometimes you'd get ahold of some old *doughty* damp wood that needed a blow torch to set it afire.

You have to take the stovepipe down and clean the soot (sut) out about once a year. That's another reason for burnin' good hardwood—pine wood builds up creosote in the pipe. A little rich pine's all right for kindlin', as the fire gets hot enough afterward to burn the creosote out. *Rich pine* is where the pine *rosum* (resin) collects and forms into a hard brittle area, usually around a pine knot. Hit shore makes good kindlin'. You can just light it with a match.

An'en you about hafta know how a wood cookstove's built to know how to cook on one. Well, the stove's made out of heavy cast iron, and sets up on legs to git it up off of the floor. The top, where you do your cookin', has round stove eyes with a place to where you can poke a *stove eye lifter* in it to pick up the eye when you need to put wood in. The eyes is right over the fire in th' firebox *(far-box)*, located on the left side. These get the hottest. They's eyes *fudder* over on the cooktop, but the *futher* away they are from the firebox, the cooler they get. Then, over on the far right side, they's a solid area that ain't got no eyes. You get your stuff to cookin' on the hottest eyes, then scoot it over to keep it cookin', but not let it git hot enough to boil over or set the grease afire.

The oven (ub'm) is in the middle next to the firebox. Some stoves has a reservoir (res'-e-voy) on the right side with a lid you can lift up to dip out hot water. We thought that was a real luxury—to have a reservoir to dip hot water out of when you wanted some. It helt more water than sev'al kittles full.

The stovepipe connects to the stove at the back, in the middle. On the back of the stove top, in front of where the stovepipe connects, is a *leever*, or damper that you push to the right or left. It regulates the amount of air that goes up the stovepipe. The stove has vents down on the side next to the firebox, and the bottom of the firebox has grates. Air comes in through the vents and grate. The vents slide open and closed. A door in front swings open to get to the firebox door and the ash bin below the firebox.

Now, if you want a roarin' fire, get the fire to going good, open up the side vents and the outside firebox door, and push the damper open. Hit'll flat out *suck the cat up the stovepipe.* But all your heat goes up the stovepipe too. You have to turn the damper down some to keep the heat in and get the stove hot.

You've got to be good at buildin' a fire in a stove, too. First, you have to put some wood in that's been split into smaller sticks, or kindlin', and then lay the bigger sticks in on top of that. You have to put the sticks in a little *catty-cornered,* one or two sticks on top of one or two, so the air can come up through 'em and they'll burn good. To get the fire to goin' good, just pour about four *tablespoonfulls* a lamp oil down through a little crack between the sticks so it'll run down onto the kindlin', *strack* (strike) a match and drop it in the place where you put the oil and put the stove eye back on. It takes about twenty minutes to get the stove hot enough to start cookin'.

They bought matches in penny boxes or nickel boxes. You had to strack a *penny match* on the side of the box, but you could strack them big ol' *nickel matches* anywhere, like on the stove top or a rock. Them nickel matches had big old red heads with a white spot on the tip end. I used to like to chaw the head off, an'en chaw on the match stick. I reckin a youngun'll chaw on anythang.

I got burnt under my thumbnail and the end a my thumb one time when I tried to strike a match by rakin' my thumbnail over the top of it like I'd seen some man do. A little bit of the burnin' tip come off, got stuck inunder my thumbnail and dist stuck 'nunder there and fizzed. Lordymercy, that hurt sump'm *vi-grous!* I *come in a bean* a-wettin' my britches.

Our stove had a warmin' closet, which is like a built in cabinet above the stove top, where you put stuff to stay warm or kep' leftovers in—if you ever had any. It had a door that opened down and made a shelf that you could set pans or bowls on while you was a-cookin'. We allus had a bread plate inside the warmin' closet for leftover bread, and a meat or "meat grease bowl." After a meal, you allus put the bread plate and meat grease bowl back in the warmin' closet and shet the door.

The first thing you done when you fixed a meal was fry some fat back or streaked meat, to get meat grease to season your cookin' with, or t'do your fryin'. Any extry grease was poured out of the fryin' pan into the meat grease bowl. It'd have little bitty pieces a meat or sausage in it. When most of the grease got used down to where the bottom of the bowl was thick with the settlin's, you took a boiled tater or piece a biscuit bread and sopped that up and eat it. I'm a tellin' you, that was good eatin'!

Another part of the bad news is that no matter how hot the weather is, if you want t'eat, you hafta build a fire and heat up the cookstove. On summer days when she thought it might be real hot, Mom put on a cake a cornbread to bake while she cooked breakfast. If they was green beans or sump'm else to fix for supper, she put them on to cook, too. When the bread got about done, she let the fire go out and the stove cool off. She turnt the bread upside down on a plate and left the skillet over it, and it stayed soft til supper time. Lots a times, we just had cornbread and milk or buttermilk for supper.

Talkin' about cookin' cornbread made me think about sump'm Bud told me about Mom a-cookin' on th' fireplace back when he was just a big old youngun. He said that one day Mom put a *corn dodger* (cake of cornbread) on in the *Dutch ub'm*. When it got done, she'd pulled it out of the fireplace, took the pokin' arn and lifted the led off and laid it down on the hearth. Then she'd gone off sumerce else for awhile.

All of a sudden, a big ol' hound dog come a-runnin' in the door, grabbed her bread right out of the ub'm, and took off with the whole thang. She got *as mad as an old settin' hen*, and started hollerin' at Bud to kill that *dadjimmed* thang. She told him to tie a rope around its neck and drag it in the creek and *drownd* it. He wrassled that dog all over the creek bank. It kep' a-gittin' away from 'im and he coutn't get it *drownded*. He fin'ly got a-holt of a stick and beat it in the head till he kilt it.

Now, it wutn't that he was a-wantin' to kill that dog, or nuthin'—he jist knowed if he ditn' do what she said do, she'd a-beat him to death first, an'en would a kilt the dog ennyhow.

His words: "An'en I had to bury the dern thang."

This is another portion I copied from my sister's notebook, with a few of my own comments:

"Us kids about always had the stove oven full of potatoes to bake, or roasting ears when they were in season. There wasn't any sweet corn then. We had ears of white corn, the kind of corn we shelled to take to the mill, to make our cornbread. It sure was good when it lay in the oven till it got good and brown."

"Then there was the parched corn and corn meal. The corn was put in a heavy iron skillet with a small amount of lard or meat grease, and heated slowly, stirring often to keep from burning. The grains of corn would plump up and brown nicely. When it got browned good, salt was sprinkled on it while it was hot. Parched corn is a very tasty treat. Sometimes some of us would go to the barn loft where fodder was stored and take our parched corn in a coffee poke, and played for hours and eat corn."

We browned cornmeal in a skillet, too, and called it parched meal. We sneaked and put a little sugar in it after it got browned, and eat it with a spoon. You had to be awful careful not to get choked on it, though.

She continues: "We made flapjacks, also. We just stirred up some cornmeal and mixed it with some water, salt and soda, and fried it in meat grease. Our corn meal had to be sifted because the corn was took to the corn mill to be ground, and had to be sifted to get the bran out. When a miller ground a bushel of corn, he would take out a half gallon or so of corn as pay for grinding your corn. When he got enough corn (toll) to grind himself a sack of meal, he would sell it to make some money."

Mom told me that years ago, when she was young, she used to run a mill. She talked about it as if she really enjoyed doing that.

I also remember the *flapjacks*, and still make them sometimes when I want a fast snack. I usually do this in the fall, when my daughter brings me some sorghum molasses from a mill over at Young Harris, Georgia. I put a little flour in my cornmeal to make them stick together better. I fry the flapjacks in butter, then put 'em out on a plate, lay another wad of butter on top, pour sorghum surp over 'em 'til they just about float, and eat to my cholesterol-free heart's content. Have a glass of milk with them, and *you're in hawg heaven.*

We woutn't a-knowed what you was a-talkin' about if you'd a-said "pancakes" to us. "Cake" to us meant it had sugar in it. ('Cept for a cake a cornbread.) The other day I was watching HGTV and this famous chef was making fritters and crepes, and a-carryin' on like they was really exclusive, Grade A, high-class gourmet delicacies. All of a sudden, I thinks t'myself, "W'y—that ain't a thang in the world but *flitters!*"

Now flapjacks hain't the same thing as flitters, *not by a long shot.* You use flour in the place of cornmeal to make flitters. When you want some bread fast, you can make them instead of havin' to make up biscuits or a cake a cornbread and bake it.

Dad was what he called *"a dabster hand"* at flippin' over flapjacks and flitters in a skillet. He didn't use a fork or nothin' to turn 'em over. He just give the pan quick jerk and a toss, and they flipped right over, *jist as purty as you please.*

If somebody described sump'm that had been mashed, or was flat—like a *flat tar* (tire), it was said to be *"as flat as a flitter."*

I'll tell ye one thang, what's a fact—if ye ain't never eat cathead biscuits baked in a wood cookstove, you jist hain't never eat a good biscuit.

Mom made what she called "choked off," or "choked out" biscuits. That means she ditn' roll out her dough with a dough roller an'en cut the biscuits out—she choked 'em off. Here's how she done it:

A-body uses a good-size bowl or a dishpan, one, and puts about four pound of self-risin' flour in it. Make a *shaller* well in the middle of the flour. Pour about a fourth of a cup of melted lard in the well and stir it into just the flour right around it. Allus leave a good inch of flour untouched next to the outside of the bowl so the dough won't stick to the sides. Then add and stir buttermilk in the middle of the well, a little at a time, til you git however big a ball of soft dough you want. They's some that mixes it in with their faingers, and some that does it with a fork.

When you git yer buttermilk mixed in and the outside of the dough coated with flour, so it ain't sticky, you take yer thumb and forefinger and choke off a wad of dough—however big you want yer biscuit. Place that'n in a greased bread pan and keep on doin' that til the dough's gone. Put 'em in a hot ub'm and bake 'em. The flour is sifted and put back in the bowl, ready fer next time.

I tell ye right now, them cathead biscuits is so good that when you put a bite in yer mouth, *yer tongue'll jist about beat yer brains out.*

CLEANNESS AND NAISTNESS

They's a sight a differ'nce in people's idy of what's considered *cleanness* (cleanliness) and *naistness* (nastiness); in other words, what's sanitary and unsanitary. Regardin' table manners, they was certain rules about what was and wudn't done. These rules might be called "How To Behave Yerself at Th' Eatin' Table," and have stayed with me (mostly). Nowadays, I guess you'd call it "Dining Etiquette." Mom might be busy, but she noticed stuff, and tryin' to slip sump'm past her was *like trying to sneak daylight past a rooster*.

Fust and fo'must, when Mom hollered "Git ready to eat," or "Supper's ready," she never meant *a'ter whahl* (after while)—you quit whatever it was you'us a-doin'. Right then. You ditn' want her to have to come and git ye; she knowed dist e'zackly how to git yore butt to movin'. O' course, we had another good reason, too—you'd better git yeself in there, or purty soon they woutn't be nothin' left on th' table to eat.

You lined yerself up at the washpan and washed your hands and face. And you better not dist dip your hands in the water and wipe the dirt off on the towel, neither. And don't go a-runnin' off a-handlin' nothin' else before you eat. You set *yeself* down in yer own place at the table and kep' quiet.

Second, but by no means secondary in importance: *keep your grubby mitts to yourself.* Don't you go and tetch nothin' that you, *yer ownself*, ain't goin' to eat. You've got your own fork or spoon. Keep it to ye'self. You don't never use it to get sump'm off of a servin' plate or out of a servin' dish. That's what the *big spoon* (servin' spoon) is in the bowl fer—to dip out the beans and taters with.

When you got sump'm out of a bowl or off of a plate, you ditn't put it back. We never cut cornbread up in fancy squares like folks does now—*No siree.* We put our faingers on the bread and got aholt of the specific piece of cornbread we was goin' to break off, and ditn't touch it nowhere else. If you broke off too big a chunk, you eat it (or *snuck* it to th' dog, one); you ditn't handle it, break some off and put the rest back. Same way with a biscuit. Be shore that's the one you want before you pick it up, for when you git it, hit's your'n. Sometimes Mom'd throw a biscuit down to the other end of the table to one of us, but nary one of us had better not try it.

They was allus a fork on the plate of fried chicken, tater biscuits and stuff to use to *fork* stuff off of the plate. Then you laid the fork back on the plate. They was allus a "jelly spoon" in the jelly or a "gravy spoon" in the gravy. You got out what you wanted with that spoon, and put it back. We had a spacial "butter knife" that was kep' on the dish with the butter, and it was put back after you got some. And God help us all if Mom looked down in the jelly jar and seen little dabs a butter in it.

I've been to folks' house and seen somebody *souze* their fork or spoon in their mouth, rub it over their tongue good an'en suck it off, an'en use it to get some butter, jelly or sump'm out of a bowl or off of a plate. Or they'd take their own fork or spoon and get a bite out a this bowl and a bite out a that bowl, a-eatin' right out a the servin' dishes. Or pick up the big spoon out of the bowl full of stuff and taste whatever was in it, an'en souze it back in there with the rest of the stuff in the bowl. That's what was called *"messin' and gommin'"* in it.

Oh, my Lord, have mercy! Hit scares the livin' water out a me dist to thank about what would a-hapm'd if one of us'd a-pulled any *sich a* trick as that. Mom or Dad, one, whichever was the clostest, would a-slapped us plumb out onto the kitchen porch, or through the wall, one, *whichever was the handiest.* At least our head would a-went.

I've seen a woman get a spoonful of stuff out of a pot to taste it, lean over and hold the spoon over the pot with part of it a-drippin' back in the pot while she slurped some of it off a the spoon. An'en dist put the rest of it back in there and stir it in. Mom allus took a clean spoon, got a little dab of stuff out of cookin' pot an'en helt it off to the side with her hand under it to taste it. And she never used it no more 'thout wipin' it off with the dishrag.

She was clean with her cookin' and she expected us to be clean with our eatin'.

Anybody a-reachin' over with their fork or spoon to git a bite out a yore plate was license to kill 'em. You might dist git a fork *stobbed* up in yer hand—a-pullin' any sichy trick as that. Same thang with yer cup or drankin' glass. You eat out a yer own plate, a-usin' yer own imple-ment, and drunk out a yer own cup or glass or jar—whichever was yourn—and nobody else's. You ditn't want to haf'ta drank somebody else's *slobbers* after they'd *stuck their bill in* your glass.

One day I went to somebody's house, and they was done'n already a-settin' at the table eatin' their dinner when I got there. One of 'em scooted back her chair and got up, and said, "Here, I'm done eatin'. You can have my plate." I wondered if I'd heard right, and thought shorely she must a-meant "place," 'stid a "plate."

Now, I could a-eat, *all right enough.* I was purty hungry. And them rations a-settin' out on th' table smelt mighty good. I was dist about to set down, but when I seen that nobody wutn't a-makin' no move to set out a clean plate—or fork—or glass—ner nothin', I commenced to *lyin' like a yaller dog.* I told 'em, "I'm not the least bit hungry, thank ye. Yuns dist go right ahead and finish yer dinner; I done an' *eat a big bait* right before I come, and coutn't hold *nary nother* bite."

I tell ye right now, hit's awful hard to get over how you was raised.

I still won't eat nothin' if I think somebody's messed and gommed in it.

And I aim t'have a clean plate.

EATIN'

Now, this here part is wrote purty clost to the way it would be spoke if you was to say it like we say it. If you don't understand what you read, try sayin' it out loud.

We had a big long *eatin' table* made out a planks and two by fours. It had t' be a good sized'un fer us all to git around it. They was a homemade bainch over next to th' wall on th' fur side a th' table, an'at's where th' littlest younguns set. We ditn't have anough chers fer ever'body t'have one, but we did have some dannymite boxes and nail kaigs fer the older younguns t'set on. They never tuk up as much room as a cher did.

Mom allus set down at th' end a th' table next to th' cookstove. She'd set th' biscuits on th' ub'm door to keep 'em warm, an'en dist tawsed one over to whoever wanted another'n, when they asted. She nussed th' baby on her lap, or set it at th' end a th' bainch next t' her when it got big enough t'set alone. She never had no high-cher. Then we'uz lined up accordin' to our age, all down the bainch, an'en on around th' table, with th' oldest'un a-settin' next to Dad, over on t'other side a Mom.

Ever time a baby got big enough t'set on th' bainch at th' table, t'other youngens dist scooted down a notch. When a youngun got to move off a th' bainch around to th' end a th' table and set'n a cher, they thought they 'uz dist about grown.

We thought th' table looked s' purty when we got a new tablecloth. Sometimes it 'us checkedy, but then ag'in, it might have perty flares or some kind a pi'chers on it, one. Hit 'uz made out a oilcloth and 'uz easy to clean off by dist awipin' a damp dishrag over it. Y' coutn't set nothin' hot on it, though, er hit'd melt 'n stick t' th' bottom a th' pot. Then when ye picked up th' pot, th' stuff'd peel off plumb down t' th' cloth backin', an' stick on th' bottom a th' pot. We used a tablecloth til dist about all th' stuff got peeled off of it, and got so full a holes and cut places that it looked plum naisty.

Mom never let us hang around th' kitchen inunder 'er feet, 'n' we never come t' th' table, neither, til she hollered, "Supper's ready." An' when she did holler,

ye'd better gitchey hands woished 'n git t'th' table. She ditn' put up with no foolishness out of us.

They usually wutn' no use in messin' up no bowls t'haf t'woish. She dist
poked a big spoon in a pot a stuff, 'n set it on th' table on a doubled-up dishrag 'r
sump'm when we'us ready t'eat. Spoons was turned upside down in a glass jar in
th' middle a th' table so we c'd 'ist reach 'n git one, 'an at's what us younguns eat
with. Th' grown people eat with forks. We ditn' eb'm have no *case knifes* (dinner
knives) in th' house. If a fork cout'n cut it, ye dis' picked it up in yer hand'n
gnawed it off.

If y' wanted more on y' plate, y' handed it down t' Mom 'r Dad, one, an' they
give ye what they wanted y' t'have. (I now realize that was the way they made sure
everybody got an equal share). Y'ditn' tell 'em what you druther have, neither.
Y'had t'eat what they put on y'plate, whuther y' p'tick'ly liked it 'r not.

Mom allus put sev'al pieces a fatback in th' soup beans, and me 'n Coonie 'n
Oval, 'spacially, dit'n like that ol' boilt fat meat. I dit'n like th' slick way it felt'n
m'mouth. They made us eat it ennyhow, whuther we wanted to 'r not. Dad liked
it, 'n we was glad, fer that meant they wout'n be s'much left over fer us t'haf
t'eat.

When we eat soup beans, we crummeled up a chunk a cornbread on th' plate
first, an'en poured th' beans 'n bean soup over top uv it til the plate was full
enough to jist about run over, but not hardly. Mom allus had t'make th' beans
good 'n soupy so they'd be aplenty t' wet down th' cornbread good. She boilt 'em
a long time so the soup would be good 'n thick.

We dist had odds 'n ends a dishes. We got differ'nt kinds a dishes out a oatmeal 'n woishin' powders an'en we had some plates made out a that speckledy
blue porcelain 'namel stuff, like th' canner was made out uv. That 'namel'ud chip
'n crack off, if it got pecked agin' sump'm, and them plates was purty banged-up
lookin'.

Th' oldest younguns said that they'd eat off of a lard bucket led a-miny a time.
We liked t' joke around 'n tell other people that we ditn' never haf to woish
dishes at our house—we dist drove a tarpaper nail through th' middle of a lard
bucket led and nailed 'em to the table all the way around, 'stid a settin' plates,
an'en dist licked 'em clean whenever we got done eatin'. When we had surp,
though, sometimes one of us'd lick til they wore the head offa the tarpaper nail,
and had to drive another'n in it. We'd *back up one another* that it was so, and
dang near have 'em a-b'lievin' us, too, til we'd git so tickled we got to sniggerin'
and give it away.

Sweetie n' Lewis brung some *luneum* (aluminum) plates, 'n spoons 'n forks 'n stuff in from the CC camps when they got out. They brung a couple a parin' knifes, too. Now, we thought that was sump'm, t'have all them thangs that woutn't rust, or th' handles rot off of, neither. Mom was still a-usin' one a them parin' knifes fifty year later.

We dist drunk out a tin cups, pint fruit jars, snuff glasses, peanut butter jars, 'r whatever was give us. I had a little tin cup with a handle that I allus drunk out of. But now, we never drunk out a tin cans like you buy stuff in. You could git tin-poisoned out a them.

You might a-hyerd th' sayin', "They ain't no use to cry over spilt milk." Well, we did. Any body that knocked their milk over got a good lickin', whuther they c'd he'p it 'r not. And I gyar-un-tee ye, they done some squallin'.

Dad and Mom had their own teacup 'n saucer that they drunk their coffee out of. (Some folks said "sasser," but they was considered kindly ignert). All a th' grown people poured some a their coffee out a their cup in to their saucer to drank it. Now they had a certain way a-pickin' up their saucer. They spread out their hand 'n tetched th' side a the saucer with their thumb and middle fainger, t' git a-holt around one side uv it, don't ye know, an'en eased their fourth fainger up 'nunder th' saucer so's they c'd pick it up to drank out of. Thataway, they ditn't stick their fainger in th' hot coffee, or be naisty about stickin' their fainger in nothin'.

The coffee'd be hot, 'n they'd pick their saucer up and blow on it—you know—t'cool it off some, before they tuck a sup. It 'us all right for it to make a little slurpin' sound, dis' as long as ye ditn't git too vulgar about it, and sound like a hawg a-eatin' slop.

That was accepted as th' proper way a-drainkin' a cup a coffee. Ever'bydee drunk it thataway.

Lots a times, I *study about* Mom and Dad a-gittin' into a big *racket* at th' table one time when we 'us a-eatin'. Dad made 'er mad about sump'm, and she dist upped and picked up 'er cup and th'owed it at 'im dist as hard as she could th'ow it. It 'uz one a them big ol' thick heavy caiffay cups, too.

Now, she tried not to cuss in front of us younguns, but she come awful clost to it that time. And hit's a good thang he dodged, for that cup went a-whizzin' right past his far'd *like a bat out a hades*, hit the door facin' and busted into a thousand pieces. It hit th' door facin' so hard that they'uz a piece of it drove up in th' wood. Hit 'us still there sev'al year later when we moved out a that house. If it'd a-hit 'im in th' head, hit would a-kilt 'im.

He dist throwed back 'is head and laughed at 'er. I thank they both liked a good fight. But hit like to a-scared us youngens t'death when that cup slammed into th' door facin' like a gunshot.

Now, we ditn' hardly ever have more'n one 'r two thangs at a time fer breakfast besides biscuits 'n butter, but at differn't times, we eat hot fruit, streak-ed meat—also called side meat, middlin's 'r fatback, one—gravy, and *aigs*. Dad liked his aigs with th' yaller runny so he c'd sop 'is biscuit in 'em. *Oncet in a whahl*, we'd have fried chicken. And *oncet in a blue moon*, we had a can or two of Banner Brand Sausage,™ and thought that was real spacial. Mom'd either put it in scrambled aigs or make gravy with it to stretch it so they'd be enough to go around. That stuff was *larpin'*.

We had jelly 'r jam til it all got eat up. Th' older younguns said that Mom used t' put up jelly 'n jam in half a gallon cans, but it still never laisted much long.

A'ter we got done eatin' ever'thang on our plate, we'd sop it clean with a piece a biscuit. In spite of what we told people, we never nailed our plate down ner licked it, neither.

When we got the dishes washed, one of us girls allus swep' out th' bread crumbs 'n dirt 'n stuff. Most a th' trash went through th' cracks before we got to th' door. But before we c'd sweep, we sprainkled water on the floor to keep th' dust down where them big ol' globs a mud'd been tracked in on them *hobnail boots* and dried, an'en got walked on and ground into *fizzle dust*.

That was when we had a-plenty a stuff. Eb'm with all a th' stuff Mom *put up* (canned), we still had some mighty lean times. They had t' sorter look ahead t' make th' canned stuff last all winter. They hatn't never eb'm hyerd tell uv a freezer, an' they never had no 'fridge'e-ator, neither. They dist *made do* with what they had. Sometimes we dis' had cornmeal mush 'r blackberry mush, one. Ever oncet in awhile, we got a box a oatmeal 'r some rice. Th' onliest way I knowed t' eat rice til I was near grown was to cook it, sweeten it and eat it like hot cereal. We had some puffed wheat ever now n' then. My great aunt liked shredded wheat, 'n we use t'snigger at 'er fer callin' it "threaded wheat." But th' only time I ever seed any a that was at Paw Taylor's.

But they was *a-many a-time* when we eat soup beans or taters, or flapjacks or dist whatever we had to eat, breakfast 'r not. And cottonseed meal or shorts mixed in with flair or meal in the bread tastes purty dang good when ye hain't got nuthin' else.

Now, we might not a-had the kind a rations back then like people has now, but Mom and Dad raised ten younguns in one of the hardest times this country has ever seen, and we never starved to death. Now, I ain't a-sayin' we had dist whatever we wanted to eat, but ever' one of us was healthy. We jist eat plain *grub* (food), like taters, soup beans, and stuff we raised and canned. Mom ditn't have no recipes for nuthin'. She never eb'm had no measurin' cups or spoons—dist put in a handful a this and a dab a that. She ditn't have no bakin' powders; she used self-risin' flour and put sodie and salt in the corn bread. It don't take no recipe to cook soup beans, taters, cornbread and cathead biscuits.

Most of the time, we dist had milk and bread for supper, unless they was beans or sump'm like that left over. When we dist had buttermilk or milk and cornbread, we *crummeled up* th' cornbread in our glass and poured buttermilk, or rag'ler milk either one, in it, and eat it with a spoon. Some of 'em'd put black pepper in their'n. Dad did, and liked to chop up a onion in his'n. When we had ramps or gyarlic, he'd put that in it. That was a good supper. As Dad would say, "good herbs."

We shore was proud when Dad brung in a bucket a *surp* (syrup), cause we hardly ever got any kind a-sweetenin'. Sometimes it 'us red Karo,™ and sometimes it 'us another kind—Dixie Dew,™ I thank it was, that was cler and tasted kindly like honey. We had a 'luneum surp pitcher with a led that raised up when you pushed down on a *leever* right above the handle, an'at let it pour out. When you got out what ye wanted, ye turnt the leever loose, the led snapped down and cut off the surp. We'd stir it up with butter an'en put a wad of it on a hot biscuit, bite that off, and load 'er up ag'in.

I've hyeard Dad tell about this man that stayed all night with us one time. At breakfast the next mornin', he dist kep' a-pourin' surp out a the pitcher and dis' *rounded his plate up.* He eat and eat on that surp, and Dad got to thankin' that maybe he hatn't meant to pour out so much, and was jist a-tryin' t'be mannerly and clean his plate up to not waste it. He was afeared the man might git sick, so he asted Mom to git him a clean plate. When Mom took his old'un and give him a clean'un, Dad asted, "Now, what can I git ye?"

I be dawged if that *jaisper* ditn' say, "If ye don't care, I thank I'll have some more a that surp." Then he picked up that surp pitcher and poured hisself out another *remption.*

Dad said he never wanted to do nuthin' so bad in his life as to jist grab up that surp pitcher and pour it all on top a that scutter's head.

A'ter it got to where they wutn' so many of us, ever oncet 'n a while Dad'd git Log Cabin surp in a square-like tin bottle 'at was painted to look dist ezackly like a little lawg cabin. A purty little thang! Hit might a-helt a *koirt* (quart), but more like a little over a pint. Ye unscrewed th' cap on top of th' chimbly to pour out th' surp. Now that was sump'm spacial, and when it got empty, we dis' set it up t' look at it. But now, them surp buckets come in awful handy.

One time we went down to Ed Lambert's on Collett Creek and watched 'em make surp. Hit shore was inter-es-tin' to see. We got some a them 'lasses and Mom made some *"'lassy sweet bread"* a-usin' 'em fer *sweetenin'*.

Mammy and Maw Hicks allus made tea cakes and sweetened 'em with 'lasses surp. Now, them thangs was good! I thank they put some ginger in 'em.

Now—we never called it "molasses"—hit was *sogrum surp, 'lassy surp* or *'lasses.* Sometimes we'd stir up a little bakin' sodie in it on our plate. Hit'd turn real pale yaller, commence to swellin' up like it was about to bile, 'n was fizzy in y'mouth when y' eat it.

Another thang we'd do wuz put a little vinegar in some water and sweeten it, an'en take and stir up a little bakin' sodie in it. Hit'd fizz and foam plumb out over top a th' glass. That 'uz Jun'lusky Co-Colie, I reckin. We *snuck around* and done it, 'cause Mom'd *git on us* fer wastin' sugar.

Back then, they called all soft dranks *"Co-coalies"* or *"dopes,"* one. I's a big old youngen before I drunk a real Co-colie. One Fourth a July, some people come by and had a bunch a *dopes* they put'n th' woishtub out at th' sprang t' cool 'em. They was one called a Or'nge Crush,™ or Nehi arnj™ that I liked the best. They called it a *"yaller dope."* They had some packs a salty peanuts, and poured a pack in their bottle a dope an'en eat 'em as they come out with th' drank when they turnt it up to drank some. I *never had seen th' like a that.*

They had some cans a Vi-anner (Vienna) sausage, *simon feesh* (salmon), sardines and some sodie crackers that they brung, too, 'n we got t' eat some a them. Them sausages and fish was good too, they was, but them sardines'd *puke a buzzard off a gut waggin'.* It smelt to me like them fish had crawled in that can and died, but Dad and them menfolks eat 'em fer chasers. Lordymercy!

Nobody but jist grown people and the biggest younguns drunk coffee. Back durin' th' war, coffee was rationed and stores sold coffee substitutes. One a them was Postum.™ Mom liked hit real good. But Dad cussed about that old chick'ry they put in Luzianner (Luzianne)™ coffee. He druther have JFG.™

I recolleck sugar 'n gas a-bein' rationed too. They had little books a stamps that Dad had to take t' th' store when he bought sump'm that was rationed. Mom never went t' th' stores in town then, that I knowed of.

◆   ◆   ◆

We never knowed what storebought tea was. We made tea out a differ'nt wild herbs and thangs, but I recolleck *sassyfack* (sassafras) and spicewood tea th' best. Spicewood is a shrubby-like tree that grows wild. You don't hardly ever see nary'n now, and most people woutn't know what it was if they seen it.

Bud dug one up for me sev'al year ago and brung it to me, and I set it out in my back yard. It's a purty good size now, and I make me some tea ever now'n'en.

You scrape off th' bark and make yer tea out a that. I trim my bush back ever' year, and use the trimmin's t'make tea. I like to brang some of th' trimmin's in and lay 'em up sumerce in th' house, or stick 'em down in a jar, one. Hit makes th' house smell s'good.

And when I set down and drank me a cup a spicewood tea, in my mind I can still see our old house 'n yard 'n barn 'n all, and all of us a-settin' around the table—dist like we use t'be.

EATIN' HIGH ON TH' HAWG

The old sayin', *"eatin' high on the hawg."* means you're a-eatin' goo-ud. When they slaughtered a hog, we shore 'nuff did eat high on the hawg for awhile. When it got cold enough in late fall to where the meat woutn't rurn, and the moon was right accordin' to th' Almanac, it was *hawg-killin' time.* It had to be done when the moon was a-shrinkin', or a-wanin', so the meat'd *draw up* (shrink) and render out a-plenty a lard 'n grease. That was real important because you had t'fry some meat t'git some grease for seasonin' and fryin' stuff before you could *set a meal on the table.* If a hog's kilt on the new moon, or when it's a-risin', that meat'll just lay there and swell up in the pan, and they won't be much grease atall.

They had to be a big pile a wood cut and everthang got ready the day before, for after they kilt the hog, they had to get the meat worked up quick so it wouldn't *spile* (spoil). They toted sev'al buckets a water and filled up the old caist iron wash pot to get it to bilin' so they could scald the hog and clean it. An'en they needed a barrel or big ol' washtub, one, to scald it in, and had to have buckets for dippin' out and pourin' water, and dishpans and big pots to put the meat in as it was cut up.

They had to get a early start on hawg-killin' day, to git done before dark. It was a hard day's work and took lots a help. I'd hear 'em talk about whether they'd shoot it, or knock it in th' head, and made shore I was out a hearin' while that went on. I never could stand to see nothin' hurt or killed.

When they got the hog scalded and scraped, they hung it up by the hind legs on a short stout pole they called a *gamblin' stick,* and poured some more water over it to wash off all the hair 'n trash 'n stuff. They cut off its head to let all the blood *drene* out a the carcass. Mom hated to clean that hog's head worser'n anything, but her and the rest of 'em liked that *souse meat* she made out of it. Dad liked it pickled. I never would eat it. I'd seen 'em a-cuttin' the eyes out a that ol' ugly naked hawg head and I didn't want nothin' to do with it.

They'us awful careful not to nick the gallbladder when they cut it off a th' liver. They said that old *gall* (bile—from the gallbladder) rurnt the meat if it got on it. The lungs, heart, and kidneys had to be cooked right away or they'd spile. They allus give *a mess a meat* to whoever come and helped 'em with it, and sent some of the parts that spiled quick to other folks around. They knowed who liked what and tried to send 'em whichever part they druther have. Nuthin' was throwed away—they used ever'thang but the squeal. They usually give the youn-guns th' bladder t' play with. They washed it and blowed it up with air, tied a strang around th' hole, and we played ball with it. Dad liked pickled pigs feet, so they was saved. They used separate pots to put meat trimmin's in for sausage, fat to render lard and cracklin's and stuff, as they finished trimmin' up the carcass and separated the hams, shoulders and middlin's.

Mom allus got some meat to cookin' dist as soon as it come off a the hog. We had frash meat for supper, breakfast and dinner for a few days, and tried to use up all the meat that couldn't be salted down before it rurnt. Fried *tenderline* (tender-loin) was Mommy's favorite, an'en she'd make *redeye gravy* in the pan. The rest of the meat would be *cyored* (cured) or salted down to preserve it and was put on shelfs to *take th' salt.*

The next day was a busy'un, too, and they used up more wood. The skin and fat and some of the fat off a the *innards* had to be *rendered out* to make lard and cracklin's, and sausage had to be made and canned. And Mom had to work up that souse meat and make liver mush. She was awful pa'tic'lar and never let nobody else fool with her souse meat and liver mush. It had to be done dist right.

We all liked them meat skins and cracklin's after they was baked good and *brickle* (brittle, crisp) in th' ub'm. I'd break one apart to see if it was good 'n brickle before I eat it. I didn't want no soft squshy fat meat, but we shore could *scrunch on* them brickle meat skins. Mom or one of the older younguns would mix up some cornbread batter, put some of them cracklin's in it and bake *crack-lin' bread.* We eat it til our belly button pooched out. We could eat a square yard of it.

Whenever anybody said meat, they allus meant hawg meat. Chicken was dist chicken. We never raised beef for meat. A cow was for milkin', and was kept til she died and was buried, or was sold, one. A family just about coutn't make it 'thout a cow. She had a name and stood up there right next to the family in importance. Now, she was took care of. A cow's kep' a-many a family from star-vation.

Everybody put a bell on their cow. Back then, people used to take their cattle they wudn't milkin' back into the mountains over toward Choga and leave them there for the summer. I remember people comin' by on the road, a-herdin' their cattle. They put a certain mark on their ear so everybody knew who they belonged to, and they all just run together back in the mountains. The cowbell helped them find their cow when they went to get her, and they knowed their cow by the sound of her bell.

When all us youngens was home, we kep' two cows so one'd still be a-givin' milk when the other'n was dry. They was bred so they wouldn't *come in frash* (bring a calf) close to the same time. We didn't get no milk for about two months when a cow come in frash. They turned her dry before the calf (kaif) come, and after it was borned we couldn't use the milk for about two weeks because she give *beaslin's* (colostrum), and you coutn't drank that.

When a cow got to *bullin'* (come in heat), one of the boys'd have to go borry a bull, or take the cow sumerce to get her bred. A bullin' cow is about the orneriest dang critter they is. They had to head 'er off and ketch her an'en do some wrasslin' to get her to lead with a rope halter.

Mom allus done the milkin' unless she was sick, but that ditn't hardly ever hap'm. She'd put dairy feed or nubbins in the feed box so the cow'd stand still while she milked her. She could squirt out big streams a milk, a-workin' both hands at the same time. I used to like to go watch her milk. I'd take my little tin cup and she'd milk some in it for me to drink sometimes, dependin' on the mood she was in. At times, she'd tell me to open my mouth, and she'd squirt some milk in it. But like as not, she was apt to draw a circle all around my face and just wash it good with the milk and not get nary drop in my mouth. She could aim it cler acrost th' stall and hit where ever she wanted to.

The milk was another thang where she was awful patic'lar about cleanness. She brung the milk to the house and strained it through a flour poke *strainin' cloth* that was kept dist for that purpose. It allus got washed out good and hung up to dry dist as soon as it was used. When she strained the milk out in big mouth gallon jars or lard buckets, she took it to th' spranghouse right then.

When she got ready to use th' milk for supper, she'd skim off most a th' cream. If she skimmed off too much cream, they called it "blue John." Lordy mercy, I loved that cream where it stuck to the side a th' jar when the milk got poured out. I'd sop the last drop of it out on my fainger and lick it off. I wisht it come in chunks so I could eat it like candy.

She saved up th' cream fer a few days til she got enough for a churnin', then brought it out a th' spranghouse and "poured it up" in th' churn. Then she'd tie a clean rag over the top a th' churn and lay a plate over that. Th' milk had to *clabber* before she could churn it. When it first started to *turn* (sour), it was called *blinked milk*, then it set up thick and clabbered. She checked it pretty clost, for she didn't want it to get too sour. It had to be jis' right.

Mom didn't want none a what she called ol' white puffy butter. She throwed off on people that made that kind a butter and said it wudn't fit to eat. She wanted it yaller and solid. When she got ready to churn, she put the *churn dasher* in the churn and pushed the led with a hole in the middle down over the dasher, then carried the churn full a milk sumerce and set down. As she worked th' churn dash up 'n' down, she had a rhyme she'd chant in rhythm: "Come butter, come; come butter, come. Ol' Saint Peter's standin' at th' gate, waitin' with a butter plate, come butter, come." In about twenty minutes, they'd be little wads a butter commence to pile up around th' hole in th' led where th' dasher went through.

She "*gathered*" the butter by holdin' the dasher kindly sideways and pushin' it around on top of the milk to make the butter stick together in a wad. When she was done with th' churn dash, she give it to one a th' youngens to lick, and give another'n th' lid. She put the butter in a big bowl, added some cold water and stirred it in to wash out ever bit of the buttermilk, then poured the milky water off. Then she put in a little salt. I liked to wait til she got th' butter *worked up* and moulded so I could git th' bowl to sop out with my fainger. I liked to watch her pack butter in the mould an'en push it out onto a saucer, and see that purty print it made on top of it. In fact, some people called it *a print of butter*. She took th' butter and buttermilk to th' spranghouse as soon as she got done.

◆   ◆   ◆

The only wild meat I remember us a-havin' was when Bud went a-squirrel or *pheasant* (grouse) *huntin'*. He liked them squirrel heads. He'd suck out the brains, and smack his lips, and make a big racket out of it, *a-showin' out*. I'd about as soon eat a housecat as a squirrel, myself. He went a-squirrel huntin' dist about ever mornin' when he was home. He loved to squirrel hunt about as good as he liked to devil and aggervate one a us youngens.

One day he went off a-squirrel huntin' and was gone a good little while. I wudn't much taller'n th' table, and was a-standin' in the kitchen by the table with my back to the op'm wender. All of a sudden I hyeard this racket like a big ol' squirrel makes when he's a-barkin', and about that time, sump'm hit me right on th' back a th' neck. Hit dist about knocked me down, and I *screamed like a river painter* (panther) when I put my hands up there and felt them thangs. Hit was three or four gray squirrels he'd shot and tied together by the hind legs, and had throwed 'em on me. They'd jist wrapped right around my neck and stuck. I like to a never got them thangs knocked off of me. Hit scared me so bad I wet my britches and th' water dist run acrost the kitchen floor in a stream an'en down through a crack, and I was so scared I dist stood there and watched it. I coutn' say a word. He jist hollered, a-slappin' his leg, 'n' *like t'died a-laughin'* at me. I's so mad I could a-kilt him. I ditn't see nary thing funny about it atall.

Once in a while, some of 'em went a-coon huntin' at night. I remember the coon huntin' because Dad had a carbide light with a reflector that he fastened on his *fard* (forehead) with a headband when they went a-huntin' at night. Flashlight batteries costed, and ditn't last much long out a-huntin' at night. I thought that light was sump'm magic. It had two metal cylinders that screwed apart in the middle where they tapered in and joined together. He poured some little gray grains a carbide in one side and added water in the other'n. It commenced to fizzin' and a-blubberin', and stunk like a rotten egg when he poured the water in it. When he struck a match and helt it up to the little hole in the middle of the reflector, it made a round flame that shot a way out.

How in the world could sump'm' burn water? I don't know, but hit shore done 'er. *I woutn' fruit ye.*

♦   ♦   ♦

I've seen TV shows and movies where they showed people in the mountains a-livin' off the land. They eat deer meat, bear and turkeys and all kinds a wild meat. They eat *high on the hawg* ever' day.

Wellsir, I got to studyin' about it, and I didn't recolleck us a-eatin' all a them thangs like that, and wondered why. So, I called my walkin', talkin' *'cyclopedie* named Bud, and asked him about it. He said that back then, they wusn't no wild game like that in the mountains around here where we lived. They wudn't enough *maist* (mast—nuts, berries, etc.) to feed nothin' after the chestnut trees all died out. Outside of squirrels, a few *pheasants* (ruffed grouse), *whistle pigs* (groundhogs), possums and coons, they wutn't nothin' much to hunt. So, outside of a chicken maybe oncet ever week or two, and fat back or streaked meat to git grease to fry in, we never had much meat except right after hog-killin' in the fall.

I tell ye, we was *pore*. P-o-o-r, pore. I mean dist about as pore as a-body can git and still make it. But we did. Somehow 'r other, Dad and Mom'd allus come up with sump'm.

I remember Mom a-cookin' some snowbirds oncet, and makin' dumplin's on 'em. It took them boys nigh onto two hours t'pick 'n clean 'em. Talk about *piddlin' business!* They wutn't a thimble-full a meat on one.

But we ditn't never eat no snakes. Or polecats.
And Dad said a dang 'possum's too naisty to eat.

RAISIN' CHICKENS

Chickens was another thing a family dist about had to have for eggs and meat. Ever'body had chickens back then, and ever'body had their favor-ite, like Dommerneckers, *Rhodollent* (Rhode Island) Reds, white, red or black *lagerns* (leghorns), and banties. We had all differ'nt kinds and mixes.

I allus loved bein' around chickens. I spacially liked to watch a big old rooster strut around and crow. Their long shiny neck feathers was so purty. Some of his feathers was so black that they looked green and shimmered when he stretched and bowed up his neck to crow. When one of 'em crowed, purty soon you'd hear another'n crow, over in Cullie's yard or off sumerce else, a-anserin' back. In books they say a rooster says "cock-a-doodle-do," but it sounded to me like he said, "Coward to come over here." You see, he ditn't want no other rooster a-comin' in his yard.

I could sound jist like a rooster a-crowin'. I used to like to devil one, and would go off out a sight behind the barn or sumerce, and crow real big. He'd crow back, and purty soon, here he'd come—a-huntin' that other rooster. Then I'd slip off and go sumerce else and crow. That ol' rooster would dist about crow hisself to death, and I'd dist about run him crazy, a-tryin' t'find that other rooster. Their eyes turns red and dist glows when they git mad, and he'd git plumb fightin' mad, a-jerkin' his head, blinkin' his eyes and kickin' up dirt.

We jist let them chickens roam wherever they wanted to, except we had to keep 'em run offa the porch—to keep 'em fum makin' sichy mess, y'know, all over the porch.

Chickens went to roost when it got dusky dark. We had *roostes* (roosts) built a way up 'nunder the raifters of the barn shed, and you'd see them chickens gether up and go to easin' up that pole ladder, one at a time. They'd jostle around and chuckle to theirself, a-gittin' fixed in their place, till they got all lined up on th' roost. Then they'd poke their head 'nunder their wing and go to sleep. I never could see *how in thunderation* they kept from fallin' off a them roostes. If we needed to ketch one, we'd wait til they went to roost, then it was easy to just pick it off the roost.

147

Sometimes a bunch'd git up in them big ol' hemlocks out at the back a the house and you could hear 'em in there a-chucklin' ever oncet in awhile, after we'd gone to bed. The foxes coutn't git 'em up there, but ever oncet in a while, a possum would climb up and git into 'em. They'd go to squawkin' and cacklin' and Dad or one of the boys, one, would jump up 'n grab the gun and go shoot that varmint out a there.

We built hen nestes all over th' place, eb'm on to the back of the house. We had t'clean 'em out, and put clean straw in their nest, or they'd get chicken lice, or mites, in 'em. I got some on me a few times. They're little ol' bitty thangs, and'll dist about eatch ye t'death.

Them chickens liked to git up inunder the porch and fluff up and waller in th' dust, and they'd be big ol' round holes wallered out all over in the dry dirt 'nunder there. People said they's a-takin' a dust bath, and done that t'keep lice off of 'em. I liked to git 'nunder there and play with 'em. They'd let me catch 'em, and I'd set in there with one of 'em on my lap, and talk to it and pet it. I loved chickens.

The hens usually started layin' about the middle a January, and started to settin' in about three months. Dad bought layin' mash to feed 'em. He'd cut up dried cayenne pepper and put in their feed to get 'em to lay. When a pullet got old enough to start to layin', her comb'd get real red. If somebody seed a girl a-actin' feisty, they'd say, "Her *comb's a gettin' red*." Bud said they was "*a-gittin' brigsome*."

We kept a *nest aig* in their nestes. That was a egg that they put a mark on so they could tell it from the frash'uns, and we'd dist leave it in there so the hen'd come back to her nest and lay some more. If you took all of 'em out, she'd leave her nest. Ever oncet in awhile, you'd hear a hen a-cacklin' and know she'd laid.

I liked to go gether up eggs. We took the egg bucket to go gether eggs in, but we kept 'em in another'n. We kept track of when they was laid, and put the frash'uns separate, so we could use up the oldest'uns first.

Sometimes, a hen'd go off and make a nest in th' weeds or sumerce to hide it. But you could watch her, and when she went to sangin', she was fixin' to go lay her egg, and you could watch where she went and foller her to her nest. When we *fount* it, usually they'd be a big pile a eggs in it. We'd put 'em in some water to figger out whichuns was rurnt. A rotten egg would float torge the top. If she'd already gone to settin', we dist let 'er set. The eggs'd be too fur gone t'eat.

She had to set three weeks before the *diddles* (baby chicks) hatched out. Now, if you know what's good fer ye, y'better leave a settin' hen alone. They'll fuzz up real big and spread out their wings, 'n fly into you, 'n' dist *flawg* the dickens out of you. They'll peck a chunk out a your arm or leg or dist wherever they can *git a purchase* on ye. They'd peck a eye out if you wutn't careful (*kyerrful*). You learn real quick what *mad as a settin' hen* means, and hit dist takes one time t'learn ye.

One time Dad put duck eggs under a ol' settin' hen. Soon's them ducks hatched out and hyeard that creek water a-runnin', they *made a bee line* fer the creek. Them ducks *like to a* drove that ol' hen crazy. She run up and down that creek bank a-cluckin' and a-callin' to 'em, and jist *come in a bean* a-drowndin' herself a-tryin' t'take *kyerr* a them diddles. And they'd be a-swimmin' and a-divin' and a-quackin' and havin' the best time you ever seed, not a-payin' a bit more a 'tention to her than nuthin'. Finally, she dis' got so out a breath that she dist give up 'n set down on th' creek bank 'n watched 'em. She had 'er mouth wide op'm and her tongue was dist a-waggin'. That ol' hen never did *have a lick of sense* after she got them ducks raised.

You had to keep a hen and diddles put up in a chicken coop at night for a while. That hen'd git them diddles out in the dew early of a mornin', and they'd *git drabbled* 'n die.

When the diddles got t'be fryin' size, we'd start to eat the old roosters and layed out hens. You talk about tough! You coutn't a drove a fork up in one a them old chickens if you was to fry one. They was *as tough as whit leather*. The only way you c'd eat one was to put it in a pot a water and cook it all day and make dumplin's on it. When they got ready to kill one, they'd throw out some chicken feed, 'n Mom or Dad one'd tell which one of the youngens whichun t' kill. They'd have t'ketch it, and wring its neck or chop its head off, one a t' other.

I coutn't stand t'watch 'em a-floppin' around a-dyin'. I got a good whuppin' one time 'cause they told me to wring a chicken's neck and I ditn'. I caught it, and kindly slung it around by the *goozle* a little bit, but not enough t' kill it. When I throwed it down, hit *took off like Snyder's pup*. They made all kinds of fun of me, n' said I's too dumb t'kill a chicken, and never did tell me to kill another'n. But I's smarter than they give me credit fer—I never aimed t'kill it. Dist druther take my whuppin'.

Dad used t'raise game roosters to rooster fight with. He'd catch the rooster he was aimin' to fight, and sharp'm its spurs. Sometimes he fastened a metal spur that he called a gaff, over its own spur so it could really cut up another'n. Other men would come and brang their caged-up roosters to our house to have a rooster fight. They'd start off a-braggin' and makin' bets on their rooster. Most of 'em ditn't have no money, much, t'bet with, but they'd bet pocket knifes 'n watches 'n stuff—likker—whatever they had. They'd pass a bottle a likker around while they was a-makin' their brags n' bets, a-chawin' 'n' a-spittin', and a-cussin' an' a-laughin' like big jacks a-brayin'.

I watched 'em one time. They was all ringed up in a op'm place out in the yard, and had put two roosters in to fight. If one rooster tried to get away, they'd ketch it 'n throw it back in, jist a-cussin', and call it a "G_d_ *kyaird*" (coward), a SOB, and all kinds a ugly names. When they throwed it back in, that other'n dist lit into it and tore it up. Blood was a-slingin' ever' wheres, with them a-beatin' their wings and flappin'. Its comb'd be about tore off and maybe a eye pecked out, and the other'n kept on til hit kilt that'n dead, an'en stood on top of it, a-peckin' its head. Then it'd rare back and crow. You never heard sichy cussin' and hollerin' and carryin' on like them men done. They had blood splattered all over 'em.

It made me sick on my stomach, and I had nightmares about them pore ol' roosters. I never watched nary nother'n. And I lost what little dab of respect I had left fer men.

How could any body be so cruel?

DISHWATER AND HOG SLOP

My older sisters used to stay in a racket over whichun was goin' to wash and whichun was goin' to dry the dishes. Dishwashin' was done with the dishpans settin' on the cookstove, so the water'd stay warm. We washed 'em in one dishpan and ranched 'em in another'n. Mom ditn' make soap. The only dishwashin' soap we had was that ol' brown Octagon™ soap, like she washed clothes with. It worked purty good if the water was real warm, but most of the time, the stove'd cooled down and the dishwater was kindly lukewarm by the time we got done eatin' supper.

We better not leave the bar of soap in the water, though—hit'd get soft and mushy, and jist be a-wastin' it. Ever time we needed more soap, we had to pick the bar up, rub it on the dishrag, an'en lay it back down. You learnt that you better get the glasses and plates first, for as the water cooled down, the grease started stickin' to the dishes after you washed a few. The soap ditn't cut grease hardly atall in cold water.

Our dishrag was a little old thin piece a flour poke or sump'm, and you coutn't scrub nothin' with it, it was so soft and flimsy. After they'd been used on the pots and pans a time or two, they looked dirty, even when they was clean. They was washed out in the ranch water, but a lot a times, they still soured. They was soaked in bakin' sodie water to get that smell out of 'em.

We didn't have no pot scrubbers, and the burnt or stuck stuff was awful hard to get out of a pan. Mom used to set the empty gravy pan back on the stove and said hit'd burn the gravy loose and make it easier to wash. It might a done it for her, but all I could tell was that it just glued it on better when it was my turn to wash 'em. Hit *made me so mad I could spit fire* when she done that. You had to use your fingernails or a spoon to try to scrape the stuff loose, and since I kep' my faingernails gnawed off to the quick, sometimes had to take the pan out to the spring branch and use sand to scrub it off.

By the time you got done with them old greasy pots and pans, the dishwater was usually cold, and the grease would be stuck in a thick waxy ring all around

151

the dishpan, with big flat globs of it a-floatin' around on top a the dishwater. Sometimes whoever threw out the water didn't get the dishpan cleaned out good. When Mom went to use it to mix up a cake of cornbread and found a greasy ring all around the inside of it, somebody *got their hin'end busted.*

I remember pourin' soapy dishwater on top a peelin's and scraps in the *slop bucket,* and stirrin' up hog shorts in it to feed the hogs. I got to wonderin' why we poured dishwater in the slop bucket, and asked Bud about it. He said it was to keep 'em from having worms and intestinal parasites and kept 'em cleaned out good.

If they was more dishwater in the dishpan than they wanted to put in the slop bucket, they just slung it out the kitchen door into the kitchen yard, where the ranchin' water, water where we washed our hands or bath'd in, and the wash water all got slung out. We ditn't have no grass in the yard next to the house, and when we run around the house, we knowed to slow up when we got to the kitchen yard. Hit was so hard packed and slick from all the greasy water throwed out on it, if you hit it on a dead run, you'd be on your backside with your feet up in the air and slid fifteen feet before you knowed what hap'm'd to you.

Sometimes, somebody or other might be a-comin' torge the kitchen door, and th' one a-throwin' out the water not be a-lookin', and they'd jist dash water all over whoever it was a-comin' in. I s'pect it wutn't allus accidental.

Mom slung a whole dishpan full a dirty dishwater out on one of Dad's old drankin' buddies one time—right in his face. Hit was dist a-streamin off a the top a his head and down his face. Hit wet the whole front of his shirt and ever'thing, too. He knowed better'n to say anything to her though, for she'd a-whupped him all over the kitchen yard. Him a-bein' a man woutn' a-made one bit a difference to her. Many a time I've seen her flex her arm, ball up her fist and shake it in the air and say, "I can outrun, outcuss and outfight any man on Jun'lusky." And she could.

And would. And did.

A man named Burchfield used to come to our house ever oncet in awhile, and him and Dad would get to drinkin' and he'd be *drunk as a lord* and coutn't go home. He stayed all night with us one time, and was purty well *tanked up* when he went to bed. We just had two beds besides Dad and Mom's, so he slept in the bed with the oldest boys.

Some time along in the night, he started in to bawlin' like a big overgrowed calf. Mom got up and lit the lamp and brung it in there to see what all the *ruckus* was about. And there he was—stuck down in betwixt the bed and the wall, *jist as naked as a jay bird.* He must a had to go outdoors and tried to get up when he fell in behind there and got hisself stuck. He was a purty good size man.

He let out another bawl, and Mommy set the lamp down and took off *dist a-flyin'* into the front room. When she come back, she had the broom. She *lit into him like a hen on a June bug,* and *jist beat the snot out of him* with that broom. She said, "I'll learn you to lay in here and beller like a dern calf in the middle a th' night, a-wakin' up ever'body in the house. Now I don't want to hear no more out a you."

Then Lewis got up and pulled him out a there and give him another thrashin'.

I don't remember if he ever stayed all night with us any more after that, but I betchey one thang—he never made no more racket at night at our house.

PLAY

BEING BORED/BEING THANKFUL

I am at a loss for words to describe my feelings when I hear a child of today say, "I'm bored."

Bored?!!!!

How on earth could anyone be bored with the mountain of toys, games, cassettes, CDs, radio, TV, VCR, computer games, movies, books, coloring books, crayons, markers, paints, brushes, all kinds of paper, pencils, swimming lessons, music lessons, sports, little league, school and church activities, and on and on, that kids have now, and take for granted? I can only imagine how I would have treasured having just one of the things they have become bored with.

You never caught one of us a-settin' around a-bein' "bored." And it *woutn't never a-done* for one of us to a-said that to where our Mammy or Pappy could a-heard it. They'd a-worked us to death at sump'm or other, til we'd a-been glad to have a minute to set down and rest. We was too glad, as it was, to get turnt loose a little while from all the work we had to do, to be bored.

My husband and I raised two wonderful children, but there were times when I found myself being upset when one of them didn't seem to appreciate something they were given. The thought would go through my mind how I would have loved that, and here this ingrate was, turning up its nose at it.

I had to learn to see things through my children's eyes instead of expecting them to see things through mine. Since they never had the experiences I had, there's no way they could appreciate things as I would.

As I have watched TV, and seen the crime and violence in the inner cities, I've gained even more appreciation for being born and raised in the mountains. You see the homeless huddled under bridges and on filthy, rat infested streets, with nowhere to go—no clean drinking water and eating out of trash cans. They live in constant fear for their lives. People are afraid to go outside their door, and can't let their children go outside to play.

We didn't have all the foods that people today consider necessary for a well balanced diet; but we didn't have to fight other people off to get to rummage through a trash can for some moldy bread or food that had been thrown away.

Even though life was hard, and we were poor, we had a security that those poor people will never know. We had acres and acres of woodlands in which to play, and clean pure water running down almost every holler. Our parents could just turn us loose and we could be gone all day, and nobody worried that somebody would come along and molest or kill us. We were more safe out in the mountains than those people are at any time.

We didn't have any locks on our doors. In the summertime, the doors and windows were all left open, and we didn't even have screens on them. We just went to bed and went to sleep without any worry. You could leave tools or anything lying around and nobody would steal them.

We didn't know we were poor. As I got older and became exposed to more things, I came to realize it, and felt badly deprived. Now that I'm a lot older, I realize that it is *because* we were poor and didn't have a lot of things, that I developed resources that I might not have known I had. We learned to entertain ourselves and develop our own imagination, creativity and talents by using whatever materials we had on hand.

I'm most thankful I learned that real happiness does not come from material possessions. It's all just "stuff." True happiness comes from being at peace with God and myself. I learned to enjoy being by myself and to be comfortable with "me," and in fact, get out of sorts when I don't get time to myself. I don't need a lot of people around me constantly, or be on the go to enjoy myself. That doesn't mean that I'm anti-social. I love being around other people, exchanging ideas and seeing how others live. If I didn't love people, I certainly wouldn't have gone into the nursing profession.

When you've been there, you learn compassion for others in similar circumstances. I was once in a nice car with someone when they passed an old battered pickup, and they said, "They ought to get that pile of junk off the road." I can't imagine such arrogance! They should be thanking God for what they have. But for the grace of God, it could be them—or me—in that old truck.

I remember an old Buick car my husband and I had when our second child was a baby. When we were first married, Van was in charge of the x-ray and lab department in a hospital in eastern North Carolina, and I had my choice of opportunities as a Registered Nurse. We bought a new car, and were enjoying having more money than what we needed for necessities. While we were happily awaiting our first baby, we had many discussions about the future, and decided we wanted to raise our family in the mountains.

We moved back home in December 1956, and he took a huge cut in salary to work in a doctor's office in Murphy, and I went to work at Andrews hospital making less than the maintenance man. Then in April, I had a Cesarean section when David was born two months prematurely, then another when Donna was born eighteen months later. I stayed at home to care for our two children. We didn't have money for any luxuries, but managed to have what we needed.

Then, the doctor Van worked for closed his lab. We couldn't afford the payments on the new car we'd bought, so we traded it in for an old '51 Buick. Something in the rear axle screamed like a lost soul as we drove along, and it had a big hole rusted out in the floor board on the passenger side, right under my feet. But it ran well, and got us there and back home. Every time Van drove through a puddle, water splashed up on my legs (or higher), if I wasn't careful to keep something over the hole in the floor. He liked to catch me off guard, and did it intentionally sometimes. He laughed so hard that I couldn't stay mad at him.

Unlike many young people today who want a home, new car and everything right now, we knew how to manage with what we had, and knew the difference in luxuries and necessities. We didn't go into debt to have the best of everything immediately. We had learned how to discipline ourselves. I made a choice, and thought being home with my babies was more important than a job to keep a new car. We could buy a new car later, but our children were only going to be babies once, and only for a short time. I've never regretted that decision. And we've had lots of laughs, remembering that old Buick.

I recently heard a man criticize people for buying shoes at a factory return outlet store. He said they were shoes somebody else had worn, then boasted, "I've never wore nobody else's shoes in my life," as he stuck one of his feet out and looked admiringly at his shoe.

He's *"like a hog under a oak tree,"* never lookin' up to see where the acorns are comin' from.

And I betchey he never went barefooted in the snow, neither.

PLAY PURTIES

We ditn't ever call 'em "toys," we called 'em *play purties*. And nary a single, solitary store-bought toy did we have. I'll tell you what we did have—we had what we could come up with by usin' whatever we could find. Nobody in this country in this day and age could imagine just how limited we were in man-made materials; but we each developed a vivid imagination and creativity as a result.

Take this one thing, for instance: Think of all that would be eliminated from today's everyday world when I say we had nothing plastic. And we never had no posterboard, paper, color *crins* (crayons), paints, glue, paste, tape, markers, books or magazines, neither. We was lucky if we had one little stub of a pencil. The only pair of scissors on the place was the haircuttin' scissors and the ones Mom used for cuttin' cloth, and she never let us use 'em for nuthin'. She woutn't eb'm cut paper with 'em—said it rurnt their adges. She took care of them scissors and kep' 'em put up.

At our house, we had the barest of necessities. Even a tin can was a treasure, as all the canned stuff we had was in fruit jars—and they got washed out and put up for next year. We better not be caught a-playin' with nary'n, for they costed too much to have to buy new'uns ever year. If a jar got chipped on the rim, we used it for a *flare pot* (vase) in the house, or drunk out of it, one.

One treasure we had was a piece of arn railroad track about seb'm inches long. That was our make-b'lieve bulldozer or roadscrape that we used to bulldoze roads out in the dirt with, to crack walnuts on, or to straighten out bent nails on with a hammer.

We made purty red pick-ups or lawgin' trucks, one, out of empty Prince Albert™ *'backer cans* (smoking tobacco tins). They was sorter flat with the sides rounded, you know, about a inch thick and maybe three inches wide and five inches high. We pulled the led off an'en pulled the end out of it, an'en pulled it apart at the seam and op'med it out flat. Then we bent it in a squared U shape to make our pick-up bed, and tacked it down on one end of a piece of board, a-leavin' a couple inches stuck out for the cab part. We nailed a tarpaper tack on the front end, where the radiator cap would be, and tied a strang around it so we could walk and pull it if we wanted to do some long-distant haulin'. We broke up little sticks and ricked 'em up on our trucks like sticks a cordwood, and hauled it to town to sell. Or used short lengths of corn stalks and made out like they was big old lawgs.

We pulled the buddin' blossoms off of *lily bushes* (Rose of Sharon) to use for "women people." The petals was spiral shaped, and the tip ends was jist a-fixin to unfold—kindly flared out like a skirt is. We set her in the truck with the man when they was a-goin' to town, to the *movin' pitcher show* at the theater or goin' off *a-loaferin'* summerce.

We made fences out a cornstalks or sticks, one, and laid out a great big farm on the ground there. We made us some men, horses, dogs and other animals out of cornstalks. Like, for a man, we'd cut a slice off of a cornstalk a little lesser'n a inch long for his head, and another piece about two inches long for his body. We cut narr' strips longways off of the tough outer peelin', an'en sharpm'd 'em on the ends to stick in the pith (soft center) of the slices to join the head and body together, and to make legs and arms. We made hosses and cows and thangs the same way. For the cows, we cut a short slice off and stuck it 'nunder her belly to make her a milk bag.

Fer some reason, I thought a zebry was sump'm I dist had to have, so I allus made me a zebry. I *never thought one breath* about it a-bein' odd to have a zebry on a farm. I made it a great long neck, and it was fun to have that zebry a-pokin' it's head up to where it could see over top a thangs where them cows and thangs coutn't.

We stacked up corncobs with the ends overlappin'—like how a log cabin's made—and built some barns, cribs, and other buildin's. We made whole set-tle-ments, an'en played like we was people in 'em. We made up tales about what-all they was a-sayin' and doin'. Like, we'd meet up out on the road in our pickups and pull over and stop. One would say, "Howdy, Roscoe, *hahyou?*" The other'n would answer back and say, "Well, Sam, *jest tollible*, I guess. My blamed ol' truck haint a-runnin' *worth a plug nickel*, and I can't *fer the life of me* figger out what'n th' heck's wrong with th' dang thang."

Then the other'n would say, "Wellsir, why don't ye jist pull off here and let's *monkey around* inunder the hood and see if we can't figger it out." So we'd pull over to the side of the road, get the cornstalk men out and lean 'em up against the front of the truck. Sam'd maybe kick a *tar* (tire), and say, "Looks like ye need a new *casin'* (tire), too. I'd be kinda *juberous* (dubious) a that'n, if I was you." An'en we'd finish actin' it out.

Sometimes we was lucky enough to get aholt of a old metal barrel ring to make a hoop (rhyme it with book) to play car with. We made a guide for the hoop out of a stout piece a wire (rhyme it with tar) about two foot long. We bent one end over to make a handle, then bent the other end over and down into a U shape for the hoop to fit into. You give the hoop a little shove to get it to rollin', an'en started to runnin' after it, and put the U down low ag'in the wheel behind it to push it along and guide it. If we ditn't have no wire, we used a stick. We'd run for miles around and around the yard, a-makin' rackets like cars a-runnin', tryin' to see if one's Ford could outrun the othern's Shivalay.

Us littl'uns would tie a strip a cloth around the end of a stick for a bridle, an'en git a-straddle of it and play like we was ridin' a hoss. We allus named 'em. We'd bray like a mule or whinny like a hoss, paw the ground and kick up dust, and jump over imaginary logs and fences. Ever oncet in awhile, we took our hoss out to the creek to git a drank a water and let it rest some.

One time Lawerence and my cousins, Buddy and Tooter built a homemade *waggin* (wagon). They took a crosscut saw and sawed some wheels off a the end of a lawg about a foot through, an'en bored holes through the middle of 'em with a auger. Then they made some axles and fastened the wheels on it with a big old nail drove crossways through the ends. The front axle would swivel around, and they'd put one foot on one side and one on the other'n, over clost to the wheels, and push on it with their feet to guide their waggin. They done a good job, and had lots of fun with it. They drug it up the steep trail torge the toilet, an'en took turns a-ridin' it back downhill.

They was a whole lot bigger'n me, and I usually dist watched 'em play, but one day they decided to be nice to me (or so I thought), and put me on it to let me ride one time. They showed me where to put my feet over on the axle next to the wheels, told me to hold on good, an'en *took a run'n go* and pushed me off real hard. I went a-clatterin off down that trail, dist a-ballhootin'. Them wheels wutn't e'zackly round, and bumped so bad hit like to a-jarred my guts out. My teeth chattered together so bad I bit a chunk out a the inside of my jaw. My feet jarred loose, and I coutn't guide it, and the first thang I knowed, I tore right through the middle of a patch a blackberry brars along the side of the garden fence. Hit fin'ly r'ared up on the garden fence and turnt over right on top of me. Them brars dist *tore me up like new ground*, and I was beat up all over. Hit *come in a bean* a-killin' me. So much fer waggin' ridin'. And good-hearted boys.

An'en one of us might say, "*less pl'like*" (let's play like) and tell the other'n what they'd thought up for us to *play like* (pretend). For instance, one would say, "less pl'like Injuns." So, we'd cut tall Joe Pye weeds, tie the tops together, stand the long stout stalks up and spread out the bottoms in a circle to build a teepee. We'd put rocks inside to make a place to set down and pull *furrins* and *pennyrile* (ferns and pennyroyal) and put over 'em to pad 'em with. We'd go to the woods, gether up a roll a sheet moss and brang it back, an'en cover the teepee up all over, and hang a flap over the door. We laid moss on the floor like a carpet. Hit was so purty and green—looked dist like sump'm out of a fairy-tale book. And, oh, I can still smell how good that pennyrile, ferrins and moss smelt when you got in there.

They was a great big ol' white flint rock that stuck a way up out of the ground, out betwixt the crib and the creek. It got warm out in the sun, and we use to go set on it and play. We snuck the hammer or the grow devil, one, out there to knock off chips of flint to use and to play with. Hit was purty just to look at. We'd strack pieces of flint together to make sparks fly off, like Injuns used to do to start a fire.

We had a old broke-off knife that we used to cut stuff with, but usually used a piece of broke glass or a sharp piece of that flint rock for cuttin' and scrapin' stuff. When we wanted to cut sump'm that we needed a good knife for, we took it to the house and got a knife and done our cuttin' there an'en put the knife back up. We ditn't take it off nowhere to lose. A pocket knife would of been a real treasure.

When we made a bow and *arr'* (arrow), we made the bow out of a green stick that would bend, but not bend too easy, and used a piece of heavy twine for the bow strang. We sharpm'd sticks for arr's. We made headbands by overlappin' ends of laurel leafs, and pinned 'em together with little sharp twigs. Then we'd go off a-huntin'. We brung back buffaloes, *dyeres* (deer), rabbits, and all kind a wild meat, to hear us tell it. We went through the motions, anyhow.

What we liked to play with better'n dist about anythang was a slingshot. Paw Taylor learnt me how to make one. Now, back in his day, they *ax'ly* used 'em to kill squirrels and birds and things with, that they eat, and to kill snakes with. They was savin' with their bullets. He showed me all about what kind a rocks to use. Paw could knock a catbird right out of his cherry tree the very first lick, and kill it *stone cold dead.* He allus kept his slingshot and some rocks ready, a-settin' on his porch in a tin can right by his cher.

I made my slingshot prongs out of laurel. Laurel wood is hard and don't break easy, and the way it grows, is easy to find the best shape of a Y. The slingshot rubbers was strips cut off of a inner tube. The best pouch in the world is a old shoe tongue, or boot tongue, one. Hit's soft enough to bend around a rock, and rough enough to let you keep a good grip on it. And the rock stays jist *e'zackly* where you put it til you let it fly. You got to have a good pouch or you can't make your rock hit where you want it to. Hit's got to stay dead center in the middle of yer pouch.

I never did kill nuthin' but snakes with it, but they was *dead meat* whenever I *cut down on* one a them. I druther to shoot empty tin cans or bucket leds, one, to git to hear the ping they made when the rock hit 'em. I got so I could dent one up purty good.

Sometimes we'd find a little limb that had the right shape to whittle out a pistol and make a bow and arr', and played like we was the Lone Ranger and Tonto©, like we'd hyeard over the radio. Then we'd ride the range and kill off all the villians (vill-e-yens). We'd hide behind bushes and trees and wait for the dirty dogs to come ridin' by, and we'd ambush 'em and fill 'em full of lead and arr's. We hollered "Pow! Pow!" for gunshots, and "Ping" for arr's, and made mouth rackets for ricochet bullets.

We made flute whistles out of willer bark and kazoos and crow calls out of laurel. Or we'd swipe some a Bud's cig'rette papers if we had a old comb that still had any teeth left in it. When you hold the paper up ag'in a comb and barely put your lips on it and hum out through your mouth, hit sounds dist like a kazoo. They was us'ally other younguns to play with us, and ever'body'd have sump'm to make a racket with—either a bucket led, old wore-out rub board, a tin can full a rocks, or dist a old rusty lard bucket to beat on with a stick. We sounded like a rag'ler marchin' band. Or would bend over and dance and skip around in a circle, a-playin' like we was Injuns a-doin' The Woar (war) Daince, a-smackin' our hand on our mouth while we done The Woar Chaint.

We *lufta* (loved to) play in the barn loft, and stayed up there fer hours on end. We watched peewee birds build their nestes up there in the raifters, an'en waited and watched for the little birds to hatch out. Ever' day or two, we'd ease up to a nest we could git to, and look in to see how thangs was comin' along. We was awful careful not to tetch nuthin', though, for they said the mamma bird could smell it if you tetched her nest, and woutn't never come back, an'en them pore little baby birds'd starve to death. We ditn't want nuthin' like that to hap'm. We learnt to tell which bird nest was which, by the kind of eggs that was in their nest—what kind of speckles and which color they was, and so on.

One time me and Oval saved up enough strang to make us a tellyphone line to reach from the crib out to the barn. We beeswaxed our strang real good, and took and poked the end through a hole we'd punched in the bottom of two tin cans, an'en tied it around a nail and pulled it up flat ag'in' the inside. A stick would a-deadened the sound, is how come we used a nail. One of us got up in the barn loft and set in the door, and the other'n got in the crib and stood at the wender. You had to hold it by jist the end a the tin can and keep the strang real taut and let it *swang* free so it wutn't be a-tetchin' nothin', so it could vibrate, an'en hold the can over your ear while the other'n talked, to make it work. *Law, me,* woutn't we a-had us a time with some walkie-talkies?

On second thought, though, we prob'ly got dist as much satisfaction—or more, out of our home-made tellyphone, a-havin' to save up strang, and figger it out, and all.

We made up all kinds a secret codes so nobody but us knowed what we was a-talkin' about, and wrote letters to one another in code. They was complicated, too, but we memorized 'em. We made ink out a pokeberry juice and made a pen out of a big rooster wing feather, cut off slianted to make a point. We wrote on a paper poke, a used en-velop, or whatever we could sneak out a the house.

One thing we loved to play with was what we called *spinners*. When Mom used all the #8 thread off a wood spool, we'd whittle it in two in the middle, an'en whittle and taper it down on that end. We'd hunt a stick just the right size to fit in the hole, push it down in it and sharp'm it on the end, leavin' about a inch handle a-stickin' up on top to git a-holt of it by. It took some practice, but we learnt how to hold it dist right between our thumb and middle fainger, an'en give it a sudden twist and turn it aloose. We'd see whose spinner could spin the longest.

We made *daincers*, too. We'd cut out a pasteboard circle, about a inch and a haif to two inches acrost, an'en punch a sharpm'd stick down through the middle of it. We spinned it jist like we done a spinner to make it daince. We'd take poke-berry juice ink and make spots on 'em to *doll 'em up*, so they'd be purty when they dainced.

We made what we called a "*zizzer*" out of a big two hole button and a strang. To make one, put a end of the thread through each one a the holes, an'en tie it in a hard knot, leaving about a ten inch loop a strang on each side of the button.

Loop the thread over each of your thumbs, a-keepin' the button in the middle. Then brang your hands about six inches apart to give some slack in the strang, and swing th' button around and around, a-twistin' up th' thread. Slowly bring your hands apart, then pull harder and faster, and this puts tension on the thread and starts the button to spinnin' as the thread untwists.

Right when the thread jist about comes untwisted, start to giving it slack again. The button keeps on a-spinnin' and twists it up again. You can do this over and over without having to rewind, just by pullin' your hands apart an'en easin' 'em back torge each other. The thang is, you can ease that button down to jist barely tetch sump'm solid as it spins, and it makes the dangdest whinin' racket you ever hyerd, "zzzizz, zzzizz, zzzizz." And hit's a real loud, high-pitched racket if somebody holds out a sheet a paper good and tight for you to make it zizz against. Sounds like a *si-rene* (siren) on a poleece car.

A neighbor up the road give me a doll when I was about five, and I thought that was the purtiest thang I'd ever laid my eyes on. I loved that doll. Suzy had on a purty dress, and a matchin' bonnet with ribbins on it that tied 'nunder her little chin. Her body was stuffed, but her head, arms and legs was made out of sump'm they called *delft*. One day I had her by one arm a-runnin' through the yard, and hit her head agin' a rock a-stickin' up, and it broke. I was plumb mortified when I seen it was holler inside, except for the parts that made her eyeballs roll down and shet. They wutn't no way to fix it, and I was heartbroke. I don't remember ever havin' *nary nother* bought doll.

The only other dolls I had was ones I made. I took a square of old rag and put a round rock or a wad a some kind a stuffin' in the center to make a head, folded and gathered up the cloth under the head and tied it, then fluffed out the bottom for its skirt. I made little'uns for babies and little younguns. Or dist rolled a little fat stick a wood up in a rag or cornshucks like a baby in a blanket.

Somebody brung in a pair of old scissors one time and I figgered out a way to cut and fold pasteboard to make little chairs and tables without usin' any glue, 'cause I ditn' have none. I usually made 'em out of washin' powder boxes. Paste-board was hard to come by, and when anything that come in a pasteboard box was used up, the box was saved. A shoebox was a treasure that didn't get cut up, though. It was used to keep stuff in. We hardly ever got one a them.

I now realize how kind some of the kids were that I went to school with. When I was in grade school, girls used to bring their paper dolls to school and play with them at recess. I thought they was so purty, and liked to watch girls play with their paper dolls. Sometimes, one of 'em asted me to play with her dolls with her. I loved that, and was real careful with 'em. I drampt of havin' purty clothes like them dolls had.

I cut women's pictures out of an old Sears & Roebuck catalog to make me some paper dolls and drawed clothes on the blank spaces of used notebook paper and cut 'em out to put on 'em. Some of the older youngens had brung home a few short pieces of throwed away *color crins* (crayons) from school and I colored their clothes with them. I sneaked off to the back room and *hunkered down* out a sight betwixt the bed and the wall, and set in there and played with 'em on the floor, afeared I'd get in trouble for cuttin' up the catalog.

Then one time, somebody give me a book of paper dolls. The dolls was printed on the cover, and was stiffer than the clothes you cut out on the inside pages. They was easier to hold and play with, and a whole lot purtier than my homemade ones was.

And you can bet I took care of 'em.

PLAYIN'

As a child, I didn't really get to know my older brothers and sisters very well, since there was so much age difference. They were busy doing other things while I was out playing. When I was born, Bud was 14, Sweetie was 13, Lewis was 11, Alma was 8 and Thelma was 7.

By the time I was old enough to remember much, the oldest four were gone. Sweetie and Lewis left home when they were around seventeen, and went to the CCC camps and stayed there til they got married. The year I was nine, Bud was caught carrying a load of liquor and served a six months term in prison, then worked away from home, off and on. Alma married at 16, and Coonie at 15. I remember them playing some of the games we played, but mostly, they were too big to play with us younger kids. There were certain games you played when you were a certain age, and once you passed that age, you were made fun of if you played them.

My aunt Cullie and uncle Jess Mathis had a bunch of youngens and they lived in the holler across the road from us. Their sons, Buddy and Junior, was closer to Lawerence's age. Their daughter Fay Frances, was a little younger than me. Everybody called her "Sister." They played with us a whole lot. Mom's brother Kermit married Dad's sister, Cora. Their boy, Tooter, was about two years older, and their girl, Harriett was a year younger than me. Tooter come to play with Lawerence and Buddy a lot, but Harriett didn't never come much. They lived on up the road above Paw Taylor's.

They was allus a-plenty of youngens to play with one another, but Sister was the only girl for me to play with much. Since I had a brother next older than me, and two younger brothers, and boy cousins near my age that played at our house, we mostly played with boys. They liked to show how tough they was, and what all they could do, but anything they could do, I could do jist as well, or better. Except fer spittin'. I never did understand why an ol' boy started spittin' ever few minutes when he got about twelve or thirteen year old—I reckin they thought it made 'em look more like a man. Made 'em look *silly as a goose* to me.

But I learnt to be tough and hang in there. I also learnt that the older boys, 'spacially Lawerence, would do the "Tom Sawyer" trick to get me to do jobs that they didn't want to do. All he had to do was put that superior look on his face, snerl up his lip, and tell me "lil' ol' silly gals can't do that," and I'd show him that this was one gal that could. It took me awhile, but I fin'ly caught on that he knowed dist e-zackly what he was doin', and I was the sucker.

I was goin' on seven when Vernon was born. He was a big chunky baby with red hair, and could bawl the loudest of any youngen I ever heard. Sounded dist like a caif a-bellerin'. Fortunately, he laughed a lot. It was my job, a lot of the time, to "watch the baby." He was Mom and Dad's pet, since he was the baby, and was a boy to boot. When he got big enough to play, though, him and Oval played together most of the time, and I played with Sister.

After supper was when a bunch of us played together outside til it got dark. Some of the outdoor games I remember us a-playin' was *Whoopee Hide*, which the *town doods* at school called "Hide And Seek," tag, Aunt Nee Over, Back Door, Red Rover, Crack The Whip, London Bridge, Drop The Handkerchief, and Kick The Can. Our favorite was Whoopee Hide. And of course, we played ball. We made our own balls out of twine wrapped around a rag or a little round rock, and made our bat out of a narr' board with the handle whittled down on one end so we could catch a-holt around it. It looked more like a thick paddle than a bat.

At school, where we had a round bat, we picked out a leader for each side, then holding the bat straight up and down, one tossed the bat to the other'n. The other'n caught it. Wherever they caught it, they would take turns puttin' their hand around the bat, one above where the othern's was, til one got so clost to the top the other'n couldn't get a hand hold and lost their chance to bat first. If they just barely could get a-holt of it, they had to toss the bat over their shoulder without any more hold than what they had. If they dropped it, the other'n won.

Another game I remember watching boys play was called Club Fist, but I don't exactly remember why they played it. What I remember is that one would get a-holt around the leader's thumb, making a fist. Then another boy would close his fist around that one's thumb, and as many as could reach in stacked their fist on. The leader would give the top one three choices: "Knock it off, take it off, or let the crows pick it off?" If he chose to take it off, the others would make fun of him for being too sissy to try to hold on. If he said, "Knock it off," the leader would try to knock the othern's fist off. Now, that could do some hurtin'. Then, if he said, "Pick it off," the leader would try to pinch a chunk out of his hand til it hurt so bad he turned loose. I don't reckin that felt none too good, neither, just goes to show how much an ol' boy likes to prove how tough he is.

We had rhymes we said to pick out who was "it." We'd get in a line and one person stood in front and pointed to each one in the line as he spoke, counting off one person for each word: "Acker backer, sody cracker, acker backer, boo. Acker backer, sody cracker, out goes YOU." That person dropped out of the line, and this was repeated til one person was left, and they were "it."

Another was: "William Trembletoe, he's a good fisherman, catches hens, puts 'em in a pen, some lay eggs, some lay none. Wire, briar, limber lock, three geese in a flock, one flew east, one flew west, one flew over the cuckoo's nest, O-U-T, out goes he, you blamed old dirty dish rag YOU."

Boys settled who went first by pickin' up a round, flat rock and spittin' on one side, then one askin', "Wet or dry?" The othern'd say which, and they'd flip the rock in the air. If the wet side landed up, the one who said wet got to go first, or choose sides first. This was like flippin' a coin for heads or tails.

Girls played hopscotch a lot. Boys would play sometimes at home with a sister or a cousin, but he ditn't let no other boys know he done it.

I reckin playin' marble was the universal game that everbody played. From the time they was old enough to learn how, boys and girls both played. Then when girls got on up a little bigger, they ditn't like to git down and crawl around in the dirt and git their dresstail and bloomer legs and stockin's dirty, plus, a-bendin over and crawlin' around, hit was hard to keep your dresstail down and not show boys your bloomers. *Nice girls keep their dresstail down.* Now I druther play marble than dist about anythang but climb, and would git down and play til I was the only girl left a-doin' that, and got too ashamed to do it at school. But I shore done it at home. I kept me some marbles hid in a 'backer poke. I remember a big ol' cream colored taw I had, and I could allus win me some marbles with that'un. I could win dist as many as Lawerence could, but he liked to sneak around and use a steel ball-bearin' and bust 'em up. I *ditn' aim to* have my marbles busted up, so I quit playin' with him.

Then there was the doodle bug holes. These were about two inch wide, cone shaped depressions in the ground where the doodle bugs lived, usually under the edge of the porch in the dry dirt. We took a little piece of straw and dist barely scratched the dirt down in the cone, to make him think a ant or sump'm was tryin' to get out of it. As we scratched, we chanted some rhymes to get him to come out. One I remember was, "Doodle bug, doodle bug, come out and git yer bread and butter."

Sometimes it took a long time to get him to come. But dreckly, you'd see the dirt commence to wigglin' in little jerks, and he'd finally wiggle on out. All of a sudden, he'd grab aholt of the end of the straw with his pinchers, and we'd give it a jerk. We didn't never kill him, but we shore jerked him out a there when he got aholt of that straw.

In the wintertime, we played Blindfold, Bum, Bum, Bum, and Clothespins. In Bum, Bum, Bum, there'd be the same number of people on each side. They'd decide what they were going to "play like" they were doing, then join elbows and go marching toward the other side. They said, "Bum, Bum, Bum, here we come" as they marched, then stopped in front of the other side. The other side asked, "Where you from?" They'd say, "Purty girls and boys station." The other side asked, "What's your occupation," to which they answered, "Most any thing," so they'd say, "Git to work."

The other side would have to guess what they were acting out. If they guessed, then it was their turn. If they didn't, then the other side got to do it again.

We played checkers and fox-and-geese on homemade boards, using grains of corn or colored buttons for game pieces. We wudn't allowed to play no kind of card games—that was a awful big sin. If Mom found any cards at our house, she stuck 'em in the stove and burnt 'em, no matter who they b'longed to.

We played "Who's got the thimble," only we used a button or a bean or sump'm for a thimble. Mom was kindly pa'tic'lar about her thimble and ditn't want it lost.

We learnt how to do all kinds of designs with a circle of string looped around our fingers in certain formations. Some of the designs we made were Jacob's ladder, cat in the cradle, and cup and saucer.

The rare times I got to go to Cullie's, though, we played rummy, gin rummy, setback, and all kinds of card games. We made them cards live hard. We used matches instead of money. When we needed to keep score, Jess had a scoreboard made out of a piece of wooden board that he made holes in with a big nail. We set matches in the holes and moved 'em down the board to count off the score by fives. That's where I learnt to count by fives and tens. Everybody laughed and cut up and we had the biggest time. I wisht we could have fun and laugh at home like that.

I shore did *luf'ta* go to Cullie's.

One time somebody give Cullie and them a bunch of high heel shoes and a poke full of fancy lookin' dresses. They give some of 'em to Alma, Thelma and Coonie. I remember one of them dresses was real bright red with big ol' yaller flares on it, and was made out of some kind a silky-like cloth. They wutn't a woman on the creek that *would a-been caught dead* in one a them thangs.

Them shoe heels was so high they couldn't hardly stand up, much less walk in 'em. They must a-been three inches high, and them heels tapered down real keen at the bottom. They kept a-turnin' over and they *like to* a-sprained their ankles a-tryin' t' walk in 'em. Fin'ly, they took some of 'em out to the chop block and chopped them heels off, and tried to wear 'em thataway.

That never worked neither. They never knowed about steel arch supports. After they cut the heels off and put the shoes on, the toe dist *dang nigh* turnt straight up and their heel set down, with the back a th' shoe dist about plumb down agin' th' ground. You ort to a-seen 'em a-cranin' their neck, a-leanin' fards, a-tryin' to walk with the toes a them shoes turnt up and them a-tryin' t'keep from fallin' backerds. They coutn't a bit more walk than they could a-flew. I dist got down and rolled, a-laughin'. *Hit beat a hen a-rootin'.*

Them shoes might a been all right on a street sumerce, but you can't hardly walk in keen heel shoes on a rough plank floor with them heels a-gittin' ketched in th' cracks, or out in the yard a-stobbin' up holes in th' dirt, one. They wutn't no use in nobody on Jun'lusky a-tryin' t'wear 'em.

Them shoes was purty, and looked *real costly*. I could a cried, a-thankin' how I'd a loved to a-had 'em if they hatn't a had them ol' high heels on 'em.

Me and Sister played dress-up and would put on a pair of them high heel shoes and one of them dresses. They was a way too big for us, but we never cared. We dist tied a belt around our waist t'hold it, 'n' *scooched up* the skirt part. We thought we was grand ladies.

She'd got a-holt of a tube of dark red lipstick, prob'ly her sister Grace's, and we painted up our lips with it. Cullie didn't care, but I made sure Dad or Mom didn't ketch me a-paintin' my lips. That was a sin, and nobody but whores done that. They called 'em *Jezzybelles*, and girls or women that painted their mouth and smyered rouge on their face was like *a bullin' heifer*, out a-lookin' for a man. And if a man give her what she was a-astin' fer, she coutn't blame nobody but herself.

They was big ol' round spots of bright or'nge powders that growed on the side of pine trees—pollen, I guess. We scraped some off and used it for rouge when we got dressed up in our fancy dress and shoes, put on our lipstick, and wore our chinkypin *joo'ry* (jewelry) that we made out like was pearls. We ditn't know what a whore was, nohow.

When we went up the old railroad grade next to the pines and picked *chinkypins* (chinquapins) in the fall, we'd brang 'em in and strang 'em up on thread and make necklaces and bracelets out of 'em. After we wore 'em a day or two, we started chawin' 'em off of the string and eatin' 'em til they was all gone. They'd keep right on if you ditn't eat 'em up, but got too hard to eat. They was *as hard as a pine knot* when they dried out. I reckin chinkypins still grows in the mountains. They was good—tasted sorter like ches'nits.

Me 'n Oval 'n Vernon had us a playhouse, too. We'd change the place where it was ever once in awhile, but we allus had one. Sister Mathis'd come and bring her little sister and brother, Frieda and Gail, to play in it with us. Sister looked after them like she was their mammy. W'y, she'd lug one of them younguns around when they was so big their feet'd *pyert near* drag the ground, but it never seemed to bother her none about takin' 'em ever'where she went. We'd just play like they was our youngens in the playhouse. We'd feed 'em and put 'em to bed and they'd go right along with whatever we done.

When Sis and Lewis' boy, Roy, got big enough, we made us a playhouse up at their house, down under the pines where the spring was. We'd stay in the play house all day, some days. Sis'd allus give us stuff t'eat. Lots a times, she'd be down there a-doin' the washin'. That's where her wash place was.

Anything broke and throwed out got looked over to see if we could use it, and usually got took to the playhouse. We made tables, chairs, benches, and a cook-stove out of rocks and old boards. We really had a good seat or table if they hap-pened to be a stump there. Lard and syrup bucket lids made good plates, and the porcelain discs out of can lids was saucers. If we got aholt of any tin cans, we used 'em for pots and pans, and glasses or vases. We gathered flares for a flarepot, and allus had one. (Any kind of flower arrangement was called a *flowerpot.*) We used short hemlock limbs or broom sage for a broom and kep' the floor swep' *as clean as a whistle.*

An old chipped teacup with the handle broke off made a good butter mold, and we used other things to mould cakes, cornbread or biscuits. We'd pack a mould full of damp sandy dirt and turn it out upside down onto a board or plate, an'en decorate it with daisy petals and things. Seed pods was green beans, round creek rocks was taters, sand was cornmeal and dirt was flour. We made up a cake of cornbread to eat with our beans and taters. We played like we cooked and baked, an'en then set down to eat.

In them days, nobody around here except peddlers ever knocked on a door—they dist come on in. If somebody they knowed knocked on the door, Dad or Mom one'd say, "Git on in here. You don't need t'stand out there a-knockin' on no door," in a tone of voice that said, "Ain't you dis' like one a the fam'ly?" like they was kindly insulted because somebody thought they had to knock.

We'd been told in school that you was s'post to knock on a door before you come in, so we tried t'act like we had good manners at our playhouse. We played like it had a door, and opm'd and shut it when we went in or out, like we was s'post to. One of us'd be *"comp'ny" a-comin',* and would knock on the door. Now, we treated our comp'ny good, I mean. The other'n inside the house would go op'm the door and ast our comp'ny in and offer 'em a cher and sump'm to eat or drank. They'd ask, "D'j'eet yit?" Then th' othern'd say, like, "Much obliged, but I *done and already* eat. I might try a piece a that cake, though, *if y'don't care."*

We'd go through the motions of cuttin' off a nice big piece a cake, layin' it out on a nice plate, puttin' a fork beside it, and take it to our comp'ny. They'd say "Thankye," or "Much obliged," and go through th' motions of eatin' it with the fork.

We talked like we'd heard grown folks talk when comp'ny come, and tell where all we'd been and what all we'd been a-doin', and ast how the *fambly* was. It was awful bad manners not to ast about their fambly. We made up some purty hairy tales sometimes, when we got to goin' good.

I musta been' up purty clost to fifteen year old when I fin'ly quit playin' in a play house.

A-SLIDIN', A-CLIMBIN' AND A-SWANGIN'

In the summertime, we hit the woods and stayed gone all we could. That way we didn't get into no trouble at the house. Just out from "The Pines," on the side of the mountain acrost the road, was a real steep holler. Some of the older youngens made 'em some homemade sleds to ballhoot down the holler on. When we could find one, we'd take a piece of a pasteboard box and slide down the holler on them pine needles. You talk about sump'm slick, now, that was slick as glass. Some of the youngens took a piece of tin over there and left it hid, so hit'd be there when they wanted to play "slide." We ruck up great big piles a leaves down at the mouth of the holler and slid inunder 'em and jist buried up over our head in there.

Ever' fall, we took tow sacks over there to fill up with leaves and carry back to the barn to put in the cow stall to make her a bed on. Before cold weather set in, we tried to get a good thick layer put down, so they would soak up the cow pee and keep it dry, and she could lay down and stay warm. We done that to the horse stall, too.

People now talk about a "branch" off a tree. We never said "branch" for a limb. A brainch was runnin' water, like a creek, only less.

They was some big old hemlocks over in the holler, and the limbs growed right down clost to the bottom of the trees and tetched the ground at the ends of 'em. I'd grab aholt of the tip end of a big bottom limb of a hemlock on the lower side of the holler, and pull it way back up the bank around the tree as fer as I could pull it, kindly like cockin' a bow to shoot it. When I'd jump and my feet come up off of the ground, hit sprung fards and give me a sling, and I'd go a-sailin' out over the holler torge the other side, then I'd turn loose and keep a-goin' til I landed on the ground over there. Sometimes my feet went to slidin' on them slick needles, and I got slung before I was ready. Then I was liable to wind up dist any ol' where down through there. We took turns a-doin' that.

We knowed where ever' grapevine was in them mountains, and played on a grapevine swing til we slap wore it out, an'en went on to another'n. One time me 'n Oval 'n Sister found one up torge Boomer Den, on the mountain above our house. I got on it and was a-swangin' acrost a steep holler, and about the time I got out in the air over the middle of the holler, that *dadgum* grapevine jist come a-unravellin' out of the treetops. When I hit the ground, I went to rollin' *head over heels* down the mountain. I was still aholt of the grapevine and all balled up in it when I finally come to a stop, a way down yander. That's another time I *come in a hair* a-gittin' kilt.

Then here come Oval, scared to death, just a-ballhootin' down the holler to see if I'd got kilt. I was black and blue all over from where I'd hit rocks and stuff, but nuthin' wutn' broke, so we never told nobody.

Now, a saplin' on the shady side of a mountain grows long and skinny. We *clim* up saplin's that was little enough around to bend over, but was still big enough to not break with you, and played "Tarzan." We'd look for a stand where they growed purty clost, but would still give room to ride one over without it a-ketchin' in another'n, and still be clost enough to git a-holt of it. When you clim to the top of a saplin' and rode it over agin' another'n, you could reach out and grab the other'n and get a leg holt. Then you could turn looset of the firstun and be over in to the top a thatun. We'd see how fur we could go without havin' to get down and walk on the ground.

I got broke like a *"suck-egg dog,"* though, from ridin' a saplin' over to the ground. I rode one over one time, and I wudn't hardly heavy enough to make it bow over enough for me to drop off to the ground. And there I was—a-hangin' up in th' air there, aholt of th' top a that bent-over saplin', dist a-swangin'.

Wellsir, I went to pumpin' my legs and got it to swangin' big, an'en fin'ly swung my legs up and hooked 'em over the trunk of the saplin' a little ways fudder from the top, and got on it, there. And there I was, upside down. I needed to git a little ways more on away from the top of the saplin' to let the weight shift, so hit'd straighten up. I was havin' to climb feet first up that tree top, a little at a time. Then when it did straighten up, hit sprung up all of a sudden with a snap that like to a slung me out of there like a rock out of a slingshot. I wutnt a-lookin' for that. Hit's a good thing I had a good *choke-holt* on it. That tree top was dist a-sprangin' backerds and fards, a-slangin' me with it. When thangs kindly settled down, *I want ye to know* I got down from there.

From then on, I just skinnied on down a saplin' when I got done playin' Tarzan.

I was like a *tree-frawg* when it come to climbin'. I could climb en-ny-thang! Ditn't make no nevermind to me whuther it had limbs on it clost to the ground or not. I could a-clim up the side of the barn if I wanted to. I useta climb up on top a the barn and set a-straddle of the roof. And I luf'ta climb the highest tree I could find and dist set up there and look down at the world all around me. W'y, they'd be birds a-flyin' around down there that wutn't near as high up in the air as I was. I coutn't git over how little ever'thang looked when you look down on top of 'em like that, and how fer a-body could see.

One day I clim a great big ol' hemlock up above the spring, and just kept on a-climbin' and a-goin' til I dang nigh got to the very tip top of it. I bet hit wutn't as big around as my arm there. It started to leanin' over with me, an'en broke off before I could back down some. I started to fallin', but kep' a choke-holt on that li'l ol' top as it come down. All of a sudden, they was a purty good jerk on it and I *come in a dab* a-losin' my holt. Hit'd ketched on a big limb *fudder* on down the tree, and there I swung, with the tree top upside down in my hands. I swung over and got a laigholt around a limb, an'en got another holt with one hand, and could turn the top loose. I *fenegaled* around til I got over clost to the trunk and clim on down.

Hit never scared me right then, but a'ter while, I *studied on it* a right smart. If I'd a-fell, they woutn't a-been nuthin' left but a greazy spot where I'd hit the ground. Dist the thoughts of it scared me bad enough to where I never clumb that fer up no more.

I've hyeard it said that *angels watches over fools and little childern*, and they must be sump'm to it, or I'd a-been kilt when I wutn't nuthin' but a little bitty youngen. I know I shore missed some good *chanches*.

SWIMMIN' HOLES AND PLAYIN' IN TH' CREEK

Back in them days, they wutn't no swimmin' pools and recreational parks nor nuthin' like they is now. We woutn't never a-got to go to one, but eb'm if we had, we'd a-been too *tard* to do anything by the time we got there. The only swimmin pool I ever knowed of when I was a youngun was down at Neal Hay's place, about two miles out a town, and we'd a-had to walk about five mile there and five back, so it woutn't hardly a-been worth it. Some of the oldest younguns went down there a time or two when they was about grown, but I never did. Mr. Hay rented out bicycles, and that's mostly what they went for. They rented one for so much a week, an'en took it back. But they never done that many times. Money was too tight.

Some time along up in the summer when the ground warmed up, we'd pon' up the creek and make us a swimmin' hole. We used the biggest rocks we could lift to dam it up. Then we pulled weeds and ferrins and dug up great big dirt clods with grass roots in 'em to plug up holes that leaked the water out. Hit took us about all day to build one. When we got it ponded up, hit looked like a great big lake to me. Now I realize that it was more like three foot deep on the deepest end.

The boys pulled off their shirts and rolled up their overhall legs to *go in a-swimmin'*. (We always said, "go *in* a-swimmin'.") Us girls dist wore our dresses. It was considered the more lady-like thing to do, to wade out first and wet your dresstail down, so it woutn't trap air inunder it and float up, a-shinin' your bloomers at ever'body. What I done, I tied my dresstail in a knot or dist stuffed it down in my bloomers, one. I didn't need no dang dresstail a-flappin' around in my way. Long as nobody coutn't see my neck-edness, I never cared one way or the other.

That creek water was so cold, you coutn't stand it to dist jump right in all at oncet. Hit'd take your breath. And you coutn't stand it but a few minutes at a time, neither. When you first started to go in a-swimmin', you had to stick y'toes in first, an'en one foot at a time, an'en wade a little, t'get used to it before you

178

jumped in. And it plumb took your breath if somebody splattered you. Of course the boys had to show out 'n dare each other, 'n done *belly busters* dist t'splatter us. That's one time I ditn't take the crazy *e-jits* (idiots) up on a dare, to jump right in. When they come out on the bank to warm up, they'd be so cold they'd be plumb blue pietted, with their teeth dist a-chatterin'.

One summer we had a swimmin' hole out behind the wood shed, and one day me 'n Oval decided we needed us a boat. We talked about it awhile and figgered out what to do. We snuck out to the spring spout and carried that big old wash-tub out to the swimmin' hole. Then we got some poles to use to guide the tub and keep it fum turnin' over, and was going to take turns "ridin' in the boat" acrost the water. Now that was tricky business, 'cause you had to set exactly in the middle, and not lean any which a-way, to keep it from turnin' over. We practiced awhile at the edge, an'en decided we knowed jist how t'do it.

I got in the tub, and just about made it to the other side, when all of a sudden the tub capsized, a-trappin' me under it. I guess the cold water took my breath for a minute, but I'd got to where I coutn't hold my breath no longer, and was a-see-ing bright shootin' stars a-comin' at me when I fin'ly got ou'fenunder that tub. That's one time I dist *knowed I was a goner.* That *scared my mule.* We never pulled that stunt no more.

I's a-scared of the water anyhow. Mommy wouldn't let us play in the water unless one of the bigger youngens was there. She was afeard of water, I reckin because her younger brother, Kermit, got drownded in Nantahala River when I was about three. I don't remember it, but I heard 'em tell about it a lot a times, and it made me a-scared a water.

Kermit was a grown man with two little younguns—a boy a little older, and a girl a year younger'n me. His family and our'n was *a-layin' out* (camping) over on the river, next to a deep hole. They was a spring over on the other side, and they had to go acrost a footlog to get water. Lewis started acrost it to go to the spring, and fell off into the river…Kermit was a expert swimmer, and jumped in to get him out, but he got caught in a sink hole that sucked him down onto the bottom and trapped him. Lewis got out, but they didn't get Kermit out til sev'al hours later. He was the only brother Mom had.

So, most of the time, we just waded in the creek, or played games like seein' who could go the fudderest up or down the creek by jumpin' from one rock to the other and not getting our feet wet. We'd find us a stick, tie a piece a string with a bent straight pin on it, and use red worms to fish with. They wutn't many fish, of the kind you could eat. They didn't stock trout streams then. We caught hornyheads and crawfish, and liked to watch the *minners* swim around in the water. We put anything we caught in a jar of water and watched it awhile, an'en poured it back in the creek.

When we was out a-huntin' red worms or playin', sometimes we run acrost *a thousand laig-ged worm* (millipede). *Igolly*, you talk about some youngens a-shet-tin' their mouth, now we did, when we saw one a them. Old folks allus told us that *if a thousand leg-ged worm counts your teeth, you'll die*. If anybody seed one, they shet their mouth dist as tight as they could shet it, and would point at that thang and try to talk without openin' their mouth, "umm-m-m-wmm!" and the rest of us knowed to shet our mouth and turn away quick. Now, we b'lieved that for a fact.

Another thing I was afraid of was leeches in the creek. They said them thangs'd latch onto you and bury their head in your skin, and you coutn't git 'em loose, and they'd suck out all your blood. When any kind a trash or anything else tetched me or stuck to my leg, I had a *heebie-jeebie fit* and got that thing offa me, right now.

I never was much afeard a snakes, though. I made 'em live hard. I've slipped up on one a-many a time and kilt it with a stick about a foot long. I never did bother black snakes, though. Dad said they eat mouses and things, and liked for one to stay around the barn. If we seed a copperhead or rattlesnake, though, we made tracks to tell some of the grown folks so they could shoot it. I didn't mess with them none—I ditn' want one *a-charmin'* me like no mouse.

People said to *never look a snake in the eye or hit'll charm* (hypnotize) *you*—that's the way they ketch rats 'n rabbits 'n thangs. And *when you kill a snake, hit never plumb dies til the sun goes down*. I know fer a fact that they'll keep on a-wigglin' long after you think they're dead. And *if you'll go back at the same time the next day to the same place where you kilt a snake, you'll see another'n*—maybe its mate. *If you hang a snake up in a tree, hit'll rain*.

They also told about a *"hoop snake."* They look kindly like a king snake, only they've got a long keen tail that's hard on the end—like a sharp cow's horn. They said them thangs'd ketch their tail in their mouth and stand up in a circle and roll like a hoop. That tail must've been sorter like a stinger, for they said if it rolled into a tree and stuck it up in the tree, hit'd kill it *graveyard dead* in a day. I never did see one, though, and I'm glad, for I woutn't want one a them *boogers* a'ter me.

One time Lawerence was goin' down the trail b'low the wood shed torge the swamp. They was a fence along there with longways poles, right beside of the trail, and a big ol' blacksnake was stretched out a-sunnin' on one of them poles. Knowin' him, he prob'ly went to devilin' it, and hit bit 'im on the arm. They tied it up in a *turp'mtine rag* for awhile, and never thought no more about it.

I don't know if it was the same snake or not, but I remember Dad a-bein' as *high as a Georgie pine* (about drunk) one day, and catchin' about a six foot long blacksnake off a that same fence. He helt it up and looked it right in the eye, and then just *up and* bit its head off and spit it out.

An'en one time I seen him ketch one and hold it, and it jist a-wrappin' and a-twistin' around his arm, a-tryin' to git away fum 'im. He *prized* hits mouth op'm, spit it full a snuff, an'en th'owed it down on the ground. Hit jist layed 'n *wharped* the ground, bit itself, and tied hitself up into all kinds a knots. I don't know if it died or not, fer I'd seen enough, and *lit a shuck* to the house.

He wutn't afeared a nothin', and was meaner'n any snake., 'spacially when he was *about half shot* (about drunk).

SCHOOL DAYS

TAKIN' UP BOOKS

In the early 1900's, when the school term began in the fall, it was called "*takin'* *up books.*" My parents went to school at the Upper Junaluska Schoolhouse, on a one acre lot owned by the county. It was also the place where they got married. They used it for a school-house through the week and for a church-house on Sundays. When they spoke of it, they called it "The Old Jun'lusky Schoolhouse." It was located right acrost the road from where I was born, but it got burnt up long before then.

They described it as a wooden frame building, and it was all jist one big room. All of the pupils set in the same room, but they was divided up into sections, accordin' to whatever grade they was in.

Paper was hard to come by, and they used a little slate to write on. They was kindly like a little piece of blackboard, and ever' youngun had their own slate. They used what they called a "Blueback Speller" to learn how to spell.

They just had one teacher. He boarded somewhere in the community during the school year, as it was so far out of the way. Mom said the teacher usually boarded with her parents. Robert Barker was one of the teachers, and he wutn't a whole lot older than they was.

They just had school through the sixth grade there, and the school term was six months out of the year. That was the only schoolin' that the biggest major'ty of 'em ever got, if they eb'm got that much. If they could sign their own name, hit was sump'm to be proud of, for they was a-many a one that coutn't, and dist had to put a X by where somebody else wrote their name for them. Back then, they thought that going through the sixth grade was a good education. I don't know how many year it took to graduate from high school, seems like it was 10, but a person could be a teacher if they had a high school diploma. Most of 'em, like Mom and Dad, only went through the third grade.

Back then, childern was needed at home. In big families like they had back then, the oldest girl 'spacially, was needed around the house to help her mammy with raisin' the family. They was allus the washin', cookin', cannin' or sump'm else a-needin' to be done. A lot a the time, she never married. It was common to see a old maid aunt that was allus a-goin' from one place to another'n—to help

185

out when a baby was borned, or some of the kinfolks *took sick*, one, and needed somebody to *wait on 'em*. When she got one job took keer of, she'd go back home to her daddy and mammy and stay there til she was needed someplace else. An'en she took care a them when they got apast goin'.

Boys had to git wood, help raise the crops, or find work to help make a livin', one. Lots a times, the oldest boy never got married neither, as he was too busy a-workin' to help raise his younger brothers and sisters. If he did marry, he usually just brought his wife there, and they helped to raise the other youngens and their'n too. Back then, hit was common to see three generations a-livin' under one roof.

To call somebody "Aunt" or "Uncle" was to show the highest respect—it prob'ly come from them havin' had a aunt or uncle that helped raise 'em, that was like their mammy and pappy.

My oldest brothers and sisters went to school at Upper Jun'lusky, too. About all that had changed was that they had tablets (a paper pad) that they wrote on, and a pencil to write with.

First one, and then another'n of the men in the community took turns a-cut-tin' firewood and haulin' it to the school house to heat with. Bud said that the lit-tlest younguns set up clost to the stove where it was warmer, and as they passed into the next grade, they got moved fudder back away from it. He said him and the bigger boys wore two pair a overhalls to school when it got real bad cold, because they had to set away back torge the back, away from the stove, and it got *colder'n whiz* in that back corner. I've got one of his old school pictures, and shore anuff, you can see two pair a overhall galluses on him.

JUNALUSKA SCHOOL HOUSE

Schools in Cherokee County hatn't been consolidated, then. They was little ol' schoolhouses scattered all over the county. Our'n was on the lower end of Jun'lusky, about three mile above town, and was called Lower Jun'lusky School. Hit wutn't much differ'nt from the one Dad and Mom went to, except when we finished the third grade, we went to "town school."

Where we lived on the head of Jun'lusky Creek was a way back in the mountains about eight mile out of Andrews, the clostest town. I allus heard that the creek was named for Chief Jun'lusky of the Cherokee Indian tribe, and that he used to live up there a long time ago.

It was a steep graded, windin' gravel road that nuthin' could travel on in bad rainy weather or when they was a deep snow. When it rained for sev'al days, the roadbed got soft and routed out and vehicles got *marred up* to their axles in the mud. They coutn't nuthin' git through except maybe a log truck, and sometimes they coutn't, neither.

The potholes was so deep that when the school bus hit one, we would bounce so high our heads jist *dang nigh* hit the top of it. The bus was flat on top, and was a whole lot lower than the ones on the road today. It made a loud "boing" noise when it hit a big pothole, where that tin top would dip down and sprang back up all of a sudden. The seats was dist long padded bainches down both sides, with a lower one in the middle where the younger childern set back-to-back agin' one another.

Sometimes the school bus coutn't get through to pick us up. We got to stay home and they never counted us absent, eb'm if they had school and we wutn't there. But I'd druther a-went to school than to a-stayed at home.

If it rained much hard while we was at school, the bus coutn't get through to take us all the way home. It usually marred up in the mud right above Wib Mosteller's place, and the bus driver dist set there and spinned his wheels. When he seen he wutn't a-goin' nowhere, he opm'd the door and let us git out and walk the rest a the way home. We had to step out in the soft soupy mud to get out of the bus, and sometimes we'd go in half way up to our knees. When we had shoes on, we'd take 'em off and tie the shoe strangs together, and throw 'em over our shoulder to carry 'em before we got out of the bus, to keep from gettin' our shoes full a mud. One time I stepped out in a suck-hole so deep hit dist sucked the shoe right off a my foot when I took a step. I had t'grub down in there with my hand to find it and git it out. Hit was buried up to my elbow. That's when I learnt I better take 'em off before I got started.

Sometimes, the bigger younguns had to carry the littluns piggyback on their shoulders to git 'em over the worst places. We looked like mud moles by the time we got home.

After we got off, sometimes, it lightened the bus enough to where the driver could git the bus to rockin' backerds and fards and ease it out of the routed-out place, or maybe git it to backin' up and back down the road til he found a turnin'-around place. But they was times when he'd have to walk, hisself, and go and git somebody to come and hook chains to it and pull it out.

When the snow in Andrews was three inches deep, hit was six to twelve up on the creek, and the temp'ature was ten or more degrees colder. The fudder the bus went, the deeper the snow. When he seen it was gittin' too bad to try it any fudder, the driver let us out to walk. Now, that tickled us youngens, to get to walk on home in the snow, usually from about four mile down the road. Of course, snowballs was a-flyin' from ever side, and we had to lay down and make angels, and roll up balls to make snowmen and stuff like that, dist ever' little bit. We'd be *wet as a dog* and half froze by the time we got to the house, but we never paid no 'tention t'that.

Our daddy and mammy ditn't encourage us to go to school, and thought learnin' to cipher your numbers and read and write some was all a-body needed. They wutn't no use for a girl to get much *schoolhousin'*, nohow. All my older brothers and sisters except Coonie quit school about the sixth grade. She finished the eighth grade. I can't remember any of the older'uns except Coonie and Lawerence actually a-goin' to school, but I do remember Thelma a-talkin' about Miss Christy, a teacher that she liked so much. They told me what all they done, and all, and what it was like at school. They let me go with 'em a day or two the year before I started, and I dist coutn't hardly wait for school to start the next year, so I could go.

Ever evenin', I'd watch, and run and meet Lawerence when he got off of the bus. He'd brang me a pocket full a acorns from them big old oak trees in the schoolyard. I can still see him a-pullin' them acorns out of his pocket, a-turnin' it wrong side out when he pulled out a big fist full. We eat 'em. Them from the school yard trees was a whole lot bigger and sweeter than them little ol' bitter'uns around our place. They was *as bitter as gald.*

I was dist a little old skinny *tow-headed youngun,* and I remember Maw Hicks a-comparin' me to my brothers and sisters in size. She said I was goin' to be the *runt a the family,* and my aunts a-settin' there on the porch, agreed with her. I ditn't know what "the runt" meant, except what I'd heard said when they talked about pigs, but they said it meant that I'd be the least'un in the family. I reckin *you can't never tell by lookin'* at a youngun, for I growed to be six foot tall.

My hair was so blonde it was almost white, and straight except for a slight curl on the ends. My skin was real pale, too, and I remember wonderin' if I really did b'long to Mom and Dad, since they both had dark curly hair. Alma and Thelma had dark auburn-brown curly hair, and Coonie's was black as a Indian's and straight as a stick. The older boys had dark brown hair too, except Sweetie's was lighter. Oval's hair was blonde, too, so I figgered maybe we did b'long to 'em, or at least Oval was my brother. An'en too, I thought, they already had so many younguns, why would they let me live there if I hatn't a-been borned to 'em?

I heard people talk about how pale I was, and Mom said that I was thataway because she was a-carryin' me when her sister Lizzie died before I was borned, and I was marked by her a-lookin' at Lizzie and her dead. I heard 'em tell about all kinds a ways babies would be marked from things that their mammy seed or from sump'm that hapm'd while they was *a-carryin' a baby.* One they told about was a baby that was borned with a big ol' bruised lookin' birth mark on it at dist ezackly the same place where a cow had kicked the woman. One woman had got bad skyered by a bear, and her baby had a patch of grizzly black hair on its back, from her a-bein' scairt by that bear. I shore was glad none a them thangs'd hap'md to Mom, but it did make me awful sad to thank about her sister a-dyin' and leavin' her pore little younguns without a mother. *I hated that.*

I remember a-hearin' Mom and some other'ns a-talkin' about my yaller hair, and they said it was a *throw-back* (genetic inheritance) from one side of the family. I thought by it bein' a *throw-back* that they thought it was ugly. I allus felt differ'nt from them, ugly and not as good as them, and since I was marked, it woutn't never be no differ'nt.

The year I started school, I thought it never would come fall, but it finally did come. Coonie was the one that *combed my head* of a mornin'. My hair was long, and I dreaded her a-gettin' a-holt of me. She'd put one hand on top of my head to hold it, and start the comb in my hair right up next to my head and give it a big rake, dist a-jerkin' the hair out with the tangles. She wutn't mad or tryin' to be mean, or nuthin', she was just a-wantin' to git it done. That's dist the way she allus was. Ever'thang she done, she *went at it like killin' snakes*.

She's still like that, too. She's *a trash-mover*. I like to *joke around with her* now, and tell her she's the very reason I'm *as hard headed as a mule*, but it's a wonder I ain't bald-headed from where she kep' it jerked out by the roots.

I was tickled to death to git on that school bus and *go it*. I liked gittin' to ride on that big ol' school bus. The driver pulled over and stopped down at Lower Jun'lusky Schoolhouse to let us littluns git off there, an'en he went on to take the rest of 'em to town school. Hit was kindly scary a-bein' left by myself with them other younguns that I ditn't know. But the teacher was good to me, and I made friends before the day was out.

Our schoolhouse was dist one big classroom with a little side room to put stuff in. They was a big ol' high pot-belly coal heater a-settin' *right smack dab* in the middle of the school room, with a great long stovepipe that run all the way out the top a the schoolhouse.

Miss Eleanor Enloe was my first teacher. We said "Miss" for a teacher's name, eb'm if it was s'post to be "Mizzis." I loved Miss Enloe. Her handwritin' was *so* purty! I wanted my handwritin' to be jist like her'n was. She give us paper and a pencil and had us do ovals and push-pulls to learn how to write our ABC's. I loved to do them, and tried real hard to make 'em perfect. In my mind's eye, I can still see that large print alphabet *all rowed up* acrost the wall right above the blackboard, and tried to make my letters like them—dist like Miss Enloe's was. She was good to us, and read to us a lot. I could a-listened all day

I hatn't never seen nary coal heater before. When the weather turned cold, we took turns a-carryin' a bucket a coal in from the coal bin outside. It took two of us first-graders to carry one. When I seen the teacher a-puttin' coal in the heater, I remember a-thankin' how amazin' that was, that you could put sump'm like black rocks in there and they'd burn! W'y, a-body woutn't never have to git out and git in farwood atall if they had a pile a coal and one a them heaters! And I never seed sich big chunks a coal in all my life. All I'd seen was them little ol' bitty pieces we picked up along the railroad track and fed the pigs. I'd seen 'em put some of 'em in the fire, but never did know they burnt 'thout wood

In the winter, Miss Enloe brung eggs from home, or we'd brang some, one, and she scrambled eggs for us in a iron skillet on top a the heater for dinner. Only, she called it lunch.

The water bucket and dipper set on a table up torge the front. Coonie'd told me they was a dipper in the bucket, all right, but we wutn't s'posed to drank out of it. We was to dip up water and pour it in our own drankin' glass that we brung from home. They was a hole in our *dest* (desk) top that was jist right t'set our drankin' glass down in.

Our teacher allus sent two of us to the sprang to carry our water back. We went up to the road and acrost the bridge, and up a trail through the woods to git to the sprang. Some crab apples growed up there, and them little green thangs was *so sour they'd make a pig squeal*, but we eat 'em anyhow.

When the weather was warm, we set out under them big oak trees in the school yard to eat our dinner. The only thing I had to take was a biscuit or two with some jelly or fat-back, one, in it. I carried my biscuits in a coffee poke, and had to double it up and take it back home to re-use. We didn't have wax paper to wrap biscuits up in, so they was just stuck down in the poke, and it made 'em taste like stale coffee. Sometimes two kids from the same family packed their dinners in a little lard bucket, and carried it back and forth. They could even pack fried 'taters in it. Some kids had a nice lunch box, and some had a little brown paper poke they called a lunch bag, and *samwiches* made with *"light bread"* wrapped in wax paper. We never had light bread at home. I'd seen some before, but folks said that a piece a that old light bread woutn't amount to enough to wad a shotgun with; hit woutn't *stick to yer ribs* atall.

I loved school, but ditn't like 'rithmetic as good as I liked readin'. I jist *pyorely* loved the sound of words. I was allus amazed at how only twenty six letters in the alphabet could be arranged so many different ways to tell anything a-body wanted to tell. I recollect our first grade book with a pichure on ever page. It said: "Mac sees Muff. Muff sees Mac. See Mac run. See Muff run." I was so proud when I could read, and read ever'thing I could git my hands on.

Livin' off up on the creek, and all, they was many a thang out in the world that I never knowed they was, til I went to school and read about 'em.

I ditn't much like old *Joggerphy* (Geography) though, as hit ditn't make much sense to me then. My world started and ended with home and the schoolhouse.

That's all I knowed...

GOIN' TO TOWN SCHOOL

Miss Enloe was my second grade teacher too, and was still there when I started the third grade. Then, my whole world changed. Three months into third grade, they closed Junaluska school and sent us to town school. Things sure was differ'nt.

I remember thinking how big I thought them two-story school buildings was. They was three of 'em: the old wooden primary, or "White Buildin'," the brick Elementary school buildin', and the High School buildin'. Over at the far side of the playground was the Rock Gym. That playground was the biggest piece a level ground I'd ever seen, other than Wilhide's corn field.

When we got to town school, they give us a test to determine our grade level. I found out that Miss Enloe had done a good job, for I come out ahead of most of the town school kids on my score. Miss Barnard was my third grade teacher. She was a good teacher too, and I really liked her.

When I think about the Elementary school building, one thing always comes to mind. Right where you started down the hall upstairs, on the left-hand side was a two story doll house settin' in the floor. It had all the miniature furnishings in it, and I thought it was the most beautifulest thing I'd ever seen. I used to just squat down there and gaze at it and let my imagination go wild, thinkin' about what it'd be like to live in a house like that. I coutn't imagine what that bathroom was like, plus the kitchen, and all that furniture, purty wallpaper and curtains. W'y, it was dist like lookin' at a real fairy-tale. I guess that was the first glimpse I had of what other people's homes were like.

What's so amazing is this: It set there for years—in reach of everybody—right on the floor in that hall, and not one child bothered it, took anything or damaged it, that I knowed of. Can you imagine what would happen if it was left unattended for just one day in an elementary school building now? Years later, when I heard that the building had burnt down, that house was the first thing I thought of, and it made me so sad.

It woutn't a took but jist one little spark to a-set it afire. The janitor, Mr. Tatham spread some kind of oil on the wood floor and then spread sawdust over it to keep down th' dust, before he took a push broom and swep' it up. But that was the customary way a-doin it then.

Miss Morton loved to teach about nature, and kept guinea pigs, white mice, and all kind a things in her room. She brung in different kinds of cocoons so we could watch the moth or butterfly emerge, and things like that, and took time to explain about anything we wanted to ask her. And not just kids in her room, but ever'body went through her room ever day or two to see what was happenin' to things. That's where I learnt about a Cecrophia moth and butterflies.

I was in for a culture shock, though, when it come to the differ'nce in Junaluska School and Andrews City School. They was more children in my third grade class than they'd been in the whole Junaluska school. I hatn't never seen nuthin' like the water fountain, where you jis' pushed a button and the water squirted right up in your mouth, or the bathrooms, where you jis' flushed the toilet and it woished itself clean. We'd had a outside toilet and carried our water in a bucket at Junaluska school, like we done at home.

It didn't take me long figger out why a lot of kids quit school after they started town school. Some of the "town kids" made fun of us that lived back in the mountains, and treated us like we *ditn't have a lick a sense.* My clothes was homemade out a flour and feed sacks, and wutn't nowhere like them storebought clothes the other girls wore. They eb'm wore shoes in warm weather. I was used to going barefooted, and ditn't eb'm have no shoes til it got to snowin'.

I'd simply not been around other kids except my family, cousins, and the kids at the old school. They'd thought, acted and dressed pretty much like me.

Most of the children ate in the lunch room. Some of 'em lived clost enough to go home to eat. I got so I woutn't take no dinner to school because I was too ashamed of them biscuits in a coffee poke, after I got made fun of a few times. I got awful hungry, but that was better'n bein' made fun of. Coonie and Lawerence had took canned stuff—apples, taters or canned stuff to school and traded 'em in for their dinner. They'd give 'em so many lunch credits in exchange for whatever they brung. They'd stopped doing that by the time I started to town school, though.

When dinner time come, I'd just file out with the rest of 'em like I was goin' to the lunch room too, an'en slip out of line and go out on the playground and play til lunch time was over. If I stayed in the room and ditn't eat, the teacher'd ast me if I was sick, the reason I wutn't a-eatin'. I remember goin' down 'nunder the trees and playin' marble with the boys at first. I was more used to playin' with boys than with girls. Boys didn't pay that much attention to clothes and goin' barefooted. Then some a the girls seen me and said hit wutn't nice to git down in the dirt and crawl around and play with boys, a-gittin your dress dirty and showin' your bloomers.

I did get to eat in the lunch room a few times, and remember how good it smelt in there. The food was good, too, and was differ'nt stuff from what we had at home. The thing I remember most was the glass milk bottle. Milk wutn't homogenized then, and it had about a inch of cream on top of it. The milk had to be shook to mix the cream up in it. It had a little round pasteboard insert that fit down into the neck of the bottle to seal it. This had to be pulled out. I remember lickin' th' cream off of the underside, then looked around and noticed that nobody else done that. Why did people make rules that kep' you from enjoyin' little thangs, when hit ditn't hurt nuthin'—dist made you feel ashamed?

I learnt one way to show 'em I wasn't stupid. We had a spellin' bee ever' few days, and most a the time, I won it. I hardly ever missed a word on a spellin' test. My fascination with words paid off there. And I'd helped Coonie study spellin' by givin' out words to her at home. I loved spellin'

We each got a pamphlet-like weekly periodical, called the Weekly Reader, that we studied. It had news stories and told about the latest in inventions. I remember how awed we all were, even the teacher, when we read the one that told about a new invention called television, and predicted that eventually every home would have one. (Am I really that old?)

I loved that *liberry* for grade school students in the Elementary building. I couldn't b'lieve there were so many books all in one place. Then our teacher took us downtown to the Carnegie Public Library, and when I walked in there, I thought they must have all the books in the whole world. Why, they had more walls in there than we had in our whole house, inside and out, and ever one of 'em covered up with books. Lord, I ditn't have no idy where to start—I wanted to look at all of 'em. I even loved the smell of it in the library. And we got to go one day a week.

One time I checked out a small children's book at the town library and someone stole it from my desk. When it was overdue, I wasn't allowed to check out any more books til I returned it or paid for it. The book cost $1.65, but might as well a-been $1,065, as there was no way I could pay for it. I knew I'd just get in trouble at home if I asked for the money, and they'd never give it to me, anyway, so I never asked. I felt so ashamed when the others lined up to go to the public library and I was sent to the school library. I could still check out books there. I guarded a book with my life after that.

I also learned a valuable lesson in how badly you can hurt a person by stealing from them. I remember looking in my desk, and looking again and again. I could just see where I'd put it and left it, and couldn't believe it was gone. I kept hoping somebody'd put it back.

Miss Barnard was the school librarian by then, and she was so kind and friendly to me. She let me help her do things in the library, and taught me the Dewey Decimal System so I could help her re-shelve returned books. She made me feel that what I did was important, and complimented me often. She suggested book titles and encouraged me to read, and thought reading was very important. It greatly lessened my guilty feelings about wanting to read so much. I will always love her for that. It was like I was just hungry for knowledge about everything.

At home, if Mom or Dad caught me reading, they scolded me and put me to work at something. So many times I heard, "You ain't a-settin' around here on your lazy hin'end *with your nose stuck in a book*, a-wastin' time," or I was accused of "tryin' to make a educated fool" out of myself. I couldn't even do homework at home, unless I slipped around and did it, for they said I was s'post to do school work at school. That's why I'd left the book in my desk at school.

Nowadays, my librarian daughter, Donna, keeps me supplied with a big bag of books on tape and books by authors that I like. Anything I want! Sometimes I go by the library and she fills a huge bag for me. I walk out a there a-feelin' richer'n a miser with a sack a gold, with my feet *dist a-hittin' the high spots*.

When school started, Dad bought each of us a nickel pack of Blue Horse™ notebook paper and a pencil, and it was s'post to last us through the school year. Of course, it didn't. I used to look at that pretty clean paper, with not a spot or wrinkle on it, and wisht they was some kind of magic I could do, so when I pulled out a sheet, it would replace itself, and I would allus have a full pack.

He made me bring all the used paper home for him to see, and it had to be covered with school work on both sides, or he said it was wastin' paper. I got in trouble if he found any drawing, even on the back side of a used paper. He even expected me to use the back side of a test paper that had been graded and handed back.

I saw other kids borrow paper from each other. If we had a test and had to have a neat paper, I'd ask another kid if I could "borry" a sheet of paper. Of course, I couldn't pay it back, so I made sure I didn't ask the same one again til I had to. But nobody seemed to catch on or to mind.

Sometimes I got paper from the trash can and erased it. When I saw a kid start to write and make a mistake, then wad the paper up and throw it away, oh, I just cringed. I couldn't imagine how they could do that. I wished at least they wouldn't wad it up when they threw it away. I could have used it.

I'd watch a kid stand there and grind a pencil down on the pencil sharpener, or toss one in the trash can when they thought it was too short. When I thought nobody was looking, I'd get it back out. Or find one on the school ground and pick it up. I didn't dare ask for another pencil, for I'd be accused of not taking care of the one I had. It was serious business to me, to lose one.

Dad said that the state was supposed to provide everything you needed for school, and wouldn't ever give us money for book fees, workbooks, or anything like that. I just wanted to die when the teacher called out the names of the children who hadn't brought in their fees.

I also dreaded picture-taking time each year. I'd seen how it was with the older kids at home. They made our school pictures, and when they came back, gave them to us to take home. I didn't know what else to do with them; I had nowhere to hide them. When they were taken home, Dad wouldn't allow us to take them back to school, but wouldn't pay for them, either. He said they were his youngens and nobody had a right to take their picture without asking him first. He said, "They're my youngens and my pictures."

Isn't it strange how certain little bits of memory can stay with us so long? It's as if the mind took a photograph. In my mind, I can still see Dad a-settin' leaned back in a straight back chair on the front porch, with the pictures a-layin' on his lap when he said that. I didn't think it was right for him to do that, but I knowed better than to say one word.

As the deadline for bringing in the money grew closer, there'd be a roll call and names called out. Mine would always be there when everyone else had paid, and I'd finally have to try to give an explanation. I was so ashamed to have to do that, and felt guilty as if I'd done something wrong.

I remember one time our teacher took us on a class picnic at the end of the school year. Everyone was supposed to bring their share of money to pay for drinks, etc. (a quarter?) There I was—no money, and no way to get out of going. Everyone was nice to me anyway, like they didn't even know it, and I remember how guilty I felt when a boy handed me a coke. I knew it would be impolite to refuse, but felt terrible about not having paid my share. I felt too ashamed to have any fun.

I was afraid to tell anybody that I didn't have any lunch. One time, for some reason, I hadn't had breakfast when the school bus came. I remember it was a Monday because Dad worked away from home through the week and came home every Friday after work. He left to go back to work early on Monday morning.

For some reason I'd walked to town with a girl friend. Mom and Dad had both told me I'd better not be caught goin' to town for any reason. Other kids didn't realize the penalty I paid for disobeying. They'd beg me to do something, anyway, and I'd give in and do it, tryin' to make friends and fit in. I covered up for Mom and Dad, ashamed of the way they treated me.

We'd just started up the street, and all of a sudden, there stood Dad—and he'd seen me. As I watched him walk toward me, I thought my time had come. The very least that would happen was that he wouldn't let me go to school any more. He asked me where I was going, then for some reason I've never figured out, asked me if I'd had any breakfast.

When I said "no," he told me to come on with him. He took me up to Owen Luther's cafe' on the corner and bought me a hot dog and a coke. It was the first hot dog I ever had. I watched 'em put mustard on it and didn't know what it was. It was also the first cafe' I'd ever been in. I was dumbstruck by the jukebox and everything in there. He made no threats, just sat there on a stool beside me, and talked with some of the men sitting around, and didn't act mad at me. I sure was puzzled, and thought about it all day.

I was in for another big surprise when I got home. Mom was furious. It seems Dad went back home and got on to her for sending me to school without breakfast. She really wore me out. She said I better not tell Dad she whipped me, either, or she'd give me worse'n that. I've wondered if he ever knew that I never did have any lunch, either.

I made friends with some good kids and had a lot of good times at school. Many of the ones I was with in the third grade were in the same room through the higher grades, and we graduated together. We played hopscotch, jump rope, and went over to the park and played on the swings and seesaws, sometimes. There was plenty of room for softball with room still left for kids to play other games on the playground. That was one time when I didn't feel so left out. When they chose sides, I was always among the first picked. I batted left handed and could knock a ball right off the playground. I could run fast, and was good at running the ball down after a player hit it, and getting it to a base to get them out. I loved softball, and made friends playing ball but I always felt like I was on the outside looking in most of the time. I watched how the other kids acted, and tried to fit in, but always felt different from them. Deep down, I knew I could never be like them.

Seems like we celebrated the coming of Spring more than we do now. One celebration at school I remember was *May Day*. I never hear it mentioned now, but it was quite an event when I was in school. The boys wore white shirts and girls wore new pastel colored dresses they'd bought or had made to wear to dance around the Maypole. They were lilac, light blue, green, yellow, pink and all shades of spring colors. Somebody put up a tall Maypole and fastened different colored wide paper streamers at the top. These were spaced way out into a circle all around the pole and fastened to the ground. As they played music over a speaker, each child picked up a streamer, and as they danced around the May-pole, went in and out and around each other, doing a May dance. The streamers were woven around the pole and got shorter and shorter as they circled it. The dance ended when they got so close to the pole they could no longer circle it, and the pole was covered with all those colors woven together, with all the kids in their pretty clothes all ringed up around it. It was beautiful to watch.

One year, the school took some of the children's art to Cullowhee for an exhibition. One of my teachers asked me to do a pastel painting to send. I had no idea what a "pastel" was, or why she thought I could do one. She sent me to a teacher named Miss Trilby Glenn, who sat me down with some colored chalk, a sheet of fine sandpaper, and a picture of an orchid to copy. Then she briefly showed me how to draw and blend the chalk with my fingers. It took me awhile to get the hang of it, but I practiced on the background first, and she was patient. I'd go work on it for an hour or so every day for awhile.

When they came back from Cullowhee, they told me my art had won third place out of dozens of entries from across the state, and they were so proud of me. They gave it to me, and I still have that pastel. I didn't remember anybody ever being proud of me before then, and it felt good.

Another time, during a program to present to the entire school in the big auditorium, I was to do a scene with colored chalk. It was large enough for everyone to see from their seats, and I had to stand on some steps to reach it. It was a scene of a big old colonial style house with a balcony, and leading up to it was a curved driveway with flowers growing all along the sides. In the driveway, a man and woman walked arm in arm toward the house. He had on a topcoat and hat and she had on a long full-skirted dress and shawl. I memorized the sequence of which to draw first, then second, etc.

I had to practice several times because I had to do it fast. A girl in my class, Elizabeth Bell, was going to be reading a poem titled "It Takes A Heap O' Living In A House To Make It Home," and it had several verses. I had to finish the drawing close to the same time she finished reading. She read slowly, and glanced over to keep up with my progress to give me time to finish. I was terrified, but got it finished on time, and it was pretty. It always scared me to have to recite, read aloud in class, or have any attention focused on me, but it was worth the ordeal of getting up in front of an audience just to get to do that drawing. I sure wished I had some colored chalk like that, and some of that nice paper.

I also enjoyed the compliments of the other children, and after that, I was recognized by everyone for my "artistic talent." They'd ask, "How in the world did you do that?" or say, "Lord, I couldn't ever do anything that pretty," and several teachers told me how "beautiful" it was. It sure was nice to feel I'd done something right and be looked up to, for a change. For me to have anything, or be able to do anything someone else admired was unbelievable. But I also knew that I'd desperately prayed for help, and knew where any talent I might have came from.

Today, whenever someone buys—or I give them one of my paintings, pottery, carvings, or whatever, it makes me so "humbly proud" to be able to create or make something that someone would like well enough to display in their home. I am "humbly grateful" to God for whatever talent I have to bring joy and beauty into another person's life.

I loved art, but back then, there was very little art instruction in school. Besides, I didn't have any materials to do art, even to draw. I studied all the pictures or paintings I saw in books, and read about famous artists. I sat and gazed at the colorful paintings of angels and cherubs, and the graceful flowing clothing in paintings of people in a big Bible. Every picture or painting I saw on a wall, even ol' George Washington, held a fascination for me. I'd lie in bed at night and imagine what it would be like to have all the materials necessary to do a painting, think what colors I'd choose to paint a certain picture, and how I would go about it, and just dream of being an artist.

Back when my children were small, there were no art supplies sold nearby, so I ordered a basic set of oil paints, brushes and some canvases from Sears. I bought some art instruction books—one at a time—from a rack in a corner of a grocery store. I played with those paints, mixed colors, and painted every time I had a few minutes, and got good enough for people to ask me for my paintings. Later, when I had a little extra money, I tried acrylics, tole and decorative painting, drawings, and watercolors.

A few years ago, I taught some art classes at Tri-County Community College. Once, when I was getting ready to go, my husband asked me, "Do you realize that you taught the first formal art class you ever attended?" I hadn't realized it, and it kind of scared me, in a way. But I knew he was proud of me, and they wouldn't have hired me if they didn't think I was capable to do the job. They had called me—and that gave me the confidence I needed. I'd also gone to the *School Of Hard Knocks* (trial and error—on your own), and when you learn thataway, you learn your subject well.

Several years ago, I was talking with a very talented artist friend, and she was telling me how poor her family was when she was growing up. She said her mother gave her brown paper bags to draw and color on, because they couldn't afford paper.

She just thought she was poor.

I didn't say anything, and just listened. But I knowed that even if I'd a-had color crins and pencils, I'd a-been in big trouble at home if I'd a-tore open a paper poke and *wasted* it a-drawin' on it.

They was to be used, not wasted.

They's more'n one way a-bein' poor.

SCHOOL DISCIPLINE

We was allus told when we started school that if we got a whuppin' at school, we'd get another'n from Mom or Dad at home. Since they was so strict at home and I was used to *mindin'* (obeying) without question, I never had no trouble at school. I had more freedom at school than I did at home.

Gittin' sent to the Principal's office only happened when somebody done sump'm real bad, and they was in trouble when that happened. I suppose the most common form of discipline was to make us write a sentence a hunderd or more times, dependin' on how ever many the teacher felt we deserved. Writin' the sentence, "I must not chew gum in class" a hunderd times was dist about a ever'day thing for sombody or other. One boy tried to be smart and use two pencils so he could write two lines at a time, but it didn't work much good. (Probably still doesn't.)

Makin' somebody set in the corner, or out the hall, was one way to make 'em be-have. And if a kid come to school with their breath a-stinkin' like ramps, they had to set out in the hall all day long. Lawerence and some of them other ol' boys eat 'em a-purpose just to git to set out in the hall.

Keeping the mischief-maker in at recess was another common form of punishment. Sometimes, somebody had to stay thirty minutes after school, maybe for two or three days at a time. I don't remember what I done, seems like it was for not havin' my homework, but one time the teacher kept me after school and I missed the bus. I was scared spitless when I found out the bus was gone and I'd missed it. I knowed I'd *git my killin'* when I got to the house, and was scared to go home, but didn't know nuthin' else to do. I started walkin' down schoolhouse hill and commenced to cryin'. When I'd about quit bawlin', I'd think about what was a-goin' to happen to me when I got home, and start in again. I cried til I got the hiccups.

I knowed hit'd be a-gittin' down clost to dark before I got to the house, and I was bad scared of the dark. There was one stretch of about four miles with no houses on it atall, away on up the creek, and nowheres to run to git away from it if sump'm was to git after me.

I kep' my head down and tried not to wipe my eyes, and kindly turnt my head away, like I was just a-lookin' around and look like I had some business out here on the road whenever a car passed by. I'd gone clost to two mile, *dist a-Cadillackin'*, and had got apast where Junaluska road branches off the main highway, when a car stopped by the side of me. It was Sweetie and Lewis on their way home from work. Boy, was I glad to see them!

When I got in the car, I told 'em what hapm'd, and went to bawlin' again. Seems like one of 'em had sump'm left in their dinner bucket and give it to me to eat, but anyhow, they got to talkin' and cuttin' up and got me to hush cryin' by the time I got home. I shore dreaded goin' in that house. Lewis went on home, but Sweetie went in with me and talked to Mom. Lord, I was so glad he done that. He could git around her better'n anybody. Well, sir, he went on home then, and it took me a while to b'lieve it, but she ditn't whup me. But she wrote a letter and sent it to the teacher the next day, and they never did keep me after school no more.

I just got one paddlin' at school the whole twelve years I went, and never oncet got sent to the principal's office for misconduct. I probably earned a few paddlin's I didn't get, but felt like I didn't deserve the one I got.

Some teachers showed partiality to the childern whose folks was what we called "*big shots*" in town. Us backwoods younguns called 'em "*town doods.*" They usually set up clost to the front, and was knowed as teacher's pets. They got by with dist about anything they wanted to.

I was often asked how to spell a word by other kids in my room, since I was a good speller. One day, one of the teacher's pets, and a girl I liked, turned around in her seat and was callin' my name in a loud whisper. She'd evidently called it sev'al times, for somebody punched me and pointed at her. When I looked at her, she asked me how to spell a word. I was spellin' it for her when the teacher called my name and told me to come up front. She give me a paddlin' right there in front of ever'body for talkin' in class, but never said one word to the girl that was turned around in her seat and called out to me to get my attention.

The girl did try to explain to the teacher, but she still give me a paddlin' It wutn't bad atall, just the embarrassment of it. It made me feel even more worthless. To me, that was a lesson in *"It's not who you are, it's who you know."* I treated her with respect due her as a teacher, but never did like or respect her after that. It's a good thing Mom and Dad never knowed about the paddlin'. That wutn't nuthin' *to the side of* what I'd a got at home.

We had a man substitute teacher that had a method of teachin' that I don't agree with. When he asked you sump'm in arithmetic and you give the wrong answer, he made you come up to the front of the class and hold out your hand. He bent your fingers back and smacked the palm of your hand purty hard with either a ruler or the handles of a pair of scissors laid flat. Now, them scissors handles hurt! How many times he smacked you depended on what he thought you deserved. I think that's a little drastic for giving a wrong answer. I got called up and smacked on the hand a few times in his class, but so did just about everybody else. He was *ugly as a mud fence*, and about six foot two, but he looked to me like he was ten foot tall and big as a toilet. It scared me bad when he called me up there and made me stick out my hand. I'd shore like to see him try to smack my hand now! I've growed a wee bit myself since then.

But he learnt me one thing that stuck with me all through the years, and is still interestin'. It's a bit of trivia about the meanin' of numbers. It goes like this: *One's a one. Two's a couple. Three's a few. Four's a plenty. Five's a pile, and six is half a dozen.*

I've been good friends since school days with one high school teacher I had, and she is a kind person. She had some unusual but effective methods of discipline, and seemed to know just how to deal with any particular student. She ditn't know then, and prob'ly still don't know I never had no dinner at school. Few people outside my family knows. I'd see kids come from the lunch room with something they didn't eat while they was at lunch, maybe some peanut butter cookies, a bananner or apple. Sometimes, they helt it up and asked if anybody wanted it. I tried to *be mannerly* and not *act hoggish*, but if nobody spoke up purty soon, I'd take it.

This one pa'tic'lar time, though, somebody give me a apple jist as we was goin' into class. I got a bite or two before everybody got settled down. Then I started sneakin' a bite behind an open book I stood up on my desk like I was readin' out of it, and thinkin' I was getting by with it. All of a sudden, the teacher called my name, and said that since I was so hungry, I could finish eating and the class would wait for me. She knew how self-conscious I was. Of course, everyone laughed and sat there a-lookin' at me. I always blushed easy, and was always bein' teased about it. I know I'd have glowed in the dark right then.

She made me stand up, and I took one bite, but just couldn't swaller no more, with ever'body a-lookin' at me, so she made me throw it in the waste baisket, and went on with the class. I wisht the ground would open up and swaller me, I was so embarrassed. And I sure did hate to throw that apple away.

Mrs. Bell, one of the cooks at the lunch room, had a reputation for her wonderful peanut butter cookies. Somebody gave me two of them once, and I thought they were the best things I ever ate. I'd never eaten a peanut butter cookie before.

I can now make peanut butter cookies almost as good as hers, and they are my son's favorite kind. He has enjoyed them all his life, and I thank God that neither of my children had to watch with hungry eyes as all the other children filed into the lunchroom.

Every time I make them, I think about that little ol' skinny tow-headed young-gun I used to be, and eat another one…or two…or three…for her.

SHOTS, ITCH AND LICE

The school nurse come around oncet a year to give vaccinations to the school children. I was absolutely terrified of getting a shot. Even if I played sick and didn't go to school, they kept a record, and that nurse allus come back to get me. Just the smell of that alcohol made me break out in a cold sweat. As I waited on my turn, I wouldn't even watch her give another kid a shot after I saw her do it one time, and it made me scared of her, too. It took two or three teachers to hold me to give me my shots. *I'd druther a-took a whuppin' dist any day.*

Ever' oncet in awhile, she give each of us a little packet that had a bar of Lifeboy™ soap, a toothbrush, and a tube of Ipanner (Ipana™) toothpaste or a little tin shaker box of Pepsodent™ Tooth Powders in it, one. Then we got a lesson on how to brush our teeth. We'd brush our teeth sev'al times a day til ever' bit of toothpaste that would come out was squeezed out of the tube, then we'd split the tube open and lick out ever' last smidgen of it. When it was gone, we never seen no more toothpaste til the next time they handed it out. For a toothbrush, we used the chawed-up end of a little green birch stick dipped in bakin' sodie on the rare occasion we did brush our teeth.

I hated my teeth, as I had a wide gap between my two front teeth. I was so self conscious about it that I'd try not to smile big enough so anyone could see 'em, or hold my hand over my mouth when I laughed, one. I felt so ugly that I never smiled when they took school pictures.

People said that chewin' gum would help keep your teeth clean, and ever' oncet in awhile we got a piece of Dentyne™, Juicy Fruit™, or Teaberry™ chewin' gum. One piece. We thought we was lucky to get that. Shucks, it took two whole packs to give us one apiece around. We'd chew it awhile, and then we'd stick it to the underside of the table or some place while we eat. Mom allus laid her'n up on a little shelf that was built into the front side of the clock. That was her place—but nobody else better not put their chewin' gum nowhere on the clock, though. We didn't touch that clock *in no shape, form or fashion.* I learnt that I better not go to bed with it in my mouth, either, or I might wake up with it all balled up in my hair, or stuck to the piller slip, one. So I'd stick it up on the head of the iron bedstid til the next morning, and try to remember to get it before Mom seen it a-stickin' up there.

Most of the time, for chewin' gum, we skint a piece of bark off of a birch tree and stripped off the inner white layer to chew on. It smelt so good, and really tasted good. Trouble was, it didn't last long., and if you chewed too much of it, it'd *bung you up* (constipate you).

Several things were a source of embarrassment to me when I was in elementary school. An incident with the school nurse was one that really upset me. The nurse came around frequently and checked children for head lice and the *eatch* (itch). Both of these carried the stigma of a person's family being naisty, and people thought it was something awful, socially, to have either.

All the girls in my family had sores on our legs in the summer. They were probably caused from gnat or insect bites and us scratching them, or getting out in the wet weeds and getting them infected. They told us to let the dog lick the sores and it'd cure 'em. I don't guess that helped none.

We dist about kept a sore on the corner of our mouth, too. Coonie was the worst for that. I've since learned that this is a symptom of vitamin deficiency. Whatever the cause, I had a few sores on my legs.

One day, the school nurse came to the classroom door and called me out into the hall. Without any explanation, she asked me to come with her. I followed her out to the stairwell, and thought we were going somewhere when she started down the stairs. Then she told me to stop, and had me to stand and wait on the top stair. She went down two or three steps in front of me and turned around. Then she said, "I'm sorry," and before I even knew what she'd said, had grabbed hold of the hem of my dress and jerked my dresstail up so far that she could see my upper chest.

I was mortified! And I started to cryin', then. I was as embarrassed for her to see my dingy flour sack underwear as much as anything. But I couldn't believe she'd do that!

She explained that she had to check it out when anything suspicious was reported to her. I wondered who reported it. It must have been my teacher, I thought. I loved my teacher and thought she was my friend, but all this time when I thought she was being nice to me, what she was really thinking was that I had the eatch. I felt so violated, and betrayed.

The nurse talked to me a few minutes to calm me down, and waited for me to stop crying. Then she had me go into the bathroom and wash my face. Then I had to face going back in the room, with everybody looking at me and wondering what the nurse had found wrong with me. They all knew that when the school nurse singled me out, she thought I had something that was "*ketchin'*." Now, I thought, nobody'd ever want to come around me no more because they'd think I was too naisty, or they might ketch something off of me, one.

I do remember us *shore anuff* havin' the eatch one time. When Mom found out about it, that very night she greased us up good with sulfur mixed in lard. That stuff *stunk like cyarn* (carrion) when it got warm. Then ever' night they brung the washtub in to the front room in front of the fireplace and put real warm water in it. One by one, Mom gave ever' last one of us a good scrubbin' with Lysol disinfectant. The oldest boys didn't go to school then, and ditn't git it, so they got by without it. I remember her a-standin' me up in the wash tub when she got done a-scrubbin', an'en pourin' rubbin' alkyhall all over me, straight out of the bottle. Talk about gittin' set afire and froze to death at the same time, now that done it! Then we got greased up again and it was left on us til the next night, when we got another round. I don't remember how many nights this went on, seems like seven, but Mom *got shed of* that eatch. I begin to think she was going to git shed of me before it was over with.

I don't remember for sure that I had the lice, but I do remember a-gittin' my hair combed out with a fine tooth comb and somebody a-lookin' my head for louses and nits. I must a-did, though, for Coonie had 'em bad—a whole lot worser'n anybody else—and Mom cut her hair off real short. She used *Oil a Sassyfack* (Oil of Sassafras) on our head to kill the louses and nits. Coonie was ashamed to go to school because she knowed that everybody'd know she had the lice was the reason why her hair was all cut off.

They had all a them bedclothes and ever'thang to wash out and bile, but they wudn't nary nother louse or nit to be found on nobody's head. When Mom got done with us, them louses had *hit Bush River* (They was gone from there).

MOM AND DAD

I done a lot of *studyin' about* whether or not to tell how Mom and Dad really was, and what all went on at our house when we was all dist younguns. I put off and put off about sayin' anything that ditn't have to be said, because I want anybody that reads what I've wrote to enjoy it and feel good about it—and I want to feel good about it, myself.

On the other hand, real life's about the good and the bad both, and you got to learn to take the bad with the good, make the best of it, an'en go on from there. I wrote and re-wrote, and put in and took out, and fin'ly decided to say just enough to tell the tale, but not tell ever' little de-tail. It would take a book bigger'n a-body'd want to tote around if I done that.

I fin'ly come to realize that I'd spent a good part of my life a-keepin' things to myself, mostly to cover up for them. I wudn't ashamed of 'em because of who they was, or nuthin' like that—but of the way they done, and the way they treated us. I've tried to look at their side and remember that times was differ'nt, people had a differ'nt way of doin' things, and that they lived in awful hard times. So, some of it I can understand. But I never have understood how they could treat us younguns like they did. And I still don't want to have to think about it no more'n I have to. *What's done is done, so let bygones be bygones.*

There's lots of things I admired about them. They was both *clever* people—good-lookin' people, and hard workers. I don't see how in the world they raised ten healthy younguns with no more'n they had, 'spacially at a time when the whole country was on hard times. 'Course, they never had nuthin' extry, and never had much, but they knowed how to make do and take care a what they did have.

They was differ'nt from one another in a lot a ways, and alike in a lot a ways. Dad was out-goin' and *never seed a stranger.* He liked a big crowd of people around, and was allus *a-jokin' and a-goin' on* with 'em. He wutn't bashful atall, and made friends with ever'body. On the other hand, Mom never did have much to say to nobody, and *kep' to herself.* She wutn't what you'd call bashful, dist not out-goin' like Dad was, and ditn't make friends easy. She was awful bad to take

what people said the wrong way, 'spacially when she thought they was *a-lookin'
down on 'er.*

Dad was a fanatic about keepin' his word. If they was one thing that made
him madder'n gittin' a *dun* (bill) in the mail, it was for somebody to call him a *lar*
(liar). He thought that sending him a dun was like sayin' they thought his word
wutn't no good, and they had to dun him like he was some dead-beat to git him
to pay what he owed. He considered that to be *a slur on his char-acter.* And if he
eb'm thought a man was callin' him a liar, Dad had him knocked flat of his back
before he knowed he was hit.

They wutn't nuthin' he liked better'n to git in a fight. He *made his brags* that
he could whup any man, no matter how big a feller he was, long as he fit with his
fistes like a man, one-on-one. Ever'body knowed to watch how they op'm'd their
mouth around Lawton, or they was liable to git it shet with his fist. He carried a
thang in his pocket a few times that he called "knucks" when he thought somebody woutn't fight fair or would gang up on him. It was a metal bar with holes
that he run his faingers through, and when he shet his fist up on it, it stuck out
apast his knuckles. He said he could shell teeth with it.

He'd tell us younguns to do sump'm that he knowed would git us hurt, an'en
laugh like it was a big joke. Bud told me how Dad *come in a hair* a-killin him one
time, when he was dist a little feller. He set Bud up on a high rock in a bank and
told him he'd ketch him, and made him jump off. Dist as Bud jumped, Dad
stepped back and let him jist go ke-whorp on the ground where it was kivvered
up with sharp gravelledy rock. When Bud cried, he'd laugh at him and shame
him fer bawlin' like a sissy. He'd set him back up there and threaten to whup him
if he ditn't jump, an'en Bud would dist *bust the ground wide op'm* agin. Bud was
black and blue and skint up all over hisself. Dad said hit'd make a man out of
him.

Dad and Mom was awful *tight on us* (strict). Back in the early 1900's, people
had a stricter code of conduct to what they do now, and kids was expected to
mind and do what their Pappy and Mammy told 'em to, with no arguin', questions or talkin' back. At our house, though, hit went a way past bein' strict. I
thought I had it rough, but my older brothers and sisters, 'spacially Bud—*bein's*
he was the oldest, had it a whole lot rougher. After I got older, they told me what
it was like when they was dist youngens. I might not a-been much size, but I
remember a whole lot a the stuff that went on.

We dreaded to see comp'ny come, for we knowed Dad would haf to *show out.*
He liked to show people how good his youngens minded him. Mom or Dad
either one would just nod or jerk their head a certain way, do their hand a certain

way, or sorter point, and we was s'post to know what they wanted done without us a-bein' told. It was our bad luck if we guessed wrong. And they *flew off the handle* if one of us asted 'em what they wanted. They considered that to be a-sassin' 'em. They hardly ever talked to us unless they was givin' us our orders, and we better not even look like we wanted to talk back to one of 'em.

When Dad pointed down at the floor, we knowed to hit it, face down. We dist fell down there on our hands and knees, then laid down and stuck our nose in a crack. And we better not move til he told us we could, neither. He'd go right on talkin' to someboody like he ditn't know we was there, but if one of us moved ary bit, he seen it, and rubbed their nose in the crack real hard or give 'em a lickin', one.

An'en he'd line the oldest'uns up and make 'em daince, and they better not slow down or quit til he told 'em they could. I remember daincin' fer people myself a few times, too. I *ditn't have a bit more idy than a goose* how to daince or what kind of daincin' it was, I jist knowed I better dance. I jist done like I seed the others do.

Sometimes when they told one of us we was fixin' to git a whuppin', they'd say, "You need a good doast of hick'ry tea," or "birch tea," one, or said we needed a big doast of medicine. They used any kind of a green tree limb to whup us with, but called it a hick'ry or a limb, one. What some folks called a switch wutn't near as big as a limb like they used on us.

Dad would give his pocket knife to whichever one was goin' to git a lickin', an'en send 'em to cut their own hick'ry. If he ditn't think the one you brung back was big enough, he wore that'n out on you, an'en made you go back and cut another'n. Now, that made it awful hard to decide on. Even a li'l ol' keen switch looked as big as a fence post when you knowed it was a-goin' to be used on yore hide, but then, you ditn't want to take no chanch on gettin' two whuppin's. And you never knowed til after he got done with it whuther he thought it was satisfactory or not.

He whupped hard, and jist as faist as he could do it. You could hear that limb jist a-whisslin', a-cuttin' through the air, with pieces of it a-snappin' off and flyin' all over the place. If we was in the house, you could hear them ends a-hittin the wall like sleet on tin. When he got done with it, a limb was too broke up to use any more—he wore it plumb down to the nub. They used the belt or a razor strop on us too, but they druther make us go get a hick'ry so we'd have more time to dread it. I'd allus druther get a whuppin' with a leather strop or belt than a limb, that is, if I'd a-had my druthers.

They never did whup us on the laigs to where other people could see it, and Dad never did whup me as hard as he did the older boys or the hoss. But still, I've had oozin' welts to stick my dress to my back where it dried, and it burnt so bad it about took my breath when it was pulled loose.

They both had a cruel streak and a bad temper. Mom was dist as quick to whup us as Dad was, and I never one time seen her take up for one of us or ast him to stop. She'd look at us like she was glad to see us a-gittin' what we'd been a-needin'. When Coonie was fifteen, she slipped off and got married and she still had big ol' whelk marks and bruises on her back from a bad whuppin' Mom had give her a week before she run off. I'd got so scared, I run and hid. I thought she was goin' to kill her.

One thing Dad liked to do was tell one of us he was goin' to give us a whuppin', an'en say he was givin' us time to thank about it. Then he'd let it go and go, and we'd live in dread about what was a-comin', but we never did know when. About the time you begin to think maybe he'd changed his mind—maybe three or four days later—all of a sudden he'd jerk off his belt, or there he'd stand with a limb in his hand, sorter whackin' it agin' his britches leg. He'd grab you by the wrist and wear you out, an'en say, "Uh-huh! Thought I fergot about it, ditn't ye? I told ye I'd give ye a lickin', and I don't never go back on my word." It was worth takin' a whuppin' to fin'ly get it over with.

We was absolutely scared to death of both of 'em, but 'spacially of Dad. He said a youngun needed a good whuppin' ever' day to loosen up their hide and make 'em grow. He stayed about half drunk when he wudn't full drunk. We never knowed when he'd take a notion to give one of us a lickin', and he allus found a reason to, whuther we'd done anythang or not. I knowed when he got that look in his eye, he was dist a-lookin' fer a excuse to whup somebody, and I dist tried to stay out a sight and be right quiet. If him or Mom either one dist started lookin' at me right straight, I knowed I was in big trouble. That allus meant I was a-fixin' to git hurt, one way or 'nother. I still get uneasy when somebody's attention is focused on me.

A lot a times, what they said to us and how they done it hurt worser'n the whuppin's. They was sly as a fox, a-tryin' to trip us up by astin' questions that needed more'n a *uh-huh* (yes), *hunh-uh* (no), or a nod. They was both expert at boxin' you in and twistin' your words around so that any *ains'er* (answer) you give 'em was wrong. If we ditn't ains'er, they got mad and whupped us for *stubbin' up*. If we did ains'er, hit better be in the most respeckful tone a voice, or they'd say we was a-bein' a smart aleck and whup us for that. Most a the time we never knowed what to say.

We was made to be humble (submissive), and told not to *git too big for yer britches*. It was only a few years ago when I realized I didn't always make eye contact with another person during a conversation, and realized why. If one of us looked Mom or Dad in the eye, especially when they were *gittin' on to us,* they took it as defiance or disrespect. We knowed we better keep our head bowed and not look 'em straight in the face. But then again, maybe the next time one of 'em got mad and *got on to me,* and I ditn't look up, they'd holler, "You look at me and pay attention when I speak to you, young lady!" But it was usually safer to keep my head down than look up.

Tryin' to describe Mom is like trying to describe the wind. You can't predict with any accuracy when it will change, how it will change, from which direction it will blow, when it will come your way, or how much velocity it will have. The only thing you can be sure about is that it will change. And it could change without your being aware of it. What she laughed about one day, she'd beat you half to death for the next.

Dad was a lot like Mom in that he was changeable. When he was about full a likker, he'd *fly off the handle* over nuthin', and was *as mean as a copperhead.* At times, he'd pick at Mom *jist for pure cussedness,* til he got a good cuss fight or argue-ment out of her. And it usually ditn' take much. They argued and *fit* about half the time—but I never knowed Dad to hit her. She'd a kilt him if he had. She wutn't scared a him 'r nobody 'r nuthin' else, neither.

If Dad done ary thang to make her mad, she'd not only be mad about that, but would brang up ever'thang else he ever done and *throw it up to him.* Ever' time. Over and over. She never forgot, and she never forgive, whuther it was Dad or anybody else. And she'd *git eb'm with 'em,* no matter who it was, how long ago it was, how long it took, or what she had to do to do it. She allus had to have the last word. Makes me think about a tale they use to tell about a man and his ol' woman a-gittin' in a argue-ment, an'en got to fightin'—sump'm about a pair a scissors. He got her down in the creek and was a-holdin' her head inunder the water a-tryin' to make her *holler calf rope* (give up). About the time he thought he'd helt 'er under as long as he could 'thout drowndin' 'er, he'd let 'er come up for air, but she still woutn't give up. Finally he helt her under a little too long, and dist as she was a-tryin' to draw her last breath, she stuck two faingers up ou'fenunder the water and worked 'em like scissors blades.

That was Mom!

She took what us youngens called "mad fits." When her and Dad got into a racket, or things didn't go to suit her, she'd *take a mad fit.* I've seen her flop down on her back, kick her heels up and down, and beat on the floor with her fists, a-screamin' and a-hollerin and cussin' and cryin', jist like a little youngun a-havin' a *hissy fit* (temper tantrum). An'en she'd threaten to kill herself. She'd say that when she was dead, ever' body'd be sorry about how they'd treated her, but hit'd *done'en* be too late, then. That seemed to be her ultimate revenge on ever'body.

At times we'd be scared so bad our chin 'ud be a-quiverin' so hard we coutn't eb'm talk. We's afeared she'd hit us if we got in reach of her, but we'd all get down on our hands and knees around her on the floor, a-cryin' and a-baggin' her not to kill herself. We *sounded like lost souls in tarment* (torment, hell). It went on like that til she wore herself slap out. And we was left a-thinkin' we better be awful careful, or *unbeknowin'st to us* (unaware), we might do sump'm to make her kill herself. And hit'd be our fault.

I've *studied about* her a lot, and admired her spunk. I can sympathize with her situation, and know there had to be *a-many a day* when she felt completely over-whelmed with work and responsibilities. I know she had a rough time and worked hard trying to raise us. I hurt to see the swollen varicose veins in her legs and her sore, painfully chapped hands. I honestly don't know how she managed to keep going day after day, year after year. But she did it in a way that conveyed, not love for us, but the attitude that we were a burden she wished she didn't have to endure, and all her troubles was our fault. Bud still has the whole body expres-sion of apology to the world for just being in it. So did Alma. And the rest of us felt that way.

We lived in fear that at any minute one of 'em would fly mad or find sump'm to whup us for. They took out their *flusteration* on us. Times was hard, but they seemed to want to make it even harder on us. They was allus a-lookin' for sump'm 'r other to growl about, and ways to put us down and shame us. Accor-din' to them, we never did do nuthin' right. Jist as shore as they seen us a-laughin' and playin' and havin' fun, they put us to work a-doin' sump'm, or said sump'm hateful. And Mom had lots of old killjoy sayin's she'd tell us, like *"laugh or sang before breakfast, cry before dinner."* I've had to learn to let myself feel joy without being afraid it's going to be snatched away from me.

I realize that back in their time, people didn't openly show much affection. And for sweethearts to act any sich a way was a *shame and a disgrace*. Why, eb'm a man and his *ol' woman* never so much as helt hands in public, much less *bussed* (kissed) one another—eb'm on the jaw. But they did talk kind to one another and showed by how they acted that they liked one another, and they was good to their younguns.

But Mom and Dad never showed us no affection—any time or any place, or bragged on us for nothin'. If one of us got hurt, we got no sympathy. As if that wutn't bad enough, they tried to turn us youngens agin' one another or make us mad at one another. Bud told me one time Mom helt him down and made Sweetie whup him, and when Sweetie tried not to hit too hard, she told him to hit harder or she'd *stripe his butt* and show him how it was done.

They'd put one of us up to watch another'n, like at school, and tell on 'em if they done sump'm they wutn't s'post to. If that'n ditn't tell on the other'n and it was found out, that'n got a worser whuppin than the one that done it. If two younguns got in a fuss, they ditn't give a dang *whose butt was the blackest* (guilty), they give both of 'em *the same doast of medicine.*

I don't remember neither one of 'em ever holdin' me on their lap, huggin' or kissin' me, or even dist a-bein' good to me when I was little—or any of the rest of us either, for that matter—except for Vernon. When Paw Taylor died, I remember a-wonderin' if anybody'd eb'm cry if I was to *up and* die. I coutn't think of a soul, and thought Mom and Dad would prob'ly be glad to git me out a their way.

I can still see the sad, fear-filled eyes and solemn faces of my brothers and sisters, like we was *all rowed up* in a line around the room. I wisht they was some way I could go back in time and gether up them pore, pitiful, *brow-beat*, defenseless little younguns in my arms, and jist love 'em.

They's one thing that allus amazed me, and that was how Mom and Dad acted around other people and other childern. Talk about *wolfs in sheep's clothes!* I felt like I was a-watchin' somebody altogether differ'nt from the people I knowed at home. I've had people tell me I had "the sweetest mother." When she talked to other people, her voice was altogether differ'nt from her usual self, a-talkin' so sweet you'd think *butter woutn't melt in her mouth.* And Dad would laugh and be *jov'al* around other people and pet other younguns, even give 'em pocket change.

Yet they kep' their own childern *all cowed down* (cowered). I coutn't b'lieve they fooled other people like they did. Hit was *all put-on.*

I learnt one thang fer shore, and that's how differ'nt things can be, from what it looks like they is.

The scars and hurts in your mind never do plumb go away. On account of how Dad and Mom done, I had a hard time a-trustin' anybody. I was allus a-waitin' for 'em to turn on me. Even after I was grown, no matter how kind they spoke, or how good our relationship seemed, I never *trusted 'em as fur as I could throw a bull by the horns.* The tension was always there, and in the back of my mind, I was allus a-waitin' for the other shoe to drop. I was afraid of both of 'em as long as they lived.

When he started workin' for the Champion Paper and Fibre Company, Dad wutn't at home with us youngest'uns as much as he had the oldest'uns, and he'd had to cut down on his drankin' to hold down his job. He wutn't as mean, and they both let up on us some after the oldest'uns left home—say, from Lawerence on down, and wutn't as hard on me and Oval and Vernon.

After he got saved, he stopped drankin' and joined the church, and I seen a big difference in Dad. A few times when he'd be walkin' past my chair, he'd stop and lay his hand on top of my head and rub my hair in a awk'ard sort of way. He had me to set down on his lap a few times, and put his arm around me and kissed me on the cheek. He treated me better'n Mom did, but I was still a-scared of him.

Dad could do about anything, I think, and was *sharp as a tack*. Whatever needed doin', he done it—from fixin' our shoes to shoein' hosses. He knowed all about gardenin' and how to raise any kind of crop a-goin' by the signs. He kept bees, and dist walked right up and got honey out a the gums with them bees a-crawlin' all over his arms, and they never stung him. He could gear up, hitch up and work any kind of work animal and doctor 'em, could carpenter, weld, oper-ate heavy equipment, was expert with explosives—powder man, they called it, or cook. Jist whatever needed doin', he *took a-holt of it*. And he done it all good, too. I'm still amazed at men that can't fix nary thang around the house, and have to call on a plumber, electrician, or somebody to come and do odd jobs for 'em.

Along about the time I started high school—about 1948, Dad and Bud built us a new house, except Lewis helped lay the foundation off and they got Sweetie to come and help Bud put the roof on. Dad jist come home on the week-ends, so Bud done most of the main work through the week, and Dad done the cab'nets and finish work when he was home. They ditn't have no kind a power (pair) tools like we have now. About all they had was a foldin' rule, level, hand saw, clawhammer, markin' pencil, and ladder. They bought their nails in wooden kaigs. They done most a their markin' by rakin' a big nail acrost the plank. Hit took a lot a time and labor to build a house, havin' to use a hand saw to saw off ever piece a lumber that went up.

When Dad put in a *zink* (sink), him and Mom had runnin' water in their kitchen for the first time in their life. They dammed up the branch on the side a the mountain and built a reservoir, an'en run a water line down to the house. I remember him a-comin' in the house when he got ever'thang ready, and turnin' on the water, and we all stood around the zink jist a-watchin' that water run. He showed Mom how to turn the fawcet off and on, an'en dist *stood there a-grinnin' like a mule a-eatin' sawbrars*. He was so proud a hisself. No more carryin' water up the hill from the sprang.

When we got *lights* (electric power) about 1950, Dad wired (wahr'd) the house his own self. Then he went to town and bought a Frigidairy (Frigidaire™ refrigerator).

Bein's as he was the baby, they treated Vernon altogether differ'nt from how they'd treated the rest of us. They was better to Oval than us, too, but they didn't pet him like they did Vernon, and made a big differ'nce in them. Back then, people went to town a-Saturday mornin' to git their groceries and feed and stuff. They never said "go shoppin'" like we say now. They said they was a-goinna "Go to town." Dad liked to keep his truck all shined up, and made me or Oval, one, usually Oval, dip water out of the creek and wash and clean it up early ever' Saturday mornin'. Then he took Mom and Vernon to town with him. Sometimes Oval got to go, but Dad would set Vernon on his lap and let him drive the truck. He was their baby, and they never tried to hide the fact that they *thought more of* (loved) him than all the rest of us put together.

They allus put me to doin' some kind a job while they was gone off to town. Most a the time, Dad told me to do the churnin'. When he wutn't around, Mom woutn't let me churn. She ditn't want me a-messin' with her churnin'. I didn't care if they did make me stay at the house. I liked to churn and was glad when they got gone, so I could listen to country music on the radio. Me and ol' Hank or Lefty Frizzell had us a sangin' good time. I had to look out so they ditn't come back and ketch me at it, though. I wutn't spost to tetch that radio. I *took and* set the churn out on the front porch in warm weather so I could hear the truck a-comin' and run and turn the radio off right fast before they got there.

After Thelma got married, that left Lawerence, me, Oval and Vernon at home. Since Lawerence was gone most of the time, and the boys was usually off a-playin', that left me mostly by myself around the house with Mom. She never did forgive Thelma for gittin' married and runnin' off and leavin' her. I think she dist about went crazy over it. I seen her wipe her eyes ever' once in a while and felt sorry for her. After Thelma got up fourteen or fifteen year old, Mom and her allus talked, laughed, and done things together, and I knowed she missed her—I did, too.

Maybe Mom being so isolated and lonely would explain some of her behavior. I tried to talk to her and be friendly, but she never let on like she heard a thang I said—like I wutn't eb'm there. She acted like it was her bad luck that Thelma was gone and she had to put up with the likes a me. But wutn't I worth nuthin' atall? Mom made it cler, that compared to Thelma, I *wutn't worth a plug nickel.*

It sounds so happy and all, to say your mother went around a-whistlin' and sangin' all the time. Well, it wutn't nuthin' like that atall. The way she whistled wutn't like where you dist pucker up and whistle a happy tune. It was a real keen shrill whistle that got on your nerves. She done itsomehow a-blowin' betwixt her front teeth, with her mouth dist pyert near shut, a-lookin' real grim and solemn. Her lips never moved nary bit. When she wutn't a-whistlin', she was a-sangin' one a them old sad mournful ballads dist about *ever' breath she drawed*—from the time she got up til she went to bed.

She ditn't want that old radio on a-makin' a racket, and if Bud or anybody turnt it on, unless it was Dad, she turnt it off purty quick—'spacially when "that ol' news" come on. She wutn't interested in nuthin' that didn't di-reckly concern her. Her sangin' and the whistlin', spacially, got so nerve-wrackin' I got so I'd go off to where I coutn't hear it. She come a-stormin' out on the porch one day and said she knowed why I'd gone off out there, and jist wait and see, one day I'd wish I could hear my poor old mammy's voice and she woutn't be here (That same old veiled threat of suicide).

She *watched me like a hawk,* and I stayed *nervous as a long-tailed cat in a room full a rockin' chairs,* afraid she'd git onto me about sump'm. I'd be a-doin' sump'm, and all of a sudden she'd *beller* out and tell me to do it some other way. Seemed like ever' time I turned around, she *give me a good rakin' out,* and said I couldn't do nuthin' right.

She had her own way a doin' ever' thing, and it was usually *backerds* to how anybody else would do it. She ditn't want nary thang changed. Ever' little thang had a certain place to be put at, and you didn't dare put it one inch away. I had to watch out ever' minute, so I woutn't break one of her rules and make her mad. One certain pan set on top of another certain pan in exactly a certain place. Or one skillet was turned upside down and another'n right side up on top of it. The dishrags better be clean and hung up at a certain place in a certain way. She got fightin' mad if the broom was stood up on the straws. That made it "git *whopper-jawed*". It had to be stood up on the end a the handle. If I hapm'd to overlook sump'm, she'd accuse me of doin' it a-purpose to spite her.

I hated the constant tension and I felt so trapped and helpless, but I shore wutn't a-goin' to run off and git married to git away, like Alma and Coonie done. Every day, I prayed that God would help me get along with her til I could make it through school.

She'd allus acted like I was sump'm naisty, but then she went to makin' me put my dirty clothes in a sep'rate pile over at the foot a my bed next to the wall, and woutn't eb'm tetch 'em. She never washed mine in with their'n, and acted like it would contaminate their clothes by puttin' mine in the same water. And after Dad bought a wringer washin' machine, she didn't want me to help do the washin', and she didn't want my clothes in it. I was told not to bother that washin' machine, and had to take my clothes out on the back porch and wash' em on the rub board.

I even had to heat water on the stove and take the washpan out on the back porch to clean up (bathe), even in the winter time, so I could throw the water out in the back yard. She didn't want me pourin' water where I'd washed my head, or my bath water neither one, in the sink. She said they was some little wheels down in the zink drain, and if hairs got tangled up in 'em, hit'd stop up.

When Dad got her a 'lectric iron, I wutn't allowed to tetch it. I had to use the old black irons that you heat on the stove.

She made me wash the dishes, but she ditn't want me *"a-messin' and gommin'"* in her cookin'. She didn't want me to tetch nuthin', like stir a pot, or eb'm lift up a pot led to look in it. She didn't want me a-tetchin' one thang that was her'n, and didn't tetch me or nuthin' of mine.

She looked for any excuse to give me a whuppin' and keep me scared of her. She kep' the razor strop hung up on the side of the cabinet in plain sight to where I had to pass right by it ever' time I went from the kitchen to the front room. Young as I was, I finally seen into it, that she liked to see me cry more'n anything. The bigger I cried, the better she liked it. Then she'd whup me again for cryin'. It made me mad at myself to give her the satisfaction of seein' me cry, so I made up my mind not to. I got to where I could just focus my mind and look sumerce else, and stand there with my arms folded up and never flinch a muscle. It was the only way I had to fight back. That made her *so mad she coutn't see straight.* She'd whup me til she was *plumb tuckered out.*

I was about fourteen the last time she give me a whuppin'. She'd wore herself out a-wearin' me out. When she fin'ly quit, I looked her straight in the eyes and calmly said, "Some day, somebody's going to have to give an account to God for the way I've been treated." Only God knows what courage it took to say that, and only God could give me that courage. I figgered she'd kill me, but she ditn't never whup me again. She still schemed ways to hurt my feelin's or keep me afraid of her. It was like she coutn't stand to see me happy.

To me, it seemed like she deliberately set out to totally destroy me. She talked like she had a direct access to God that nobody else had. That really crushed me. I knowed by now that if she had any influence with how God felt about me, I *was a goner.* She told me, and for a long time dist about had me b'lievin' that she could read my mind. That's where she *dropped her candy.* I knowed that coutn't be so, for she 'cused me of thinkin' about and doin' thangs that I never even *drampt* about, much less done. It was dist meanness she'd drawed up in her own mind.

Not long after I decided I wanted to be a nurse, she overheard me talkin' about it with one of my friends. One day in the dinin' room, she told me I couldn't never be no nurse—nurses was clean, and I was too naisty to make a nurse. That remark hurt so much that I can still show you exackly where she was standin' when she said that.

When I told Dad I wanted to be a nurse, he about had a stroke. He asked me if I knowed what nurses done. I sort of did, and when I started tellin' him, he said, hell no, the only thing nurses was there for was for the doctors to "fool with" any time they took a notion to, and I wutn't goin' to be no nurse. He better not hear no more about it. You'd a-thought I was goin' into prostitution full time.

From then on, I kept my mouth shut. I couldn't talk to 'em about nuthin' without them a-turnin' it around and makin' it into sump'm filthy.

But God and I had other plans. I didn't know how He would do it or how long it would take, but I knew that's what I was going to do with my life. And I wasn't going to let their dirty minds destroy my trust.

◆   ◆   ◆

They had to know where I was and what I was doing every minute. I felt like a prisoner. Even if they let me go anywhere up on the creek, Dad sent Oval and Vernon to watch me. He told 'em if they seen me "git into any meanness," they better tell him, or he'd give 'em a good thrashin'.

One time my aunt Bea gave a party for the teenagers up on the creek. She come up to the house and talked Mom and Dad into lettin' me come. She'd planned some games and fixed treats for us. I coutn't believe they'd let me go—just like that. Sure enough, they sent Oval and Vernon along to watch me and tell ever'thing I done, 'spacially if I went outside in the dark with a boy.

They knowed they wutn't invited, and nobody ditn't want 'em there, but knowed they better do what they was told to. Can you imagine how much fun I had with them a-settin' there *solemn as a judge*—four big tattle-tale eyes and ears glued right on me, a-watchin' ever move I made, and wonderin' if they'd take anything I done as "meanness?" Dad and Mom had made it sound so sneakin' and dirty that I felt sick to my stomach to dist think about kissin' a boy, even in a game of Post Office or spin-the-bottle.

I never stayed long, for they'd told me what time to be back at the house, and the party was dist a-gittin' started good when I had to leave. And I think Oval and Vernon was glad to git away from where they wutn't wanted. I never went to no more parties.

◆   ◆   ◆

Back when the older boys was home, Dad allus made one of them git up and build the fire of a mornin'. After they was all gone, sometimes Dad made me do it. When he called my name, I knowed I better fall out a there and he'd better not have to call but one time. It was allus real early—usually between four and five o'clock. A few times, it was three in the mornin' when he hollered at me to get up and build the fire.

The house got cold purty fast when the fire died down, and by mornin', it was freezin' cold. I had to put on my short sleeve cotton dress in the dark when I got up, for the only lights was the overhead lights after we got power, and they ditn't want no light a-shinin' in their eyes. Hit dist about took my breath when I set my *bare-necked* feet out on that cold linoleum floor. I never had seen a housecoat or bedroom shoes then, except for them little felt shoes Mammy wore.

After I got the fire to goin' good, I filled up the coffee pot with water and set it on the heater so Dad could put his coffee in it when he got up. It woutn't a-been so bad if I could a-gone back to bed and a-got warm while the house heated up, but Dad woutn't let me. I had to stay up and keep the fire a-goin'. I got awful cold before the heater got warmed up. I had to set there in a straight back chair and not make no racket that might wake them up, or he'd a-come out a there and give me a good thrashin'.

I never had no radio or TV to keep me comp'ny, and not eb'm nothin' to read—just set there and listen to that old clock a-tickin' away—tick-tock, tick-tock, tick-tock. It made me so sleepy, an'en when I started gittin' warm, sometimes I'd doze off in spite a ever'thing. I sure did come alive, though, when I heard Dad's heels hit the floor. I can still hear that thunk, an'en his pocket change and keys a-jinglin' as he pulled his britches on. The fire better be a-goin' good and I'd better not be asleep when they got up. They still woutn't let me go back to bed.

It was warmer in the front room, anyhow. In the winter time, Mom put whatever cover she wanted me to have on my bed, and that was all I could have. She had a big stack of extry quilts in the back room, but when I asted her one time if I could put another'n on my bed, she'd said they wutn't no use a-dirtyin' 'em all up. I knowed better'n to ast her the second time.

She was *warm natured*, sorter heavy-built and solid, and wore short sleeve dresses in the winter time dist like she did in the summer time. She didn't put a whole lot a kivver on her bed, and slep' in her *petticoat tail*, but Dad was kindly bony, and slept in his long-handles. Their bed was in the middle room and the heater was not more'n ten feet away from it, in the front room. My bed was in the room fudder on back, and it got awful cold back there some nights. The covers even felt kindly damp and cold to my naked arms and legs when I got in the bed, and seemed like it took forever to git warm enough to go to sleep. I'd dist lay there in my petticoat tail and shiver, sometimes. They was dist barely enough cover to keep from freezin' to death, but not enough to stay good and warm.

I don't know why, but when I lie down and get still awhile, my temperature and pulse rate drops. It's like I go into a mild state of hibernation, and sometimes get cold, even in the summer. My husband used to laugh and tease me about it. He said if he came that near to being dead when he went to sleep, he'd be afraid to go to bed.

I tell you one thing for sure: I don't lay there and shiver in a cold bed now. I have a heated mattress pad *and* an electric blanket on my bed. And that pad stays on my bed the year 'round. I don't use it on hot summer nights, of course, but I know it's there. If I get cold, all I have to do is click that sucker on and turn it up on "broil" if I want to. I have stacks of quilts that Coonie and I and others have made. And pretty soft cozy blankets. If I want one, I get one—and don't worry about it gittin' dirty. I've got me one a them there automatic washin' machines and dryers, too.

Sometimes in cold weather when I start to bed, I think about them long cold winter nights up on the creek, with the wind a-whistlin' around the corners of the house and moanin' through the cracks. I snuggle down in my toasty warm bed and whisper a heartfelt, "Thank You, God," as I pull the covers up over my *years*. (Literally.)

◆　　　◆　　　◆

When I think about Mom and Dad, I feel so sorry that they never knew the indescribable joy of loving and being loved by their children. It's so sad to think about what a loss that was, to have never felt or given that love, especially when they had ten golden opportunities. You may be *pore as a church mouse*, but *it don't cost a thin dime* to give a youngun a hug. And that's the most precious gift you can give them.

I've felt pure joy surge through my very soul when I'd pick up one of my babies and they'd snuggle against me and say, "'love you, Mama." Nothing could make me intentionally destroy the love and trust I saw in those precious eyes. I couldn't bear it if I thought they feared and felt about me as I did about Mom and Dad.

My son was describing someone's personality once. He said they looked so soft and sweet, like a wild kitten that you couldn't resist reaching out to pet. But when you reached out your hand, you got it shredded.

I immediately thought of Mom. Through the years, sometimes she did some unexpected kindness, or acted friendly for awhile. I'd begin to think maybe we could at least be friends. Then, like the wind she'd suddenly change, and like the kitten, would shred, not my hand, but my heart. And I'd never know why.

I think Dad tried to make up for his past mistakes before he died in 1957, and we had a good relationship. But I never stopped being afraid of him.

I wept when Mom died at age 95, but not just because she had died. I realized that I had kept on hoping that we could somehow still have a loving mother and daughter relationship.

Sometimes I weep now because I know it will never be.

PAW AND MAMMY

My mother's parents were:

Memory Allen Taylor, 20 April, 1878—15 August, 1943, and

Emer Lavada Stephens Taylor, 16 April, 1879—27 October, 1949.

Everyone outside the family called them Uncle Mem and Aunt Emer. We called them Paw and Mammy. My memories of them are good ones.

A few years ago, I realized that I knew very little about Paw in his younger days, and asked Mom about him. This is some of the things she told me:

Paw's mother was Mary Ann Burch Taylor, and they said she was a full blooded Cherokee Indian. After raising her family, when her youngest daughter Martha got married, she went home with her to Tellico Plains, Tennessee and lived there the rest of her life. His father, James Thomas Taylor, came and lived with Paw and Mammy after his wife went to Tellico.

Mom said Paw and Mammy was allus good to her and her brother and sisters. She said that Mammy spanked her a few times, but Paw never did.

When Paw went off to the woods and found some berries to pick, or needed a container for something he wanted to bring home, he made a birch bark bucket to carry them in. He was good at working with his hands and used to play the banjo. He was a member of the Odd Fellows Lodge, and belonged to another group called Farmer's Union over at Aquone. He was the "whistle blower." That meant he had a cane whistle that he blew at their meetings, I guess to call them to order. He did several different jobs, but always farmed. One of his jobs was overseer on road construction, and was a Deputy Sheriff for a while. He also wrote some poems.

When I think of Paw, I have a mental image of a tall, stocky-built man, bald on top with a fringe of white hair along the lower sides and back of his head. And I remember his kind voice. He used to sit in the sun out on the porch steps to eat an apple. Since his teeth weren't good enough to bite an apple, he cut the apple in half, and used a special spoon with a sharp edge to scrape out the insides of his apple to eat it. He made it look so good, the way he ate it. Sometimes he'd give me a bite. Of course, he give me one for myself, but mine wudn't near as good as his was (I thought).

He had the biggest hands. Sometimes he'd pick me up and set me on his lap and rub his hand down over my long hair. He could put his thumbs together at my waist in front and touch his fingertips at my back. He called me "Trigger," and pronounced it as "Treeger."I don't know why he called me that, but I remember him hugging me and saying "Dear little Trigger," whenever I went there. He was always so kind to me, and I loved him better'n anybody.

They lived about half a mile up the road from our house. The thing I remember most about Paw and Mammy's place was the fruit trees all over their place. They was all kind of apple trees: Early Harvest, Ben Davis, Limbertwigs, sweet apples, two kinds of June apples, Winesap, Golden and Red Delicious, Pott's apples, and others I can't remember the names of. There was one which had enormous green colored tart apples, about the size of a small cantaloupe. He called 'em Horse apples. I never have seen a apple like that since. One apple would easily make a big pie. There was also sarvis, plum, cherry and pear trees. One cherry tree had big ol' yaller sweet cherries on it, and they was so good. The reduns was sour, and smaller. A few of the old apple trees, and one pear tree is still there, and bears fruit.

A big old tree that they called a "*peekin*" (pecan) tree grew in their yard. It tasted something like a white walnut, had a hard shell but was smooth like a pecan, yet it wasn't shaped like either. It was rounded on one end and pointed on the other, and was about the size of a pecan. The inside of it didn't have the bitter membrane that a pecan has, but was segmented like a black walnut. I'd never seen nuts like that until about two years ago when a friend who taught Agriculture told me they were heart nuts, and gave me a basket full. It was like going back in time.

Their house was built right on the creek bank. The kitchen and kitchen porch was on the side next to the creek. You could look straight down into the creek from the kitchen window and off the porch. I thought their toilet was really something. You could go out the door at the lower end of the kitchen and down the steps outside, then go through a side door underneath the kitchen to the toilet he'd built in there. The creek eddied sideways there and run right under the toilet holes where you set. You could set on one hole and watch the creek run down under the other'n. They wudn't no stink about that toilet, 'cause ever'thang got washed down the creek.

They was a small porch on the upper side of the kitchen—and just beyond that, below a steep bank, was the springhouse. You could dist about step off onto its mossy roof from the edge of the porch. One thing that still amazes me is that the whole side of that steep bank was a huge log that was buried except for that side of it. What you could see was at least four feet, top to bottom. And it wutn't rotten. You don't never see trees that big around here no more.

Some sarvis trees growed right up agin' the springhouse. Paw had a straight chair on the porch where he set with his slingshot and kep' the birds run out of his cherry and sarvis trees. He picked up just the right sized rocks to use in his slingshot and kept 'em in a big tin can a-settin' by his chair, then stuck his sling-shot down on top of 'em so he could git to it easy. When he saw a bird light in a sarvis tree, he eased his hand over to the tin can, got out his slingshot and a rock, and shot that bird right out of there. Usually he just scared one a-purpose, but sometimes he hit it and give it to the cat. He helped me make a slingshot, and I got so I could hit *pert nyear* anything, but I coutn't stand to kill no birds. I dru-ther target shoot at a tin can or sump'm.

Their spring was jist beyond the springhouse. You had to go out from the porch steps and down a trail that circled around to get down to the spring. They was a circle of the biggest ol' hemlock trees all around the edge of the creek and over the spring with their tops so close that they was like a roof. You coutn't see the sky when you was down inunder 'em. It was so shady and cool, and I loved to go in there and just set and listen to the creek run. The ground was covered with needles from the trees and smelt so good. Some rock steps went down to the spring, where they dipped the water out with a big tin dipper they kep' a-hangin' up on a laurel bush.

They had it fixed up down by the creek for a wash place, with a big old black cast iron wash pot and a homemade bainch to set the tubs on. Wash water was dipped out of the creek. They kep' the washtubs hung up on the side of them big hemlock trees.

On past the spring was a foot log with a hand rail over the creek, and a slatted gate on the other side. They had to cross the foot log to go over to the mailbox. Pink climbin' roses growed all up and down the creek bank over there, and you could smell 'em all over the place when they was bloomin'.

They was a garage (grodge) over by the road that had belonged to my uncle Kermit before he died. One time Dad and Mom got in a big racket, and Mom upped and took us younguns and moved out and left him. I don't know how old I was at the time, but I must of been five or six. I don't think Vernon had been born yit. I remember Dad askin' each and ever' one of us if we wanted to stay with him or go with Mom. *Not nary a one* of us said we would stay with him, but I do remember me a-goin' off to myself and cryin' because he was by hisself. I don't care what kind a daddy a youngun's got, he's still your Dad.

Mom moved us into Kermit's old garage. It was built out of sawmill planks, had one little wender in the back, and a dirt floor in it. Lucky, it was summertime, so we stayed warm, and slep' on a pallet on the floor. The bigger youngens slep' outside inunder the yaller cherry tree. They done the cookin' outside on a fire. We thought it was fun—like *layin' out*, sorter.

I remember somebody with a log truck a-brangin' Daddy up there. He had a twenty-five pound sack of flour and some other stuff up on the bed of the truck. That's another mental picture I have of Dad. I can still see him a-climbin' up on the back of that truck and handin' down stuff to the big younguns. My head wasn't as high as the bed of the truck.

I don't know how long we stayed there, but it wutn't long til Dad come a-baggin' Mom, then stayed all night, and *finegaled* her into movin' back to the old house where I'd been borned at. He promised her he'd quit drankin', and she was real *tickled about that*. But he never done it. Inside of a week, he was drunk as a dawg. Jist like a dang drunk—they'll *promise you the moon and give you a punkin'*. I remember them a-quarrelin' over him not a-keepin' his promise. But she'd done and already moved back, then.

They was three rooms with a full length porch on the other side of Paw's house. He had a wide board nailed up between two porch postes to to make a saw rack, and called it his "saw sharp'nin' board." It had pieces of wood on it with slots where he put his saw with the teeth up, and used his saw sharp'nin' tools to sharp'm it. I remember a tool he called a spider that he set down over the saw teeth, a gauge, and a little metal hammer he pecked on the saw teeth with. He had files of different shapes and sizes.

I loved to go to Paw and Mammy's, but wutn't allowed to go much. Usually, I was sent for some reason when I got to go. They sent me up there one time to get some milk. It was in a gallon glass jar, and heavy for a little girl to carry. It was sweaty from being in the water in the spranghouse. I'd dist got started down the road good, when it slipped out of my arms and busted all to pieces on that graveldy road.

I never did make no racket when I cried, 'cept for snubbin' an' snifflin', and big ol' tears a-streamin' down. Well, I was standin' there *a-squallin'*, and lookin' at that broke glass, afear'd to go home. I knowed fer shore I'd get a bad whuppin' this time, for we got one at home if we eb'm jist spilt our milk at the table. Paw must a been a-watchin' me, for he come across the footlog and walked down the road to where I was a-standin'. He told me to "Hush, now; we'll jist go git another'n, and nobody won't know nothin' about it." He got me by the hand and led me back over to the springhouse and give me another jar a milk.

Another time, I started down the road to go home, and got right below the place where I'd broke the milk jar. It was dusky dark, and I was a big ol' *fraidy-cat* after dark. I heard some kind of animal make a racket, and dist stopped and stood there, afear'd to go on. He called out to me from his kitchen porch, and I hollered back that I heard a *booger* (sump'm that'll git you).

He come over to where I was a-standin', and started walkin' down the road with me. We got down the road a little ways when I heard it again, and he told me I was hearing some hogs a-gruntin' down in Henry White's hog pen. He walked on past the hog pen with me, though, told me to go on home, and I know he stood there till I turned off down the trail torge our house, for I kep' a-lookin' back to see.

His apple house was right acrost the branch from the lower side of his house. I can *squanch up* my eyes and dist about smell them apples when the door was opened. They was big bins in there where he stored apples that he gathered off a the trees. They was so purty—yaller'uns, dark red'uns, green'uns, streaked'uns, ever one in hits own bin. Paw ditn't care if you got a apple, if you wanted one, but it was hard to make up your mind which'un you wanted, sometimes. Them apples must've kep' about all winter, 'cause I remember us a-havin' some at Christmas. They was Arsh taters, sweet taters, and punkins in bins, too.

Mammy subscribed to some magazines, and Paw took the newspaper. They was stacked in there so Paw could use 'em to wrap up the purtiest apples in paper to keep. I used to go in there and set on the floor by the wender and look at them magazines. Seems like the one I liked was called Home Comfort. It had good stories in it. Some of the magazines had continued stories in 'em. I liked to read the Grit paper, too, and the funny papers they got with the newspaper. They didn't care if I read 'em, but I couldn't take 'em home, 'cause Mom and Dad didn't let us set around and read. I could of lived in that apple house.

I don't know where it come from, but they was a half-grown, part bainch-laigged feist dog that come to our house and took up, and he took up with me. He follered me around ever'where I went. I called him mine, and named him Joe. He was so smart. I talked to him all of the time. I remember a-slippin' him in the apple house with me, and he'd lay down with his head acrost my laigs or lap, one, and I petted him while I read. I loved that dog. I never did have nothin' I could call mine before.

Mom *thowed off* on it and said it was a *dadblasted* sorry dog and wutn't worth the rations it took to feed it. I coutn't see that, for he ditn' eat nuthin' that wutn't throwed out anyway. They wutn' no sichy thang as buyin' dog food back then. W'y—people'd a-laughed you out of the country if you'd a-said you bought dog food. I jist tried to keep Joe out of her sight, and we stayed off away from the house as much as we could.

Then one day, he wutn't there. I went all over the place and called and looked, and looked and squalled, but never did see him no more. Nobody knowed a thang about it when I asted. I *ort to a-knowed better*. Years after that, I fin'ly found out that Mom'd had Bud to kill it. It took me a long time to forgive them for that.

Paw talked about the Lord sometimes, and always *"said the blessin"* at the table. I memorized it. It was: "Our Heavenly Father, we thank You for this table which has been prepared for the needs of our bodies. Forgive us our sins, and save us for Christ's sake. Amen." Both of them read the Bible some every day, and Mammy loved for me to read it to her.

I don't know the year they started it, but Thelma and Alma went to Paw one time and asked him to start teachin' Sunday School. Once in awhile, Mom and Dad let them walk down to Valleytown Church to Sunday School, but it was a long way there and back, and they couldn't go much in the winter. It was too far for us littluns to walk.

Paw started conductin' Sunday School in his apple house, and us youngens and some of the neighbors went to it. I remember Paw a-holdin' his songbook, leadin' the sangin', and us a-sangin' the song, "The Eastern Gate." The chorus says "I will meet you in the morning, just inside the Eastern Gate over there; I will meet you, I will meet you, I will meet you in the morning over there."

I don't remember a time when I wasn't aware of the existence of God, and always just talked to God about things. At Sunday School, I learnt that's what "praying" is. I loved learnin' about the Bible in Sunday School. Many times I've thought how Paw never had no idy of the far-reaching influence that one thing he did had on my life.

The best smellin' place I was ever at, in my whole life, was the "back room" at Paw and Mammy's. That's where they kept what they put up and dried, and pickled, and stuff. There wasn't no bed or nothin' in there, but dist tables and banches and shelfs, and nails drove up on the wall to hang thangs up on. You went through the front room and the middle room to the back room, and made a right-hand turn to go in to the kitchen. The back room collected all of the smells from the kitchen—of wood smoke and meat a-fryin' at breakfast, along with all of the other good smellin' stuff in that room.

Paw made some wood frames about three foot square and tacked screen wire over 'em to lay their apples on to dry 'em. He laid them on some tables over clost to the wender where the sunshine would come in and hit 'em good. Ever' day, they'd turn the apples over. When it dried out enough, Mammy put it in flour sacks an'en put some dried sassyfack bark in with the dried fruit to keep the bugs from botherin' it. Then she tied the flour sack tops up in a knot and hung 'em up on nails around the wall, out from where she hung up their leather britches. It smelt so good, and sometimes she'd get down a sack and untie the knot in the top, and give me a little handful of dried apples to eat. You could taste the saasyfack in 'em.

But the best thang any body ever stuck a tooth in, was them dried fruit pies that she fried in butter. She'd fry up a big plate full, and put 'em in the pie safe in the corner of the kitchen. It had punched tin on the doors, that let air in, but kept the flies out. She usually had some tea cakes in there, too.

I hadn't never heard the word "applesauce" back then. Cooked apples was called "*fruit,*" and dried apples was "*dried fruit.*" I was grown before "fruit" meant anything besides apples to me. Other fruits was called by their name, like plums, pears, or oranges, one. I still think cooked apples in my mind when somebody says "fruit." They made apple butter from fruit, with cinnamon, allspice and cloves in it.

Then they made what they called "bleached fruit." They took a clean empty bee gum and set it out in the yard away from the house. Then they put racks of peeled, sliced-up apples in the bee gum, an'en *jacked it up* on one side a little bit, and set a saucer with some burnin' sulfur 'nunder the bottom, so the fumes would go up through amongst the fruit to bleach it. You didn't want to be a-breathin' them fumes, they'd choke you to death. They preserved the fruit, and no insects didn't get in it. It dried so pretty and white, and had a different taste from plain dried fruit, which turned a light brown color. But it didn't taste nothin' like sulfur smells, though.

An'en there was the churn jars full of stuff. Besides pickles and thangs, they was churns and jars full a dist about any kind of homemade wine that was made. And that was jist the way it was. They didn't think a thing atall bad about a-body a-drankin' a glass a wine if they wanted to. Hit was good for the stummick. For us youngens, less than half of a jelly glassful was about right, just don't go and overdo it.

And Paw had built him a place, sorter like a closet with deep shelfs, into one corner of the back room, where he kept his cured meat on the shelfs. The meat was packed with salt to preserve it. He used some bought stuff out of a box, called "Morton's Sugar Cure," and put it on some middlin's to make bacon, and used it on hams. It tasted a right smart better'n plain old fatback, and it sure smelt good a-fryin'. You could smell that in the back room, too. That back room sure had lots a inter-estin' smells.

The front room had a full size bed on one side of it where Mammy slept, and a cot on the other side where Paw slept. His'n was in the opposite corner, with the head turnt around so he could see her. He laid a bee gum on its side under the wender, between his bed and the stove, and used that for a seat. And they was a ladder back chair, Mammy's rockin' chair, and a dresser in there.

Paw made cat holes in the front room and kitchen doors. He cut about a six inch square piece out of the bottom corner of a door, then made leather hinges and tacked on to the piece, then tacked it back in the hole on the door. Since the hinges would bend, the cat could push it open, and come and go as it pleased.

Mammy saved the good parts of old clothes and other remnants an'en tore 'em up into narr' strips, or strings, sewed 'em end-to-end, and rolled 'em up into big ol' balls. Then she knit 'em into strips from five to seven inches wide, and sewed 'em together longways to make a bedspread. That made all colors of stripes, with the colors all mingled together, and that was the purtiest thang. They was warm, too. That's the only kind of bedspread I knowed they was.

She said that when she was a girl, her family raised sheep and sheared 'em for the wool, and told me how they done ever'thing. She learnt how to knit "boggins" (toboggans), mittens and socks when she was a little girl, and learnt me how to knit.

Paw whittled down some hickory wood sticks and scraped 'em real smooth, and made some knittin' needles for her. His father lived with them for a few years, and he had a old umbreller that he give Paw to take the ribs off of to make some knittin' needles out of. I've got a pair of 'em, and a pair of the hickory ones that he made. Mammy give 'em to Mom and she give 'em to me, and I still use 'em. My sisters never did knit.

Mammy was a small boned woman. She had smooth, fair skin, snow white, naturally wavy long hair, and the bluest eyes. She said she had auburn-brown hair when she was young. Before she went to bed ever' night she combed out her hair good, and platted it into one long plat a-hangin' down. She had a fine-tooth comb, regular comb, and big celluloid hairpins that she used when she put her hair up in a bun, or topknot, as she called it. She always looked neat and well groomed. She had a pert little turned-up nose, and I thought she was purtier'n a doll. I've heard some of the older members of the family say that she had a bad temper, and I seen her lose it a few times with Dad, but she was good to me. Mom described her as a "sweet mother."

When I told her about something good I'd done, or when I did something she thought deserved praise, she said, *"Well, give you a button!"* I didn't think about the meaning of her words then, just knowed from the way she said it that I'd done good. Since then, I've come to think "giving a button" was the equivalent of pinning a medal on someone, or giving an award.

She wore long sleeved dresses that come down to her shoe tops, with what she called "aperns" over her dress. Her aperns was more like a pinafore, and about six inches shorter than her dress. She dipped sweet snuff, and carried her little snuff-box and haincher in her apern pocket. She always wore a wide brim straw hat outside if the sun was out.

She had a wide brim black velvet "Sunday" hat, with feathers and a veil on it, that she kept hangin' on the wall. Her "little black satchel," where she kept her money, hung on a nail above her bed. Once in awhile, not real often, she'd tell me she'd give me a *brownie* if I'd do something for her, like take her spit can or chamber out to the branch spout and empty it and wash it out. She had me stand on her bed and reach her little black satchel down to her, and she'd take out her little leather snap-top change purse and get out a brownie and give it to me. A brownie was what she called a penny. When she said something *hain't worth a brownie*, that meant it was *awful sorry* (good-for-nothing).

Once in awhile, when she asked me to "fetch" her some water, she'd give me a brownie. Fetchin' her some water meant taking a quart jar—about as big as I could carry without it a-gittin' too heavy—and walking clost to half a mile up the old wagon road bed apast Kermit's old house to his spring to get it. She'd got so she wouldn't drink no other water. Young as I was, I somehow realized that the water had something to do with the fact that it came from her dead son's spring, and that's why she wanted it. She'd talk about Kermit sometimes, and cry.

When Dad found out about it, he *cussed a blue streak* and told me he'd *skin my hide* if I went up to that spring ary other time and got water for her. Him and Mammy despised one another, but she wouldn't say one thing bad about him to us. I'd slip off and go get it anyways, 'cause I wanted to do what she asked. Then, too, I was more afraid of her a-dyin' from not havin' no water than I was of him, although that was *a right smart*.

One day he caught me with the water just as I got back into her yard. He never went about Mammy's place, and I never expected him to be there. He was standin' by the front porch there, *dist a-turnin' the air blue a-cussin'*, and started pullin' off his belt to whup me because I hadn't minded him. I stood rooted in my tracks, just about scared plumb to death. I just knowed he'd cut the blood out of me this time.

All of a sudden, there was Lewis a-standin' between me and Dad. I remember gettin' behind him and huggin' around one of his legs with one arm, aholt of his britches leg, and lookin' around at Dad. I just knowed Dad would kill him when Lewis told him to leave me alone, that he wasn't going to whup nobody. I thought I must be dreamin'! I didn't think that even God would dare to stand up to Daddy and sass him.

Lewis reached down and took my hands loose from his legs and told me to take the water and go on in the house, and I took off in the house and stayed with Mammy. I don't know what happened after that. I was scared Dad would kill Lewis for sassin' him, and was too afraid to look out there, but in a few minutes, Lewis come on in and said it was all right. Dad never said no more to me, and nobody got nary whuppin', and after that I went and fetched water whenever Mammy wanted some. Lewis told me I could.

Mammy was allus *kindly sickly*. She said her legs didn't work right. From the time I can first remember her, she used a walkin' stick. Then she used a light straight-back chair to push along in front of her to hold onto as she walked. You could hear her a-walkin' through the house—scrape, bump, scrape, bump as she went along. She wore felt bedroom slippers with soft leather soles all a the time, and I thought her little feet looked so pretty in them. She ordered 'em out of a catalog.

Mom said that when she was a little girl Mammy had to go to Knoxville, Tennessee one time, and stayed gone for three months. She had to have some sort a female operation done, and was never strong after that, and couldn't hold her water.

She took "smotherin' spells," and set out on the porch in her rockin' chair to get air, and somebody'd have to set and fan her. Sometimes her spells lasted for hours. Every time she breathed out, she said "uuh," in a high pitched voice. She said she was "sufferin'," but I didn't know what she meant by that. She took Tincture of Lobelia, (Teencher a Lobelie) for her asthma (azmie), and allus kep' a little bottle of it. They bought it at the drugstore and put some in a bottle an'en poured a certain amount of white liquor in to dissolve it.

One of the older youngens, usually Coonie, stayed with them at night, and sometimes come and got Mom when Mammy had a bad smotherin' spell. Dad would get mad and cuss. He said she was dist a-puttin' on, that they wutn't a thang in the world wrong with her, and she was just a-usin' that medicine as a excuse to take her a drank a likker. He'd tell Mom she wutn't a-goin' up there, but Mom went on anyhow, and when she got back, they'd get in a big racket.

Then, about a month before my ninth birthday, on August 15, 1943, some-body come to our house and told Mom that Paw had done something they called "committed suicide." I didn't know what that meant, and when I asked, they said that he had shot hisself in the temple with his pistol, out on the front porch. I still didn't realize what had happened. I didn't know what a temple was, or where it was at, either. But from the way everybody was actin', I knowed something awful had happened to Paw.

Back then, when a dead person was embalmed and put in their casket in their buryin' clothes, they was said to be *"laid out."* Then they took them to their home and put the casket to where people could view the body. That night, they said the dead person *lay corpse*, and people come to *set up* with the casket that night. Folks come and went, neighbors come a-brangin' food, and ever'body allus eat a midnight supper. When somebody come in, it was customary to offer 'em something to eat, and they was took on back to the kitchen and fed.

They didn't use a lot of cosmetics on a corpse then, neither. When they got the casket in place, they took me with them up to Paw's house to let me see him. They'd took out his cot, and put the casket where it was. I was just tall enough to tiptoe and look over the edge to see inside. When I looked in, I was lookin' right at the side of his head where the bullet hole was—where the bullet had went in—and that's when I knowed he was dead. He was the first dead person I ever remember seein'.

I don't remember anything at all about the funeral, where it was, or if I even went to it. I just couldn't believe that he would kill hisself and leave me on pur-pose, or that he didn't want to live, and wondered if I'd done something to make him mad at me, or hurt his feelin's, one. Didn't he know how much I loved him? To this day, when I hear a gunshot, a firecracker, a backfire or something, I flinch and immediately recall that bullet hole in Paw's head.

I wrestled with many a question for years, and still wonder about it. I've heard people say he was murdered, that his billfold was never found. But Mammy said that he come into the kitchen and said, "Brace yourself," to her before he went out through the back room onto the front porch. In just a minute, she heard the pistol fire and went out and found him a-layin there. France Postell happened to be a-passin' by in a log truck over at the road, heard her a-hollerin', and went over to see what was wrong, then went and got Mom.

I've wondered if he was depressed from having lost four out of his five chil-dren. One of their babies was stillborn and was buried over on the mountainside across from Junaluska church. And I know I saw Mammy cry lots of times, when she'd talk about her little girl, Mary Etta (Mary Etter), that died of diphtheria when she was four. After all those years, she still had a flowerpot of dried golden-rod on a table in the middle room, that Mary Etta had picked for her a day or two before she died. Kermit had been their only son, and was their pride and joy, and they never got over their grief after he drownded. Their other daughter, Lizzie, died at age 32, leaving seven young children. Mom was the only one a-livin'.

And, he must a-felt awful bad about Bud a-bein' in prison for gittin' caught a-carryin' that likker. Bud was a-brangin' it to Paw for him to try to make a few dollars off of it, since him and Mammy was dist about down to their last *greenback*. Seemed like they wutn't no other way a-gittin' what they needed to live on and pay their tax and stuff. Most of the time, it was politics that decided who got on Welfare, they said. They'd got turned down, and they wutn't no Social Security back then.

His reason for doing what he done is something I will never know on this earth. And they's people that says they's no forgiveness from God if you commit suicide.

But the God I know is a loving and compassionate God.

And rememberin' Paw a-sangin' that song in Sunday School has helped me a whole lot—for I know he meant it when he sung it, and I really do b'lieve I will meet him in the mornin' over there.

STAYIN' WITH MAMMY

I don't remember the exact sequence of events after Paw died, but I'll relate a few of them. They built a good-size room on the upper side of our house and brung Mammy down there to stay with us. She hatn't been there long, though, til her and Dad *got into it* one night. She got mad and commenced to *raisin' Cain* (or *cane*) to go to her house. It was a way up in the night. Dad was *about half shot*, and was *dist a-cussin', and a-rarin'and snortin', and a-stompin' around* the whole time they was a-gittin' her gone.

They lit the lantern and went to the barn and geared up Old Nell, our part Shetland pony, and hitched her up to the buggy. That was the only way they had of taking Mammy home. Then they set her in a straight-back chair and carried her out, chair and all, and loaded her up in the buggy, and took her home.

I thought Coonie was so lucky to get to stay with Mammy at night and git away from home. I wisht I could go and stay 'stid a her. Then after she run off and got married, I did git to. By the time I started stayin' with her, she'd *done'n got* plumb a-past walkin'. The last time she walked was the New Years' day after Paw died.

She coutn't control her water, and we had to keep what she called "piss pads" inunder her. They was old doubled-up sheets, or some quilted pads Mom had sewed together and made. We hung 'em up to dry out when they got wet, and used 'em til they got to stinkin' too bad, an'en Mom washed 'em out.

She coutn't go to the toilet, so they took the seat off of a straight chair, cut out a round hole in a wide board to make a toilet seat an'en nailed it on the chair. Then they sawed out a rung on one side of the chair and fixed a shelft, so we could stick her chaimber under there for her to use, an'en git it out to go empty it. The potty chair allus set right ag'in the side of her bed. I had to help her get up, an'en partly lifted, and partly let her pull on me to get her over on the chair when she needed to use her chaimber. I put the led on it when she got done, and looked to see if she needed a dry pad on her bed. I had to take her chaimber out to the brainch to empty it out and wash it ever' mornin'.

I helped her get ready to go to bed, even if she did stay in it most of the time. She kep' a straight chair in the bed 'nunder her pillers, so she was about half way

235

a-settin' up all of the time. The front of the chair was turned down torge the mattress, with the chair legs a-stickin' up in the air at the head of the bed and the back of the chair a-pointin' down torge the foot. Then her pillers was laid on the back of the chair for her to lean back ag'in. Ever' piller had a certain place to be put, and I had to put 'em jist right to git her fixed so she could sleep good.

She had to have some water, her spit can, and a orange colored box of Luden's™ cough drops a-settin' by the bed on her little table. Sometimes she give me a cough drop. She tried some other kinds a few times, but ditn' like 'em. One kind was Smith Brothers™, that was black and tasted sorter like *liquish,* and Vicks cough drops™, but they was pretty strong.

Sometimes she took her finger and got a little dab a pneumonie salve (Vicks Vaporub™) out of the jar and put it in her mouth or up in her nose, one, to o'm up her nose.

Her dresser set over a little piece from her little table, and she had some bottles a medicine a-settin' on that side of the dresser. One was Tincture of Lobelia, that she took ever' day for her asthmie. I fixed it and give it to her if she needed a doast at night. Another thing she took ever' night was Black Draught (drawft)™, that kept her bowels thin. The other'n was antiacid powders that had to be stirred up in water and drunk before they settled. She allus kept a bottle of Camphor. It come in little solid squares that was dissolved in alkyhol. She rubbed that on her fard when she had a headache, or on her wristes if she felt faintified.

The lamp set on the dresser, and Mammy wanted it kep' a-burnin' all night, but was turnt down (the wick) so it dist barely was lit. I kep' a piece a pasteboard scotched up between her medicine bottles on the dresser and the lamp so it wouldn't shine in her eyes.

I slep' on Paw's cot. Lots of times, before I *turned the lamp down,* I laid there with my head propped up on the foot of the cot to be closter to the lamp, and read to her. She liked for me to read books and stories to her. I brung liberry books home to read out loud to her while I read 'em myself. She liked to hear the Bible, too, and had me to read her favorite passage in the fourth chapter of II Timothy, where it says, "I have fought a good fight, I have finished my course, I have kept the faith." She knowed lots a verses by heart. When I spelt a word out to her that I didn't know, she told me how to pernounce it and explained what it meant.

She ditn't care if I read to myself, neither. I laid there a many a night and read til ten o'clock (way up in the night!). It was so quiet with no sound nowhere but that ol' mantel clock dist a-tickin' away. It sounded so loud when it struck that I'd jump.

Some nights, we jist talked, and she told me about when she was a young girl. She told about where they lived over at Aquone before the lake covered it over in water, about them a-havin' to move, and move the graveyard before the water covered it over, and about her kinfolks that had lived there. It made me sad that her old home place was under water, and she never could go see it no more.

She told about ghostes and haints, too, and could tell some hair-raisin' tales. And *painter* (panther) *tales*! Lord, I'd get *goose knobs* all over me a-listenin' to her tell some of 'em. She said when a painter hollered, hit sounded dist like a woman a-screamin'. They was one tale she told about a painter a-follerin' her, that had dang near got her.

She'd been to somebody's house one time, and was late a-gittin' started on home, and hit was a-gittin' down clost to dark when she headed out. They never had flashlights to carry around with 'em, like we do now. All they had was a lantern, and it jist barely give enough light to walk by—and she never eb'm had no lantern. The trail went through a field, an'en she had to go through some woods around the side a the mountain. Her mammy and daddy lived in a holler a good ways over on the other side. She'd done and gone acrost the field, and when she got in the woods, hit was purty dark, but she knowed the way, and went ahead on in the trail around the mountain.

Then she got to noticin' that ever' time she took a step, she could hear dry leafs a-crunchin' down real soft, where sump'm else was takin' a step—right out from her. When she stopped, hit stopped. When she took a step, hit took a step. She'd figgered it must be a painter, and was scared to death it was a-goin' to jump out any minute and tear her all to pieces. Them thangs was mean—big ol' thangs, with great big paws. They could rip a sheep apart in no time.

She tried to think what to do, but they wutn't nothin' fer it but to dist keep a-goin' and pray she could make it through them woods into the clearin'. They was a big old tree ahead that lent over the trail, right above her head, and she had to go inunder it. She jist knowed that if it ditn't get her before then, that's where that painter would jump up and stretch out on that tree, and be a-waitin' to jump down on top of her as she went 'nunder it.

Jist as she got clost to the tree, she heard a sheep bleat, off down b'low the trail. She heard that painter give one big leap an'en hit the ground twicet before it went out a hearin' down torge where she'd heard the sheep. And she *lit a shuck* fer home. She said she knowed that sheep saved her life.

Staying with her was *a way yon* differ'nt from the way it was at home. I never did git to stay up til no ten o'clock there. They considered that a way up in the night. We had to be in the bed by eight o'clock ever' night, regardless—and sometimes before the sun went down good. Nobody'd better not make no racket a no kind when we got there, neither, not eb'm a whisper.

And they shore wudn't no bedtime readin'.

I never would a-gone home if they hatn't a-made me. A few months after Paw died, Lewis and Sis moved in the house with Mammy and lived there. Lewis had bought the place, but she had a life estate on it. I still got to stay at night and sleep in the room with her. She needed somebody with her at night. Man alive, I felt like I had it made, a-stayin' with Mammy, and Lewis and Sis too. I've allus felt they was more like my mother and daddy than a brother and sister-in-law. That was the happiest time in my life when I was a-growin' up.

My knees used to hurt a lot when I was dist a youngen, and people said it was "growin' pains." At home, they said they wutn't nary thang wrong with me, I was dist a-puttin' on a-tryin' to get petted. If I could dist git to go up to Lewis', though, Sis'd give me a aspern and have me to lay down on her bed (in the day-time!) and wrap up a jar of hot water for me to put ag'in the knee that hurt. I remember one time both of my knees swelled so big that I couldn't bend 'em far enough to do more'n jist barely walk. Back McClain set me on the bank b'low the house and had me to climb on his back and carried me piggyback up to Sis' house, and she took care of me. Mom dist went on about her business and never paid no attention to it.

Sis was so good to me 'n Mammy, and was so purty. Her name is Virginia, but she was the only girl out of a bunch of boys, and they called her Sis. She had beautiful long raven-black hair and the darkest blue eyes, and is the most gentle, lovin'est person I ever seen. I shore do love that lady. She knows a whole lot about herb doctorin' and home remedies, and "mothers" ever'body and ever'thang that comes along a-needin' it, includin' animals. One time their old rooster got his comb frost bit, and she brung him in the house and kep' him in a box behind the kitchen stove and doctored it til it got better. He was only one in a long line of lucky critters, people and younguns she doctored and give love to, that needed it. And I don't care if they was mean as a striped snake, she'd allus find sump'm good about 'em.

When she fixed breakfast, she fixed my egg jist like I liked it. She made me my own spacial biscuit over by itself at the end a the breadpan to where it would git real crusty brown all over, and gimme coffee ever' mornin' in my own cup. And allus saved me the fryin' pan with all a them little browned bits in it, to let me sop it out with one a her good ol' biscuits. Til yit, when I go to Sis'es house, I haf to have me a "Sis biscuit"—and my husband and younguns did, too.

There was a window at the head of the cot where I slept, and it was left raised up in the summer. I remember one night I woke up cold, and was going to pull the kivver up on me, but they wudn't no kivver there. I looked inunder the bed and everywhere for it, but coutn' find it nowhere. Hit *scared the everlastin' far (fire) out of me.* I thought a booger had *retch'd* in through the wender and snatched at me, and dist got my kivvers. I couldn't think of nowhere else it might a-went.

Sis heard me movin' around in there, and hollered and asted me if anything was wrong. I told her I couldn't find my kivver. She said she'd heard me come into their room and go back out a little while ago. I didn't know nothin' about that, but went on in there anyhow to look—and shore 'nuff, there on the foot of the other bed was my kivver all in a pile. She said I'd been a-sleepwalkin'. I never knowed I done that!

I never had nobody to be any better to me as her and Lewis was. He'd allus been my hero. He had the biggest ol' muscles in his arms, and I thought they looked like Popeye the sailor man, in the funny papers.

He was 'leb'm (eleven) year old when I was born. They said that when I was a baby and cried, Lewis would git me and lay me up on his chest and I'd go right off to sleep. I slep' with him when I was little, and shore did miss him when he left home for the CC camps. I was dist seb'm (seven) year old when he got married.

He went to Valleytown Church. When I was jist a little gal, I remember the older youngens a-gittin' to walk down there and back, but they said I was too little to walk that far. It was over five mile down there. When Lewis got a car, he took me with him a few times. He even bought me a new dress to wear to Sunday School. Now, *I thought that was sump'm.*

Jobs was still skerce in this part of the country, so Lewis got a job in Tennessee and they moved off over there. Mom put Mammy in the county home at Murphy. She hadn't been there much long when Mom *harred* (hired) a man to take her down there to see about her.

I bagged so hard, she let me go with her. And *if I live to be a hunderd,* I won't never fergit what I seen that day.

It was a big ol' white, two story Colonial style house with lots of rooms. It had banisters all around the front porch where you went in, and was a pretty place. They didn't know we was comin'. We went in the front door, and didn't see nobody nowhere, and started to set down and wait, but then we jist barely could hear Mammy somewhere in there a-hollerin', "Help me! Somebody help me!"

Mom took off back through there with me right behind her, and when we found her in this room a way back in the back of the house, there laid my Mammy—*naked as a jay bird*, with not nary a thing on on her bed but the mattress and a dirty, wet, wadded-up sheet off over on the corner of it.

We could smell when we went through the door that she'd messed on herself. It was smyeared all over her hands and arms and hair, and had been on her so long, it was plumb dried. Hit was even caked up 'nunder her fingernails. And the mattress was soakin' wet.

They'd took the scissors and dist hacked about all of her purty white hair off. It was all *haggedy-lookin'*, and dist a-stickin' up ever whichaway.

It was cold in there, and Mammy was about froze. The only heat in there was a little ol' fireplace about eighteen inches wide. It had five or six corncobs in it, about half burnt, but they'd gone out, and you could tell by it not a-havin' no ashes in there, that they hatn't been no fire in it lately. Even in her condition, though, she was a-raisin' cain, and started tellin' us what all they'd done to her, and said they hatn't give her nothin' much to eat, neither.

That was one time I was glad to see Mom take a fit. She went back in there and found some woman and made 'em bring her a pan of hot water, a cake a soap, a washrag and towel. We cleaned Mammy up the best we could, and Mom made 'em bring Mammy's clothes. We put 'em on her, gethered up her stuff and took her with us.

We took her to her sister Zora White's house at Peachtree, and she lived there about a year before she died. They had her funeral in the little wooden chapel at Valleytown cemetery, and read her favorite scripture from II Timothy. She was buried in a lavender dress. I still think of her when I see a lavender dress.

Aunt Zora and Uncle Will was good people. I got to go see Mammy once while she was there, and she seemed to be satisfied, and said they was good to her. It was good to see her white hair a-growin' back out and lookin' purty again.

I've heard other people tell horror stories of how old people were treated in those county homes. That's where they put old people who were penniless and had no family that could or would take care of them. Most of the time, they knew that nobody cared enough to be checking on them, so they got away with the abuse.

That stigma still lingers, and many old folks today think that's how it is in a nursing home. They think it's like an old timey "pore house," or county home They'll do just about anything to make it at home rather than have to go to one.

Whenever I go into a sparkling clean modern facility and see clean, well groomed patients, the beautiful color coordinated decor, and notice the lack of offensive odor, I thank God that it's a lot different now.

GOIN' TO MEETIN' AND LEARNIN' MUSIC

After Mammy made 'em take her back to her house that time, the back room she'd stayed in at our house was empty. Bud stayed in it when he was there, and we called it Bud's room, but he'd gone off to work summerce—down in Arkansas, I think it was, after he got out of prison. Sweetie, Lewis and Alma was married, and our family was gettin' less and less.

Since Paw Taylor died, Sunday School wutn't held in the apple house no more. I don't know whose idy it was, but they made some bainches for people to set on, and put 'em in our back room, and started usin' it to hold *meetin'* and Sunday School in. Then, they started havin' Wensdy night prayer meetin' in first one, and then another'ns house ever week. Differ'nt people took turns conductin' prayer meetin'. Didn't make no differ'nce who they was if they was willin' to do it. When somebody led prayer meetin', that meant that they was responsible for pickin' out Bible verses they'd study that night, and explain what they meant. If they ditn't want to do the prayin' out loud their own self, they could ast somebody else to lead 'em in a word a prayer.

I remember how flabbergaisted I was when I found out that Dad and Mom and Cullie and Jess *sung by notes* out of a songbook. When Dad asted Cullie to sang alto on a song with a leadin' alto part, she dist belted it out like nobody's business, and I dist dang nigh fell off a the bainch. W'y, I never drampt she could do that!

I thought he'd said "o-w-l, owl toe," and puzzled about that til I finally learnt better. And I found out, too, that they's a sopranner, or "lead" part, and a tenor and a bass part to a song. They'd learnt how to sang "shape notes." at sangin' school in the old school/church-house, back when they was young. The name of the songbook they'd sung out of was "Temple Bells."

But I dist thought I'd heard it all. When they cut loost to sangin' a song with the name of the notes 'stid a words, my mouth flew op'm like a big bear trap—dist a-suckin' up gnats. Well, if I had t'die! I hatn' never hyeard the beat a that!

242

Dad sung bass or *ary other* part he wanted to, Jess sung bass or lead, Mom and Cullie sung alto, and Grace sung lead or high tenor. Len Morgan got to comin' then, and they got her to sang sopranner…She had the highest, keenest voice I ever heard come out of anybody's mouth! Lord, I coutn't even a-screamed that high-pitched. Now, she could flat-out sang that sopranner part!

One song they was allus a-sangin' was called "The Promised Land." Hit started off: "On Jerdun's starmy bank I stand, and cast a weashful eye—to Cain-un's fair and happy land where my por-sessions lie." Us youngens dist sung what-ever part come out of our mouth, a-tryin' to listen and learn the words and the tyune, all at the same time.

Sometimes somebody helt up the lamp so they could see the pages of a song book better. They ditn't have but two or three books, so Dad had Mom to order six song books from R. E. Winsett Company, and they used them, then.

All a my life I'd hyeard Mommy around the house, a-sangin' old sad, *tear-jerker* ballids, like Barbry Allen. In one of 'em, I don't know the name of it—but Willie asted this ol' gal to marry him and she flat out turnt him down, so he left, all long-faced. Next mornin', pore ol' Willie was dead—"drowned in a pool by the mill; and close to his pale lips he held a white rose he took from her hair." Then the gal goes to carryin' on, a-slingin' snot and cryin', "Oh, Willie, my dar-lin', come back, for I love you far more than my life," after she'd done'n turned 'im down the very night before—but he'd done'n went off and drownded hisself.

I cried then, never could sing it for cryin', and would still cry now, if I was to hear anybody sang "Mary Of The Wild Moor." It had the saddest, mournf'lest sound to it of any song I ever hyeard. It starts off: "Twas on a cold wintry night, and the wind blew across the wild moor, when poor Mary came wandering home with her child, till she came to her own father's door. Oh, Father, dear Father, she cried, come down and open the door, lest the child in my arms should perish and die from the winds that blow across the wild moor."

It goes on and and tells how the father was deaf to her cries; not a sound of her voice did he hear, "Though the watch dog did howl, and the village bell tolled, and the winds blew across the wild moor."

The next mornin' he found 'em huddled up agin' his doorway, with the pore little thang wrapped clost in hits dead mother's arms. Then it tells how the old man with grief pined away, and the child to its mother went soon. And no one, they say, has lived there to this day and the cottage to ruin has gone. But the vil-lagers point out the spot, where the willows droop over the door; And they tell how that night Mary suffered and died, From the winds that blow across the wild moor." It makes the cold chills run over me to hear it.

Stuff like that. Somebody allus got hung, shot, stobbed, drownded, run over in a stampede, went down in a ship, was mashed up in a train wreck, died too soon, got kilt or kilt somebody else, loved somebody that didn't love 'em back, either died with a broke heart or went through life a-grievin' with one, kilt theirself, or sump'm else bad.

Back then, too, dist as shore as some big tragedy hapm'd, or sump'm like you'd see in a newspaper headline now, somebody wrote a song about it, and by the next week, they'd have it on the radio a-sangin' about it. I remember they was sev'al about the Titanic and how that great ship went down. And one about a little girl that fell in a well and died; the Wreck On The Highway, and about some bad train wrecks—like The Wreck of Old Ninety-seven, and John Hardy. They was a-carryin' on the tradition of tellin' stories in song, dist like people done with them old ballids, a hunderd year ago—or more. And they was dozens about cowboys and tumbleweeds, and western kind a stuff, that told about 'em a-ridin' their hosses on the range and herdin' cattle, and all.

Now, I love to hear a ballid (ever' year or two), and appreciate their history, but when them ol' sad'uns is all you ever hear all day long, day after mournful day, hit gets awful depressin'. I dist coutn't understand why Mom wanted to sang them old sad mournful thangs all the time, when they was so many happy'uns she knowed that was a whole lot purtier. I *pyorely* love them old toe-tappin', foot stompin' songs like Ol' Joe Clark, Cindy, Comin' Round the Mountain, Sairwood Mountain, Sally Goodin', and a whole bunch a others that make you feel so good you dist want to dance and sang. Some a them cowboy songs was gooduns, too. Dist so they ditn't drag on all day, a-mournin' and a-whinin' around.

The kind a sangin' they done when they had meetin' was a whole lot differ'nt. I wanted to learn to sang ever last one a them songs about God and His love, Heb'm (Heaven), and joy, and faith, and meetin' your friends and loved-uns over yander in Glory-land, and all a them happy soundin' songs that moved right along and ditn't *waller around* all day.

They was a old junk car that set out behind the barn. I remember me a-takin' a song book out there, and climbin' up on top a that old car, and settin' up there a-readin' the words and makin' up tunes to go with 'em. I learnt a lot of 'em by heart.

I'm shore glad I learnt them songs. They's been lots of times when things wutn't a-goin' too good fer me, that I'd jist let one of them songs run through my mind to git it off a my troubles. They helped me remember that God loves me, no matter what. Purty soon, I'd feel better.

Dad pointed out and showed me the differ'nce in the shape of the notes, told me it's name, and sung the scale to show me how it was s'posed to sound. I thought it beyond belief that you could tell how a song went by follerin' them little black thangs on lines a music.

Oncet I learnt to sang the scale and base a song on the first note, "do," I knowed that "re" was dist a little dab higher, then "mi" a little more, and so on, and got so I could hum around til I learnt enough by seein' the way the notes went up and down on the lines and lookin' at the shape a the notes, till I could look at pyert near any song and get the gist of how hit'd be sung.

Jess picked a banjer. He used to bring it around there from his house, and set on the bank in the shade over at the edge of the pines acrost the road. He picked what he called "clawhammer banjer pickin'." He usually had a pint likker bottle leaned up agin' his side. Ever' so of'en, he'd screw off the cap, turn the bottle way up, and take a snort. Then he'd say a big whispered "Ahhh!," smack his mouth real big, give it a swipe with the back of his hand, an'en screw the led down, lean his bottle back up agin' his side, pick up that banjer and frail th' dickens out of it. If a strang broke, he dis' kep' on a-pickin' and pattin' 'is feet and sangin'.

Even when I was a little bitty thang, I loved to be around Jess. He was fun. I remember a-crawlin' acrost the footlog and goin' over there to set on the pine needles with him and watch him pick his banjer. He'd pick that banjer, pat both of his feet, laugh and sang all kind a funny songs. One of 'em was "You git a line, I'll git a pole, honey, we'll go down to the crawdad hole, honey, baby, mine." His favo-rite song (I don't know the title) said,"Troubled in mind, I'm blue; But I won't be blue always, for the sun's gonna shine in my back door some day."

We had us a ball, til somebody missed me a-bein gone out of the yard and started hollerin' fer me. I got my butt busted for slippin' off a many a time. But ever time I hyeard Jess a-pickin, I went to 'im—jist like the Pied Piper. He must a found out about 'em a-whuppin' me, fer he got to where he brung his banjer over on our side a the creek, and he'd set out there on the chop block by the woodshed and pick and sang. I liked it when he tuned it down into E, and picked one where he made one strang give a funny whaing when he turnt the tightenin' key up and down.

I absolutely loved anything that made music, even beatin' time on a lard bucket with a stick. I'd heard Ike Winfrey play the fiddle at Mom and Dad's dainces, and wisht I had one. Mom had allus wanted to play some kind of musical instrument, and said lots a times that she'd give anythang in this world to make music on sump'm. But she never could play a note on nuthin'. She 'spash'ly wanted to play a fiddle. She got one, one time, and kep' it a-hangin' up on the wall. I wanted to play that fiddle so bad I could taste it. I just knowed I could. She woutn't eb'm let me tetch it, let alone hold it in my hands. Nobody in my family ever learnt to play that fiddle. Hit dist hung there.

First one and then another'n had a gittar, and I was keen on learnin' to pick a gittar. The very first thang a body tried t'learn to pick was "Wildwood *Flare* (Flower)." Mother Maebelle Carter was said to be the best at pickin' that'n. When you got to where you could pick that, hit was accepted that you could pick a gittar. One of the older youngens'd managed to get aholt of a gittar sumerce, and had a little instruction book that showed the chords. I reckin all the older'uns except Coonie learnt to pick the gittar some, but they wouldn't eb'm let me handle it. I reckin they thought I was too young t'learn, or woutn't take keer of it.

Lewis had the purtiest gittar I ever seen. It had F holes, 'stid a one round'un. I don't know how it hapm'ed, but it got cracked real bad. He was going to finish bustin' it up and throw it away, but I bagged 'im so hard that he give it to me. I felt like somebody'd handed me the key to the Kingdom a Heb'm. And it was mine!

My cousin, Buddy Mathis—Sister's older brother, showed me how to use the chord chart that showed where to put your faingers to make chords. I took that old cracked gittar and the little illustrated instruction book, and set out on that old car behind the barn, and anywheres else that nobody'd bother me, and practiced for hours on end. When I coutn't *actiously* be a-pickin' with my faingers, I was a-pickin' in my head. I made blisters on the end of my faingers that burnt like fire, but I gritted my teeth and kep' on a-pickin'. They peeled off, an'en they got callused—but I learnt to pick that thang. I eb'm learnt t'pick "Wildwood Flare." And I's allus a-grinnin' when I's a-pickin'.

I hummed along as I picked, then got that old songbook out and learnt to pick and sang at the same time. I don't sang like no bird, but I can sorter carry a tune in a bucket.

Somebody'd left a country and western music magazine there, and it had words to sev'al differ'nt country and western songs in it. I learnt Red River Valley, When The Work's All Done This Fall, Come a Ti-yi-yippee Yippee Yea, In The Pines, Down In The Valley, and all them old'uns. I picked and sung dist about ever country, western and folk song I heard. They had some old Carter Family, Roy Acuff and other records, and I learnt all a them, too.

Dad liked to play the radio at night when people come in to listen to th' Grand Ole Opry and radio station WCKY in Cincinnati, Ohio, or the one in Del

Rio, Texas. Later on, Hank Williams was my favorite country sanger, and the Chuck Wagon Gang was allus my favorite gospel sangers. I liked the Delmore Brothers and the Louvin Brothers, too. I never could stand Kitty Wells, though; she was too whiney fer my likin', eb'm if she did make a hit song out of Honky-tonk Angel.

Through the years, I learnt to play twelve different musical instruments—not expertly, but enough to enjoy them myself and play along with other people. And I could play Wildwood Flare on every one of 'em. I've always been thankful for that talent, and the joy it gives me. There's just something about makin' music that I can't resist, and I feel music plumb down to the very bottom of my soul. My gittar is still my favorite instrument. And I betchey I could still pick Wildwood Flare if I wanted to.

LIVIN' IN THE APPLE HOUSE

I'll tell this story as Mom and my family has told it to me, and some of the events as I recall them. I never knew any of the reasons behind it.

In the fall of 1943, Daddy went to work for the Champion Paper and Fibre Company. Their main office was in Canton, but they had jobs in progress all over western North Carolina. Dad could do whatever come handy, and they sent him wherever they needed him at the time. He done differ'nt things at differ'nt jobs. He scaled wood, run a jackhammer and drilled holes for dynamite, was a "powder man," run a dozer, or whatever—it never made no differ'nce to him. He was a good cook, and even cooked at some of their work camps. It was a good payin' job and he liked it. He stayed with them til he died. Best of all, he quit drinking so much. He was away from home through the week, as he left early a-Monday morning, or sometimes a-Sunday evening, and come home on Friday after work.

In the fall of 1944, Dad was working at Highlands. I was around ten year old. One day, *out of the clear blue*, Pa and Ma Hicks come up to our house, and Pa jist up and told Mom that he wanted us off of his property. He'd never had made out a deed for the place like he'd said he would, accordin' to his agreement with Paw Taylor. I don't know what his reasonin' was, but he give us a certain amount of time to be out of the house. It made Mom so mad she packed up our stuff right then and we moved into Paw Taylor's apple house, leaving what little furniture they was in the house. Dad didn't even know we'd moved.

Next evenin' late, us youngens went down there to ketch our chickens. We had to wait til along about dusky dark to ketch 'em when they come to roost, an'en take 'em up to the new place. So we'd gone on down there with our tow sacks, and some of us was over in the yard in front of the barn a-waitin'. Thelma was a-standin' over at Cullie's mailbox, a-talkin' to Cullie and some of 'em. Then, here come Pa and Ma a-walkin' up the road with their walkin' stick.

I seen 'em come up to Cullie's mailbox and stop, but don't know none of the other de-tails first hand, for I was over in the barn yard across the creek. Thelma told later, that when they come up to where she was, over at the road, Pa said he thought he told us to get off his property, and asked what business we had, and what we'us a-doin' there. They got into a fuss, and Ma Hicks was aimin' to give Thelma a whuppin' for sassin' 'em, and started torge her. She shoved Ma Hicks away from her, and Ma lost her balance and fell backerds down in the ditch.

I could hear 'em a-talkin' purty loud, and they sounded awful mad to me. When I seen Ma fall down, I got scared, and took off, a-takin' it two rows at a time up the trail torge Lewis' house. (My first reaction, as always—when in trouble, head for Lewis.)

He told me to stay at his house with Sis, and took off a-runnin' down the road to where they was. Later on, I heard that Pa Hicks had got his knife out, and while Lewis was tryin' to take it away from him, Lewis got cut on the top of his head. But he got Pa's knife away from him, and kep' it. I guess they've still got it.

I don't remember if we ever did get our chickens or not, but none of us wutn't allowed to go back down there, or go to Pa and Ma's house for years. I wutn't never around 'em much. I dist knowed 'em when I seen 'em, and knowed who they was.

When Dad come home that weekend, he found us moved out. He come on up the road a-huntin' fer us and found out where we was. They went to town and got a bed and dresser *on th' credit*. Back then, *a man's word was his bond*, and ever'body knowed that Dad *was as good as his word*. Lewis put in some windows, got some lumber and built a bedroom, kitchen and porch onto the side of the apple house. Mom put up wallpaper that had big ol' green ferrins printed on it. She put it up with wallpaper tacks drove through the middle of some thin round metal disks about the size of a quarter. Wallpaper then was sorter like the paper that brown paper pokes are made out of now, only it was light gray or tan with prints on it.

The apple house was a whole lot nicer house than the one we'd left, and Mom liked livin' there. She acted the happiest there I ever seen her.

One day somebody said they'd seed a load a *house plunder* turn into the road to our old house. Pa Hicks had rented the place to Len and Arthur Morgan, and they'd moved in. They'd been a-livin' at the old Jake Abernathy place down the road a ways. They was good people, and friends with our family. They lived there sev'al year.

After we'd been there awhile, Dad took Mom with him over on Fires' Creek to the loggin' camp to cook for the men. They took Vernon with 'em, and they'd be gone from Sunday to Friday evenin' after ever'body left out of the camp and went home. Us youngens stayed there by ourself, but Sis and Lewis lived right on the other side of the branch in the same yard, and Thelma was about grown then.

We had a radio Bud had got from Paw Taylor, and we made up for lost time, a-listenin' t'that radio. Around noon we listened to the Cas Walker show on a Knoxville station where they played all a them country songs by sangers that was pop'lar back then. And we laughed at ol' Hot Shot Elmer and Molly O'Day, and sometimes Minnie Pearl, and a bunch of them funny'uns that was on the Midday Merry-Go-Round. Ever night, we listened to one of them radio shows, like the Lone Ranger, Beulah Show, Amos 'n Andy, Henry Aldrich and some other'ns—I fergit now, what all.

The Creaking Door was a scary mystery story that come on, I fergit how many nights a week, but you talk about a bunch a youngens a-gittin' quiet, now we did. We set dist as clost up to the radio as we could get, so we'd hear ever word, and all a them eerie background rackets. When the show come on, hit sounded like old rusty door hainges a-scrapin', as the door s-c-r-e-a-k-e-d op'm real slow. That man that told what all was a-goin' on talked real deep and made th' goose bumps stand up on me to listen to him. If sump'm had a-made a racket all of a sudden, or a-hollered "boo," we'd a skint our head a-divin' inunder th' bed.

We dreaded to see Mom and Dad come home, for we'us a-havin' a high ol' time, but *that put the quietus on* our stayin' up a-listenin' to the radio. Mom stayed home a week or two ever now and then, and made a little extry money a-makin' blackberry jelly and sellin' it to th' camp. She said them men shore did like her blackberry jelly with their biscuit for breakfast, and they *bragged on it* and said her'n was the best they ever eat. Now, that pleased her. We got out and picked ever' berry we could find for her to make jelly out of. And, along with the berries, got us a load a chiggers to scratch.

We'd lived there a year or so when Bud come home. He'd been a-workin' and stayin' with Alma and Had in Arkansas, where they lived then. Dad was makin' good wages, and had commenced to buildin' a new house on the land Paw Taylor had give us. Lewis helped him get the foundation laid and git it started. When Bud come home, he started workin' on it. Dad helped him on the week ends, and it was a-comin' along purty good.

In the meantime, Len and Arthur Morgan kep' a-lettin' folks use the back room at our old house for a meetin' place, and they'as a-gittin' to be a good-size crowd. Lizzie Mae and John Ledford, my uncle Elden and Aunt Bea and their youngens, Dugan and Bunt Shields and Christine and Harold, their girl and boy, Sweetie and Ruth, Cullie and Jess and their youngens, the Mostellers, McClures, Morgans, our fam'ly, and some other'ns was a-comin' to Sunday School and meetin', and started talkin' about raisin' money to build a church. Dood and Bunt said they'd donate the land to build it on. They talked about differ'nt kind a ways to make money for the new church, and ever'body started astin' ever'body they knowed for donations.

One a the fund-raisers was to make a quilt top t' raffle off. I think Lizzie Mae bought the white cloth and cut out sixteen squares, and differ'nt women took one to work on. Their name was to be embroaderied in the top left corner of the square, to show whose work it was. Thelma, Mom, Sis and me all took one of the squares. Ever'body that give a dime would git their name embroaderied on the square. When they was finished, they'd sew all the squares together to make a quilt top. Then all the names'd be put in a hat and a name drawed out to see who'd git the top.

We'd all got our squares done and they was all sewed together. The names was embroidered in all different colors, and it was inter-estin' to see all the differ'nt handwritin' on it, where the women had wrote the names. This pa'tic'lar Easter Sunday, April 21,1946 was goin' to be the day to draw the name for the top. I wanted to go to Sunday School to the name drawin' so bad I could taste it. I'd watched Cullie, Sis and Mom, and learnt how to embroider. I'd worked hard on my square, and wanted to see who got to keep the quilt top.

Dad was still drinkin' some, and liked to go over to the lake on a-Sunday. He drove a comp'ny truck home on the weekends, and sometimes on a Saturday night we'd load up and go over to Chogie and *lay out* (camp). One time we was a-layin' out over there next to Chogie Creek, and the gnats got to bitin' us awful bad. We'd rubbed gnat oil all over us, but we might as well a-rung the dinner bell and hollered, "Dinner's ready," to them gnats for all the good it done us. They eb'm got up 'nunder our clothes inunder the kivver. You could hear first one, then another'n of us, a-scratchin', kickin', a-slappin' and thrashin' around, a-snortin' and blowing 'em out of our nose, and sayin' "Phew!"

All of a sudden, Dad give a big sling and thowed his covers back and hollered out, "Let's go to the house," dist as loud as he could holler! That sounded like the best idy I'd ever hyeard in my whole life. *I'd about enjoyed all a that I could stand,* too. We tore out a them beds, jis' a-swappin' ends, thowed our stuff on the truck bed any old whichaway, clim up on top of it all and lit out fer home about three o'clock in the mornin'. We shore was glad to git t' th' house.

Now, back to the church business.

Dad wanted to go to the lake that Sunday. I told him they was going to draw the name that day of whoever would win the quilt top. When I asked him if I could stay home and go to Sunday School, he went to cussin' and said no, I wutn't a-goin' to do it, I was goin' to the lake with them. He still cussed every sentence he spoke. I coutn't help but cry a little, but I was afraid of makin' 'im mad if he seen me, so I dist turned my head off, and never said nothin'.

When we got back, the quilt top was at our house and somebody told me they'd drawed my name. I coutn't b'lieve it! I happened to look at Dad, and still remember that look on his face. He looked surprised, too—and *sheepish*—and for dist a minute, for the first time in my life, I think I seen him look a little ashamed of hisself. I begin to understand, then, how the Lord could work and bring about changes I didn't dream was possible. Ever day, I prayed harder'n ever that Dad would make a change and quit drankin' and cussin', and bein' so mean.

The total amount of money we made was $58.80. It don't sound like much money now, but back then, it was a whole lot. Ever'body was tickled about it That'd buy a whole lot a lumber and nails. The least amount of money made on a square was $1.15. There was two with $9.00, and the rest was in between. I made $3.00, which was pretty good for an eleven year old with no way to go nowhere to solicit donations. Folks up on the creek woulda give more, but they dist ditn't have much.

I've kept that quilt top all these years. Ruth and Sweetie kept it for me while I was away at school, and for several years after that. Mom quilted it a few years ago. I thought that might stabilize it. About three years ago, I gave it to Lewis' youngest son—my nephew Melvin, and his wife Ramona. They and their children live on a part of the old Paw Taylor property, and are members of Junaluska Church. I knew they'd appreciate its history. I leave it to their good judgment as to whom they will pass it on.

They's one dandy story I've heard told about the fund-raisin' for the church. I enjoy it so much, I just have to pass it on.

It's about Dugan (Fred) Shields, who donated the land for the church and later became a dedicated preacher and pastor, and Lawerence. At the time, neither one was a church member.

Dugan was a nickname that most a the time was shortened to "Dood." Well, he was down at the buildin' site a-clerin' trees and burnin' brash one day, and Lawerence was a-helpin' him. Back then, when somebody was out in plain sight, hit was the same as a open invite to people a-passin' by to *stop and howdy* a while. Most menfolks did.

They'd hatched 'em up a scheme to raise some money, and figgered what all they was goin' to do, and how they's a-goin' to work it, and Dood give Lawerence two greenbacks to keep in his pocket, so he could go along with it.

Shore 'nuff, hit wutn't long til somebody stopped over at the road, and this man come over to where they was, and wanted to know what was a-goin' on that they was clerin' off land there. Dood come out with the sad story that they was tryin' to get up enough money to build a little church house up here on the creek, but the funds was a-tricklin' in awful slow. He laid it on thick and said we shore needed a church house bad, so's them pore little ol' youngens up here that never had been to church, and prob'ly woutn't never have no other chanch to, could go to Sunday School and learn some Bible.

When Dood had laid it on thick enough, Lawerence commenced to diggin' around in his pocket and come a-haulin' out them two wrinkled-up dollar bills. He said he'd been a-workin' and savin' up his money for a long time to buy some shoes before it snowed, and it was all he had, but he wanted to give it to Dugan to go on the church house.

Dood made a big show out of it, a-gazin' sideways over torge the top a th' mountain, like he was a-tryin' not to pucker up and cry, blinkin' his eyes, pullin' out his haincher, shakin' it out and doublin' it back up, and blowin' his nose, and actin' like hit was dist ever'thang he could do to keep from bustin' out to bawlin'.

Ol' lanky Lawerence was grubby and dirty, and looked ever' bit the pore skinny boy he was. He growed so fast his britches legs was allus too short.

The man was so tore up over seein' sichy pore young boy a-givin' the last dime he had in this world that he'd worked out to git shoes with, that not to be out-done, he brung his pocketbook out a his hip pocket and give Dugan a donation, too.

They worked that routine on sev'al folks. I don't know how much money they got, and they won't nobody else never know neither, for they prob'ly *ground squirrel'd* the biggest part of it, a-knowin' them two.

Dad, Bud, Lewis, Sweetie, Jess, Dugan and some others worked along as they could to build the church house. The old Junaluska schoolhouse where I'd started school was being tore down, and they got some of the lumber and desks out of it. They took the desk tops off and fastened the seat parts together to make some pews. They built a pulpit (lectern), and a table to put in front of it to set the waterbucket on, and mounted little shelves on the wall between the windows to set the oil lamps on.

Dad brought an old train bell in that he'd got somewhere where he was wor-kin', Canton, I think, and they made a belfry and hung it inside it. They tied a rope to it and run it down through a hole in the loft so they could pull on the rope to ring it.

They got the church finished and the dedication service was held on September 15, 1946.

Later on, Dad and Lewis bought Aladdin lamps for the church. Several years after they got electricity, I was a Sunday School teacher there, and found one of the old lamps in the teacher's stand in a Sunday School room. I asked the church to let me buy it. They brought it up in a business meeting and voted to give it to me.

Several years ago, I gave it to Roy, Lewis' oldest boy, and his wife, Betty.

Old Junaluska Church

There's a small country church I'm remembering today
Where I went as a child, and I learned how to pray;
And the Sunday School teacher who helped me to see
The wonderful Love that God has for me.

The structure looks plain, til you look at the giving
And you know of the love that went into the building;
The men and the women who gave of their labor
And worked on the Church House alongside their neighbor.

The seats are not purchased, or fine, padded pews,
But made from the desks of an old torn-down school;
And fashioned with hands that were rough as the boards,
But were built with love for the House of The Lord.

There's no air conditioning, but on a warm day in spring
When the windows are open, you can hear the birds sing
As if praising our God from their place in the trees;
While inside, the preacher leads prayer on his knees.

The most beautiful chimes in the world can't compare
To the old train bell ringing in the clear mountain air;
When it peals out its tones—so loud, and then soft
From a rough rope that's run through a hole in the loft.

Some of my friends don't attend any more.
They're living with God now, and sing in His choir;

And through Heaven's window, they're watching for me
To enter The Gate, where in God's church we'll be.

-Cleo Hicks Williams-
© 1978

In loving memory of a plain mountain people
In a plain mountain time
Who worked together to build
A plain mountain church.

LITTLE CHOGIE

When we lived there in the "apple house," Thelma started courtin' and then married Cooper Ferguson from over at Little Choga. He was a little older than Dad, and was considered a well educated man in that day. His place was way on back in the mountains on a windin' gravel road full a switchbacks, at least five miles on past our house. He lived with his mother Arzelia, who was a granny doctor, but she was gittin' on up in years, and had quit granny-doctorin' by then.

They had a house that was painted white, and was real nice *to the side of* lots of other people's houses back then. They wutn't nobody much had a upstairs, but that house had two upstairs rooms. And they was a separate dinin' room. Law, me, I hatn't never seen nobody have a whole room that all they used it for was to eat in, with a nice big round storebought wood table and fancy high back chairs that was varnished, and a great long cab'net lookin' thing in it that they called a buffet. And they was doors that you could shet in betwixt ever room. Lordy, we never had no inside doors atall, dist a doorway you went through. I never seen so many nice doors, and they all had doorknobs on 'em, and a key hole, too. Real fact'ry made doors. And big ol' tall heavy wood bedstids with carvin's all over the headboard and footboard, and big ol' soft thick feather ticks. We had mattresses at our house now, but they wutn't nuthin' like them feather beds.

They had a awful purty place that took up the whole valley, with sev'al acres of fields, apple trees, and pasture land. I remember seein' big ol' round corn shocks and hay stacks a-standin' in the field. That was the biggest, nicest barn I ever seen, too, with a great big hay loft and all kind a gear a-hangin' in the hall way. They was a little branch that run between it and the house.

It use to be a good size community through there. When they built the dam that made Nantahala Lake, the roads was cut off except for that windin' round-about Little Chogie road, and people had moved off and jist left their homestids a-settin' there. They was a few old abandoned homestids still scattered about, with the houses and outbuilding' a-standin' empty, and their rooftops a-rottenin' and cavin' in. Old gnarly, moss covered fruit trees stood in fields that was all overgrowed from where they'd been untended.

They was a little country church just up the road from their house, standin' unused, with a little graveyard off to the side of it. Wild gooseberry, buckberry and huckleberry bushes growed along the old road a-goin' up to the church. Me and Thelma'd go up there to pick some in the fall when they got ripe. Sometimes we set down on the church steps to rest awhile, or wandered through the old untended graveyard with its simple rectangular white marble tombstones, and read the names and dates on 'em.

They was rows of tombstones, some evidently from the same family. I noticed one in pa'tic'lar. It was a row of five little younguns, their graves a-startin' out short with a baby, a-gittin' longer on down the row. The dates of death was dist a few days apart. How awful! It made me feel so sad I could a-bawled. We figgered they must a-died in a epidemic of some sort.

I remembered Mammy a-tellin' me about epidemics. They was one that was the Flu, another'n that was the Smallpox and another'n that was Diphtheria. She cried when she told me about how her little girl, Mary Etter had died in a Diphtheria epidemic. She said that Diptherie caused a youngen to have a sore throat that kep' a-gittin worser 'n worser, and it got so hit coutn't breathe on account of a thick membrane that come in their throat, and they coutn't swaller. They'd cough awful hard, and try so hard to breathe in that it sounded dist like a rooster a-crowin'. They'd finally git real weak from not bein' able to git no nourish-ment down 'em, and their throat jist kep' a-closin' on up to where they coutn't git no air in, til it fin'ly kilt 'em. She'd burnt the lamp and set up night after night with Mary Etter, a-rockin' and bathin' her face and puttin' poultices and stuff on her, and tryin' to give her broth out of a teaspoon, but she died in spite of ever'thing.

Can you just imagine bein' stuck a way back off to yourself in a place like that with no close neighbors, no power, telephone or means of transportation except a horse, and your sweet little youngun a-layin' there a-sufferin' and sick enough to die, a-knowin' all the time that they wutn't a thing on God's earth nobody could do?

I know that prescription medicines is real costly now, but when I hear some-body a-growlin' about the price, I wonder what them people back then would a-give for a chance to save one of their childern's life. Diphtheria is a thing of the past in this country. We have vaccinations now, and all kinds of "miracle drugs." But best of all, we have hope that they can recover.

Just down the road, not far from the lake, is Glen Choga Lodge. It was a large country inn, well used and loved in its day. It's an impressive structure, built of logs and natural materials, inside and out. Old moss covered statues and yard ornaments still stood around here and there on the grounds. Cooper and Thelma were caretakers of the place, and when they went to check on things, they let me explore everything in the place. It still had lots of furniture, books and things in it, and an old Victrola and some records. The bedrooms had handbuilt commode chairs, with a chamber pot down inside 'nunder the seat, and a little closet that they set it back in and shet the door on when it wutn't a-bein' used.

It's hard to describe how the whole area made me feel—mournful, I guess, is the word that fits the best. Mammy had told me about my ancestors who had lived in the area, and where she was raised, and the old home places and deep hollers and coves now covered up under water, forever gone. There'd been a mill owned and run by a man she called "Uncle Dave Howard," whose wife was a close relative of hers. All the folks for miles around took their corn there to get ground into cornmeal.

I thought and wondered about the people who first moved in here when it was a mountain wilderness. So many questions ran through my mind. Where had they come from, and why had they come? Was their ancestry Scotch, Irish—or what?

I imagined the hard work, clearing the land with an axe and mattock, and plowing with oxen or mules. Or did they have horses? They grubbed out stumps and roots, set out and tended fruit trees, raised crops, and built their outbuildings. I wondered where and how they got the materials to build their houses. What kind of tools did they have, and where did they get them? How in the world did they bring things way back in here? If they used a wagon, how long did the trip take, and how many trips a year did they make? What if they got sick or hurt?

How many years or generations of hard work did it take to make these places into homes? They were still beautiful home places. How many harsh winters had they endured, and how did they ever survive in this cold, high mountain country? Where are they now? I wondered if they ever got homesick.

They surely had many memories of the years they lived and raised their families in these homes they loved. When I thought about them having to move away and leave them, even having to move the graves of their family, it was as if I felt and shared their grief. I still feel that way when I go there. I wonder if there's such a thing as "genetic" emotions or memory.

It was so "silent." No sounds could be heard except the birds, the soft wind in the trees, and running water from Little Choga Creek that meanders through the valley.

And I now wonder if anyone ever stops and thinks, or even knows about the sacrifice those people made so that we can enjoy electricity.

Or ever realizes what untold stories lie buried in the deep, dark water beneath them as they zoom along in their high-powered speed boats.

I learned firsthand to appreciate how hard it is to live in almost total isolation that far back in the mountains. My experience was very little, though, compared to Thelma's lonely life back on Little Chogie. I thought the head of Jun'lusky was isolated, but at least we had kinfolks and neighbors close by, and people passing by on the road at least once a day.

She didn't have nobody to talk to. It was a rare occasion for anybody to pass by on that road. The mailman, Arnold Rowland drove down as far as their mailbox on weekdays, only stopping a minute to open and close the box. For weeks at a time, he'd be the only other human she saw. Cooper's mother had moved out. Cooper was a cook and went off to jobs at different locations, and was gone for long periods of time. When he came home, he only stayed a few days or weeks before going off on another job.

She ditn't have no power, telephone or car. She was stranded except for walkin', or ridin' Old Lou, the horse. She had to be there to take care of the cow, horse, pigs, and chickens, and done the gardenin' and ever'thing else that was needed to keep up a place. She had to milk twicet a day and take care of the milk and butter, a-takin' it to the spring, and done the churnin'. And done it all by herself. She carried water from the spring, and had to go acrost a footlog way over on the other side of a field, on over in the edge of the woods to get a bucket of water. She caught her wash water out of a spout in the branch between the house and the barn.

Sometimes, she'd write Mom a letter and ask her to let *one a-t'other* of us come over. She was good to us, we allus had a good time, and I was allus ready to go to Thelma's when they'd let me. Sometimes Mom let us, and sometimes she didn't. At times me and Lawerence went, and sometimes me and Oval, or one of us went by ourself. We could catch the mailman in the evenin' and ride over there, or we could walk. It took about two hours, but we didn't think a thing in the world about strackin' out to walk over there. We enjoyed gittin' turned loose to walk it.

The house was *struddy-built*, but awful hard to keep warm with a fireplace. She had to cut enough wood for it and the cookstove, too. I got out and helped her when I was there. That way, we could use a crosscut saw and saw down some bigger trees so she woutn' have to chop down so many and drag 'em in. We could saw it up an'en she could bust it as she needed it.

Some narrow steps led up from the side of the fireplace to two rooms upstairs. Over on the side walls of the rooms were little doors that opened into storage space out toward the eaves. I liked to prowl in there and look at things. Cooper's mother had put old catalogs, high top buttoned shoes, her side saddle, and other stuff in there. An antique dealer would lose his mind to see all those things now. I thought they were real antiques back then.

One thing I loved was the old pump organ that had been Arzelie's. It was a big old purty thing, with carvin's all over it, and round shelfs on each side where you could set your lamp to see by. Thelma let me try to play it, and I treated it with respect. It had a whole row of stops that I liked to pull out or push in, one, to see how it changed the sound. I liked a meller tone. That's where I first learnt to play anything with a keyboard. Ma Hicks had a organ, and she played it one time when I was there. I was dist spellbound a-listenin' and watchin' her, but I'd a been skint alive if I'd a tetched it.

It wudn't long before I could play a few songs by ear. Since I'd learnt chords on the gittar, I fooled around with the keys til I found the chord I wanted. I ditn't know what key it was. Then I fooled around some more til I found the chords that went with it, rememberin' how many keys up or down to move my fingers when I wanted to change chords. Then I figgered out the melody part with my right hand. I learnt one song at a time. Trouble was, I'd git so busy a-playin' that I'd forgit to pedal with my feet, til the sound started fadin' away, an'en I'd git to pumpin' agin.

I ditn't hardly know what to make of Cooper. Mom and Dad hadn't wanted Thelma to marry him. Sweetie was in the Army, and had wrote her a letter a-baggin' her not to marry him. They thought he was too old for her. People said he was so stingy he'd *skin a flea for its hide and taller*. And of course, I'd heard all a that. He was allus good to me, but I wutn't used to no attention and couldn't figger out why he paid attention to me. He was always a perfect gentleman with such good manners, and he learnt me a lot, especially table manners. I never eat with nuthin' but a spoon before.

Whenever I stayed a night or two with them and he was there, he seated me at the table, pushed my chair in before he sat down and noticed everything I eat. He said I needed more meat on my bones. They had a lot more different kinds a stuff to eat than we did at home, and I had to eat a little of everything. He put what he thought I ort to eat on my plate, and I might as well go ahead and eat it, for he woutn't let me leave the table unless I did. He made me eat the first asparagus I ever saw. They raised it.

I was scared of horses. Old Lou was a gentle old mare, and Cooper'd pick me up and set me up on her back, and lead her around to let me ride, to help me get over bein' afraid. I'd hang onto her mane for dear life, but Cooper laughed and cut up so big I learnt to relax and enjoy riding. He had me use his mother's side-saddle.

When I had to come home, I was too scared of boogers, painters and bears to walk all the way out a there by myself. I'd catch the mail boy and ride out to the gap of the mountain where the road forked, as that was where Arnold turned right to go back toward Aquone, where he lived. Then I made tracks the rest of the way home. If two of us was together, we walked out and cut across through the "Silvey Fields," a old abandoned farm, and that knocked about three mile off of the distance home. But we never lost no time a-goin' through there, for they said that old house was hainted, and we b'lieved it.

One day, while we was still livin' at the apple house, I was out runnin' and tried to jump over a old piece of heavy tin that theyd laid over a chicken coop. The end flipped up and caught me on the top of the toes, dist about cuttin' off one a my toenails.

That thing hurt bad, and a few days later, the whole toenail come off. It was all swelled up and *red as a possum's butt in pokeberry season*, and wutn't eb'm *tied up* (bandaged), but Mom never paid it no mind. Cooper stopped by one day, and when he seen that toe, his mouth dist gaiped op'm, and he told Mom "Lord have mercy, that toe is bad infected and has got pus a-comin' out of it. She's liable to lose it, or worse." I ditn't really understand what was going on, but he told Mom to brang him some Lysol and warm water in a wash pan, and some clean white rags.

He had me to set down in the doorway, set the pan of Lysol water on the porch floor, and had me to set my foot down in it. He got down on one knee and took a rag and started to cleanin' up my whole foot. Then he'd pull the rag up out of the water and let one corner hang down so the water'd run off of it in a little stream, right onto my toe. He done that over and over till he'd washed all a that dried pus and dirt and stuff off of it. Then he tore a piece a cloth off and made a clean bandage for my toe, wrapped strips on up around my foot to hold it all in place, and tied it around my ankle.

He told me to keep it clean and dry, leave that bandage on, and not to be a-botherin' it or pickin' at it with my fingers. He come back the next day and brought something to put on it—Proxide, I think it was, to soak the cloth loose. He went through that cleanin', washin', and tiein' it up again. He come back ever day for a few days, an'en spaced it out till it ditn't need a bandage no more and a new toenail had started to grow.

I still ditn't know what to think about him a-payin' all that 'tention to me. I reckin it was because I thought he was so smart and knowed so much, was why I was so backerds around him. He'd allus told me I was smart, and bragged on me, and wanted me to stay in school and git a good education. But I knowed I was plumb ignert to what he was.

Then he done something else for me that I never got over to this day. It was in my junior year of High School. Orders had been sent off for our class rings, and they'd come. I knowed I ortn't to expect to be able to get one, but I wanted one so bad I could taste it, and thought that maybe I could find some way a-payin' for it. I think it was twenty six dollars I had to have. Anyhow, I'd ordered the cheapest'un they sold.

Back then, a man could cut locust posts, or stakes, we called 'em, and get eighteen cents apiece for 'em. Bud done that sometimes. Some man with a truck would come by and pick 'em up and pay for 'em. I thought and thought, but didn't know of nothin' else I could do to make any money, but figgered I could do that if I kept at it hard enough. I'd need to cut 145 postes to have enough money to pay for my ring.

I took the axe and went way off up on the mountain where they was a bunch a locust trees, and chopped down some, and trimmed 'em up. An'en tied a rope around one tree at a time and pulled 'em down into the field at the back of the house to where we had a saw horse.

I took one of the handles off of Dad's crosscut saw to make me a buck saw. I'd wrassle a tree up on the sawhorse, measure the length I needed, and saw it off. Now, if you don't know nuthin' about differ'nt kinds a wood, they ain't no way for you to imagine how hard locust wood is. Or how heavy. I'd saw awhile and rest awhile, but after while, I'd get a length sawed off. Then I'd scoot the pole over on the saw rack, measure it off, and go at it again. A few times, when I got to the very last stick, it'd *like* (lack) maybe a couple a inches a-bein' long enough. I could a cried. That meant cut another tree and drag it in. They had to be dist exactly standard size.

After I got the trees sawed up, I had to split 'em into stakes, a-usin' big iron wedges and a grow devil. You talk about slow, tough goin'! Locust wood is made out of long, tough, stringy fibers. I'd get the pole to splittin' good and a bunch of them stringy fibers off a one side would hang on to the other side. I'd have to get the axe and chop 'em apart to finish bustin' it.

And the way the grain run, some of 'em'd be too crooked to sell after I'd done and worked 'em up and got 'em busted.

I'd come in from school and work til dark. I'd be so tired and sore it hurt to move, and them blisters on my hands hurt and burnt like fire, til I made calluses.

And I was allus a-skinnin' my knuckles or gittin' splinters in me some where or other, and mashin' my toes or barkin' my shins, one.

Finally I got 100 postes cut and sold. I still needed 45 more, or eight dollars. But the money had to be turned in by the coming Monday, or they'd send the ring back. I dist coutn't stand to think about that. I finally got up enough nerve to ask Mom if she'd ask Dad to let me have the money when he was home that weekend. I was afraid to ask him myself. When I asked her, she didn't say nothin', so I just took it for granted she would, or she'd-a-said "no."

She allus sewed a little pocket on the left-hand side of her petticoat top, and kept their foldin' money in it, fastened up with a big latch pin. When Dad got paid and paid his bills, he give her money to keep in her petticoat pocket, to save. Saturday, I seed him give her a fifty dollar bill, and when she unfolded the other money out of her petticoat pocket to add that one to it, I seen that she had to have at least two hundred dollars in there. I just knowed he'd give her the money I needed a-Monday mornin'.

Well, I thought, she might be keepin' it, afraid I'd lose it. Then Monday morning come, and she didn't give me no money. When I waited as long as I could and finally asked her, she said she wutn't a-givin' me no money for no ring. It was about ten minutes before school bus time. I was simply crushed. If she'd just a-told me one way or the other, I'd a-asked Dad myself, and now it was too late. I still don't know if she even asked him. I'd worked so hard, and still wasn't going to get my ring. Silently, the tears poured down my face.

Along about then, a car stopped over at the road, and it was Cooper. He come to the house and on in to the kitchen. He spoke to Mom, and then to me. He seen I'd been a-cryin'. I don't know why he asked, unless Thelma had mentioned it to him, for I hadn't seen him. But he asked me if I had the money I needed to pay for my ring. I told him I needed eight more dollars, and this was the last day before they sent it back. He pulled out his billfold and handed me eight dollars. I couldn't believe my eyes! And I couldn't believe that he'd even come to see if I had it, let alone give it to me.

Of all people! Cooper! Who everybody said was so stingy! Through the years, I've learned, and still marvel at how God provides for my needs—and even my wants, a lot of times—sometimes in the most unexpected way conceivable. And at the right time—every time. And I have to relearn that every once in awhile.

Cooper could be so kind at times, yet he expected so much from Thelma. He was old-fashioned and expected her to obey him as if she were his child, made her wear old-fashioned clothes, and wouldn't let her wear any make-up or cut her hair short. He never gave her money except for bare necessities when he was gone, or let her go to town to buy anything. And she done the work of a man every day, besides all the women's work she done.

She stayed on Little Chogie by herself til she got close to term expecting their first baby. Our second cousin and her husband, Hazel and Chuck Dillard had moved into an old house on up the road above the church, and they checked on her and helped her do the heavy work. When she went into labor, Chuck rode Old Lou out and got a granny doctor at Andrews to go deliver the baby. After several hours, they knew she was in trouble. Chuck rode Old Lou out to our house again, and got somebody with a car to go in there and get Thelma. They took her the twenty or more miles on to Murphy hospital, the only one in the area at that time. Her son, Norman, was born there and they were both fine. But *it's a thousand wonders* they both didn't die.

She lived there and had three more children, all born at home. When Norman, then Brenda, and then Lanny started to school, they had to go all the way over to Nantahala School, since they lived in Macon County. It was *a way yon fudder'n* it was to Andrews. They sent a small school bus all that distance in there to get them. Them poor little youngens had to leave before daylight and didn't get home til nearly dark. They missed school a lot in the winter because the bus couldn't get in there to take them.

Her baby girl, Faith, was a little over a year old in 1959, when she got sick. They had a car then, and were getting ready to take her to the doctor when Faithie just gasped and stopped breathing. We never knew exactly what caused it.

Thelma was almost overcome with grief and never again acted like her old self. Before long, she took the children and moved out, then divorced Cooper. She moved to Georgia and lived there til she died at home in bed from a sudden heart attack in 1978. She was 51.

OLD TIMEY PREACHIN',
PRAYIN' AND SHOUTIN'

Please know that this narrative is not intended to be disrespectful, judgmental, or demeaning in any way. I'm just tellin' how things was seen through my eyes at the time, with the understandin' of a little ol' ignert mountain girl. I loved that little country church, and those dear people had a lasting positive influence on my life. I still miss them and the sense of family we shared.

The customs at Jun'lusky Church was *purtnear* the same as they was at other country churches back then. A few of 'em today is still *mightnear* like they was back then.

When Junaluska Baptist Church was finished and dedicated, they needed a pastor. Preachers then didn't go off to school to learn how to be a preacher. They felt a call from God to preach, an'en dist started preachin'. People felt that God would teach 'em whatever they needed to know from studyin' the good ol' King James Bible, if they truly was called of God. Of course, town churches wanted a educated preacher to pastor their church, but that wutn't necessary to pastor a little church like Jun'lusky. Town churches called their preacher "Reverend," but we dist called 'em "Preacher."

Back then, the church members got together and prayed about it, and asted God to lead 'em to whoever He wanted to be their pastor. Then when they asted the preacher they felt led to, he prayed about it, an'en told 'em if he felt a call to come. If he did, then they brung it up before the church and voted whether or not to elect him.

They elected Preacher Weldon West for their pastor. They didn't know much about proper church procedure, but "Little Weldon," as they called him, had lots of experience, and knowed all about stuff like that. He learnt 'em how to conduct business meetin's and communion service, and the proper way a-doin' things. He was a tall, skinny, well respected man that *knowed his Bible.* He was a good preacher and a good man.

A white shirt was called a "Sunday shirt." Men ditn't never wear one except to be buried in or wear to church, if they had one. Only, people ditn't call it "church." Hit was called "Sunday School and preachin'" on a-Sunday mornin'. Any night service was simply called "meetin'," either prayer meetin' or revival meetin', unless it was a "sangin'." A teacher once overheard me say I'd been to meetin' and corrected me; she told me to say "church," 'stid a "meetin." She prob'ly went to town church, and ditn't know how we done thangs.

And they never did button up the cuffs on their shirt sleeves, they dist turnt 'em back a couple a turns, and that way, they woutn't git dirty. Usually, dist the preacher wore a necktie. Dad wore a necktie ever oncet in a while, but he never pulled the knot up tight or buttoned up his top shirt button. He jist done it mostly to show out n' be funny.

He liked to wear one a them big wide flaredy neck ties, with the biggest ol' brightest colored flares he could find on one, 'spacially red. He'd put one on, *rare a way back an' rub it down*, jist *a-grinnin' like a basket full a possum heads*, an' say, "Boy, don't I look sharp?"

Although they was s'post to be a time for a service to start, nuthin' never follered a exact schedule. Things was informal, and went "accordin' to how the Lord leads." People come early, and gathered up in little bunches *hyere n' yander, around and about*—out in the churchyard, on the porch, or a-settin' in differ'nt bunches inside—to talk awhile before Sunday School, a-gittin' caught up on one other's news. You could hyear first one an'en another'n a-sayin', "D'jew hyear about so-and-so?"

Folks jist mingled about. Ever oncet in awhile, when somebody'd hyeard ever'thing one bunch said, and so as to *not to slight nobody*, they moved on to the next bunch to hyear what they said, til they'd got around to ever'body and hyeard all the news. Church folks was jis' like fam'ly.

They wutn't nobody come in and *set humped up* in one place, like they ditn't want nuthin' to do with nobody else, like some folks does now. And people ditn't jist come to Sunday School an'en up and leave before preachin' started, or come a-stragglin' in dist barely in time for preachin'. Hit dist wutn't done. Sunday School and preachin' went together *like Karo with surp*.

The first thing some of us youngens done was to go down to Dugan Shields' sprang to ranch out the water bucket and brang back a bucket a frash water. The water bucket and dipper was kep' a-settin' on a table in front a the pulpit, and ever'body drunk out a the same dipper.

When the bell rung, people gethered in, and the sangers (the choir) went on up to the front to sang a few songs. They had a custom at Jun'lusky that I ain't never seen nowhere else. The sangers all stood around the pianner with their back to the congregation.

When they thought they'd sung enough, and started layin' their songbook down, the pastor'd stand up and say, "Let's have a word a prayer." The ones that was Christians, and able to git up and down, got up from their seat and come up front to "kneel at the altar," which was anyplace down on the floor in front of the pulpit. This showed they was humble before the Lord. Lots a women had 'em a haincher in their hands, or had one handy in their pocket, one, in case they needed it. Men usually kneeled down on one knee, but women had to put both of their'n down to keep anybody from seein' up their dresstail. That bare wood floor shore was rough on knees. If they could get to it, they would turn around and prop up their head on the seat of the front pew, or they'd set on the adge a the stage, one, an'at made it better.

Now, if you ditn't go up and join in prayer, don't think it went unnoticed. That meant you was a sinner or was out of fellership, one, and was targeted for the *altar call* later on.

Maybe the pastor would lead prayer, or would ask "Brother" somebody to lead prayer. Women ditn't never lead prayer. As soon as he said two or three words to start off, other people joined in, a-prayin' out loud, and some of 'em cried as they prayed. Hit was real, heartfelt prayer. After while, the voices begin to fade out as one after the other'n quit off. Everbody stayed on their knees till the last'un finished, an'en ever'body said "Amen." You could hear one after the other'n blow their nose as they got up to go to their seat. If you've never experienced this kind of prayer, you've missed a real blessin'.

But sometimes, somebody'ud dist go on and on a-prayin', like they was a-preachin' a sermon 'stid a prayin'. More'n likely, it was a visitin' preacher. I allus thought that was a mighty pore time to go to preachin' a sermon. If a-body wanted to preach, he ort to at least be decent enough to let folks get up off a their pore ol' knees and set down.

Then the Sunday School Sup'intendant "opm'd up Sunday School." That meant that he made whatever announce-ments they was to be made, read some scripture verses, and "said a few words." Lots a times, them "few words" turned out to be the first preachin' of the day. They was a few times that we never did git around to havin' no Sunday School.

After Sunday School was over, whatever time that was, they had a ten to fifteen minute re-cess. They was two well separated toilets up in the adge a the woods behind the church, one for men and one for women. Ever'body that smoked got a chanch to smoke a cig'ret or two, or git a chaw a t'backer, one. And the women that dipped snuff had a chanch to reload if they wanted to. Nobody *never thought nuthin' about it.* And *like as not*, the preacher was *the biggest duck in the puddle.* In fact, sometimes one of us girls would bum a *weed* (cig'ret), or maybe a couple of 'em, off of our Sunday School teacher or somebody, and we'd take off up behind the toilet to smoke. We'd pass one around and take turns a-gittin' a drag off of it. I had to be careful not to let Dad ketch me at it, though, or he'd a-made my hin-en smoke.

When they rung the bell for preachin' to start, the sangers begin to gether up on the stage behind the pulpit. Somebody'd holler, "Let's git started. Ever'body that can and will, come on up and help us sang." Little youngens was welcome, and visitors was invited while they handed out the song books. Ever'body dist stood wherever they wanted to. Back then, they never much liked for nobody to pick a gittar in church, for that was too much like what *them Holinesses* done, and it wutn't done much in a Babtist church.

Before we got a pianner, the sangin' leader give everybody "their note" by sangin' "do, mi, sol, do" up the scale, then "do, sol, mi, do" back down it, before he landed on the startin' note. Later on, Dad bought a tunin' fork sumerce and brung it in and give it to the sangin' leader to use. He'd give it a whack, cock his head sideways and listen to git the right key, an'en sang it out to where ever'body could hear it. Everybody sung their note, an'en they'd cut loose t'sangin'.

First one, and then another'n would call out a number, and they sung however many they wanted to. If some of 'em ditn't know their part good, they stood next to somebody that did, and learnt how thataway.

Somerce along in there, they "took up a collection," or "passed th' hat," one. We ditn't have no offerin' plate. Dist whoever had a hat or cap handy let 'em use their'n. Usually, Bass Mosteller or Collin Morgan was the only ones that had a hat. Most men wore caps with a bill, or one a them stripedy railroad caps, one, but it never made no differ'nce whichun they used.

Little youngens was usually give a penny to take to Sunday School. Their mammy tied it up in the corner of a haincher fer 'em so they woutn't lose it. Now, that penny was mighty important. *Sunday School money* went to pay for cards for the Card Class, or lit'ature or any other expenses the church had.

That was Sunday School money. This here was a *love offerin'* to pay the preacher with. Lots a people dist give two or three pennies, or maybe a nickel or dime, if they had it. The whole collection usually run from a few cents to two, maybe three dollars, if hit was a good'un. The preacher wutn't paid no salary. The Bible says, "If a man won't work, neither let him eat," and a preacher wutn't no better'n nobody else to have to git out and work for a livin'. But they did think they ort to help him pay for his gas and stuff, to come and preach.

After ever'body set down, the pastor got up to preach. They was a few preach-ers around the country that wutn't called to no church right then, or was dist a-learnin', maybe, and they'd visit differ'nt churches, or might fill in if a pastor was sick. After the pastor preached, it was the mannerly thing for him to do, to ast if ary one of the visitin' preachers had anything to say. So, on top a his preachin', they might be another'n or two preach. They was expected to testify but keep it short, not to be a-takin' over, don't ye know, but they dist went by how the Lord led 'em. An'en, it was usual to ast "if anybody's got anything they want to say before we close." Usually, somebody did, and here come another sermon. Lots a times, we never got out til after one or one-thirty.

Preacher West was a soft-spoken man with a high voice, but he talked loud enough for ever'body to hear him. And he wutn't *long-winded*. But some a them preachers was, and they ditn't jist preach loud, you could hear 'em a-hollerin' plumb over at the road. The way it us'ally went, a preacher allus started off a-rea-din' his Scripture, dist a-talkin' purty quiet, when all of a sudden, he'd holler out a word real loud Then he'd commence to goin' in a sing-song *chaint* for a little bit, an'en would beller out one word and draw it out real long, an'en chaint again for awhile. He'd git louder and louder, till it got so he was dist about a-hollerin' out all of it. Ever' little bit, one of the men hollered "A-man." An'en sometimes, somebody—usually one of the older women, would cut loose to "*shoutin*'." Then, maybe two or three more would start, with people a-hollerin' "Aaa-man!" and "Praise the Lord" all over the place. They called it "gittin' happy." And they was.

When the preacher got to goin' real good, he'd run around 'n stomp, beat on the pulpit with his fist, and wharp his Bible down flat to where it sounded like a gun shot a-goin' off in there. And some of 'em hollered so loud that their face got purpledy-red and their neck veins stood out like ropes. That neck tie got jerked loose and throwed down, or stuffed in his side pocket, one, where the end of it stuck out and flapped around. They might git so carried away that they'd jump up and stomp on a bainch, or leap frawg over it, maybe. He was really *on far* (fire) when he done that.

When I first started goin' to church, all that hollerin' scared me. I thought they was mad about sump'm. I knowed when somebody got mad enough to start hollerin', they was mad enough to fight—or whup somebody, one. Then I seen nobody else was worried, so I settled down. I got used to it.

Mostly, back then, preachers preached hell fire and brimstone, and about peo-ple a-bein' so *weak-ed* (wicked) that God was a-goin' to have 'em throwed into a lake of everlastin' fire and tarment for punish-ment. Sounded to me like God went around a-watchin' for thangs to git people for, and a-body'd better be awful careful. As the old song said, "You Can't Do Wrong And Get By." And preachers was really agin' doin' any work, or enjoyin' "worldly plasures"—like huntin', goin' a-fishin', shootin' a gun, settin' off farcrackers or makin' any big rackets on a-Sunday.

I wondered lots a times if a preacher thought his wife was a-sinnin' when she'd got up early that mornin', carried in frash water, done th' milkin' and feedin', built a fire and fixed ever'body's breakfurst, woished up th' dishes, laid out his preachin' clothes, got th' youngens ready for Sunday School, busted up some wood, ketched, kilt and cleaned a chicken and cooked dinner before she got herself ready to go to Sunday School and preachin'. Did he really not know all that stuff had to be done? Or did women not count?

(And wonder how much cussin' he'd a done if she'd a-got up a-Sunday mornin' and dist set down with 'er hands all folded up, a-prayin' 'n readin', and never strack a lick at nuthin', like he done?)

An'en they was real bad to preach about what women ort not to do. One a the sinfulest thangs a woman could do was to powder 'n paint up her face like that *strollop*, Jezebel—and looky what hapm'd to her. She went'n *dolled* herself *up*, and was throwed out of a real high wender, 'n her blood jist splattered all over the street 'n the horses 'n ever'where. An'en the dogs eat 'er.

Hit was a sin and a shame to wear shorts, and they wutn't no decent woman ever wore britches, neither. Pants was men's clothes, and it was forbid in the Bible for women to wear men's clothin'. And they wudn't s'posed to bob their hair off short—that was their glo-ry. MAN was the head a the house and the woman done what he said do, and ort not to question his a'thor'ty.

Women was to keep silent in church. Now, I never could understand why they said that, but still she could teach Sunday School, be secretary, treasurer, or sang in the choir. I reckin'd that meant for women to keep their nose out a the men's business, an'en let them take credit for all that got done. The way I seen it, if it hatn't a-been for the women, the church woutn't a-never got built in the first place, and *a-pracious little* would ever git done if ever'thang was left strickly up to the men to do it.

When he preached agin' sump'm that ever'body knowed somebody there was guilty of, like went to a pitcher show or a ball game, one, they said he was *"a-steppin' on their toes"*, or *"a-skinnin' 'em,"* one. Some folks thought that was real preachin'. I got tard a that kind a preachin' purty quick. I b'lieve in preachin' the Bible, and lettin' God handle the rest. The way I seen it, folks had more'n enough troubles to *plague 'em* all week long, and needed help and straingth to git 'em through the next'un. In other words, like the Bible says, "Feed my lambs."

One day we'd got to the house, and Dad was a-braggin' about how the preacher'd "shore skint 'em today." Now, I had to be awful careful that Dad didn't think I was a-sassin' 'im, but me, I was kind a *put out* about it. I *studied about it*, and decided that quotin' th' Bible woutn't be a-sassin' 'im, and told him: "Dad," I said, "My Bible says 'Feed my sheep,' not skin my sheep." He looked at me awful straight, and I thought for a minute there I'd *done 'en stepped in it*, but then he dist walked off. And I never did hear him *a-handlin' any sichy talk* as that no more.

Now, I ain't a-sayin' all preachers done that. They was many a good ol' preacher that when he started preachin', you could tell right off that he truly was "*a man of God.*" He knowed his Bible, and teached it, and you could feel the Spirit movin' when he preached. Now, he *done good,* an' made you feel good, too. You left there ready to tackle *the ol' Devil* the next week.

It was customary for the preacher to go home with somebody for dinner, and people seen that he was asted by somebody. They wutn' a-havin' no preacher a-goin' home hungry. If his wife and younguns was with him, they was made welcome, too. He went home with first one, and then another'n, so as not to be partial to nobody. People usually had fried chicken with gravy and biscuits, a cake or pie, and whatever else they had to fix.

They never was a set number of nights for a revival to run. It also run for "as long as the Lord leads"—up to two weeks—or more, sometimes. The preacher allus *give a altar call* after he got done preachin'. Then he called for a verse of song, and ever'body stood up. They'd start a invitation song while he pleaded with sinners to come up to the altar and be saved. If somebody come up and kneeled down, the sangers kep' on sangin' as long as they was up there. One would come, an'en after while maybe anothern'd come, and they might be eight or ten before it was all over. The preacher jist kep' on a-pleadin' for them to come up. Lots a times, that "verse a song" turned out to be ever' verse a that song and sev'al more too. An'en they was times when we sung ever' invitation song in the song book, an'en went back and started all over.

They was lots a shoutin' and praisin' the Lord at a revival. When somebody come up off a their knees and said they'd been saved, or come up a-shoutin', one, somebody else might cut loose to shoutin', or some woman scream out like a river painter. They'd be people a-gittin' happy all over that church house. The first time I seen that, I's about ready t'crawl inunder a bainch, hit scared me so bad. But as I understood more, I felt real joy for them. I still love to see a person saved, but it's been a long time since I seen sich a vict'ry celebration as they had.

The business of "gittin' saved" was all real confusin' to me. People started comin' up to me when the altar call was give, a-cryin' and baggin' me to *go up* and git saved. I sure didn't want to die and go to hell—dist the very thought give me *the cold chills.* So I *went up* sev'al times. I done all I knowed, and ditn' know nothin' else t'do, but nothin' never did happen to me like I'd heard other people say it did to them—like lightnin' a-strackin' 'em, sump'm gittin' a-holt of 'em and makin' 'em want to shout, and all kind a things like that. I finally dist told 'em I was saved so they'd let me alone.

Well, they turned right around and set up a *babtisin'*, and I was *in a fix* then. I was scared to death a deep water, and that lie I'd told *wutn't a-settin' none too good* with me. I knowed *good 'n well* I'd git drownded dist as shore as they souzed my head inunder the water, and knowed, as the preachers said, I'd "bust Hell wide op'm" for lyin'. But they wutn't no way around it, so I went ahead with it.

They *ponned up* the creek to use for a babtisin' hole down there in front of Miss Piercy's place, out from where Ruth and Sweetie lived. Hit was deep. And cold! Ooshie! That water was colder'n whiz. And I was shamed enough to want to *crawl off in a hole and pull it in behind me* when they lent me backerds to put my head inunder, 'cause one a my legs flew up and my big toe poked up out a the water. I thought I was a-fallin', and dist knowed I was a-gittin' my drowndin' so I tried to ketch myself, but they ketched me and hauled me back up. Ruth 'n Sweetie hapm'd to snap a pitchure and got me with my toe stuck up. Ever'body laughed, but I was too glad to git it over with and not git drownded to let it bother me much.

They was a bunch of us got babtized. It was October 20, 1947. I was a month over thirteen year old.

I'd read the Bible a lot, and memorized sev'al chapters, Psalms and differ'nt verses but I still hatn't never figgered it out about bein' saved, goin' by what preachers and other people said. It was really a-*worryin' the life out of me.* One night I was layin' in the bed *a-studyin' about it,* and it *come to me* that from what I'd read, the Bible was about God's love. The only real constant love I'd ever felt in my whole life had come from Him. I made up my mind that I was a-goin' to take what the Bible said, the way I understood it, and quit bein' scared to death all the time about what people said. I'd trust God, and live my life the way I thought He wanted me to, no matter what nobody thought. And when I done that, I felt such a deep joyous peace flow through me that I just laid there with the tears a-pourin' down the side of my face. I knowed ever'thang was all right.

Not a burnin' bush. Not thunder or lightnin'. Not mighty rushin' wind. I knowed it was the "still, small voice" I'd read about in the Bible. After a while, I turned over, scrooched up against Oval's back, hugged him up and went to sleep.

That peace and joy has never left me. When I've been in tough situations, and almost ovecome with grief or fear, that still small voice has always guided and comforted me. I can look back now and see God's guiding hand in my life, taking care of me even when I least deserved it and wasn't even aware of it.

A few weeks later, Preacher France Postell was holdin' a revival over on Little Chogie. Our church went a few nights, and one night Dad got saved over there. I dist about coutn't believe it. Finally! He was indeed, a changed man after that. I was still afraid of him, but he did stop drankin' and cussin', and was a whole lot easier to git along with. To me, it was nothin' short of a miracle.

He was workin' at Canton, and when the church decided to get a piano (pea-anner), he got one at L. J. Ward Piano Company and brung it in on the comp'ny truck. He'd made arrange-ments for them to make pay-ments on it, however much they could, when they could. Len Morgan could play a organ, so she played the piano when she was there. But she was *gittin' on up in years*, and coutn't come ragler.

After I'd heard the piano player from Valleytown church, I wanted to play one *so bad I could taste it*. They had a piano in the front of the auditorium at school, and lots a times when we was waitin' on the bus after school, some of us'd go in there and peck around on it. One or two kids knowed some little ol' jigs like "Coonshine" or "Heart and Soul," and learnt 'em to me. One of us would play on the bass side, and one would play on the other side. *Tickled me to death!*

I thought playin' a piano would be the grandest thang a-body ever could do. I'd lay in the bed at night and my faingers'd dist go to twitchin', a-thankin' how it'd feel to play one. But I knowed they wutn' no use in me a-wishin'. As Mom allus told me, "*Wish in one hand and mess in the other'n, and see whichun gits full the quickest,*" only she ditn't say "mess." Even if we had one, it'd be like that fiddle a-hangin' on the wall—I'd never git to tetch it.

A girl at school said she was takin' piano lessons, so I asted her who give her lessons and how much it costed. When she said her piano teacher lived right over at the edge of the school yard, I thought how great it'd be to walk over there after school and take lessons. Dad'd said he was makin' good money now, and they might let me practice on the piano down at the church.

When I asted, Dad or Mom neither one woutn't let me. Lewis even offered to pay for my lessons. Him and Sweetie was both a-workin' at Teas Extract, and they both offered to come by and git me and brang me home when they got off, but they still woutn't let me. They said they wanted me on that school bus, and that's what had better hap'm. And when they said "No," it was allus th' end a that. They wutn't no talkin' about it, and they wutn't obliged to give nobody no reason.

Dad had been to Ward's sev'al times a-buying song books, and made friends with Mr. Ward. Nobody ditn't know he was goin' to do it, but one Friday evenin' when he come home, he brung a piano that he'd bought. I dist coutn't b'lieve my eyes. Maybe I could learn how to play one now, eb'm if I coutn't take no lessons. I didn't know one thing about how to relate notes on a page of music to keys on a piano. The only person I'd seen close up that could really play a piano a-goin' by music, was Miss Hudson in Glee Club at school.

I found out right quick that it didn't work to hold the keys down and play it like a organ, but I pecked around on it anyhow, a-tryin', and was learnin' a little bit. Then Lawrence Anderson teached a *"shape note" sangin' school* at our church. I learnt the name a the notes, about lines and spaces, and that where ever you seen the "do" on a line or space, that was the key the song was wrote in. He showed me on the piano where middle C was, and I took it from there. I figgered out the chords that went with the key of middle C (the chords you mostly use a-playin' the gittar—C, F and G), and learnt to play a song wrote in C. Then I learnt the key of F, an'en G. Then I started up the scale, one note at a time, a-tryin' to learn ever' one of the keys. Other than knowin' enough to tell what key a song was in, I didn't know music, and played by ear. I didn't know nuthin' about sharps, flats, rests, or what time it was wrote in.

Bud got so tard a hearin' it that when I'd start, he'd go to growlin' about it, an'en git his gun and take off to the woods a-squirrel huntin'. Mom might a-did, too, but since Dad wanted me to learn, they knowed better'n to say anything.

By now, Dad was big into goin' to church and sangin's. We hatn't had the piano long, and he'd heard me sorter peck out a few songs, a-tryin' to learn 'em. He rec'anized the name of 'em, and thought that if I could play one song in one key, I ort to play any song in any key, dist whatever was called out. He ditn't understand it when I tried to tell him, and said it was good enough to where I could play at Sunday School.

Next time they bunched up to sang at Sunday School, he jerked his head sideways torge the piano and up and told me to git over there and set down and play that thang. When Dad told you to do sump'm, you done it. I knowed him well enough to know I better do dist ezackly what he said do, so I set down and fumbled through the best I knowed how. I hatn't learnt all the keys yet, so I jist picked out a key I'd learnt that was the clostest to the key the song was wrote in, and played it by ear. It's a good thing I loved music and had some natural talent, or I'd shore *a-been in a bind.* You talk about prayin', now, I done it. I still can't b'lieve I done that. It had to be answered prayer.

It kindly *turned the damper down* on me a-bein' so tickled about havin' a piano when I understood that he expected me to play out in public—at Sunday School and preachin', and sangin's and ever'thang—without no lessons, or givin' me time enough to learn how, neither one. Now, that was what you call *bein' betwixt a rock and a hard place.* I never was real good at it, though, and was ashamed that I coutn't play as good as other piano players, but I done the best I could.

Sunday evenin's, different churches from all around come and brung their choir, quartets, trios or duets. They took turns a-sangin' for awhile, an'en ever'body sung together. Then we'd go to one of the other churches the next Sunday evenin' for a sangin'. I sung in duets, trios, and quartets, as well as with the Jun'lusky sangers. I'm still amazed at how good the girls on the creek could sang. They had a natural ear for harmony. We'd hear a song, write down the words, and two or three of us'd get together and decide whichun was goin' t'sang what part. We ditn' know what else to call 'em, so we called it "high, low and lead" parts. I'd learn it on the piano, and an'en we'd sang it. It was usually me, Harriett and Sister, and sometimes, Christine Shields or Mae Mosteller. And we sounded about as good as anybody from the other churches did.

That piano instrumental tune, "Down Yonder," by Dell Wood, was real popular at the time. It was fast-movin', foot-stompin' square daince music like I liked. Bud liked that'n too, and I heard it on his radio sometimes. Somebody was a-playin' it on the piano at school one day, and showed me the basics of how to play it. I coutn't wait to git to the house and learn it. Mom ditn't never ast me no questions about what I's a-playin', and never did let on like she even heard it. But Dad was differ'nt. If he ditn' know, he'd ast me what it was, and it better be gospel music. He said it was a bad sin to go to them ol' dainces, where ever'body was a-drankin' and a-*hoo-rawin'* around, a-feelin' a women's titties and ever'thang, and he wutn't a-*puttin' up with* me a-playin' no daince music.

I got Down Yonder purty well down pat while he was at work, though. Some of us girls got to the church early one Sunday mornin', and they dis' kep' on a-wantin' me to play Down Yonder. I told 'em Dad'd kill me if he heard tell of it, but bein's as nobody else wutn't around yit, I'd do it. So they all ganged up around me, and I was really *a-gittin' with it,* a-tryin' to sound like Dell Wood did on the record.

All of a sudden, here come Dad dist a-bouncin' down the middle of the church, a-swangin' his hips and clickin' his faingers, and grinnin' all over hisself, like a mule a-eatin' sawbrars. When he hollered out, "Let's sang a verse a that," I jist about pyorely fell off a that stool with a heart attackt. I was dumb-struck! The girls started hum-hawin' around, an'en one of 'em spoke up real quick and told him it was dist a song we'd hyeard and ditn't know the words to it. We started grabbin' song books off of the piano, passin' 'em out, and handed him one t'git his mind on sump'm else real quick. Boy, that was a clost-un!

When it was Jun'lusky's turn to host a sangin', we had *"all day sangin' and dinner on the ground."* Bud woutn't eat at th' church house. He said it was ag'in' Bible teachin'—it put the poor to shame, and we had houses to eat in. He allus *went to the house* before dinner.

Mom usually fixed fried chicken and made a 'nanner puddin', a cokernut cake, or one a them stack fruit cakes, one, and differ'nt kinds a pies and stuff. We set it in pasteboard boxes and put a cloth over it to keep out dust and flies when we got ready to go.

We never had no powdered sugar or Kool Whip, or nuthin' like that, to make icin' for a cake or pie. It was made out of beat-up egg whites. We ditn't have no egg beater, and ditn't know what a whisk was. Now, if you ain't never tried to beat egg whites up with a fork til they git stiff enough for frostin', you don't know how tard your arm can git. That's one time Mom let me help her.

They never bought Co-Colies and soft dranks like we do now. They dist took jugs a water or Kool-Aid™, one, or maybe somebody'd make some lemonade to take. Some people said that ol' Kool-aid™ was hard on your kidneys, but us younguns shore liked it. Then Dad *took a notion* to take a wash tub and drive down b'low town to the ice plant and git a big fifty pound block of ice so people could put some in their dranks. He put a tarpoleun over it to keep it from meltin'. People would chip pieces off of it with a ice pick to put in whatever they was a-drankin'. They thought that was really sump'm to have ice in the summer, and he thought he'd done sump'm big when he done that.

Then he brung home a good-size wooden whiskey barrel, and had found a wooden spicket that fit the bung hole down clost to the bottom of it. He drove the spicket in the hole to where it fit good and tight, and that way, it could be turned off and on to fill up a glass without havin' to dip stuff out a the barrel. Dad was shore proud a that barrel. He brung in a bunch of lemons and made lemonade. Then he put a big chunk a ice in his barrel and poured lemonade in it, and set it on the end of a table. People thought that was sump'm, now, dist to hold their glass 'nunder the spicket and turn the handle to let run out however much lemonade they wanted, an'en turn the handle to shet it off. It kep' flies out of it, and they wutn' no dipper to haf'ta fool with.

They was sev'al a us girls in Bass Mosteller's Sunday School class. Some of us got to talkin' and decided we'd like t'have us a picnic that evenin' after the sangin' was over. We had it all thought out. Bud had a car, and we'd ast him if he'd take us. He tried to act tough sometimes, but the girls bagged 'im into goin' along with what we wanted to do.

They was a big ol' poplar log a-layin' on the ground, right out from where they had the tables set up. Women set their boxes in behind that log out a the way when they got their stuff set out on the tables. Well, us girls mingled around a-fillin' up our plates, and I filled up my plate and went t'set down on the log t'eat. That was what it was s'posed to look like, anyhow. I was a-slippin' stuff off a my plate and stickin' it down in a box we'd stashed in behind that log. Then, one or two at a time, the girls would sidle over to where I was a-settin'. When we thought nobody wutn't a-lookin', one of 'em would swap plates with me. Then I'd ease stuff off a th' plate, a little at a time, and poke it down in th' box. Then another'n would trade plates with me. We had that box plumb cram-full a fried chicken and cake and stuff.

After dinner was over, we had to go on in th' church house for sangin', and Bud snuck back down there and got our box, after the crowd thinned out some. They was one last problem. We'd made it up to tell Dad and Mom we wanted to go ride up the road with Bud. I hardly ever got to go anywhere, and ditn't know if they'd let me or not, but they did let me, since it was dist Bud and some girls, and no boys.

Bud had our box in th' trunk and we set in each other's lap and scrouged in his car. Six in the back, and three besides Bud in front. Bud took off up to the "Cold Spout" on Little Chogie road, and I'm here t'tell ye, we had us one more picnic. We laughed and giggled and had us a big time a-talkin' about how we'd pulled that'un off and nobody a-ketchin' us at it. Bud laughed and had a good time, too, even if he had acted like we'd dist drug him off and made him come.

One thang Bud remembers and laughs about is what Sister Mathis done. When we got up to th' cold spout, we started *showin' out* and *cuttin' up*. Sister grabbed Bud's cap and stuck it up 'nunder her dress to make her belly stick out like she was "expectin'." She'd hold her hands spread out acrost each side a th' cap, kindly double over and holler "Ooooohhhhh! Ooooohhhh! Junior's a-comin'!" She'd look cross-eyed and loll out her tongue, and make the awfulest faces you ever seen. We laughed at her till we cried, an'en her pains'd kindly ease up and we'd go back to eatin' and talkin' about sump'm else. But ever oncet in a while, Sister'd cut loose again, "I'm—oh Lord, a-tellin' ye, oh, uh, Junior's a-comin', Oooooohhhhh!" and we'd have another big laugh.

I reckin we all had the silly giggles, for ever'thang anybody said or done was funny to us. Hit's a good thang they wutn't nobody around to hear us a-carryin' on like *eadiets* (idiots), or they'd a-thought we'us all drunk and a-*called the law on us*. We eat some, an'en we'd cut up some.

Like I said before: They say God takes care of fools and little childern. I reckin I'll have to add thiefs, now.

Hit's a thousand wonders we ditn't git food pizenin'.

MY FIRST JOB

It was a perfect summer day in the mountains. Puffy white clouds drifted along in the sky, and the air smelled so clean and fresh you could almost taste it. The sun was warm on my back as I watched the butterflies flit lazily from flower to flower, slowly opening and closing their showy wings to flash their brilliant orange, black, yellow and blue colors. From high up in the trees overhanging the banks of the creek, a joyous chorus of bird song could be heard above the rush of the cold clear water as it ran merrily on its way down the mountain.

The water was icy cold to my bare feet, and it felt so good to step up onto a big flat sun-warmed rock in the middle of the creek and let them warm up. I stood and watched the *snake feeders* (dragonflies) dart and zoom back and forth, like playin' a game of tag. The water spiders skittered and skated across the silvery-blue surface of the water where it eddied into quiet glassy pools.

I looked down toward the lower pasture, and wondered if Sister had left a letter in our mailbox. "Sister" was the nickname of my cousin who lived up in a holler about a quarter of a mile down the road. We'd hollered out a little place in the ground next to the corner fence post in the pasture and laid a flat rock over it, and called it our mailbox. It was our own secret place. We wrote a letter to one another and checked our mailbox oncet, or maybe twicet a day, if we needed a anser real soon. Sometimes, if they was sump'm we didn't want nobody else to know about, we'd say in the letter what time for us to meet and talk, so we woutn't take the chanch of nobody else a-gittin' holt of a letter.

She *minded* her little brother and sister all the time, and could go anywhere around clost to home dist as long as she took 'em with her. I wutn't s'post to go no fudder than the pasture fence, so when we needed to talk, she'd come on up there and we'd act like we dist hapm'd to be there at the same time.

We had a certain way of doublin' up our letter so we'd know if anybody else had found it and read it. My little brother Vernon was sure to swipe any letter he seen me hide, and tell on me, so I had to watch out for that. I thought he b'lieved the only reason he was borned was to spy on me and tell Mom ever'thing I done. But most of the time, him and Oval was out sumerce a-playin' together, so I'd slip off while he was busy at sump'm else.

I loved to go to Sister's house to see my Aunt Cullie, but hardly ever got to. I remember one year I asted Mom and Dad to let me go to Cullie and Jess's house, and let that be my Christmas present. I knowed I woutn't git nuthin' else, nohow. But that's what I got! Two whole hours! Tickled me to death! Me and Jess played a game of fox and geese, and we all eat cokernut cake and peppermint stick candy. One of 'em had got a jack-in-the-box that played "Pop Goes The Weasel," when you turnt the crank on it, and we sung that song while Cullie cranked it. We had us a merry ol' Christmas, but I had to watch about gittin' back to the house when my time was up. Them two hours dist flew by before I knowed it.

I wisht I could a-stayed all day, but I'd done and been told oncet, and ditn't need to be told no more, to be at the house when I was s'post to. One time before, when we lived acrost the road in the house where I was borned at, Dad had let me go to Cullie's house and told me I could stay a hour. A few minutes later (it seemed to me like) I heard him a-hollerin' at me. When I took off down the trail torge our house and seen him with the leather strop in his hand, I knowed I was in big trouble.

He bellered out, "I thought I *towjew* (told you) not to stay but a hour. What's the matter? Can you not tell time?" I knowed right then I was in for a good whuppin'. With my head bowed, I squoze out a little scared "No, I can't." He retch out and grabbed my arm and took me in the house. Then he drug a straight-back chair in front of the fireplace, turnt its back around to it, and told me to git up there on it. I knowed I wutn't s'post to stand up on no chair with my feet and ditn't know if it was to make it easier for him to wharp me with the leather strop, or give him excuse to whup me twicet, or what, but I knowed do dist ezackly what he said do.

After I clim up on the chair, he pointed to the clock on the mantel and said he'd learn me how to tell time. It was a old pendulum clock with a one inch cut-out pitchure of my aunt Cullie in the corner of the glass front. He told what the numbers and the little hand and big hand meant, and how to tell time. "Next time I tell you to be back at the house, young lady, ye dang well better be here when I tell ye. You won't have no excuse." I sorter understood how the clock business went, but he'd sounded so hateful I'd been too scared to pay full attention. I slipped around later on, and asted Coonie questions to make dead shore I knowed how. And that's how I learnt to tell time.

My feet had got warm now, and I thought I might jist ease on down to the mailbox and see if I had a letter. I snuck on down-stream, a-wadin' around slick rocks, creepin' back into the shadders in amongst the bushes, or a-hoppin' from rock to rock. I was watchin' for any unwary water snake stretched out over the water on a piece a driftwood, a-sunnin' hisself. I'd sorter "borried" Lawerence's air rifle and slipped around the house and off over the bank so nobody woutn' see me a-goin' to the creek.

I loved to shoot a air rifle, and water snakes was a perfeck target. I had t'ease along real quiet, like a Injun—and slip up on 'em, for if I made the least little racket, or moved too quick, they'd be a splat in the water and that snake was gone. I waited real patient til I got a cler shot at his head, and he was dead meat.

Deadeye! That was me!

I loved to show Lawerence that I could shoot better'n him, because he thought a boy was *a way yon* more superior to any gal, and a younger sister was about the most useless thing a boy could have, that is, unless he wanted to *devil somebody*, or wanted sump'm done, one. After I beat him a-shootin' a few times, he *stubbed up* and quit lettin' me shoot his rifle, and would be *ill as a settin' hen* if he found out I'd borried it.

They wutn't no way in my family, though, that a *girl* could have her own rifle. I'd allus heard that *what ye don't know won't hurt ye*, so I figgered that what he ditn't know woutn't hurt him, neither. I knowed Mom would take his side, because she learnt us not to bother nuthin' that ditn't b'long to us, and to *keep our faingers to ourself.* But the temptation to borry it was *too much sugar fer a nickel, and not enough fer a dime.* They wutn' no use in lettin' it lay there and rust. And these days, all he had his mind on was courtin', so I figgered he woutn't never know about it, nohow. He'd *took a shine* to one a them Kyle gals, and was *half addled in the head.*

All of a sudden, I re'lized they was a car a-comin' up the road! Nobody up here on the head of the creek had nary'n. Usually the mailman's car was the only one on this road through the week, but it wudn't time for him, ner the day of week for the store truck to come, neither.

I started to duck down and hide behind the bushes, but re'lized that me *a-wool-gatherin'* (daydreaming) and the sound of the water both, had let the car git too clost for me to hide without them a-knowin' what I's a-doin'. I ditn't want to look plumb ignert, a-hidin' and all, and they'd done 'n already seen me. So I let on like I didn't see nuthin' atall, a-thinkin' hit'd pass on by and keep a-goin'. But Lord help us, hit begin to slow down, an'en stopped in the dusty road above me. Ah, shoot!

They was a middle-aged man and woman in the car, and soon as the dust settled down a little, she rolled down her wender and spoke to me. She interduced herself and her man, an'en said, "We're looking for a girl named Cleo Hicks."

I dist stood there dumbstruck! Natcherly bashful from the way I was raised, I was *plumb beat* (embarrassed) for them proper town folks to see a fifteen year old gal out here a-totin' a rifle and wadin' around barefooted in the creek, with a ol' faded, wore-out dress on that wutn't fit fer a dog bed, much less wear. *I wisht the ground would jist op'm up and swaller me whole.*

I reco'nized the name, for my friend Rose Ella, a girl that lived a little fudder on up the creek, had told me about Mr. and Miz Christy. They sometimes harred (hired) her to stay with 'em to help look after Miz Christy's mother, and help out around the house some. She'd told me how good they was to her, and she loved to stay with 'em.

Rose Ella had five brothers and sisters, and her dad was a Babtist preacher that cut cordwood for a livin'. They lived over acrost the creek in Cora and Kermit's old house. Hit was dist a little ol' three room house, built out of rough sawmill lumber, and they had to dip their water up out of the sprang with a dipper and tote it about a koiter (quarter) of a mile.

It was *a whole nother story* at the Christy's, though. She said they lived in a big ol' nice two-story house, and she had the whole upstairs to herself, with her own bedroom and bathroom and ever thang, when she stayed there. What all she told me sounded like sump'm you'd read about in a fairy tale book, 'stid a bein' real. She eb'm walked to school like town kids did. On top a that, they give her three dollars a week to stay with 'em, and she could spend it dist however she wanted to. I'd seen some stuff she'd bought with her money, and thought how lucky she was to git to do that.

But how'd they know *my* name?

After a minute, *I come to myself* and said, "I'm Cleo Hicks." Oh, Lord, how backerds they must think I am, I thought—dist stand here *like a knot on a lawg* and can't eb'm speak back to folks when they speak to me, 'thout me actin' *sillier'n a dern goose.*

But the lady spoke with courtesy and respect. She explained that Rose had been staying with them, but for some reason, couldn't stay the next few weeks. They'd planned on going out of town to visit their son, and needed somebody to stay with her mother while they were gone. They wondered if I could come and stay with them a few days so I could get to know her and become familiar with the household routine before they left, and then stay while they were gone. She said that Rose had recommended me as a reliable person and I would be doing them a tremendous favor.

All at the same time, I was surprised, delighted......and terrified! *I dist ditn't know about that!* Miz Christy was a school teacher, and Mr. Christy was a office manager in Andrews. I was awful bashful. I'd lived all my life up here on the creek, and never was around other people much, let alone town folks like them. I hatn't never been nowhere except to school, and when school was out, never went nowhere til school started back up. I hardly ever seen anybody all summer long outside a my family or church. I wutn't atall easy in my mind, 'cause I ditn't know how to talk or be-have around people like them.

They sounded like honest folks, and *give their word* that if I didn't like to stay, or got homesick, one, they'd bring me right back to the house. I was awful tempted, but thought I dist better not, since I was so backerds, and all. But I was too timid to tell 'em "No." .

An'en, *I thinks to myself*—'Mom won't let me go, nohow,' so I told 'em I'd have to ask my mother—*that'd put the qui-e-tus on that.* She woutn't let me go nowhere.

They parked their car and walked up to the house with me, interduced their-self to Mom, and told 'er what they wanted. *Well, I be dawg'd* if she ditn't say I could go! I'd never a-thought it!

They waited on me and talked to her while I got my clothes and stuff together. I felt like I's a-dreamin'. One minute a-wadin' in the creek, and the next'un, a-leavin' home with dist the same as strangers! And Lord, what would I take? But they wutn't much choice in the matter. Outside of a few old ever'day clothes, I dist had two *changes of clothes* that was decent enough to wear to school. If I wore a totally clean dress to school ever day, I had to wash it in the evenin' and iron the one I'd washed out the day before. I dist had one old pair a shoes that I'd wore to school and saved 'em to wear when I went somewhere, as I usu-ally jist got one pair a year. Since the school year had just ended, they was about wore out.

Lucky for me, I did have one dress I thought was nice. I made it in Home Economics class out of some cloth my teacher had give me. I'd sewed it real care-ful, with pintucks acrost the bodice, and gathered the skirt real full. It also had a high enough neckline so that dogged flour sack petticoat didn't show. I'd never had a bra.

I drampt of havin' one a them soft sweaters like other girls wore to school but knowed they wutn't no use in me a-dreamin'. Ever'thing was bought for how long it lasted, and they thought a sweater woutn't last no time atall. Girls would ast me to pick fuzzballs off their sweater, and I was tickled to do it dist to git to touch their sweater. 'Course they thought I's dist a-bein' nice.

I also had two pairs of cherished *jammers* (pajamas), the only ones I'd ever seen outside of a catalog. Mammy's cousin had brung her some clothes she'd out-growed, and since she didn't want 'em, she give me the jammers. I washed off at night and put on my jammers, like I'd read in stories that people done, stid a sleepin' in my petticoat tail. I liked to look at myself in the lookin' glass a-wearin' em. Made me *feel like somebody*. They was so soft and cozy.

In a few minues, I'd put my stuff in a brown paper poke, put on my shoes and socks, and was ready to go home with the Christys.

When we got to the edge of town, Mr. Christy turned off onto a shady, tree-lined street and drove past a bunch a big old purty Colonial style, two story houses with level, grassy yards and flairs and all differ'nt kinds a purty bushes in 'em. He pulled the car up in the driveway of a nice big two-story house set back away from the street, and declared that we was home.

When we got in the house, they interduced me to Miz Christy's mother. Her name was Miz Fisher. She was a elderly lady with a sweet expression and I liked her *right off the bat*. Then Miz Christy took me upstairs to show me my room and let me put my poke down. Lord, I ditn't know what to think about all a them stairs!

If I had t'die, that was the beautif'lest room *I'd ever laid eyes on*, outside a the time my teacher took me to her house and give me that cloth. And was the big-gest thaing! W'y, hit was pert nigh half as big as our whole house was! It had two beds in it, and they was made up nice with the pertiest matchin' bedspreads you ever seen, tucked back 'nunder the pillers and all. And the room was so light and airy. I never seen the like a wenders in one room, and ever' one of 'em had real thin curtains that let daylight in good. And they was wender screens on 'em, too. Them curtains kindly billered out when the breeze blowed in, and was so white they'd about put your eyes out! Lookin' out in the top a them trees outside made it seem sorter like bein' up in a treehouse or the barn loft, one.

Miz Christy told me this room had b'longed to her two boys as they was growin' up. I coutn't imagine what it would be like to live my whole life in a place like this. And all this room for jist me by myself! I don't reckin I ever had slep' in a room by myself. And had a door that you could shet and fais'en it! *Now, if that don't beat all!* Rose shore hatn't been *a-stretchin' it* (lying). Ever' thang was jist like she said, only they wutn't no way she could a-made me see it like it really was. Hit shore anuff *wus* like sump'm' you'd read about out of a story book.

An'en she showed me the bathroom, and said it was for me to use. They, My Goodness, you reckin they was another'n in the house besides this'un? Two bath-rooms? Now, that did *cap the stack!*

I know I must a-went around a-lookin' like a big-eyed boy at a picnic, with *my eyes stuck out on stems so fur you could a-knocked 'em off with a stick*. All the rest a that day, I dist follered her around a-lookin', and tryin' not to let on that I was. Ever'thing was so nice that I was about afeard to tetch it.

Hit's a good thing I was bashful and ditn't start right in to eatin', because when we set down to supper, ever'body put their hands in their lap and bowed their head while Mr. Christy *said grace*. At home when Mom hollered, "Supper's ready," we set down at the table and dist *fell in* and eat, but Paw Taylor said grace before meals, so I knowed what was a-goin' on. We dist had sandwiches, bein' it was Sunday, but they sure was good. I liked that light bread. They eb'm had a toaster and toasted it. But hit was all I could do to keep from rubbin' my hand over that purty wood that the table was made out of. I hatn' never seen nuthin' so fine *in all my born days*. Not nary a scratch nowhere, and *all shined up like new money*. Hit was too purty to eat off of.

When I started upstairs that night, Miz Christy showed me where the light switches was, and turnt the light on for me to go up the stairs. They, Lord Have mercy! Dist "snap," and the whole place lit up like daylight! Of course, we'd had power put in about a year ago, but we had to pull a chain that hung down by the overhead light bulb to turn on the light—wutn't no light switches.

That night I took a real bath in a real bathtub. I figgered out how to stop it up, an'en ditn' hardly know what to think about me a-runnin' however much hot water I wanted out of a spicket—and not havin' to carry it in and heat it up! I felt kindly funny *a-strippin' off buck naked* and gittin' in the water, though, afeard somebody might walk in and ketch me, and me with no way a-coverin' up. I seen that the door was fais'ened good though, and got in there and lay back and soaked and smelt that nice smellin' soap til I got plumb pruney. I dried off with a great big ol' soft towel, dusted on some a them bath powders Miz Christy had said I could use, an'en put on my jammers. I still think of that bath when I smell Cashmere Bouquet™ soap.

On top a ever'thing else, they was all kind a good books and magazines to read if I wanted to. Bud had the only ones they was at our house. Like me, he loved to read, and sometimes brung *funny books* (comics), Big Little Books, True Story or Westerns home, that he'd swapped with Cullie or somebody. I di'n't never bother 'em unless he told me I could, but he usually let me read 'em after he got done with 'em. Trouble was, I had to sneak around to do it. Mom and Dad thought hit wutn't nuthin' but pure laz'ness to set around with your nose buried in a book.

When I started to go to bed, it was so purty and smooth and smelt so clean, I thought maybe I ortn't to sleep in it. I hated to git it all wrinkledy or dirty it up. But I got me one a them books and got in the bed. I felt dist like a princess in a fairy tale—*all decked out* in my jammers, a-layin' there a-smellin' so good, and propped a way up high on them big ol' soft pillers in that nice bed, a-readin' me a book.

Next mornin', when we went in the dinin' room to eat breakfast, the table was already set, and ever'body had their own place mat with the purtiest plate on it—and a table knife, and a fork, and a spoon, all, a-layin' on a napkin by the side of it. They was a little glass of arnj juice by our plate. At home, we never got no oranges except on Christmas Eve. We never got no arnj juice, any time. I'd learnt about place settin's in Home Ec, but at our house, we never eb'm had no case knifes, ner napkins, ner place mats neither one. We done good to have enough forks and spoons to eat with if somebody come. I ditn't know how to use a table knife. Heck, it was awkerd enough for me to eat with a fork, because I hardly ever eat with one. I eat with a spoon, mostly.

I eat real slow and watched and done however they done, a-tryin' not to *show my igner'nce*. I don't thank they noticed, for Mr. Christy devilled me about boys, and *first one thing and another*, and laughed at me for blushin' so easy. I could see the devil-ment in his eyes, and could tell he was dist a-tryin' to be friendly and all. He was funny.

Their butter was in little long, square sticks, like that there margarene we got back durin' the war, that come with a little pack a yaller colorin' to mix up in it.

Mr. Christy went to work after breakfast, and I helped Miz Christy wash up the dishes. I was scared to death I'd drop one of them purty dishes and break it. I ditn't know what she'd do if I did, because I got a whuppin' at home if I broke one, or spilt my milk.

Then we made up the beds and tidied up the house. Miz Christy was good to me, and showed me dist ezackly how she wanted things done. I felt sorter out of place, and wudn't used to bein' treated respectful or havin' any attention paid to me unless I was in trouble for sump'm. I *settled down* after while, but was still *kindly skittish*. I dist knowed that sooner or later I'd *foul up* and make her mad at me and maybe they'd run me off. But it never hapm'd.

I hadn't never seen sich fine furniture. It was a joy to run my hand acrost that purty wood and polish it til it shined. You could dist about see yeself in it. That furniture polish made the whole house smell nice by the time I got done. She said I done a good job, and I was glad of that.

We talked to one another, with her mostly a-doin' the talkin', and I watched her while she ironed a few pieces. She talked real soft and quiet, and asted me questions about myself: What kind a stuff did I like to do? Did I like school? Was

I aimin' to finish high school, and what did I want to do after I graduated? I said either a artist or a nurse, one, but prob'ly a nurse.

She told me to let her know if I wanted her to, and she'd help get me a scholarship. A scholarship! A scholarship? What on earth was that? I *ditn' rightly know*, but never wanted to *skin my igner'nce* by astin' her.

I thought them was the cleanest clothes *I ever did see.* After I watched her awhile, she let me iron some pieces. That shiny clean 'lectric iron felt light as a feather and was dist like playin' to how I done it at home. I loved ironin' them purty things! I thought these folks must be awful rich! Ever' day, they took things for granted that I never knowed to exist.

Next day, she asted me if I wanted to take a walk, and maybe go to the post office and mail a letter for her, if I did. It was a good thing I'd gone to the post office with a girl friend a few times, so I knowed where it was and how to mail a letter. I told her I'd be glad to. She had it all ready except for *backin' the en-velop* (writing the address on it), so she went ahead and *backed it*. Then when she give me money for a stamp, asted me if I had money to get a coke. When I said I didn't, she give me a extry dollar and said it was mine, I'd *done and already* earned it. Mankind alive! Here I was, goin' to town by myself, trusted to do it right about mailin' her letter, and had money I earned my own self. Talk about *feelin' like some body*, now, I did!

After I got done *mailin' off* her letter, I stopped at the drugstore and bought me a cherry smash for a nickel, a toothbrush, and a tube of Ipana toothpaste—and still had money left. *I thought to m'self* that now I could feel good and clean *shore enough,* after I took a bath and brushed my teeth, and all. She'd done and give me some Prell shampoo and I'd washed my hair like it said on the bottle to do, and it looked lots shinier and cleaner'n it had.

Then ever' evenin about one o'clock, after dinner was over, she said I could go ahead and take a walk, and had me go to the post office to call for their mail. She told me to take my time and enjoy it, and I did, and got to look at all the stuff in the store wenders. I never had been allowed to be in town by myself before. An'en when I got back, I got to go upstairs and read some. I did after supper too.

W'y, I *never done enough work to break the Sabbath.*

Mr. Christy had some sisters that come and eat with us one time, so I knowed who they was. One of 'em was Miss Jean Christy—the schoolteacher that Thelma loved so much. That was a su'prise. They'd check on us while the Christys was gone, in case we needed anything. Miz Christy wrote down their telephone number, and showed me how to call 'em if I needed 'em. The next week, they left to go on their trip and stayed gone three days, a-leavin' me with

Miz Fisher. She was real easy to please, and we got along fine. When the Christys come home, they was real pleased, and told me they 'preciated me a-doin' such a dandy job while they was gone.

They took me back home that week-end. Rose Ella was a-comin' back the next week, so I never got to go back no more. I was sorry, in a way, but glad in a way, to be back up on the creek a-runnin' around barefooted and doin' like I knowed to do—like snake huntin', choppin' up stove wood, and hoein' corn, and stuff. But I never did forget how good they was to me, and what it felt like to live in that nice house and all, where ever'body got along good. And let me read and look at books. Made me feel good that I'd done a good job, and all the more determined that one day, I might could live like that, and do what I wanted to do. And not have somebody *a-growlin' at me* all the time, and bein' afraid they'd whup me.

The Christys give me six dollars for the two weeks I stayed with them. One thing I got that I woutn't never a-had otherwise, was a short sleeve pullover nylon sweater. I'd seen one in Fisher's store wender on my post office trips, and when I got my money, I went in and bought one. It costed $2.98. That year, the fashion was them new "glow colors"—pink, lime green, or yellow. I picked out a glow color lime green'un. I totally cherished that sweater. I dist coultn't b'lieve nuthin' could be so soft, outside of a *baby diddle* (chick).

Not knowin' how to take care of one, I wrung it out when I washed it, and it got all wrinkled up. I laid it out flat on the table and started to iron it, but the very minute that iron tetched the sleeve, that section jist melted away.

I was heartbroke. But I figgered out how to fix it. I cut it a little bit and turned the damaged place back inunder and sewed it down good to where it woutn't ravel, and made a sort of cap sleeve. Then I done the other'n the same way, to match it. I never had seen one that looked like that before, and knowed it looked kindly odd, but I loved it anyhow.

Hit shore beat nuthin'.

HIGH SCHOOL DAYS

I started high school in the fall of 1948. In Elementary School, we just had one teacher and stayed in the same room all day, so I enjoyed changing classrooms and teachers for each subject. Mrs. Aline Bristol was my home room, English and Latin teacher, Ruth Hamilton taught P.E., Meredith Whitaker taught Home Ec, Annie Ruby Barnett taught Chemistry, Dale Starnes taught General Business, and Jean Christy had study hall.

At the time, I couldn't fully appreciate them, but through the years I came to realize the positive influence these wonderful teachers had on my life. Once I got as far as high school, I began to dare to hope, then believe that I could finish school and have a better future. I also had a few good friends who accepted me as I was, helped me feel I was a person of some value, and helped me learn to laugh.

When I was around twelve, I started growing. And growing. By the time I was thirteen and going into high school, I was about five inches taller than any of the other girls, and as tall as or taller than most of the boys. I was so skinny that people said I needed to stand twice in the same place to make a shadow, and that made me look even taller. I'd always felt ugly with the awful (I thought) gap in my teeth and mole beside my nose, and my shabby clothes. But before then, at least I could mingle with the group and not feel so self-conscious. Then suddenly, here I was—with my head a-stickin' up like a bean pole above everybody else and no way to hide. I felt like I *stuck out like a sore thumb*—ugly, awkward, and different from everybody else.

Why, God? Things were bad enough before. I wished I could just be invisible.

P.E. was a required course. Imagine my dismay when I went to P.E. and was told that I'd have to wear gym shorts. I wasn't allowed to wear pants, much less shorts. On top of that, they cost three dollars. I didn't want to even imagine the fit Mom would take if I asked for money for a pair of shorts. I finally got up the courage to ask her, and explained that it would be only in the gym where we did all kinds of exercises and played basketball, and everybody wore shorts. After going on about so much unnecessary foolishness at school, asking what good was that going to do me, and telling me it was a sin to wear shorts, and what kind of women did that, she finally said she'd order a pair of britches out of the catalog and I could wear them. Dad said I wudn't never goin' to be wearin' no shorts, and would get wore out with a belt if I ever did, even if I was a grown woman.

When I told Miss Hamilton that Mom and Dad wouldn't let me wear shorts, she agreed to let me wear jeans or pants. I would have loved a pair of blue jeans, but what Mom ordered was some navy blue linen-like ladies slacks. No girl my age would have been caught dead in them. They cost $1.98. I hated them cuss-ed "slacks."

Miss Hamilton must have seen my dilemma, and offered to let me work for the money to buy a pair of gym shorts. I know now that she invented little jobs for me to do to earn it. Then there was the problem of a tee shirt. When I told my friend, Barbara Mosteller about my problem, she brought me one of her tee shirts. It was blue and white striped. Thank goodness it was loose and thick, and I was flat chested, for I didn't own a bra.

Now I still had a problem. What was I going to do with the shorts? I couldn't take them home. And what was I going to do about the slacks? If I didn't take them to school, Mom would start asking questions. I hid the shorts and shirt here and there at school, and carried the slacks back and forth, so Mom would think I was wearing them. And prayed that nobody found out and told on me for wearing shorts at school.

I loved basketball and was very good at it. Miss Hamilton begged me to play on the school team, even offered to take me home after practice. I knew there was no use to ask Mom and Dad, for they'd never let me wear shorts in public. Even if I played basketball, I already looked odd enough without being the only one on the team wearing slacks. When I told her they wouldn't let me play ball, she offered to go to the house and talk to them and assure them she'd look after me. Oh, Lord, no! Not that! I wanted to play basketball as much as I'd ever wanted anything in my life, but couldn't tell her that. They'd find out I wore shorts at school and would kill me, or make me quit school. I told her I had too much work to do at home after school.

I was fascinated with typing and shorthand. I longed to take it, but it was hopeless for me as there was a typing fee. As I walked by the typing classroom, I slowed down so I could see them type a little. Barbara's older sister had taken typing and shorthand, then got a job as a secretary in Washington, D.C. It sounded like a dream come true.

Miss Whitaker let me do jobs for her to pay my Home Ec fee.

Mom let me take a piece of flour sack to class to use to learn how to hem a handkerchief. I made an apron from a feed sack. Then I had another problem. In order to pass Home Ec, we were required to complete a garment of some kind.

I'd have to ask Mom for money for pattern, fabric, thread and buttons. I knew she'd never give me the money, and if I did get any fabric, it would be whatever she wanted me to have—probably feed sacks, white thread and buttons cut off of something else. I'd never be allowed to choose. I dreaded the ordeal, and kept putting it off. I hated feeling like I always had to beg for everything I needed, then settle for whatever she said.

One day, Miss Whitaker handed out pattern books and told the girls to select a pattern for what they wanted to sew. Then, while they looked them over, she took me downtown to her home. I'd never seen such a fine house! I'm sure I must have gawked. She took me upstairs, where she had a big trunk with several pieces of fabric stored in it. She opened it and told me to choose anything I liked. I was overwhelmed by all the beautiful fabrics. I felt they were all much too nice for somebody like me. She finally chose one for me, with matching buttons and thread. I thought it was the prettiest fabric in the trunk.

Then she helped me select a dress pattern. I hated to cut the material, afraid I'd ruin it, but she assured me I could do it. I loved handling and sewing the fabric and loved that dress. I did a good job and was so proud of it. I've always been grateful to her, and never forgot what she taught me, for I not only developed a love of sewing, but learned what a difference one act of kindness could mean in someone's life.

I took two years of Home Ec, and especially liked the cooking and nutrition classes. I tried to tell Mom about new and useful things things I learned, but she wasn't interested. She took it as a personal insult to her way of doing things, and said I was *actin' uppity*, and *tryin' to get above my raisin'*. She wasn't "a-wastin' no money" on unnecessary ingredients to try new recipes, or even let me try anything different with what we had. I was to keep my naisty faingers to myself in her kitchen, unless it was a specific task she told me to do, and I had to do it it exactly how she said. I just couldn't understand anyone who wasn't interested in learning anything new.

A group of friends and I were talking at school one day, and we began discussing what we wanted to do when we left school. Various girls told what they wanted to do, and Christine said she wanted to be a nurse. That just absolutely rang a buzzer in my brain. A nurse! Yes! That's what I want to be. That's when I first had a goal in life other than get a good enough education to leave home and support myself.

I was in the ninth or tenth grade when they had a special assembly to give special awards to students on the honor roll, for perfect attendance, etc. They called name after name, and the student went up front, up the stage steps, across the stage to the center, accepted the certificate, then went on across the stage and down the steps on the other side.

I was sitting way in the back, a-mindin' my own business when the Superintendent started talking about a student who was so helpful to the teachers, was so courteous, and some more good stuff. I really wasn't paying much attention, but by the time he said the teachers had selected this student for special recognition, I was wondering, 'Golleee! Who in the world could that be?' when he said my name.

I didn't think I heard right. Everybody was clapping, and kids started craning around to look at me. I didn't know what to do, and finally stood up to acknowledge the applause, then started to sit back down. My knees were rubber. He told me to come on up, he had a gift of appreciation for me from Miss Hamilton and Miss Whitaker.

I just thought a row of corn looked long. It seemed to take forever to get up there and walk across that stage. Everything seemed unreal. I just wanted to grab the gift and run, and was flustered when I realized he was extending his hand to shake hands with me before giving me the gift. My face must have been blazing. Then I had to walk the forty miles back to my seat with everybody looking at me.

I didn't think I deserved any kind of honor—they were the ones who had been so good to me. Besides, I'd just as soon not have everybody lookin' at me. It near scared me to death. At the same time, it made me feel so good that the teachers liked me and approved of me. And had Mr. Hudson really actually shook hands with a nobody like me? Just like I was some body!

When I finally got back and collapsed in my seat, the kids around me started telling me to open my gift. It was a billfold with three one dollar bills inside. Most all the other girls had one, but I'd never had a billfold before. And that three dollars looked like a fortune to me.

Barbara Mosteller was one of my best friends. She lived on the lower part of Junaluska Creek. Her parents had five girls. I thought she was the prettiest girl in school with her dark naturally curly hair, and a smile that lit up her whole face. She was as sweet natured and kind as she was pretty. I could never see why she wanted me for a friend, but felt so lucky that she did. I felt like she was all the things I could never be.

Her daddy gave her a dime every day for lunch money. She went to the drugstore in town instead of eating in the lunch room. I don't know when or how it started, but she invited me to go to the drug store with her. I wanted to go with her, but hated to go and just sit there and look at her while she ate, since I didn't have money to buy anything. She said she didn't want to go by herself, and talked me into going with her.

When we got to the drug store, she got a coke from the icebox and asked for two cups of ice. A cup of ice was free. I didn't know that! She got two straws from the counter. Then she got a pack of six double crackers with peanut butter in between. When we sat down in a booth, she gave me three of her crackers, poured half the coke in my cup of ice and handed me a straw. She was very matter of fact about it, as if she were returning the favor of me coming with her.

This went on awhile, then Faye Ensley started coming with us. She also got a dime every day. She bought a coke and crackers, and like Barbara, shared them with me. So—we each had four crackers and they each gave me part of their coke. I thought it was the height of sophistication to go downtown every day for lunch and sit in a booth sipping coke through a straw.

Both of them seemed happy to share with me, just to have me come with them. I never felt like a "charity case" with either of them. But always in the back of my mind was the fear that Mom and Dad would find out what I was doing, and probably wouldn't let me go to school any more.

We had a lot of fun together. There was one male teacher, Mr. Starnes, that we liked to joke about and pull pranks on. I don't know why we chose him. Who can figure a kid's mind? Maybe it was because he always seemed so composed and in control. He was good to us and was really a nice person. He also drove our school bus.

We decided to try to upset his composure and felt that some ramps in his desk just might be the trick to do it. Anyone who ate ramps had to sit out in the hall in disgrace, and nobody was allowed to talk to them. We certainly were forbidden to bring them to school. Nobody but ignorant hillbillies had anything to do with ramps.

I brought some ramps from home and when we got to school, we made tracks to get in his classroom before he got the bus parked and the other students started coming in. We shoved the ramps in a lower desk drawer and got out of there.

It was way up in the day, and the ramps were livin' up to their reputation. Mr. Starnes asked if anybody had been eating ramps, but no one had. He finally found them in his desk drawer. We were right. It did upset his composure. Considerably! He tried his best to find out where they came from, but nobody knew a thing. He said they hadn't come in on his bus or he'd have known about it. That automatically excluded us angels. We sure wudn't about to tell him any different.

Kids gave me paper to do cartoon-type drawings on for them. I could draw Popeye, Olive Oyl, Swee'pea, Dagwood, Blondie, and other comic strip characters. Then I made up some characters and started drawing my own comic strip. I gave myself the name "The Junaluska Kid," and Barbara was "Black Bart." I did one just about every day. I didn't put any real names in the comics, in case a teacher got hold of one, but drew caricatures of both Mr. Starnes and Mrs. Bristol so closely that the kids knew who they were anyway. I did a comic strip about Mr. Starnes finding the ramps in his desk, and I think it was passed around to every kid in high school. They went into hysterics laughing. I'd discovered a talent, and learned that people could laugh with me, not at me.

A ventriloquist once brought a "dummy" and entertained during an assembly program. I was really impressed. One day, we were goofing off and I decided to be funny like the dummy. I could look cross-eyed, and make some weird faces. I changed my voice, moved my mouth like the dummy, assumed the cross-eyed look and addressed everyone as "Howdy, Podnuh." and did some funny oneliners. First it was a couple of girl friends, then other kids started asking me to make that funny face and say my lines. They laughed til they cried.

I could also instantly assume an innocent dead-pan face. Sometimes in class, one of my friends would look at me, I'd look crosseyed or do that weird face, and they'd start giggling. Immediately I'd assume the dead-pan look, in case the teacher looked up, and that just made them worse. When the teacher looked up, there'd be four or five kids giggling, and there I'd be, studying my book, innocent as a lamb; the most well-behaved girl in school.

About the time I started high school, Mom and Dad started going to church regularly. Around the tenth grade, Faye Ensley started coming to our church, then coming home with me to spend the night. We were best friends. She wasn't intimidated by Mom and Dad, and often talked them into letting me go home with her to spend the night. She could charm a snake. She and Barbara quit school around the eleventh grade, but Faye and I still saw each other often, and remained the best of friends.

My last two years in school, us Junaluska girls became friends with our bus driver, Paul Anderson. He knew we were good girls, just having fun, and laughed along with us. Dugan and Bunt Shields' daughter, Christine started playing hooky, and spent about one day a week with my sister-in-law Ruth, or Ruth's sister, Thelma McClure, who were her cousins. She begged me to come with her. When Christine started in, you might as well go along, for she didn't know what "no" meant.

I wasn't too hard to convince, though. Pretty soon it was me, Christine, Sister and Harriett. We'd go spend the day with Ruth, Thelma, or my sister Alma, who lived in one of the Extract houses right up from Ruth's sister, Thelma. We helped them fix dinner, wash clothes, or whatever they were doing, played with their youngens, sat around and sung, and had the best time. It was good to just have fun and see how other people lived. Paul said he'd never tell on us. We'd tell him where we were going that morning and he'd let us off the bus, then stop and pick us up in the afternoon. We'd go home on the bus, like good girls were supposed to do.

I didn't know Ruth very well. Even though she was my sister-in-law, I hadn't been around her much. We had a lot of fun at her house, and I got to know and love her and my nephew Ronnie, who was a sweet little boy between two and three. She didn't tell on us for playing hooky, and invited us to come back any time.

I practiced writing like Mom and learned to be such a good forger that nobody caught on when I wrote my own excuses. Back then, they used pen and ink. When I got my report card, there would be some days absent on it, so I put a tiny bit of clorox on the days absent square and bleached it out before I showed it to Mom. No such a thing as White-Out then. One thing about being too strict on a child—it doesn't make a good child, it makes a deceptive child.

All through school, I never went to a ball game or any school activity outside of school hours on school grounds, didn't go to the junior or senior banquet, prom or senior trip, and never went out on a date. I went to school and came home. Period. (Except for playing hooky.)

When Mom and Dad started going to church, at least I got to go to church. Dad never met a stranger, and was always inviting the preacher or somebody home with us on Sunday. After Mom started seeing people and getting out some, she started acting better, and didn't act like she was mad at me all the time. They bought a few inexpensive clothes for me, too, I guess because when they went to other churches, they were ashamed of how I looked compared to other girls. I still didn't get to choose anything I wore.

When Lawerence was eighteen, he married Roberta Passmore, who was fifteen. She was and is one of my favorite people. We've always been good friends. She is quiet, soft spoken and shy—the opposite of Lawerence. All the young folks (except me, of course) went to the *show* (movies) on Saturday evening. They always showed a Western and a continued story. A few times Roberta invited me to go to town with them, and they took me to the show. Preachers preached about that being a awful bad sin, but I didn't see nothing wrong with it.

Every time I passed from one grade to another, I gained more confidence that I just might graduate from High School after all, if Dad and Mom didn't make me quit. My dream of becoming a nurse began to seem like a possibility. I asked

God to make it possible, if that was what He wanted me to be. I thought about Mammy, and how I'd loved helping take care of her, about my uncle Dewey, a diabetic who died with gangrene of his foot, about Thelma and what a hard time she had when Norman was born, about my aunt Lizzie who had died from malnutrition, and how it might have made a difference if someone had known what to do for them. I wanted to learn about medicine and how to help sick people get well.

As graduation finally approached, I knew I had to make some decisions, and prayed for guidance. I'd heard preachers say God "gave them a calling" to preach. I felt that my calling was to be a nurse. I thought that to be able to relieve suffering and help people get well would be the most wonderful thing I could ever do. I was determined that regardless of what Mom and Dad said, with God's help, somehow, I was going to be a nurse.

A girl I knew worked as a nurse's aide in the hospital after school. I asked her questions about her job, and she told me what she did there. Dr. Van Gorder's step-mother was a teacher in study hall and I asked her how to get a job at the hospital. She told me I needed to go down to the hospital and talk to the administrator, a woman named Mary Willie Gentry.

I left school early one day in time to get back and catch the bus and walked down to the Rodda—Van Gorder Hospital and Clinic. I talked with Mary Willie, and to my amazement, was hired on the spot. She answered my questions and explained everything to me. She said I'd have a day and a half off a week, and would be paid sixty dollars a month for three months, then be raised to eighty-five. They would train me to do whatever I needed to learn. I would start on Monday after graduation on Friday.

She told me I'd need to wear a white uniform, hose and shoes, that Nichols' Store sold them, and most of the nurses had a charge account with them. They'd let me get what I needed and I could make payments later.

I left there practically walking on air. At long last, I could see a way beginning to open up for me. I was so surprised at how friendly Mary Willie had been, and how she had treated me with kindness and respect. I surely must be dreaming—everything was too perfect!

I hadn't said any more to Mom and Dad about being a nurse. I dreaded the time when I'd have to tell them. I knew I'd have to leave home if I took the job, and was going to leave anyway, but didn't know if they'd ever have anything else to do with me, beat me to death, or what. But this time they were not going to ruin things for me, no matter what they did or said. I couldn't face staying at home any more, regardless of what I had to do to get away.

Except get married. I wasn't about to exchange one prison for another. Of course I felt like any other normal girl, and noticed boys could be pretty interesting. I'd even tried "smoochin'" a time or two. At one time, I was sure I was in love, but when I thought about my sisters and other young girls who'd married at a very young age, boys lost their appeal to me. Being barefooted and pregnant was one thing fer shore I didn't want nothing to do with. I was not going to have a baby every other year, have to give an account to some man and ask his permission for every move I made, and be totally dependent on him. I'd made up my mind and vowed that I would not be dominated by, or dependent on anyone ever again.

Maybe some day, after I got to be a nurse and could be independent, I might meet someone I trusted enough to consider marriage. Or maybe not. I was going to leave that in God's hands. I was going to have to trust men a whole lot more than I did then.

I couldn't wait to tell Ruth and Sweetie I had a job at the hospital. I don't remember exactly how it came about—either they told me I could, or I asked them if I could stay with them when I started working. I offered to pay them board. They said for me to come on, I could have my own room at their house. I'd never been so excited about anything in my whole life.

I was also scared to death. I had many unanswered questions. Am I really smart enough? What if Mom was right when she said I was "too nasty" to be a nurse? What if people didn't like me, once they really got to know me? I didn't feel like I was as good as other people, and wasn't worthy of anything good. I'd always felt like I was on the outside looking in, and didn't truly belong anywhere.

I needed to get my uniforms and be ready to go to work, so the week-end before graduation, I told Mom and Dad about my job and my plans to stay with Sweetie and Ruth. To my great surprise, they stayed calm and didn't offer any objections or say anything. Dad even took us to town that Saturday and Mom went to Nichols' store with me. Mr. Nichols set me up an account and the saleslady helped me select two uniforms, nurse's shoes, hose, a garter belt and white shoe polish. And I finally got a real honest-to-goodness storebought slip and underwear. But Dad and Mom didn't even offer to help me pay for my things. I got them on the credit in my own name, with no money down. They didn't set any certain amount to be paid or any certain day to make a payment. I found it hard to believe the store owner had confidence in me and trusted me enough to earn the money to pay for them later. Surely God was working things out.

I was puzzled about them actin' so nice to me, though. Then I figured they probably thought I'd make a fool out of myself and come crawlin' back home in disgrace—as the old saying goes, *"Give him enough rope and he'll hang hisself."* Then they'd have me right where they wanted me.

The Friday I graduated was the happiest day of my life. With God's help, I'd done it! My whole being was shouting, "Thank You, Lord!" to think that after a lifetime in prison, the doors had been thrown open and I could just fly right out.

Actually, they had. And there were many doors ahead just waiting to open and let me walk through.

Faye gave me a nice graduation card with three dollars inside for a graduation gift. After the graduation ceremony, I went to the late show with her and some other girl friends to celebrate. I never had got to go to the show and stay out late before. I remember almost dancing for joy down the sidewalk toward the theater. The expression, "floating on air" closely describes the way I felt.

After the show, Christine and I went to Sweetie and Ruth's and spent the night. When I went home the next day, I started puttin' my stuff in a paper poke to be ready to leave after preachin' the next day.

Sunday evenin' about two o'clock, Sweetie, Ruth and Ronnie came to get me. I had my clothes and stuff all packed up and ready to go.

And I never looked back.

MORE THEN AND NOW

I think I should take a little time here to again reflect on the comparison of then and now, and being thankful for what we have now.

I'm sure there are needy children now, just as there was back in the 1930's and 1940's. The definition of a "need," however, has changed drastically from the 1940's to the present day. Even low income children of today are rich when compared to most children of that time. There are many social and economic resources available now that were unheard of then.

For example: Is it possible that today there could be any child go through the entire twelve years of school having no lunch, and no one be aware of it?

If a child came to school without shoes or even a sweater when it was cold and blowing snow, never had paper, pencil or other school supplies, day after day, year after year, would nobody notice? Or investigate? Or get help for them?

Children who lived within a mile of the schoolhouse walked to school back then. The rest rode the school bus. I don't remember one student who drove their own car to school. Most of the teachers didn't even have a car. When you drive by a high school today, the large parking lot is filled with late model cars. I'm sure they don't all belong to the teachers.

Children then wanted what other children had or wore, whether it was a certain style of clothing, toy, or whatever. They wanted to fit in with the group. But there wasn't near as much "stuff" for them to demand as there is now. Today's children also want whatever is in vogue, whether it's a certain style of notebook or a certain brand name of jeans, shirt, pants or shoes. Many of them also have their own room at home, a TV, computer, electronic games, CD's, stereo, telephone, and spending money. Some of them spend enough on junk food, recreational activities and cars to support a small family.

I wonder if they appreciate what they have—and if it's good for them to have so much simply given to them without their earning or contributing anything.

On the other hand, I wonder how many times a week they sit down together as a family and share a meal. How many of them have a stable family and someone who cares enough to see that they are taught any kind of moral values? Or will take time to listen and help them with their problems? They face incredible peer pressure related to things we never even thought of .

They are blessed with many opportunities, however, that were unheard of in my time. Many young boys and girls left the mountains because there was no hope of a good future if they stayed in this area. Cutting cordwood just didn't pay enough to raise a family. My brothers all left the area to find work. Three went to Georgia to work as soon as they were old enough, and never came back here to live.

A good future is almost taken for granted for any child who wants to take advantage of their opportunities—and a girl's future doesn't have to mean being *barefooted and pregnant*. They can make choices now. If they don't get a good education, that is their choice.

Thank God that at least they have hope, and can find help if they need it.

ON MY OWN

SETTLING IN AND
STARTING TO WORK

Ruth and Sweetie lived on Slaughter Pen Road, about a mile from town. The paved street, cracked sidewalk and far spaced street lights ended at the park, just a little ways off Main Street up the road toward their house. They lived back out of sight in a holler, on a routed-out dirt road. A car could usually make it in and out all right, but after a rain it was too slick to risk sliding off into a rut and getting stuck or damaging a car. Sweetie had no problem going in and out with his pickup, though.

They had a living room, kitchen and two bedrooms, with a full length front porch and a smaller back porch where the wringer washer sat. The spring was down a little trail behind the house. They had a nice big garden on the hill above the house. Sweetie was a good gardener and loved to work in it. He had to have his corn patch, tomatoes and okra.

Ronnie was just a little feller, and slept in his bed in the room with them, so they let me have the back bedroom. I thought it was the height of luxury to have my own room and could put my stuff wherever I wanted it. Not that I had much stuff to put anywhere, though. All I had was a few clothes, my two new uniforms and nurse's shoes. Everything I owned could have been put into two grocery bags. At home, Mom had assigned me one drawer of a dresser in the middle bedroom to keep my things in. It was never crowded.

Not only had I never had my very own room before, it was the first time my bed was the only one in the room. And the room had a door. At Dad and Mom's house, Oval and Vernon's bed was right beside mine and I could look right over the foot of my bed and see Mom and Dad's bed in the other room. There was no privacy, as there wasn't an inside door in the house. I undressed in the dark and slept in my petticoat. (Women used to say they slept in their petticoat tail.)

I still couldn't believe I was a high school graduate. I was the first one in my family to finish school. I'd heard that my first cousin, Ray Hicks in Tennessee, had graduated from high school, and he was the only Hicks in my grandpa Hicks' family ever known to finish high school. Boys usually quit school along about the fifth or sixth grade, and before my sisters and many other girls got to be my age, they were already married and had one or two younguns.

My hope of being a nurse began to seem like a possibility now, and I was excited and anxious to get started to work. At the same time, I was cautious about being too hopeful. Mom had drummed that into my head all my life with all her fatalistic and pessimistic sayin's, like, "*Laugh before breakfast, cry before supper.*" I'd always had the feeling of standing outside and looking in while others enjoyed life in a world I could never enter. Good things happened to someone else, not me.

Most people thought that nobody but outlaws and bootleggers lived up on Junaluska Creek. Did I dare hope that other people might treat me as their equal? I knew I was at least of average intelligence, but hadn't had enough social contacts to know how to interact with other people except kids at school. Could an ignorant girl from Junaluska Creek ever really amount to something, and be like other people? Many times, trying to finish high school had prompted the question, "Just who do you think you are?" Or brought the accusation of "tryin' to get above your raisin'," or "makin' a educated fool out a yerself."

Just getting away from home changed my whole outlook. Sweetie and Ruth seemed glad to have me with them, and made me feel welcome. In the relaxed and easy-going atmosphere of their home, it was like living in a different world. I began to feel good about the possibilities in my new life.

The next morning, as I got ready to go to work, it felt so strange to get dressed in my new storebought underwear, slip with lace at the top, uniform, white hose and shoes. I had the sensation of standing over in a corner watching me pretending to be somebody else. That couldn't be me! Ruth kept telling me I'd do fine, and Sweetie said not to worry, I'd catch on.

After breakfast I rode to town with Sweetie in his pickup truck as he went to work. I had to be there by 6:30. When I got out of his truck and he drove off, leaving me standing there on the street corner in the early morning daylight, I felt a sudden panic, and asked myself the same question General George Custer probably asked himself right before the arrow hit: "What am I doin' here?"

The town of Andrews had three *red lights* (traffic lights). The Rodda-Van Gorder Hospital and Clinic was located upstairs in a corner building at the middle red light, over Nichols' Clothing Store. The entrance was on a side street. Steep, dimly lit stairs about five feet wide curved up to the waiting room, or lobby. There was no elevator. The only other entrance was from the fire escape in the back alley.

Today, a building like that would never be approved for a hospital; such a thing as a building code was unheard of then.

It's hard to describe my feelings as I went up those dimly lit, creaky stairs. The only time I'd ever been inside a hospital was when I'd come to the front office and applied for a job. I had no real idea what to expect. I was scared to death, yet excited, and wondered: Am I smart enough to do this, will they like me, do I look all right, am I too tall, clumsy, and ugly? I was so bashful around people, would I seem ignorant—or—maybe—maybe I just better turn around and get out of here before somebody sees me.

For a few moments I'd forgotten what had helped me get through those years at home and finish school: Ask the Lord's guidance, then keep on truckin' and keep on trustin'. It seemed that God had worked miracles just for me, personally, to get me this far. This was the only way I knew how to get beyond my past. I could face dying easer than going back to what I'd left.

I'd found it wasn't very helpful to me to set a certain time to pray, and then go on about my business. I never knew what was going to come up, and I needed to know He was right there with me all the time. It had become second nature to me to talk to God silently from my heart as I went along, just to reassure myself that He was with me every minute.

I found myself asking from my heart, "God, oh God, please, please help me. Make them like me. Please, Lord…help me to learn, and be a good nurse, and make my life count for something good in this world…Lord, are you there? Are You listening?"

Mary Willie had showed me where to go when I was there before. As I was sending up my silent, urgent prayers, I slowly kept climbing the stairs, and when I finally reached the top at the lobby, went straight on back to the nurse's desk.

Everyone was friendly, introduced themselves to me, and welcomed me. They looked so clean and neat in their white uniforms and shoes. For the first time in my life, I felt that I was dressed as well as anyone else in the group, and that made me feel good. My uniform was as nice as anyone else's, and it made me appreciate the people at Nichols store for their kindness and help.

The tired, sleepy looking night nurse was getting ready to give the morning report. It was almost like hearing a foreign language as I watched her turn the cards on the Kardex and give the morning report. Each patient had a card with their name, age, diagnosis, medications and treatments, and any special instructions on it. As I listened to her report about each of the patients and heard the others' comments, my mind started buzzing with one question after another. What was an OB? Did she say…"catheter?"…What in the world is that? And cc's output? What did that mean—answer a buzzer? HS medicine? PRN? BID? TID? A dram? Every patient had a diagnosis, but what's that? Every time somebody said something, I had a question.

Of course, I had enough sense not to butt in to ask. But I'm sure I must have looked like a big-eyed boy at a picnic—with his mouth hung wide open.

After report, one of them told me to go along with her and work with her today. Before long, a buzzer rang in the hall. She told me to come on, and was off like a shot, with me right behind her. As she passed a numbered panel on the wall, she pushed a button that made an arrow disappear behind a number. She went to that room number and asked if she could help them. Oh! So that's how you answer a buzzer.

Right by the desk was a thing I heard them call "a dumb waiter." One of the nurses put her head inside the dumb waiter hole and hollered "Hazel," and in a few seconds, "Hazel" answered, "Yes?" The nurse told her what she wanted her to know and Hazel answered, "O.K." Huh! What a trick!

I learned that Hazel Wilson and Kate Wooten worked in the kitchen and did all the food preparation. The kitchen was on the first floor underneath the nurse's station, where the shoe shop used to be. The entrance was from the side street, on down from the main entrance. There was no way to get from the hospital into the kitchen without going down the stairs to the outside and down the street, and there was no telephone connection. The dumb waiter shaft served as an intercom.

The dumb waiter operated by pulling one of two strong, heavy ropes to make it go up or down. In a few minutes, I heard a rubbing noise and saw the two ropes by the dumb waiter moving, and somebody said, "The trays are out!" When the dumb waiter stopped, there were two shelves—like in a box on its side, with two breakfast trays on each shelf.

I'd never imagined such a thing! Boy, howdy, wouldn't me'n Oval'n Vernon a-had us a time, if we'd a had one of them thangs out in the barn loft?

One of them started getting the trays off the dumb waiter and handing them out for us to take to the patient rooms—called "out on the floor," then when it was empty, pulled overhanded on the rope to let the dumb waiter back down for more trays.

As we passed out trays, I learned how to roll the patients up in bed, help them wash their hands and face, and position the bedside table for them so they could eat. The beds were all manually operated, probably army surplus.

As I worked, I began to learn the layout of the hospital. There were eight patient rooms and twenty one beds in the hospital. The rooms were located around the corner perimeter of the building, with windows overlooking the street. The row of rooms on the side facing main street was separated by a lobby in the center from the row of rooms facing the side street. One small private room was located on past and behind the nurse's desk.

The nursery was also on past and behind the desk, in the corner of the building. It was a cubicle just large enough to walk around and between four bassinets and a cart full of diapers, baby clothes and bottles.

You went to the right through the swinging doors on toward the back to the doctors' private office, operating room, and scrub foyer. Make another right turn through some more swinging doors to go through the linen room, lab, x-ray, office, and clinic. These areas were located in the interior portion of the building, parallel to the patient rooms.

There were no private bathrooms. A small bathroom with a sink and commode was at the far end of the hall next to the clinic, for the patients on that side of the lobby. A larger bathroom, with an old clawfooted bath tub that set on the floor, was near the nurse's desk for the patients on this side. Storage shelves on the wall above the tub held supplies, such as toilet paper, white enamelware enema cans, red rubber hot water bottles and ice collars.

Patients were checked at intervals to see if anyone needed help with eating or wanted more coffee. The ones who couldn't manage were fed. Coffee was brought to the patient in either a small stainless steel insulated container or a small ceramic pot, to keep it hot. We'd never heard of styrofoam at that time.

It was strange, and different from the way I was raised, to see toast on the breakfast trays and "light bread" or rolls on the dinner and supper trays, instead of cathead biscuits or cornbread.

I learned first thing that coffee and cigarettes were considered a necessity for most nurses to keep going. Just about everybody smoked. There was an ashtray on the nurse's desk and others here and there in the area. Each shift got coffee from the kitchen, and the coffee pot was always hot. Everybody had their own cup and could get a cup of coffee whenever they had time. They had coffee and cigarettes and chatted while the patients ate.

As soon as the patients finished eating and we'd sent their trays down to the kitchen on the dumb waiter, "A.M. Care" was given. Patients able to do their own bath were rolled up in bed or sat on the side of the bed and given a basin of warm water, soap, wash cloth and towel. Everyone was asked if they wanted their back washed, or were given a back rub. Others were given a bed bath by a nurse. Linen was changed wherever needed. I learned what a draw sheet is, and how to use one to pull a patient up in bed or turn them over.

The "linen chute" was most interesting. On past the nurse's desk, on the outside window sill, was built what looked like a wooden box with a door about eighteen inches wide and two feet high. To put something in the laundry, the window was raised, the door of the box opened and the dirty linen put into the opening, where it fell down out of sight. When you looked down from the window, you could see that the wooden box was actually the top of a metal-lined chute connected to the roof of a small building down on the street—not much bigger than a dog house but about six feet high. The laundry landed down there in the little building, and a man in a cleaners' van picked it up every day from down there.

Later on, I heard a loud commotion and hollerin' from down there. Somebody had throwed a big armload of laundry down on top of the man's head while he happened to be in there picking up the laundry. From the laughter up here, and the thumpedy-bump and hollerin' from down there, tryin' to get out of the tangle in the dark, I realized it wasn't always an accident. I *betchey* eight or ten bedsheets does hit a man's noggin purty hard a-fallin' from that distance.

After A.M. Care, all the pitchers were filled with fresh ice water. Mr. Bill Webb, "the ice man" had an ice plant over at the edge of town. Every day he delivered big blocks of ice to the hospital, drugstore and other businesses in town. They were probably about eighteen inches square. He delivered the ice from the back of his pickup truck, which was lined with a heavy tarp under and over the blocks of ice. He used some huge ice tongs to handle and pick up the blocks. He was a familiar sight, coming in with a wide grin and hello, carrying a big block of ice. We had a metal lined ice cart which held one of the big blocks, and when we needed ice, used an ice pick to chip off small pieces to put into a glass or pitcher.

In the afternoon, one of the OB's couldn't void and had to be "catheterized." I wasn't quite sure what they were talking about, but was told to come along to observe and help with that. So—I learned that an OB was a woman who'd had a baby, and now she couldn't pee, or "make water," only they called it "void." I learned how to feel to see if the bladder was distended; how to massage the uterus and tell the difference in the uterus and bladder. But I was totally amazed when the nurse put the catheter into the urethra and urine started running out.

Well, I'll be doggone! I didn't know there was two openings down there! I'd just supposed a woman peed and had a baby through the same opening—I guess I'd never really thought about it.

It may sound hard to believe how totally ignorant I was, but I was *dumb as a rock*. A person's "privates" was simply not talked about when I was growing up.

And I was almost eighteen years old!

I was kept so busy on my first day that it was gone before I knew it. Everyone was patient with me, and the nurse I worked with that day explained what things were, how things were done, and answered my questions as we went along and did our work. I learned how to fold and tuck a sheet to make "hospital corners" on the beds, give a bed bath, put people on bed pans, do a catheterization, measure urine in cc's (cubic centimeters), and any number of things. Even with her explanations, I'm sure I must have asked dozens of questions. I learned that the medical profession had a language all their own.

Later, when I was in Nurse's Training, I was astounded at what I'd been doing in the hospital by the end of my first week there. I was doing unsupervised procedures that a third year student wasn't allowed to do.

When I got off work that afternoon, I was fairly exploding with excitement at the the realization that I really and truly had actually worked all day in a hospital. My vocabulary had expanded by at least fifty words. And how I had enjoyed it! My spirit was singing with thankfulness that things had gone so well. I knew that the Lord really had been listening to my silent, desperate prayers as I'd slowly climbed those stairs this morning.

Was that only this morning? I'd worked my tail off, and was tired, but it was a happy tiredness. The patients had seemed to appreciate little things I did for them. They encouraged me, reassuring me that I was doing "great," and was going to make a "fine" nurse. This first day, I'd learned that patients usually returned kindness with kindness. I found that everybody in this town including hospital personnel, knew everybody else, knew I was new on the job, and wanted to help me.

This shore was better'n gettin' out a-stubbin' my toes and steppin' on sharp rocks a-hoein' corn barefooted, 'n choppin' wood 'n makin' blisters 'n gettin' splinters in my hands. And feeling isolated, hopeless and powerless.

And nobody growled at me about nuthin' or give me one single silent, disapproving glance.

In fact, everybody acted as if they liked me, and we'd had such fun working together. When it was time to go home, everybody gave me a big smile, and told me "'Bye. See you tomorrow." Tomorrow! I can't describe the joy those words brought. They seemed to be glad that I was coming back tomorrow. Me! And I could hardly wait to come back. I wanted to learn more, and loved being with such nice people.

A totally different girl came bouncing down those stairs that afternoon. I was so excited that I forgot about being tired. I took off toward home almost at a lope. I couldn't wait to get there and tell Ruth and Sweetie all about my day. For the first time in my life, I think, I didn't dread to go home.

It was so good to have somebody who acted as if what I had to say was worth listening to. I was still a little hesitant, and watched what I said. But I was finding that I could tell them things without worrying about having everything I said picked apart and scrutinized, then finding myself being made fun of, or being reprimanded for saying or doing something wrong, and wondering how I'd got myself into this mess.

I still couldn't quite believe they could be this happy all the time, and weren't going to suddenly get mad at each other or at me for something.

Most mountain men took great pride in showing their woman and everybody else *"who wears the pants around here."* A woman was supposed to *stay in her place*, keep her mouth shut and told, *"ask me no questions and I'll tell you no lies."*. If there was any bossin' and braggin' to be done, he'd do it.

I soon found out that things were a lot different around here. Sweetie was always laughing and joking about something, and was always teasing Ruth. But when she'd had enough of his clownin' around, all Ruth had to do was say, "Ah, Sweetie!" in a fake reprimand. He might laugh a little as a way of response, but he was immediately under control.

I didn't know which was the funniest—to see that little five foot woman boss around a six foot two man, or see a big husky six foot two man let a little five foot woman boss him around. They both knew who wore the pants around here, and both enjoyed it. One thing was obvious—they loved each other.

They'd lost two babies before Ronnie came along, and he was the light of their life. Ruth devoted herself to him, and kept him spotlessly clean. She was one of these rare women that always looked neat and clean, even when she was dirty. I told her she always looked like she just came out of the beauty shop, and she did. With her naturally curly black hair and brown eyes, she was a beautiful lady—inside and out. She was quiet and easy-going, had a soft voice, and I never heard her raise her voice and sound angry.

She was also a great housekeeper. I don't remember her going around cleaning all the time, but their house was always neat and clean. She just seemed to have a knack for it. Unfortunately, I never learned her secret.

I bought some hair curlers to roll my hair. They didn't make it as kinky as the homemade strips cut off a tobacco can. My hair looked a lot better now that I had some shampoo and could wash it whenever I wanted to. Then I decided to cut my hair. I'd wanted some bangs since I was a little girl. Coonie'd had bangs, but I didn't.

Since I couldn't afford to go to the beauty shop for a permanent, and wouldn't know how act or what to say if I did, I decided to do it myself. I bought a Toni™ home permanent and read the instructions through several times. The instructions even told you how to cut your hair. Ruth helped me, and we cut some bangs and cut my hair medium short, then put in the permanent. Lord, I thought them curly bangs was purty. Made me think of Shirley Tample. I was beginning to look and feel like a different girl.

I figured Mom and Dad would "have a fit" when they saw me, as I'd always been absolutely forbidden to cut my hair, especially to have bangs, and I was still scared of what they might do. I'd sneaked and cut my hair some when I was in about the tenth grade, and didn't ever do that again. Now that I was getting a taste of living my own life, I intended to continue. I'd do what I could to keep peace with them, but was determined to never let them dominate me again.

Sweetie and Ruth got their mail at the Post Office. I thought it was real "citi-fied" to go to the Post Office and call for your mail, like I'd done for the Christy's. They told me I could do it myself, if I wanted to. That absolutely thrilled me to death.

I didn't expect much mail, but went down and told the Postmaster I'd like to call for it, instead of having it sent up on the creek. That may not sound like a big deal to anyone else, but it gave me such a sense of freedom to know I could get mail and Mom couldn't open it and read it first, and pry into my business. I knew she'd burnt some letters addressed to me a few times, or tore letters up and throwed 'em in the creek because they were from somebody she didn't like.

Gollee—this was better'n me and Sister a-havin' our mailbox under a rock down in the pasture. And it didn't have to be kept secret. Here at the Post Office, I could get mail from anybody, and nobody could get it but me. It made me feel like a reg'lar person to walk up to that Post Office window and get my mail just like other people did.

Sometimes I had to stand in line, but I enjoyed it, as other people talked to me while we waited. I got acquainted with a lot of people that way. Andrews was a friendly town. It felt so good when I met somebody and they'd smile and speak to me like an old friend the next time I saw them. I was proving to myself that I wasn't the kind of awful person Mom had made me think I was.

After a few days, I didn't even have to say my name at the window. When one of the postal clerks saw me, they'd say "Hello," and either tell me I didn't have any mail or just reach and hand it to me.

I also learned that, in fact, it was against the law for anybody, even Dad or Mom, to get my mail and open it.

Goody Ha Ha Ha!

◆   ◆   ◆

If The Great Physician had written a prescription for me for what I most needed at that time in my life, I'm sure the names Sweetie, Ruth and Ronnie would be written in the space for the prescribed therapy.

Then again, maybe He did do just that.

They gave me exactly what I needed. I don't think they ever really realized the extent of the healing they helped bring about in my life and in my heart.

GETTIN' TO KNOW PEOPLE

The names I recall were Wilma Crawford, Lucille Holland, Mae Wooten Griffith, Audrey Cole, Judy Hawk, Ruth Mashburn, and Artie McConnell. Wanda Hardin was a high school girl who worked from after school til eleven. Wilma and Lucille were two of the most fun persons I was ever around, yet probably had the hardest life of anybody there. When Wilma laughed, it was like a man's deep hearty guffaw. Mae was a small, pretty woman with dark brown eyes and black hair. She was quiet and gentle, and had a soft, soothing voice. She reminded me of my sister-in-law Ruth. She could calm a patient by simply talking to them, and was good with sick babies.

Artie was an older woman, and her children were older than me, but she could sure turn out the work. She was a regular "trash mover." She knew more old timey home remedies than anyone I've ever known—and they worked, too.

Judy printed faster than many people can write. It looked like typescript, or slightly back-slanted calligraphy, with each letter perfectly formed. It was so beautiful that I liked to just look at it. I'd watch her print and was amazed that someone could do that so easily. Her husband, Mickey Hawk was a policeman. Ruth Mashburn was married to Fred, who worked in the office. They were very religious, but not in a condescending, pious manner, just good people. She was kind and easy-going, and always had a laugh just ready to bubble out from under her smile.

Audrey was a widow, but was cheerful and a good worker. She'd have made a great stand-up comic. She had one story she told that gave us all stitches. When she started it, she'd fling out a hand, palm side up, with her thumb across it, and say "Pea-orly, and there stood Grady......with his eyes...lookin' like two blubbers in a pee-pot." The last line said something like "And there I was, settin' a-straddle of a bob-wire fence, both feet on the same side, and that's the last I seen of Sal."

At shift-changing time when a bunch of them were together, it sounded like a big party going on.

Charles "Bud" Jones was the orderly. He was a tall, lean colored man who was called upon whenever they needed a man to do something for a male patient, plus run errands for the doctors—not always pertaining to hospital work. He was always pleasant and quietly went about doing whatever it was he did. I soon became good friends with him. We always found something to have a good laugh about. He could make a funny comment that summed up and capped any situation. He called me "Highpockets," and I told him all he ever done was stand around a-holdin' up the walls. We both knew that was a joke. They kept him busy. But he did love to fish, and sometimes sneaked off and went.

Ruth Neal and Betty Wood were R.N.'s who worked with the doctors in the clinic and operating room. Betty's sister, Martha Caldwell, and Jean Stewart, another R.N. from Robbinsville, also worked there during the time I was there.

The lab technician was Frances McPherson. "Miss Frances" was a tiny, feisty little elderly lady who seemed to never run out of energy. Janice Barton helped her in the lab. Kenneth Ledford, the x-ray technician, also worked in the lab. The only people I remember from the office was Mary Willie Gentry and her brother, Fred Mashburn.

It was common for them to call most everybody by their last name. I was "Hicks." (Ruth) "Neal" was the "head nurse" in charge of nursing personnel. She made out the work schedule. She was a petite woman with red hair and was the perfect role model as a competent, intelligent R.N.

The nurses' aides were called "nurses" by everyone, so I will refer to them by that title. None of the nurses in the hospital had any formal training. They had been hired when Dr. Van Gorder and Dr. Rodda started the hospital, and learned how to do things as they worked on the job. They actually performed on the level of a RN—and beyond. They mixed medicines into, started and gave IV's, gave medications, assisted with deliveries, took care of the mothers and babies, changed dressings and did whatever else needed to be done.

After the clinic closed in the afternoon, they evaluated any patients that came in and most of the time, went ahead and treated them and gave them medication to do them overnight until the clinic opened. They taught me a lot about first aid. I'm still amazed at the size of a cut that can be closed with some steri-strips and adhesive tape by someone who knows how to do it.

The RN's were only there during the day, and then they worked back in the clinic and operating room. A patient needed very special skilled care if one of them came out on the floor. They and the doctors came back at night only if there was an extreme emergency.

Everybody supposedly worked eight hour shifts, and worked a rotation schedule of one week 7-3, one week 3-11, one week 11-7, then a week on relief—which was two days 7-3, two days 3-11 and two nights of 11-7. We got a day and a half off each week. In order to get two days off together, we could trade around and take one day off one week and two the next, as long as the shifts were covered. Those were standard working hours in 1952. I quickly learned to sleep when I had the chance, regardless of the time of day or night.

There were two people on each shift. They had to take care of the hospital patients and nursery on day shift, and take care of outpatients and help with deliveries on 3-11 and 11-7. Each shift had definite responsibilities and nobody left work undone from their shift to carry over to the next. Most days, we worked overtime at least an hour. It wasn't that we didn't work hard—there was usually just too much to finish in eight hours. There were so few of us that sometimes one of us had to stay and work another shift if someone was too sick to come in. We didn't have maids. When a patient went home, we stripped the bed and cleaned the room as soon as possible.

I was paid a salary of $60.00 a month and promised a raise to $85.00 after three months if my work was satisfactory. That was the most any of the nurses made. Out of this amount, I had to buy my uniforms, hose and shoes. I paid Sweetie $20.00 a month for board.

That salary may not sound like much, and it wasn't enough for the work we did and the unpaid overtime we put in, but there were no other jobs available back then.

I thought I was lucky by comparison to the others. I don't see how some of the women made it. Almost all of them had small children. One of them had a husband who laid drunk all the time and contributed nothing—and tried to steal what little money she made for them to live on. Two more of them had left their husbands and were raising their children alone. One was widowed. As I picked up trays after the patients ate, I saved any unopened milk or food they could use for them to take home to their children. After all, anything returned to the kitchen was supposed to be discarded. Why not put it to good use?

You'd think they'd be a bunch of complaining, hard-to-get-along with women, with all the troubles they had, but they were wonderful people to work with. I really liked everyone who worked there, and they took me right under their wing. We had fun together, even though we stayed on the run most of the time. Somebody always had a good joke to tell, and there was much laughter and easy banter. It probably relieved the pressure from the hardships in their lives and the things we encountered at work. They all worked well together, and helped each other. Through the years I've never known a more compatible and good-natured group of workers.

I was timid about asking questions at first. I'd always been told that it was bad manners to ask people questions. In school, I was too bashful, and didn't want any attention drawn to me. Mom got aggravated if I asked her questions, so I'd long ago stopped asking her anything. I'd learned to just watch and listen, and most of the time I found out answers without having to ask. I had to ask questions here, though. Everything was totally strange and different, and I needed to know what I was doing in order to give good patient care. They seemed glad to answer my questions and volunteered information if they saw I was hesitant. Soon I was learning all kinds of new things.

I was also learning how to start a conversation by talking with the patients and the other nurses, and wasn't as self-conscious here.

When I started to work, I thought I could just work at the hospital and learn to be a nurse. I hadn't realized that the "nurses" I worked with were really nurse's aides. Wilma later got her LPN license through a "grandfather clause," which allowed a person with a lot of experience to take a test and get her license. After that one time, though, a person had to finish a course of training at an accredited school of nursing in order to be licensed.

When I learned the difference in a nurse's aide, LPN, and RN, I began to wonder where to go to school and how on earth I could ever get enough money to go. I wanted to be a real nurse. I wanted to learn anatomy, how the body worked and all about medicines—everything there was to learn.

I'd seen how Neal signed her name with a comma and R.N. after it. That's what I wanted—I wanted to be a registered nurse. I wanted to be the best RN in the whole state of North Carolina. I decided that after I got my raise, I'd start saving a little money each month so I could go to school, no matter how long it took. God had got me this far, surely there was a way. I'd long ago learned just to keep quiet, *tough things out* and keep on hoping.

I'd already made getting my teeth fixed my first priority, however. I think I must have been born with the toothache, and was so self-conscious about that ugly wide gap between my two front teeth. I must have inherited that gap from my aunt Cullie. Both teeth on each side of the two front ones were badly decayed, and I needed to have some others filled. I had no idea how much it would cost, but I'd have the work done as I could afford it.

I was scared to death of a dentist, but really wanted to get my teeth fixed. I went to see Dr. Charles Almond. He examined my teeth, told me what I needed done, and how much it would cost. To my surprise, he told me he'd start working on them right away, and I could pay a few dollars, or whatever I could afford each month. I was so happy and anxious to begin, and he was so nice to me that I wasn't so afraid then.

Paying him five dollars a month was going to be the most I could pay. He said that amount was fine. I was already committed to Nichols store for five dollars a month, although they didn't set any amount to pay or any time limit to pay it. This meant that I would have less than thirty dollars a month left from my paycheck of sixty dollars before taxes. That was lesson #1 on time payments.

I think it cost somewhere around two dollars then to have a tooth pulled. Dr. Almond made dentures and partials himself in his little lab in the back of his office. I went each week and he worked on what I needed to have done. When he was finished with that, he planned to pull my six front teeth and put in a partial immediately. He said they'd look like natural teeth. That made me so happy—it meant that those dreadful gapped front teeth would be gone forever. I could hardly wait for that to happen.

He was kind and friendly to me, and during my office visits in the following weeks, he asked me questions about myself. We had many discussions about getting an education to better one's self in life. He told me he'd come from a poor family and had a hard time trying to get through dental school. He gave me lots of encouragement, and said I was too intelligent to settle for a high school education and being a nurse's aide the rest of my life. I was really impressed to think that somebody with his education and reputation would think I had the ability to amount to something, and would take the time to talk and listen to me.

When he finished with the other work, he made the impression for the partial for my front teeth. I'll never forget his delight—and mine—when he put the partial in place and handed me the mirror. When I smiled, I couldn't believe it was me. My delight must have shown on my face, for he reached out, put his arm around my head and hugged it against his chest. I could feel the vibrations in his chest as he chuckled to himself. It was all either of us could do to keep from crying out loud for joy, and we both had tears in our eyes. When I left that day, I don't know which one of us had the biggest smile, but I sure felt better about mine.

I loved that man, not only for what he did, but for realizing what it meant to me. I don't know if it was an adolescent image I had of myself, or if I was truly that ugly, but getting my teeth fixed made a tremendous difference in the way I felt about my appearance. I still didn't think I was pretty, but I had a lot more self-confidence, and didn't try to hide my mouth any more when I smiled.

I was slowly beginning to find that there really were a lot of good people in the world, and true friendship went deeper than my physical appearance.

It felt so strange to make my own decisions, and it was more than a little frightening. I'd never been allowed to make any decisions on my own, even small ones, and was always told in no uncertain terms what I could and could not do.

Getting my teeth fixed was a decision I never regretted.

◆   ◆   ◆

I had a hard time realizing that Sweetie and Ruth didn't expect me to ask their permission for anything. They treated me as a responsible adult, and it was wonderful to be trusted. At first, when I worked late, I worried and half expected them to demand to know where I'd been and what I'd been doing. But they didn't seem to mind my coming and going at odd hours. I quietly slipped in and out of the house and they never complained or told me if I disturbed them. If they went to bed, I could go in my room and read half the night if I wanted to. I was really enjoying this new freedom.

I was working the night shift, and one afternoon when I got up, Ruth apologized and said she knew I couldn't have got any sleep. When I asked her why, she said she couldn't keep Ronnie quiet. He'd stayed inside all day, and had made a lot of racket. She was afraid I'd get too hot if she closed my door. I was so surprised—and touched by her thoughtfulness. I hadn't realized she'd been trying to keep things quiet for me when I was sleeping in the daytime. I'd slept like a log and hadn't heard a thing.

If she only knew how much I enjoyed just lying in my bedroom and hearing the happy sounds of him playing around the house, and of her going about the house, doing the housework, cooking, or whatever. (And not whistling or singing old mournful ballads.) I was so grateful just to be allowed to be a part of their family.

I felt bad to think that Ronnie couldn't run and play in his own house because of me. I apologized to her for not realizing that she was trying to keep things quiet, and told her to please just go about her business and let Ronnie make all the racket he wanted to make—it really didn't wake me or bother me…

A few days later when I got up, she said, "Don't tell me you didn't hear Ronnie today. I think he was trying to wake you up so you'd get up and play with him." He'd run back and forth through the house pulling his wagon, making a racket like it was a car, and every once in awhile, would make a sudden turn into my bedroom, circle around and run back out. He got so fast one time he turned it over and spilled out his toys right by my bed. When she looked in, she saw that I was still *sawin' the logs*. I hadn't heard a thing. I never did, unless she called my name, then I was awake in an instant. I'm glad I learned to be able to turn my thoughts off and sleep, for sometimes I witnessed things at the hospital that were hard to get out of my mind.

There was always something good to eat in the kitchen and they wanted me to help myself. I enjoyed helping Ruth with the cooking, washing, house work and taking care of Ronnie when I was there, and they seemed to appreciate it. Ruth was a good cook, and could make the best fudge anybody ever ate.

Sometimes Sweetie cooked up one of his concoctions, which usually had something to do with kraut, pickled corn or beans, green tomatoes, or ramps. He made what he called a "Mulligan stew." Whenever I tasted what he'd cooked and said it was good, he'd break out in a big grin. He always made everything fun. It was a wonderful feeling to be in the kitchen cooking, eating, laughing and talking together. We made some big messes sometimes, but he'd say "Don't worry about it," and help clean up after we finished. I was beginning to feel that maybe I might actually be somebody that other people liked to be around. We sure had fun together.

We had the best time just doing ordinary things. Ruth had a wringer washing machine out on the back porch, and I helped her do the washing when I was home. It was a big job just to carry the water up from the spring to fill the washer and tubs of rinse water. When I wasn't there, she washed my clothes right along with theirs. My uniforms had to be starched and ironed. She used real starch and it didn't stick to the iron like the flour starch Mom used. But having only two made it a constant hassle to keep one clean and ironed. I was going to get some more when I could afford them.

Ronnie was so cute, and was the best behaved little youngen. I loved playing with him. When I came home from work, he'd come running to meet me as fast as his little legs could carry him. One day, he came flying toward me so fast that I didn't catch him, and he bumped his head on my hip bone. I was skinny as a rail, and my hip bones stuck out like handlebars on a bicycle. (Well, maybe not quite that bad.) He started crying like his little heart would break and went running to Ruth, hugged her around the legs and told her I had a rock in my dress and it hit him in the head. After much petting and persuasion from us both, I finally got him to feel my hip to see that it wasn't a rock, and I hadn't hurt him on purpose. Before long, all was forgiven and he was playing with me again.

He taught me to be careful what I say to a little youngen. I teased him and threatened him with all sorts of outrageous things, like pull his nose off and put it back on upside down, pull his ears up and tie them in a knot on top of his head, or chop his head off. We'd wrestle around and I'd tickle him and pretend to chop off his head with my hand. We'd have a big laugh, and the more outrageous it was, the bigger he'd laugh.

The house was built on a slope along one side, and Sweetie had his chop block and axe underneath one corner of the house so he could go in there and chop kindling and keep it in the dry. One day, Ruth let Ronnie play under there awhile. When she went to check on him, she found him with the axe, and he was laughing real big about something. He'd found a litter of kittens under there, carried them over and put them in a pile by the chop block, and had chopped one of their heads off. He didn't realize that he had done anything wrong. After all, I'd laughed when I threatened to do it to him. Poor ol' Ruth was just sick about it, but she never acted like she blamed me.

I never dreamed he would take what I said literally. From then on, I was careful what I said to Ronnie or any other child.

◆   ◆   ◆

At the hospital, I was learning new things every day and loving it. Each thing I learned made me want to know more. I felt as if my mind was starving for knowledge. And deep within, for the first time in my life I had the satisfying feeling that I was exactly where I belonged, doing exactly what I'd been born to do.

I really paid attention and tried to do a good job at whatever I was asked to do. At first, it kind of scared me and was hard for me to accept that the people I worked with had so much confidence in my ability and trusted me to do things right. But I sensed their approval and acceptance that what I did was as good as anybody could do, and felt that I contributed my part.

We tried to get everything done as soon as possible, unless it was something ordered for a specific time, for I soon learned that the old adage of "*The best laid plans of mice and men*" was certainly true in a hospital. Patients are still human beings, and all are individuals, and have individual needs. What took five minutes for one patient might take fifteen for another. If we got on the ball and stayed caught up, then anything extra that came up could be easily handled without us getting so far behind.

One thing we had to be careful about was to do Clinitests on time. At that time, I'd never heard of testing blood for blood sugars outside of the lab. Diabetics had a Clinitest done three times a day before meals and at bedtime. This was a urine test for sugar. A certain number of drops was put into a test tube and a Clinitest tablet was dropped into it. It fizzed a minute, then the color changed. The color was compared to a color chart to show how much sugar was in the urine. Results were recorded as O, trace, or 1+ to 4+, and Insulin was given according to what their Clinitest showed.

SETTIN' UP AND PASSIN' OUT MEDICINES

They showed me how to do a procedure once, and the next time, I was expected to do it myself. I could always ask, though, if I was unsure of something. The second day I was there, I was showed how to "set up" and "pass out" medicines and give shots. The third day, I was told to do it by myself.

The medicines were kept on open shelves built into the wall on one side of the nurses' station. The area was about six feet high, three feet wide, and had about seven shelves. On the bottom was a row of big tall dark red glass jugs that held two to three gallons each. These contained Mineral Oil, Milk of Magnesia, Cascara Sagrada, Elixir Terpenhydrate, Cheracol Cough Syrup, Castor oil and maybe some others I have forgotten.

I remember one big red jug with a thick creamy laxative (Creomulsion?) in it—an emulsion of Castor oil. They gave it to patients who were having gallbladder x-rays, or others who needed to be "cleaned out good."

It was also used to speed up an OB's progress. They poured a good sized paper cup about half full of it, then poured several glugs of mineral oil on top of that, and gave it to an OB to drink, to start labor. After an hour she was given an HHH, or "three-H enema." When I asked what the "HHH" stood for, I was told "high, hot, and a hell of a lot." They alternated the laxative and the HHH enemas hourly. After a doast or two of that and the HHH enemas, she was ready to deliver something.

The medicines were arranged in alphabetical order on the shelves, and were mostly single file across each shelf. There probably wasn't more than forty different medications, including aspirin and vitamins. These doctors really believed in giving vitamins. We dispensed a lot of them, orally and I.V.

I forget the name, but there was one quart sized bottle of liquid vitamins formulated in a wine base, and every once in awhile (not every day), Mary Willie would come back and say she needed a "shot" of vitamins and got the big bottle down and poured herself a generous shot on some ice chips. I tried it one day, and man, that stuff was good! But I didn't want a rerun of the time I got drunk when me and Lawerence stole some of Dad's corn liquor, so I left it alone and kept my mouth shut.

The two pills I remember most were Dramamine™ and Delkadon™. Dramamine, a yellow tablet, was for nausea, and had a slightly sedative effect. Delkadon, a large bright red coated tablet, was called a "nerve pill."

The nurses didn't bother the doctor with every little complaint a patient had. I soon learned that they used those two pills to give to a patient when they complained of something and didn't have a PRN (whenever needed) order, or when they didn't quite know what else to give. The pills looked quite impressive, lying there together. They probably never heard the two high-falutin' words, "placebo effect," but I saw those two pills and a good "snake doctor" sales pitch work wonders lots of times. Fortunately, they were also about the safest thing you could take.

If a patient had cold symptoms, they were given some Coricidin™ tablets and a bottle of cough syrup. That's still a good choice.

Over in the corner at the nurses' station was a rectangular shaped stainless steel sterilizer on a stand, which was kept about half full of water and constantly simmering. We had to wash and clean medicine glasses, needles and syringes, and used the sterilizer to boil them in.

There was a handle on the side of the sterilizer which raised the lid as it lifted the perforated bottom liner up out of the water so you could use forceps to get things out. The syringes were glass and had at least a five or six digit number printed in small numbers on both the barrel and the plunger. The numbers on each had to match in order for them to fit. Sometimes there'd be eight or more in the sterilizer at one time. That meant sixteen syringe pieces to sort through besides the needles.

I learned to pick up the barrel first so I could hold it in my hand, then pick up the plungers one at a time with the forceps until I found a match, then insert it into the barrel. If they hadn't been cleaned good, they stuck and had to be thrown away. Occasionally, the barrel got a little crack, and finished breaking apart in my fingers when the plunger was inserted.

Once the two pieces of the syringe were fitted together, forceps were used to sort through the needles to find the one you needed, according to what you were going to give. A little short #25 needle was used to give a pain shot. (Any injection was called a "shot.") The longer and larger ones were used for IM (intramuscular) injections. Those #18's were mean looking rascals, mainly used to give blood.

The needles were used, cleaned and resterilized, and sometimes had to be sharpened and the barbs filed off the tips. Even with that, they got pretty dull after tumbling against the metal sides and bottom of the sterilizer while being boiled.

The only antibiotics I remember us giving in shots was Penicillin G and Streptomycin. The Penicillin came in powder form in a multi-dose vial. A certain number of cc's (cubic centimeters) of sterile water, or diluent was added to the powder to mix it so that one cc contained 100,000 units of Penicillin. We drew out 100,000 units from the multi-dose vial and gave it every four hours around the clock. Their hips got awful sore from all those shots. A few years later, the dosage was measured in millions of units, came premeasured in a sterile, disposable syringe (with a sharp, new needle) in a slow release base. Sure saved the patient a lot of stickin'.

The Streptomycin powder was slightly yellow and was really sticky after mixing. It looked like syrup. You had to use a big needle to give it. It took so much force to push it out of the syringe, that if you didn't hold the needle onto the syringe tip, it would fly off and the Streptomycin would squirt all over the place. Then you had to do it all over. It squirted out on my hands one time and almost took the skin off my hands wherever it touched. The patients said that stuff hurt, and I sure believed them after that.

Then there was the "mycin" antibiotics—Aureomycun and Tetracycline.

The locked narcotics cabinet was mounted into the wall in the hall next to the buzzers. At the end of each shift, each container was opened, the pills were poured out in your hand, then counted as you put them back. The count was done by two people—a nurse going off duty, and one coming on. Each had to sign the book to certify that all were accounted for. Nobody left the building until all were accounted for and each drug signed out by whoever took it out of the narcotics box.

One person carried the narcotics key during their shift, then gave it to the nurse coming on. There was one—and only one—narcotics key. That way, everyone was sure that only one person on that shift had access to the narcotics. That was a big responsibility. I don't guess there ever was a nurse who didn't, at least once, forget she had the key and took it home. Back before everybody had telephones, it wasn't long before someone was sure to be beatin' on your door.

I learned how to sign out for whatever I removed. The name of the drug, the dosage, date and time administered, patient's name and the doctor who ordered it all must be recorded. When I opened the container, I had to count the number of pills or capsules it contained and check the book to see that the number was correct. Then I signed out for what I removed, and recorded the number left in the container.

The narcotics for injection were in the form of tiny little pills: Morphine, Dilaudid™, Pantapon™, Phenobarb and Codeine. The prescribed pill was shaken out of the pill bottle into your hand (think of how many hands that pill had touched), dropped into the syringe barrel, the plunger replaced, and Sterile Saline or Water for injection pulled into the syringe through the needle to mix with the tablet. Sometimes it took a bit of shaking to get it dissolved. No, we didn't boil it to sterilize it. Or nothin'. Just give it. Never had an abcess. Honest!

Demerol was a clear liquid, sealed in 100 mg. glass ampules. We scored the ampule near the top with a small file, then snapped the top off and drew the desired amount from the ampule into a syringe. If the order was for 50 or 75 mg., you withdrew the correct dosage and set the rest on the shelf for awhile in case somebody else needed some. Sometimes there'd be two or three partial ampules sitting there. If discarded, two nurses had to sign—one as a witness for the other, that it had been "wasted."

I shudder to think what would happen today if an inspector found them.

One of the nurses showed me how, and had me give her a shot of sterile saline. I thought I'd be squeamish about giving shots, since I'd always been so scared of them, but I was O.K. with it—it wasn't my hide getting' stuck. Seriously, though, just stickin' somebody to be stickin' 'em, and doing something to help somebody made all the difference. It thrilled me to death when a patient complimented me on how "easy" I gave their shot.

The oral narcotics were PAC with Codeine, Phenobarbital tablets and several kinds of sedative capsules—Napental™, Nembutal™, Carbitral™, Seconal™, and Amytal™. There was a six ounce red colored bottle of Elixir Phenobarb for children, and a larger bottle of Elix Terpenhydrate with Codeine™ for coughs. Every patient got a "sleeping pill" at bedtime unless ordered *not* to get one.

One of the nurses showed me how to "set up" medicines to give to the patients, by taking each prescribed pill, capsule or liquid from its container and placing it in a pill holder or medicine glass on a "medicine tray." They saved the little peel-off rubber caps from the tops of IV bottles to set on the medicine tray to put pills and capsules in. They didn't use medicine cards, and at the time, I'd never heard of them. To set up the medicines, the nurse went down the Kardex one card at a time to see what medicines were ordered for each patient. She put the capsules or tablets in the rubber cap or poured liquid medicine into a medicine glass for one patient and set them on the medicine tray. Then she flipped the Kardex over to the next patient's card and set up those medicines. She just lined everything up on the tray as she went through the Kardex. There was no patient's name, room number, medication, dosage or hour written anywhere on anything.

Alcohol sponges were made by packing a jar full of cotton balls and pouring alcohol over them. If a patient got a shot, it was laid on the tray with an alcohol sponge wrapped around the needle.

When she finished with the bottom card on the Kardex, the medicines were all set up, and they were ready to be "passed out" or "give out."

I giggled to myself, to think how the definitions in my vocabulary were changing. Back up on the Creek, a "dram" or a "shot" was what they called a drink of likker. And I'd heard men talk about "settin' up" when they played poker, "passin' out" when they got too drunk, and bein' "give out" the next day.

My third day at work, they told me to give medicines. One of them watched me set them up, then told me to go aheaad and give them. By the grace of God, I must have given the correct medicine to the correct patient. At least no one had a reaction, complained, or died. But it worried me. I had a hard time remembering which little cap of pills or shot went to which patient, but having them lined up in the order of their room numbers helped.

Still, I just thought that was the way everybody did it, so that was the way to do. I didn't know any better. From then on, I was on my own, unless I needed to ask about something.

I had to learn fast, and it wasn't long before I was doing just about anything that was needed. I was starting IV's by the end of the first week. One day I'd just finished giving medicines when one of the OB patients rang her buzzer. She and another OB patient in the same room said their pills had been mixed up. Each had been given the other's pills. I thought I'd die of heart failure. I had no idea what the pills were for, or what they'd do if given to someone else. I took off to tell the older nurse and ask what to do. I ended up having to go tell Dr. Van Gorder what I'd done. Then I was in double heart failure. I was in total awe of him. I'd barely seen him a few times, and didn't know how mad he was going to be. I might even get fired. But I'd rather get killed than kill somebody, so I hurried back and told him what I'd done. I was so scared my voice was shaking, and my knees a-knockin'.

He musta seen how terrified I was. He said it wasn't serious—one of the women was taking a pill to dry up her breast milk; the other pill was standard medicine to keep an OB from bleeding; so no harm was done. Just be more careful next time. I got weak in the knees with relief. Then I had to go admit my mistake and explain to the women.

I simply hadn't seen the medicines enough times to be familiar with them. But I knew for sure that I didn't ever want to feel that horror again, and am extremely careful about medications to this day. Thank God I've never had to have that feeling again. Maybe it was a good thing I made that medication error with one that caused no harm, for it made a lasting impression on me as to what could have happened if it had been a medication that could have harmed or killed someone.

I didn't realize it at the time, but that was the first of many times in years to come that I would run to Dr. Van for help. I may have been scared to death at the time, but learned that he would be kind and always take care of the problem. He always took the time to explain and teach me what I needed to know. He trusted me, as he knew I would always tell the truth and put the patient's welfare first. And I didn't go running unless I was desperate. In later years, I had the same kind of relationship with Dr. Blalock. At times, I thought they trusted me too much.

We used refillable *fountain pens* at that time. From then on, whenever I gave medicines, if it was for more than one patient, I wrote the patient's last name beside it in ink on the white porcelain enamel medicine tray. I didn't care if nobody else did. I didn't want to kill anybody or make them sicker than they already were. Fortunately, the rubber caps didn't slide around to get mixed up. And an alcohol sponge wiped the ink right off the tray when I was finished.

Another thing happened that left a deep imprint in my mind of what a medication can do. One day a lady named Billie Sheidy, in her early thirties, was in the clinic and was given a shot of Penicillin. She stopped at the office window, paid them and walked down the stairs to the street. When she got down on the street, she collapsed, and somebody carried her back upstairs, yelling for help. They put her on a hospital bed and somebody called for me to come and help get her clothes off. I could see her flesh swelling as I worked. In that short span of time, her eyes were swollen shut, her lips about an inch thick, and she was having trouble breathing. Her ankles were swelling out over her shoes. When we got to her girdle and started peeling it down, you could see an imprint of the fabric and the swelling rise behind the girdle as we rolled it down off her body.

Fortunately, the doctor gave her something that counteracted the Penicillin reaction, and she was all right after that. After witnessing that, you better believe I never forgot to ask about allergies before I gave any injection. And made doubly sure I gave it to the right patient.

That lady had four little children, and they came mighty close to being orphans that day. Later, we became good friends. I was teasing her one day and told her not to even ask me for a drink of water—I wasn't giving her anything after they way she'd scared me. We had a big laugh, and I found myself thanking God that she was alive and able to laugh.

The names of medicines always fascinated me. There was a "drug room" back in the clinic where medicines were kept, and the shelves were full of samples that drug salesmen left. When I had time, I'd go back to the drug room and get down different containers and read the labels and inserts that came with them. I really learned a lot by doing that. I began to associate certain drugs with the conditions they were prescribed for.

I enjoyed working so much that I didn't care if I never got a day off. As soon as I learned enough to handle it, I worked for anybody that needed a day off, or was sick. I didn't get paid extra, but their paycheck was never short because they missed a day.

That made me happy. I knew they needed every cent on their paycheck.

LEARNING ABOUT DOCTORS

There were three doctors: Dr. Charles O. Van Gorder, Dr. John S. Rodda, and Dr. Joseph Stickley. Dr. Stickley left Andrews not long after I started working. Then Dr. Floyd E. Blalock came. Dr. Van Gorder and Dr. Rodda had served together in combat in World War II. Dr. Van Gorder came to Andrews first, then contacted Dr. Rodda and convinced him to come. They had a lot of trauma experience and were both surgeons. Dr. Van Gorder was also trained in plastic surgery. Dr. Blalock was a Navy man, and is one of the kindest, most compassionate people I ever met, as well as a great doctor. Children and the elderly, especially, loved him. Ruth thought he was wonderful with Ronnie.

Dr. Rodda was a brilliant doctor, and very handsome. I always thought he resembled Omar Sharif. He had a trim little mustache and piercing brown eyes that seemed as if they could look a hole right through you. He appeared stern, with a military bearing, very seldom smiled, and was always perfectly groomed. All the nurses were scared to death of him. They'd go to any lengths to keep from having to call him at home. One would beg or bribe the other to call him when they had exhausted all other resources, and had no other choice but to call him.

Of course, it rubbed off on me before I ever met him. Although he never did or said anything mean to me, I steered clear of him, and quickly ducked out of sight when I saw him coming. One day I was hurrying through the clinic and pushed the swinging door back fast—and it hit somebody. OH NO! It was Dr. Rodda! I stood there as if made of stone, and if he'd a-said "boo," I'd probably have jumped through the ceiling. He very calmly reached out, put his hand under my elbow as if to steady me, slightly tweaked his mustache on one side and said, "Young lady, you need to slow down."

Then he lightly flicked his hand against his jacket sleeve once, as if removing a dust particle that had dared to get on him, shrugged himself into that military bearing and regally walked away. From then on, when I approached the swinging doors, I always glanced down through the space at the bottom to see if I saw Dr. Rodda's immaculate feet before I pushed it back to go through.

Dr. Van Gorder was as jovial as Dr. Rodda was solemn. He usually wore an OR scrub suit top or a lab jacket. He loved to pull pranks and pick at nurses. Many times, you couldn't tell when he was serious and when he was joking.

The doctor always wanted a nurse to accompany him when he made rounds. One day Dr. Van came out on the floor as I was passing by, and asked me to go with him to check some patients. We went into the four bed men's ward. When one of them told the doctor that his back wasn't feeling any better, he turned to me and said, "Cleo, how about putting a board under this man's bed."

That request was a new one on me. I wondered why he wanted a board under the man's bed—but I sure wasn't going to ask him. Then I thought, maybe he's going to do something with it later. Ah, heck, I didn't know! Anyway, he was the doctor—if that's what he asked for, that's what he'd get. After he left, I asked Bud Jones where the bed boards were kept, went and got one and—oh yes I did—I put it under his bed. Laid it right on the floor. Scooted it a way back inunder there so nobody wouldn't be a-stubbin' their toe on it.

Can you imagine how mortified I was when one of the nurses came along and found it, wondered what it was doing there, then told me it belonged under his mattress?

I was to be reminded of that for many a year to come, just to keep me humble, you know. Especially by Dr. Van. Some smart aleck had *run and blabbed* to him.

In return, when one of the others teased me, I'd tell them something like, "That's O.K. Just go right ahead and run your mouth. You just wait. One of these days I'm goin' to go off to school, and when I come back I'll be your boss. I'll see that you get paid back for gettin' smart with me."

I'm sure I taught them a few things, too, like when dealing with a kid frash out of the woods and dumb as a rock, be explicit in your instructions, and don't take nothin' for granted.

There were many other incidents that were hilarious. One of them happened the night Artie and I were in the linen room putting away the clean linen. Artie could tell it funnier than I, as she was mostly the observer.

The linen room was located just across from the scrub area in front of the OR. Beyond it was the lab and clinic. Inside the operating room was a side door that opened right out onto the metal fire escape in the alley behind the hospital. The doctors always used this entrance, and when we heard the metallic ring of footsteps on the fire escape, we knew we better straighten up and fly right.

Sometimes we "cut up" a little—and giggled a lot. This particular night, Artie was unwrapping and sorting the bundles of clean laundry, and I was putting it where it belonged on the shelves. She came across a pair of men's long-handle underwear that had evidently got mixed up in the hospital laundry and sent to the cleaners. Artie, a short woman, held 'em way up above her head and said she bet them things was long enough to fit me.

I said, "Well, we'll just see if they are," and started pulling them on right over my uniform, stuffin' it down into them. About the time I got the top started up over my shoulders good, we heard a loud metallic racket out toward the fire escape. Dr. Rodda was on call, and Artie said, "Oh, Lord, here comes Dr. Rodda!"

You talk about gettin' in high gear!

Quick as lightnin', I started tryin' to jerk them longhandles off. I finally got my arms out of 'em, and started slidin' 'em on down, but my shoes got hung up in them *doggoneded* legs and I couldn't get 'em out. And there I was, all hobbled up and couldn't step more than a foot at a time. The straddle of them underwear come just below my knees, and I was gittin' all tangled up where their arms were floppin' around my feet. I'd a-swore they was a dozen arms on them underwear and ever' one of 'em was out to tie my legs up.

Mankind alive, I was dancin'! I twisted, undulated and hip-hopped, while I reached around a-huntin' for armholes as I realized I'd have to pull them long handles back up before I could walk, an'en I'd have to pull my shoes off and start from the bottom to get 'em off of me. Artie was going into hysterics laughing at me.

As I took off through the dark lab and clinic rooms, I didn't turn on any lights; Dr. Rodda couldn't see me in the dark. As I did a fast shuffle across the clinic, I was reaching around my backside and holding on to the top of the long handles with one hand and tuggin' 'em up between my knees with the other'n.

I was trying not get all tangled up and fall down till I could get across there to the bathroom over next to the patient's rooms. If I could just get in there, I could lock the door, nobody'd see me, and I could get these cussed things off of me. Just as I finally reached the hall door, I managed to get the shoulders of the long-handles up over me, leaving the arms empty and flappin' around.

I let go of the underwear, and was fumblin' around in the dark a-tryin' to find the door knob and get the door open to the hall, when all of a sudden, it came open and I shot out into the hall. There was just enough light from the street light to see how to get into the bathroom. I barely glimpsed a patient coming up the hall as I raced inside and quickly shut the door.

I leaned back against the door, took a few deep ragged breaths and turned on the light. Then I sat down on the commode, finally got my shoes off, got my feet out of them underwear legs and pulled 'em off.

I rolled 'em up in a wad and stuck 'em over in a corner, so it would look like a patient had left 'em in there. Then I straightened myself up and came out walking very businesslike—in case Dr. Rodda was out there lurking about somewhere.

In the meantime, while I was in there getting out of the underwear, I'd heard a buzzer cut loose and it sounded like somebody was holding the button down, which meant they wanted somebody fast. In a few seconds, I could faintly hear voices and knew Artie was taking care of it.

Artie came back to the linen room where I'd gone, and started just a—cryin' out loud, I mean, but trying not to, and just bent plumb over a-holdin' her belly. Just for a minute there, I thought something was bad wrong with her. Then I realized she'd laughed til she was cryin'. In between sobs, gasps, and giggles, she finally managed to say, "I've-peed-my-britches."

When she got so she could talk, she could only say a few words at a time before she went to laughin', and then back to cryin' again. She finally managed to tell me that the patient in the hall had seen me a-streakin' out of that dark doorway at the end of the hall and thought I was a ghost.

Or something.

She didn't exactly know what she'd seen, but it shore 'nuff scared the livin' daylights out of her.

The racket we heard must have been a dog a-knockin' over a trash can out in the alley, for Dr. Rodda never showed up.

It's a good thang for us.

And it's a good thang that patient ditn't have a weak heart.

T & A SEASON

I'm going into such detail here to illustrate the difference in surgery, anesthesia, and post-operative care then and now.

We all know of the four seasons. When I went to work, I heard the nurses say that they dreaded "tonsil season." I came to know exactly what they meant, and I'm so glad it has now gone the way of the horse and buggy. In the summertime, almost every day, one, two or more kids had a T & A—medical jargon for tonsillectomy and adenoidectomy, or *having their tonsils took out*. This was classified as minor surgery. Back then, it was common practice for doctors to recommend a T & A for any child who had persistent chronic sore throat. The Polio epidemic had been a very recent threat, and it was thought that having a T & A might also help prevent polio.

The child was admitted early in the morning, having had nothing by mouth since midnight. After they took it to the O.R., we went in and elevated the foot of the bed and made a "tonsil bed" to be ready when they came out. We had a suction machine all ready on the bedside table.

As an OR nurse in later years, I never put a child on a stretcher and strapped it down; to me that was heartless, frightening to the child—and not necessary. I tried to go in and visit a few times to get the child used to seeing me, then carried it in my arms to the O.R.

When the child was placed on the OR table, a sheet was wrapped snugly around it from the neck down to serve as a restraint. Four inch wide webbed straps, attached to the underside of the table, were brought up and buckled over their body to further restrain them and keep them from sliding off the table. Even with this, a nurse had to hold down the child at the shoulders until the anesthetic took effect. It could suddenly squirm free if someone didn't keep the sheet in place and restrain it. When I took a child from its mother and father and put it on the table, restrained and held it down during induction with it screaming "Mama" in my ear, I felt like a traitor. Poor baby.

The table was positioned at a fairly steep slant during surgery, the head lower than the feet. This was so any fluids would drain from the mouth, and keep the patient from aspirating blood and/or vomitus.

Back then, just about everyone who had general anesthesia was given Ether. An Ether mask has a metal frame, with metal screen mesh in the mask area. A few layers of gauze were placed over the screen and fastened in place by a flexible wire coil spring that fitted into a depression around the outside of the mask. The excess gauze at the edge was then cut off.

Ethyl Chloride, a fast acting Ether-type general anesthetic, came in a dark red glass spray bottle. When turned upside down, a lever was pushed down and the contents sprayed out in a fine mist, like a frozen vapor, and the frost covered the Ether mask held on the child's face by the doctor. This was used as an induction, just to get them to sleep, since it acted faster than Ether.

After three or four good breaths of the Ethyl Chloride, you could feel the child relax. A few more, and the Ethyl Chloride bottle was set down, an airway inserted and "drop Ether" started.

Ether came in a small metal bottle, about half the height of a 12 ounce Coke can. The "cap" part of the bottle was a dome shaped insert of lead (I think—at least it looked like lead and was soft like lead). A medium large safety pin was fastened through the soft metal cap, from side to side. When the can was inverted, the doctor slowly dripped the Ether from the back end of the safety pin onto the Ether mask. This part took about twenty minutes.

The doctor kept a close check on the patient's eyes. The amount of pupil dilatation indicated what level of anesthesia the patient was under. When the patient was under deep anesthesia, the mask was taken off, the airway removed and a "mouth gag" retractor was inserted. The retractor was a hinged semi-circular device with padded places for the teeth to fit in, when placed in the mouth. A ratchet on the side held it open after it was inserted, and it was opened as wide as necessary to hold the mouth open during the T & A.

A metal nipple with a hole in the center which pointed toward the throat was built into one side of the gag, and rubber tubing was attached to the outside end of it. The other end of the tubing was attached to a clear glass bottle of Ether attached to the side of the suction machine. The amount of Ether coming through could be regulated, and the machine sprayed the Ether through the nipple into the patient's mouth. Every time the patient breathed, it inhaled the prescribed amount of Ether.

The doctor wore a headband to which a small spotlight was attached in front. This spotlighted the mouth and throat area. First, the adenoids were essentially shaved off with an instrument called an adenotome. Then the tonsil was grasped with a long instrument with teeth (tenaculum) to elevate it, then the mucous membrane around the tonsil was dissected with a long handled tonsil knife.

Another long instrument with handles (a tonsil snare) had two small holes in the other end. One end of a strong, small gauge (tonsil) wire was inserted through each of these holes, making a loop. When the handles were slightly squeezed together, the wire retracted inside a sleeve, making the loop secure. The wire loop was passed down over the tenaculum and pushed into place under the tonsil. When the snare handles were squeezed hard, the tonsil was cut free with a snap, as the wire retracted into the handle.

Bleeders were tied off or sutured, or if small ones, cauterized with a Bovie™ machine needle (electrocautery). A round tonsil sponge was inserted into the tonsil cavity and held for several minutes. Then it was removed and the throat inspected to see if the bleeding was under control.

One major problem with this method was that if much bleeding occurred, the throat could fill up pretty fast. Endotracheal tubes were not used. I never even saw one there. I've seen blood suddenly spurt up and spray onto the doctor's face. Then the suction machine had to be used to keep the blood from going down the throat when the patient breathed.

The bleeder had to be quickly clamped off because during suctioning, the Ether was being drawn out through the suction tip, the anesthesia would start wearing off and the patient would begin to wake up. If that happened, a tonsil sponge was applied and held under pressure, and the suction taken out of the patient's mouth long enough for them to get a few breaths of Ether to put them back under.

When the procedure was finished, the patient was carefully observed to be sure the bleeding was under control before they discontinued the Ether and took them off the table. They were carried directly from the OR to their room, still asleep. We had no recovery room. They were put with their head at the foot of the bed, positioned on their belly across the knee hump so their chest was higher than their head, and their head turned to one side so they wouldn't aspirate drainage.

One of us had to stay with them and use the suction, if needed, until they "reacted," or regained consciousness. That's one job I continually prayed through, and the only thing I ever really, truly hated to do. I stayed scared to death until they woke up enough for me to see them swallow. Then I watched to see if they were swallowing too much, indicating that they could be swallowing blood.

I usually had to watch them from one to two hours. I wiped the little face with a cool damp washcloth and kept talking, or had its mother talk, to try to keep them quiet. Bloody drainage ran from the side of the child's mouth, and I kept it wiped off. Standing right over the T & A patient, the Ether and blood scent mixed together came right up into my face. It nauseated me and I got a headache from smelling and breathing the Ether fumes. It's highly volatile and explosive, and I think it's illegal now to even have Ethyl Chloride or Ether stored inside a hospital.

When they started reacting, most of the time the child would suddenly start vomiting, and bloody green vomitus with an Ether odor gushed out all over me, the bed and everywhere. But once they got rid of all that stuff, they started feeling better.

Poor little youngens! They'd wake up crying and *sick as a dog*. As soon as they were awake enough to take a few ice chips and swallow, I let the Mama hold the child on her lap to help it feel more secure. We always put one of those red rubber refillable ice collars around their neck. I was never so relieved as when I put the youngen on her lap and could get out of there to breathe some fresh air and relax.

They had to stay overnight, and were allowed ice chips for a few hours, then Jello. They were given Aspergum for the pain. That's just what it sounds like—Aspirin in chewing gum.

Often, I'd hear one person ask another if their youngen was having surgery, and if it was serious. They'd reply, "Oh, no. They're just gettin' their tonsils took out."

Now maybe my opinion don't count for much, but to me, having a T & A is serious business, and is major surgery in my book. I've worked in surgery many years, and have assisted with all kinds of major and minor operations. I'd still rather help do any kind of surgical procedure than a T & A under the conditions we had back then. I dreaded one from the time I saw it on the schedule and worried til they went home, and *many's the time* I've whispered a heartfelt "Thank You, Lord," as I watched 'em leavin' to go home.

WORKIN' THE NIGHT SHIFT

I even loved working night shift. Perhaps it made me feel more independent and satisfied some of the adolescent rebellion I'd built up through the years. We always got up early, and never took a nap or slept during the day. To work the 3-11 shift and stay up late, then sleep late the next morning, or work the 11-7 shift, stay up all night and sleep all day, was a totally foreign experience. I'd always had to go to bed with the chickens—along about dark. I remember lying there in bed in the summer; looking out the window, listening to the crickets and katydids (kittydids) and watching it get dark.

I walked home from work in the daytime, but the hospital had a taxi escort service that took us home at eleven, or came and picked us up when we worked night shift. The taxi driver's name was "Fodderblade" Conley. I always walked down to the main road to meet him so he wouldn't have to drive his car over the rutted road at night. I was still scared of the dark, but Sweetie let me take his flashlight, and Fodderblade was always there at exactly the time he said he'd be there. I remember the relief I felt when I saw his headlights turn into the drive-way and stop, so I could get in his car out of the dark.

Back then, I was quite a comic around friends I was comfortable with, and on slow nights, we'd get in a silly mood lots of times, trying to stay awake. Ruth Mashburn always wanted me to sing that old Gene Autry song, "Just A-Bummin' Around," or I'd pretend I was pickin' a banjer, pat both my feet at the same time, and sing "The Crawdad Song," like I'd seen my Uncle Jess do. It still felt strange for me to have someone's attention and still be at ease with them. We had lots of fun together.

When the census was low and we had a few minutes' break, or while making tonsil sponges, Artie and I used to sit on the window sill at the laundry chute and quietly sing gospel songs. I sang soprano and she sang alto. Our favorite was "Bound For The Kingdom." We always kept one ear tuned for a buzzer, though. We may have clowned around sometimes, but that bunch of people was dedicated to their job and to the patients. When a buzzer sounded, one didn't wait for the other. That buzzer got answered immediately. And they helped each other. If one started to go change a bed, the other offered help. One didn't go off duty and leave the other to finish any work.

There were several jobs that night nurses routinely did in addition to taking care of the patients. When somebody used a rubber glove, they tossed it into a basin of green soap and water. One of our jobs was to wash the dirty rubber gloves. After washing and drying them, we inspected them for holes by blowing them up to see if any air came out a hole anywhere. Then they were powdered and sterilized to be reused.

We had a handmade wooden box for a glove powderin' box. It had glass in the sides so we could see what we were doing inside the box, and had holes in the end to put our hands through. We poured about two inches of glove powder in the bottom, stuffed several gloves in, then put our hands through the holes to fluff 'em around and coat 'em with the powder; then turned 'em and fluffed 'em again to coat the other side. The box kept the powder contained so we wouldn't breathe it.

There were glove wrappers made of double layers of heavy cotton material, sewed into a rectangle which had been folded to make a pocket on each side to hold a glove. We folded a cuff down on each glove, put one in each pocket of the glove wrapper, added a little packet of glove powder, taped the edges closed, and wrote the size of the gloves on the tape. Then we stacked them ready for the RN's to autoclave (sterilize with steam under pressure).

When wearing a pair of gloves, if one of them got torn, only the torn one was discarded. Any odd ones that were left were washed and tossed in a box to be used for rectal exams, etc.

With today's threat of HIV and other diseases, I bet one hospital employee uses more disposable gloves in one day than we used in a whole week. And I bet the Health Department would close the place down now if they even thought gloves were reused.

Even when we had a chance to sit down, there was always something to do on night shift. In the summertime, we stayed busy trying to keep up with the demand in OR for tonsil sponges. We made small, medium and large sizes. We took a 4 x 4 gauze sponge, put a number of cotton balls in the center, according to the size we wanted to make, folded each corner over to the center, rolled and bunched it up neatly to make it rounded, and sewed it together tightly with heavy black thread, leaving a long tail of double thread about eight inches long. Then we tied two knots in the end.

The long tail was always kept outside the mouth so the sponge couldn't dislodge and go on down their throat. The doctor pulled on the tail of the sponge to remove it. We made sure they were securely sewed. We didn't want one coming apart or the thread coming loose and a sponge getting sucked down a child's throat.

Today, they are purchased by the gross, sterile and ready to use.

◆　　◆　　◆

Each patient had a chart inserted in a metal chart cover which hung on the chart rack. A chart is considered a legal record of each patient during their hospital stay, and it is very important to be clear and accurate when writing on a chart. In those days, we used refillable ink pens to write in a chart. Each person recording anything in the chart must sign their name, date and time of the entry.

We had to think carefully what we were going to write before we wrote it on the chart. It is illegal to erase or mark out any entry to make it unreadable. If you made an error, you drew one line through the error, made the notation, "error" above or beside it, dated and initialed it.

We were supposed to print instead of writing.

Three ink bottles always sat on the desk. Each shift used a different color of ink; 7-3 used blue or black, 3-11 used green, and 11-7 used red. You could tell what shift I was working by the color of ink on my fingers, as I always got ink on my fingers when I refilled a pen.

Another responsibility of the night shift was to add additional chart pages if needed, such as Nurses' Notes, or Bedside Notes, Progress Notes, or Doctor's Order sheets, and make new charts to have ready when a patient was admitted.

Imagine what you would think if you were working with a nurse and she said, "I've got to go draw the midnight lines." I guess you'd be as puzzled as I was, until you saw it done. When midnight passed, after the last notation before midnight on the Nurses' Notes, a line in red ink was drawn all the way across the page. Centered directly under it was written or printed the day of the week, month, day of the month, and year—for instance, Wednesday, February 12, 1952. Then another line was drawn across the page directly beneath the date. That was the midnight line. It signified the beginning of a new day.

I have a nice thought about that, if we could just do it in life. When the day's over, and the midnight line is drawn, it's history. As with the legalities of charting, we can't erase or change a thing. It's done. We can only initial our mistakes as errors and accept the responsibility for them, then move on and try to do better next time. You can't carry one word over beyond the line—it's a fresh, new blank space for the coming day.

Just try to keep it neat.

◆   ◆   ◆

The babies took a lot of time. We had to check often to keep them clean and dry. Each newborn was carefully watched to see if they voided and had a BM (bowel movement), and this was carefully charted. We had to record the number of BM's and the time, color and character of the stool. This was important, as this indicated that all their "plumbing" was working normally. Another night duty job was to fold and stack diapers. We didn't have disposable diapers. Soiled diapers were thrown down the laundry chute.

We gave each baby a complete bath each night. We also recorded the time and amount of each feeding. We usually got a baby out of the bassinet and rocked it while we fed it, but sometimes when we had two or three and they all cried at the same time, we'd prop their bottle and watch them all eat at the same time. Then we'd check their diapers and bassinet to see if everything was nice and dry. If we were getting low on clean bottles, we washed and sterilized some more, and made formula. We sterilized the bottles, nipples and caps in a big pot on the hot plate.

Today, formula comes ready to use in sterile disposable bottles, and a modern young nurse probably wouldn't know what a reusable diaper was if she saw one, or how to fold it and put it on a baby if she did.

Every once in awhile the patient census got down to three or four, with no babies in the nursery. If a nurse had a headache, cramps, or didn't feel well, sometimes she'd lie down an hour while the other one took care of things. I didn't like to go into an empty patient room and get on a bed. I got a blanket and pillow, went into the bathroom and climbed into that big old claw footed bath tub to take a nap. It was close to the nurses' desk and everybody knew where to find me if they needed me. Nurses get so tired sometimes that they can sleep anywhere. I know.

Back then, there was no traffic on the street after around eleven o'clock. We used to say *they rolled up the sidewalks at eight o'clock.* On the rare occasion when we heard a car, we listened to see if it stopped down at the entrance, and gave a sigh of relief when it went on by.

At about the same time every night during the early morning hours, you could hear the Greyhound bus slow down at the corner drugstore at the middle red light, where people were supposed to wait if they wanted to get on the bus. Then you'd hear the driver let off the air brakes and speed back up as he went on through town. I'd wonder where the people on the bus came from and what it was like there, where they were going, and how it would feel to just get on that bus and go. It made a lonely sound as it gradually faded away into the night, headin' out of town.

The dimly-lit town was deserted and still, and I felt like we were the only people awake in a sleeping, silent ghost town, guarding a building full of sick people. It gave me an eerie, sort of sad, lonely feeling, along with a huge sense of responsibility for the patients.

On a dark stormy night, it got plumb scary upstairs in that creaky old building when the wind blew and I could hear things banging around out there. As I looked out a window, I could hear the wind whistling and moaning around the street corners, and see small bits of paper and trash swirling and dancing about in dust devils down on the street. When a big gust of wind came, you could feel when it hit the building. It swayed and creaked and the windows rattled. At times, brilliant flashes of lightning made the lights flicker as the sound of thunder rolled back through the mountains.

As I walked through the halls to check on the sleeping patients, the bare wood floor *screaked* lightly with each step I took. I carried a flashlight and kept it aimed at the floor so I could ease in and listen to each person's breathing without turning on a light. I quietly made the rounds and checked each one every hour when I wasn't too busy with a critical patient or an OB.

◆   ◆   ◆

When a patient came in at night, the more experienced nurse took the patient on back into the clinic and checked them out. It might be a sick baby or child with a fever, somebody with a pain in their belly, or any number of things. The older nurses knew what medications were needed and permitted, and usually dispensed them without calling the doctor. It was a real life-and-death emergency when a doctor was called. They needed their sleep, too. I watched and learned.

If a baby had a fever of 102 or above, we gave them baby aspirin and bathed them in cold water to cool them down. Sometimes we put alcohol in the water to give them an alcohol sponge bath, or wet a sheet in cold water and wrapped them up in it if their fever was dangerously high. Poor things would just shiver all over.

I remember that Bismuth was one of the standard medicines we gave to babies and young children for upset stomach.

Many of the old-timey mountain folks were really superstitious. A thick volume could be written about them. I already knew a lot of their ways, but learned a lot more working in the hospital.

I learned to listen carefully to a patient's history. It was common to run into cases where people had been treating kids or each other with old-timey home remedies, which worked a lot of the time, but sometimes we heard about some strange practices. One night, there was a couple discussing what they thought had made the child sick. One told the other, "I told ye that a-body ain't s'posed to eat fish and drank milk together. Hit'll make you sick ever time." I've heard that said several times since.

It wasn't unusual to see a baby with a well-worn little homemade cloth bag of asafoetida, or "fittidy" as they called it, on a string tied around their neck, or wearing poultices of groundhog oil, bear oil, onions, or other folk remedies to cure the croup.

Among all the odd, strange and curious things I've ever heard, one stands out in my mind above anything I ever heard before or since. This was in the new hospital about 1965. Billie Reighard was working with me that evening on 3-11, and was assigned to the E.R., when a poorly dressed, not too clean young woman came in, carrying a child about eighteen months old. We took it into one of the ER exam rooms, checked its temperature, looked in its ears and throat, listened to its chest and asked the usual questions about when the baby got sick, if it was eating, vomiting, coughing, etc., and made notes.

The baby had diarrhea, a high temperature, and appeared to be dehydrated. It was pale, had dark circles around its eyes and was a mighty sick-lookin' little youngen.

When Bille asked the mother what treatment she had been doing at home, she answered that she had been giving it "chicken tea." Billie looked at me, and I looked at her, and we didn't exactly know if we'd heard right. Billie said, "You mean chicken broth?" and the woman said "No. Chicken tea."

Billie said "Chicken tea? What's that? How do you make chicken tea?" The woman answered, "It's where you gather up—you know—some, uh, dry chicken turds, and some of it's dark and some of it's white. You pick off the white part and put it in some boiling water and make tea out of that." We just stood gaping at each other in amazement for a long minute as we thought, 'Huh? Come again?'

Poor little youngen! No wonder it was sick!

And guess which doctor was on call.

Billie had to call and tell him about the baby and describe the treatment over the phone. You could practically see that phone jump and vibrate as he vented his rage over somebody being that stupid (expletives deleted) and doing that to a baby. Standing beside her, I could hear it all clearly. That was one very angry doctor.

But he came on down, examined and treated the baby with gentle kindness. It was a different story with the mother, however. When he got done with her, she knowed better'n t'give chicken tea to a youngen, next time.

◆   ◆   ◆

A common treatment for a baby who was dehydrated, and couldn't retain oral fluids, was to give it a "clysis," an abbreviation for hypodermoclysis, meaning "under the skin." I hated that about as bad as watching a T & A patient.

We had to use a long, thin needle to slowly inject from 25 to 50 cc's of Saline just under the skin, usually on the back, right under the shoulder blades. We had to inject about 2 cc's at a time, partially pull the needle out, change the direction, advance the needle and inject some more. The Saline made hard, raised welts in the area until it was all absorbed. The baby screamed and kicked, and I know it must have been painful.

Sometimes, we dripped it very slowly through a needle under the skin on the baby's thigh from an IV (intravenous) bottle on a pole.

But this was a procedure that people unskilled in starting an IV on a baby could perform and the baby usually improved rapidly. It was very rare to see an IV started on a baby.

◆   ◆   ◆

There were a few patients who came in often, with various vague complaints. When they came in, they were referred to as "one of the reg'lars." I soon learned who they were.

One night, a man I recognized as "one of the reg'lars" came in about two A.M. His complaints had always been vague and varied, and the nurse had told me he *didn't have good sense* (was mildly retarded). She always sealed up some kind of pill or other in one of the little dispensing envelopes, probably the old stand-by, Dramamine and Delkadon, and gave it to him. Then she'd tell him to go home, take the medicine, and go straight to bed.

Wellsir, this time, the other nurse was busy and I checked him out. He said he couldn't see good out of his eyes, and was having trouble with 'em. I had no idea what I was looking for, but used the ophthalmoscope to look in his eyes, just to impress him that he was being checked. I didn't see anything wrong, of course. His blood pressure and temperature were O.K.

I thought about his complaint, then realized—he was alone and didn't drive. He lived about a mile out of town. How had he managed to get here and then walk up the dimly-lit stairs in the middle of the night if he couldn't see really well? Big deal!

I decided to give him a sleeping capsule to take home. I chose Seconal™ because it was a bright red and would look more impressive than a green Napental™ or yellow Nembutal™. When I got the one and a half grain capsule out, I decided he was a big man and got out two. Yeah, that ought to do it.

I replaced the container, locked the cabinet and signed out for them, putting the name of the doctor on call in the space "ordered by." Then I sealed them up in a little envelope and took them back and gave them to him. I told him to be sure and wait til he got home and ready to get in bed before taking them; they'd make him awful sleepy, but they should take care of his eyes. Just to be on the safe side, he should come back the next day and let one of the doctors check him.

About three days later, I was starting across the street when I heard him calling out my name. I stopped and waited as he *come lopin'* up to me. He said, "I just want to know…what'n the name a God did you give me the other night." I said they were pills for his eyes, and asked him if they helped .

He answered, getting faster as he talked, "Well…I went home…and took them pills just like you said to…An'en I got 'n the bed and went to sleep and slept all the rest of the night and all day the next day. Along about dark, I woke up dist about bustin' to, uh, you know, uh, go to the bathroom, and got up and went to runnin' sideways acrost the room and run into the door facin' and knocked a knot on the side of my head……(face screwed up and rubbing head) I got me a big drank a water 'n come back, laid back down and slep' all th' rest a that night 'n woke up th' next mornin' dist starved-to-death, and m'mouth felt dry as cotton…(Pause for a big breath)…Now, I want ye t'know, I eat a break-furst."

I really had trouble keeping a straight face, but asked him if his eyes were better. He answered heartily, "I ain't had nary nother bit a trouble out a them eyes."

I said, "Well, good. The pills cured 'em, did they?" And he said, "They shore did! Thank ye."

And I knowed it was time for me to walk on before I *busted a gut* a-tryin' to keep from laughin'. But I made a mental note to limit how many sleeping pills I handed out next time, in case the house caught afire, or sump'm.

And nobody wouldn't be a-knockin' no more knots on their head.

◆   ◆   ◆

Another time, way in the night, an old pick-up came to a stop down at the front. I could hear somebody slowly climbin' up the stairs, just a-gruntin' and blowin', so I went out to see if somebody needed help. A past middle-aged man slowly came on up the stairs and stopped on the landing. I asked if I could help him.

He was obviously agitated, his face red, and his trembling voice seemed to indicate severe pain. He would drop his hands down toward his pants pockets a little, then jerk them back up, then rub them up and down each side of his hips. I asked him to come on back to the clinic with me, and noticed that he walked all spraddle-legged with real short steps.

When I asked him what his trouble was, he cleared his throat a couple of times, started to talk, then stopped and cleared his throat again. He said he'd like to see a doctor. I told him I had to know what to tell the doctor on the phone or he wouldn't come.

Finally, he asked me if there wasn't one of the older nurses there. Feeling slightly insulted, but very courteously, I told him yes, there was, and I'd go get her.

Mae Griffith was working with me that night, and she went back to see if he would let her help him. I could hardly wait for her to come back and tell me what on earth was wrong with that man. I'd never seen nobody act so strange.

When she came back, she gave that quiet little laugh she had, and told me what happened. It turned out to be funny, only it wasn't so funny.

Somebody had been stealing the man's coal. He'd stood his shotgun up against the wall by the door, put out the light so they'd think he was asleep, eased off his pants and laid down on the bed a-listening for any racket out there at his coal pile.

After awhile he heard something, jumped out of bed in the dark and was going to catch that booger in the act. He was in such a hurry that he got turned around and tangled up in the dark and ran astraddle of the still almost red-hot coal heater, and him in just his shirt tail.

I don't guess I need to say exactly where he got burnt, do I?

After I found that out, I realized that this was a good old decent mountain man that had too much respect to go *"a-handlin'* that kind a talk" around a young girl, much less show her. I cringe to I think of the pain he must have been feeling. And so humbled by his integrity.

But Mae had put an anesthetic ointment on the burn that stopped the pain, wrapped up everything and padded it good with bandages so his clothes wouldn't rub against it, and had given him a tube of ointment to take with him. He left feeling considerably better than he did when he came in.

And I learnt to investigate a little further before I went to gettin' my little feelin's hurt.

◆   ◆   ◆

I also learned that a couple of the nurses liked to have *a little nip* now and then. One night, the nurse I worked with must have had *a big slug* right before she came on duty, for she was *as drunk as a skunk* by midnight. Along about two in the morning, I discovered that an elderly patient in the farthest room on the other side was having trouble breathing. He looked awful. I ran back to the nurses' desk to get the nurse and she said we needed to put Oxygen on him. Back then, we used Oxygen tents. I'd seen the big ol' Oxygen tanks on a dolly, but never had put an Oxygen tent on a patient.

I got the tent and took it to the room, then hurried back for the big tank and rolled it out in the hall by the desk. She got up to go with me. She was so staggery she couldn't walk without runnin' into the walls. She held on to me, and I held on to her with one arm and pushed the tank with the other. She mumbled a few words and then just *turned the air blue* a-cussin' as she stumbled along. Every few steps, she'd cough real big, stop and say, "Cough-and-pee, cough-and-pee!" (not the exact word) and then cut loose to cussin' some more.

We finally made it across the lobby and down the hall to the patient's room and I set her down in a chair. She told me how to put the tent on the patient, turn on the Oxygen and how many liters to set the gauge on. The man's blood pressure was very low, skin cold, pale and clammy, and his pulse was weak and thready. I really thought he was dying.

She said he needed a shot, so I led her back to the desk and set her down. She told me what kind of a shot to give him. I think it was Coramine, a cardiac stimulant. That's what they usually gave somebody as a last resort when they thought they were dying. Anyway, I took it and gave it to the poor old man and stayed with him, checking his blood pressure every few minutes.

And did a lot of silent desperate praying. I was absolutely scared to death, but I kept my voice calm and talked to the old man, held his hand and patted his arm to let him know I was there, and kept him quiet and calm. I don't know if she called the doctor, but after what seemed like hours, the nurse sobered up enough to come back.

The old man was still alive when I left that morning, but I was worried about him. I woke up every now and then all through the day, wondering if he'd died, and said a little prayer for him. When I went back, he was a lot better, and was discharged a few days later. You can't tell me and make me believe that God doesn't hear desperate prayers.

I never reported her or told anyone about the incident til now. I didn't know enough at the time to realize just how serious her actions had been. After all, she was the older nurse, and I didn't question what they did.

I also understood how she could feel that she had to have a drink once in awhile. She'd told me about her family life, and it seemed like all she'd ever had in her whole life was hard times. If I'd had to live the kind of life she was living, and didn't know God, I'd probably have killed myself.

Besides, all my life I'd been around drunks a whole lot worser'n her.

◆　　　◆　　　◆

Wilma was one of the most intelligent, interesting, and unusual people I ever met. She had a lot of good common sense. Her father was "Doc" Morrow, one of the old doctors in Andrews. I'd heard about him since I was just a little girl. He was much loved and well respected, and had died before I met Wilma.

Wilma had a very low-pitched, almost masculine voice, was one of these happy-go-lucky people with an outgoing personality and infectious laugh, but she didn't *put up with no foolishness* out of nobody. She was good to the patients and went out of her way to do things for them, but if somebody got out of line, she could flat-out straighten 'em out.

If she heard a patient or visitor giving one of the other nurses a hard time, she went back in the clinic, got Neal's RN cap, put it on and came struttin' out like she owned the place, gruffly demanding to know "What's going on here?" That never failed to *put the quietus* on the trouble-maker.

I found her to be a fun person and just loved to work with her. She made me feel secure, as she always knew what to do in any given situation. We made a good pair.

We were always laughing about something. She was a "cusser." She wasn't necessarily mad—it was just something she did. I'd heard Dad cuss all my life, so it was nothing new to me. And she liked a little nip every now and then, too.

I couldn't understand why Wilma took a liking to somebody as ignorant and countrified as me, but lots of times when we were working the same shift, she invited me home with her to spend the night. She seemed to like having me keep her company, and was good to me. We had fun, just talking and laughing together.

She loved to play cards. Now, that was one thing Mom didn't allow in her house. She said that playing cards was a sin—as she said about most anything that was fun.

Well, if she could only see me now! That summer, I'd go home with Wilma and as soon as we got there, she put her on a pair of short shorts (a sure sign of a *strollop*, or prostitute, so Dad said). We'd fix us something to eat and she'd give me a soft drink and ice, or make lemonade for me, and put some Bourbon or Vodka in Coke or Seven-up for herself. She got out the card table and cards, laid out a pack of cigarettes and matches, and set an ashtray over on the corner, and we'd get our drinks and settle down to a long session of card playin'.

We played Rummy and Gin Rummy, and she taught me how to shuffle cards, and then how to play Set Back and Poker and Solitaire, and all kinds of card games. I got so I could shuffle them things like a pro. I loved to just shuffle cards, and found it soothing when I was worried or upset to just sit down and shuffle a deck of cards over and over while I thought things through.

We didn't do any gambling. As far as I'm concerned, if we'd gambled for money that would've been the only part that might be classed as "sin". We just kept score, and used matches or pennies as part of the game. And she provided all the pennies, anyway. In those days, folks didn't have TV, and it was a pleasurable way to spend an evening.

Wilma had a little girl, Joan, who was there most of the time, and I loved to read to her and play with her. But after Joan went to bed, or if she spent the night with a little friend or Wilma's sister, we set up and played cards til ten o'clock sometimes.

She never tried to get me to drink, and she didn't get drunk—just sipped her drink along every once in awhile. She didn't urge me to smoke, either, but told me to help myself if I wanted to. And I did.

It was an education to me to see how other people lived. Most of what I knew about how other people lived was from what I read about in books. It was hard for me to imagine. As I sat there and played cards and smoked cigarettes with Wilma sitting around in shorts, I felt deliciously wicked when I thought of how Dad and Mom would have a fit if they knew about it. Only they didn't. One reason it didn't bother me any was that I felt that the things they called a sin was nowhere near as bad as the things they did and said, and the way they treated us. Even if I'd got drunk and cussed like a sailor, it wouldn't have been any different from what I'd seen right in my own home all my life. And Wilma sure didn't beat on little helpless youngens.

I still love a good game of Rummy. And sitting and talking and laughing and relaxing with friends, without somebody "a-rainin' on my picnic." I could play all night.

And I still like to just shuffle them cards sometimes—just because I can.

◆   ◆   ◆

Sweetie and Ruth smoked, and I'd have one of theirs ever once in awhile. When I could afford it, I'd buy me a carton of Cavalier™ cigarettes. Mankind alive, I felt rich, havin' a whole carton of cigarettes. They lasted me two months or more.

Bud was serving a six months' prison sentence over at Peachtree, where Tri-County Community College is now located. Sweetie, Ruth and I went to see him about every other Saturday afternoon. We'd go in together to buy him a carton of Camel™ cigarettes and take to him. They cost two dollars a carton then.

◆   ◆   ◆

Telling about Wilma drinking reminded me of how we used to treat DT's when a patient was admitted to the hospital to get over a binge. At home, when a man was suffering from a hangover, he thought *"a little doast of hair off the dog that bit me"* was what he needed to ease the symptoms of a hangover.

In the hospital, though, he got IV's full of vitamins. If he got a little too rambunctious, he got Paraldehyde. That was a volatile liquid that tasted so bad that if I'd a been a drunk, I'd a quit, afraid they'd give me another dose of that stuff. I'd say it came real close to drinking pure gasoline.

This certain man owned a prosperous business in town, and was a good old man, but ever so often, he'd go on a drinking spree and have to come in to get back on his feet. He was the only patient I ever knew to ask for Paraldehyde when he got the jitters, only he called it "F'mal'ahyde." I'm sure he didn't know that Formaldehyde is used to preserve tissue specimens, such as an appendix, to send to the pathologist. I thought it was so funny when he asked for his F'mal'ahyde and giggled to myself as I thought, "Mister, you're already pickled enough."

It usually took awhile to coax a patient into drinking all the prescribed dose—about two ounces. We mixed it with enough orange juice to dilute and tame it down some, and poured it over ice, filling an eight ounce cup. The ice made it kind of gel. If they wouldn't drink it all, or started vomiting, the "fun" started. We used a rectal tube and Asepto syringe, and gave it to them rectally. That flat-out laid 'em in the shade. You could smell it on their breath within five minutes.

Using a 10 inch rectal tube inserted about four inches creates the necessity of getting up close and personal to administer it. How come me to know just how volatile and awful Paraldehyde is, was a first-hand experience. One night I'd just about finished giving some to a woman when she suddenly stiffened, gave a hard push, and it exploded out—right into my face. From the way it smelt, she must a-been eatin' boiled eggs with raw ramps for chasers.

I learnt that they's one thing that can make Paraldehyde worse than it already is in a cup. I'll leave it to you to guess what that could be.

And that stuff makes your eyes kindly smart, too.

OB'S AND THE DELIVERY ROOM

There were three beds in the OB ward of the hospital. We didn't have a labor room. When an OB patient was in labor, she stayed in her bed in the ward until her *labor pains* got fairly close together. The floor nurses timed the contractions, did rectal exams, listened to the baby's heart, and kept track of her progress. When labor progressed to a certain stage, she was taken by stretcher to the OR, which was also the delivery room, and preparations were made to deliver the baby.

One part of getting an OB patient ready for delivery was to "prep" her. We prepped her by lathering her up with Gamophen soap and shaving off all the hair from the lower abdomen on down. We used a straight razor. You talk about a ticklish job—now, that was one more ticklish job. Things just didn't work the same on this end as I'd seen Dad and the boys do when they'd pull their jaw or mouth to the side to take out the wrinkles when they shaved. Anyhow, it wasn't long before I could take that straight razor and whisk that hair off before you could whistle Dixie. With nary a nick.

When an OB patient came in and I got her into bed, I got that prep job done right away. It didn't take me but one time trying to prep a squirmy OB when she was in active labor to learn to get the job done before she got so far along that she couldn't be still.

We tried to time when to call the doctor so he wouldn't have to wait more than ten minutes before the baby came. We wrapped flat, red rubber hot water bottles in a blanket and put them in the bassinet to have the baby's bed warm. We put the OB's legs up in stirrups and had everything all ready for the doctor when he got there. He was usually tired from working all day, and didn't like to have to sit there and wait. And we'd just as soon not have a tired doctor under-foot, either. If he was up most of the night, he still had to work the next day. If things slowed down, he went into the lounge to take a nap until he was called.

Since there was only two of us on duty, one had to stay with the OB and the other had to take care of the floor. Many times, I'd be watching an OB who was up in stirrups when the other nurse would bring a tray of food, set it on the end of a stretcher and push it halfway into the OR to me. I pulled down my mask and ate with one hand, with a rubber glove on the other, just taking my eyes off the patient long enough to get a bite off the fork or spoon. Nurses also learn to eat whatever, whenever and wherever they can.

When the labor pains got hard enough for the woman to need help with the pain, we gave her Demerol and Atropine IM. When she got almost fully dilated, we gave her some anesthesia by mask. The Trilene mask was a hand-held chrome cylinder with a thick black rubber mask connected to it. It had a wrist strap attached to one side. We poured a certain number of cc's of Trilene, an anesthetic, into the cylinder. Then we put the cylinder in the patient's hand, strapped it to her wrist so she wouldn't drop it, and let her inhale through the mask as much as she wanted.

Letting her do it herself was a safeguard to keep her from getting too much. If she got enough to put her under, her arm would drop and the mask came off her face. When she woke up enough to start crying out, we'd put it back in her hand for her to use. During delivery, we held it on her face and kept her just awake enough to push when she was told.

Most of the time, we went ahead and did a sterile prep and draped her to have her all ready. To do a sterile prep, we used a sponge forcep to hold a folded 4 x 4 sterile gauze square, dipped it into a pint sized basin of Mercurochrome and used it like a paint brush to swab the solution on. She was a brilliant glow-color orange-red from her lower abdomen almost to her knees. And that stuff didn't wash off; she wore it off. Then we draped her with sterile leggings and sheets.

One night not long after I started to work there, Dr. Van came out on the floor from the delivery room and called to me to come and help him. The patient was having a difficult delivery and needed more anesthesia than the Trilene mask.

When we cleaned at night, I'd noticed the anesthesia machine with the tanks attached to the side but had no idea how it worked. Dr. Van Gorder pulled it over to the patient's head and briefly explained that he wanted to give her Nitrous Oxide (also called "laughing gas"), and told me how how to do it.

He explained how to inflate the breathing bag with Nitrous and Oxygen, in order to give twice as much Oxygen as Nitrous. Each tank was connected to the anesthesia machine and had a little lever. When he held the lever down, I could hear and see the bag inflate. He held the Oxygen lever down about twice as long as the Nitrous lever to fill the bag. Then he showed me how the mask attached, how to fit it to the patient's face, and hold her chin up to keep her tongue from falling backwards and cutting off her breathing.

Each time the patient breathed, the bag deflated some. When it deflated to less than half, I was to push down the levers and keep it refilled. No mention was made of the use of an airway. I wouldn't have known what one was if I'd seen it.

But he didn't have time to give me a full crash course in anesthesia. This instruction took less than five minutes.

Leaving me to do my thing, he went around to the foot of the delivery table. I now realize that he was using forceps to turn and deliver the baby. In a few minutes, he laid a squalling, kicking baby on the woman's belly and told me to take the mask off her face. When he got the cord tied and cut, he handed me the baby to take out to the nursery.

After I went away to school and started learning about things that could go wrong, I had mental nightmares when I thought about this and many other things I'd done when I worked there. Truly God had been looking after me, the doctor—and especially, the patients.

What I've described may sound primitive, or even barbaric, but think of what could have happened if the hospital and Dr. Van Gorder had not been there. Though primitive by today's standards, it was a vast improvement from the then recent past of having a baby at home, way back up on a mountain in a dark holler by lamplight, with no sterile field or instruments, and only a granny doctor in attendance. Those old midwives did a marvelous job when you consider the conditions and the limitations they worked under. But they were poorly equipped to deal with serious abnormal circumstances.

The patient would have had nothing for the pain, risked serious infection, and maybe had a leaky bladder for the rest of her life…if she and the baby survived.

In the hospital, the woman had several options to make her delivery as pain-free as possible. There were several ways to use local anesthetic by injection, plus drugs for pain control.

When a laceration, or tear, happened during birth at home, it was not sewed up or repaired, and was left open to heal on its own. It also left everything open to infection. With the poor sanitary measures available then, women sometimes died from infection. It takes weeks or months to heal, and weakens the musculature that holds the uterus in place. It was a common sight then to see older women with a prolapsed uterus and bladder or loss of bladder control. I was shocked the first time I saw a patient with a prolapsed uterus, scheduled for surgical repair. I thought it was a tumor—the entire uterus was almost completely outside her body. Think of the years of suffering that poor lady had endured.

Another advantage is that if serious complications develop during labor, we simply take the patient's legs out of the stirrups to lay her flat, open a sterile field and instruments and do a Cesarean section (delivery through an abdominal incision). Dr. Van and I, with one scrub nurse, have done many of these in less than three minutes—starting time until the baby is out. We never lost a mother or a baby.

After delivery, "perineal care" was given on each shift. This was done by putting the woman on a bedpan, pouring a pitcher of Potassium Cyanide solution over the area as an antiseptic, and inspecting the sutures for redness or possible infection. Bottles of Cyanide Solution were left in the patient's room to be available when needed. A portable infra-red light, or heat lamp was used on the suture area at least twice a day for twenty minutes to keep the area dry and promote healing.

We bathed the newborn with mineral oil and cotton balls, and put an alcohol dressing on the umbilical cord with a belly band to hold it in place.

The identification bracelet was made of little square white beads on a string. One side of each bead had a black letter printed on it. From a box, we picked out the beads to spell the last name and strung them on in correct sequence, using blank ones on either side to make it fit. An identification card was filled out and put in the metal holder at the foot of the bassinet.

This was the only patient identification of any kind used on anyone in the hospital.

Back then, it was rare to see a mother who worked, and most women breast-fed their babies. The ones who didn't breast feed took a pill called Stilbesterol to dry up her breasts. We put a breast binder on her to compress her breasts and keep them from filling up. This was a wide piece of strong cotton fabric that covered her whole chest. We pulled it as tightly as possible and pinned it in place with a row of safety pins, pulling and pinning about an inch and a half apart all down the front.

One thing that really surprised me was the practice of getting a new mother out of bed within eight hours after delivery, and helped to walk around the room. Then every shift got her up and walked her at least once. When I was growing up and babies were born at home, a new mother stayed in the bed and wasn't allowed up for nine days. I learned that early ambulation prevented blood clots from forming in their legs, a condition that had killed many women in the past.

Oh, yes, I was learning!

The mother and baby usually went home on the third day. Male babies were circumcised before they went home, or came back in a week to have it done. That's another practice I don't like. As I said about the T & A's, my opinion may not count for much, but I have one, and it's a strong one. I've lived long enough to know that medical opinion, like everything else, changes. I think, and hope, that some day in the future, they'll stop doing "routine" circumcisions.

Doctors said the baby's nervous system isn't well enough developed for the baby to feel the pain of circumcision. That makes about as much sense to me as the theory of evolution. Big Question: Then why do you have to put the precious little feller on a board and securely restrain all four limbs? And when he's lying there sleeping peacefully, why does he start kicking and screaming until he almost loses his breath when the circumcision clamp is put on? And for two days, why does he scream like boiling water is being poured over him when he wets his diaper? Duh!

It hurts, that's why.

I'm also old enough now not to care if folks think I'm old and timey and out of step with modern times. I don't believe in this kind of "routine" surgery. If it works, don't fix it, then you don't have to worry about complications.

They say a circumcision is for the purpose of cleanliness. When our son was born, and the time came, we didn't have him circumcised. We *stuck to our guns* and said that if he didn't have enough IQ to keep himself clean, we'd be the ones taking care of him and we'd do it for him.

And there ain't nobody goin' to hurt my baby and me stand there and let 'em, unless it's for something he needs a whole lot worse than a routine circumcision.

Poor little fellers has got enough misery to go through in this old world without addin' something that ain't even necessary.

HIJINKS AND MYSTERIES

It's been interesting to me to see the change in the way people feel about going into a hospital, or having a member of their family in the hospital. Back then, when someone was told that a person was in the hospital, that was mighty close to saying they were dying. They'd ask, "Do you need me to come and set up?" This was probably a carry-over from the old custom of "settin' up" with somebody when they were "bad off."

When somebody was brought into the hospital, just about every close relative they had came too. It just wasn't considered the right thing to do to go off and leave them in there by theirself. Many times, that presented a real problem in caring for the patient. It was hard to maneuver around in a room full of people with them watching every move you made. If you asked them to step out while you did something for the patient, when you opened the door, there was a hall full of people standing there ready to flock back in.

Probably another reason they did it was that very few people had telephones and they wanted to keep up with what was happening. Many times at night, we had to ask them to wait out in the lobby so their relative and the other patients could get some rest. It wasn't unusual to see a visitor go from room to room and patient to patient, easing up to the bed and peering intently into their face to ask "What's wrong with you?"

Sometimes the lobby was full all night, with all the seats full, people sprawled out all over the place, and sleeping on the floor. They'd sit and *spin yarns* (tell tall tales), smoke, dip snuff, and spit chawin' t'backer all night. It was a real social event. I didn't mind, if they were quiet, but sometimes they'd get so rowdy that one of us had to go out and ask them to please be quieter so the patients could sleep.

It was a constant effort to get people to realize that it wasn't necessary for everybody to camp out there, yet do it in a nice manner. Some nights, I felt like I was wading over, around and through people to get through the lobby to take care of patients on the other side.

I got acquainted with a lot of people there in that old waiting room, though. Lots of people knew me from the church singings. I never learned the names of a lot of people, but recognized their faces as belonging to a certain patient's family. But they remembered me and hollered at me when they saw me on the street, like I was an old friend. So I must have handled the problem tactfully enough.

They had to clear out of the lobby the next morning when the clinic opened, to make room for the clinic patients. They were seen on a first-come basis; no appointments were made. Sometimes, the lobby didn't have enough seats for all the clinic patients to sit, and sometimes they'd have to wait all day before they saw a doctor, or even have to come back the next day. I felt so sorry for them. If I could find an extra pillow, or even a bath blanket, I'd take one to some person that looked so tired and sick, so they could lean back against the wall and be more comfortable.

Many patients were from the Robbinsville area—at least fifteen miles away, over a winding road across high mountains. Andrews was the closest hospital, and Bryson City was the next. People today think nothing of driving fifteen miles, and on today's roads, it's no problem. Back then, most roads in this area were narrow two lane roads with sharp, improperly elevated curves, and if you got a little too fast, you'd lose control and go over the edge, and plunge hundreds of feet down a steep mountainside. It was doubly treacherous in the winter. At times the road was impassable and there was no Rescue Squad to transport patients then.

There were occasions, though, when the lobby was empty. One night, me and another nurse was coming across the lobby past the snack vending machines and she said she wished she had a bag of them peanuts. Neither one of us had the right amount of change. Back then, machines didn't take dollar bills.

Out of curiosity, I looked the machine over to see how it worked. I got down in front of the machine and peered up under the front edge of the recessed area where the snacks came out. Hmmm! Each item had a little door that lifted up to let the candy bar, crackers, gum, or peanuts fall out when the money tripped the release. I poked my long skinny fingers up in there and managed to get the peanuts door raised up a little bit with one finger while I poked another finger behind the end of a pack and gave a little flip—and out flew the peanuts! Hot dog! Have some peanuts! EVER'BODY have some peanuts!

I found that the wrapper on the peanut butter cheese crackers would come apart with a little manipulation. I could get the wrapper open and flip out the crackers one at a time, then pull the wrapper out. Anybody want some crackers? Hey! We've got 'em!

Them three color striped cokernut candy bars look kindly thin............I wonder......? Well, look-y here! Ain't you a purty little thing?

The news got around and other nurses were so proud of me that I never even thought about it being stealing. Anyhow, we never *acted hoggish*, and left some in there for other folks.

One day I heard Mary Willie mention that something was wrong with the snack machines; the money and the stock tally didn't come out right. I just about suffocated trying to keep a straight face, but knowed I better.

I don't recon they ever did figger that'n out.

◆   ◆   ◆

The kitchen always sent up food for the night shift. They must have run out of ideas, for it got so it was nothing but pimento cheese spread and bread to make sandwiches almost every night. Wilma bein' a big "cusser", one night she said she was getting tired of that G-D pimento cheese every night and wished she could get into that kitchen—she'd get her some ice cream.

I don't remember whose idea it was, but the end result was that I got on the dumb waiter and curled up and she let me down into the kitchen. I used a flashlight so no one from outside could see a light, and Wilma told me where the ice cream was located. I not only got us a big bowl of ice cream, but found some strawberries and got us some of them, too. And maybe some other stuff......

I put the loot on the dumbwaiter and pulled on the rope to send it up. After Wilma unloaded it, she let the dumbwaiter back down for me, I crawled back in it, and she hauled me up. We laid back and enjoyed our strawberries and ice cream and stuff.

That was the first of many a good midnight snack.

They never did solve that mystery neither.

◆   ◆   ◆

I had my own mystery one balmy summer evening while working the 3-11 shift. It was getting along toward sundown and all the windows were open. We got a good breeze up there on the second floor, and I could smell the honeysuckle from a field along the back side of town. I'd put some dirty linen down the chute and stood there a minute, dreamily enjoying the honeysuckle scent in the evening breeze. I was snatched out of my daze by a high pitched, far off voice calling, "Cleeeeooooo!".........."Cleeeeeeooo!" Then there was silence. I looked out over a peaceful sunset scene from the window; couldn't see a thing going on down there. Then the voice started calling again. Then silence.

Now, I never believed in ghostes and "haints" but I sure was beginnin' to wonder what in this or the other world was goin' on here. Then, the voice floated up again, "Cleeeeoooo!" It started on a really high note and fell about five notes until the end of the name, when the "o" sounded like "ew." I'd only known one other person named Cleo, and she sure wasn't nowhere around here. I'll have to admit I was getting a little uneasy, maybe even feeling a few goosebumps.

As I stood and puzzed about it, I couldn't think of any logical explanation. The thought crossed my mind that maybe one of the patients was dying and their spirit was calling out to me for help. I turned around, thinking I'd just quietly go check on the patients, when the other nurse came in. I was afraid she'd think I'd been into the vitamins a little heavy-handed, or had a loose screw in my head, or something—but I just had to know. I knew I'd heard that voice. I asked her if she heard somebody calling my name. She looked at me and saw I was serious, then listened a minute. Then she went over to the window. Sure enough, we both heard "Cleeeeoooo!"

She started laughing, and told me it was one of "the Fisher girls" calling their dog.

Calling their dog??? What'n the wooly-wide world you mean—callin' their dog? Ohhh——the DOG's named Cleo...Yeah......Right! O.K.! I was so over-come with relief that she'd heard it too, that it took me a few seconds to process the information.

The Fisher sisters, Mabel and Margaret, were genteel ladies who lived in the big old two story house across the field from the back of the hospital. They'd never married, and when their father died, had inherited Fisher's Clothing Store in town. Every evening, they let their beloved little dog, Cleo, out to play awhile, and called her to come in when it started getting dark.

Their speech sounded like a slight British accent crossed with Southern belle. You know—very prahpah.

I sure was glad that mystery got solved right away. Of course, the story got spread around and everybody got a good laugh on me.

But that was O.K. We were laughing together.

◆   ◆   ◆

Another night I was coming across the lobby after giving a shot. I still had the alcohol sponge (cotton ball) in my hand, and, I don't know why—to see how far I could throw it, I guess—I just *rared back* and throwed it at the ceiling way up there over the stairwell. Like a baseball pitcher throwin' a fastball—whoosh! That thang give a soggy thud and stuck like glue.

I didn't quite know what to think, but it hit me as funny, the way it went all that distance and splatted and stuck. I laughed out loud.

Next time I came across there, I wondered if another'n would stick.

Shore'nuff.

Like a tick on a dog.

After a few weeks of that, Mary Willie had her another mystery when she noticed sump'm strange a-growin' all over the ceilin' up there. Some kind of fungus? Or what?

She had a man bring a big long ladder to climb up there and check it out. He hollered back down and told her it was cotton balls.

COTTON BALLS!!? How on earth...?

Hmmmmmm?

Another unsolved mystery?

Wellsir, I'm afraid I got caught on that'n. Mary Willie wutn't no dummy, and knowed somebody had to a-put them cotton balls up there, and started askin' around. When she got around to askin' me, I owned up to it—I wutn't a-goin' to lie. But Mary Willie got too tickled to get mad at me—just told me to cut it out.

I ditn't really want to, but I did.

◆   ◆   ◆

When a patient came in for elective surgery or some kinds of x-rays, they were kept on a clear liquid diet and we had to give cleansing enemas after supper, and sometimes again at 6 A.M.

It was usually the men who objected to the bouillon/Jello supper.

The old story goes, that a man came into the hospital to have tests done the next day, and refused the liquid diet when it was served to him at supper. In a little while, the orderly came in and gave him an enema.

During visiting hours, a friend came and visited awhile. When asked what they'd been doing to him since he got there, the patient said, "I'll tell you one thing right now—when you come to this hospital and they bring you soup, you'd better drink it."

GETTING SERIOUS

That summer, a couple of things happened that really upset me, and made me do a lot of thinking about some of the horrible and tragic things I might see as a nurse.

Tuberculosis, or TB, wasn't at all rare in the early fifties. There was a sanitorium at Black Mountain where patients from this area went for treatment.

I don't know why this patient was in the hospital instead of being sent to the TB sanitorium—maybe he was too sick or waiting to be transferred—anyway, he'd been admitted with the diagnosis of TB. He was in isolation, and the principles and importance of isolation had been explained to me.

So far, the patients I'd encountered had been easy to please, except for the occasional cranky one. Even they usually apologized for getting cranky. I found that even nice people sometimes get cranky when they don't feel well. That was O.K. Nuthin' personal.

But this patient was different. Nobody could get a civil word from him and he was constantly rude, complaining and cursing. He cussed even worse than Dad used to cuss, if that's possible. I was shocked to hear in the report that he claimed to be an atheist. I'd never even thought about there being anybody that didn't believe in God. Even the worst old drunk I'd ever seen set around and cried and talked about God.

One day he rang his buzzer and I went to the door to see what he wanted. In a loud voice, he hollered, "Give me some water!" He seemed agitated, and was acting strangely, repeating his demand for water as I quickly put on a mask and gown and went in to take him some water. I saw that he had water in the pitcher and glass on the bedside stand, and thought "How peculiar—why is he asking for water when he has some?"

I filled a glass about half full of fresh water and held it out. He acted as if he couldn't see it, or even knew I was in the room, so I told him I had him some water and helped him raise up, and held the glass to help him take a drink. The glass had no more than touched his lips when he screamed and threw his arms up and backwards, knocking the glass from my hand and causing the water to spill across his shoulder, arm and chest. He screamed again, saying, "Oh, God, I'm on

363

fire," and started trying to knock the water off him, then swinging his hands as if they had fire on them. He acted as if the water was burning gasoline everywhere it touched him.

He started rapidly kicking his feet, still screaming and saying, "Oh God!" over and over. I noticed that he was starting to have some bloody froth in the corner of his mouth. I was afraid he'd fall off the bed and hurt himself, and was having a hard time trying to keep him in bed. He didn't seem to hear me or see me when I tried to calm him, his wide eyes darting around as if he saw something that he was terribly afraid of. He was saying something, and I finally understood a part of what he was saying as, "Oh, God, I'm burning in hell."

I can't describe the horror I felt when I realized what was happening in his mind. I didn't know what to do to help him. I finally just bent my body across his chest to keep him from falling out of the bed. The other nurse had heard the screaming and came running in. Just then, he gave another horrendous scream and lunged toward the edge of the bed, then suddenly became limp and still, lying partially on his side across the bed, with an arm dangling and his head slightly hanging over the edge of the bed.

I straightened up and looked at his face. His eyes were wide and staring. Bright blood oozed and dripped from the corner of his slack, open mouth. I knew he was dead.

That was one of the worst things I ever witnessed. And one of the saddest. How terribly sad to have lived his life denying the existence of God, then calling out His name as he was dying. I wondered if his spirit was calling out from Hell before his body actually stopped breathing.

And I still think about him and wonder.

◆   ◆   ◆

The second incident left a permanent mental image of how horribly a person can be injured in an accident. I'd seen a few minor injuries—cuts, fractured arm, sprained ankle, etc., but nothing really life-threatening.

One day I heard loud men's voices coming from the street down at the entrance. I looked down from the lobby window onto the street below and saw some men milling around a big log truck, and heard the sound of heavy footsteps running up the stairs.

As I looked down, I could see that something was laid across a huge tire on the back of the truck. Then I could see a man's head dangling from the edge of the tire, almost touching the truck bed. Behind me, I heard a man tell Mary Willie that they had a man hurt bad down there on the truck.

She came out of the office and pointed to some portable army stretchers mounted on the wall of the stairwell and told them to get one of them to use it to carry the man upstairs. The man grabbed the stretcher down and raced back outside.

The men climbed up on the back of the truck and were bent over the injured man so close together that I couldn't see as they moved him onto the stretcher. Then they lifted him off the truck and came up the stairs. Somebody said for them to take him into x-ray, and I went over to hold the swinging doors open for them. I had to move on back into the small room, as there was no way to get around them to get out.

I heard one of the men say that the man had been operating a crane down on Valley River below town, and it had turned over into a gravelly ditch full of water, crushing him under the crane. As they lifted him off the portable stretcher onto the x-ray table, I saw that he was a colored man, and as they slid him over on the table, his body bent in strange places where there were no joints. I could see his muddy shoes and pants legs, and his legs and feet were unnaturally positioned. Dr. Van Gorder came in and immediately said he was dead—there was nothing he could do for him.

When he said that, everybody just sort of stepped back a little. Standing pinned against the wall, I suddenly had a clear view of the mangled body there on the table, about three feet away. I was too horrified to look away; just looked in disbelief as my eyes traveled across him, then back again.

He was still wet and muddy, with dirt, mud, pieces of gravel and debris, even dead leaves and small sticks ground into his torn flesh, which looked stark white against his dark shredded skin. One of his eyes was almost out of the socket and the rest of his face was lacerated, mangled and distorted.

And I smelled that sickening scent of human blood and traumatized tissue. That smell was to become so familiar in the years to come. I was never bothered with that smell in surgery, however. This particular smell, as on that day, comes from bleeding and trauma, as from an auto accident victim, when the blood is several minutes old. Many times when I would be in the Emergency room working on a patient in an enclosed area, that smell would bring back memories of my first encounter with it.

Later that day when I sat down to eat dinner, I looked at my plate and had to quickly get up and leave. They had Spanish rice.

Fifty years later, I still think of that poor man whenever I see Spanish rice.

THE SUMMER OF 1953

One thing about being a nurse, it's never boring. No two patients ever react the same way to the same treatment, and nothing's ever the same two days in a row. When you're inside those walls, you're in another world. You may go home dead tired at the end of the day, and although there are many things beyond your control, you have the deep satisfaction that you made a difference to someone.

By the end of 1952, I was still loving the work and still determined to go to school, but hadn't been able to save but a dollar at a time, here and there. Every time I saved a few dollars, something came up and I had to spend it. My white hose got runs in them and I had to buy a new pair every few days, .and I had to buy a few clothes now and then. We were allowed to wear white sandals to work so I finally got a pair.

I reasoned that I'd been getting along on sixty dollars a month, and when and if I got my raise to eighty five, I could save at least fifteen to twenty dollars a month. The next month would be December, and if I worked one more year, I would have enough saved to go to school. But I still hadn't got the promised raise.

But how much money would I need? And how would I go about getting into school? And where would I go? I was discussing this with Wanda Hardin one day and she said she had an aunt who lived in Knoxville, and Fort Sanders Hospital had a School of Nursing there. She was thinking seriously about going there for nurse's training.

Early in the spring of 1953, a new RN started working in the clinic. Each school of nursing had their own distinctive nurse's cap, and you could tell which school a nurse graduated from by the cap she wore. I admired her cap and asked her where she graduated from, and she said Fort Sanders. Could this be possibly be just coincidence?

I asked her how to get admitted and how much the tuition was. She didn't know how much tuition was now, but I'd need to write and ask for an application form to fill out and send in. I would be given an appointment for an interview and then be notified if I was accepted. I could find out about tuition when I went.

I got the address and wrote, asking what their requirements were and asked for an admission form to the School of Nursing. When I got a reply, I learned that I had taken the required courses in High School. I filled out the form and sent it back. Then I got an appointment for an interview.

Wanda said she would go with me for the interview. We could go on the bus and spend the night with her aunt, go to the interview, then come back that afternoon.

I still didn't have very many clothes, and had nothing fit to wear to Knoxville for the interview. Back then, proper young ladies wore a hat to town church and for all special occasions. I wanted to look my best, so for the occasion, I bought a pretty little hat with a veil for $1.98, a nice new dress for $2.98, and some beige colored nylons. At that time, nylon hose had a seam up the back, and women checked often to see if their seams were straight and centered.

That was my first bus ride, and the farthest I'd ever been away from home. We went through Robbinsville, and the winding road seemed to go on forever. When we finally came into Knoxville, I was amazed at all the cars, trucks, buses and vans, and all the big buildings. I'd heard the joke about the country boy who went into the city for the first time and sunburnt the roof of his mouth walking around with his mouth open, looking up at the tall buildings. I sure could identify with that.

Wanda had written her aunt and told her what time the bus would get into Knoxville, and she met us when we got off at the bus station. My goodness, there were people all over the place, waiting for a bus. It sure was a lot different from the street corner at the drugstore in Andrews, where a person would set their suitcase down on the street and lean against the light post while they waited for the bus.

Wanda's aunt was a sweet lady who seemed glad to have us. They lived right on the outskirts of the city, on a street with houses that looked pretty much alike all around. I'd never seen so many houses, street after street, and wondered how on earth anybody ever found their way home in this maze.

She went with us the next day to help us get around. Her aunt wore a hat and gloves, and I was glad I'd splurged on a hat, so I didn't feel so much like a country bumpkin. We walked up the street to a bus stop to catch a city bus. She explained that we had to wait for the correct bus to take us to the hospital. We watched several buses go by, then finally she said this one was ours. When we got on the bus, she bought the bus tokens and we took a seat and headed for downtown. I could never have imagined what a city was actually like. This city bus business was amazing. I don't think Wanda had ever been on her own in a city before, either. I sure was glad we had somebody who knew their way around.

The lady who interviewed me was pleasant and helpful in explaining what I needed to know. It was a big relief to learn that student nurses lived in a nurses residence on the hospital grounds. I knew that if it was up to me to get around here, I'd get so lost nobody'd ever find me.

Wanda's aunt took us to lunch, then to the bus station and saw that we got on the right bus to go home. I was already getting homesick.

I must have done all right on the interview, for I soon got a letter saying I'd been accepted into their School of Nursing. For a few days, I was on cloud nine. Then when month after month passed and I didn't get a raise, I began to get worried about money for tuition. I was supposed to have got my raise on September 1, 1952 but was too timid to ask about it. I wondered if my work was satisfactory. If it wasn't, nobody had said so, and I knew they sure were getting their money's worth out of me.

Berkshire Knitting Mills had come to Andrews, and several girls I knew worked there. They all told me I ought to quit working at the hospital and get a job at Berkshire. I couldn't believe how much money they made—at least three times what I made! Plus, they got off on time every day and had weekends off. Every time they got a paycheck, they bought pretty new clothes, went to the show, and bought hot dogs, popcorn, and stuff.

I only got paid once a month and never had an extra dime. Every time I got my check, I hopefully looked for my raise, but the amount was always the same. I knew I was going to have to do something different. I needed $125. to pay my first year's tuition, $75. for the second, and $50. for the third. That was an impossible amount to save on my salary.

It was along toward the middle of April when I decided I was going to go to Berkshire to work. I could work my notice, work at Berkshire from May through August, giving me four months to make the money for my tuition. It broke my heart to think about quitting, but I could see no other way. I was going to nurses' training or die trying.

It took me a few days to get up enough courage to talk to Neal about it, but knew I had to work a two weeks' notice and had better get it done. When I told her I was going to quit, she wanted to know why, and I told her. She said I was one of the best workers they ever had and didn't want me to quit, but I told her I had no other choice.

I went on about my work, relieved to get it over with, but wanting to cry when I thought about leaving. About an hour later, Neal came out on the floor and told me Dr. Van Gorder wanted to see me in his private office. It scared the daylights out of me. What on earth had I done wrong? The only time I'd seen anyone summoned to the private office was when they got fired or were in big trouble for something—I felt like a kid going to the Principal's office.

I hadn't been around Dr. Van enough to get to know him, and was totally in awe of him. When I went on back to his office, the door was open and he was seated behind his desk. He smiled and spoke to me, calling my first name, which surprised me, and told me to come on in and have a seat. I went in and gingerly sat on the edge of the chair, scared to death. It had to be something big and terrible for him to take time to see me so formally in his private office! Oh, Lord, help me—what have I done? It must have been a bad mistake this time.

He said, "Neal tells me you're going to leave us." I said "Yes, Sir." He said, "Would you mind telling me why?" I told him I'd been working a year trying to save enough money to pay my tuition in nurse's training. I hadn't had a raise, and hadn't been able to save enough. I wanted to get a job at Berkshire so I could save enough money to begin fall classes in September .

He said, "You're too good a nurse to work in a plant." That surprised me a lot. I had no idea he even knew my name, much less know if my work was good. Then he asked me where I planned on going to school, and I told him I'd gone for an interview and been accepted at Fort Sanders.

He said, "If I were you, I'd reconsider going to school in Tennessee. If you plan on working in North Carolina, you need to go to school in this state. You'll come nearer learning what you need to know to pass state board exams and get your license. I'll tell you what—Sam Hunt, the administrator of Memorial Mission Hospital in Asheville, is a good friend of mine. If you think you'd like to go there, I'll give him a call and see what you need to do to get you in school out at Asheville."

I told him I'd appreciate all the information I could get. He looked up a number and placed a call to Mr. Hunt. As I waited, I wondered why, and couldn't believe, he'd go to all this trouble for me—even making a long distance phone call! He was too busy and too important to be wasting all this time on me—and paying for a long-distance call, too. The phone call lasted a few minutes, and he made notes on his memo pad as he talked, then asked me for my mailing address.

When he hung up, he told me Mr. Hunt said there would be no problem, he'd take care of it, but I'd need to get my application in soon. He tore off the memo sheet and handed it to me. It was the name and address of Elizabeth Parsons, Director of Memorial Mission Hospital School of Nursing. He had given Mr. Hunt my name and address, and said I would soon get a packet in the mail with an application form, the requirements for entry, and information about the school and the curriculum.

I told him I'd still have to go to Berkshire to earn tuition money. He said, "If you'll stay on here til time to start school, I'll let you have the money to pay your tuition." I thanked him and told him he might have to wait a long time before I paid him back. He told me that the only thing he asked was that when I got through school, if I came back to this area to work, I'd give him first chance to hire me. I promised him I would. Gosh, he sounded like he had no doubt I'd pass all my studies and graduate.

Everything seemed unreal. Then, the reality of what had just happened seemed to suddenly penetrate my consciousness. I could have fallen right down on the floor and kissed his feet. Not twenty minutes ago, I'd come through that door feeling like I was facing the executioner. I'd quit my job, my mind filled with trying to find a way to go to school, and maybe having to wait another year. But now—after years of hoping and praying, working and trying to save and getting nowhere—everything had suddenly fallen into place and I was really, truly, at long last, going to Nursing school. In a little over four months! I was simply overwhelmed.

Thank You, oh, thank You, God! And thank you Dr. Van Gorder!

He stood up and extended his hand. I stood up, and we shook hands. Determined to keep my composure, I thanked him again, and left. By the time I reached the hall, though, tears were streaming down my face. I had to go into the bathroom and cry awhile. I sank down on the commode seat, sat there and sobbed with relief, joy and gratitude. I wanted to fly home—running was too slow—to tell Ruth and Sweetie—and shout to everybody, "I'm going to school! I'm going to be a real, live, honest-to-goodness Registered Nurse, oh yes I am!"

And I didn't have to quit right now. Right now, I had to dry my eyes, wash my face, get out there and finish my shift.

In a few days, the information packet arrived. There were pictures of the hospital and nurses' residence, and other pictures of interest. The tuition was the same as at Fort Sanders. I would live at Latta Nurses' Home, right across the street from the hospital on Tunnel Road, and have all my meals in the hospital cafeteria.

All student nurses were required to live there during the entire three years of training. They didn't admit married students. No one was allowed to get married until their last six months of training, and then only with written permission from the Director of Nursing. Uniforms would be issued to me, and free laundry service was provided for them. I was responsible for my shoes, other clothing and personal needs.

There was a physical form to be filled out by a doctor, a dental form to be filled out by a dentist, and an application form. I also needed a transcript of my high school records and the names of three personal references.

There was a list of what I was allowed to bring with me—mostly a few clothes, pajamas or gowns and personal items, and a radio if I wanted one. I'd need an alarm clock. A bath robe was on the list, and I'd have to buy one. I'd never owned one, and had no idea what kind to get. I picked out a navy blue plisse' one from the National Bellas Hess catalog, got a money order and ordered it.

When I got my next paycheck, my raise was on it. I went to Battle furniture and bought an Arvin radio. Just think! Less than a year ago, I wasn't even allowed to turn the radio on. Now I had my own radio, my own room to put it in, lived in a house where people were good to me, people on the job who liked me, was doing what I loved—and now everything was all set for me to go to school.

I was proving that Mom and Dad were wrong about me and about nurses. Both Neal and Dr. Van Gorder had said I was a good nurse. Imagine that! And Dr. Almond had said I was intelligent. And the nurses at work said they knew I'd do good in school. These were all people I'd learned to respect. With God's help, and the help of all these new friends, I'd earned these compliments through my own hard work and making my own choices. I was even beginning to like myself a little, now that I had a chance to make my own choices and find out what kind of a person I really was.

You can bet I didn't hesitate to get right down on my knees by my bed that night and joyfully thank God for everything. Then I got into bed, turned my radio on real low, and laid there in the dark and smiled as I listened and thought about the future.

A few days after I sent in the required forms and information, I got a formal letter from the Director of Nursing who said I'd been accepted for admission to their September class. I didn't even have to go for an interview.

I wore that letter out, getting it out and reading it, folding it up and putting it back. It was reassurance that good things were about to happen. I'd worked so hard and waited so long that I just couldn't quite let it soak into my brain that I really truly was going to school soon.

◆   ◆   ◆

That was to be a very eventful, busy summer.

Dad and Mom didn't say a thing when I told them what had happened. I was still going to church and playing the piano except when I was working 7-3. When I'd gone to work, Dad told me he expected me to be in church on Sunday morning. He came to Sweetie's house to get me the first time, then told me to be waiting down at the road on Sunday mornings at 8:30. I *reckinned* he didn't want to waste time with them. He'd be there to pick me up and I'd better be there.

When I worked nights, I barely had time to get home, change clothes, and grab a bite of breakfast before time to hurry down to the road. Sometimes, I just grabbed one of Ruth's good old cat head biscuits, put an egg or some jelly in it, and ate it as I went.

It was the same as before I left home. I had to do exactly as I was told. I was too afraid of Dad to even say I was tired. It wasn't that I didn't want to go to church; I was always there when I wasn't working. I was resentful that I had no choice and felt forced into it. The fact that I'd worked all night and was tired and sleepy, or worked 3-11 and didn't get home til one in the morning, and had to be back at work that evening at 3 PM or eleven that night, didn't make a dab a difference to Dad. He was always at the church house by 9:00 and liked to stand around and talk to the other men before services started.

Preaching lasted til anywhere between twelve-thirty and two o'clock. I had to be careful to stay alert to hear that phrase "while we have a verse of song" and be ready to get up there on that piano bench for the long invitation. And I was so tired and sleepy. Most of the time, I was lucky to get three hours sleep on Sunday.

Back then, I just thought he didn't care how I felt, and it was partially true. But now, years later, I realize he'd die rather than admit it, but I think he missed me. And he was so proud of my playing the piano that it made him feel important by association, to be my Dad. He really was trying. I'd seen some big changes in him and was so glad. He was just used to being the boss and giving orders, like he always had.

He was finding out that other people spoke well of me, and I could tell he was proud, but he never told me. He spoke kindly to me, but I was careful not to do anything he disapproved of, at least not so he'd find out about it. I was still scared to death of both Mom and Dad.

Mom was friendly, and good to me during that period of time, but I never got to the point where I took it for granted. I had to have my appendix and an ovarian cyst removed in the fall of 1952, and Dad said I was coming back home when I got out of the hospital. Mom took good care of me and was good to me.

That's just the problem—I never knew if their actions were because they cared about me, or if they were trying to keep me under their control. And every time I went back home, in my mind I was still that helpless, frightened child. The awful suspense that one of them would suddenly fly mad at me was always there. I hated being so suspicious, but had learned my lessons well, and never let my guard down for an instant. I went back to work a week to the day, and sure was glad to be back at Sweetie's.

Lawerence and Roberta's first baby, Randy had been born in 1951. He was a sweet little boy and I just loved him. I liked to go to their house and see them and play with Randy. He was so well behaved that I could take him anywhere with me, even to the show, and he never cried.

I stayed with them a couple of months during the time when their second baby, Vickie was born. Lawerence was working away from home, but came home and stayed the week she was due to be born. Then he had to go back to work. A day or two later, Roberta went into labor. We were staying with Ruth and Sweetie that night. I'd worked 3-11, came home and got in bed with her. She woke me up a little while later and told me she needed to go to the hospital. Sweetie took us down there and I stayed with her til Vickie was born.

Roberta still laughs and tells about how she couldn't believe her eyes when she was lying there on the delivery table and saw me come walking in, eating an apple. It wasn't anything new to me by then. I was hungry, and had found an apple, and was used to eating anything, anywhere, anytime.

◆   ◆   ◆

My best friend in high school, Faye Ensley, was still my best friend. We got together often, and had some good times. She dated boys from time to time, but never got really serious about any of them. Then she started telling me about a boy she'd met and really liked. She went to his home and met his family, and told me all about them. They were nice friendly folks. She thought I'd like them, and wanted me to go their house with her and meet them. They had a dairy farm on Bluff Road in Marble.

She told me about each one of them, and kept telling me that her boyfriend's brother, Van, was "a perfect match" for me. She said he was a nice person, a lot of fun, and real good-lookin'. I wasn't at all keen on having a boyfriend. All I was interested in right now was going to school and didn't need a boyfriend to complicate matters.

I thought boys my age were silly, boring and full of baloney. They had no idea what life was all about. All they wanted was a good time. My idea of a good time was totally different from theirs. I was asked to go out on dates, and liked to look boys over and talk, as any normal girl does. I'd dated maybe three boys, and hadn't been much impressed with their adolescent behavior. I'd rather be home cuttin' my toenails than to have to wrassle with some over-eager Romeo, trying to keep his hands out from under my clothes. I described them as foreigners—with *Roman hands and Russian fingers.* If that's all they wanted, they could just hit the dusty trail. I double-dated some, but decided I wasn't going out by myself with a boy again.

Then, my last double date had turned out to be a dud. One of my old girl-friends talked me into coming on a blind date with her. I trusted her absolutely. They'd just picked me up and we started to ride around, when I found out his name. I hadn't known him, but I sure knew his wife. Take me home, or stop and let me out!

Men! Who needs 'em?

I always believed that love and sex should be like different sides of the same coin, they couldn't be separated. I'd seen a few fourteen, fifteen and sixteen year old girls drop out of school to get married, thinking they were in love and not knowing *the difference between bein' in love or bein' in heat.* In two year's time, they changed from a pretty, laughing young girl into a stoop-shouldered, sad-faced young mother with an air of defeat in her whole bearing. To be trapped in the situation of being "barefooted and pregnant" must be a miserable existence.

In fact, I didn't like anyone—male or female, putting their hands on me in any way, even lightly touching me on the arm during a conversation. I was uncomfortable when anyone got too close to me. I liked to keep my distance. In retrospect, I imagine it was because the only time I remember being touched as a child was when I was held and punished; or the pretended affection they showed when they were trying to find out something to punish me for.

And I didn't trust a man *as far as you could kick an anvil.*

When I met Faye's friend, I agreed with her that he seemed nice and fun to be with. He was a real good-looking feller—tall and slim, with light hair, long thick blond eyelashes and blue eyes. I thought she'd hit the jackpot this time, and was happy for her. I agreed to go with her to meet his family next Sunday, but just forget about the "brother" business.

On Wednesday before I was to go, the clinic was covered up with patients, and Neal came out and asked me if I had time to give diathermy (deep heat) to a man with a strained back. It involved putting him under the diathermy machine, setting the control and watching him for twenty minutes so he didn't get burnt. I was glad to do it and take a break.

When I went into the treatment room, the man was on the table behind the curtain, and I picked up his clinic card to see what his name was. It was Van Williams, age 30, from Marble. Oh—'Is this Faye's boyfriend's brother?' I wondered. I said, "Hello! You must be Van," as I pulled the curtain aside.

He smiled up at me and said, "I'll have to plead guilty," and laughed. Many years later, when he told anyone how we met, he'd look at me with a teasing smile and add, "And I've been pleading guilty ever since," and laugh that wonderful, contagious laugh.

We talked during the treatment, and to my surprise, I found myself enjoying the conversation very much. He told me he'd been helping his Dad and brothers build a tobacco barn and had hurt his back. He told me about his family, called their names and gave a description of each of them, how they'd moved here from Haywood county, and how the dairy farm was run. I learned that he had been in the Army and was still living with his parents. I'd known his younger sisters, Anniebelle and Betty, in school. They were so cute, and I thought it was unusual how they had other friends, but seemed to be each other's best friend. If you saw one on the schoolground, the other one was with her.

He was a talker. It's a good thing I'd set the timer, or I might have fried him right there, we were so busy talking. After he sat up on the table, we continued our conversation. He said that Faye had told him about me, and added his invitation to hers, to come to their home and meet his family. I told him I planned on coming this next Sunday afternoon after church.

He perked up, and said, "Let's pull a joke on her." His big idea was for me not to tell Faye I'd met him, then when we got out of the car, he'd come running out and we'd grab each other and hug like he was an old friend that I didn't know what had become of, and watch her reaction.

Huh-oh! Not another'n. Ah, heck! And I'd really liked this'n.

I was easily intimidated, and hadn't learned how to disagree with anyone. He must have seen my reaction on my face, though, for he quickly said, "If you want to, that is. But I think it would be fun to pull a little joke on her." I didn't know what to answer, so I didn't say anything. Then I said I had to be getting back to work in the hospital or I'd never get caught up, it had been nice meeting him.

When he stood up, I was pleasantly surprised. He was about three inches taller than I was. For some reason, ever since I'd got old enough to notice, it was always short men who made a pass at me. They'd sidle up like a *little banty rooster* and look up at me with a "pleased-with-myself" expression that said, "Well, looky here what I found!" And it seemed to me that the tall men always chose a little short woman. Go figure!

I'd just thought his brother was good looking. Oh my gosh, just look at him! Tall, dark-haired, lean and tanned from being out in the sun, and what a wonderful smile. I thought he was as handsome as Clark Gable in a rugged sort of way. He definitely got my attention. And there was definitely something different about him.

He gave me a cheerful "See you Sunday," and I was gone. I didn't think he'd see me, but…then again…maybe he would.

I couldn't get him out of my mind all the rest of that week, and was in a quandary over what to do. I finally told Faye about meeting him, what he'd said and I didn't think I wanted to go with her. But I did. As usual, Faye used her skillful art of persuasion, assured me he wasn't like "that," and I agreed to go. I'd found it interesting to have a man talk so lovingly about his family instead of being so full of himself. And I hadn't been been self-conscious with him at all til he came up with that "huggin'" business. What to do, what to do?

When we got there, most of the family came out and Van's mother and sisters hugged Faye. When she introduced me, they hugged me too. Then Anniebelle and Betty were talking about knowing me from school. With everybody talking and hugging, it eased the strain of the situation, somewhat. I found that this was a whole family of "huggers."

I immediately liked them, and was enjoying getting to know everyone. Van's dad was named Lee, his mother, Lizzie. Ruby was the oldest sister and was unmarried. Van was next, and was the oldest son, then Bobby, Grover, Lewis, Anniebelle and Betty. Grover's wife was named Edith. Bobby was mentally disabled and couldn't talk, except to say Mommy, Daddy, and called Van "Donny." He was like a child and had a doll and some toys. They said he had been injured during birth. I could see that his disability made him no less a member of the family.

Before long, Van invited me to come into the hall with him to see his gun collection. I figured he was just trying to get me off to myself, but didn't want to seem rude in their home, so I went with him. When we got in the hall, he apologized to me and said he realized he was practically a stranger to me, and was sorry if he seemed out of line. He'd been thoughtless of how I might feel.

Now this was better. He seemed to genuinely understand how I felt. I accepted his apology, and he showed me his guns, but for the life of me, I couldn't have told you whether he showed me guns or fishin' poles. I was too busy watching him and trying to figure him out. He was highly intelligent and there was definitely something different about him, and I was definitely interested in finding out what it was. In fact, he was the most interesting person I'd ever met. And I was a little bit scared about the way I was feeling.

I was working 3-11 the next week, and guess who showed up at the hospital close to quitting time one night, asking if he could walk me home? I told him I didn't get off until after 11:00, but he said he'd wait out in the lobby. I couldn't believe he could be interested in me. You'd think such a good looking man with such a great personality would have women lined up just waiting to grab him. Why wasn't he married? Had he been married before? If so, scratch that'n off. Maybe there was something wrong with him. But surely Faye would know. I decided I'd just have to find out for myself, and then I'd know.

When we started up the side street where the lights were far apart, he reached over and got my hand, saying something about being careful not to trip on the dark sidewalk. I thought to myself that holding hands was one thing, but that better be all. Then I noticed that the sidewalk was kind of broken up in places. Maybe he is just being a gentleman and seeing that I don't trip. I hoped so, for I found myself enjoying holding hands as we walked. It just seemed a natural thing to do. I hoped nothing would spoil it.

I found myself talking easily to him, and we talked non-stop til we got to the park, then sat down in the swings, side by side, and talked some more, getting to know each other. Then he got up and walked around behind me, and I thought, here comes the hands. Time for me to get going.

I felt the chains move as he took hold of them, and to my astonishment, he said, "Do you like to swing?" then started pushing the swing, slowly at first, then higher. We were like two kids laughing and playing on the swings. Then he let me slow to a stop and we sat and talked some more.

After what seemed like maybe thirty minutes, I looked at my watch. Oh, my goodness! This couldn't be right. It was almost three o'clock in the morning. Ruth'd be worried. We hurriedly walked the rest of the way home. He asked permission to kiss me good night, and kept his hands where they ought to be. He said he'd like to come back Saturday, and I said O.K. Then he left to catch the bus to Marble.

I was a long time going to sleep, even at that late hour. My mind was spinning. I felt as if I'd known him all my life, yet at the same time, there was something so mysterious about him, and so much I didn't know. I knew a lot about him now, though, after the four hour talking session. I found myself looking forward to seeing him again, and hoped Saturday would hurry.

I'd told Ruth and Sweetie about meeting him at the hospital. Now I had a lot more to tell them, and couldn't wait for them to meet him. They laughed when I told them about us swinging in the park at three in the morning, like two little kids. I'd stopped expecting them to reprimand me, and told them things as if they were my two best friends. They knew I wasn't going to do anything drastically wrong.

Sweetie was studying for his GED and I was helping him study. He caught right on to long division and the other assignments. He passed his test and was so proud—and we were proud of him. By then he was better at math than I was. He was very intelligent; he'd just never had a chance to get any education beyond the sixth grade.

When I got to work that afternoon, the girls wanted to know if that good-looking man they'd seen me leave with the night before was my boyfriend. I said "yes" proudly, then thought—oh, my gosh—is he really? And found myself hoping that he was. What a change one day can make!

When the night shift came on, they asked me if Mr. Williams had found his son. I didn't know what they were talking about, and asked. Wellsir, it seems that Van's Dad had got worried about him and came to the hospital about three in the morning, asking if they'd seen him. They told him Van had left with me after I got off at eleven. *Oh, my word!* My name's mud, now.

When I explained it, they all laughed, kidded me and said I shouldn't have kidnapped him. They treated me just the same as they always had. But I was worried. Van's Dad must think I was awful, or a strollop, staying out that late at night with a man. How could I ever face that family again? I shuddered to think what I would have been accused of, and what would have happened if it had been my parents. Oh, Lord, don't let them find out! I'd be branded forever—if I survived the punishment I was sure to get.

Like most other people at that time, neither Sweetie or the Williams' had a telephone. To my surprise, Van showed up late the next Saturday morning. When I asked if his Dad was upset, he laughed and said, "W'y, no. They didn't know you were working til eleven, and wondered what had become of me. After Dad found out I was with you, he went on home." He went on to say he'd been seriously wounded in the Army, and they'd been protective of him ever since he'd come home. He told me his Dad was a good judge of people, and after I left their house last Sunday, had remarked, "I like that girl. She's got her feet planted square on the ground." I liked him, too. We'd sat on the front porch and talked while I was there. He was an interesting person, was *sharp as a tack*, and I'd enjoyed our conversation very much.

Sweetie and Ruth got to meet him and I could tell they liked him. Sweetie had also been injured in the Army in WW II, so they had a common bond.

It was getting close to noon and I'd cooked dinner that day. I was *as fidgety as a hen on a hot rock* when I saw that Van had made himself at home and apparently expected to stay and eat with us. I don't remember what else I cooked except gravy and biscuits. There was a good reason to remember that. I'd got up from the table to put some more biscuits on the plate, and was so jittery that I bumped a couple of biscuits off into the gravy. I could have died with embarrassment. Van asked me if the biscuits were so hard that I had to soak 'em in the gravy and gave that booming laugh of his. It took a minute for what he'd said to sink in, and by then Sweetie and Ruth were laughing too.

That's the way he was—his laugh was so hearty and genuine that everyone else around him laughed, too. Then he said he didn't mean to embarrass me, he was just teasing, and the biscuits were as good as any he'd ever eaten. By then, I'd regained my composure, somewhat, and we all laughed and went on eating. I barely ate; it was hard for me to swallow.

That's all I remember about dinner, except that he thanked us and complimented me on how good everything was. I was afraid he'd think I was the worst cook he'd ever seen. He'd already bragged several times about what a good cook his Mom and Ruby were, and I already felt intimidated. You'd think, from the way he talked, that his sister, Ruby practically walked on water. She was an expert cook, seamstress, or anything else. I could throw a plain old supper of beans and taters and cornbread on the table, but didn't think I could ever measure up to "my sister, Ruby."

We walked downtown in the afternoon, and planned to go to the movies. Again, he got hold of my hand as we walked, but when we got down to main street, I pulled my hand away. I was somewhat embarrassed, and afraid somebody would see us and report to Dad. I liked him a lot, but wished he'd just keep his hands to himself. At least out in public. He had no idea how afraid I was that Dad himself might see me. Nothing would please him more than to take his belt off to me right there on main street.

He said he wanted to show me something in the window at Dorsey's Jeweler's. We walked down the street and stood outside the window, looking at the display. He pointed to a gold filigree pendant necklace with a large sapphire colored stone in the center, and asked me if I liked it. I told him it was beautiful. He reached and got my hand again and told me to come on, let's go in. As he opened the door and held it for me, I got my hand back.

We went in and he told Mrs. Dorsey we'd like to see the sapphire pendant. She got it for him, we looked at it, and he told her he'd take it. At the time, I wasn't thinking clearly, but he must have already been there and made arrangements, for she put it in a little bag for him and we left.

When we got out on the street, he wanted me to wear it. He was as excited as a little boy. I was hesitant and didn't really want to accept it. I hadn't had a chance to refuse it in the store without causing him embarrassment. After all, I barely knew him, and didn't want to feel obligated in any way. He looked into my eyes like a lovesick cowboy and said he wanted to get it for me because it was the color of my pretty blue eyes. I was so flustered and confused that I could feel myself blushing. He said, "Please let me give it to you. I want you to have it. There's no strings attached." I thought, "I swear, I'm going to have to be careful. This man can read my mind." I wasn't about to let any man get any strings attached to me. I thanked him and told him I loved it—it was my favorite color, and my birthstone. He fastened the clasp when I started to put it on. I'd never owned a nice piece of jewelry before.

It must have been pretty good quality, for in June, 2003, I had it fifty years. It hasn't yet turned my neck green—and I cherish it and the memory.

After we were seated in the theatre, he put his arm around the back of the seat and laid his hand on my shoulder. A few minutes later, he reached over and got hold of my hand. I was scared somebody would see us and tell Dad. Going to the show was a sin, so the preachers said, and to be seen holding hands in a theatre was a sin and a shame. Nice girls didn't do that.

He held my hand again as we walked home, then suddenly said, "I love you." I stopped, looked at his face and saw that he was serious and thought, '*Whoa, Nellie! You're plowin' just a little bit too fast for me.*'

I said, "But you don't even know me yet. This is only the second time I've been out with you." He said, "I know it sounds crazy, but I feel as if I've always known you, and have always loved you. I've waited all my life for you to come along." I told him I liked him a lot, but would never tell him I loved him unless I was absolutely sure. I still had a long way to go to trust him, and still wondered if he was really serious or just feedin' me a line.

He said that was good enough for now, he could wait. He wasn't going to put any pressure on me. Just let him keep on seeing me.

I just couldn't understand how a man as sophisticated, intelligent and handsome, who'd been in the Army and travelled to so many places in the world could be interested in an ignorant mountain girl like me. I'd never been anywhere or done anything worth tellin' about, and I was sure he'd met a lot of women who were much prettier and smarter than I'd ever be.

We were at the park again. I decided it was time to get it over with. I'd let him see the real me, and let him know what kind of family I'd come from—then see how long he wanted to hang around.

Not looking at his face, I told him what my childhood had been like, and of my determination to go to school, be able to take care of myself and never be dependent on anyone ever again. I had a hard time trusting anybody. If my own mother and daddy didn't love me, I couldn't expect anyone else to.

I looked straight into his face, expecting to see rejection, but to my astonishment, saw that he had tears in his eyes. I said I didn't want his pity; I just wanted him to know what I was really like before things went any further. I wasn't good enough for him, and never could be.

He swallowed hard, then stood where he was and held out his arms. And I walked into them. He'd been waiting for me to make the first move. We stood there a long time with our arms around each other, and cried.

It's hard to describe how I felt, but I found myself feeling so safe—as if finally, at last, I'd come home.

I'd heard songs about kissing tears away, but didn't think it actually happened. But that's exactly what happened. After awhile, he put a hand on each side of my face, and kissed my eyes and cheeks where the tears were running down. "How could anybody not love you?" he said, then told me again, "I love you. With all my heart and soul, I love you."

I thought, 'I can't believe this. I've never seen anyone so kind or humble.'

And, right then, I *almost* believed him.

TIME OUT

I decided to take a little "time out" here to try to give some insight to the changes that were going on in my mind and life. It would take a big volume to contain the questions I had, explain and give insight into all the changes that occurred in my life from May, 1952 through September 1956.

To say I graduated from high school on Friday, left home on Sunday, and began work on Monday, is such a short summary of leaving my old life behind and beginning a new one. It was far from the end of a story; it was just a turning point.

We've all heard the expression, "a storybook ending." Fairy tales and story books often end with one sentence: "And they lived happily ever after." Or as Roy Rogers and Dale Evans did in Western movies and stories—"They rode off into the sunset."

This implies that problems, troubles, heartaches, emotional wounds, and financial needs are things never to be confronted again. It leaves the reader or viewer with a good feeling to a happy ending.

In real life, however, when you reach that last sentence, you are just beginning to live with the reality that your past isn't something you can just let blow away in the wind—pouf, it's gone.

When you are a child who has been abused since birth, has never been shown love—even very little kindness, from your parents, and have been told, shown and made to feel that you are worthless, nothing but a burden, and even resented for being born, you face a lifetime of trying to overcome it. I observed this in my own family.

Although you grow up and leave, you take those memories and emotional problems with you. Only after you are separated from the source by time and distance can you begin to recover. Some victims of abuse learn from their experiences and use the wisdom they gain as a foundation to build a better life. Some never learn to deal with it, and build the walls of their own prison, never realizing what they're doing to themselves and others.

Some of them react by going through life being abusive, belittling others, bragging, and putting on a big front. They're tough. Nothing's going to bother them. They may become financially well-off through their ability to take advantage of other people. They have to be on top.

They make it hard for others to even like them, and may end up as an alcoholic and die early and alone. They can't bear to let anyone see the vulnerable child behind the tough exterior they present. And God pity the person who makes the mistake of loving them. They seem to try their best to bring that person down and keep them down. When the person who loves them finally can't take it any more and breaks away, they have proved to themselves, "See, I knew they didn't mean it. Nobody loves me." Many times they leave emotionally scarred children behind.

Others simply accept as truth that they are no good, feel unworthy of anything good, and constantly search for approval and acceptance. Their mind has been conditioned to expect and allow other people to dominate and treat them as a subordinate. They have a "learned" sense of hopelessness. Their spirit has been crushed so many times that they reach the point where they feel that there's no use in trying to have or be anything better. With this attitude, they never succeed at anything.

They go through life with self-defeating behavior, filled with self-pity and self-loathing, always looking for the worst to happen so they can reinforce their feeling of "See? I knew it. Nothing good ever happens to me." I call it the "poor little me" syndrome. If they marry, their partner is constantly having to face the challenge of proving their love and trying unsuccessfully to build their self esteem. My wonderfully wise husband described them as someone who would rather have pity than love. Pity doesn't require any response or responsibility from them.

Then there are those who feel that just because they had a hard time growing up, the world owes them some sort of atonement.

There are other people who live their lives making sure they "never go hungry again." They buy what I call "stuff." Their whole life is centered around making money and what it will buy—a big house in the elite section of town, the best of furnishings, a new luxury car, expensive clothes and jewelry, and eat at the most expensive restaurants—all the outward signs of wealth. They are uselessly trying to feed their hungry spirit.

Of course, I simply hadn't had enough life experience at the time to see that some people never realize what they do to themselves and others. During that period of time in my life, I did a lot of thinking, soul-searching, meditation and prayer—though I didn't even have the knowledge then to put a name to what I was doing.

I was just starting to begin preparation for what I thought I wanted in my future, and thought I finally had things going the way I wanted them to go when out of the blue, there was Van. At that time, the way I saw things was "either" or "or." I could *either* go ahead with my plans for school, *or* I could get married. Period.

Going to school meant learning, expanding my mind, making my own decisions, being independent, and "*being somebody*" through my own efforts. Marriage and children might be possible later.

Or—getting married, on the other hand, meant having a husband to take charge of my life and make every decision for me, with my whole life having to revolve around him and what he wanted. I'd have to give up school, stay home and spend all day every day cooking, cleaning and keeping house; make a garden, have a baby every year or two and raise a house full of kids. I loved kids, but knew I wasn't ready for marriage and children.

When a woman had children, it left her vulnerable to having to submit to abuse for the sake of her children being clothed and fed. I wasn't willing to make that sacrifice. From the time I can remember, I vowed that I'd never bring a child into the world to be treated as I was. Back then, women had nowhere to turn for help. There was no child care assistance, shelters for battered women, or jobs to enable them to support themselves.

Then there was the problem of trusting people, especially men.

I'd learned that God was all you could really trust. A verse in the Bible says, "Trust in the Lord with all thy heart and lean not unto thine own understanding. In all thy ways acknowledge him and he shall direct thy path." That's direction and promise, and I'd found it to be true. I couldn't understand many things, but believed that God was directing my path through life. I'd come to believe that life in this world is really a school for learning, to make preparation for the next life beyond.

I'd learned to look for the lesson God thought I needed to learn in whatever happened to me, good or bad. I'd already seen how my past helped me to be more understanding and compassionate towards others as I took care of patients in the hospital and listened to problems people told me about. I wanted to get more education so I could be better able to help others and myself.

I remember distinctly lying on the bed after I had my appendix out, and thinking about how individual people play certain roles in the world. I wondered: if we all have a soul, or spirit, and the body is just a house for it, why was my soul/spirit placed in my particular body at this particular time? I'd heard the words, "But for the grace of God, there go I."

But for the grace of God, I could've been in the body of that poor colored man draped across the big old tire on the back of that truck. Or one of my sisters or brothers. Or an Indian, or a Negro in Africa. God must have a reason for placing my soul/spirit in my particular body at this particular time.

I wondered what it was.

MAKING SOME MAJOR DECISIONS

That raise really helped. I was watching my pennies and paying off everything I owed. I didn't want any unpaid debts left behind. I knew I would have no income to make payments once I went into nurse's training. I went to see Dr. Almond to get my dental form filled out, and waited to ask about the balance on my account until he filled out the form. After he handed me the form, he turned and went into the back of his office, then came back out with a sheet of ledger paper with some writing on it. He held it facing me so I could see that it was a record of what he had done, and the date and amount of payments I had made. The last entry showed there was still a balance of around $38. To me, that was a bunch of money.

He looked so solemn that for a minute, I thought he was reminding me of my debt to him, and was shocked that he might ask me for it now. Then, as he held it up in front of him, he told me he wanted to give me a going-away gift. He tore the paper from top to bottom, then into smaller pieces, and I watched as they fluttered down into the bottom of his waste basket.

I sat there stunned—my mind racing. This was too much—he'd already done so much for me. Did he realize what this meant to me? Now I could pay off Nichols Store when I got my next check, and maybe even get a nice new pair of nurse's shoes. Mine were looking pretty worn, and I would need some to take to school. I could use some other clothes, too, but I was going to school even if I had to wear tow sacks. Paying off my debts came first.

He came around beside the chair and put his arm around my shoulders, laid his head on top of my head, gave me a hug and said, "I'm so proud of you." And that's one hug I deeply appreciated and needed. I had come to think of him as a good friend, and really respected him.

I was still learning! Thank You, Lord! And thank you, Dr. Almond! I won't disappoint you. And that's a promise.

◆   ◆   ◆

Van was coming around a couple of times a week, now. Sometimes he borrowed his Dad's truck. Other times he caught the bus to Marble and walked the mile home from there, or got a Taxi to take him home. We talked for hours on end, and the more I was with him and learned about him, the better I liked him. I thought he was just too good to be true. I'd never met anyone like him.

We both liked to be outside, and spent a lot of time just walking and talking. Alma lived in the first house on the row of Teas Extract houses, and we walked around that road to her house a time or two. I'd come to know her a little better from the days I'd spent with her when I played hooky. I thought her kids were so pretty that they didn't look real. I loved to play with them, or just watch them play.

Van invited me back to the Williams' home and I went to visit them a few more times that summer. I loved the family, and loved the place. When you turned off of US 19 and went up the mountain on the winding gravel Bluff road, you'd think you were going to end up on the top of the mountain. About a mile from the main highway, just as you thought you were reaching the top, you suddenly found yourself looking at a beautiful, peaceful valley.

They had about 150 acres which ran from mountain top to mountain top. A small stream meandered down the center of the valley. Fat, sleek cattle grazed on rolling, green pasture land, and there were well tended fields on each side of the branch. A roomy new tobacco barn was situated on the far side of the branch, toward the upper side of the valley.

Looking straight ahead at the end of the dirt road, on a small hill across the branch sat a "homey" looking, welcoming, white two-story farmhouse with a chimney and tin roof. Behind and below the house was the milk house, with a weathered gray barn and crib at the edge of the woods. Surrounding the whole valley were layers of hazy protective mountains. When I went there, I had the feeling that I'd gone into this peaceful, secluded place and closed the door behind me, leaving the whole world outside.

You could tell from looking that it was a well kept and much loved place. I was impressed to learn how much hard work it takes to run a dairy farm. It's a seven day a week job—long days that require everyone's cooperation and help. They had milking machines, but it was still a major chore to do the milking twice a day.

There was always something needin' to be done—from fixin' fences to gath-erin' eggs. They raised their own pigs, and also raised strawberries that year. A farm tractor helped with the farming. Their tobacco allotment, which involves a lot of intensive labor, was their cash crop in the late fall. It made the FHA mort-gage payment and paid for their Christmas.

Chickens and guineas had the run of the place. Van's Dad saw to it that a weed didn't dare poke its head up in one of the neat, perfectly straight rows in his huge garden. His mother and Ruby kept the household humming with activity, and there was always the smell of something good cooking.

One day, Van and I walked down to the lower end of the pasture to the edge of the woods. We came to a low barbed wire fence, and he astonished me by swooping me up and setting me across it. He laughed at the stunned look on my face. Then we walked on over toward the sound of rushing water, and we were at the top of a beautiful, high waterfall over to one side of the Bluff. It was so cool and peaceful here. Van told me that he and his family used to come there in the evening after working in the fields, and go down under the waterfall to take a shower. That must've been some shower after coming right out of the hot sun.

Incidentally, right now I'm sitting in our home at that exact location, looking down the mountain from the edge of "the Bluff". We built our house, spent many happy years, and raised our family here by the waterfall, where its soothing sound is constantly heard.

Grover and his wife, Edith lived in the house with the family. They had been married about two years and didn't have any children yet. Grover had been work-ing on the Biltmore Estate in Asheville, but came home to help run the farm. They needed everybody's help to keep it going. Ruby worked on a job in Andrews. Van was living at home and helping with the things he could, but couldn't do a lot of heavy work because of his chest injuries.

He told me about his injuries in the War and his mother told me her side of the story. He was in Germany during the worst part of the war and during a bat-tle, a shell exploded right in front of him. It blew him back into the side of a half track, breaking almost every bone in his body, including head injuries. His ribs were fractured and pushed back into his lung on one side, with multiple rib frac-tures on the other side.

There were only three survivors in his outfit, and his headquarters was destroyed. After they got him to the hospital, they put him in a whole body cast, which he wore for eighteen months. He lost down to around 110 pounds. He was in the hospital for several months, and for a long time, his family didn't know if he was dead or alive. He couldn't come home during all that time, but was finally discharged and sent home. He would never fully recover from his wounds, and made several trips to Winston-Salem related to frequent severe headaches. He went by bus, a long trip there and back. The doctors finally clipped a nerve to relieve the pain. Now I understood why they were so protective of him. They still celebrated his homecoming.

It seemed like just about every week, some of the Williams family from Haywood County came for a visit. Back then, it was the customary thing for relatives to come and stay from a few days to a week or two at a time. Van had a large extended family of aunts, uncles and first cousins, and the house was always bursting at the seams. They just came right in and made themselves at home. The rafters seemed to vibrate with everybody talking and laughing at the same time, but Lee and Lizzie always seemed happy to have them. She'd *kick up a fuss* if they started to leave after just one night.

When they got a meal ready, it looked like enough food to feed an army. And they could flat out put it away, too. Lizzie fussed at me because she thought I didn't eat enough. She sat me right between her and Lee so she could see to it that I ate. I soon learned that nobody could ever eat enough to satisfy her. And Van wasn't exaggerating when he bragged on what good cooks they were.

I found that each person who came there was hugged by each one of the family. And not just when you came. You got hugged when you came, you got hugged when you left, and several times in between. I could see they loved each other, and weren't the least bit self conscious about showing it. And Lizzie always kissed me too. I didn't know women kissed women. I could see that I was going to have to do a lot of getting used to this family if I stayed around them.

Now I saw why Van was always reaching out to touch me. He'd been used to it all his life. It was just an involuntary gesture and part of his personality. I couldn't imagine being raised in a family like this. He couldn't possibly know how much I envied the loving relationship they had with each other.

Sometimes when he came to see me, we went into "Ma" Woods' Cafe' on the corner at the middle red light, sat and drank cokes or coffee, had a hot dog or hamburger, and played songs on the juke box. Two of my favorites were The Wayward Wind© and a piano instrumental called Coconut Grove©.

One evening about six-thirty, as we were just coming up to the corner at Ma Woods' Cafe', a car pulled to the curb and stopped. Mary Willie and her husband were inside. We chit-chatted a bit, and they invited us to get in and ride around with them for awhile. We got in, and when the light turned green, her husband made a right turn, heading toward the upper end of town. When we came to the intersection to go up Junaluska Creek, we made another right turn onto McClelland Creek Road.

We'd gone about a mile when Mary Willie asked if I'd like to drive by Artie's house and see where she lived. I said yes, so we made a left turn onto a pretty gravelled lane. Artie's was the first house, and when we got there, several cars were parked around her yard. Mary Willie wondered what was going on. When we stopped and got out of the car, hospital people came pouring out yelling "Surprise!"

It was the biggest surprise I'd ever had! I had no idea they were giving me a going-away party. Everybody was there except the doctors, and two nurses who were holding down the fort at the hospital.

I had no experience in social situations, and was uneasy as to what was expected of me. That was probably the first real party I'd ever gone to. Being with Van eased the tension, though, and I was soon enjoying myself. Van, as usual, made himself right at home. He was relaxed, talked and laughed easily to everyone, yet still stayed close by and was attentive to me. Was there no end to the pleasant surprises I was learning about his personality? He could talk to anybody about anything. I'd seen college graduates that didn't have half the vocabulary or knowledge he had. What a kind, generous, compassionate, intelligent, well-read, interesting, fun-to-be-with, person he was. I found myself warning "Cleo" that she was getting to like him just a little too much—she was no where near his league.

They gave me some nice gifts. I got a nightgown and pajamas (I was going to have to buy some), stationery and stamps, and some other things that would be useful. Jan Barton gave me a pair of baby doll pajamas, the "in" thing at the time. I had a great time, and was so touched that my friends liked me well enough to give me a party and gifts.

After the party, they helped me put my gifts into the trunk of Mary Willie's car, and her husband drove us to Sweetie's house.

That night, I thought about how easily and completely Van had kept the surprise party a secret from me. I hadn't suspected a thing, even the coincidence of having me right there on the sidewalk at the right time for Mary Willie to pick us up.

And chided my suspicious mind for wondering if he had any more secrets I didn't know about.

I still had a lot to learn. And trust was the biggest thing.

◆   ◆   ◆

They started running a revival up on the creek. I could go and be there every night—if it didn't run too many nights, when I'd have to change to 3-11 shift. Nowadays, you hear churches advertise three, five, or seven night revival services, with the opening and closing dates scheduled well ahead of time. Back then, they'd start praying for revival, then when he felt it was time, the preacher would announce the beginning date. A closing date was never mentioned. It was for "as long as the Lord leads us." That could be two nights or two weeks—or more.

The revival had started, and Van had invited himself to come and take me on Saturday night, "if that's all right with you." What could I say? It made me happy that he volunteered to go to church with me. Chalk up one more plus on his side. Church was very important to me. But the problem I had was that I knew Dad would be there, it being a week-end, and knew that neither he nor Mom would be be happy about it, to put it mildly. I introduced them before church, and could see Dad's hackles rise, and Mom gave me that "you've messed in your britches" look, but they didn't say anything.

After the service was over and we were leaving, Dad walked right up and told us, "I'd better not hear tell about yuns a-parkin' along the road nowhere." It embarrassed me to death, made me mad, and hurt my feelings, too.

As we were going down the road, I apologized for Dad and told Van I envied the trusting relationship he enjoyed with his parents. Mine always acted like they couldn't trust me out of their sight, and I wished they wouldn't always think the worst of me, as I'd never given them any reason not to trust me. I was so upset, my voice trembled and I was on the verge of crying. We were going past the Ledford Fields and he pulled over to the side of the road and asked me if I was crying. I was trying to tell him not to stop, but before I could say anything, headlights pulled up behind us.

Van rolled his window down when I said, "Oh, Lord, it's Daddy." He came up to the window and said, "Uh-huh. I knowed it. I knowed youns'd be parked jist as soon as you got out a sight a th' church house." I was mortified—and per-trified with fear. I was praying that Van wouldn't say anything to make him mad or Dad'd drag me out of the car and they'd get into a fight.

Van calmly said in a clear strong voice, "Mr. Hicks, you might like to know that the reason I stopped was to try to get her to quit crying because she was so hurt by the way you treated her. Now, we've not done anything wrong, and don't plan on doing anything wrong. If you're going to be mad at somebody, get mad at me. I was the one who stopped." I felt like the time Lewis stood up to Dad for me. I just knew he'd kill both of us.

They looked straight at each other for a few seconds, then Dad said, "All right. Go on. But you'd better not be a-gittin' into nothin'," and turned around to go back to his truck. Van turned to me and asked me if I was all right. I could only nod yes, and he shifted gears and pulled back into the road. He reached over and took my hand, could feel me still trembling, and said, "It's all right, sweetheart. It's all right. He's never going to hurt you again." He apologized for stopping, when he knew Dad specifically said not to. He just couldn't imagine being that afraid of my own Dad, even after what I'd told him, but now he'd seen for himself how things were. He assured me it made no difference in how he felt about me.

A few days later, I somewhat hesitantly took Van with me to their house. I thought if they knew him better, they couldn't help but like him. They were as friendly to him as to anyone else who came there. Dad never mentioned the incident, and they both acted as if nothing ever happened. Of course, Van was his usual relaxed talkative self. Oval and Vernon were used to the silent, unsmiling, strained way it was at home, and sniggered about how much he talked. Next time I saw them, as brothers do when teasing their sister, they elbowed each other and asked me when I was goin' to bring "Ol' Windy" back. I refused to take the bait for a fuss. I just chuckled. It didn't matter to me what they thought.

I kinda liked "Ol' Windy."

◆   ◆   ◆

Time was running out, and I was trying to be sure I had everything I needed to take with me, as I didn't know how long it would be before I came back. One day when I was up on the creek, I mentioned to Mom and Dad I was going to have to get a suitcase. Back then, folks always said "suitcase" for any kind of luggage. They had two Army lockers that Sweetie had left there. Mom kept her stuff in them and I'd always been forbidden to "bother" them. Imagine my surprise when they said I could take one of them with me to school, "But you better take care of it." I thanked them as I was leaving, taking the locker with me, and said now I recon I had everything I needed except a Bible.

Dad went into the middle room and picked up the "good" Bible off the dresser. It was one they'd bought from a Bible salesman a few years back. I liked to use it, as it had a dictionary, maps and study helps. It was exactly what I'd have liked if I could afford one. He handed it to me and told me I could take it. He had a smaller one that he carried to church. Again, I heard, "But you better take care of it." I just couldn't believe they'd let me take that Bible!

I "took care of it," all right. I read that same Bible almost every day all through school and through the years since. When I took it back after I got out of school, they told me to keep it. It's still my favorite Bible. I wish I could find another one like it. It's been rebound once, and the pages are yellowed, worn and loose again now. It's still the Bible I pick up and read first thing every morning.

And it reminds me that maybe they did care about me more than they let on. After all they gave me their best Bible.

GETTING THINGS STRAIGHT

I was sad to be leaving Sweetie, Ruth and Ronnie, all my old friends, my friends at work, and the people at the little Junaluska church. I'd been the church Secretary a long time, in addition to playing the piano. Sweetie was the Treasurer. I'd miss being in Bass Mosteller's Sunday School class. He was the *sangin' leader,* and had taught the Young People's class for several years. I learned a lot from him and came to love him dearly. He was the most humble, non-judgmental person I ever saw, and loved us young folks.

He dispensed good old down to earth wisdom about everyday problems without getting preachy or laying a load of guilt on you. He talked to the Lord in an easy natural way, like you'd talk to your best friend. A few years ago, I was thinking about Bass and wondered what it was that made him so special. I realized it was because he made people feel good about themselves.

How many people do you know who does that?

Sweetie never "preached," he was always kind, and helped me learn to laugh—a wonderful gift. Lewis taught me a lot, plus being a good example by the way he lived. Before I got to know Sweetie and Ruth, Lewis and Sis were probably the only example I'd known of a loving, ideal relationship in a marriage.

I desperately wanted to believe that Van was sincere, but still thought he was just too good to be true. He was the most wonderful person I'd ever met, but I couldn't understand why he would want somebody like me. I believed the old sayin', "If it looks too good to be true, it prob'ly ain't."

Whenever I looked at him now, I felt such a surge of pure joy that it just made me catch my breath. I loved to be with him, and couldn't ever seem to spend enough time with him. The thought of leaving him behind made me want to cry. What was I going to do about him? That question and many others kept running through through my mind.

Was this love? Would it last? Did I even know what love was? Could he really love me? Was he really as wonderful as he seemed, or was it just wishful thinking on my part? I knew that marriage would be the next question to answer if I told him I loved him. Would he expect me to let him run my life? Could I still go to school, or would he expect me to cancel all my plans?

Was it fair of me to ask him to wait three years? If he did agree to wait, I'd have plenty of time to find out if this was the real thing. If he didn't, it would break my heart, but I was going anyway. I knew what I wanted to do, and wasn't going to be tied the rest of my life to a man who didn't care what I wanted, no matter how much it would hurt to let him go.

And what about his health? His mother had expressed her doubts that he'd ever recover enough to take on the responsibilities of a wife and family. If I went on to school, that wouldn't be a problem because I'd know how to take care of him if he became disabled in the future.

I'd found that I could talk to him about any trivial little thing and he never treated it as silly. He seemed to understand me better than anyone I'd ever met. So afraid of what I would find out, but realizing I had to, I finally decided to honestly discuss these questions that were constantly running through my mind. We would settle everything one way or the other.

Oh God, help me to say and do the right thing. I don't think I can bear to lose him, but help me to know if this is the real thing, and is part of Your plan for my life. I need to get my priorities in order.

Next time he came, as we walked up the street toward home, I stopped under some big oak trees just below the park. I told him I had something I wanted to discuss with him. My well-rehearsed speech was supposed to begin with: "I think I love you, but…"

I found myself hesitating, and when I looked at him, suddenly I just knew, and said, "I love you" instead. I can't describe the joy I saw on his face, or the joy and love I felt when I saw it. There was not a shred of doubt now that I loved him, but I had to know more.

When he asked me to marry him, I told him I needed him to answer a question before I answered. I asked him if he would be willing to wait three years. And I mean wait about everything, with no hassle about it.

He said of course he would. He'd waited all his life for me, and he'd wait forever if he had to, because there'd never be any one else he'd ever love. He wanted me to get my nurse's training, for if we got married and I didn't, I might be happy for awhile, but later regret not having gone to school. I might even come to resent him, and he couldn't bear that.

I told him I still had one more thing. I wasn't asking, or preaching, and would never tell him again. I just wanted him to know that if he ever came home drunk, no matter what the circumstances, or how much I loved him, he would never come home to me again. He said he understood why I felt that way, and that was one thing I'd never have to worry about—he didn't drink.

Now we both knew how things stood. What a relief! I could hardly bear to think about leaving now, but for both our sakes, I knew I had to.

Young and inexperienced as I was, I believe God gave me the wisdom to know that I still had a lot to learn about life and about myself before I could commit to a marriage. I felt so grateful to Van for the freedom and time he was willing to give me to do it. I could be getting my nurse's training while I sorted it out.

GOING TO ASHEVILLE

Sometimes, when I look back, I'm amazed at the faith and courage I had back then. I knew beyond a doubt that this was what the Lord wanted me to do. I didn't know how He would provide, I just knew He would. I said goodbye to everyone beforehand, then went alone, bought my bus ticket to Asheville, got on the bus and left.

I had no idea where the hospital was located, or how far from the bus station it was. Thank goodness, I'd made the trip to Knoxville and saw how the bus station operated there. I figured Asheville was about that size.

I'd cried when I left Ruth and Sweetie's house. I knew I'd miss them so much, and that Ronnie was too young to understand it all. I didn't want him to miss me too much, but didn't want him to forget me, either. He would do a lot of growing in three years.

I was feeling sad at leaving everybody, Van in particular, but refused to let my mind dwell on it. I was more than a little bit scared at being totally on my own in a strange place. But mixed with all the other emotions, was the excitement of being finally, really, truly, on my way. It was like riding an emotional roller coaster as the big old Greyhound bus ate up the miles on the crooked, uphill-downhill road through Nantahala Gorge toward Asheville.

Many times, when I'd heard the muffled sound of the Greyhound bus echo through the deserted streets in the early morning darkness, I wondered what it would be like to be standing there waiting, and when it stopped, just climb on, let the doors close behind me, and leave everything behind. Now that I was actually doing it, everything seemed unreal, as if I were dreaming. Again, I had that feeling of being apart from, and watching myself.

That sense of unreality was mixed with excitement, curiosity and a sense of freedom as the bus wound around the curves, going farther and farther away from all that was familiar to me. After it pulled into the bus depot and parked for a rest stop in each town, the bus driver stood up, faced the passengers, announced the name of the town and told them how long we would be there. Then he swung down onto the street and left the door open so the passengers could go and come as they pleased. I stayed on the bus and watched what everyone else did at first, afraid I might get lost and not get back on the bus in time, and be left behind. After seeing that everyone was back on the bus and waiting before the driver got back on, I began getting off to take a break with the others. I tried to act casually, as if I were an experienced traveller, but inside, I was bursting with excitement, and more than a little scared.

When I got off the bus in Asheville, the bus driver opened the luggage compartment on the side of the bus, and set my trunk out on the sidewalk. I thanked him, picked it up, and started walking over toward the Yellow Cab stand. I had seen how that was done on my trip to Knoxville. A cab driver saw me coming and got out of his taxicab to take my luggage, which he stowed away in the trunk of the cab. Everything I owned was in that Army locker, but the things I treasured most was my Bible and the framed 8 x 10 picture of Van in his Army uniform. He'd given it to me a few days before I left.

When I told the cab driver I wanted to go to Latta Nurses' Home, he said, "Oh, sure, that isn't far," opened the door for me and I got in the cab. When we got there, he opened my door for me, got my trunk out and set it by me on the sidewalk. After I paid him and he left, I found myself suddenly feeling very alone and anxious.

I had less than ten dollars left. And that was all I had—with no cetainty of getting any more. Just enough to buy a return ticket to Andrews if I needed one.

I've thought back to that time and asked myself if that wasn't a foolish thing to do, and where I got the courage. I'd just the same as stranded myself out here alone in a strange city with no money. Then I'd remind myself that I hadn't been alone. God knew exactly where I was; I was just exactly where I was supposed to be, at just exactly the right time. I had my orders and was reporting for duty.

I stood there on the street and looked around me. A four foot high stone wall edged the sidewalk next to the narrow front lawn of what seemed to be an ancient brick building. Huge trees grew on the well-kept grounds. An opening in the stone wall had smoothly worn steps leading from the sidewalk up the path to the solid-looking, ivy-framed front entrance. It looked like something out of an old English novel. A large weathered stone set above the door was engraved with the reassuring words, "Latta Nurses' Home."

As I stood there and looked, I became a little more anxious, and found myself thinking, 'what if they've changed their mind, or misplaced my application and don't know who I am, or—or—or, what'll I do, if...?'

Quickly in my mind, I told myself, "Cleo! Cut it out!" and didn't allow myself to start thinking any more foolishness. I firmly picked up my trunk, carried it up the steps to the door, set it down and rang the doorbell. A thin, primly dressed, white-haired lady opened the door. I told her my name and that I was a new student nurse. She gave me a friendly smile and said, "Oh, yes! We've been expecting you, Miss Hicks. I'm the housemother, Mrs. Whitmire. Please come on in," as she opened the door wide, stood aside and beckoned me inside.

Boy, was I glad to hear that! The relief made me go weak in the knees. She asked me to come with her and she would show me to my room, and said she hoped I would be happy here. As we made our way upstairs to my room, she talked in a friendly manner, pointed out the bathroom and other things along the way, and told me a few things I needed to know about living in the nurses' home. When we reached my room, she unlocked the door, opened it, and handed me the key. She told me I could go ahead and start unpacking, and someone would be by later to show me the way to the cafeteria. If I needed anything at any time, either she or someone else would always be downstairs at the front desk. Then she quietly left.

The room was small but nice. It had an Army cot style bed, large chest of drawers with a mirror over it, a small upholstered chair, a desk with a straight chair, and a closet. I looked at the key, then squeezed the hard cold metal in my hand to be sure I wasn't dreaming. I couldn't believe I really was here at last, had my very own room and was holding the key to it! The key was solid proof that I belonged—I had a place here.

There was a tall, heavy-framed window in the center of the wall facing the street. It had a wide windowsill with a steam radiator underneath. I walked over, sat on the windowsill, and looked down below me. The hospital was right across the street, set back into a wide lawn. It was an old building, and looked huge to me.

As I watched, I saw a small group of student nurses come out of the hospital entrance and start walking down the sidewalk toward the Nurses' Residence. They were talking and smiling, and looked very neat and professional in their uniforms and caps. In the late afternoon sun, their snow-white nurse's caps gleamed like halos on top of their heads, and the edges of their crisp white pinafore skirts fluttered out and blew back with each step, like wings waving in the breeze as they walked. To me, they gave the impression of angels floating along as they came down the walk. From years of habit, I found myself wishing I could be......

I drew a sudden intake of breath as the realization hit me: I'm one of them now!

Gosh, I'd better start unpacking!

GITTIN' SOME MORE BOOK-LEARNIN'

The next day, all the incoming student nurses met in the conference room. I think there was thirty-one of us, and all of us were female and white. We were told the rules, regulations, dress and uniform codes, house rules inside the Nurses' Residence, and what kind of behavior was expected of us. An outline of college courses, special courses of study at the School of Nursing, and the different departments we would work in during our three years there were all gone over, questions answered, and explanations given.

They made certain that we understood what was expected of us, and told us what we could expect from them. The rules would apply equally with no exceptions. Anyone who broke them would be sent home immediately, and would never return.

We could have no visitors or go home during our first month in training. During our three years there, first year students had to be in the nurse's residence by 9 P.M. through the week and on Sunday. We could stay out til 10 P.M on Friday or Saturday nights. Second and third year students had to be in by 9:30 P.M. through the week and Sunday, and 10:30 on Friday or Saturday, but seniors could be out til eleven on Friday or Saturday. Everyone had one twelve o'clock leave per month, a one o'clock leave per year, and one two-night weekend pass per month. No male visitors were permitted beyond the reception room just inside the front entrance, which was always in sight of the housemother.

If we were sick, we would remain on the premises and be seen by a doctor at the hospital. If hospitalized, we would be hospitalized at Memorial Mission under their care. In other words, we were under their direct supervision for three years.

We would have one week of vacation after we'd been there a year, and two weeks during our second and third year. We would have days off for the major holidays, but we may not get them on the holiday. Hospital patients must be cared for on holidays just the same as any other day. But they would try to give the holiday as near to the actual date as the scheduling would permit.

Back then, it was called a "Nurses' Home," or "Nurses' Residence." A "dorm" was housing at a college. All students were required to live at the Nurses' Home. Married students were not accepted, and no one could get married until their last six months—and then only with written permission from the Director of Nurses.

We were introduced to Mrs. Diora Russell, the night housemother. She was a tall pleasant lady, a few years younger than Mrs. Whitmire. First, in the house rules, there was a register at the housemother's desk near the entrance of the nurses' home, to be used by all students when they entered or left the premises. There were spaces to write the date, student's name, destination, time you left, and time and signature when you returned. This procedure was to be followed, even if you were only going to run down to the corner drugstore and come right back. Failure to comply would be grounds for dismissal. Anyone who signed in or out for another student would also be dismissed. They were to know exactly where we were at any time of the day or night.

A young person now would probably find that too restrictive. For myself, it was far more leniency than I'd had at home. I could at least go out without having to ask permission, and no one was going to tell me "no." I could spend some time out without telling anyone exactly where I was going—I could write "downtown" or "movies" on the register. No one would ask where I'd been or what I'd been doing when I returned, just so I got back at the proper time.

There was to be no loud noise, music, talking or carousing around in the nurses' home, to keep from disturbing students who would be studying, working at night and sleeping at different hours. First year students had to have lights out and be in bed by 10:00 P.M. on weeknights. The housemother checked to see if lights were out, and everyone was in their bed. The door was unlocked whenever we were in the room, and she quietly opened it to peek in as she made her rounds. She could see inside from the dimly lit hall.

We seldom came into contact with the older students, as they were working different shifts and had different classes. It lent a mysterious air to wonder what they were doing, as we would eventually be doing the same things.

I was practically in awe when a group of seniors rustled by in their crisply starched uniforms and caps with a black stripe across the band. They looked so fresh, clean and self-confident as they walked briskly along. From a window, I could look down and see them coming and going from the hospital to the Nurses' Home. At night, they seemed like beings from some other world as they appeared to float in and out of the darkness from lamp post to lamp post.

Then we were measured for uniforms (I was 20 inches around the waist). Each of us would have uniforms made to our measurements, and issued to us. They were ours to keep, and were to be sent to the hospital laundry when they became soiled. They would clean, press, and return them to us. We wouldn't need them for awhile, as we had to do some preliminary studies before we could go into the hospital for on-site training and practice.

During the six months probation period, we were called "probies," and wore a short sleeved, straight cut narrow blue and white striped uniform with two roomy pockets. They buttoned to below the waist and were so long that they came down to about four inches above the top of our shoes. It had no waistline, but had a separate, straight, two inch wide belt that buttoned in front, made from the same striped fabric. We laughed and called them prisoners' stripes.

The uniforms weren't as stiffly starched as the detachable white collar and cuffs. They were starched as stiff as cardboard and ironed flat. The boardlike collar was bent around the neck and fastened at the top button on the uniform. It was so stiff that it rubbed my neck raw on each side.

The three and a half inch wide cuffs were bent around and two headed buttons pushed through the buttonholes where they overlapped. To keep them from sliding down the upper arm, they had a small buttonhole on the inside edge that corresponded to a button on the uniform sleeve. I pinched the inside of my upper arm a few times trying to get the small button on the uniform to go through the stiff buttonhole on the cuff before I learned to button them before putting it on.

We had to wear a hairnet if our hair was long enough to touch our collar. The only jewelry we could wear was a very necessary waterproof watch with a second hand. Incidentally, all watches then were the kind that had to be wound. The finishing touch was a name pin. Mine said "Miss C. Hicks." Every once in awhile, someone teasingly called me "Miss Chicks."

◆   ◆   ◆

In 1953, the stylish skirt length was thirteen inches from the floor. Full circle skirts were 100 inches around the hem and multi-layered, ruffled net half-slips were worn under them to make them stand out. Flat ballerina shoes were popular, and "see-through" blouses were the "in" thing.

Flowing, "drapey" coats with wide, turnback cuffs and collar or "poodle coats" were in style. Circular corduroy and pleated wool plaid skirts with pullover sweaters were worn in the winter. We still wore bobby socks with saddle shoes or penny loafers with Capri pants or blue jeans.

◆　　◆　　◆

I was going to have to do a whole lot of studying in the next six months, and needed several books. I wrote to Mary Willie and told her what books I had to buy and the amount of money I was going to need. It was somewhere around seventy-five dollars.

I really had a hard time writing that letter. I wished I didn't have to ask and feel so much like a beggar. But Dr. Van Gorder had volunteered to let me have the money I needed, and told me to write Mary Willie when I needed it. I regarded it as a loan, and told myself I would repay it when I finished school and got a job. That helped my feelings somewhat, but I was only going to ask for money for what I absolutely had to have to stay in school, nothing else. I guess my problem was that I was *as independent as a hawg on ice,* as the old sayin' goes.

Right now, the coat my teacher gave me in the tenth grade was beginning to look rather outdated and worn. It was a double-breasted, straight-cut Chesterfield style, but at least it kept me warm—a new one wasn't a necessity. I'd worn worse than that, or gone without, all my life. Long ago, I'd learned the valuable distinction between a want and a necessity. I'd manage.

Although Dad had a good job and could afford to help me, he never offered. I'd do most anything rather than ask, since he'd given such a sordid description of what a nurse was, back when he found out I wanted to be one. I was determined never to ask or feel obligated to them for anything ever again. If they cared enough to want to help me, they could offer.

Then, too, I'd heard them both make the remark, "Uh-huh, I knowed it," whenever one of my sisters was having a hard time, as if taking great satisfaction in being able to say that. They'd made their life miserable at home, then acted as if they'd done something disgraceful when they married and left. They didn't worry about her little youngens being cold and hungry, so why would they care what I might need?

I wouldn't mention it to Van, either. I didn't want him to feel responsible for me in any way, and I wouldn't accept anything from him until we were married. It was enough for me just to know he was there.

We'd promised to write every day, and I could hardly wait to get a letter. Sometimes it was hard to find the time, but I wrote him a letter every night, and missed him so much I could hardly keep from crying each time I wrote—and sometimes did. I was so glad I had his picture. It was the first thing I'd unpacked. I just tried to keep my mind on what I was doing here, and told him all about it, trying to be cheerful when I wrote, yet not so cheerful that he might think I wasn't missing him.

I was getting to the point where I realized that just having to have a three cent stamp every day was going be a problem. Ninety cents a month is a lot when you have no income.

I'd been writing to Ruth every week, and always wrote something to Ronnie. I missed him and Randy more than anybody in the family. When Ruth wrote and told me that Ronnie cried just about every day and kept asking where I was and when I was coming back, it just broke my heart. But I knew she was a wonderful mother and would find ways to keep him busy and happy. Roberta was a natural mother, and Randy had a little sister now.

A week after I mailed the letter to Mary Willie, I got a letter from her, with a check enclosed for seventy-five dollars. I sure was glad to see it. The books I had to buy were Nursing Arts, Chemistry For Nurses, Biology, Anatomy and Physiology, Taber's Medical Dictionary, and Pharmacology and Therapeutics. We would have a course in Ethics, but didn't need a book. I had a couple of much needed dollars left. Postage stamps were one thing I was going to buy.

◆   ◆   ◆

During the next six months, we would spend the morning studying Nursing Arts in the School of Nursing classroom, and the afternoons at Asheville-Biltmore College.

They gave us an IQ and aptitude test. I don't remember what my IQ was, but remember being complimented on my score by the Educational Director during one of my evaluation sessions. It made me happy to know that somewhere it was written in black and white that I wasn't stupid.

We rode a bus up the winding road to Asheville-Biltmore College, located on top of Beaucatcher mountain. The bus was owned by the hospital. They had a driver who drove the bus there, waited, then brought us back to the Nurses' Home. I was impressed by the ancient-looking buildings covered with English Ivy, surrounded by spacious, well tended grounds and beautiful old trees.

The college courses we studied (that I remember) were Anatomy and Physiology, Chemistry For Nurses, Biology and Microbiology. They were wonderful instructors who made their classes interesting.

I also remember how sick I got, smelling that pungent Formaldehyde while we dissected the frogs which were preserved in it.

I was, and am still fascinated with Anatomy and Physiology. To this day, I can sit and read an Anatomy book with the avid interest of reading a novel. To me, it's miraculous how the separate body parts and systems are made, function, and interact with each other to keep the body performing properly. Things we take for granted every day are marvels of design and function.

We studied History of Nursing, and learned all about "dear old Flossie" Nightingale, Clara Barton and other outstanding names in history.

We learned about the different kinds of employment opportunities we might have as RNs—Education, Public Health, the military, doctor's offices, and the various departments and specialties in a hospital.

Miss Fuller taught Nursing Arts, which consisted of several things nurses shoud know. We would have theory and instruction in the many different procedures we needed to learn in order to give basic care, then to practice under supervision on a patient in the hospital.

We were given a checklist of all the different procedures we were required to learn, such as a bed bath, turning a patient, giving enemas, applying a bandage, giving intramuscular injections, etc. (We were not allowed to start an IV or blood!) Each procedure had specific "1, 2, 3" instructions. As we studied the procedures, we and a RN had to initial that we had been instructed and understood the instructions. We were taught and supervised, then did the procedure three times, getting it initialed as having been done correctly by whatever RN was in charge at the time. After that, we could go ahead and do the procedure without supervision whenever it was ordered.

When a patient went home, we had to clean every square inch of the room except the ceiling. We used a sanitizing cleaning solution and wiped down everything—the bed, including the springs, top, bottom, and around all sides of the mattress, bedside table, overbed table, inside and outside the locker or closet, and the walls. When that was finished, we mopped the floor.

We left the bed unmade an hour or longer to air the room and let everything dry, then went back and made the bed. The room was thoroughly inspected. Miss Fuller had a white glove that she put on, then ran her hand along unlikely places in the room, like over the top of the window frame, the top of the locker, and underneath the bedsprings. If any dust or dirt showed on the glove, you did the whole thing over.

She wasn't doing this to be mean, or making us do it just because she said so; we were taught the reasoning behind it. A thorough cleaning was necessary for the protection of the next patient.

I done'n seen that if I could make it through three years a-trainin' in this place, I could say I had some dandy nurse's trainin'.

LEARNING ABOUT DISABILITIES

At times when Van wrote, he sounded somewhat depressed and it bothered me. I didn't have money for a bus ticket every month on my week-end off and had only been home once. The bus ride took three hours, and I didn't get there until Saturday afternoon. Then I had to catch the last bus for Asheville at 2:00 P.M. on Sunday in order to be back by 9 P.M. That didn"t give me much time to visit anyone.

Once he wrote, saying he missed me, and referred to my obsession to be a nurse. He said that if it was another man, he might know how to handle it—but how do you compete with a little white cap? That really upset me, and I thought, "O.K. Here comes the other side. I knew he was too good to be true."

If he started pressuring me, he'd find that it didn't work. And the "pitiful act" wouldn't work either. I was staying right where I was. I'd made certain that he knew exactly what to expect from me, had given him a choice, and he'd made promises I expected him to keep, or it was all over. I knew it would break my heart if he changed his mind, but I'd understand that it was too much to ask. No matter how much it hurt, I'd give his ring back. I knew he'd been right when he said I might spend the rest of my life being resentful and regret giving up all I had worked so hard to accomplish.

And spiritually speaking, I had reported for duty, still had my orders, and the only thing that was going to stop me was to drop dead. I knew I was exactly where I was supposed to be and doing what I was supposed to be doing. And that's a good feeling.

I knew I needed the freedom to learn about life on my own, and to overcome my fear and mistrust of people, but I didn't want to go to the other extreme and be gullible. I needed experience in being able to assess people and situations for myself in order to make the right choices for me. I had a lot of conflicting emotions to resolve and was beginning to make progress, but I needed time.

Another reason kept nagging me in the back of my mind—what Van's mother had said about him never being able to live a normal life. I really didn't understand to what extent his injuries would affect him. They were so protective of him, did they not expect him to live long—or what?

At the VA Hospital in Oteen, I got a glimpse of what kind of life a disabled veteran might have, and gained some valuable insight that has been of tremendous help ever since.

Several organizations in town had various veterans programs, visited and spent time with them. Students were encouraged to visit and help them pass some time while they were there. There was a large recreation area with bowling, pool tables, all kinds of games and occupational therapy available. Students usually went in groups, and spread out among the men to play games or just talk. Many of them chose a specific veteran to spend time with, to help him feel he had a friend in this area, and cheer him up.

I felt so insecure and awkward in social situations that I didn't go with them at first. A lot of the girls didn't, so I didn't feel pressured. When the ones who went came back after a visit, I listened as they talked about what they did and sometimes told what some of the men had experienced. Some of their stories were heartrending.

I had become best friends with Bettie Davis, a friendly, funny girl from "Naw-fuk," Virginia. We laughed a lot about each others' accent and the differences in the way we talked. One day, I was talking and mentioned a "poke full" of something. She looked puzzled, then when I explained, went into hysterical laughter and said, "Oh, you mean a sack!" To her, a poke meant getting jabbed with a finger.

Well, it did to me, too, but I thought everybody knew that a "poke full" of something meant there was a *right smart* of stuff in a poke, like maybe a grocery bag, but not a whole sack full of it. To me, a sack was a tow sack or feed sack—something big. A sack, to her, was any size of a paper bag.

She'd been going to the VA hospital and became friends with a veteran from Tennessee. She said she enjoyed going, and had a good time. One night, she came in and told me he had a car and they were planning to take another veteran friend to a drive-in movie the next night. His friend was depressed, and he felt that getting him out of the hospital environment might be good for him. She said they were from east Tennessee, and talked and acted a lot like me.

She invited me to go with them. Well—that was different from being in a whole crowd of people, and having to get all dressed up and know all the social "p's and q's." I just never did like being in a big crowd. After some persuasion, I agreed to go.

I'd heard the descriptions, but was totally unprepared for the reality of what I saw when I walked in there. All around me were young and middle-aged men with one or both arms or legs gone, a missing eye, all sorts of disfigurements—in casts, on crutches, and in wheelchairs. One was in hospital restraints to keep him from falling out of his wheelchair, his face a blank stare, head tilted to one side, and drooling from his mouth. But several appeared normal.

I was almost overcome with emotion—rage at war, compassion for these young men who had to face the rest of their lives living with disabilities, and try-ing to imagine how their family and friends felt when they saw what had hap-pened to them. Most of them had left home as healthy, vital young eighteen year olds and came back like this—their lives forever changed.

We went to the drive-in, and soon we were talking, laughing, having a good time and enjoying the movie. But as I listened to bits and pieces of the men's conversation with each other, I remembered some of the things Sweetie had told me. I began to learn that some disabling after-effects of being in a war couldn't be so easily seen. I began to understand a little of what Van and his parents had gone through, and the mental adjustments they were still having to make.

Intending to help give him more confidence for his future, I told the friend that I was engaged to a disabled veteran. He replied, "You're too young to get yourself tied down to a man like that. You don't know what you're getting into." I had no idea what his injuries were, but saw that he felt it was too much for a veteran to expect to have a normal life again. I realized that not all his injuries were visible. It gave me a lot to think about.

Bettie's friend generously insisted that we take his car back to the Nurses' Home, then we could come back the next evening. Bettie agreed. I remember my surprise that she had a driver's license. Among my girl friends back home, not a single one of them had a driver's license, and very few women in Andrews did.

Back then, here in the mountains, women just didn't get out and drive around by themselves. They'd have been the talk of the whole country. The man did the driving, and if a woman went anywhere, he drove her. If it was somewhere he didn't want to go, she had to stay at home or find another way to go. For this man to just offer his car to a girl and let her drive off in it was something I'd never have imagined.

A few days later, our VA friends went home to Tennessee.

After that, I did a lot of thinking about the young veterans I saw at the VA Rehab Center. I knew that they would be subjected to rude stares and comments from insensitive people who will stare at a handicapped person and make unkind, rude remarks. They act as if they think the person intentionally did something to cause themselves to be as they are.

The problems I had experienced were nothing in comparison to theirs, but I'd also felt the humiliation when someone looked me over as if examining a circus freak. It seemed as if I could feel their eyes rake over me until they exposed the exact spot where I was most vulnerable. And felt the hurt when some otherwise kind person thoughtlessly made an unkind remark about my height. But that was so minor when compared to the veterans' disabilities, and the comparison made me thankful for my strong healthy body.

There have been times when I wondered if I grew so tall by sheer will power, to be big enough to defend myself from abuse. It's more common now, but back then it was very rare to see a six foot tall girl. Unless you are one, you can't imagine how it feels to walk into a room and have someone walk all around you, pointedly looking you up and down as if they couldn't believe their eyes, then exclaim, "My God! How tall are you, anyway?"

I'd been subjected to unkind remarks about my height since I was about twelve. Most people would agree that being a dwarf is a handicap, but they never consider that being an extremely tall girl is one also. For a very tall person, living in an "average" world is like living in a world full of children's furniture and ill-fitting clothes. Back then, there was no tall size in clothing stores. Fortunately, I became an expert seamstress and love to sew my own clothes.

Lawerence was six foot six, and just laughed about it, but people seem to admire a tall man. But I was more easily intimidated. I'd be so embarrassed that I'd wish I could just shrink down and become invisible, but seemed to become taller, more conspicuous and awkward instead.

For awhile in High School, I'd slumped, trying to look shorter. Miss Hamilton, my PE teacher, who also was tall, but two inches shorter, talked to me about standing straight, and told me to be proud of my height. Then I noticed how otherwise pretty girls looked with that hunched-over, slouchy posture. I realized that I might not be pretty, but it only made me look worse to slouch, even if there was nothing I could do about my height or my clothes.

I was the tallest girl in high school, including my teachers, and was the tallest girl in the whole school of nursing. Only two other girls came close—they were five foot ten. Several times through the years, some woman has said that she wished she was as tall as me—perhaps trying to make me feel better. I know she would soon change her mind if the wish became a reality.

One day in Home Ec, I was standing at the sink doing something, and Miss Whitaker was sitting in a chair at a table over to the side. Out of the blue, she said, "Cleo, you have such small feet."

I looked down at my feet in surprise, but they were still the same ol' feet, then looked at her and said, "Small?" She said, "Yes. In proportion to your height, you have very small feet." I thanked her for the compliment, then got to noticing other girls' feet. To my surprise, I found that what she said was true.

But I never made fun of little girls with big ol' feet. I knew that just like me, they were the way God made them, and there was nothing either of us could do about it.

People also make unkind remarks to overweight girls and women, and I sympathize with them. But there's always the possibility that they can lose weight and look more "normal." I'm six feet tall—and there's not a thing I can do about it.

I came to understand one reason why big girls wanted to look smaller. Petite, cute little girls get petted and babied, and not as much is expected from them—from their parents or their teachers. I saw how they got away with things in school, just because they were little and cute. Since then, I've also seen how unprepared for life they were after graduation and felt sorry for them when they discovered they had to grow up and live in the real world.

I've also learned that short people, especially petite women, sometimes feel intimidated by me because of my size. When I sense this, I go out of my way to make them feel at ease with me.

Just because I'm taller than a man doesn't mean that I don't like for him to show me courtesy, or open a door for me. Inside, I'm as feminine as any woman, and love soft sweaters, lacy underwear, flowers and Valentines. That was something I'd found so different about Van. I loved the way he was always courteous, protective, and treated me with such gentle kindness and respect. The way he acted, I almost believed he was proud to be seen with me. He made me feel beautiful and special to him.

Even now, just when I begin to think I'm not really so much different from other people, someone comes along, catches me off guard with a rude remark, and *I allow them* to make me feel ashamed of my height.

Most importantly, I've learned that most people make derogatory remarks about others because of their own feelings of insecurity. They erroneously try to gain status and "stature" by trying to make others—not just me—appear to be of less value than they. I've found that the ill-mannered man who keeps picking at me and making remarks is usually an immatue, insecure "little" man, regardless of height or size.

Van gave me valuable insight by helping me see that people who tried to make me feel inferior were actually envious of me. That was hard for me to understand, because I felt that I had nothing anyone could possibly envy.

I've seen handicapped people who were highly successful—maybe not in spite of their handicap, but because of it. They've learned how to be disciplined and find a way around their handicaps.

In spite of what I've learned, it's still hard to remain friendly and courteous to people who, every time I see them, try to intimidate me with their actions and rude remarks about my height as if insinuating that I belong in a circus side-show.

But I try!

BIG CHANGES

Van's next letter was full of apology, asking me to forget he'd ever said anything. I was only too happy to do that.

A few days later, he wrote—saying he was thinking about applying to Dell School of Medical Technology in Asheville for training to be a lab and x-ray technician. First, he'd need to get his GED. I was thrilled to death! I knew he could do it.

He went to Cullowhee, took his GED test and passed it. Then he came out to see the school, had an interview, and put in his application. He was accepted, and was to come to Asheville the last of December.

That was right away! We were both so excited. We could see each other often when he came to Asheville.

The people at Dell School had given him the address of a boarding house over on Riverside Drive, and he made arrangements to live there. We both felt better about things now.

"Lord, had that been a little test?"

◆　　◆　　◆

As a sign of respect, when a doctor walked up to the nurse's desk, all nurses, aides and ward clerks stood at attention, as if in the military. If he didn't sit, no one sat, not even the tired old grey-haired nurse old enough to be his grandmother. They remained standing until he walked away.

I still feel a shock (and give silent applause for both) when I see a doctor walk up to the desk and the nurse glances up and says, "Good morning, Doctor," and goes on with her paperwork or whatever, while everyone else elbows around him and goes on about their business. Good riddance of a stupid tradition!

Certainly, doctors should be respected, but "my opinion is" that patient care should come first. I've been in situations where I've had to stand there, so tired and sleepy I could drop, the hall lit up with call lights, maybe have a patient waiting for pain medication, the charts not done—while "himself" decided what he was going to do. Baloney! At least, he could've said, "I don't need anything"—or something—and let everybody get on with their business.

If he needs help, all he has to do is ask. I've yet to see a nurse that wouldn't immediately drop everything to help a doctor.

Besides, we've got women doctors now. (Applause and cheers!) That was rare in those days. I think we had only two on the entire hospital staff at Memorial Mission.

◆   ◆   ◆

Then suddenly, things started to change. First, we got the surprise of our lives. We were required to observe three autopsies during training. They weren't done very often. One day, when I had been there about two months, an autopsy was scheduled to be done, so we were taken to observe it to get one of them behind us. My classmates were girls right out of high school, and most of them had never seen anything more than a cut finger or a nosebleed.

It was a small room, and they lined up all us little probies in a circle around a stainless steel table, on which was a sheet-covered body. The pathologist pulled the sheet off, exposing the man's nude body, and explained that the suspected cause of death was a stroke or aneurysm.

The doctor put on gloves and a long protective gown, then rubbed his gloved hands together as if in anticipation as he looked at the man. We could see that the table was surrounded with a built-in trough, and realized its purpose was to serve as a drain to catch blood and body fluids. I looked on with disbelief as he picked up a scalpel and in one swift motion, whisked it across and through the man's scalp from behind one ear to the other. Then he dug his fingers under the top edge of the scalp and pulled it down over the man's eyes and nose, freeing it from the skull with a scalpel as he went. Next, he pulled the back part of the scalp down toward the back of the man's head, exposing the skull. He said this would keep from disfiguring the face, and the scalp would hold everything nicely in place when he was finished.

Then he picked up a hand-held circular saw. The saw blade was about four inches across and flush with one end, and he held it by the handle on the opposite end. He turned it on, revved it up, looked around the circle of wide-eyed innocents, and gave a big wide-lipped smile.

Then he proceeded to begin sawing around and through the skull as if making a cap from the skull at the top of the man's head. Before we knew what was happening, small pieces of flesh and bone went flying through the air, hitting us all over. It looked like small bits of hamburger. The tiny sharp bone fragments stung when they hit our skin, and just stuck to us wherever they landed.

Some of it hit a pretty blonde girl in the face. She put her hands up over her face and ran horrified, almost screaming, from the room. The pathologist didn't seem to notice, but went right on sawing until he lifted the circular piece of skull off and held it up like a trophy. It looked like a turtle shell.

I won't go into detail about the whole autopsy, but the rest of us stood there and watched it all. I can see that we probably could have learned a lot about the human body later, but not before we even began studying Anatomy. I never understood why they did that to us so early in training.

When we got back to the Nurses' Home, some of us went by to check on the girl who'd ran out. She was still crying, her face red and wet with tears as she frantically threw her clothing and belongings into her open luggage on the bed. She'd already called her mother. About fifteen minutes later, her mother came and got her, and we never saw her again.

◆　　　◆　　　◆

Construction was underway across town for a new five story hospital on Biltmore Avenue, just up the hill from Biltmore. It was the site of Victoria Hospital, and part of the old hospital would be kept, with the new, larger construction built onto the front. It would combine three local hospitals into one—Memorial Mission, Victoria, and Aston Park.

We were to have a new Nurses' Residence, and there would be two students in each room. I would have to adjust to having a roommate. All the girls were wondering who their roommate would be. When it was announced that we would be allowed to choose, Bettie and I signed up to be roommates.

When Bettie went home for the Christmas holidays, she came back changed and sad. The young man she was engaged to had really got to her, saying how much he missed her, he couldn't live without her, and begged her to come back home. After a week of indecision, she packed her bags and went back to Virginia to get married.

Van had moved into the boarding house over on Riverside Avenue, and was enjoying lab school. He would take lab a year, then x-ray for three months. By the time he finished, I'd be half way through school.

From the new hospital, the boarding house was about a mile and a half away—within walking distance—or he could catch a city bus. We walked all over

Asheville and Biltmore and got to know where everything was. And we were getting to know each other better.

He made good friends with two of his fellow students, Bob and Rena, and we double-dated with them a lot. Bob also lived at the same boarding house. He had a car, and the four of us went to the drive-in several times together, or just rode around exploring the surrounding area. There were miniature golf courses all along the highway then and we enjoyed stopping and playing on a sunny day.

They had to study a lot, and so did I. Lots of times, we just parked somewhere and the three of them studied together in the car, or sat under a tree while I did my studying. Bob and Rena were always asking Van questions. His mind was like a tape recorder, and he'd tell them what they wanted to know as if he were reading it right out of the book, or explain to them how to do a certain lab procedure. It was amazing. He was the smartest person I ever knew, but he didn't make a big show of it or act superior to anyone.

◆   ◆   ◆

We were the first students at the new Memorial Mission Hospital. The building was beautiful. They had a large veterans memorial plaque in a walled courtyard just outside the lobby and snack bar, and the names of servicemen from Western North Carolina who died in WW II were engraved on it. I was so grateful that Sweetie's or Van's name wasn't on it.

Everything in the hospital was so new and clean. Those shiny-floored halls looked a mile long. I was to find out that they felt like they were a mile long, too. It would be interesting to know just how many thousand miles I hurried up and down them. There were five floors, with a different service on each. Before I left there, I would know every nook and cranny in the whole place.

The new Nurses' Residence hadn't been completed when we moved patients to the new hospital. Until it was finished, the students would be housed in former patient rooms on the third floor of the old Victoria part of the hospital. I was glad when we got to move out of there. There were no locks on the doors, and it made me a little uneasy. The Emergency Room was on the ground floor right under us, and we could hear people talking loudly below the windows. Sometimes they sounded as if they were drunk and fighting.

It reminded me of Saturday nights in the hospital at home. Every Saturday night, it seemed, we got somebody in from Graham County a lot of the time, who had been in a wreck, fight, stabbing or shooting. Here, lots of them were from Madison County.

In the new Nurses' Home, students were grouped together in areas according to their seniority. The probies were in one section, the second year students in the next area, and finally, the seniors together. It was a good arrangement. It was nice for our class to be close together so we could run in and out to discuss things or ask questions of each other without disturbing the older students.

Male nurses were something new on the horizon. There was one male student in the class ahead of me—a veteran using GI bill benefits, then two came in with the next class after mine. They didn't have to live in the Nurses' Home, and one of them was married.

We had a lounge with—would you believe it? A black and white TV! Watching television was a new experience for me. Very few people owned one of them, at least back home, they didn't. Girls went around whistling the tune from the Andy Griffith show. As the lounge was used by all students, it was interesting to sit in there, watch TV and listen as the older students told about an interesting patient, or discussed what they'd done that day. I looked forward to knowing what they knew, and doing the things I heard them talk about.

The laundry room was next door to the lounge. There were sinks where we could do hand laundry, and washers and dryers. The washin' machine was one of them newfangled front-loader automatic washers, with a round glass window in the door so you could see the clothes tumble around in there. Just put the clothes inside, add some washin' powder, close the door, set the control, and go in the lounge and watch TV or do whatever you want to while the clothes were being washed. What a way to live!

I'd never used a clothes dryer, either. I was amazed at how smooth the clothes came out. Well, *looky there*! Most of 'em had less wrinkles when they come out of there than the clothes at home had after I'd rubbed 'em off with them old flatirons. And there were ironing boards and electric irons.

Around the corner was a small snack kitchen with a round table, four chairs, a refrigerator and toaster. There was always some bread and peanut butter on a shelf. Each day, bacon, eggs, cheese and tomatoes were put in the refrigerator for the night shift. The students could eat before they went on duty or make their own breakfast when they got off if they wished. The rest of us left their food alone. We knew they'd need something to eat before going to work at eleven, or come off duty tired and hungry at seven AM.

We had to walk over to the hospital cafeteria to eat during the designated hours it was open, as it was closed between times. If you didn't get there, you had to wait til the next meal. It was all right during our first year, but when we started working night shift, it presented a problem. We had a hard time getting enough sleep. We ate breakfast when we got off at 7, then maybe we'd have a class from 9 to 10, and another from 1 to 2, or 2 to 3.

If we got lunch, we had to be in the cafeteria during the time from 11:30 til 1:00. Supper was from 4:30 til 6. We'd no more than get undressed and sleep an hour or so, when had to get up, dress, and either go to class or to eat.

We were each given a key to our room. Rooms were to be kept neat and clean and were inspected once a week. Only approved items could be kept in the room. We weren't allowed to keep food in our rooms, except maybe a candy bar or an apple—no big stashes.

Our bed was to be neatly made at all times when we were not in it. We stripped our bed by a certain time on a specific day of the week and placed the neatly folded used linen, towels and washcloths on the floor outside our door. A maid collected, counted and noted each item on her clipboard as she pushed the linen cart down the hall. If she didn't collect any, you didn't get any, and it was reported. When she returned later to pass out linens, she let herself in with her pass key and laid the clean linen on the bed.

No visitors were allowed on second floor, as girls would be going in and out of their room, to and from the bathrooms in various stages of dress (or undress) at any time. There were no private bathrooms. A large bathroom was located at each end of the hall. Each one had several compartments for commodes and shower stalls. Each compartment had doors that locked.

If someone had a visitor, or a telephone call, it was announced on the intercom. If it was a visotor, we had to go down to the housemother's desk to greet them. Also, the one telephone for students' use was a pay phone at the foot of the stairs. We weren't allowed below second floor if we weren't fully dressed and presentable.

There were sofas and chairs in the downstairs reception room just inside the entry. We could receive visitors and sit in there with them. The reception room was situated directly across from the housemother's desk and anyone in there could be observed through the wide, open doorway.

If it was a male visitor, you better believe you were being kept under constant surveillance. We were expected to conduct ourselves in a ladylike manner—no necking or even hand-holding. Any man who escorted us home at sign-in time was expected to leave us at the outside door.

Incidentally, we had a student council, and students could be brought before the student council for violation of any of the rules. For each infraction of the rules a student was given a certain number of demerits. If you reached a certain number, you were expelled. I got called before the student council once, toward the end of my second year. I'm serious, and wouldn't you know it—somebody saw me and Van holding hands. I was almost twenty, and engaged to him. I was given some demerits and cautioned to never let it happen again.

We were allowed to smoke in our room, and no one treated us like lepers if we did. When we were on duty in the hospital and had a break, we could smoke in the nurses' lounge or in the dining room. I liked Cavalier brand the best. Trouble was (or maybe good for me), I didn't have the money to buy many.

Patsy Humphrey was almost as tall as I, and we became good friends. We signed up to be roommates, and I found her to be a compatible one. She was from West Asheville, knew her way around town, and taught me a lot about city life. Her father died when she was a little girl, and she had lived at an orphanage until her mother remarried and got her three children back.

Our second year, her parents gave her an old 38 Ford, and when we had gas money, ran around everywhere in it. We went to her home on Michigan Avenue a lot. She was my roommate all during training, and we had a lot of good times together.

She brought me one of her swimsuits and we went out to Beaver Lake several times. She had some experience as a lifeguard, and with her help, I overcame my fear of water enough to swim on my back almost as fast as she could swim. But when I turned over and looked at the water, I went down like a rock. We went all over the lake with our feet hooked on each side under an inner tube. I'd pull her awhile and she'd pull me awhile.

Occasionally, we'd get a wolf whistle from some man at the lake. At first I put it down as "boys will be boys," who would whistle at any girl—or thought it was for somebody else. When I realized they were meant for me, I was embarrassed. I wondered if they thought as Dad and Mom did—women who wore shorts were out lookin' for a man. Why else would they whistle at me?

When I looked in the mirror for an objective analysis, I saw that I was no *ravin' beauty*, but maybe I didn't look too bad, after all. At least I didn't see myself as *ugly as a mud fence* any more. Huh! Maybe I was just a "late bloomer."

But Van was always telling me I was beautiful, and he made me feel beautiful, even though I knew I was nowhere near the "beautiful" category. Thanks to him, at least I was no longer ashamed of myself. Whatever men thought was their problem. Just let 'em whistle. I was having a good time, and sure didn't need a man to louse things up. Besides, I was engaged to the best, most handsome, most wonderful man in the world.

◆   ◆   ◆

One day, Humphrey and I went window shopping, and were admiring the new fall coats in the window at Bon Marche'. A "poodle" coat caught my attention. It was a warm medium dark brown, with a hint of rust in the textured surface. It was the latest style, with a shawl collar, wide turn-back sleeves, and draped gracefully in the back. I said I sure wished I could afford to buy that coat.

My same old coat was not only pretty well worn, but totally out of style. I just wished I could find a way to earn some money to buy a new one. I'd already told the Lord I didn't want to seem vain, but was gettin' pretty tired of that old coat. Was there any way He could help me get a new one? It didn't have to be nothin' fancy, just decent.

Some of the students got a dollar an hour baby-sitting for one of the doctors once in awhile. But they usually asked for the same girl when they called, so that was all pretty well sewed up. Besides, I wouldn't know how to act in the doctors' fancy homes.

Every once in awhile, I got a chance to "sit" with a patient. It was actually private duty, but as a student, we couldn't call it that. We were paid five dollars a shift, and thought that was good money.

Humphrey told me I could probably get the coat and make payments on it. I was somewhat doubtful, being a student with no income, and from out of town, too. But she said it would probably be easy; other students had accounts there. I thought, "Well, it wouldn't hurt to ask," and I'd just like to feel the fabric, anyway—that wouldn't cost nothin'.

We went inside, and I looked the coat over. It was fifty dollars—a lot of money! But I thought it was the prettiest coat I'd ever seen. When the sales lady came over, Humphrey asked her for details about setting up a charge account for me. When I told her I was a student nurse, she said, "Oh, that's no problem. We'd be happy to set up a student account for you."

I tried on the coat, and when I looked in the mirror, was astonished at the difference in my appearance. I looked so elegant when I turned up the soft warm collar. If I had this coat, I could wear it as a cover-up over my other old clothes, and nobody'd even notice them.

Next thing I knew, I was walking out of Bon Marche' with my beautiful new coat. I felt like a princess. I wasn't worried about the five dollars a month payments. God had provided everything I needed so far—and He'd do it again.

Besides, I just kind of felt like He'd set up this whole thing. I was never late with a payment.

That was probably the best bargain I ever got. I wore that coat for years. The material was soft and drapey, and so cuddly warm. On a cold day when the kids were babies, I put it on, tucked one or both of them in next to me and wrapped the coat around us. They called it my poodle-dog coat. When they were napping away from home, I used it as a blanket, and even put it down outside for them to sit on several times. I thought I might as well just wash it and use it for that, as Van had given me a new cashmere coat. But it came out good as new, so I just ironed the lining and wore it some more.

For a few years, it went out of style, and hung in the closet. When that style came back in fashion, I got it out and wore it some more, and got many compliments on it. About fifteen years ago, when they came into fashion again, I ran across some of the same fabric in a different color. I reluctantly took the old coat apart to use as a pattern, and made a new one.

◆   ◆   ◆

Having grown up in such isolation, it was quite an education to be among so many girls with so many different backgrounds. It had been a new experience to meet so many people at the hospital in Andrews, and to have made so many friends, but they were mostly small town people and we had similar ways and speech.

The Nursing students were from the country, small towns, big cities, and even different states. Some of our patients came from or had lived in different parts of the world. I loved to hear about the places they lived and discover the cultural differences in people.

When anyone asked me where I was from, and I told them "Andrews," they usually asked,"Where's that?" Most people seem to think North Carolina ends at Asheville—or did, until there was so much publicity during the manhunt for Eric Robert Rudolph. "My opinion is" that Asheville is just the place where the best part of North Carolina starts. The western Smoky mountains. Home.

Another thing of interest to me was how many different denominations of churches there were. We had a short course in religion in order to help us understand our patients' religious affiliation. Speakers from different denominations came to explain their beliefs and customs of worship. A Catholic priest explained about last rites, religious icons, a rosary, etc., so if we came across one while caring for a patient, we'd know what they were and leave them where we found them.

I came to realize that it isn't true that if you're anything but a *hard-shell Baptist*, you're on your way to Hell. God has some good people everywhere. I was learning a respect for other people's beliefs, and that the denomination wasn't what took you to Heaven. Because someone's opinion, background or ways were different from mine didn't make them wrong—just different. My world was expanding and my interest in learning more about it was growing. I was feeding that hunger for knowledge, and savoring every bite.

GETTING MY NURSE'S CAP

We had regularly scheduled private evaluation sessions as we went along, and the areas that needed improvement were pointed out. If we weren't performing at a satisfactory level at the end of six months, we'd be sent home. Those who made it would be given their nurse's cap and get to wear a white pinafore-like bib and apron which covered most of the blue striped uniform.

I spent two hours a day on the hospital wards now. We made beds, fed patients, gave A.M. Care, and I got to do a procedure often, checking off one after another. I was anxious to get all the required ones in so I'd be sure to get my cap at the end of six months.

Finally, the six months' probation was over and most of us earned our much-coveted nurse's cap. Now I could wear the white pinafore type apron over the striped uniform, and look more like a real nurse. I was so excited I could hardly eat or sleep.

They had a beautiful traditional capping ceremony for us. We were told to invite our family and friends, but Van was in school, and there was nobody else for me to invite. For the first time, we wore our new white aprons. The lights were dimmed and we walked single file down the center aisle, carrying a lighted candle in a candleholder that was a replica of the one Florence Nightingale carried through the wards. We alternated turning left and right until we were lined up in front. There was now fourteen of us.

We had memorized, and now recited the Florence Nightingale Pledge. It was an oath we took: "I solemnly pledge before God and in the presence of this assembly." To summarize it, we pledged to practice our profession faithfully, with loyalty to aid the physician in his work, and not knowingly take or administer any harmful drug.

Then the Director of Nursing Education came along and placed a nurse's cap on each of our heads and congratulated us. We were so proud of our cap. By then we had definitely earned it.

Getting dressed now was quite a bit more complicated. The buttons were the removable kind. The ones on the cuffs and apron were two-headed, or two-sided, and the ones on the uniform were the kind with a metal shank on the underside, with a little pin—like a small bobby pin or cotter pin which went through the hole to fasten the button on. I think it took about sixteen altogether. It took awhile to get all that buttoning done. I learned to button the cuffs on the blue striped uniform first, then do as much buttoning as I could while I could get to them easily, and leave just enough unbuttoned to still be able to put it on. I fixed it way ahead of time, and hung it up ready to put on.

The apron was in two parts—a bib and a skirt that buttoned together. The bib part had long wide straps that went up across the shoulders, crossed in the back, and buttoned onto the waistband in back of the skirt/apron piece. The skirt/apron was so stiff it would stand alone on the floor and not bend or fall over. It met in the back and buttoned at the back waistband. With every step I made, it rustled, and if I walked fast, the edges popped as they fanned stiffly out and back.

We had the option of buying a nurse's cape. It was made from a finely woven heavyweight Navy blue wool fabric, had a bright red lining, gold military type buttons, and a mandarin-type collar, with the gold embroidered letters "MMH" on each side. A student looked sharp as she walked along in her uniform, the front edge of the cape blowing open and turning back just enough to glimpse a flash of bright red. I didn't get to buy one til toward the end of my second year. I still have it.

In addition to polishing my shoes every night, I had to wash and iron my cap often. It had to be stiffly starched, and great care had to be taken not to scorch it. Proud as I was of my cap, I hated the way our caps were made because they were so hard to iron. They were made from heavy cotton fabric, and yellowed fast.

The band was flat, easily ironed, then folded over to where the back part was sewed on. The back part was gathered very full where it was sewed to the band, especially in the center area. I had to get the tip of the iron down into every little gather and try not to press them flat. The bottom of the back had a drawstring which was pulled to gather the bottom of the cap after it was ironed. When the string was pulled, this made the middle part fan out and stick up into what reminded me of a turkey's tail.

It stood up a good three inches where it was gathered and sewed to the edge of the band in front. This "turkey tail" part was almost right on top of my head when I put the cap on. I was always and forever bending over and hitting it against a bed, wheelchair, or something, and knocking it crooked. It seemed like I had to straighten it every few minutes.

After having to adhere to such a strict dress code for so many years, don't you know I felt like I was going to work in my p.j.'s when nurses started wearing scrub suits in recent years? And socks. And soft comfortable shoes. And no more garter belt or girdle and white stockings to keep clean. Just think how many hours of my life I've spent washing and ironing starched white uniforms, washing white hose, white underwear, white shoestrings and polishing white shoes. I'm happy to slam the door on them "good old days!"

After we moved into the new hospital, the cap design changed, much to our approval. Since Memorial Mission had combined three hospitals, the band edge had two slight indentations, making three slight scallops, signifying the three hospitals that combined into one. It opened out flat, and took only one small button in the back to hold it into the proper shape after bending it around. Best of all, they were permanently starched and perfectly smooth. Goodbye to ironin' "ol' turkey-tail!" And good riddance!

Anyone could tell how advanced a nurse was by her cap. Students wore a plain white cap til we began our second year, then wore a stripe all the way across the edge of the band. Now I couldn't wait til I earned my "stripe-" a five-eighths inch wide black velvet ribbon across the band of the cap.

The night before we wore our stripe, we had a giggling good time helping each other put our stripe the exact distance from the edge of the band and finding a way to hold it in place. I found that KY lubricating jelly made the perfect glue. It was water-soluble and the stripe came right off when the cap needed washing.

When a senior graduated, it was customary for her to leave her stripe to an underclass student. This showed that she thought that person would be an outstanding nurse, and was her way to bestow an honor on them. Emma Jean Elliott thrilled me to death when she gave me hers, as I really admired her. I gave mine to Hazel "Priceless" Price. When we graduated, we would wear a three-eighth inch stripe at a right angle on the outside corner of the band, and would wear a gold MMH pin on our uniform.

This all may sound like being in the military service, compared to today's nursing education experience. Actually, the program was designed to teach responsibility and self confidence, and instilled pride in belonging to the nursing profession. The priviledges and recognition we were given at intervals along the way gave us goals to work for, and made us feel that they were rewards we had earned.

The whole atmosphere at the School of Nursing was what could be called a combination military and religious school. They even rang a vespers bell and held vespers at sundown.

These traditions also gave us a sense of history. At times like during the capping ceremony, I had a sense of being in a long line of dedicated nurses, reaching through time beyond the battlefields of World Wars I and II, the cold, harsh

Crimean war and Florence Nightingale. When I had this mental picture, I was always facing them, so I must be following, instead of being in front.

I could imagine the primitive conditions of long ago hospitals or barracks, where nurses faithfully served through long sleepless hours in spite of cold, hunger and few supplies. I tried to imagine the frustration and despair they must have felt to watch their patients suffer and die with very little means to give them comfort and relief. But they never gave up trying.

I was so proud and humbled to be in the same profession as these women who had so nobly served and sacrificed, and resolved to live up to the heritage of what I felt to be the best profession anyone could choose.

But times change, and values change—there's a lot to think about. Living in today's modern world of science and technology, I feel some reluctance to write these feelings, as I might be considered more than a little *"sappy"*(very idealistic and sentimental). If I am, I've been that way for many a year, and can't see that it's ever done any harm. In fact, maybe more folks might just need a little doast of "sappy."

After all, where would this country be today if our forefathers had lacked that characteristic?

Where are all the heroes (and heroines) of today—the people who inspire us to be something better than we are by following their example?

GETTING DOWN TO BUSINESS

In six months, we'd finished our college courses, and would take the remainder of our classes in the Educational Department on the ground floor of the nurse's residence. This was where the School of Nursing office, classrooms, a fairly large auditorium and the office of the Educational Director was located.

A reel-to-reel projector with slides and a few anatomical models were the only audio-visual aids we had available at the time. We had a life-size dummy to use for practice when learning to give a bed bath, correctly turn and lift a patient, or do other procedures.

We would spend only about two hours in the classroom each day, and work in the hospital the rest of the day. As we took classes in a subject, we would work in that section of the hospital. We'd have three months in each service, except for only one month in the Special Diet kitchen. We'd have a full course in Diet and Nutrition, and also had to rotate through Central Supply Room (CSR).

We wouldn't have classes the last few months, but were supposed to be able to choose where we wanted to go for more experience in that area. I chose Pediatrics, but of all places, they sent me to OR. That would have been my last choice. Made me wonder if a certain Doctor back home didn't do some meddlin' into my business.

On the first floor at the front of the hospital building was the main entrance, Admitting, Business offices, Medical Records, Lobby and Snack Bar. Urology and Orthopedics was located beyond that, on a first floor wing of the hospital. I wondered what on earth Urology had to do with Orthopedics, and when I walked down the hall, I found out. Just about every patient had a catheter bag hanging on their bedside. People with fractures, injuries and Orthopedic surgery can't get up and go to the bathroom.

Second floor was Obstetrics, Labor and Delivery, Newborn Nursery and Premature Nursery. Services were still segregated. The "colored section," called "Second South," was in the old part of the building which was formerly Victoria

Hospital. There was a long corridor between the colored and the white patients, so the two never saw each other.

Third floor was pre and post-op Surgical patients, Operating and Recovery Rooms. Fourth floor was Medical patients and Central Supply Room (CSR) Fifth floor was Pediatrics. The cafeteria, main kitchen, diet kitchens, x-ray, lab, and Pharmacy were all on the ground floor.

The ER and Outpatient clinics were on the ground floor of the old part.

The CSR in 1955 was a drastically different place from the CSR of today. Having to clean, re-sterilize and supply the whole hospital made the CSR a busy, busy place. The whole hospital depended on CSR to keep it running smoothly. Offhand, I don't remember any prepackaged sterile items except IV solutions, IV and blood administration sets, surgical knife blades, some sutures, catheter bags and tubing.

The ever-increasing use of plastics has made a dramatic change in the hospital. Today's CSR is mostly a place for storing and dispensing prepackaged sterile disposable supplies. Bedpans, urinals, wash basins, thermometers, soap dishes, water pitchers, drinking glasses and other things that we had to clean and re-use are now issued to each patient individually, and either taken home or discarded. Syringes, needles, medicine cups, razors, drapes, gowns, towels, surgical sponges, all kinds of tubing, stomach tubes, catheters and supplies for OR and Delivery Room are prepackaged, sterile and disposable, intended for one-time use.

We used disposable blades but re-used the razor handle. In my third year of training, hospitals had started to buy a few presterilized and disposable items, like catheterization trays. Even then, we had to sterilize the catheters and add them to the tray. Now, even suture or clip remover trays, catheter and prep trays—along with the instruments, catheter and razor, are disposable.

CSR was divided into four areas. First was a dirty area where used items were returned for cleaning, then they were taken to the clean area where they were re-packaged and re-sterilized. Most items were sterilized in an autoclave. An autoclave is like a barrel lying on its side, except it is thick, heavy stainless steel, with an inner and outer jacket. It has a heavy rack which pulls out on wheels for loading, then slides back inside with the supplies on it. It's about three feet across and six feet deep from front to back. We had some smaller ones for small items. They were all kept running.

The thick, heavy round autoclave door in front was closed and fastened by swinging it closed, then turning a wheel (like a steering wheel) which caused heavy bars to slide out into place inside a recessed area in front. When pressure started building, the door was automatically locked in place and couldn't be opened as long as there was any steam pressure inside. After the contents dried and cooled, they were taken out and stored in the sterile storage section.

The remaining section was for unsterile reusable equipment which needed to be cleaned, sanitized and stored until requisitioned—such as Wangenstein and regular suction machines, Oxygen tents, vaporizers, croup tents, bedpans, wash basins, enema and douche equipment.

Back then a stainless steel dressing cart on wheels was kept on each floor. It was stocked with sterile supplies for dressings or to remove sutures and clips. We used stainless steel cans with lift-off lids as containers for sterile supplies. CSR filled each of them with different sizes of gauze squares, fanfolded sterile towels, tongue depressors, cotton balls, applicators, etc., taped the lid on, labeled and dated them, then autoclaved them. A stainless steel bucket for soiled dressings hung on one end of the cart. Soiled dressings were wrapped in newspaper, put into paper bags, then sent to the incinerator. Before plastic came into common use, paper bags and newspapers served many purposes. The dressing carts were regularly taken to CSR to be cleaned and restocked.

Absorbable suture came in prepackaged sterile peel-open packs, but cotton, silk, and braided nylon suture came on spools. We wound it off onto half of a tongue depressor in about two yard lengths, then autoclaved it in small paper autoclave envelopes.

To prepare suture needles for surgery and ER, roll gauze was wrapped around a four inch square piece of thin cardboard. Then assorted sizes of half circle and three-eighth circle cutting and plain tip needles were fastened through the gauze to hold them in place. A few straight skin needles were added at the bottom. Then they were wrapped, labeled and autoclaved. After they were used, they were not thrown away unless they were broken or badly bent. They were carefully washed, put back on the gauze in the proper place, and re-sterilized.

Sterile suture needles now come in all sizes with all types of suture bonded into the eye end of the needle (called atraumatic). There is less trauma than suture threaded through the eye of a needle, which makes a larger hole in the tissue. Some suture is smaller than a hair. If suture is opened and put on a sterile field, it's all thrown away if unused.

Needles for injection were returned to CSR after being used, and had to be washed, rinsed and inspected. Each and every one—separately! A stilette was used to ensure they were not stopped up. If the needles were dull, they had to be sharpened. There were different types, like spinal needles, and several sizes of each type. It took hours just to do the needles.

We had no plastic or nylon flexible catheter type needles like the ones now that are left in a vein for a few days. We used a large-gauge stainless needle, like the ones we used for shots. When a patient had an IV, the arm was firmly fastened to an armboard so the elbow couldn't be bent, and they had to lie still until the IV finished. If they needed more IV's, we had to start a new one every twelve hours to avoid infection. We had no Heparin locks to keep blood from clotting and stopping up a needle. The IV tubing came loose easily from the metal needle and had to be carefully taped. If the needle came loose from the IV tubing. the patient could lose a lot of blood from the backflow through the needle, if not discovered.

Everything was marked with an expiration date, three months from the sterilization date. After that, they had to be re-dated and re-autoclaved. It was a huge job just to label the little autoclave envelopes and put the expiration date on them. The envelope or bag had to be labelled before the item was put in, or the (new ballpoint) pen would punch a hole in the paper. Anything with the tiniest hole in the wrapper was considered contaminated, or unsterile.

The envelopes and bags had stripes or bars that changed color in the autoclave, and the autoclave tape used to seal them turned a striped brown, indicating that it was sterile. Syringes, medicine glasses, adapters, clamps, and other small reusable items to be put on a sterile field were sterilized the same way as suture.

We made our own solutions, such as Sterile Distilled Water, Sterile Saline, liquid Furacin (for burns), Mercurochrome, Merthiolate, Iodine, etc. Salt came in tablets, Furacin came in concentrated solution, and the others came in crystals. We had to learn how many salt tablets to use in a certain number of cubic centimeters (cc's) of water to make Isotonic Saline, and how to measure the others and mix to the proper strength. Liquids were put in 500 or 1000 cc. glass beakers and a gauze cover was taped around the top. This was to allow for expansion to keep the beaker from exploding from built-up pressure inside the autoclave.

We had to learn how to fanfold leggings, lap sheets, drape sheets, towels, surgical gowns and other things so they could be picked up by a corner and unfolded without touching the sterile field area. All the drapes were heavy cotton fabric, fan-folded and wrapped individually or made into packs and sterilized. Lap packs are sterile drapes used in surgery, and OB packs are for the delivery room. The contents of each pack had to be put in a certain order as we folded and stacked them. Then they were wrapped in double thickness pack wrappers, which also were inspected for holes.

We had to inspect each piece for tiny pinholes. If a hole was found, it was circled and sent to the sewing room to be repaired. The people in the hospital sewing room sewed and made all these different things from bolts of closely woven cotton fabric. I think they made everything except surgical gowns and scrub suits.

After cleaning, in CSR, rubber items such as urethral catheters, stomach tubes and other items that weren't to be autoclaved were soaked in a germicidal solution in stainless covered containers called boats. They were emptied, cleaned, and the solution changed periodically, according to what germicidal agent was being used. They were more particular in surgery, and ran these articles in the autoclave for three minutes. If you ran them any longer, they fused into a mass of melted, steam-cooked rubber, and had to be thrown away.

I found that out in surgery one fine day, when "The Celebrated Surgeon" needed a T-tube, a rubber drain used in gallbladder surgery. T-tubes were the most expensive kind, and I'd thoughtfully put in a whole bunch so "Himself" could have a nice selection to choose from. Every few minues, the scrub nurse asked if the autoclave had *come down* (finished its cycle), and finally somebody checked the autoclave when something started smelling like hot rubber. I'd accidentally set the timer for thirty instead of three minutes.

I found out that it kind of stinks the place up to do that, and it didn't make me real popular, neither.

MEDICINE AND SURGERY

When we were sent to Medicine, or fourth floor, we studied Pharmacology, Drugs and Solutions, and learned how to give medications correctly and safely. I learned many little tricks to avoid medication errors.

We used medicine cards, and each patient had an identification tag on the door and foot of the bed, and wore an ID bracelet. In addition, the person's name was called to verify that it was the correct patient, unless they were unconscious.

It gave me nightmares to think about how we gave medicines in the Andrews hospital. And when I learned the effects drugs had on the human body, it made me shudder to think how I had dispensed, and seen others dispense medications, with no idea of what action, interaction or side effects might occur.

On the other hand, they were doing the best they could with what they had. What if there had been no medicines at all available to people in that remote mountainous area? They had no means to go anywhere else.

It was fascinating to learn what the proper medication in the proper dose can do. I was also even more scared to death of medicines now that I knew about side effects and how dangerous they could be, and handled medicines with a healthy respect. If I had any question, I went to the original order the doctor had written on the chart, no matter how rushed I was.

By the time we left that floor, we were able to give total patient care including medications, except for starting IV's and giving a blood transfusion. No student was allowed to do venipunctures. We were shown how, but only RN's did them.

Huh-oh! I didn't know it was that big a deal. How many hundred had I started on patients in Andrews? *And here I had* even gone a way back on Nanty-haley by myself one time and give a woman a IV.

"Thanks, Lord, for taking care of me AND the patients, even if I was a-breakin' the Law."

Come to think of it, I bet the Law's got sev'al fractures where I broke it. I'd bent it awful bad sev'al times, too.

◆   ◆   ◆

I got to wondering just when Penicillin was discovered—I've forgotten. I pulled out my old Pharmacology and Therapeutics book that I studied in school, and began looking at it. It's a sixth edition, copyright 1952, with fairly big print. When I looked up Antibiotics, there was a grand total of thirteen pages, including pictures, with all the information for all antibiotics in use at that time. The Antibiotics were Penicillin, Streptomycin, Aureomycin, Chloramphenicol, and Terramycin. I've seen more information today in a drug insert for one antibiotic drug than is given for all those listed in the book. There's simply no comparison to the number and type of drugs available then to what is used now.

There was a separate six pages about Sulfonamides, listed as "Anti-infectives," and only four were listed. I'd forgotten about the existence of several of the diseases listed in the book—as well as most of the medications.

I thought it was so funny when I read the chapter titled "Purgatives," and found that there are twelve pages devoted to them in comparison to thirteen pages of Antibiotics. I didn't remember us a-thinkin' *a good cleanin'-out* was so important, either. Now, the next time you go to take a doast of Castor Oil, I want you to remember that the book says, "It should be given ice cold on an empty stomach."

Did you know that you can buy odorless and tasteless Castor Oil now? What'll they think of next?

And if you went and got overdoasted on them Morphine pills, in amongst the other pleasant little things you'd get to counteract it, would be a purgative. Remember? Good ol' Castor Oil? And a hot coffee enema.

It says so *ratchere* in this book. Page 182.

Want t'borry it?

◆   ◆   ◆

When we went to the Operating Room, as always, we had a check list, but it was much longer than the others. We had to learn instruments, techniques, and several surgical procedures. We had to first be instructed, then observe, assist with supervision, then satisfactorily perform the nurse's duties for a certain number of different operations. Each procedure had to be checked off and signed by the supervisor that it was done on a competent level of performance.

We learned the names of instruments as we cleaned them, and learned to assemble different instrument trays according to the procedure they would be used for.

Students observed several times, learning sterile technique, what supplies and instruments were used, then how to either "scrub" or "circulate" on each surgical operation. Our basic knowledge of Anatomy, Physiology and Microbiology was a necessary part of understanding what was going on.

Reading about something in a book and actually seeing it are two very different things. I've had people ask me if it didn't bother me to work in surgery and see all that blood. My answer is—it depends on your reason for doing it. I'm sure I'd be horrified to see someone cut another person in a fight. In surgery, however, you are trying to help someone get well, improve their quality of life, or even save a life.

This is a more graphic example. Helping with Orthopedic surgery was not one of my favorite things to do. Sawing, nipping off bone, drilling holes, putting in screws and driving in pins or nails is not my cup of tea. Leg amputations were done with a saw that looked like a small handsaw. An orthopedist once had me saw a leg off, just above the knee. I did it, as I knew the man would surely die if he didn't have the leg amputated—and I wanted to stay in school. I couldn't refuse. In those circumstances, of course I did it, but I can't imagine doing that under any other circumstances.

Each surgeon was different, as are people in everyday life. Some were helpful by explaining things, others cussed if you didn't already know. Everyone knew that the surgeon was the person in charge here, but some of them took great delight in reminding everyone that he was the star of the show. At times, they cussed and threw things on the floor or across the room, like a kid throwing a temper tantrum. Then it was amazing to watch what a beautiful job that "bratty kid" did, once he got everyone's attention, their inferior status established, and settled down to business.

Sometimes, I felt that the surgeons thought the students were there for the sole purpose of having someone on which to vent their frustrations. Some of them were really mean to us. I would have felt bad if it had only been me, but anyone was a likely target, even the RNs.

I learned a lot in the OR, but didn't like surgery because I never got used to the tension. I'd been raised to know that when somebody got mad, somebody else (me) got hurt. I knew there was nothing I could do or say in my defense, as I couldn't risk being sent home. But I vowed that when I got out of school and on a job, no doctor would ever treat me that way again and get away with it, even if

I was fired. I could find another job. I might just give him lessons on how to throw things and cuss. I'd learned how to cuss before I could walk.

Fortunately, not all of them were like that.

Memorial Mission Hospital had the privilege of having Dr. Hillier, a brilliant neurosurgeon, on the staff. Right before I went there, he'd performed a total hemispherectomy, which is removal of one entire side, or half of the brain. It was the first one ever recorded where the patient survived.

"Neuro" is one of the most interesting things I ever studied. The neurosurgeon was good to the students and saw that we weren't put aside so we couldn't see. He invited us, one or two at a time to come right up to where he was working, and explained what he was doing and why. I scrubbed in with him a few times. I'd have loved working with him.

Sometimes the anesthesiologists were about as mean as the surgeons. There was one skinny, white haired one that everybody loved, though. He was always pleasant to work with, and gave great anesthesia. His name was Dr. Nelson Bell. He'd been a missionary in China, and had a daughter, Ruth, who was a nurse. I'd heard some of the older students talk about what a sweet person and good nurse she was. She'd married a young preacher named Billy Graham, from out around Montreat. He was just getting his Crusades For Christ going good, and his name was beginning to be recognized in other places.

One thing I especially appreciated was anesthesia for T & A patients. After induction, they were intubated with an endotracheal tube. This is a semi-flexible tube that is inserted into the trachea, then a balloon on the end is inflated so it can't come out, and basically, the lungs are sealed off so a patient cannot aspirate anything into them. Their breathing is controlled at all times by the anesthetist.

The anesthetic agent and Oxygen is administered through the tube, and we could suction as much as needed without pulling the anesthetic out through the suction. I wasn't scared to death all the time with this type of anesthesia. And the kids weren't nearly as sick post-op. And wouldn't you know it—I was assigned to assist with so many more T & A's than was required that I filled up all the allotted space and finally just stopped recording them on my check-off list. Man, I was tired of them things!

The last time I worked in an OR, it was illegal to have or store Ethyl Chloride or Ether in the hospital building. So many more safe anesthetic agents as well as drugs have been developed, and an anesthetist has many IV drugs at his disposal to induce anesthesia. He or she simply injects it right into the IV tubing, and immediately—the patient is out like a light.

A patient always goes into the recovery room until they are awake and aware of everything. Any needed equipment and trained personnel are immediately available. The anesthetist or doctor is in hearing distance. It's rare for a patient to experience nausea. If they do, fast, effective medication is injected right into the IV tubing.

Another thing that wasn't so good about working in the OR was that you had to wear shoes with special soles to prevent sparks from static electricity. They could cause an explosion of the anesthetic gases. Those "cuss-ed" shoes felt like they had metal soles, they were so hard and stiff. We even had to wear cotton underwear.

On the rock-hard concrete floor was a hard tile made specifically for OR use. With all the Ether, Oxygen, and volatile gases floating around next to the floor, we sure didn't want any sparks from static electricity. Each piece of equipment in there had to be grounded by a piece of metal chain attached to it and touching the floor at all times.

At the end of a long day on my feet in the OR, my feet and legs hurt too bad to cry. The regulation nurses' shoes with hard leather soles we had to wear every day weren't much better.

Now if there's anything that'll make you 'preciate havin' them good ol' soft, air piller, cushion-insole walkin' shoes like I wear now, that'll do it. Just a-thinkin' 'bout them ol' stiff hard-bottom shoes makes me want t'grab up ever pair I've got an' hug 'em real good. I love them thangs.

◆   ◆   ◆

I learned how to take care of patients in the Recovery Room, and found that I liked it, once I was trained to do it properly and knew that help and proper equipment was always available.

Then, when we went out on the Surgical floor, it was easier to know how to give good post-op patient care, as we knew what had been done to the patient in Surgery. We knew what signs to watch for to signal something was wrong after they were taken out on the floor from the Recovery Room and knew how to do specific dressings, according to the operation they'd had.

Then, as now, it was heart-breaking to do burn patients' dressings. Sometimes it was so painful that they had to be taken into OR for debridement (cleaning off the surface) and dressings under anesthesia. Burns are easily infected, and back then, we didn't have the antibiotics and treatments for burn patients that are available now. I'm so thankful for the Shriner's Hospitals and burn care centers we have today.

Our third floor supervisor was a "Mrs. No-nonsense." I wondered if her face would crack if she smiled. I thought she singled me out to follow and check everything I did just so she could find something to get onto me for. I made sure she didn't find much. If she was as mean as she looked (to me), I sure didn't want no trouble out of her.

My last week on Surgery, I was scheduled for my last counselling session before I left her floor, and dreaded it, for I just knew she'd have a whole bunch of "constructive criticism." When it was time for my scheduled appointment I went to her office as if someone were pushing me from behind. The door was open and she was sitting behind her desk.

I about had a heart attack when she looked up, smiled broadly, and kind of chuckled like she knew a joke. She said, "Well, Miss Hicks!" She was practically beaming. What in the world? She must've found a big 'un this time.

I must have had a funny look on my face, for she actually laughed. She did! Then she told me she knew I probably thought she was the meanest person in the world, but I had the ability to be an exceptional nurse if I applied myself. If she hadn't stayed after me all the time, I'd goof off and not be the nurse she knew I was capable of being. When she went over my assessment sheet, it sounded like Ol' Flossie Nightingale 'stid of me.

Dearie me! Who'd a thought it? I'd not only made the grade, but got a smile and laugh out of her, to boot.

◆   ◆   ◆

I find it interesting how certain things evoke certain memories. For instance, hearing a certain song brings back a memory of a certain time, place, or person. Or a color reminds me of something. When I hear a dove, I think of the baby noises our tiny son made when he discovered he had a voice. When I see a toy tea set, I think of tea parties Donna and I had in the afternoons, when she was a five year old "lady." My senses of sight, taste, hearing, and touch trigger memories for me, but it seems that I tend to relate more to certain smells, or scents—to people, places and events.

Occasionally, in the spring, I catch a certain refreshing, slightly sweet smell, combined with a "ferny," faint spicy scent, that reminds me of going outside and smelling the early morning air deep in the mountains. The smell of frying bacon and perking coffee reminds me of cold mornings when I slid in beside the woodstove in the kitchen and sat on the stovewood to get warm. Old English Lavender™ makes me think of the soap in Dad's shaving mug. Windsong™ perfume was what Wilma Crawford always wore. Old Spice™ makes me think of Van.

When I smell Chanel # 5™ I'm reminded of a woman dying with cancer on the third floor of Memorial Mission Hospital.

Students used the side door entrance down on first floor, opening into the stairwell. When I walked inside the stairwell I could faintly smell the terrible odor of decaying human flesh coming from the end room on the third floor. Nothing they tried could completely mask the odor.

She was one of my assigned patients—her name long ago forgotten, but I will never forget the beautiful, meticulously groomed lady in her thirties. She had Ca (cancer) of the lower colon and the surgeon had done a colostomy, removing everything inside the rectal and vaginal area. It was left open (?) to heal. After I gave her a bed bath, she always had me powder her with Chanel # 5™ bath powder. Then she'd dab the perfume on her wrists and behind her ears. She loved her pretty, lacy satin nightgowns, and I always put them on her, although a hospital gown would have been easier and more sensible.

At first, I loved the scent of her perfume and bath powder. Then, as she lay there day after day, the cancer kept eating away, and the odor became stronger. I knew she had no way to escape the odor of her own decaying body. Each morning, I had to irrigate and cleanse the area of raw unhealed flesh, then put fresh gauze packing in before I gave her a bath. As I watched her grow weaker day by day, I still used the bath powder and perfume on her, and tried to make her feel fresh and clean despite the odor.

She was a sweet, uncomplaining person, and although I tried to be extra gentle, I could tell she had terrible pain with each movement she made. Her husband visited often, and it was obvious that they deeply loved each other.

I think it was about three months before she finally died. Maybe it was my imagination, but long after she was gone, each time I opened that door to the stairwell, I seemed to catch a scent of Chanel # 5 mingled with Ca.

And sometimes, when in a crowd, I smell Chanel # 5 and think of her.

It's so tragic to think that with today's modern treatments and early detection methods, she might have lived a normal life and helped her husband raise their children, or even have lived to play with her grandchildren. Even if the Ca can't be cured, modern pain medications can control the pain so much better.

◆   ◆   ◆

When I was in school, Memorial Mission was considered the most up-to-date and well-equipped hospital in Western North Carolina. As I learned about medicine and surgery, I thought about people I'd known as I grew up, and how their lives would have been changed drastically, or even saved, if they'd had access to the medical and surgical treatment available here. I especially thought of many people, some now old or dead, who had birth defects that were never corrected, and the untold heartaches that would never have been suffered if they'd had some simple corrective surgery.

When I graduated, I remember the confident feeling I had that I knew all the latest, most up-to-date things in Medicine and Surgery. It was true then, but when compared to today's knowledge, "I hadn't seen nuthin'."

At that time, a case of polio still cropped up now and then. I learned how to operate an iron lung and care for the patient. There's probably medical professionals nowadays that don't even know what one is. Thank God!

I remember taking care of post-op cataract patients. As they came back to their room after a long tedious operation, great care was taken in transporting and transferring them. Their bed was kept in a rolled-up position with sandbags on each side of their head. They weren't even allowed to turn their head to either side. We had to feed them, put them on the bedpan, and treat them as total invalids for several days. Even after they were allowed up, they weren't allowed to bend over for about two more weeks.

Eye surgery was performed by the ophthalmologist, Dr. Weisenblatt. She was a tiny little German lady, and was considered the best. I remember a treatment she gave to help avoid infection and speed healing by causing a Protein reaction. It was milk injections. Yes! Plain old cow's milk! She was very specific in her instructions about how to prepare it. Using low heat, a small saucepan, and a thermometer, I had to slowly heat the milk to a certain degrees F. for a certain number of minutes and let it cool. Then I took it to the patient's bedside where the doctor drew up a certain number of cc's into a syringe and gave it deep into a big muscle.

The last time I worked in OR was in 1992. Cataract patients came into the unit that morning on an outpatient basis. They put on a patient gown, were put to bed, vital signs taken, and eyedrops and medication were started in the admitting ward. As soon as the few minutes' time was up for the drops to dilate the pupils, they were moved over to a preparation area next to the OR, where I started an IV, put a monitor on them, and assisted the anesthetist with a local anesthesia block. Once the surgeon began, it kept the whole staff working to have another patient ready by the time he finished with one after another, after another—all day.

They were taken directly back to the admitting ward from OR, given breakfast or lunch, got dressed and went home. They went to the doctor's office the next morning for a brief exam to see if everything was O.K. Some patiens no longer required glasses.

What a difference forty years can make!

Surgical procedures, instruments and equipment are light years away from what they were as recently as twenty years ago. I was shown through an operating room about ten years ago and was amazed at the things they were using. I'm sure a lot of those are obsolete by now.

My tour guide/friend laughed when I said I'd have to have a whole lot of book learnin' to operate all this newfangled computerized machinery. I was used to "ON" and "OFF"—or toggle switches.

◆   ◆   ◆

In about 1966 at the new hospital in Andrews, I became the OR supervisor at the urging of Dr. Van Gorder, and simply because there was no one else trained for the job. I had forgotten a lot, and he was patient as he instructed me how to prepare and assist him in operations. Before we began any procedure, he explained in detail, and even drew diagrams of the procedure, the sequence, what instruments and suture he needed, and what I needed to do to help him. He explained and taught me as we went along. I loved working with him. He treated me more as a colleague than an OR nurse.

Dr. Rodda wasn't doing surgery any more at that time. I scrubbed and assisted him on only one operation, and he was absolutely textbook perfect. Dr. Van Gorder gave spinal anesthesia for most of his operations to free up a doctor, but Dr. Rodda gave anesthesia a few times before he stopped working in the OR altogether. I was still nervous around him, but surprised at how helpful he was in teaching me things I needed to know. Then Dr. Blalock gave anesthesia whenever he was needed, and did emergency surgery when he was on call. He didn't do extensive major surgery, but could expertly do an appendectomy and take care of fractures and trauma patients. Occasionally, he did breast biopsies and other operations.

I considered working with those doctors an honor and a privilege. I loved it. They were kind to me, and took time to answer any question I had. I learned that I need not hesitate to discuss any problem I might have. I knew their primary concern, like mine, was for the patient's welfare. I tried not to call unless it was necessary, but I always knew that if I became worried about a patient, all I had to do was call either of them—day or night.

I found the relaxed atmosphere entirely different from when I was in training. Dr. Van was always laughing, and pulled jokes on me and everyone else. Dr. Blalock was quiet and easy-going. Dr. James Stephens, a M.D. from Robbinsville, did minor surgery from time to time. He came by just about every day to stand in the door and chat awhile with Dr. Van while he was doing surgery. He always left us laughing. He is a wonderful doctor as well as a man of integrity, and for many years, filled the great need for a doctor for the people in Graham County.

When the hospital opened, and for many years after, there were very few RN's in the area. I was on call for thirteen years straight, not only for surgery, but also for difficult deliveries, auto accidents or other emergencies. I stayed at the hospital many nights to comply with the legalities of the hospital always having a RN in the house. I slept on a cot, and they woke me if they needed me. I wasn't paid for being on call, and didn't get paid any overtime for several years. My salary was much less than it would be in a larger hospital, but I had the deep satisfaction of being where I was needed, and making a difference for good in many people's lives.

We trained Polly Pack and Wilma Reece, two nurses' aides, to work in the OR, then Bertie White, who had worked there before, came back. We had a great team. They took turns being on call, and were competent, caring and dependable. We had a lot of fun working together through the years, and I loved them as if they were my sisters.

I consider Dr. Van Gorder and his family among my dearest friends. Although I repaid the loan, I hope I somehow returned some interest on his investment in my education.

◆　　　◆　　　◆

While writing about the years I worked in Andrews hospital, and thinking about "Gratitude For Shoes," another memory came to mind.

Around 1969, a new two story addition with new offices, kitchen, dining room, CSR, x-ray and lab, Labor, Delivery and Nursery was built onto the hospital, making a total of sixty patient beds,

At that time, I was Director Of Nurses, still on call around the clock, OR Supervisor and surgical assistant to Dr. Van Gorder, and was in charge of the Housekeeping department. I had to make out all the work schedules for all those employees. We used time cards, and each pay period, I had to use a pencil and a calculator to figure up each person's time, and fill out their time sheet to turn in to the office for payroll.

I was essentially doing at least four jobs, plus being on call. We had only four RN's besides myself, and two of them were part-time. The LPN's were lifesavers, doing the work of RN's, and the aides went far above and beyond the call of duty. We all pulled together, helped each other, and took excellent care of the patients.

At home, I had a partially disabled husband, a twelve year old son, and an eleven year old daughter. I felt guilty because I couldn't spend as much time with them as I'd have liked. When I came home, I was dead tired, and still had to cook, clean and do housework. But Van was wonderful with the children. I knew they were with him or his family, so they were being loved and cared for. He never complained about my job having so much priority. But I was their mother, and wanted to be there, too.

Needless to say, I was stretched pretty thin, and beginning to feel the effects of all the stress. Still, I didn't think I could just walk away, with the need for nurses so great and sick people needing to be cared for.

Even with the low wages in this area, the working people had made a commitment and had money deducted from their paychecks to help build the desperately needed hospital. These people were family, friends and neighbors. When a car or ambulance pulled up in the Emergency entrance, I never knew who would be in it, needing medical care. Our three doctors were devoting much of their lives to keep the hospital running. I was only a nurse, but I could make their jobs easier.

I became so fatigued, and wanted so much to be with my family more. Also the salary was so much less than I'd be paid almost anywhere else. I found myself thinking more and more, that I would like to find a job with less demands and more money. When I discovered that an untrained maintenance man was making more money that I was, I was crushed, incredulous, then angry.

A RN friend had gone into Public Health and I was astounded when I learned her salary, plus vacation time, retirement and other benefits. She worked five days a week (never overtime), had all holidays and week-ends off—and was never on call!

A few days later, I saw an ad for a Public Health nurse in the area. I asked about the requirements and found that I was qualified. I became so excited, just thinking about it, but was torn between a new well-paying job and leaving the hospital. I began asking God to help me make the right choice.

I had an appointment for an interview and written exam at Western Carolina University at Cullowhee at eight o'clock on a Saturday morning in one of the campus buildings. My friend said there was nothing to it—I'd do fine. I bought a new outfit and some nice new shoes, so I'd look my best.

It was cold that morning when I got up early and left for the long drive. I turned the car heater up on high, and the hot air felt good on my feet. Still plagued with uncertainty, as I drove along, I renewed my prayers, asking God to help me make a good impression and pass the exam—IF it was what He wanted me to do. That was still my #1 priority. But, I reasoned, why can't I have things a little easier and make more money at the same time? And I wasn't getting any younger. I thought of some of the nice things we could afford, places we could take the children to and couldn't imagine how it would feel to be free (not on call) when I wasn't working. But I couldn't quite squelch the guilty feeling that maybe I was being a little materialistic.

As I got near the campus, I became aware that my right foot seemed a little loose in my shoe, and wiggled my toes around. What in the world? When I parked in front of the building, I had a closer look. Sure enough, the sole on my new shoe had apparently been glued on, and the heat had melted the glue! There was definitely about an inch gap there. I thought, well, maybe nobody'd notice, and I'd go on in.

When I set my feet out onto the cold pavement and stood up, the whole side of the shoe opened up, and half of my foot just scooted sideways out on the pavement. There was no way I could walk and keep my foot inside my shoe.

I got back in the car, shut the door, put my head down on the steering wheel, and began to cry. Then, I thought about the times when as a child, my well-worn shoes would come apart like that. And I remembered how God had brought me from hopelessness and nothing to getting a good education. And my reason for going into nursing was a desire to serve others, not for monetary gain.

Wasn't that exactly what I was doing?

In addition, I was married to the most wonderful person I ever met, had two healthy, happy children, and they were surrounded by loving grandparents, aunts, uncles and cousins. Our needs were supplied—we had a nice home down by by the waterfall, with a whole valley where all the children in the family could safely run and play. And all around, the beautiful safe haven of the surrounding mountains. How blessed I was!

Then I laughed out loud at God's sense of humor. I'd asked for unmistakeable evidence of His guidance. What more fitting, personal evidence could I have than my big foot a-stickin' out the side of a brand new shoe? Again, I thanked God for my shoes—all of them. Even the ones with the flappin' soles.

I had that same feeling I'd had all those years ago when I'd left Andrews alone on a bus for Asheville. I knew I was exactly where I was supposed to be, and doing what I was supposed to be doing. I'd simply forgotten where my real treasure is.

I tossed the shoe over on the floor of the passenger side, laughed again, and turned the ignition key. I could hardly wait to get home and tell Van of my experience. I could just hear his booming laugh. Van...still my husband, my best friend, and the longer we were together, the more I loved him. He'd understand, as always.

Besides—my reward is yet to come. One of these days, I'll wear the ultimate in brand-name shoes—a pair of "golden slippers," so they say. And I betchey they won't never come unglued......or need no half-solin'.

Wonder if they'll let me play "Wildwood Flare" on one a them harps?

◆   ◆   ◆

When I walk through the familiar halls of the hospital now, I have a vague sense of unreality when I see all the strange faces. Very few people recognize me. If I start to feel a little nostalgic, thinking of my old friends and co-workers no longer there, the feeling is quickly replaced by a feeling of gratitude that there are fresh young hands and minds to replace our old tired, worn ones. We gave them a good foundation to build on.

I'm always amazed at the state-of-the-art equipment and the well-trained personnel who use it. It's good to see all the modern equipment they can use to save more lives and help more people recover faster than we ever dreamed possible. One example is the fully equipped modern ER, ICU and CCU.

I was there even before they had monitors—when the only cardiac equipment nurses had was a stethoscope, an attentive ear, and observant eyes.

And I'm not THAT old!

LABOR AND DELIVERY

I enjoyed Labor and Delivery. At school, they basically used the same drugs and anesthesia as at Andrews, but the facilities were much larger and completely up-to-date. The concept of "natural childbirth" was becoming popular, and classes were held to teach that method. Breast feeding was declining, as more women worked.

After I studied Obstetrics and learned about complications that were possible with both mother and baby, I realized that the OB's in Andrews had been getting the best of prenatal care from the doctors, so that possible complications were found before they were ready to deliver.

Good prenatal care was crucial then as now, but we had no fetal monitors or modern methods for early detection of problems, such as we have now.

Back then, the only methods of contraception were condoms, diaphragms and spermicidal foam, and many unwanted pregnancies occurred. Abortion was illegal. There were a few doctors who had the whispered reputation of performing abortions. Doctors who performed a few too many D & C's were scrutinized. "D" is for dilating the cervix and "C" for curettage—scraping the lining of, or emptying the uterus. Occasionally, there was suspicion when the reason charted for doing a D & C was to clean up after a "spontaneous" abortion. I sometimes saw the dangerous consequences of attempted abortions by non-medical persons—everything from their using coat-hangers to drinking different concoctions to get rid of the pregnancy.

Back then, the most disgraceful thing a girl could do was be unwed and pregnant. No "decent" person would have anything to do with her. It was still common practice for parents to conceal the pregnancy and force a girl to give the baby up for adoption.

One evening, we got in a young unmarried woman in labor. I still admire the compassion her doctor showed. He came in, grouped the supervisor and other personnel together, and said firmly but kindly, "I don't want to hear of anyone making any untoward remarks to this patient, or being unkind to her in any way. She's a good girl from a good family. We need to realize and accept that the sex

445

urge is a biological fact, and is stronger even, than hunger. Who are we to judge her?"

That was an unheard-of philosophy in those days.

I've weighed the pro's and con's of abortion many times and still have mixed emotions. I never approved of abortion as a means of birth control. Even when a D & C was classified as necessary, it was sickening to me to see tiny little hands, feet, arms and legs, and maybe even little entrails dangling as they emerged after being torn from the tiny body.

On the other hand, I assisted with a delivery once that left me sickened and angry. A young mentally retarded girl, maybe fourteen, came in for delivery at term. She had no idea what was going on, and screamed and cried for her Mommy. She was terrified, being tied down on a table in a room full of strangers with masks on their faces, doing things that hurt her. Can you imagine her terror?

Should she have had an abortion before it got to this stage?

I wonder what happened to the baby.

I'm glad God didn't leave the judgin' up to me. If He had, angry as I was, I'm afraid the father of that baby would've been publicly, roughly and permanently relieved of his source of testosterone by an executioner with an old dull, rusty pocket knife.

◆   ◆   ◆

Today, they're called African-Americans. I know they've been called a lot of other names, but generally, when I was growing up, they were called "colored people." Without any intentional disrespect, I am writing about them using the terminology which was in use in 1955.

I think there were only two colored doctors and one colored dentist on the hospital staff. Occasionally, a colored nurse's aide worked the night shift, but usually there were no colored nurses working on the white patient floors. They worked in the colored section of the building. There were no colored girls in nurse's training. Colored people at the hospital worked as maids in housekeeping, helpers in the kitchen, laundry, and sewing room, or as orderlies.

When I trained in Public Health, their prenatal check-ups and Well Baby Clinics were held separately from the white clinics.

The "colored" Delivery Room was on one side of the new Labor and Delivery department. It was smaller, and although nice, it didn't have as much equipment and lighting as the "white" ones on the other side of a wide hallway/scrub area.

One evening on 3-11, we'd been so busy we hadn't had time to even slow down to eat, when two nurses from Second South came hurriedly pushing a colored OB on a stretcher through the double doors. She was crying out in pain. I'd already had experience in Labor and Delivery, and knew to get her on a delivery table so she could be checked. Fast!

The Supervisor had left the area for a few minutes, maybe gone to check someone out on the floor. We still hadn't cleaned the colored delivery room, and the only available clean room was on the white side. I told the nurses to "bring her in here." They helped me get her on the delivery table and left.

Just as I got her positioned and the safety strap in place, the supervisor came through the door, and I could tell by the look on her face that she was furious with me. She said, angrily, "You're in big trouble, young lady. You know better than to bring "her" in here." Her tirade was interrupted as the patient screamed out again, and her abdomen tightened in a hard, long contraction. I automatically reached out and placed my hand on her belly to time it.

It was lasting a long time, I thought. Suddenly, her whole body went limp. She wasn't breathing! The supervisor grabbed a stethoscope and heard no heartbeat. She yelled at me to page a Code Blue in Labor and Delivery.

While I was doing that, she put the resuscitator on the patient, then almost immediately we had people coming through the doors. One was a chest surgeon and one was an obstetrician. I opened the delivery and cardiac arrest trays and just stood back out of the way. I knew I was in way over my head. In seconds, the chest surgeon had the chest open and started massaging the patient's heart.

An anesthetist was there by then, to intubate the patient and get her oxygenated. The Obstetrician was trying to get forceps around the baby's head to deliver it. Fortunately, it was down and in proper position, ready to deliver. Soon, the patient's heart was beating on its own, and she was trying to breathe. The Obstetrician delivered a big ol' kickin', squallin' baby. The anesthetist gave the patient enough anesthesia to keep her under while her chest was being closed and the obstetrician finished up.

After it was all under control and the doctors were finishing, I found myself feeling weak with relief, and so thankful that things had ended so well. "Thank You, God!"

I thought about all the "what if's" related to this patient. What if the nurses had got her there just three minutes later? What if I'd been too afraid to value the woman's health over fear of any punishment I might get for putting her in the white delivery room? What if the supervisor had been there? What if if she had been put in the colored delivery room where there was no resuscitator and other needed equipment? What if there had been no doctor immediately available? A variation of less than three minutes time in any of these "what if" situation would have resulted in an entirely different ending.

Not only was there a doctor, but a chest surgeon and an obstetrician, an anesthesiologist and other trained personnel—exactly what was needed! And the right equipment, instruments and lighting that were needed. There was no way I could have moved all that equipment across the wide hall and into the room without making several trips. By then, it would have been too late.

I heard the chest surgeon say he had his hand on the outside door knob ready to leave when he heard the page. It seemed more than coincidence that everything had happened the way it did. I felt that God had placed them, as well as me, in the right place at the right time. Was there a reason?

As far as I was concerned, this was a miracle, and I was grateful to have been a small part of it. I didn't care if they did send me home. Deep down in my heart, I knew I had done the right thing—there was a living, breathing young mother with a healthy baby to prove it. It was reward enough for me when I visited the mother a few days later, and saw the loving look on her face as she was feeding her baby, although she didn't know who I was, or the part I'd played in her delivery.

She recovered and went home in a week. No one ever mentioned the incident. I was neither commended nor reprimanded.

But maybe, just maybe, this event had been instrumental in getting a few people to realize how wrong it is to have different standards of care, and place a greater value on one human life over another.

Or would they continue to risk or lose a patient's life for want of a few pieces of equipment from right across the hall? Just because of the color of their skin.........

◆   ◆   ◆

I liked Pediatrics, but somehow it was harder for me to accept illness in a child than in adults. It was especially hard for me to see birth defects and children who were disabled or disfigured from trauma of some kind. I became especially attached to an eight year old burn patient named Juanita. She was a little colored girl with pigtails, who had a smile that melted my heart. She'd been burned from her neck down, and had one operation after another for contractures and skin grafts. She seldom had a visitor. I think her mother had to work long hours and had several other kids to care for. I went back to see her and spend time with her until I left training. I got her up, held her on my lap in a rocking chair and read stories to her. She stayed there for months and months.

It was fairly common to see a very sick, even an obstructed child with worms. Early one morning as I started into a Pediatric ward, the six foot-three male "probie" almost collided with me—running out past me with one hand held high and danging something from a finger and thumb, a stricken look on his face. He took off down the hall, repeatedly yelling out the supervisor's name and adding, "Lord, God, A'mighty!" each time.

As I went in, I noticed that the steam radiator was hissing, and the windows were fogged over from the cold outside. A little two to three year old girl in a crib bed next to a window was standing up, holding onto the side rails of the bed, and crying. I started toward her, intending to pick her up and hold her, but as I got closer, I noticed several streaks on the window. At first I thought they were drops of water forming and running down. Then I could see that they were long white looking streaks—and one of them fell off!

No wonder that poor baby wanted out of there! It was worms she'd passed in her diaper. They'd crawled all over her bed, up the window, many had fallen, and the window sill was almost covered. I looked down, and I bet there was thirty or more on the floor around her bed. Let's don't even talk about the odor.

◆　　　◆　　　◆

When I worked in Premature Nursery, a baby under three pounds wasn't expected to survive, but some did. They were kept til they weighed five pounds. I fell in love with a little red-headed "preemie" from Bryson City. He weighed a little over two pounds, but he was hanging in there and beginning to grow and gain weight. Already, I could see evidence of his personality.

Of course, I said prayers for each of them but there was just something special about this little'un. After I left the Nursery to go to another department, when I had to go to another part of the hospital on an errand, I "re-routed" and went by the nursery to look in through the window to see how he was doing. I could see that tiny patch of coppery hair and know he was still hanging in there. I watched him gain and grow, and was so thankful when he was discharged in excellent condition. I told Van all about him, and said I hoped some day we'd have a little red-headed boy.

We did. When we took him home at seven days old, David Van weighed three pounds, seven ounces. He was born two months prematurely, and Asheville had the nearest premature nursery. Since I had so recently worked in Premature

Nursery, the doctors felt he would have as much chance to survive at home under our care as he would if we took him there.

To make a long story short, he's now a *strappin'*, healthy six foot three—but still our precious "little red-headed boy." I'd described both our children in detail before we were even married. I hadn't asked for them to be premature, but the most important thing remains—we got to keep them.

Van always had something humorous to say. When our beautiful, blonde-haired "Daddy's Little Girl" was born, he remarked, "I swear, Honey—sometimes I think God just sits up there, waitin' for you to send in an order."

Well, of course I don't send him orders, but He sure does take requests.

If Van hadn't been the wonderful, caring person he was, I couldn't have managed to give David the care he needed. For several weeks, we had to feed him every hour. I was recovering from the surgery, and was still weak. Van worked all day, then took turns with me feeding the baby at night. He changed his diaper or whatever was needed at the time. I've never seen a man any more proud of his son. His face practically glowed when he held him. Ruth and Ronnie came and stayed with me during the day til I got back on my feet.

In my Dad's generation, a woman took care of the baby. A man would have been embarrassed and ridiculed if someone had seen him changing a diaper. He'd have been called "henpecked." That feeling had changed little when our children were babies, but Van said it was his baby, too—why should he not share the responsibilities? He didn't care who saw him.

Today, I can't believe I'm the same person who went into the Premature Nursery, put down a feeding tube slick as a whistle, and fed them, easy as 1-2-3. I relieved the night R. N. two nights a week for three of my last six months in training, and wasn't at all uncomfortable doing it—just careful. Then raised our own two preemies.

These days, I'm scared to death of a newborn. I'm so afraid they'll get choked. I don't even want a mother to hand me a bottle to give to a fifteen pound baby. I love to hold them, but if they need to be fed, I just hand 'em right back and say, "You do it." Time sure has changed this old girl.

It's amazing how God gives us the strength and courage we need, when we need it.

◆   ◆   ◆

In April, 1955, Van finished X-ray and lab school. I was so proud of him. He went to work for a Dr. Williams in Forest City, and liked the doctor, his co-workers, and his work. He was the kind of out-going person who does so well in a job dealing with the public.

He bought a 1953 Chevrolet, and came up to Asheville on the week-ends I was off. By then, I was working different shifts, and was on duty except for one week-end a month. On Saturday morning, if I wasn't on 7—3, he drove up to Asheville, stayed a couple of hours, or maybe we went somewhere for lunch. Then he drove on to Marble to spend the night with his family—another two and a half to three hour drive. He came back by to see me awhile on Sunday afternoon. I missed him, just knowing he was gone from Asheville.

On the weekends I was off, he picked me up and we came home together. He took me to Sweetie's or up on the creek, and went on to Marble. We loved those week-ends, because we had more time together. Sometimes, I visited with his family a little while. In December,1954, Grover and Edith had a little girl, and they named her Cathy. She was spoiled by the whole family, and Van's parents loved being called "Pappaw and Mammaw."

If I stayed at Sweetie's, I always went by to see my friends at the hospital. When I walked down the street, somebody usually hollered at me, and I'd stop to talk a few minutes. One time, somebody hollered at me, and Dugan Shields came hurrying down the street toward me. We shook hands, and he told me he was so proud of me. Then he took three rumpled one dollar bills out of his pocket and insisted that I take them—he wanted to help me, and apologized that he didn't have more. He said he'd be praying for me.

I was very close to tears. I realized that like him, there were a lot of these old mountain people who wished me well. And I'd seen how hard he had to work to get what little money he had—snakin' cordwood down off the mountain. Sometimes when I got depressed, I thought about those people at home, rooting for my side, and it helped tremendously. And that three dollars was a lot of help to me then. I'd been *broke as a convict*.

That's how I made it through school—a dollar here, a dollar there, and the occasional five dollars a shift I earned from sitting with a patient. Every time I got broke, or close to it, and needed money, something came up.

Van and I enjoyed having the car, and he encouraged me to learn to drive. He just turned it over to me and let me drive. A few times, we went out to Canton, in Haywood County, to visit with his cousin Vaughn, and his wife Agnes. They lived in a renovated old log house, and had it wired and plumbed and fixed it up nicely.

Van had talked about them ever since I first met him, and I felt as if I already knew them when I met them. Van felt as if Vaughn were another one of his brothers. They were close in age, were together a lot as children, had both been in the Army, and had a close bond.

I immediately loved Agnes. She was the sister of Edith, Grover's wife. Agnes was one of these bubbly, talkative, friendly people who loved everybody, and always had something good to say about them. *Her heart was big as a punkin'.* She was also a good listener. I was completely at ease with her, and we giggled like two school girls. I felt as if I'd gained two good friends in my future in-laws.

They always made me feel welcome and I enjoyed going to their house.

KEEPING A BIG SECRET

I finally understood why I was so afraid to love Van or anyone else. Loving some-one meant they had the power to hurt me, and I didn't want any one to have that ability. I truly did love my parents, and the way they treated me hurt so much. They'd shown me over and over that they didn't care how much they hurt me, even seemed to derive a perverse pleasure from it. How I felt didn't matter. I'd tried so hard not to let their way of thinking become my way of thinking, and had endured their abuse with the hope of one day being free.

Now that I was free, I realized that they were still controlling me and depriv-ing me of happiness because of the fear that others would hurt me as they had. And I was allowing it. Once I realized that, I had to decide if I was going to spend the rest of my life holding other people at a safe distance and never really know-ing true friendship or love, or risk being vulnerable by allowing myself to care without setting limits.

I realized that I was making others pay for things they didn't do, by withhold-ing genuine friendship and affection. In the process, I was also making myself pay, by building a wall around me, making myself a prisoner.

I was holding the key to my own prison in my own hand, and that key was love. And only I could use it. But from understanding something, and putting it behind you takes time. I'd already learned to love and trust Sweetie and Ruth, and other people I'd met and become friends with on my own, to a certain extent. I treasured their friendship, and could see that I needed them. They'd helped me feel that I did matter.

I learned to love and trust Van more each time I saw him. He never again even hinted that I quit school, and had shown beyond a doubt that he really loved me, and wanted me to be happy. He'd been waiting over two years, willing to take whatever time I had to be with him—and never complained.

We seemed to have mental telepathy. When I walked into a crowded room, I could spot him instantly; the instant I looked at him, he looked straight at me as if I'd touched him. When he looked at me, I could see the change of expression on his face, and the absolute devotion in his eyes. And through the years, it never changed, even for a second.

At times now, I was the one who reached and got his hand. When I did, the look on his face was pure joy. It was getting harder and harder to see him leave. That empty feeling I had when I wasn't with him was getting bigger and bigger. When he was ready to leave, many times I felt like just getting in the car, going with him, and chucking the whole thing. But I knew I couldn't do that.

After all this time thinking things through about his health, I decided that the sensible thing to do was finish training, then I could take care of both of us if he became totally disabled. I knew it might be hard, on down the road, but not marrying him was out of the question. The next time his mother mentioned his health, I told her that it didn't matter to me—I'd rather have two weeks with Van than a long lifetime with anyone else. I'd treasure each day we had for as long as God let me keep him. She never mentioned it again.

We planned on getting married around the first of April—after getting permission from the Director of Nursing, of course—following all the rules. That would leave about six months til I graduated.

Around Christmas time in 1955, I learned that I had to go to Torrance, Pennsylvania for three months of Psychiatric training. I had to leave about the middle of February, though, and that blew our plans out the window. The thought of not seeing each other for three months, and being that far away was just about more than either of us could bear. We decided to get married the next week-end, and keep it a secret. At least we'd have more time together before I left.

Psychiatry was the last requirement in training, and if we could just make it through that, it wouldn't be long til graduation. We started making plans.

Another rule was that when a student went on a week-end pass, we had to state where we were going. It had to be with someone on a previously approved list, such as family, or must have written permission from our parents to go to a specific place on a specific date. Then that person had to mail a letter within a week, stating we'd been there on that date.

How much more innocent could it be than to say I was going to spend a week-end with my brother Bud, and his wife, Mae?

He lived at Union Mills at the time, and I wrote him a letter telling him of my plans. He wrote back that he would cover for me, just let him know the dates and when to write. I knew he'd never tell. I was afraid if Dad found out, he'd be so mad that he'd tell on me, and I'd be sent home.

◆   ◆   ◆

January 27, 1956 was the longest day of my life. I was working 7—3, and was so nervous that I couldn't do anything right. I dropped a bedpan (full of *slop*) flat on its bottom and that stuff just shot straight up out of it, splattering me from my bib down, and went all over the floor. I never did that before or since. After cleaning up the mess, I had to go to my room, clean my shoes, shower, dress, and go back to finish my shift. Van was getting off early to pick me up at 3:30.

We already had our marriage license, and he'd made all the arrangements. When he had told the staff at the doctor's office what we were going to do, they insisted that they be part of it, and planned the wedding. The nurse and receptionist attended the Presbyterian Church at Forest City, and arrangements were made with their minister to be married at their church. We were thrilled to death. Neither of us had wanted a "Justice Of The Peace" wedding, but hadn't seen any other way.

Van went to a clothing store and was measured for a suit. They called his measurements to the tailor so the alterations would be finished in time. But there was a glitch in that plan. Van was so broad through his shoulders, and slim around his waist and hips that they didn't believe the measurements. With the delay, his suit hadn't come, so the clothing store owner loaned him one for the ceremony. The jacket was one size and the pants were another, but they fit fairly well. As for me, I didn't care if he wore blue jeans and a tee shirt. We'd been waiting too long to postpone things for lack of a suit.

Van had given me the money to buy my clothes, and told me to get whatever I wanted and not worry about how much it cost. I took Humphrey with me, went to Bon Marche' and bought a nice suit and blouse. It was tailored to perfection and was the most expensive thing I'd ever owned. It was around ninety dollars. (Incidentally, our daughter, Donna, wore that suit as she left on her honeymoon in 1978. It was right in style, and fit her perfectly.) I borrowed a pair of medium high heels from Emma Jean Elliott, to have the "borrowed" part of my clothes. Of course, she didn't know where I was going to wear them.

When I got off, I hurried to my room and changed clothes. I'd already packed my things. Humphrey knew where I was going, but I knew she wouldn't tell. She was excited and happy for me. When I got back downstairs, Van was waiting out front in the car. He *lit up like a Christmas tree* when he saw me, and got out to put my bag in the car. We felt like two kids keeping a secret from the grown-ups, and were the two happiest people on earth.

The wedding was beautiful and perfect. They'd placed fresh flowers around the altar in the church, and the minister performed a beautiful candlelight ceremony. The office nurse and receptionist signed the marriage certificate as witnesses.

As we had no family there, it was a very small reception, but the table, flowers, cake and refreshments were lovely. They even made pictures for us. Van's friends seemed to like him a lot, and were very friendly to me. I was touched by their thoughtfulness and effort to make our wedding special.

I looked forward to becoming friends with them after I got out of school and came here to live.

When the reception was over, we had to go by the boarding house to let Van take off the borrowed suit, so it could be returned later. I waited in the car while he went in to change. When he came hurrying out, he had on a bright red corduroy shirt and jeans, and looked more like my Van. He was so handsome, and my heart fairly burst with joy when he opened the car door and said, "Hello, Wife," and I realized he was my husband. No one ever loved any one more than I loved him—my best friend, and now my husband. My everything. And now when he told me he loved me—I believed him. He'd shown in so many ways that I was the most precious thing in his life.

Now I'm really going to be classed as out of step with modern times. Young people today think they can't wait. They rush into marriage with the thought that if it doesn't work out, they'll just get a divorce and move on. Or will live together first, and see how it goes. Many go from one sexual partner to the other with very little or no commitment. Too late, they find that this lifestyle only brings heartache and leaves emotional scars. When the bills start coming in, or an unwanted child gets in their way and they've discovered that life is not all romance, the relationship dissolves.

By the time Van and I got married, we knew each other so well that we not only loved each other, but were best friends. Forever. We waited until we were both sure of what we wanted, and the time was right. It wasn't easy—we were normal in every respect. But each of us put the other's welfare first. That's real love. And it lasts a lifetime. Through leaky houses and rusty old cars and sick children and dirty diapers and sickness and medical bills and anything else life can throw at you, we only grew closer. Now I know that even after death, I still feel that love.

We discussed many times how strange it was, that when we were having things the hardest, that was when we were the closest. Of course! Each of us was giving the other strength and trying to protect each other.

Our wedding day was the happiest day of my life. We drove to nearby Chimney Rock and spent our wedding night, then went home to his family in Marble the next day. Everybody was waiting, and had to hug and kiss and *carry on* awhile to welcome the new daughter-in-law. I knew I was the luckiest girl in the entire universe to be married to Van.

I didn't have to be back til eleven on Sunday night. That time when he left, we knew that from then on, whenever he came back, I could go with him and stay with him until he had to leave. That was good enough for now.

Bud wrote the promised letter, saying he'd really enjoyed my visit. And we looked forward to "visiting him" again.

Nothing like a brother to *stick with ye, like Karo with surp!!!*

◆   ◆   ◆

The plane left Asheville airport for Wheeling, West Virginia. There we changed to a larger plane to fly on into Pittsburgh. I knew the three months would be slow in passing, but was excited, as this was my first time to fly. I thoroughly enjoyed it, and wasn't afraid at all.

A bus met us at the airport, and as we rode, I could see the dirty black smoke billowing out of smokestacks around Pittsburgh. It was a long bus ride that gradually took us out through beautiful farmland and mountains. I began to wonder where in the world we were going to end up, when we passed a small sign that told the name of the town. It was just a wide place in the road, no bigger than Marble.

About three miles further, we saw several large two and three-story brick buildings built closely together, like a compound. We pulled up and stopped at strong-looking locked metal gates with an eight foot high chain-link fence on each side enclosing the buildings and many acres of grounds. The gates were opened and we went through. They were locked behind us. We were at a State Hospital.

It's a good thing that this was my last subject to study, or I'd have been out thumbin' a ride to North Carolina before the end of the first week. I found out immediately that I was no psychiatric nurse. The actual study of Psychiatry was extremely interesting, and I studied and read everything I could get my hands on. But in my mind, I could never separate impersonal theory from actual practice.

I hated that place and everything about it. It was out in the middle of nowhere with no place to escape. I think maybe it was the sense of confinement that I hated. The nurses' dorm was right next door to the Admissions building, and all through the long night, we could hear the muffled sounds of people at the windows, crying and screaming and trying to get out.

There was such an atmosphere of sadness and hopelessness on the wards. We were separated into small groups of two or three when we went into one of the buildings. Every door we went through was unlocked to let us through, then locked behind us. None of the students had a key. As we were escorted through one door after another, I felt that I was going deeper and deeper into a place of nameless horror, and had to fight the impulse to turn around and run to get out of there. An attendant was with us all the time, but when I looked at the blank expressionless eyes and insane faces surrounding us, it scared me to death.

And the smell! I can't describe the odor that permeated the place. In the morning, when the attendant opened the outside door to take us in, that sickening odor came right out into my face and nauseated me. It was the smell of human sweat, excrement, and some kind of cleaner that only mixed with it and made it worse.

We had to help give showers to the women. We'd have a dozen at a time to take off their shapeless cotton dresses with no buttons, then escort them single file down the corridor to the showers. We lined them up in front of the row of shower heads before the water was turned on. The shower heads were high enough to be out of reach of a patient, and the water hit them on top of their heads. An attendant controlled the water flow and temperature from a control inside a locked recessed area in the wall, over away from the showers.

There were no doors or partitions. The large stone-walled and floored room was totally bare except for the shower heads protruding from the wall. It reminded me of a dungeon in a horror film. The students and attendants spread apart, staying alert and keeping each woman in plain sight. We were cautioned that some were suicidal, others homicidal, and to never get out of sight of each other or let a patient get us alone. This was a State Hospital For The Mentally And Criminally Insane.

One woman ate everything she could get her hands on, regardless of what it was. We couldn't let her have soap, and had to watch her closely when she had a washcloth. She even got down on the floor and picked up and ate the loose hair that didn't make it through the drain—or dead flies—or whatever. They said she had "an oral fixation." Later, when we took them for a walk, she tried to pick up night crawlers off the warm sidewalk, things in the grass—or anything. She had a stack of x-rays a foot high where they'd x-rayed her for things she'd eaten.

When I read their case studies, I cried, I was so sorry for them. Some of them had endured unbelievable horrors. Some were murderers. A few talked so intelligently that I thought they must have made a mistake when they put them in here. But then I saw the other side of them a few times.

One man believed that electricity could travel through the air from wires or fixtures, affecting people, and would not walk under an electric light fixture. When he very carefully explained his theory to me, I found myself almost believing him, he made it seem so logical.

The nurses' stations were behind unbreakable glass enclosures. We were told that when a patient became "disturbed," to get in there, lock the door, and stay until we were told to come out, no matter what happened. Don't try to help—you'll only get hurt or be in the way. Everything would seem to be going well with a group of patients, then suddenly, one would literally "go crazy." Attendants appeared from nowhere and subdued the screaming, fighting patient, wrapping them in a cold wet sheet to restrain and calm them. They were given Thorazine injections to sedate and keep them calm.

When we escorted them to the dining room, they were each given a spoon (never a fork or knife) as they went in; the spoons were counted, and the count recorded. The doors were blocked and no one left till all the spoons were collected. Remember—we did not have plastic dinnerware then. One day, a woman climbed up onto the middle of the table and defecated, then started cursing and throwing it all over the other tables and patients before the attendants could reach her. Of course, some of the others reacted with anger and were trying to get to her to fight with her. I was terrified. That was literally like the old sayin'—*When the (you-know-what) hit the fan.* Fortunately no one was injured, just needed a shower and clean clothes.

Most of the patients were given tranquilizers to keep them sedated. Electric shock treatment was used a lot. Many of them cried and begged the attendants not to shock them, and tried to get away. I had to learn how to restrain a patient and hold them while this was done, and use a gauze wrapped tongue blade to keep them from biting their tongue during the convulsion that followed. How I hated that!

I tried to learn to see the patients from an objective viewpoint and with clinical detachment, but it didn't work for me. I was so sorry for them. One patient had bedsores so large and deep that the bones of her spine, hips, heels and elbows were exposed. She was so thin you could count her ribs. Her face looked like a grimacing skeleton with thin, sallow skin stretched over it. She couldn't walk, and stayed in a rigid, half-fetal position. If she were put on a flat surface on her back, she'd have rocked; she didn't straighten out or bend. She was kept nude, and placed in a one foot deep bed of cedar sawdust inside a wooden box.

One day I helped an attendant lift her into the tub, and she almost got away from us, trying to put her head under the water to drown herself. She cursed at us for pulling her head up. I was *wet as a dog.* When I closed my eyes at night, I could see her. Poor thing! I'd probably try to drown myself too, if I was like that.

I cried every day, and sometimes several times a day, while I was there. I missed Van so much, and got so homesick, and there was no place to go to get away from this nightmare. When we could, we got out and walked, or caught the bus into town, just to get away for awhile. But there was usually deep snow on the ground, and when that got down to where spots of ground could be seen, they'd run another foot or two on top of it.

Many times I sat cross-legged on my bed, shuffled cards and played Solitaire when I couldn't concentrate enough to study, trying to ignore the muffled screams from admissions. "Thank you, Wilma. Neither of us dreamed our card playing would help me so much, back when you were teaching me."

In May, on the last morning I was there, we had to go in at 7:00 and work til 9:00. Another student and I had to make forty patients' beds in a large ward before we could leave. They were low tubular metal cots, side by side in long rows. I went through them twenty beds *faster'n a whirlwind in a corn patch.* I's a-headin' fer th' hills down in good ol' North Ca'liner.

I was one more happy girl amongst a whole plane load of happy girls on that plane. A spontaneous cheering and clapping burst out of us as the plane circled Asheville airport getting ready to land.

One more week a that business, and I'd a-j'ined them patients.

I don't give up easily, but my experience with the mental hospital left me feeling so frustrated—knowing that there was nothing I could do to alleviate the anguish and suffering of those inmates. I was emotionally drained. I didn't even know how to pray for them. I had to revert to the technique I'd learned growing up. When anything is too painful to think about, and you know there's nothing you can do about it, think about something else—and let it go.

Whenever I see a Mental Health sign in a rural community, I wonder how many people realize the vast difference in the way mental patients are treated now. When I was growing up, there were no local mental health facilities to help. A person only got help when it was almost too late—only when they were sick enough to be *sent off* (committed) to a state mental institution. Then, forever after, they carried the shame of having been in the "crazy house" or "the nut house." The word, "Morganton," here in Western North Carolina, meant "the crazy house." We never heard the words, "mental health."

If people could only understand. Everyone can see that someone has a fracture by the cast on his arm. It wasn't necessarily his fault. Because a person has no visible evidence doesn't mean that their mental illness is less real—and also is not necessarily their fault. They also need a "cast," or support—so they can heal.

Modern medicines make it possible for mentally ill people to work and function normally, and nobody even knows. There are laws now to prevent people from being sent to a mental institution against their will, and a limit as to how many days they can be kept, even when the court orders them there for evaluation. There's still a minor social stigma, but nothing like it used to be.

I have such admiration and gratitude for those people who have the fortitude and skill necessary to help them.

◆   ◆   ◆

When we got back to Asheville, they let us off through the week-end. Van came and picked me up, and we had our first long week-end together at the rooming-house where he lived in Forest City. We'd made it! Four more months and I'd be finished. We were on cloud nine.

Next time I was off, we went home. We still hadn't told any of my family we were married, except for Bud and Mae. We went to visit Lewis and Sis. We hadn't been there long, and the first time I was alone with Sis, she surprised me by asking me how long we'd been married. I should have known I couldn't keep a secret from her. Sis knew me better than anybody.

I wrote a formal letter to Mrs. Parsons, the Director of Nurses, requesting permission to be married in June. Less than a week later, I got a letter with her permission, congratulations, and blessing. So—my first week-end off in June, I was officially married, as far as the school was concerned. It felt good not to have to keep it a secret any more.

I didn't enjoy my one month's stay in the OR any more this time than I did the first time. I'd never have believed that Surgery was where I would spend most of my nursing years. But working with Dr. Van Gorder was a vastly different experience from working with the surgeons in Asheville.

I spent my last three months working night duty float. This meant that I relieved a night charge nurse on her two nights off, and was responsible for a whole floor of patients that were totally new to me. By the second night, I was more familiar with the patients and more at ease. Then the next two nights, I would be in another department with more new patients. I worked in all departments, relieving the RN's. That was a tough assignment, and was a real test of whether or not I'd been trained well enough to be a competent RN.

◆   ◆   ◆

In the meantime, Dr. Williams decided to go back to school to specialize in Psychiatry, and closed his office in Forest City. Van had a good job offer and went to work as Director of Lab and X-ray at Franklin Memorial hospital in Lewisburg, about thirty miles east of Raleigh. Neither of us realized just what the position would demand of him.

Back then, in that area, we didn't have the luxury of calling the Red Cross and having the blood delivered. He had to run his own blood bank in addition to the hospital work. He kept a list of possible donors and their blood types. When a patient needed blood, he typed their blood and began trying to locate a donor to come in to give a unit. Then he had to crossmatch the donor with the patient. It was a good-sized hospital, and the area was pretty heavily populated. Hardly a week went by that someone didn't need blood, many times at night.

The lab also did EKG's. The machine had arm, leg, and chest leads that had to be run individually, taking about thirty minutes to do an EKG. The corrosive gel had to be carefully cleaned off the metal leads. The fun was just beginning—the EKG was recorded on a roll of film that had to be developed in a developing solution in the darkroom, and hung up to dry. X-rays were developed using the same procedure. This all took a lot of time, plus the added job of having to drain, clean and put fresh solution in the developer vat periodically.

The new machines recorded an EKG directly on a strip without having to develop the film, but the hospital administrator denied the request for one. Van finally got so frustrated that he parked the old machine on the top stairwell landing in front of the door, gave an orderly ten dollars to just take off through the door and slam it open, and then keep his mouth shut. Of course he was at the nurse's station on another floor when it happened. By the time that old relic hit the bottom of the steps, there were pieces of it scattered all the way to the basement. He got a new one.

Today, it only takes a jiffy to stick the self-adhering, snap-on EKG leads on a patient. At the push of a button, the machine automatically does an immediate, complete EKG, recorded on a strip that can simply be torn off and put on the patient's record. Of course, the leads and wires are disposable, and all that gook doesn't have to be cleaned off them.

We'd never heard of a cardiac monitor.

When X-rays are taken now, in seconds they are ejected, dry and ready to read. No muss, no fuss. We won't go into all the things we have now that go way beyond the simple EKG and x-rays we had then. It would fill books. We'd have thought we were reading science fiction books if we had read about the things that we have now.

Although Van had an assistant, he was still considered on call whenever he was needed. He had stipulated when he was hired, and was promised that he would have one week-end off a month. Sometimes, though, his assistant was sick, or they'd have a critical patient or pending surgery, and he couldn't just walk off and go five hundred miles away. So his one week-end off a month wasn't always possible.

When he did get to come, he got into Asheville on Saturday evening after a six to eight hour drive, and possibly having been called back during the night. There were few four-lane highways then, and it was a long drive through small towns on two-lane roads. If you got behind slow-moving traffic, you were stuck. Then he had to leave on Sunday morning to get back to Lewisburg before dark. By then, the hospital would be waiting with work to be done as soon as he got back. He didn't have to make the trip but a couple of times, though—graduation was approaching.

Finally, at long last, it was September, 1956. Our graduation ceremony was held on a Friday evening at 8 P.M. on the front lawn of the nurses' residence. Vaughn and Agnes came out from Canton. They were the only family or friends I had who attended. Van couldn't get off from work that day. On Saturday morning, I had my bags all packed and was ready when he came to get me.

We packed everything in the car and I gave one final look back at the hospital and nurses' home. I was grateful for all they'd taught me, and to God for making it possible. But I was more than ready to get in the car with Van and head for our first home together. We made a vow that from now on, nothing short of death would ever separate us again. We were the happiest two people in the world.

This was the first time I'd gone to Lewisburg, and I thought we'd never get there. After hours and hours of driving, we finally arrived. At the edge of town, Van drove into the driveway of an old two-story Colonial style house with huge pin oak trees shading the walk and front porch.

Mr. And Mrs. Sykes, the well-past-middle-aged couple who owned the house, lived downstairs and Van had rented the two room upstairs apartment for us. It was furnished, had one large room which served as living room and bedroom, with a small kitchen/dining room back under the slope of the roof. The bathroom was in the hall just outside our door. They occasionally rented a room to an overnight guest, and we would have to share the bathroom. We didn't mind. To us, it was wonderful just knowing that neither of us would have to leave the other, other than going to work.

I planned on getting a job, but Franklin Memorial where Van worked—like most other places, had a policy of not hiring both husband and wife—however, I could do private duty. We decided that would be better, anyway, and I could work just when I wanted to. I needed a break. We could live on Van's salary.

We got out and rode around after work, so I could see what kind of country this was. It was *flat as a flitter* as far as I could see. The town and the people were typically Southern, and spoke with a more distinct Southern accent than people in Andrews. They were nice, friendly folks, and the most civic-minded people I ever saw.

But I felt plumb naked without the mountains. I kept scanning the horizon and just couldn't believe there was no mountain to be seen anywhere. The lazy little stream they called a river was the color of uncreamed coffee, and ran so slowly that you couldn't see it move. It was warm as dishwater. Van took me fishing one day, and I thought I got my hook caught on a small stick of wood or some trash. When I lifted my line up out of the water, it was a fish Van called a chain pickerel, about eight inches long. It just hung there—*limber as a dishrag*. I thought something was wrong with it, but Van said no, that's the way they are.

Compared to wading out and catching a trout on a dry fly in the swift clear water at home, I couldn't believe this. Nary a wiggle out of that thing. I just eased it back in the water. It wutn' no fun to ketch a fish that was so near dead I felt sorry fer it, and I dang shore wutn't a-goin' to eat the thang.

He went fishing several times with one of his friends, but I didn't go again.

I never imagined a place could be so hot, either. Folks didn't have air conditioners, like they do now. Upstairs in that apartment, even with a big fan going, it stayed close to ninety degrees with no breeze. And it didn't cool off much at night like it did at home. Van brought a big block of ice home every evening, and we put it in a washtub set across a couple of kitchen chair seats. He put the fan behind it and aimed it so it'd blow across the block of ice toward the bed at night. We lay on top of the cover to sleep.

When we'd been home and started to leave, Van's mother had loaded us down with canned stuff. I'd already learned that you didn't leave her house unless she gave you something, and you might as well take the first thing she offered, for she'd just hunt out something else if you didn't.

We would put a quart can of peaches in the refrigerator to chill, then eat the whole can that night. They were so good. But we both realized that what made them so good was because they were from home. In my mind, I could see the front porch with a big washtub full of luscious, golden, red-blushed peaches, and smell their fresh aroma as they were peeled, seeded, sliced and packed into Mason jars. And see the look of pride and satisfaction on her face as she set rows of shiny quart jars of peaches on shelves in the can house.

You could close your eyes and just smell the freshly baked peach cobbler as she pulled it out of the oven, and taste the mouth-watering, sugar-coated flaky crust, covered in thick rich cream from the milk-house.

She made "chow-chow," a relish type mixture of coarsely chopped cabbage, cucumbers, onions, peppers, corn, and whatever else she wanted to add from the garden. Sometimes we sat propped up in the bed to read, and one of us would go get a can of Lizzie's chow-chow and a spoon and wedge it into a nest between us. We took turns eating it right out of the can until the last bit was gone.

The last time we went home was around Thanksgiving, and they'd butchered a fat hog. The house was bustling with activity. The family was busy making cracklin's, rendering lard, making liver mush and souse meat, salting away and curing bacon and side meat, and making pork sausage. It made me *hungry as a bear* when we opened the door as we came in out of the cold and smelled all that cooking going on in the house.

Van's Dad did the grinding and mixing, and added the sage and seasonings for the sausage. He said it had just enough fat meat in it to make it have a good flavor. I washed my hands, joined in and started making sausage patties. We fried some to sample. He was 100 per cent correct. That was the best sausage I ever ate. The outside was crispy, the inside juicy and flavorful, with just the right amount of seasonings and sage.

They canned the pork sausage, and of course, we had to take some home with us. I've never before or since tasted sausage that good.

I could easily see where Van got some of the characteristics I loved about him, and found so interesting. I found his Dad to be one of the most knowledgeable, interesting people I'd ever met. He'd done all kinds of work, and could tell stories in detail of things he'd done, and about his family. He never ran out of something to talk about, and I could listen for hours and be held spellbound. He had a gift for story-telling. He was down-to-earth and understanding, yet conducted himself with the dignity of being truthful, honest, hard-working, and at peace with himself, his fellow man, and with God. He loved his family and was proud of them.

Van's brother, Lewis, wasn't home now; he'd joined the Army. Everyone else had a job to do, and was busy. His mother bustled around, and kept everything humming with clockwork precision. It seemed as if the greatest joy in her life was doing things to provide for her family. The wood cookstove was kept *chunked up* with stovewood, and Grover kept the woodbox filled. The stove top was covered with the canner, various pots and pans, while the oven baked big breadpans full of sausage patties.

Somewhere along in there, Ruby and Edith had made a huge pan of biscuits and a big bowl of gravy. Everyone was going around with a biscuit full of something, or had a plate of gravy, eggs, sausage, tenderloin or something good. We were sure *eatin' high on th' hawg.*

In October, I had to go to Raleigh for three days to take State Board Exams. I didn't have a driver's license, but had been driving ever since Van bought the car. I did as Van had instructed me while learning how to drive, and by now, knew how to put on a big front, not look guilty, and keep my cool when I met a Highway Patrolman. Each day, I drove right up to the Sir Walter Raleigh Hotel just like I owned the place, and took my exams. Now I had to wait to see if I passed.

I enjoyed meeting the people Van worked with. I did some private duty and made twelve dollars for an eight hour shift. That was more than staff nurses made—their salary was around $225. a month before taxes. Getting overtime pay was unheard-of.

The difference in income was another example of the discrimination shown between men and women. Van spent one third of the time a nurse spent in training and had much less responsibility, yet he made almost three times their salary. Many times, he commented on the unfairness of it.

I'd go by the lab and help him when I got off. I washed test tubes and slides, and did other little jobs so he could get finished to go home. It was interesting to see what he did. I watched him do blood counts, using a microscope and a manual counter. He showed me what the different blood cells looked like under the microscope, and how to do a Urinalysis.

Meanwhile, I was having problems with a stuffy nose. When we got near Statesville on the way to Marble, my nose opened up and I could breathe through it. On the way back, it stopped up again just after we passed Statesville. This was getting to be a problem. There was just something about this flatland country that didn't agree with me. Van had occasional asthma attacks, and I was concerned about his old chest injuries.

I'd begun to suspect there might be a little more than a stuffy nose going on with me. In mid-November, Van made me an appointment with a doctor he liked, and I kept the car that day to go for my appointment. Sure enough, I was pregnant. I was so indescribably happy, I think I floated out of that doctor's office. I couldn't wait for Van to get off work, so I went by the hospital. As soon as I walked in the lab, he asked me what the doctor said. I told him, "We're going to have a little red-headed boy in June." He grabbed me and hugged me so hard I was afraid it might be sooner. I've never seen anyone happier.

Soon I had more good news. I had passed State Boards and was a genuine, honest-to-goodness, flesh and blood Registered Nurse: Cleo Williams, R.N. At long last. I sat down and wrote my signature over and over, just to look at it, and enjoy how good it felt to write it.

"Thank You, Lord, for sticking with me through it all."

We traded in the 1953 for a 1956 four-door Chevy, and I took the test for my driver's license in the new car. We hated to see our old Chevy go, but it had so many miles on it, we didn't want to be stranded on the long trip home. We'd soon need a four-door car when the baby came.

It was getting harder and harder for Van to get any time off. Then, too, I didn't have morning sickness—he did. I never felt better in my life. Bless his heart, he was having a rough time. I knew that happened on rare occasions, and wished I could have it instead of him. Fortunately, it didn't last long.

He had to go back to the hospital a lot, and wasn't getting enough time off to rest, as he was officially on call half the time. Back then, a pager was unheard of. Wherever he went, he had to call and tell the hospital where he was, and be available at all times in case of an emergency. It got to the point that when we went to a movie, the owner would just wave us on in, we'd had to get up and leave so many times. They finally just made a card with his name on it, and flashed it on the screen when the hospital called.

We was jist a-startin' to learn that some folks *"don't worry 'bout the mule—jist load the waggin."*

Now that we were expecting a child, we needed to think about how we wanted to raise him, and make some plans. Living here, we had the opportunity to make a lot more money than we could ever make at home. We'd met several people we liked, were becoming good friends with some of them, and beginning to feel like a part of the town. I could get a job at another hospital or doctor's office and we could easily buy a place of our own. But in the meantime, our children would be growing up. We wanted more children, but if we both worked, we'd never get to spend time with them. I'd have to leave our children with a baby-sitter.

I know it's not possible for every mother to stay home with her children. Some have to work, and circumstances differ. But if there was any way possible, I wanted to stay home with mine. I realize that part of that feeling stemmed from my own need to have a home and family of my own. I wanted to be there, and not miss a minute of it. I could always go back into Nursing when they got in school.

More and more, our conversation turned to the things we loved about the mountains. One of our favorite things to do was walk in the woods at different seasons of the year. In spring, the sweet scented Trailing Arbutus was the first thing to bloom—about the time folks went back in the mountains to dig ramps. Trilliums, May Apples, ferns, and other plants native to Western North Carolina grew in the shady leaf-mold soil in the woods. In sunny places, large patches of earth was carpeted with blue, purple, yellow and fragrant white violets.

Later, the Rhododendron, Mountain Laurel, Dogwood and Sarvis trees covered the mountainsides with masses of blooms, signalling that the cold winter was almost over. We'd have a few short cold snaps around Easter, then Dogwood winter, and Blackberry winter. It would be time to get taters in the ground and gardens ready to plant. When it came a good warm spring rain, it seemed that the whole world popped out overnight in dozens of shades of green, while a chorus of peep-frogs filled the air.

Then there would be the smell of blooming fruit trees and newly-mown grass wafting through the air, along with the droning of bees and insects, as all sizes and species of butterflies flitted and flashed their glowing colors. All the kids would be gleefully kicking off their shoes, running around barefooted and splashing through mudholes.

We talked about catchin' lightning bugs to put in a jar, splashin' and playin' in the cool, clear water of branches and creeks that ran down from icy-cold springs far back on the mountaintops. Sometimes they cascaded into waterfalls that few people even knew were there. And listening to the doves calling to each other, Whip-poor-wills coming to life along about dark, the scrooch owls and hoot owls echoing up and down the hollers on a clear night.

Of sitting on the porch and eating watermelon, watching dusk come, then night fall when the moon would slowly rise in a star-filled sky above the soft, gentle curves of the surrounding mountains. Of being so spellbound by it all that one hesitated to turn on a light and spoil the night's natural beauty.

Of waking up in the morning with the cool night air still lingering, and watching the sun come up over the purple, hazy mountain tops, as birds filled the air with songs of delight at the coming day. And smelling the damp earth of freshly plowed fields through the open window.

Van loved camping and fishing, and I teased him about hearing "the wild goose call," in the fall, and having to go when the wild geese flew over the mountains in the crisp, autumn air on their annual migration. He loved to go hunting, but mostly, he went as an excuse to get out in the mountain woodlands and enjoy the solitude. Something in his spirit seemed to require it. I understood.

He told me about walking deep into the Snowbird mountains to camp and fish with his Dad, brothers, or a close friend. They only took a piece of salt pork, some flour, cornmeal, salt and coffee, and ate wild berries, grapes or whatever they found, and what fish they caught. I understood that this was as necessary to him as food, air and water. I loved him just as he was, and wanted him to be happy. When we had some children, we'd take them and teach them to enjoy the mountains, and learn how to survive in the wild.

He talked about his childhood home in Haywood county, and a place called Shining Rock, where they went to pick huckleberries. It was a huge white rock cliff covering the side of a mountain. and where the sun glinted off the surface, giving it its name. During a thunderstorm, lightning often struck, and sent huge boulders hurling through the air, exposing a fresh shiny surface. He told me of the close knit community of Sunburst, where he was born. It was a logging operation run by Blackwood Lumber Company, and his dad worked in the shop as a welder til they closed down operations there.

The winters are cold, but the snow is so beautiful. I loved to get out and walk in the new-fallen snow and see the pines, leafless trees and bare branches transformed into a breathtaking scene of beauty in a peaceful, silent wonderland of snow. On the way back, to see the smoke rising from the chimney made me anticipate the snug, safe haven of being inside in the warmth, with the smell of hot coffee to greet me when I opened the door.

The more we talked it over, the more we realized that we loved the mountains so much, we couldn't bear to think that our children wouldn't be able to call the mountains home, or get to know our families, the mountain people and their way of life. What could money buy that would take the place of that? We decided we were going home. And we were going now! Van needed a day off through the week when offices were open to look for a job.

"Lord, please find a way, and make it possible for us to go home, so we can live and raise our children in Your beautiful sheltering mountains."

Van didn't ask this time. He told them he was taking the next Friday, plus his week-end off, and was going out of town—they'd just have to make arrangements for the hospital to be covered. They knew he meant business, and got a lab technician from out of town to come and work that week-end.

When we got home, Van asked around, and learned that Dr. Whitfield in Murphy was looking for an x-ray and lab technician for his office practice. (Coincidence?) Van went to see him, really liked him, and although the salary was much less, took the job. His work load would also be much less, with every weekend and all holidays off—and no being on call. That alone was worth more than half his salary.

Andrews had just opened their new hospital and jumped at the chance to hire me. RNs were hard to find in this area. First, as I'd promised, I went to Dr. Van Gorder, Rodda, and Blalock's new offices at the Valley River Clinic and told Mary Willie I was available if they wanted me to work there. She said I'd be of more help to Dr. Van Gorder at the hospital, so I accepted that job. I was to start right after Christmas, 1956, when Van finished working his notice. My salary would be $225. a month. We went ahead and rented an apartment at A.B. Chandler's so we'd have a place ready to come back to.

When we went back to Lewisburg this time, Van gave his notice. And as so often happens, after a place has *worked a good horse to death*, they offered to give him a raise, get help for him, and gave him all kinds of incentives to stay. But some things are worth more than money, and we were just too homesick for the mountains. And I was awful tired of trying to sleep propped up on two fat pillows to breathe through my nose.

The evening before we were to leave, Van's sister Ruby, his Dad, and Anniebelle's husband, Andrew Miller showed up to help us move home. I had already packed most of our belongings. We borrowed a rollaway bed, made a bed on the couch, and managed to fix everybody a place to sleep. Ruby slept with me, Van slept with his Dad, and Andrew got the couch. We were too excited to sleep much.

After breakfast the next morning, we washed and packed up the dishes, and packed both car trunks and the back seat of our car full. It was around nine o'clock when we headed for the mountains. Andrew was a truck driver, and was used to lettin' the hammer down on them big eighteen wheelers, so we followed him. We stopped and ate lunch, and took a couple of breaks on the way, but didn't waste any time. We wanted to get home.

As always, when we got past Bryson City and headed down Nantahala Gorge, we could feel the cool air coming off the river, like nature's air conditioning. We rolled down our windows to let the breeze blow in our faces as we breathed the fresh clean mountain air.

Always before, when we started through the Gorge, we knew home was just a few minutes away. This time, though, we were staying. My entire being was filled to bursting with gratitude and joy, and we were both *grinnin' like a basket full of possum heads*.

"Thank You, Lord! You've really done it this time!"

Beside the highway, the cold rushing water of Nantahala River looked like flowing liquid fire from the reflection of the sun setting behind the towering, smoky-blue and purple mountains. The golden-red glow was right in our eyes. But we didn't mind.

That sure looked good to us. West was home, and we were coming.

And just as in the Roy Rogers westerns, we rode off into the sunset.

MY MOUNTAINS, MY PEOPLE

Sometimes when I see an elderly person, I wish I could just look inside their mind to read the rich history and knowledge they have stored there. Every few days, I hear of one of them passing away, and think regretfully of the valuable lessons they learned and the things they knew, forever gone. Theirs is a vanishing culture in these mountains, and things are rapidly changing as more people are moving in. The terminology, phrases and words I heard as a child are seldom heard any more except from the very old. Many of their customs are gone. Most of their morals were vastly different from those of today.

When I was a teenager and full of the "superior knowledge" that teenagers are sure they have, my friends and I sometimes poked fun at the quaint speech and mannerisms of the older folks. We thought they were highly ignorant! Now that I'm older and a little better educated (not all from book learning), I have learned immense respect for them.

I've learned that there is a vast difference between ignorance and stupidity. Theirs may not be the grammatically correct English we were taught in school, but their speech and customs reflect their ancestry. Some of the language reaches back to the Elizabethan era, and sometimes you can detect a touch of Scotch, Irish, American Indian, or other language of their ancestors. We were so isolated that changes came slowly. Few outsiders moved here to live.

If you want to *git my dander up*, just let me even think I heard anyone make a derogatory remark about our customs, mannerisms, or speech. You may laugh with us, not at us. I don't get as upset about it now, however, as I once did. I've come to realize that people who come here from some other part of the country are simply reflecting their own upbringing, and are displaying their ignorance of our unique heritage. They don't understand that our speech, or language, is as valid as any other language. They wouldn't dream of going to Italy and making derogatory remarks about Italians speaking the Italian language. After all, that is their native language. But they think it makes them look smart to treat ours with derision.

I've made friends with people who came here from other places, and some have asked me why they can't seem to fit in. For a long time, I avoided giving an answer, for fear of offending them, then decided to try to "educate" them by trying to explain mountain ways as tactfully as I could. Maybe it's one of the signs of my getting older, but my patience isn't as long as it once was. Now I just let them have it with both barrels.

People create their own barriers with their attitude. A condescending, "superiority" attitude shows! Outsiders often mistake old-timey good manners for stupidity. Most all the old mountain people will quietly listen, and patiently wait for you to get done "runnin' yer mouth," go on about your business and leave theirs alone. But when one tells you they've had enough, or tells you to leave, I'd advise you to do just that. They simply say what they mean, and mean what they say, in the fewest possible words. The "pushier" you get, the less respect they have for you or anything you might say, and the deeper they dig in their heels.

I love the Bible verse in Psalm 121 which says," I will lift up mine eyes unto the hills, from whence cometh my help." I feel such a deep sense of awe and security when I look up and see the beautiful hazy blue mountain tops which surround me. I am filled with gratitude to God for letting me be born here and giving me the privilege of living in these mountains.

When I lift up my eyes and see the skyline of a beautiful mountain top which for hundreds of years, not only I, but my ancestors and native Americans before them, have gazed upon and revered, that is now being denuded, leaving raw earth exposed, jagged scars and erosion from slashes of roads across the mountainside, I think of a non-healing cancerous sore. I am filled with grief. That malignant cancer is slowly killing a beautiful, living thing.

I don't mean to sound blasphemous when I say that I also think of another Bible verse which says, "Father, forgive them, for they know not what they do."

I cannot understand why people see our beautiful mountains and want to live here, then come and set out to destroy that very beauty which attracted them.

I say to you who feel you can't fit in: If you want to fit in, build your home in the community, and make yourself a part of the community. Treat your neighbors with respect for what they are instead of what you think they should be. Sitting up there on your own piece of property on the mountain top with No Trespassing signs on your driveway and looking down on the community will assure that you will never fit in. That's like accusing your neighbors of being thieves and vandals and not worth knowing before you even meet them.

Take the time and make an effort to be a good neighbor, listen and learn, and you may be pleasantly surprised at what you might discover.

And please, please, preserve the beauty of our mountains for ourselves and future generations.

WESTERN NORTH CAROLINA MOUNTAIN TALK©

(Mountain Speech, Mountainese)

*The name I call the language spoken in the North Carolina mountains.

These definitions include words and phrases found in my book, Gratitude For Shoes, and are given to show the meaning of a "mountain talk" word or term. The word or phrase is listed alphabetically, according to the way it is pronounced by the mountaineer. Standard dictionary definitions are not generally included in this glossary.

Words are defined, and sentences are given as examples to help the reader understand the context in which they might have been used, as well as the meaning.

Much effort has been made to adhere as much as possible to the way the language was spoken in my region of the mountains of Western North Carolina in the years around the mid 1930's through the mid 1950's. We must realize, however, that words and phrases spoken in one community might vary somewhat from those spoken in another, although they might be similar. Even some families spoke words and phrases that were not heard in another family, kind of like an "inside joke."

At times, (probably, most of the time) you may think I have misspelled a word, when I have simply used an opportunity to show a pronunciation. Words ending in "ed," for example, are often pronounced as if they ended with a "t," so I write the "t" ending instead.

Old-timey mountain words, expressions and *"sayings,"* (also known as *"saws"*) are written in Italics, and are included as much as possible. Pronunciations and explanations are in parenthesis.

A

a (uh, uv)**:** of. Example: A bucket *a* (of) water. Five pound *a* lard. A quart *a* honey.

a-: put in front of a word to show action, as **a**-goin', **a**-comin', **a**-talkin', etc.

aah-ite: all right.

a-barrellin' and/or **a-stavin'** (stay'-vin) Similar meanings, but *a-barrellin'* means to come or go real fast, like dist *a-barrellin'* down the road. *A-stavin'* means that you come *a-barrellin',* but would be a-stompin' around like you was mad or something was bad wrong, as: *a-stavin'* like a mad bull. See *ballhootin'.*

a-body (a-bye'-dee)**:** refers to a non-specific person. Example: *A-body has to work if they expect to eat.* Or: *A-body ortn't to be a-carryin' tales* (spreadin', or *peddlin'* gossip).

above: value yourself more, or think you're *above* (better than) something or another person. When a person thinks of him/herself as *"too good"* to do something they think is demeaning to their own perceived status, they are said to be *above* it. For example, back then a man thought he was *above* washing dishes or changing a diaper. Some people thought they were *above* us and *looked down on us* because they were *better off* (had more money, social status, etc.) than us.

above yer raisin': When home folks think you're actin' like you consider yourself above the people and circumstances you grew up with, they say you're *"gittin' above yer raisin'."* See *biggety, hi-falutin', big shot.*

acrost: across

acrost the waters: overseas

act a fool, act a gump: behave in a foolish or playful manner; act like a comedian; to *"cut up."* If we got to *cuttin' up* and acting silly, Mom said for us to *quit actin' a fool,* or *actin' a gump.* And, no, we *hatn't never heard tell* of Forest Gump back then. **Act a fool** is also the same as *showin' out,* or *showin' your butt,* which is to make an unfavorable or foolish spectacle of yourself

actiously: (ax'-shush-lee) actually

adge (age)**:** Mountain talk for *edge*

addled, addlepated: (1) off in the head; *tetched in the head*; crazy. He was about half *addled.* (2) dizzy, off balance. It sorta *addled* him when his mule kicked him up agin' the barn door.

afeared, afyered: (a-fyerred') afraid

afore: before. *Don't go countin' yer chickens **afore** they hatch out.*

aggervate: aggravate, pester, annoy. When somebody said they were doing or saying something to somebody just to ***aggervate*** 'em, that meant they were just teasing—not being malicious. It was done jist fer ***aggervation;*** they never meant no harm.

agin': (1) against. The shovel was *lent up **agin'** the* barn. (2) pronunciation for *again.*

agg: (aig) (1) an egg, like a hen lays. (2) to ***agg*** somebody on is to enthusiastically encourage somebody to fight or do mischief of some sort. Abet. They ***agged*** Bud on to steal one of Paw's chickens.

aimin', aimed to: intend to, or planned to do something; to *have your mind set on it.* See *fixin' to.*

ainser: answer, reply.

ain't/hain't/never done it: did not do it. He said he ***never done it***, and I believe him.

ain't/hain't: isn't

air: means air—like we breathe, but it's how we sometimes say *are* and how we allus say *hour.*

airish: cool, coolish; a little bit too cold for comfort.

allus: always

altar: A designated place in front of the church pulpit, where people *go up* to pray. There may or may not be a *mourner's bench* there. Toward the end of the sermon, the preacher urges sinners to come up to the ***altar*** and repent. This invitation is called the ***altar call.***

Aman: Amen

an'at: and that. ***An'at's*** all they is to it.

an'en: and then; ***an'en*** on the other hand.

arn: iron

arnj (one syllable)**:** orange

around and about: just here, there and yander—no place in pa'tic'ler.

arr': (are) arrow. Pronounciation as in *harr* (harrow), *narr* (narrow) *spar* (sparrow). Sometimes pronounced ***arrer*** (are'-rer).

Arsch: (one syllable) Irish, as in ***Arsch*** *taters* (Irish potatoes).

ary, ary'n, ary other'n: any, any single one, any other one. See *nary, nary'n, nary nuther'n.*

ast, asted: ask, asked. *Ast me no questions, and I'll tell ye no lies.* See *axed.*

atall: (a-tall', said as one word) at all

awful: (1) terrible (2) very. The extreme degree of what is being described, as *awful* slow, or *awful* good. That was a *awful good* pie.

awkerd: awkward

ax, axed: ask, asked. He *axed* me what my name was. See *ast, asted*.

axe handle: a unit of measurement, meaning as long as an average *axe handle*. A "fleshy" lady is described as being three *axe handles* acrost her hin'end (or as broad as a gover'ment mule).

B

back: To write the name and mailing address on an envelope is to *back* it. After she *backed* the envelope, I took the letter to the mailbox.

backerds: (1) backward. Opposite of *fards* (forward) or *face fo'must* (foremost). (2) bashful; not very polished and smooth in the social graces. (3) not quite mentally retarded, but mighty close to it—*a little bit backerds*. An old expression: "*so backerds he couldn't pour pee out of a boot with the directions on the heel.*"

backin's: what you get when you add some water to make the last run of likker in the still. Poor quality stuff, *weak as stump water*.

back room: usually meaning the bedroom at the back of the house, as opposed to the front room or kitchen. The *back room* was usually a bedroom, where the younguns slept. If there was two back rooms, one might be used for storage, or used for what people now call a "pantry," where they kept their dried stuff, canned stuff, pickled beans, corn and cucumber pickles, kraut, side meat, wine and home brew. It was unheated and things were kept cold. See *front room*.

bad agg (egg), **bad apple:** A person who is dishonest, lies or steals, and can't be trusted *(rotten to the core)*.

bad cold: A cold is never simply called "a cold," it's called "*a bad cold.*"

bad off: (1) sick enough to die (2) to be in extreme financial difficulty, as: Their family is *bad off*.

bag : beg. He kept *baggin'* her to marry him.

bail: (1) The heavy wire handle fastened on each side of the top of a lard bucket, iron pot, etc. to pick it up by. (2) Money that has to be put up before they'll let you out of the calaboose.

bainch: bench

baisterd: A youngun that nobody knows who its pappy is. Syn: *woods colt*

bait: (1) what you use to fish with, or *bait* a trap with (2) tempt (3) When eating, it means that when you've eat ever bite you can hold, you've *eat a bait*.

ballhootin': travellin' fast. A great big log a-sliding down a steep mountain would be *ballhootin'*.

banjer: (bain'-jer) banjo. A person who plays the banjo is a ***banjer*** *picker*.

bank the fire: Use a shovel to place fine white ashes over a fire until the flame dies down, covering the live firecoals so they will smoulder and keep hot, but not burn up the wood. The next morning, the coals are stirred up, kindling placed on them, and the fire will once again blaze up and burn.

bark: usual meaning, but also means to scrape off some skin, as: I ***barked*** my shin.

bath: bathe. The word bathe is said as "bath," as in: She ***bath'd*** the baby.

bawl: (1) to cry, shed tears; *sling snot* (2) The noise a cow or calf makes.

beaslin's: colostrum; the first milk a cow produces after a calf is born. People don't drink ***beaslin's.***

beat: embarrass. As: It ***beat*** *him to death* when he looked down and seen his pants were unzipped *(his hoss was gittin' out of the barn)*.

beat around the bush: *hum-haw* around instead of coming right out and telling it like it is.

beat his time: When a boy wins the affection of another boy's sweetheart, he is said to have ***beat his time.*** Example: Joe went and ***beat*** ol' Jake's ***time*** with Mary.

bedstid: bedstead. Just the bed frame, not with the straw tick.

beholden, be beholden to: grateful; owe somebody a favor; to feel obligated to return a favor done for you. Mountain folks don't like to ***be beholden to*** nobody.

bein', bein's as: (be'-in) Since; because. As: ***Bein' as*** how you're going to the store, how about bringing me back a box of snuff. *Seein' as* is used the same way.

belittle: "put down" a person, treat them as unimportant or try to make them feel insignificant. See *cowed down.*

beller: yell; bellow. ***Bellerin'*** *and bawlin'* is descriptive of crying. As: That youngen jist stood there *a-***bellerin'***. See *bawl.*

better, or best: A warning, as in: "You'd ***better/best*** get back to the house by dark."

better off: have more wealth or possessions in comparison to others around you...

betwixt: in between. as ***betwixt*** *a rock and a hard place.*

bib overhalls: Overalls with a bib and galluses.

biggety: act *hifalutin*, like *a big shot*, or as if you *think you're better'n ever'body else.*

big-head: To have the ***big head*** is to have an inflated opinion of yourself. See *biggety, hifalutin'.*

big shot: somebody who acts as if they think they're more important and better than anyone. A showy and boastful person. See *biggety, big-head.*

big spoon: what we called any large spoon or serving spoon. Also called a *table spoon.*

bigun: an outright lie. He *told a bigun* on her.

bile: (1) boil, as in cooking (2) a painful, purulent lump under the skin (3) the green stuff in a gallbladder

biled: boiled (boilt)

bind, in a bind: Financially strapped, as: He didn't buy it because he was *in a bind* right then. In a difficult situation, as to be *in a bind* whether to go or stay.

birch tea: (1) tea made from birch bark, used to stop diarrhea (2) Since it was common to use a birch limb to give a youngun a whuppin', a parent would threaten to *give it a doast of birch tea.*

blackguard: (black-gyard) To *handle* (speak) filthy talk, especially around women and childern.

bless/blest: Of course, they asked God to bless them when they prayed, meaning it in the usual way. But when they was mad, *bless* was used as a substitute cussword. Most of the time, **blest** meant *damned,* as in: "*I'll be blest* if she ditn't take ever last dime I had." **Blessed 'em out** means that somebody got a good cussin'.

bless his/her/their heart: This phrase is a preamble to a criticism, put-down, gossip, or something bad the speaker has to say about somebody. Saying this is like "baptizing" what they were going to say, as: "I don't mean no harm…but *bless his heart…*" as if this gave them license to cut loose with the bad things they would say. It implies a kindliness or sympathy toward the other person, but is malicious. For instance: *Bless her heart,* she's so ugly she'd snag lightning. Or, *bless his heart,* he can't help hisself, him bein' *dumber'n a rock.*

blockader: somebody who has an illegal moonshine still in operation.

bloomers: women's knee length underpants. The legs were wide with elastic in the hem.

blubbers: bubbles

blue law: the law that prohibits selling alcohol on Sunday.

blunderbuss: shotgun

bob, bobbed, bobbed off: (1) cut short. A man had a haircut or a hair trimmin', a woman had her hair **bobbed**. Religious zealots said it was a sin for a woman to have **bobbed** hair. (2) chopped off. They had to **bob off** a chicken's head so they could have fried chicken for dinner.

bob wire: (bob wahr) barbed wire

boggin: toboggin, a knitted cap. No, we never heard of calling a sled a *toboggan.*

booger (buh-ger): (1) something to be afraid of. A **booger** will *gitchey* in the dark. (2) a wad of half dry mucus in or from the nose. (3) word used to refer to a child, pet, or something little, as: He's a cute little *booger.* See next 2 entries.

booger at, got boogered at: become wary or afraid of, as: The mule *got boogered at* the new gate.

boogered, boogered up: messed up; tore up something. Example: He *boogered up* the side of his car when he sideswiped the bridge. See *bollux*

booger man: Satan; the devil. Kids were warned that the *boogerman* would get them for lying, stealing, cussin', etc.

boomer: a red squirrel

bollux: make a mess of something. "That carpenter sure **bolluxed up** that house." See *boogered.*

bosom: In general terms, the *bosom* is the chest. As: She laid the baby's head on her *bosom.* **bosoms**: the polite way to say breasts, or *titties.*

bother: (1) aggravate or annoy somebody (2) touch, handle or move something that's *none of yer business.* When we went some place, we knowed not to **bother** (or mess with) *nuthin'.*"

bottled in bond: storebought liquor, made at a legal commercial distillery.

bow and scrape: (bough 'n scrape) be submissive and defer to another person, as: She was expected to *bow and scrape* whenever her mother-in-law was around. (I wonder if this is sarcastic terminology referring to the custom of bowing and giving a curtsy to royalty as a sign of respect.)

bowel complaint: (bal complaint) diarrhea

bow up: (boe up) Just quit and do nuthin'. As: That old mule just *bowed up* and woutn't pull that plow another step. See *stubbed up, humped up.*

box: (1) the old mountain term for *havin' a prize fight* (boxing match). (2) But the term **box** was also used in another way that is very rare. When I was a child, I overheard a conversation between an old man and one of my brothers, in which the man was talking about his wife's *box.* I was totally puzzled, as I could not connect what he said to any box she might have. Later, when I asked my brother about it, he told me the word meant vagina. (Except he *put it in plain English*). I've never again heard the word used in that context (probably since I am a girl), and decided it must be just a word he made up as a substitute. I recently remembered that, and told a friend who has studied the derivation of words peculiar to Appalachia, and she said it is still a common word used in that context in Wales and Scotland.

boy: son, regardless of age. He's Aunt Marthey's *boy.* See *girl.*

brag/bragged on: (braig) Give a compliment to or about someone or something. We never say, "praised," we **brag on** *'em.*

brainch: branch; stream of water smaller than a creek.

brang/brung: Pronounciation for bring/brought. A bred cow was said to be *going to* **brang** *a calf.* After it's born, you'd say, *"She* **brung** *a calf."*

brar: briar. Them blackberry **brars** scratched our arms all over. Also, *sharp as a* **brar** (or tack) means highly intelligent; clever.

brash: brush. People swept their yard with a **brash** made out of a tree limb. Or: He burnt that **brash** pile out in the garden. Sometimes pronounced as "bresh."

break: to train or tame, sometimes by using force or punishment, as to **break** a horse, mule or oxen to work. One old theory about raising children was that parents needed to **break** them from unwanted behaviors, instead of training them to have acceptable behavior.

break a sweat: work hard enough at something to cause you to sweat.

brick sidin': A popular covering for the outside walls of a house in earlier days. It came in rolls like tarpaper, with colored sand imbedded or glued in a brick pattern on the surface. It not only improved the appearance of the house, it made it much warmer by covering the cracks.

brickle: brittle

brigsome: like, feelin' your oats; wantin' to go a-courtin'—*feelin'* **brigsome.** See *bullin'.*

britches: pants

brogans: heavy high-topped work shoes.

brogue: walk heavily, as if wearing brogans. He woke up the baby when he **brogued** in.

brow-beat: to mentally "beat" on somebody; nag, harp, put down, or make them feel worthless.

brownie: a copper penny

brown new/brown spankin' new: Brand new. Right out of the store.

brung: brought

bull-headed: awful stubborn. Same as mule-headed.

bullin': in heat, as a **bullin'** heifer

bum: ask somebody for something, as to **bum** a ride or **bum** a cigarette.

bumfuzzled: puzzled, confused. She had him *so* **bumfuzzled** *he didn't know which end was up.*

bunged up: constipated Probably derived from the use of a cork (bung) to stop up the the hole (bung hole) near the bottom of a barrel where liquid is withdrawn.

bung hole: (1) the hole in a barrel or (2) butt hole (anal opening)

bureau: a chest of drawers or dresser

business: (1) your own affairs. Pertinent words and phrases: *tend to* (or *mind*) *my/your own* **business;** *take care of* **business;** (2) *do your* **business** is to have a bowel movement

buss: smooch, kiss

bust: (1) burst (2) split, as to **bust** wood. (3) breast, bosom, or the front part of your chest.

bust a gut: to overdo something. To **bust a gut** eating is to glut yourself. You can work so hard that you **bust a gut** trying to get it done.

button: (1) the usual meaning, but also a short, narrow, flat piece of wood nailed through the center to the door facing. When it is turned sideways, it **buttons** or fastens the door shut. (2) a figurative medal or award. When a person did something worthy of recognition or award, they said, *"Well, give 'em a **button.**"*

bydee: body

byerr: (say "yer" with a *b*) beer. Blockaders made *"stillhouse **byerr.**"*

byerr joint: one of them ol' *caiffays* or *honkytonks* where they sell *byerr* (beer).

by note: To sing or play music as it is composed or written, opposite of "by ear." Sometimes, it means to sing the melody using the name of the note (do,re,mi, etc.) instead of the words.

C

cabbage: (1) to steal. He didn't buy it, he **cabbaged** it. (2) cabbage, like you make slaw out of, is a plural word. Them fried **cabbage** was shore good.

caiffay: (kaif-fay) cafe. If they also sell beer, it's a *honkytonk* or *beer joint.*

cake: (1) A **cake** is sweet and sometimes has frostin' on it. (2) However much dough it takes to fill up the breadpan makes a **cake** of bread.

calaboose: (cally'-booce) jail. They put the thievin' rascal in the **calaboose.**

calamity: sudden, loud racket or ruckus; clatter, as: The **calamity** starts when my sister hits the kitchen to fix a meal. Or: They was a **calamity** when the fox got into the chicken house.

calf: pronounced "kyaif."

calf-eyed: (kyaif-eyed) how a boy looks a girl, or girl looks at a boy that they're *struck on.*

calfrope: (kyaif-rope) The words a person hollers out that means "I give up," as in wrestling. City speech is "Cry Uncle."

call: reason. "He *ditn't have no **call*** to treat her like that."

cankered: (cain'-kerd) spoiled, but not yet rotten, like meat that's been hung when the weather's too warm.

caps the stack: The last word—the very most in degree, probably derived from the cap of a haystack, being on top. *Beats all; takes the cake.*

care: pronounced "keer" or "kyerr."

carryin' on: *bawlin' and cryin', wringin' yer hands and "slingin' snot" all over the place.* **carterges:** (car'-ter-jiz) cartridges; gun shells

case knife: dinner knife. We had **case knifes,** like you eat with, an'en we had cuttin' knifes, like a pocket knife, parin' knife, butcher knife, Dad's knife and Cob Handle. The test of a man's ability to *sharp'm* (sharpen) a knife good is if he can shave the hair off his arm with it.

casin': (kay'-sun) casing or?caisson; a car or truck tire.

casket: a coffin

cast (kyaist): (1) made out of cast iron (2) a hint of a color, as a "grayish cast."

casterated: (kyaist'-er-a-tid) castrated, neutered. *"Cut."*

cat head biscuits: Big ol' biscuits, big as a cat's head. They are so light you have to watch or they'll float off the plate. They're also what we call "choked out," or "choked off" biscuits because the amount of dough for a biscuit is choked off between the thumb and index finger.

catty-cornered: uneven, not centered, as, putting a quilt on the bed *catty-cornered.* See *slaunchways.*

cattywampus: see *catty-cornered, slaunchways.*

caul: also called a "veil." The amniotic sac or membrane surrounding the fetus before birth. *If a baby is born with a section of the **caul**, or veil, covering its face, it is a sign that the baby will have good luck all its life.*

celloid, cetalloy, cilloid: celluloid, an earlier plastic-like material which was used to make combs, doll parts and similar items before plastic came into common use.

chafted, or **galded:** (chaif'-tid) chapped; made sore by rubbing, as in riding a horse. *Galded* is a worse condition than *chafted.*

chamber: (chaim'-ber) a portable "potty," manufactured for that purpose. It was shaped like a bucket with a bail and a lid, and made of porcelain enamel. It was commonly referred to as a *piss pot.* Many women and children used a lard bucket for a *pee bucket.* A man didn't use one unless he was bad-off sick or there was a deep snow on the ground. A common expression, referring to someone with little money or possessions: *"He's so pore he don't even have a pot to pee in."*

chanch: chance

change of clothes: clean clothes from the skin out.

char-acter: (care-ac'-ter) Character; a person's integrity or honesty. It was serious business to *put a slur on* a man's *character*…or his dog, wife, or kinfolks.

charm: superstitious belief that someone or something can *put a spell on you* or *charm* you.

chaser: something (like a pickle) eaten or taken right after having a drink of *likker.*

chaw: (1) chew, as in eating (2) enough cut off of a plug of tobacco to make one cud (rhyme with good), a *chaw,* or cheek full. That big *chaw* of tobacker made him look like a ground squirrel.

chawin' gum: chewing gum

chawed off, bit off: (1) Bit something off (2) Take something upon oneself to do, as, He's *done'n bit off more'n he can chew.*

chawin' th' fat: talking or gossiping; same as *chawin' th' cud or beatin' yer gums.*

cherr: Rhymes with err, byerr (beer), dyerr (dear), cler (clear). Chair.

chifferobe: (shiff'-er-robe) a moveable closet in which to store clothes—a separate piece of furniture. Usually there were two doors, behind which were drawers on one side and a place to hang clothes on the other.

childern, chile: children, child. The word *child, son* or *daughter* was rarely said. They said my/your/their *young'un, little boy or little girl.* When they got older, they were simply referred to as my/your/their *boy* or *girl.*

chimbly: chimney

chinch: a bedbug

chinkypin (chinquapin): a native tree bearing small round nuts covered with a burr which opens when mature to allow the nut to drop out. The round nuts are a little bigger than a large pearl and have a taste similar to a chestnut. They are close to the same color and texture as a chestnut, and have a similar skin and burr covering. The tree is more like a large shrub, however—nothing like the size of a chestnut tree.

choked-out/choked-off biscuits: see *cathead biscuits.*

chop block: a short length of a large diameter hardwood log, stood upright on the ground. It was used as a base for chopping or splitting wood or whatever needed chopping, so the axe wouldn't hit the ground and dull it. It also kept the chopper from having to bend over so far.

chuffy, chunky: A person who was a little overweight was described as being *chunky* or *chuffy,* as a *chunky* gal. A more overweight person was described as being "flashy." (fleshy)

chunk up: To *chunk up* a fire is to add more firewood (chunk of wood) to the fire.

cipher: to work arithmetic problems. See *sipher.*

clabbered: thickened up. Before churning, milk went through a procession of changes—from *frash* milk, to *blinked* milk (when it starts *turning,* or becoming sour), to ***clabbered*** milk, when it thickens and is ready to churn to make butter. An old saying, said in fun (usually) to a youngun was, *"I'm gonna **clabber** up and rain all over you."*

cleanness: cleanliness, the opposite of *naistness* (nastiness).

clean your plow: If somebody tells you they aim to ***clean your plow,*** you better either run or git ready to fight.

cler: (clerr) clear

cler light: completely, totally. I ***cler light*** forgot about it. Syn: clean, plumb

cler to: all the way. He walked ***cler to*** town.

clever: Intelligent. It implies that a-body can work real good with their hands, too.

C'liner: Carolina

clim, or **clum:** climbed

clodhoppers: heavy work shoes, like one would weqr while plowing. See *brogans.*

close-mouthed: (cloce-mouthed) having very few words; keeping information to yourself.

clost: near, close

clost akin: nearly, almost, as: ***clost akin*** to bein' naked, or ***clost akin*** to tellin' a lie.

cloth: any kind of fabric.

clothes pack: the place where a family's clean clothing was folded up and stored—usually on plank shelves nailed up on a wall in the back room. Each person had an assigned place in the ***clothes pack*** for their clothes. The family also had a *quilt pack.*

coat suit: People used to refer to a woman's two-piece suit (jacket and skirt) as a ***coat suit.***

cobbled up: botched; made a mess out of a job (usually carpentry); *by the quickest way done.* See *bolluxed.* **Co-Colie/Co-Coly:** Originally a Mountainese word for Coca-Cola, but we called any kind of fizzy soft drink a ***co-coalie*** or *dope,* one.

cold as kraut: as cold as it gets, unless it's *colder'n a well digger's butt in Alasky.*

come agin: One of several expressions which mean "Huh?" What did you say? Would you repeat that? *Shot who? Run that by me one more time.* See *Do what?*

come in: (1) come on inside (2) When a cow gave birth, or *"**come in,**"* she was said to have *found a calf,* or ***come in*** *frash* (*fresh, frush*).

come in a bean/come in a dab: too close for comfort. He *come in a bean* of kil-lin' hisself.

come to me:(emphasis on *to*) remembered; or: It **come to me** as a sudden thought, insight or idea.

come to myself: (emphasis on *come*) suddenly realized what I was doing.

common: usual. The question, "How are you?" is usually answered with, "About like *common*."

confounded: (1) bewildered, confused (2) a synthetic swear word. That *con-founded* mule kicked me flat of my back.

conjure: one method of removing warts was to have somebody *conjure* them off.

conniption: tantrum. *Have a conniption* means the same as *take a fit* or *have a hissy.*

consarned: mild expletive. See *confounded, dang.*

corn dodger: a cake of cornbread, regardless of size.

corn shock: When the mature corn plants are dry and harvested, they are gath-ered, stood on end and leaned together vertically into a cone-shaped *shock of corn.*

corruption: Purulent drainage. *Corruption* is a sure sign of infection in a wound.

cort: quart. A *cort* fruit jar.

corter: quarter.

countypin/counterpin: counterpane; a bedspread. See *coverlid.*

court; go a-courtin': to woo or romance the object of your affection; go *a-spar-kin'* or *scooter-poopin'* (family definition, I think) See *brigsome, struck on.*

coutn't: couldn't

coverlid: coverlet, bedspread

cowed down: cowering or cowered. The younguns were so scared that they were all *cowed down* over in the corner. A dog that has been beaten *cows down* when he sees someone with a stick. A person who has been belittled or abused all their life is *cowed down.* See *brow beat.*

crabbed, crabbedy: (crab'-bid) mean-tempered, hard to get along with. Such a person is described as *"having their butt (or drawers) in a bind,"* or *"their tail in a crack."*

crank: to start a car or other motor. We say *"crank it up"*—probably a holdover from the first cars ever made, which literally had to be cranked to start them.

crazy: insane Syn. *tetched in the head; not right in the head; messed up in their head; out of their mind.* When a person *went crazy,* or *lost their mind,* they were *sent off* to the **crazy** house, or asylum, and/or they *locked 'em up.* When said in a joking manner, or to mean that somebody was just peculiar in their ways, they were said to be *"as **crazy** as a louse,"* or *"as silly as a goose."* See *quare*.

creases: edible, much prized wild watercress, which grows along damp branch banks or in damp areas. Also called *creasy greens*.

crins: crayons, commonly said as *"color **crins**,* or *colorin' **crins**."*

crippled up: disabled, regardless of the cause. I'm all **crippled up** now, and can't make a garden.

crooked pencil: Someone who *figgers up (or totes up)* a bill owed to them might make a (intentional) mistake and make the sum bigger than it really ought to be. If they do this, they are said to use a **crooked pencil**. See *figger up*.

cubbert: (1) culvert (2) cupboard

cuckold: When one man *messes around with* another man's wife, he is said to **cuckold** the other man.

cud (cood, rhyme with wood): (1) what a cow chews on (2) enough chewin' tobacco to make a *"chaw,"* or **cud**.

cuss, cussed, cussin': (1) curse, to use profanity, or **cuss** *words*. He **cussed** *a blue streak*. To **cuss somebody out** is *to give 'em a good* **cussin'**. (2) a stubborn old man is a ornery old **cuss**. See *blackguard, bless*.

cussed: (cuss'-ed) accursed. Also a mild expletive. That **cuss-ed** old mule jist stubbed up.

cussedness: Do something for pure lowdown meanness.

cusswords: Profanity, especially *usin' the Lord's name in vain*.

cut: castrated (caster-ated)

cut down on or **at:** if throwin' rocks, means you let 'em fly as hard, as fast, and as clost as you can throw 'em. If shootin' a gun, means you *drawed a bead* and shot right fast. See *cut loose*.

cut loose: to start all of a sudden, jist as fast as you can.

cut your water off: (cuh-chore-water off) make you stop whatever you're a-doin'. See *put the lid on it, put paid*.

cut off: turn something off, whether you *mash a button* or turn off the switch.

cyaird: coward

cyard: card

cyarn: (kyarn) listed as "carrion" in the dictionary. It is sump'm that's dead and rotten, like what buzzards circle around. Expression: *Stinks like **cyarn***.

'cyclopedie: encyclopedia

cyore/cyored: (1) cure, remedy/cured, healed. (2) To salt down or treat meat to preserve it. My grandfather used Morton's Sugar Cure on his hams to cure and preserve them.

D

dab: a very small amount. Usually said as *"a little dab."* See *smidgin, dob, painch.* To **just dab around** is a half-hearted or feeble attempt to do something. See *lick and a promise.*

dad-blamed: a mild expletive

daft: (daift) lost their mind; *crazier'n a bat, sillier'n a dern goose.*

damp'm: dampen. We'd **damp'm** the floor down before we swept so we wouldn't stir up dust.

dang, danged, dern: synthetic swear words, to keep from jist coming right out and cussin'. Other examples: *bless-ed, consarned, confounded, cuss-ed, dern, dog-ged, dad-blamed, dad-blasted.*

dang sight: a whole lot. It's a **dang sight** better to sleep in a bed than on a pallet.

dannymite: dynamite

daresn't: dare not. I **daresn't** open my mouth (say anything) around her or she'll git mad as a wet hen. Sometimes **darren** is said instead, as: I'm **darren** to open my mouth around her.

darren: take a dare; to dare to the point of a compulsion to do something. He's just **darren** to go take that job in De-troit.

days on end: day after day for several days

dead-beat: Somebody that wont work, or *strack a lick at nuthin'.* A sorry, low-down rascal that *ain't worth the powder it'd take to blow his brains out.*

debidy: deputy, the sheriff's helper

deb'mport: (davenport) sofa, couch. Often referred to as a *settee.*

decent: Descriptive of a good woman or man, clothes that ain't too shabby, or good behavior. Anything nobody had to be ashamed of.

decked out: all dressed up in your *Sunday best, lookin' sharp.* See *diked up, dolled up.*

Decoration Day: Now called Memorial day. The last Sunday in May was a very important day. Everybody took their tools to the graveyard on Saturday, cleaned off the graves and graveyard, and put fresh flowers or crepe paper flowers on the graves so they'd look nice for Decoration Day. The whole family went and stayed all day.

deef: deaf

dern, derned: darn, darned. Substitute cusswords. See *dang.*

devil: (1) Noun. Satan; the Boogerman. An old saying: *An idle mind is the* **devil's** *workshop.* (2) Verb. To tease, or "aggervate" somebody in a playful way is to **"devil** 'em." One favorite way men had of **devilin' one another** was to *tell tales,* or lies on each other—so *outlandish* that nobody in their right mind could believe them. And if one happened to do something embarrassing, somebody'd tell it on him, and they'd *stretch it* (exaggerate as far as their imagination could go) from one tellin' to the next. Sooner or later, though, the one who started it got paid back. *What goes around comes around.* They'd begin the tale as: "I got a goodun on ol' Jake (or whoever)!"

devilish: (1) mischievous (2) aggravating.

devil-ment: (devil-mint') something *done out of pure lowdown meanness* to hurt somebody, different from just *aggervatin' 'em* or *devillin' 'em for fun.*

dickens: (1) more socially acceptable word for *hell,* or *the devil.* Examples: You scared the **dickens** out of me! *As mean as the* **dickens.** (2) Scolding; hard time. She *give him the* **dickens** for coming in late.

diddle: a baby chick

diddly-squat: the equivalent of nothing; *blank betwixt the ears.* Examples: He *don't know* **diddly-squat,** or: That *ain't worth a* **diddly-squat.**

dido, cut a dido, done a dido: (die'-dough): a dance, do a little dance; dance a jig; *cut a shine; take a fit.* Example: She **cut a dido** when she found that $50. bill.

dike, diked up: (dyke) Dress or dressed up finer than usual (usually preceded by "all"). All **diked up**. Syn: *decked out, dolled up.* When a woman is primping, she's **dikin'** *herself up.*

dis', dist, 'ist, jis', jist: Just. Also describes increments of exactness, from 'ist to *jist exackly.*

disheartenin': discouraging. It's **disheartenin'** to plant your beans twicet an' have the frost git 'em both times.

dist about: just about; almost; *pyert near*

div: (rhyme with give) dived, dove

doast: dose. Plural: **doastes** (doast'-es) as in: Two **doastes** a day. Past tense: **doasted.** He **doasted** up on cold remedy.

dob: (1) a medium amount, more than a dab. A **dob** is a wad or amount you just reach and get in, or with, your hand—like put a **dob** of lard in the flour for biscuits. See *smidgin, dab, painch.* (2) apply in a patting manner, as to **dob** salve on a sore. (3) **All dobbed up** means constipated. (4) **dobbed up:** daubed, or filled a space, as **dobbed up** the cracks in the chimney.

dog fit: For whatever reason, dogs used to take *fits,* or seizures, thought to be because they were wormy.

dolled up: fixed up purty; cleaned up good, and dressed up nice—*all* **dolled up.** See *diked up.*

done: (1) cooked enough (2) finished a bowel movement.

done and/done'n: has already, as "He's **done'n** gone." See *went and.*

done it: gone beyond what is allowed. You've done'n **done it** now!

dookey: noun or verb. Feces; a bowel movement, or to have one. Syn: *hockey*

doornail: I don't exactly know what a ***doornail*** is, other than a nail in a door, but *dead as a **doornail**,* or *stiff as a poker* means something is *stone cold dead,* or *graveyard dead.*

dope: (1) any brand of soft drink (2) somebody that *ain't got many smarts.*

double up: fold. Men like to get aholt of money they can ***double up*** and put in their pocket (*foldin' money,* or *hip pocket money*).We ***doubled up*** our clothes to put them in the clothes pack.

doughty: (doe'-tee) partially decayed wood. Old ***doughty*** stovewood *don't burn worth a flip.*

Do what? An answer meaning, "repeat that," given when the question is not understood or is beyond belief. Same as: Huh? *Come agin! What jew say? Shot who? Run that by me one more time.*

drank: (noun) drink. The liquid that you're *fixin'* to *swaller* is a ***drank***, like a ***drank*** of water. After it's *swallered,* then you've ***drunk*** it.

dramp/drampt: dreamed

drap: drop

draw a bead (on): take careful aim over a gunbarrel; ready to shoot.

drawers (drorz, one syllable)**:** underwear, or *under-drawers.* When telling somebody not to be hasty, they're told, *"Now, keep ye **drawers** on."* When a person got awful cranky, they were said to *have their **drawers** in a bind (or wad).*

dreckly, di-reckly: directly. The usual meaning, but "dreckly" means *in a little while,* or soon, as "I'll be there ***dreckly***." See *three shakes of a sheep's tail.* **Di'-reckly** means "*dist e-zackly*" (just exactly), as when you hit yourself ***di-reckly*** on your thumbnail with a hammer.

drene: drain.

driv: driven—past tense of drive. A nail ***driv*** up in the porch post. Or, He ***driv*** his car.

dropped yer candy: When you've ***dropped yer candy***, your secret's been found out, you've let a good thing go by, or made a big mistake with bad consequences. You were having a good time til you ***dropped yer candy*** *in a cowpile.*

drownd: drown; past tense is (got) **drownded.**

drugs: dregs; the settle-ment on the bottom of a liquid.

drummer: a travellin' salesman

druther: rather; would rather.

druthers: choice. If I had my ***druthers,*** I'd *druther* ride instid of walk.

duck: (1) a fowl that quacks. (2) A cigarette butt. If you was about broke, and had to be savin' with your smokin' tobacker, you took a few draws (drags, puffs) off of your cigarette and **ducked it** (extinguished the fire). Later on, you took the *duck* out of your pocket and smoked it. (3) slang word for a male urinal.

dun: Noun. A bill, or statement received in the mail, showing how much money is owed to the sender. Verb: to ask somebody for money that they owe you is to *dun* them.

Dutch oven: A fairly large flat-bottomed cast iron pot which is used in the fireplace or on a camp fire to either boil, roast or bake. Mine has 3 legs on the bottom, about an inch long, which allows the pot to set on top of live coals to heat the bottom. The lid has an outside rim to hold live coals on top of the lid in order to to heat the top of whatever food is inside, like brown the bread.

dyerr: (rhymes with err) (1) dear: The first word in a letter, as in *Dear* Mom. (2) deer: The four-legged animal that you hunt in the woods.

E

eatch: itch
eatin' table: the dining table
eb'm: even
embroadrey: embroidery
en-velop: (in'-vel-up) envelope
expectin': pregnant. See *knocked up.*
ever,. ever' last one: every, every last one, meaning all.
eyelasher: eyelash Plural is *eyelashers.*
ezackly: exactly

F

face fo'must: face foremost; forward or facing forward. See *fards.*
fainger: finger. Also, if something is said to be *made with the faingers,* it is handmade.
fallin' out: Had a *fallin' out* means they had an unreconciled disagreement and ain't friends no more.
fall pinks: chrysanthemums
fambly: family
fam'ly jewels: testicles (what it takes to get a family)
far, farplace, farboard: fire, fireplace, mantel
fard: forehead
fards: forward, *face fo'most;* opposite of *backards* .

Farris wheel: Ferris wheel

farner: foreigner; anybody who wutn't borned around here

fawg: fog

feel like some body: (equal emphasis on some and body) to not feel inferior. To feel as if you are a *ragler* person, or of some worth. See *some body.*

feller: (1) boy. He was just a little *feller.* (2) boyfriend. Her *feller* took her to the show.

fell in: started doing something. He just *fell right in* and helped us.

fell off, or fallin' off: lost, or losing weight, versus *picked up* or *pickin' up*, which means gained or gaining weight. A person who *fell off* so much that they got real skinny was said to be *"as pore as a snake."*

fer: for. Also, the pronounciation for far, as in distance—*fer* off (far away.)

fertilize: Noun. Fertilizer. We put *fertilize* in the garden.

fetch: bring, as to *fetch* me a drink of water. Also, if you sold something and got a good price, it *fetched a purty penny.*

fetch and carry: an expression meaning to wait on somebody and let them order you around all the time, *a-fetchin' and carryin' fer 'em.*

figger: figure

figger out: to come to a logical conclusion

figger up: to cipher, or calculate the total

fillin' station: a gas or service station

finegal: (fin-e'-gull) (1) manage to persuade, by fair means or foul, trickery or otherwise, as: A slick-talking salesman will *finegal* you out of your money. (2) manage to do something requiring unconventional methods of trial and error, as: I *finegaled* around til I could get a-holt of the tree trunk to climb down. (I've no idea where this word came from, and never heard it anywhere else.)

fit: (1) fought (2) seizure (3) conniption, make a big fuss. (4) Saying *take/took a fit* or have/had a **fit** can describe when somebody is either mad or glad. Example: She just *had a fit* when he came home. (She was tickled to death to see him). Or: She *had a fit* when he come home drunk. (Now, that's a whole different story).

fix: (1) verb. Repair (2) A difficult situation. Syn. a bind. He's got hisself *in a fix* now.

fixin', fixin' to: about to or getting ready to do something, as, *fixin'* to cook supper.See *aimin' to.*

fixin' up: (1) primping, gittin' *all dolled up*, puttin' on your Sunday best (2) improving something or cleaning it up, as *fixin' up* a house to move into it.

'fize: if I was (were). *'Fize* you, I'd sell that *dadgum thang!*

fizzle dust: is the description of something almost nonexistent, or as finely ground as possible, as: He ground that cornmeal into *fizzle dust.*

flabbergaisted (flabber-gyaisted): totally amazed; speechless with amazement

flapjack: cornmeal stirred up together with a little flour, salt, bakin' sodie, and enough water or milk to make a fairly thick batter, then fried like a pancake. When it gets brown on one side, it is flipped (flapped) over in the pan by holding onto the handle and tossing the *flapjack* into the air to turn it. Hot *flapjacks* is a real treat with butter and *surp* (syrup)on them. After I got grown, I heard people call them hoecakes. See *flitter.*

flare: (1) a roadside or railroad torch to show danger (2) to flame up (3) flour (4) flower

flash, flush: flesh

flashy, flushy: (1) fleshy; overweight, fat; meaty.

flat out: (1) plainly evident, as *He just flat-out lied.* (2) do with all your might, as: *He flat-out laid one on her* (kissed her).

flawg: (1)flog—how a hen scratches you and beats you with her wings if you bother her littluns. (2) give somebody a *good lickin'.*

flitter: I guess this is what *farners* call a "fritter." *Flitters* is made by stirring up flour, salt and bakin' sodie together with enough water or milk to make a batter, then fried like pancakes, only they're thicker. They're sometimes made in place of biscuits when you want some quick bread. *Flatter'n a flitter* is a term used to describe something as being very flat. See *flapjack.*

flivver: a car

floozy: a woman with a bad reputation, like one that hangs around a *beer joint* or honkytonk.

flusterated: flustered, frustrated

fly offa the handle: suddenly get very angry; lose your temper.

fodder: dried blades (leaves) of the corn plant, used for livestock food. See *corn shock.*

fool or **foolin' around with:** *Fornicatin'* with somebody.

foolish: to be very fond of. In courtin', a boy would be *plumb foolish about* a girl, meaning he liked her a lot, or was *struck on her.*

foolishness: noun. Anything that *hain't worth a dime to nobody,* whether an object or something somebody said; usually said as *"dang foolishness.".*

fool-like: (emphasis on *like*) Act foolish. *Fool-like,* I sold my best piece of land.

fo'most: (foe-must) foremost, in front, first. The calf was borned *head fo'most.*

fork: (1) To reach over and gouge a fork into food to put it on your plate, or to jab someone with a fork. He *forked* him a biscuit.

fork over: hand over, give. He *forked over* forty dollars for it.

fornicatin': Having a sexual relationship with somebody you're not married to. See *foolin' around.*

fouled up: failed to do something, or messed it up, one. He tried to fix it, but jist *fouled it up.*

foundered: To eat something until it makes you so sick you don't never want no more of that. Livestock can get *foundered* and die. May come from the word used when a ship fills with water and sinks.

fount: found

fractious: (frack'-shus) Mean-tempered; awful hard to get along with. Fretful, if a baby.

fraidy-cat: someone who's afraid of everything. What one boy calls another who won't fight him. Syn. *scaredy cat.*

Franch harp: French harp; harmonica

frash, frush: fresh. In the springtime, them *frash* greens taste awful good.

frawg: (1) frog. We don't just say *frawg*, we say whatever kind it is, like *toad frawg, tree frawg,* or *bullfrawg. If a toad frawg pees on your hands, it makes warts on them.* (2) When somebody hits you on the upper arm and makes a knot, he's *frawgged* you, and the knot is a *frawg.*

frawg hair: When something's as fine as it can be, it's said to be *as fine as frawg hair (split down the middle).*

frawg strangler: a real heavy rain. Also called *a chunk floater* or *a gully washer.*

froe: a tool used to split wood to make shingles. It was left dull on the edge so it would not cut the wood fibers, just separate them into shingles when the *froe* was struck on the top edge with a mallet. Hence the saying, *"Dull as a froe."*

frigidaire, frigidairy: (frigid-air', frigid-der'-ry) What most folks call a refrigerator, probably because one of the first ones manufactured was *Frigidaire* brand. Also called a *fridge-e-ater.*

front room: The room that people call their living room now. Back then, they had a bed in it, and a few extry chairs or nail kaigs (kegs) for comp'ny to set on. *See back room.*

fruit: cooked apples (what Yankees call "applesauce"). Dried cooked apples is *dried fruit.*

fruit cake: a cake with several thin layers sweetened with molasses. *Dried fruit* (apples) spiced with cinnamon and nutmeg was spread between the layers and over the top.

fruit jars: glass canning jars

fry'n'size: An almost full-grown chicken—just right for frying.

fudder, fudderest: farther or further, farthest

fum: from

funnybook: comic book

funnypaper: the comic strip section of the newspaper, or, "the funnies."

fur: (1) a pelt (2) far; distant. A *fur* piece means a long ways off *out yander* (yonder).

furnichure: (fern'-e-chure) furniture. See *house plunder*.

furrer, or **fur':** furrow

fuss: what you do before you start fighting...you get in a big *fuss,* or *git'n a big racket.*

'fyownto: If you want to

G

gaff: (gyaiff) a metal spur fastened to the leg of a rooster to be put into a cock fight.

gaint: gaunt

gal: girl; female. See *girl.*

galded: a worse condition than simply chapped, or "chafted." Made sore or irritated by rubbing or staying damp and sweaty, as, when you ride a horse a long ways, your thighs get *galded.*

galluses: suspenders; the straps on overalls that go over the shoulders to hold up the bib.

gamblin' stick: When a hog was slaughtered and they were ready to clean (gut) it and drain the blood from the carcass, they needed a means of hanging, or suspending it by the back legs. A short stout pole long enough to separate the legs and strong enough to support the weight of the hog was cut, then tapered and sharpened on each end. This was called a **gamblin' stick.** A slit was cut in the hog's hind legs, down next to the foot, between the main leader (tendon) and the bone. The sharpened end of the **gamblin' stick** was pushed through the slit in each leg. Then the hog could be raised and hung by pulling on the rope or chain attached to the center of the **gamblin' stick.**

gen'ly: generally, usually

genuwine: (gen-u-wine') genuine

ghostes (go-stes)**:** more than one ghost

girl or **gal:** daughter. She's Uncle Joe's *girl.* The word, *daughter,* was seldom heard. Instead of saying a *girl* was some boy's girl-friend (in today's language), they said she was his *gal.*

git: get

git around: know how to get away with something and not get into trouble. That boy knowed jist *ezackly* how to butter up his maw and *git around* her.

gitchey: get you or get your, as: "*Gitchey* britches on." But when a grown man or woman said. "*I'll gitchey,*" or "*gitchey back,*" they was dead serious, and meant that they intended to "*git even*" or "*pay you back*" for something bad you'd done to them, only they'd do *worser'n that* to you. No idle threat!

git hitched: get married. Also, *jump the broom.* See *go to Georgie.*

git into it: (git in' to it) get into an argument or a fight. They *got into it* over their property line.

git ketched: (1) be caught, as by the law, if a man (2) get pregnant, if a woman.

git onto you: reprimand, nag, scold. Syn. *growl atchey (growl at you).*

gittin' up in yers: getting on up in years; getting old

git-up: (git'-up) (1) unsuitable or odd clothing or outfit (2) ambition; desire to work or get ahead. Somebody that won't work *don't have no git-up about 'em.*

give 'em license: gave someone permission or freedom to do something, as: Just because he's kinfolks don't *give him license* to come in and take over.

give some sugar: let somebody kiss you

give their word: When mountain folks *give their word,* it's as good as a legally signed document. *A man's word is as good as his bond.* They never went back on their word, whether it was a promise or a threat. If one of them told you he was going to kill you, *you best make yeself scarce* (stay out of their sight). See *shake on it.*

glut: (1) a wooden wedge (2) overeat—*stuff yer gut.*

gnat smoke: A small bundle of rags burnt to make a smoke to repel gnats and *'skeeters.* The rags are folded and made into a roll tight enough to smoulder but not loose enough to blaze and burn up.

go see: visit. People used to *go see* one another more'n they do now.

go to Georgie: One way to propose was to say, "Let's *slip off and go to Georgie.*" To avoid the waiting period in North Carolina, a couple could go across the state line into Georgia and get married right away. They usually went to Blairsville (the closest town) to a Justice of the Peace, so they sometimes said, "Lets go to Blairsville."

goin' by the moon: many things were done according to the phase of the moon, called *goin' by the moon, goin' by the signs,* or *going by the almanac.* See *signs.*

go it: Words that were said to a child who had permission to go somewhere.

gom: make an untidy or dirty mess; usually said as "messin' and gommin'." A youngen would make a *gom* a-tryin' to cook a meal.

gone and: words added between the person and what they did. She's **gone and** done it again. See *took and, went and.*

good'n well: good and well; perfectly well. You know **good'n well** what I meant.

go on with: joke around with

goody: nutmeat; the part of something you eat (the good part).

goose: (1) (noun) a goose (fowl). To be *as dumb as a* **goose** is to be as stupid as anything or anybody can possibly get. Example: He didn't have *a bit more idy (idea) than a* **goose** what he was doing. Also, to be *as silly as a* **goose** is to be as silly as you can get. (2)(verb) To **goose** somebody is to *poke 'em (job 'em) in the ribs.* One feller would let his buddy know that he was going to tell everybody a bigun by **goosin'** him with his elbow just before he told it (like giving a wink). But don't never tell a farner about **goosin'** somebody—*that's a whole 'nother story.*

goose knobs: gooseflesh; chill bumps; cold chills

goosey: Somebody that's real ticklish is said to be **goosey.**

goozle: (goo'-zel) windpipe. When they wrung a chicken's neck, they got the chicken by the **goozle.** Also, a man's Adam's apple is called his **goozle,** and if somebody got choked, they said, *"I got sump'm hung in my* **goozle.**"

go to the house: go home.

got religion, got saved: became a Christian, *made a change,* or was *borned ag'in.*

gourd: The fruit of a gourd vine—not fit to eat, but dried for making dippers, birdhouses, etc. When somebody is inexperienced, they are said to be *as green as a* **gourd.** Somebody that ain't real smart is called a **gourd** *head.*

grabble: verb. To dig potatoes from the ground using just the hands or a small implement to rake them out without damaging the roots of the potato plant. Possibly derived from the word *grapple.* We had a big old handmade fork that we used for a **"tater grabbler."**

grannies, granny: menstrual period. *The monthly's.* She's *got her* **granny/grannies** *on.* A

granny rag was a folded piece of cloth which served the purpose of today's sanitary napkin.

granny doctor: a woman who delivers babies; midwife.

graphone, graphophone: (graf'-fone) a *talkin' machine* or record player; Syn. Victrola.

grass widder: woman who don't live with her old man.

graveyard: a cemetery is referred to as the **graveyard.** The dead is described as **graveyard** *dead,* or *stone cold dead.*

grease (greez) **your chin,** or **grease your whiskers:** Like when a man is eating meat (like from a *whistle-pig*) with his fingers, he gets grease on his chin or whiskers.

greenback: a dollar. It is referred to as a **greenback** *dollar,* but the term generally includes all paper money, which is printed in green ink on the back. When somebody says, "*I don't want your* **greenback** *dollar,*" they mean that they don't want your money for any reason—they ain't for sale.

green poultice: dollar bills, or compensation for an injury or pain a person says they have. An old Doc said, "*The only cure for a deadbeat's back is a* **green poultice.**" See *hippoed.*

grin and bear it: Accept things as they are and make the best of a given situation. *Ain't no use in cryin' over spilt milk.*

grine, grind: (rhyme with fine) groin

grined, grinded, grounded: ground. Usually said as **grined up, grinded up,** or **grounded up.**

grit: (1) verb. To grate. The tool used for **gritting** is called a **"gritter."** (2) noun. Sandy particles, like on sandpaper (3) Courage, fortitude. To endure, as to *grin and bear it.* As: It *took some* **grit** to hold still when the Doc set my arm. I had to **grit** *my teeth* to stand it (like *bite the bullet).*

grits: coarsely ground corn, cooked and eaten as a cereal or as a side dish with gravy over it, sometimes served with eggs. Contrary to the belief that **grits** are a staple in the south, I didn't know what **grits** was until I grew up. We did, however, have Cream of Wheat.

gritted: grated

gritted bread: cornbread that is baked with *gritted* (grated) *corn* in the batter.

grodge: garage

ground-squirrel: save, or hide away, usually referring to money. He **ground-squirrelled** most of his *payday* (wages). Derivation obvious.

groun'hawg: a groundhog—called a woodchuck by Yankees. We call 'em a *whistlepig.*

groun'hawg day: Old **groun'hawg day** was February 14; now it's February 2. The legend is told that *if the groundhog comes out of his hole on* **groundhog day** *and sees his shadder, they'll be six more weeks of winter.*

groun'hawg oil: *Groundhog oil* is rendered out of a groundhog, and is used for medicinal purposes. One use is to grease the chest with it to *break up the croup.*

growl, growl at: complain about, criticize, grumble, find fault with, nag or harp on somebody. His *old woman* was allus a-**growlin' at** him about something.

grub: (1)food. They had good *grub* at their camp. (2) dig hard, as in *grubbin' out* tree roots.

Guess What: A *Guess What* was the brand name of a piece of candy with a small toy or prize contained inside a paper wrapper which was twisted on each end to secure them. It was labelled: "Guess What" on the wrapper.

guts, feathers and all: The whole thing; all of it, as: He eat that pie—*guts, feathers and all.*

gyape: gape; to stare. Usually descriptive of being astonished or speechless at what you are seeing, like *standin' there like a mule a-gyaipin' at a new gate.*

gyarb: (1) a whole lot (large quantity). He raised a *gyarb* of taters in that one little patch. (2) The clothes a person is wearing, usually descriptive of mismatched, odd or outlandish clothes. Are you aimin' to wear that *gyarb* to Sunday School? See *git-up.*

gyarden: garden

gyarter: garter

gyerr: gear for a horse, mule or steer.

gyerr up a hoss: gear up a horse; put the harness and working *gear* on the horse.

H

had a time: Had a lot of trouble or difficulty with, or took a lot of effort to do something. He **had a time** a-tryin' to plow that new ground. He **had a time** a-workin' up that locust wood .

had (me/us) a time: had a good time Now, we *had us a time* while we was there.

haf, hafta: have, have to

haf-to case: a have-to case; an absolute necessity to do something or for something to be done.

haggedy: looking rough, *not up to snuff.* She looked awful *haggedy* while she had the flu.

hah you, hah yuns? How are you? How is your family? (*How are yuns?*)

haincher: handkerchief. Pronounced either *hain'cher* or *hain'-ke-cherr.*

hain't: ain't, isn't; are you not, or have you not, as: *Hain't* you got no sense atall?

haint: a ghost, sometimes called a *haint,* as: A *haint* lives in a *hainted* (haunted) house.

Haird: Howard

half-shot, half-way shot: About half drunk. *Higher'n a Georgia pine, about half lit, three sheets in the wind.* *Shot* is when they're plumb drunk, or *drunk as a dawg.*

hame: part of a harness

handle: to use a certain kind of speech, usually vulgar or profane. You ortn't to be *a-handlin' that kind of talk* in front of women and childern.

hanker, hankerin': to want or crave something. Women have a *hankerin'* for odd stuff to eat *when they're in a family way.*

handy: (1) convenient. As *handy* as a shirt pocket. An habitual liar *"just told whatever was handy."* (2) able, or has the know-how to do anything easily. He's right *handy* around the house.

hapm'd: happened

hard-shell Baptist: A strict Baptist through and through.

harr: (rhyme with car) (1) *Verb:* hire (2) *Noun:* harrow A heavy metal frame with spikes that's drug over plowed ground to break up the dirt clods. Or, *verb:* the draggin' of it.

hate, hated: regret, to be sorry. I *hate it* that their house got burnt down. In the usual meaning of the word, when they hated something or somebody, they said "despised."

have a fit: See *take a fit.*

haul off: take action. She just *hauled off* and *barked his shin.* See *upped and.*

hawg: (1)*Noun:* a hog (2) *verb:* act like a *hawg;* try to take more than your share. **Hawgish** means to make a glutton out of yerself, or try to take more than your fair share of anything; act like a *gray-eyed greedy gut,* a taunt that a kid sometimes yelled at another kid.

hawspiddle: hospital

hen a-rootin': the description of something utterly ridiculous. Example: Well, *if that don't beat a hen a-rootin'!*

het, het up: heated

hick'ry: (1) hickory, a native tree that bears hickory nuts (2) a limb or small branch (from any kind of tree) which was used to whip children was called a *hickory.* Syn. a withe See *lickin'.*

hide: (1) animal skin; leather (2) your skin. *Pokeroot tea will take the hide off of you if you get it too strong.*

hidey-hole: When kids played *whoopee hide,* one would try to find a *hidey-hole* where they couldn't be found. A bootlegger found *hidey-holes* for his bottles or jars of whiskey.

hifalutin', highfalutin': acting like you're the very cream of high society (when you ain't). Act *biggety.* When a person was actin' *hifalutin',* somebody'd usually say about them, *"They make my hin'end crave buttermilk."* See *big-head, big shot.*

hike up: to pull or raise up, as to *hike up* your britches, or *hike up* one side of something.

hin'en (hine-en'): your butt, or rear (hind) end. He said he *aimed to kick some-body's **hin'end**.*

hippin': a diaper

hippoed: (hip'-pode) when a person says or thinks they are sick or injured and there's no proof, he or she is said to be **hippoed**. See *greenback*.

his'n, her'n, their'n: (hiz'-en, hern, thern) his, hers, theirs. Some of the young-uns was **his'n**, some was **her'n**, and some was **their'n**.

hisself: himself

hissy: temper tantrum. See *take a fit*.

hit: (1) it (2) To get on with it, begin something fast, as when your Dad said, "*Hit* that cornfield."

hit bush river: git gone from here, git outta sight; vanish.

hobnails: Short nails with big thick nail heads which are driven into the bottom of heavy shoes or boots to keep them from sliding on slippery surfaces. Syn. hob-nail boots.

hockey: Noun or verb. A bowel movement, or to have one. We never heard of a **hockey** game. Sounds like a big mess (pun intended). See *dookey*.

hold with: go along with or agree with some opinion; take sides with

holler: hollow. Also means to yell out or call out to somebody.

holped: helped

honkytonk: (hawn'-ke-tawnk) A place of business that may or may not be a full-service cafe, but where beer is sold and there is music and dancing. *Decent people* don't go into one.

hooraw: (hoo'-raw)? hurrah. Cuttin' up and havin' a big time is *havin' a* **hooraw**.

house: home. People usually say they *went to the* **house,** instead of saying they went home.

house plunder: furniture and other stuff needed to set up housekeeping.

hunh-uh: No. Opposite of yes.

hum-haw: beat around the bush; say whatever comes to mind while avoiding the real issue.

humped up: All pouted up about something. **Humped up** *like a big frog*. To *stub up* and not talk to nobody or have nuthin' to do with nobody. See *mumped up*, *stub up*.

hunnert: hundred

hyerd: heard

I

ice tags: icicles

idjet, eadiet: (id'-jet, ead'-e-yet) idiot

idn't: isn't (the more genteel way to say "ain't").

idy: (i'-dee) idea, as: I got a good *idy.* Sometimes means to be thinking about, as: *I got a good idy to go down there and give him a cussin'.*

ignert: ignorant

Igolly: By golly—another cussword substitute. Also, *Igosh.*

ill: mean-tempered; quick to fly off the handle. She was as *ill* as a hornet (or as an ol' settin' hen).

I'moinna: I'm going to. *I'moinna* set down here and rest awhile.

infernal: another word used to avoid cussin'. That *infernal* woman would *drive ol' Satan to drank!*

J

'jammers: pajamas

jarfly: I think they're called a *cicada* in the *'cyclopedie.*

jasper, jaisper: another name for *feller* (fellow). I've also heard a wasp (*wasper*) referred to as a *jasper.*

jawg: jog

jawin': talking sociably. Also called *chawin' the fat, chawin' the cud, runnin' yer mouth.*

'jeet, or 'jeet yit?: Did you eat? Did you eat yet?

Jerdan: (Jer'-d'n) Jordan—the river. *We have to cross Jerdan alone when we die.*

'jew, or d'jew?: did you?

jifflin' rod: a pole or rod used for leverage

jine: join

j'int: (rhyme with pint) joint. She had arthuritis in her *j'ints.*

job: pronounced the same as the place where you work at, but it means to *jab* or *job,* like *job* a stick up in the ground, or to get a splinter *jobbed* in you. See *poke, stab, stob*

joo'ry: (jury) jewelry

jov'al: (joe'-vul) jovial. Friendly, cheerful.

juberous: dubious. Doubtful, suspicious. See *sheepish.*

Juice harp: Jew's harp. A small metal musical instrument that is held between the upper and lower front teeth. It's got a thin bent piece a-stickin' out the side of it that's plucked with the finger to make a twangin' sound.

juked: one side a little higher than the other, as: Her skirt was *juked up* in the back.

jump the broom: get married; *git hitched.* See *Go to Georgie.*

K

kaig, nailkaig: keg—a small wooden barrel. Nails used to be sold in **nailkaigs.** Lots of folks used upside-down empty **nailkaigs** to set on. They had about a half inch raised rim, or edge, and there was an expression, "*Got a ring on his hin'en* (butt)," meaning he'd *been a-settin' on a* **nailkaig.**

kainky, kainked-up: kinky, full of kinks

keer, kyerr: care

kep' to her/hisself: bashful; a little *backerds*. To **keep to ye'self** means you *druther be by yerself.*

keep it to ye'self: to not tell nobody nuthin'—keep a secret.

keep yer nose clean: *Keep your nose out of other people's business* (and it won't get bloodied).

ketch: catch.(1) A door fastener (2) deliver a baby

kewpin: (cue'-pen) coupon. Coffee **kewpins** was saved up and sent off to get a prize of some sort.

kewter to: (cue'-ter) "cater" to every whim, as to spoil a baby. She **kewtered to** it, and grabbed it up ever' time it cried. If a man *let a woman lead him around* (tell him what to do), he was **kewterin' to** her. See *fetch and carry.*

killin' snakes: To go at anything with vigor and speed. Everything she does, she *goes at it like* **killin' snakes.**

kilt: (1) killed (2) a skirt like them Scotchmens wears

kindly: (1) kind of, sort of, similar to (2) a word meaning, "Please be so kind as to," when used before a request (instead of *please).*

kinfolks: relatives

kittle: kettle

kivver: cover

knocked up: pregnant, *expectin'*, or *got ketched.* See *praignet.*

knowed: knew, known

kotex: Everybody used to call sanitary napkins **kotexes,** probably because that was the brand name of the only ones they knew about at that time.

L

laid by: After the corn had been hoed three times, it was said to be **laid by** (not hoed again).

laid in the shade: (1)finished a task. I got that patch a corn **laid in the shade**. (2) *got* **laid in the shade** meant that somebody got knocked out.

laid out: (1) camped out (2) stayed out all night (3) all fixed up in a coffin, ready for burial. See *layed out.*

laigs: (lags) legs

lamp oil: kerosene oil; oil to burn in a lamp.

lap it up: to really enjoy something, like a hound dog *laps up* his grub. And: The woman flirted with him and he really *lapped it up*.

lar: (larr) liar. Somebody that *goes out of their way to tell a lie when the truth is handier.* See *bigun.*

larpin': tastes extra special good. As: That nanner puddin' was *larpin'*. Or, as the old saw goes: *As good as snuff and not half as dusty.*

'lasses: (lais'-sez) molasses. *'Laissey sweet bread* is gingerbread with *'lasses* used for the *sweetenin'*. Molasses is spoken of as if plural—*them molasses.*

latch pin: a safety pin

laurel: To us, rhododendron is *laurel. Laurel* is called *mountain ivy.*

law: any member of law enforcement, whether city police, sheriff or deputy is "*the law.*"

law, law me, lawsy me: An exclamation. To keep from speaking God's name in vain, people said, "*Law,*" instead of "Lord."

lawg: log

lay around: stay, or hang around—doing nothing in pa'tic'lar. It's common to hear this exchange when a person is leaving somebody's home: First person, leaving: "You better jist come and go home with me." Second person: "Aah, I guess I better jist *lay around* here."

lay corpse: be prepared for burial and placed in a coffin. He **lay corpse** for two days.

layed out: A hen that's quit laying eggs is said to be *"layed out."* See *laid out.*

lay with ye: (emphasis on *with*) (1) Someone who will stick with or stay by you will *lay with ye*. To endure something to the end is *to lay with it*. (2) *stick to your ribs,* as: eggs, gravy, sausage and biscuits will *lay with ye* til dinnertime.

learnt: (1) learned (2) taught. I *learnt* my ABC's. Or, The teacher *learnt* me my ABC's. See *teached.*

learnt by heart: memorized

leather britches: green beans that have been strung up on a piece of thread, then dried.

led: lid. He was *so sleepy he had to prop up his eye***leds** *with match stems.*

leetle: little. Just a *leetle* bit.

lent: leaned. He *lent* his shovel up agin the barn. (2) loaned

let (it) alone: means don't bother, touch, or mess with it *in any shape, form or fashion.* Same as *leave it alone.*

let on like: pretend

lick and a promise: to barely begin to do something (hit it a lick), then quit (the *promise* to do better *if* there's a next time). See *strike a lick.*

lickin': a whipping (*whuppin'*) The word is used two ways—when a man won a fight, he give the other'n a **lickin',** or *whupped* him. The same word was used when a youngun got a **lickin',** or a *whipping.*

lick your calf over: you need to do something again—you didn't do a good job of it the first time.

light: the glass in a window, called a *wender* **light.**

light a shuck: Get a move on, or cause somebody else to get a move on. Example: Granny's going to **light a shuck** 'nunder your tail if you don't shake a leg. *Lit a shuck* means to take off quick—as in: *took off like Lindbergh, took off like a bat out of hades,* or, *took off like Snyder's pup.* Now, I don't know nuthin' about *Snyder's pup,* but I do know he was *takin' it two rows at a time* when he left here. He *lit a shuck,* or *run like a scalded dog.* See *run.*

light bread: storebought loaf bread. It won't *stick to yer ribs* like biscuits or cornbread will.

lightnin' bug: Yankees call 'em *fireflies.* Younguns were told to be careful, for **lightnin' bugs** *like to crawl in holes, and they'll crawl into your ears.*

lights: (1) referring tp eletrical power. We got **lights** up on the creek about 1950. An electric power bill is called a **light bill.** (2) a hog's lungs.

like as not: more than likely. **Like as not,** he stoled that chicken.

like Karo got with surp: To be inseparable. Karo is the brand name of a syrup, with the words *Karo* and *surp* used interchangeably. The saying, *I'll get with you* **like Karo got with surp** is usually said as a threat, but the meaning varies according to the context in which it is used.

like to a, like to of: almost, nearly. He **like to a** cut his thumb off.

likker: (corn) liquor made in a still. **Likker** bought from a store is called *bottled in bond.*

Lily bush: A Rose of Sharon bush

limb: (1) branch off a tree (2) term used for any kind of tree branch used to whip a youngen with

limber: limp. **Limber** *as a dishrag (or wet strang).*

line: loin

light a shuck:. Get a move on, or get somebody else to movin' on. Example: Granny's gonna **light a shuck** *'nunder your tail* if you don't *shake a leg.* (2) Take off quick, a-going somewhere, usually said as, *He took off like Lindbergh.* Or, *took off like a bat out of hell.* Or, *He took off like Snyder's pup.* (I don't know nothing about *Snyder's pup*—I just know it means he was *takin' it two rows at a time* when he left here.) See *run, running.*

liquish: licorice

lit out: Took off. See *light a shuck.* Example: He **lit out** when Granny *lit a shuck* under his tail.

little bitty: very small

littluns (lit'-luns)**:** little ones, babies

loafer: (verb) get out and go nowhere in particular. A dog that won't stay at home is a **loaferin'** dog. When a man just wants to get out away from the house, he *goes a-loaferin'.* See *strollop.*

lollygaggin': Loaferin' about, not working at or doing anything worthwhile. See *piddlin', strollop.*

longhandles: (called a pair, or set) long-sleeved, knit men's winter underwear. There were two kinds. One kind was two-piece, and the bottoms was called *drawers.* The one-pieced kind was called a *"union suit."* See *union suit.*

longways: lengthwise. Opposite of crossways (crosswise).

long-winded: description of a preacher that don't know when it's time to *go to the house.*

look: to sort through and examine for unwanted material, as to **look** dry beans or to **look** somebody's head for lice.

look down on: To consider yourself better than someone else. People **looked down on** him because he was from Mud Town. See *above.*

loudmouth: all talk and no action (or the means to prove what you said is true).

lope, lopin': walk like you was *walkin' in plowed ground,* only faster.

love offerin': a voluntary donation of money. Instead of paying a preacher a salary, they *passed the hat* in church every Sunday and took up a **love offerin'** for him.

low-down: good-for-nothing; description of a dead-beat. To call a man a **low-down** *dirty dog* is about as bad as you can say without cussin' him.

lower the boom: To turn loose and give 'em punishment (or whatever they've got a-comin'). As: She put up with his mouth as long as she could, then she **lowered the boom** on him.

low-rate: (verb) belittle. Example: She **low-rated** him right there in front of ever'body.

luf'ta: love to, loved to. She **luf'ta** make quilts.

luneum: aluminum

M

mad: angry. There are several descriptive phrases: *Got yer tail in a crack; somebody stepped on your tail; you throwed a shoe (as a horse); Got yer bloomers (or drawers) in a wad; all clouded up like a thunderstorm.* And dozens more. Also: **mad** *as a wet hen,* **mad** *as a bull,* **mad** *as the dickens,* **mad** *enough to a-kilt somebody.*

made tracks: got gone

mad fit: temper tantrum Telling somebody to calm down was said as:*"Don't git ye bowels in a uproar."* Or: *"Pull yer drawers outta yer crack,."* etc. See *conniption, crabbed, drawers, mad.*

make do: to get by with what you've got. *Make do or do without.*

make yer brags: Go around bragging about what all you're going to do (or think you can do).

make/made out like: pretend, pretended, as, He **made out like** he was sick to get to stay home.

make up: to mix ingredients to make up biscuits or cornbread. She knowed how to **make up** biscuits that *tasted so good yer tongue'd beat yer brains out.*

mammy: mother, mommy, your maw (ma). Sometimes called "Mam." *Your* **mammy** *and your pappy* is your mother and father.

marked: Abnormal marking or deformity in a newborn baby. *If a woman gets bad scared or real upset about something while she's expectin', the baby might be* **marked** *as a result.*

marred: (1) mired, as to have your car **marred up** in the mud.

mash: (1) ground up, sprouted corn used at the stillhouse to make corn likker (2) cornmeal and malt soaked in water and used to make stillhouse beer (3) press or push, as to **mash** a button to turn something on or off (4) what somebody does to your nose if you poke it into their business.

mast: (maist) naturally growing food in the wild for animals and birds to feed on, as acorns, hickory nuts, berries, etc.

maters: tomaters, tomatoes

matterss: (mat'-terse) mattress

mawk: mock, make fun of. Them smart-aleck Yankees tries to **mawk** us a-talkin', but they can't come clost to sayin' nuthin' like it ort to be said.

Mayday: The first day of May. Children celebrated it at school as the coming of spring. A tall Maypole was erected and they danced and sang around it.

meanness: (1) a character trait—plain ol' mean or bad-tempered, as: He whupped his younguns out of *pure lowdown* **meanness.** Or: That youngun's just full of **meanness.** (2) devil-ment. To do something to aggervate somebody is to do it for devil-ment or **meanness**. (3) *Tastin' forbidden fruit,* as when a boy and girl slips off together, they're liable to git into **meanness.**

meddle with: see *mess with.*

meetin': What we call a church service, home Bible study or a *prayer* **meetin'.**

meller: get more ripe and softer, like an apple or cantaloupe. There's also a threat, said as: "I'll **meller** *yer head* fer ye." *Mellerin' yer head* usually meant rubbin' it real hard with the knuckles, but could be a lot worse.

melt: a hog spleen

merr, merra, merrer: mirror; *a lookin' glass*

mess: (1) enough of some food to make a meal for ever how many you have to feed, as pickin' *a* **mess** of *poke sallet.* The quantity you have may be described as *a little* **mess** which is *a spoonful all around,* a **mess,** *a big* **mess** (more'n a-plenty), or *a whole* **mess** *(a big bait).* (2) something very untidy or dirty. See *mess (in or on).*

mess about: do nothing in particular—do this awhile, then do that awhile. See *piddle.*

mess around: (1) see *piddle* (2) two-time, or cheat on your spouse. See *fool around.*

mess (in or on): Have a bowel movement. A baby is said to **mess** *in* its diaper, as opposed to *wettin'* its diaper. To **mess** *on yourself,* or **mess** *in* your *britches* means you've had a acci-dent.

mess, the whole: every bit, or all of it

mess with: (1) to meddle with or bother something that's none of your business. (2) do something to make somebody mad (angry), as "Don't **mess** *with* me or you're liable to wish you hatn't."

messed up: (1) ruint (rurnt) (2) not right in the head (mentally ill), said as: *"His head's all* **messed up.***"*

might nigh, mightnear: close, approximate. It was **might nigh** dark when he left here. Same as **mighty nigh** or *pyert near.*

mighty pore: see *pore*

milk: (Pronounced "me'-oke") milk.

mind: (1) obey (2) **mind,** or take care of a baby (3) *got a good* **mind** *to* means you are strongly inclined or intend to do something.

Miz, Mizrus, Mistrus: Mrs.

monthly's: When a woman was having her menses, she was having *the* **monthly's.** See *grannies.*

moonin': When a boy or girl thinks they're in love and just sets around thinking of their sweetheart, they're said to be *"settin' around a-***moonin'.***"*

mouses: more than one mouse

movin' pichures, movin' pitchure show: movies. Commonly said as *"goin' to the show."*

mumped up: all huffed up and pouting about something. See *humped up.*

munts: months

mushmillen: a muskmelon. We called cantaloupes *mushmillens,* too.

mushrat: muskrat

N

naistness: nastiness—not being clean or sanitary. It also means the thing or things that are nasty, or filthy dirty. As: The floor was plumb *kivvered up with naistness.* See *cleanness.*

Nannyhaley, or Nantyhaley: (Nan-ne-hay'-lee) Nantahala. Indian word meaning "Land of the noonday sun." You go up Jun'lusky Creek acrost the mountain *torge* Kyle and Aquone to get there.

narr: narrow

nary, nary'n: (ner'-rey) not one, not a one. As: They wudn't *nary* one left. See *ary, ary'n.*

nary nother'n: (ner'-rey nuh'-thern) not another one, not any more. As: You won't find *nary nother'n* like that'n.

necked, neckedness: (neck'-ed) naked, nakedness. *As necked (naked) as a jaybird.* A person's genitals (*private parts, privates*) is called **neckedness** (a noun), as: Don't show *your neckedness.*

neenta: need not to. You *neenta* deny it; I seen you do it.

nest egg: an egg or an artificial egg that is marked, and left in the nest when the fresh eggs are gathered. Marking the egg to be left in the nest ensures that you will not get a bad egg. If all the eggs are taken (*robbin' the nest*), the hen will leave and find another place to nest.

nestes: nests, more than one nest

never: didn't. "He *never* done it." (didn't do it)

new ground: land that has never been plowed before.

Newnited States: United States.

nigh, might nigh, right nigh, well nigh, dang nigh, purt' nigh: approximately, close to, near. It was *gittin' well nigh* onto dinner time. The spring was *right nigh* the house. That horse *dang nigh* kilt him. The gas tank was *purt' nigh* empty. See *pyert near.*

nit pick: Probably derived from having to closely scrutinize a person's head in order to find all the nits on it when they had lice. To take something apart, physically or mentally, and scrutinize it in minute detail, whether it be an object or something said. A person who habitually does this is called a **nitpicker.** Example: Every time she said anything, he began to cross-examine her, so she just didn't say anything in order to avoid his **nitpickin'.**

noggin: your head. *Use yer **noggin** and figger it out.*

now: A word said to draw attention, or announce that something important was going to be, or had been said. The speaker usually paused after the word. Example: ***Now***—I'm telling you the truth. Or, I'm telling you the truth, ***now.*** It's sometimes used at the beginning or end of a sentence, with no definite meaning, as: ***Now,*** what's he up to? Or: ***Now*** look what you done!

nubbin': immature or small ear of corn. Used for cattle or hog feed.

nuss: hold a baby or someone on the lap

'nunder: under, in under

nuthin', nuttin': nothing

O

oats: what we call oatmeal. When we fed the hoss ***oats,*** it made him frisky, so I guess that's what folks meant when they said of a frisky man, "*He's feelin' his **oats.**"*

obliged: (1) thankful. Instead of saying, "Thank you," a man sometimes said, "*Much **obliged.**"* (2) feel obligated to *pay back* someone in return for something they did for you. See *beholden.*

of course/a'course/'course: A term used when futher explanation is added to a statement, said as, *'**course, a'course:*** of course. As: I never seen him, but ***a'course*** I wutn't a-lookin' for him. The cow didn't come—***course,*** I never called her, neither.

Ol': descriptive word put in front of a pet's name, as ***Ol'*** Rover. It was put in front of a person's name to indicate a buddy, or when telling something funny about ***Ol'*** John, or whoever. Also indicates something or someone is dear to them, as this ***ol'*** house, or my ***ol'*** Granny.

ol' lady, ol' woman: wife; his woman

ol' man: husband; her man

oosh, ooshey: It's awful cold!

op'm: open

one a-tother: one or the other

oncet: (wonst) once. ***Oncet*** is half as many times as *twicet.*

o'nery (oh'-nry), **orn'ry:** ornery, stubborn. Examples: *As **orn'ry** as a mule. He's so **orn'ry** that if he was to fall in the river, he'd float upstream.*

ort, ort to of: ought, ought to have, or should have

ortn't, ort not to of: should not have

ouchander: out yonder

ou'fenunder: out from (in) under. The dogs run **ou'fenunder** the porch a-barkin'. A snake crawled **ou'fenunder** that rock.

ourselfs: ourselves

outdoors, go outdoors: (1) outside; go outside (2) the toilet; using the toilet. *"I've got to* **go outdoors***"* was the term used when a person needed to use the toilet. ***Goin' outdoors,*** or ***went outdoors*** was the act of using the toilet. A person could get scared so bad he might *"**go outdoors**" in his britches.* Another term was *"doin' your business."*

outgoin': friendly, makes friends easily; extroverted personality.

out of the way: (1) descriptive of vulgar language, as talking **out of the way** in front of women and children. (2) not convenient (3) **go out of the/his way:** make any effort to do something. Example: He won't *go* **out of his way** to help nobody.

outin': outing, flannel fabric

overhalls: overalls—the kind with galluses

overhall britches, overhall pants: ones made from denim fabric

overhall jumper: denim coat or jacket. They had metal buttons.

P

pack: a designated place where things were kept, as a *clothes* **pack** or a *quilt* **pack.**

pack it off on: Lay the blame on. They **packed it off on** Tom a-bein' the baby's daddy.

pag: peg

painch: (1) pinch, the usual meaning, like when you **painch** up some skin betwixt your fainger and thumb (2) a very small amount. See *dob, dab, smidgin.*

painter: a panther

pallet: a quilt or padding put on the floor to sleep on when all the beds is full.

pappy: daddy, father, papa, pap, pappy, or your paw (pa). Also said as "poppy."

parafeen: paraffin wax. Some uses: To seal jelly in jars, to dip crepe paper flowers in to waterproof 'em, to rub on the sole plate of an iron to make it slide good.

pare: power

parterge: (par'terj) partridge…a ruffed grouse, or what we call a pheasant.

passel: (another name for parcel?) a *whole bunch, a remption, slew, or sled load* of people or things.

patch: (1) a small piece of fabric sewn over a hole in a garment to repair it (2) a small parcel or plot of ground, such as a *tater* **patch.**

pa'tickler, pa'tickly: particular, particularly. Somebody that's **pa'tickler** is a hard to please person.

payday: Noun: wages. I got my **payday** today and it's already spent.

peckerwood: what we call a woodpecker

peddler: (1) somebody that travels around a-selling stuff (2) somebody that goes around spreadin' gossip, true or untrue (*a-peddlin' tales on people*). See *tattle-tale.*

pernounce: pronounce. I now **pernounce** you man and wife.

pert near: See *pyert near.*

petticoat: a woman's undergarment, or slip. *In her petticoat tail* means that's all she has on.

pheasant: We call a ruffed grouse a **pheasant** or a partridge (*parterge*), one.

pianner: (pee-an'-ner) piano

pickin' up: gaining weight, opposite of "fallin' off."

pick: (1) pluck off the feathers, as to **pick** a chicken. (2) play, as to **pick** a guitar or banjo. (3) a tool to *bust up* rocks (4) a tool to *bust up* ice.

pick at or **pick on:** to cruelly tease

pickayunish: (peek-a-yune'-ish) very particular; discriminating. If a youngun got sick and wouldn't eat but certain things, it was said to be **pickayunish** *about its eatin'.*

piddle: not actually working, just puttering around—or pretending to work at nothing specific.

piddlin': of very little value, as, "I got a **piddlin'** little pile of taters out of the whole garden."

piece: (1) Verb. To sew pieces of fabric together to make a quilt top. She **pieced** a quilt. (2) When washing clothes, any article of clothing is called a **piece.** (3) Measure of distance, as: He walked a right smart **piece** (a pretty good **piece,** or a right far **piece).** Or: It was just a little **piece** from the house to the barn.

pietted, pieded: (pie'-did) spotted. Probably a derivative of *pied.*

piles: hemorrhoids

pilfer: usually means to *swipe* (steal) little ol' stuff that ain't worth much, but also means to slip around and *riffle* (prowl) through somebody else's stuff to see if there's anything worth stealing.

pillin's: peelings. We fed our tater **pillin's** to the hog.

p'int blank: (pint blank) eyeball to eyeball, as, I looked him **p'int blank** in the face. Also describes confronting a problem—to look **p'int blank** at it.

pitcher: (1) pitcher (2) picture

pity-sakes, take or **have pity sakes:** sympathy; feel sorry for, have compassion, or *take pity on 'em.* He *took pity sakes* on the pore ol' starvin' dog.

pizen (pie'-zen)**:** poison

plague: aggravate, be a bother, or burdensome. As: They've got enough troubles of their own to *plague* 'em without you addin' yours to 'em.

plain talk: Say it just like it is without *beatin' around the bush. Plain talk is easy understood.*

plars: pliers, as in *"wahr plars"* (wire pliers).

play/played hob with: ruin/ruined; tore something up; done mischief to. (a hob is an elf or goblin).

play purty: Any toy is a *play purty.* We used to make our own *play purties.*

p'like: play like, usually said by children, as: Let's *p'like* we're Injuns.

plumb (plum)**:** completely; very. The bucket was *plumb* full. That gal was *plumb* purty.

plunder: (1) Noun: "stuff." Household items, goods or furniture. See *house plunder* (2) go through somebody's stuff and take what you want, like Sherman did on his march through Georgia.

poke: paper bag, or small cloth sack. (2) prod, as to *poke* somebody in the ribs (3) a wild green, known as *poke* sallet. *A pig in a poke* means not knowing what something is (the pig is hidden).

pokin' arn: a poker, like you use in the fireplace.

polecat: a skunk. They ain't nuthin that stinks as bad as *a polecat.*

politely, p'litely: to be up front or confrontational, as: She *politely* walked right up to him and asked him what his business was. Or, "I *politely* told him to mind his own business."

pone: farners say we say, "*pone,*" or "corn pone," but I never heard the word til I was grown. We call it *a cake of corn bread* or a *corn dodger.*

ponned: To make a small pond, as: We *ponned* up the creek and made us a swimmin' hole.

pore: (1) poor, as in *"Pore as a church mouse."* (2) thin and bony; *"Pore as a snake."* **Mighty pore** means not very good. *He was a mighty pore excuse for a man.*

pore house: A place or home for penniless, homeless people. Also called *the county home* or *the county porehouse.*

porely: feelin' awful bad, *sick as a dawg.* See *puny.*

pore-mouth: When somebody come around a-*poor-mouthin',* they was puttin' on like they ditn't have much of nothin' in order to get sympathy or get somethin' give to 'em for nuthin', one.

Post Toasties: cornflakes (any brand).

potlicker: a hound dog

pot likker: (liquor) the flavorful liquid in the pot where you cook vegetables, greens, cabbage, etc. The way to eat it is to crumble up a chunk of cornbread in a bowl or on a plate, then pour enough *pot likker* over it to make the bread good and soupy, and *sprankle* it good with black pepper.

praignet: pregnant; *knocked up*, or *expectin'*. They *got ketched.*

preachin': The part of the church service following Sunday School. Modern terminology is "Worship Service."

present: a gift. We never call it a gift, we call it a *present.*

privates: male or female reproductive organs. See *fam'ly jewels.*

prize: pry. She had to *prize* the lid off the jar.

prize fight: A boxing match. The participants are *prize fighters.*

proper: correct, as in the usual meaning, but we mean it as referring to the actions and speech of people who are better educated or more well-mannered than us. They talk and act *proper.*

proposition: when a boy or man with ulterior motives asks a girl to slip off with him, he has *propositioned* her. See *slip off.*

proud: (1) to have self-respect and dignity; to have pride (2) pleased, glad, as: I'm *proud* to be an American. I'm mighty *proud* you come to see me. Also, (3) if something was overpriced, it was said of the seller, "He's *mighty proud* of his coffee (lard, sugar, etc.)."

prowl: to look at, or *prowl* around in things that *ain't none of yer business*, like go to somebody's house and go *a-pilferin'* through rooms, drawers and containers without permission. Or, you might go *prowlin' around* out behind the barn, in the corn crib, canhouse and other places when you think they don't know about it. This is one thing that's liable to *git you a load of buckshot in yer hin'-en* if you get caught at it.

puke: throw up, *vomick*, get sick on, or to, your stomach. An old expression: *It'd puke a buzzard off a gut wagon.*

pulley bone: The wishbone from the breast of a fowl. The *pulley bone* is prized for foretelling luck. A person catches hold of a prong on one side of the *pulley bone,* and another person holds onto the other prong, and they pull until one prong breaks off (probably where it got its name). The person who gets the short piece will have bad luck, the other, good luck. The whole bone is carried for good luck.

pull the wool over, put one over on: (1) deceive (2) to trick successfully. It's usually purty easy for a woman to *pull the wool over* a man's eyes.

pummies: pulp; if making juice, *pummies* is the pulpy part of the berries or fruit left after the liquid is drained from them.

puncher: puncture. A hole in the inner tube of a tire (or, casin') causing a *flat tar* (flat tire). People used to get a *puncher* just about every time they went somewhere. They carried a *puncher kit* which they used to glue a patch over the hole in the tube.

punkin: Pumpkin. Girls are warned, *"He'll promise you the moon and give you a punkin.* The description of a two-faced person is: *They've got a face like a punkin—one for whoever's looking at 'em from any side.*

puny: (1) feelin' bad or porely (poorly). (2) runty, as: That's a mighty *puny* lookin' pig. (3) a pitiful small amount, as: That's a *puny* little mess a beans.

purchase: get a good hold on. If he got a *purchase* on it, it wudn't a-goin' nowhere.

purt near: See *pyert near.*

purty: (1) pretty. *As purty as a speckled pup under a red wagon. **Right purty*** was a little more *purty* than just *purty,* getting close to being *real purty,* or *plumb purty.* (2) a *play purty* is a toy (3) *be purty:* what we were told to do when they wanted us on our best manners and best behavior, as in church: "Set there and *be purty,* now." Opposite of "*being ugly,*" or misbehaving. (4) A descriptive term used for measuring degree—somewhere in the middle between *fair* and *very.* If food was *purty good,* it was fairly good, but less than *extry good. **A purty good piece*** or *a purty good ways off* was a *right smart* distance away.

put-down: to demean, slander, or low-rate somebody; *put them down* to a low level of respect.

put on: (1) to get to cooking, as to *put on* supper (2) pretend, pretended. He *put on like* he was sick to get out of going to school. Or, if somebody showed a different side of theirself than what they really was, it was a *put-on.*

put up: (1) lay out your money on a bet; do what you promised. A common expression: "*Put up or shut up.*" (2) put something away for safekeeping. (3) to can, as to *put up* tomatoes.

put up with: to tolerate, as, "she *put up with* his meanness for forty years."

put the lid (led) on it: closed it up; put a stop to it. See *put paid, quietus, turned the damper down.*

pyert: pert, or peart; looking good; looking lively, alert. A girl **pyertened up** when she seen her feller a-coming.

pyert or pert near or **pert nigh:** *purty* + near; purty close to, about the same; the same meaning as "*might nigh.*" That boy is **pyert near** as tall as his pappy, and he's *might nigh* six foot.

pyore: pure

Q

quare: (quair) (1) not ordinary or normal; strange, queer. To be mentally ill is to be *quare.* To *feel quare,* when speaking of one's health, means that something just doesn't feel quite right. See *crazy.*

quart: is pronounced without the *U*: Said as "cort." A *corter* is a quarter.

quietus: (kwi-e'-tus) To *put the quietus on it* means to tone down or stop something. A teacher coming into a disruptive room full of kids would *put the quietus* on them. See *put paid.*

quilt pack: The place in the house where folded quilts are stacked and stored.

quirled, quiled: (kwirled, kwiled) curled or twined; coiled. A bean vine was *quirled* around the cornstalk. A big snake was *quiled* up 'nunder that rock.

quittat: Quit that!

R

rabbit feet: *to get rabbit feet* is to *get boogered* and run like a rabbit or to back out of a deal. As: He was aimin' to ask her to marry him, but he got **rabbit feet.** (2) the left hind foot of a rabbit is supposed to be a good luck charm when worn or carried on the person. See *boogered.*

racket: (1) any kind of loud noise or sound (2) fuss, verbal fight. He come home and started trying to *raise a racket* with her.

ragler: regular. To say a man is *a ragler feller* means that he's *a purty good feller…*

railin': *having a fit* about something; **rantin' and a-railin'** (or ravin'), *carryin' on,* **raise (or raisin') cane (? Cain):** throw a fit, verbally attack. Same as raise the devil, raise the dickens, raise sand, raise a ruckus (roo'-kus). See *carryin' on, railin'.*

raisin': the manner in which you were reared, or raised. *Don't try to git above yer raisin'.*

rake out, rakin' out: When you severely reprimand (*rake out*) somebody, you are giving them a *rakin' out.* Today, people call it a chewin' out.

ramp: an edible, pungent, native woodland bulbous plant which has an odor similar to garlic. The bulb, or underground part looks like a young onion, but has broad, flat edible leaves.

ranch: (1) wrench (2) rinse, like to *ranch* the soap out of your clothes.

rank: strong, pungent, terribly bad odor. Example: Them sweaty socks smelt *rank* a-hangin' in front of the fire. Or: Ramps smell awful **rank** on your breath after you eat 'em.

rantin': see railin'

rared: reared; raised. Examples: His horse **rared up**. He **rared back** his fist like he was going to hit him. The snake **rared up** his head.

rarin': anxious. He was **rarin'** to go.

reckin: reckon

recolleck: recollect, remember

redeye gravy: When meat is fried, there are small browned bits stuck to the pan. While the pan is hot, some coffee is poured in, and the boiling loosens the bits, incorporating them into the liquid. *This is **redeye gravy**.* See *sawmill gravy.*

red light: Any traffic light is called a **red light.**

remption: a *whole lot, a whole mess,* or large quantity of something. Same as a *slew, passel,* or *sled load.*

rest easy: relax, settle down. To **rest easy** *in your mind* means that you are comfortable with a decision, event, or something that had made you uneasy before.

retch, retched: (1) tried to throw up (2) reached

rich pine: a portion of pine wood with a heavy accumulation of resin, usually close to a knot. It can be set on fire with a match, and, other than lamp oil, is the best thing available to start a fire.

ridin' the saw, ridin' the handle: A crosscut saw has a handle on each end, requiring two people to use it. When one person kinda leans on his handle, they're said to be **ridin' the saw.** This makes it mighty hard on the other feller to pull it to him.

riffle: (riff'-ful) to rummage through somebody else's stuff. Probably comes from the verb, rifle, which means "to ransack." See *pilfer, prowl.*

right off the bat: right away; at once; at first opportunity.

right smart: a *whole lot*; a goodly amount or quantity. Opposite of a *piddlin'* amount.

rile: presumed to be *roil.* (1) To make muddy or cloudy by stirring up mud or sediment from the bottom. (2) to make or get angry, as: *get all **riled** up* about it.

rime: rind; peeling

riz: rose, arose. The bread **riz** good. He **riz up** out of the bed.

roas'in ears: (roce'-in-yers) roasting ears; mature ears of corn with the kernels still soft and juicy.

roastes (roast'-es)**:** (1) more than one roast (2) cook by roasting He **roastes** taters in the ashes.

roostes: (1) more than one roost (2) roosts. The chickens **roostes** up in them big pine trees.

rosum: (raw'-zum) resin, rosin. They gathered *pine rosum* to make salve. Another kind of *rosum* is the kind a fiddler uses when he *rosums* up his bow.

rounder: somebody that likes to party and don't take things serious; likes to laugh and have fun. Also called a *corker, a caution, or a catbird.*

rowed up: placed in a row or in a line. As: He *rowed up* some tin cans to use for targets.

rub their nose in it: find a way to further humiliate someone after they have already been humiliated. Also, when a child wet the bed, somebody, usually their mother, *rubbed their nose in it.*

ruck: raked. He *ruck* some hot coals out of the fire.

ruckus (roo-kus): (1) big fuss or fight; (2) clatter; loud noise or *racket*

rulin' days: It is said that what the weather is like on each of the first 12 days of January rules, or foretells what the weather will be like for each of the 12 months of the coming year.

rummage through: To look through items to see what you can find. See *riffle.*

run: (1) In stillhouse terms, what they made at one time was *a run* of likker. The act of making it was called *runnin' it off.* (2) ran; the act of running. Descriptive terms (past tense): *lit out in a run; run like a deer, fox,* or *scared rabbit; run like a scared haint; run like the devil; take it two rows at a time.*

run 'n go: To back up to get a good start and gain momentum as you run. For instance, if somebody was to try to jump over a fence or high bar, he'd back up and take a **run 'n go** at it.

run your mouth, run off at the mouth: verbal diarrhea; told something that should not have been told, or *spoke out of turn.*

rurn, rurnt: (say *urn* with a *R* in front) ruin, ruined.

S

sack time: bed time. I am assuming this came from a remark the old folks used to make. When it got bedtime, one of them would say, "Well, it's time all honest folks was in bed and the rogues had their sack."

sair, sare: sour. *So sair it set your teeth on adge* (edge). *So sair hit'd make a pig squeal.*

sallet: some folks think we're saying *salad,* but we ain't. *Sallet* is cooked greens, like poke *sallet,* sprang *sallet,* etc.

salt shake: salt shaker

sang: sing, present tense. As: Listen to the birds *sang.* Past tense is *sung.* She sung like a bird.

'sang: ginseng

sangers: the choir, or people a-*sangin'* songs.

sangin' leader: the choir director

saplin': A young, supple tree. A youngun that's growing fast is said to be *growin' like a saplin'.*

sass: (saiss) talk, or talk back to someone with disrespect. Don't never **sass** yer mammy.

Sassyfack: Sassafras. **Sassyfack** tea is made from the root bark.

savin' with: To be frugal with something, as: We was **savin' with** lamp oil.

saw: noun. An old *sayin';* proverb. See *sayin'.*

sawgy: soggy. The ground's too **sawgy** to plow now.

sawmill gravy: Meat is fried, leaving hot grease and browned bits in the pan. Flour is stirred into the fat, then water or milk is added until the **sawmill gravy** is the desired thickness.

Say? (pronounced sigh'-e) When someone was asked a question and didn't answer, and the questioner (usually a parent) was determined to get an answer, they repeated, *"Say?"* in an intimidating, demanding tone of voice until they got a response. (An exclamation point might be more suitable to follow the word.)

sayin': (noun) something said that is passed down from one gereration to another, as a proverb, sage advice, omen or forecast. *An old saw is the same thang as an old* **sayin'.**

sca'ce, skyerce: (pronounced both ways: scase or skyerce) (1) scarce, *hard to come by* (obtain). *"As* **skyerce** *as hen's teeth."* (2) *To make yourself* **scarce** meant to stay out of sight.

scald: to pour boiling water over, or dip something in it. A chicken is **scalded** so the feathers can easily be pulled off. A hog is **scalded** after butchering to make it easy to scrape off the hair. Also, articles—like clothing or dishes, were **scalded** to sanitize them. An old expression: *Run like a* **scalded** *dog.*

scarch: scorch

scared: (skyerred) Sometimes pronounced *"a-scairt."* Syn. *Afeared,* meaning afraid, timid. Descriptive terms: **Scared spitless:** a nicer way of saying it than if you changed the second letter in the second word. Or saying something **scared** *the spit out of* (me, you, them, it). **Scared witless.** *Scared the water out of, scared the livin' water (or spit) out of;* so **scared** (I, you,he,she) *was shakin' like a dog a-spittin' a peach seed.* The usual thing said was **scared** *to death* or **scared** *half to death.* **Scared my mule:** (Think about this one a minute.)

scare up: forage around to find what you need to do something with. Examples: I better go **scare up** some supper. Or, I'll see if I can **scare up** enough boards to make some hen nests.

schoolhousin': (school'-how-zin) gittin' or got an education. My grandpa never got much *schoolhousin'*.

scorpin: (score'-pen) not really a scorpion, but *scorpin* is what we called them little *blue-tailed lizards. Them blue-tailed 'uns is poison, and will kill a cat or make it awful sick if it eats one.*

scotch: noun An object used to keep something from moving, as a rock placed behind a car wheel is used for a *scotch* to keep it from rolling, as: He *scotched* the wheel with a rock.

screak, screech: To squeak, or creak; the sound made by something that needs oiling, like a *screakin'* barn door.

scrooch: get close to; huddle together. *Scrooch up* together to keep warm; *scrooch down* to hide or not be so obvious. On a cold winter night, we *scrooched down* inunder the quilts.

scrooch owl: a screech owl—different from a *"hoot owl,"* or *"hooty owl."*

scrouge: pack closely together. Ten of us youngens was *scrouged* up together in two beds.

scutter: rascal (man or beast)

see'd: saw, seen. As, I **see'd** it with my own eyes.

seek: (seek) (1) Sic or sick. Give a command to a dog to attack or chase. Examples: He come out of the house and told the boy to *seek* the dogs on the bear. (2) To urge. The other boys *seeked him on (or agged him on)* to get him to fight the newcomer.

sent off: got admitted to a mental institution.

serenate: (sir'-en-ate) probably derived from the word, *serenade*. There was once an old mountain custom to *serenate* a new neighbor to welcome them into the community. The first night they moved in, a bunch of neighbors got together and waited until the lamp went out. Then, in the dark, they sneaked quietly into the yard and surrounded the house. At a prearranged signal, everybody cut loose to screamin' and hollerin' and makin' all the racket they could make. Some beat on a bucket, some rung cowbells, some raked a stick acrost a rub-board—just using whatever they could find to make a racket with. The new family got up, lit the lamp, opened the door, and everybody went inside and visited awhile. It was expected the first night, but after that, you better not be caught a-sneakin' around nobody's house after dark, or you might lose some tail feathers from a load of buck shot.

set: When a hen *sets*, she sits on a nest of eggs to keep them warm, or incubate them.

settee: (set'-tee) couch, sofa, davenport

settin': sitting, as in **settin'** down. Also whatever number of eggs are put in a nest for the hen to set on, or incubate, is called **a settin' of eggs.**

settin' hen: A hen that's sitting on top of, or incubating a *settin' of eggs* until they hatch. If you get too close, she'll peck the blood out of you, hence the term, *as ill as an ol' settin' hen.*

settle-ment: (set-ul-ment') community

set up housekeepin': When a couple got married and went to live in their own place, they were said to *"set up housekeepin'.* Even a proposal sometimes was made by the boy asking the girl if she wanted to *set up housekeepin'.*

set where you're put: When we were younguns, we were *set* down and expected to stay set down in the exact place where we was put and told to *set where you're put.*

sev'al: several

shadder: shadow

shake a leg: get to moving quick. See *light a shuck.*

shake on it: shake hands on a transaction. Mountain folks set great store by their word, and even borrowed money at the bank on a handshake. If they *shook on it,* it was as good as a surety bond or signed contract. Quote: *Let your word be as good as your bond.* See *give their word*

shaller: shallow

shank's mare: when you walked somewhere, you *rode shank's mare.*

shape-notes: music written by using the different shapes of the notes instead of round notes.

shape-note sangin': when the names of the shaped notes are sung instead of the words in a song.

share down on: do something as forcefully as possible. For instance, if one youngun *shared down* on the other'n with his teeth, he bit the blood out of him. And, if you want to tighten a bolt real good, you have to *share down on* that wrench.

sharp'm: sharpen

shed of: (or shet of) get rid of, one way or another, as: He got *shed of* that old mule.

sheepish: (1) looking guilty, embarrassed. (2) being dubious or suspicious of something, as: *It looks kinda sheepish to me.*

Sherf: (shurf) Sheriff

shet: shut. Keep your mouth *shet or git it shet for you.*

shinny: come down or move easily, as, to *shinny* on down a tree.

Shivalay: Chevrolet

shock: Noun. Stalks of corn grouped together and stood upright into a cone shape are called a ***shock of corn.***

shoe last: a piece of cast iron shaped like a shoe sole on which shoes are mended. It fits over the top of an upright flat iron post that is fastened down so that both hands can be used.

shoo mossey: (mah'-cee) an expression meaning: That stinks! or, Something stinks! For instance, when a woman unpinned a diaper and found a mess, she'd say, ***"Shoo, mossey!"***

shore 'nuff: sure enough!

short end of the stick: sorta like drawing straws to see who loses. The one *with the **short end of the stick*** is the one who got the bad news, or lost.

shorts: *("hog shorts")* ground grain, such as wheat, used for animal feed.

shot: (1) a little drink of whiskey (2) plumb drunk; inebriated; *so drunk he couldn't hit the ground with his hat. About **half-shot** is about half drunk.*

Shot who?: an expression said when asking someone to repeat what they just said.

show: picture show; the movies.

showin': effort, or the result of effort. Example: He made a good ***showin'*** for his day's work. (You could easily see what he had accomplished.)

show out: misbehave in front of people, be a show-off. Usually, it's a *loudmouth* that ***shows out***. See *act a fool.*

shuck: (1) shook, as in ***shuck*** hands (2) take off, remove, as: He ***shucked*** his shirt when it started getting hot. Or, ***Shuck*** the beans out of their hull.

shucks: the covering, or husks on ears of corn

shucky beans: green beans that have some overly-mature beans in them, so you have to shell (*shuck*) them out of their tough hulls. A few of them are still green and tender enough to not have to hull, but they are mixed with the others and all cooked together. Sometimes called ***"shelly beans."***

shy: (1) short, lacking a bit, as "He was a little bit ***shy*** of six feet tall." (2) We allus called it "bashful."

sich, sich a, sichy: such, such a (an). I never said any ***sichy*** thang.

sight, a sight: (1) something to look at, not always viewed favorably. A mother might say to her boy, as she looks at his muddy clothes, "Now if you ain't a ***sight!***" (2) Or it can be something or somebody *outstandin'* good. Seeing you after a long time, a friend might say, "You're *a **sight** fer sore eyes!*" (meaning they are happy to see you). (3) **A sight** of anything means there is a whole lot of it, or several. As: He raised *a **sight** of* beans this year. Or: They was *a **sight** of* people in town yesterday. See *remption.*

sigogglin': (sigh'-gog-len) Out of kilter. See *slaunchways*

Singer sewin' machine: When something runs well or operates smoothly, it is said to *run like a Singer sewin' machine.*

sipher: (si'-fer) siphon. He *siphered* some gas out of his car. See *cipher*.

skeeter: mosquito. She had *skeeter* bites all over her arms.

skid: see *snake*.

skinflint: somebody that's *so stingy they'd skin a flea fer it's hide and taller.*

skint, skunt: skinned

skin yer igner'nce: Embarrass yourself, or show how ig'nert you are.

skittish: to be *juberous* (doubtful) or uneasy about something.

skivvies: drawers, underwear, longhandles

skyerred: scared

slaunchways: unevenly crosswise; Same as *sigogglin', yantygogglin',* See *catty-cornered, cattywampus, whopper-jawed.*

sled load: a whole bunch; large quantity. See *remption, slew* and *passel.*

slew: usually said as "a whole *slew*," meaning a "whole lot" or large quantity.

slick as a whistle (or button): When somebody done something "*slick as a whistle*," that means they done it as *quick as lightnin'* and *as easy as fallin' off a log.*

slight somebody: to snub or overlook somebody, whether deliberately or unintentionally.

slim pickin's: not having much of anything to choose from. They had *slim pickin's* for supper.

slingin' snot: bawlin' and squallin'; shedding crocodile tears in a big way (for show).

slip off: One way of proposing to a girl was to say, "*Let's slip off and go to Georgie.*" However—if he just said, "*Let's slip off,*" he had something else on his mind—a proposition, not a proposal.

slobber, slobbers: drool, salivate; saliva, slavers. *Don't let yer slobbers run back into the dipper when you're drankin' out of it.*

slow as smoke off a cold…: To finish, add *cowpile*, manure, or worse. As slow as it gets.

slur: a remark or action that is insulting or damaging to one's reputation or character.

small-boned: of a slight physical build. Opposite of heavy-built. Someone that is firm, with a blocky build (stocky) is said to be *built like a brick toilet.*

smart aleck: a person who is rude, shows no respect, and usually *loud-mouthed.* See *show out.*

smidgin: just a teeny little bit, or *a dab.* Sometimes called a *smidge.*

smush: to mash something. See *sqush*.

smut: soot. See *sut*.

smyerr: smear

snake: (1) snake, like one that'll *strack* at you (2) pull a pole of wood or something on the ground with a rope or chain, or to hook a horse, mule or steer to it and let them *snake* it.

snake feeder: dragonfly

snatchin' and grabbin': going uninvited from one thing to another a-pickin' up things that you ortn't to, *snatchin' and grabbin'* up things in your hands .

snerl: See *snurl*.

snigger: give a half-hidden laugh in a giggling manner, intended as a put-down or to shame another; snicker

snipe: sneak around and steal something, sometimes with knowledge of the one stolen from. Different from downright stealing. Dad used to *snipe* a chicken from *one or t'other* of our neighbors when they were going to have a dance at our house. People planted extra corn so anybody who needed some could **snipe** a few ears all along. See *swipe*.

snipe hunt: Men would talk and get a young boy all excited about taking him *snipe huntin'*. Then when they got way off up on the mountain, they told him to stand and hold a tow sack open. They said they'd go on up ahead and run the snipe down the holler, and the boy was to to be ready to catch it in the sack. Then them devilish men would slip on back to the house and leave him a-standin' there in the dark a-holdin' that sack til he finally *smartened up* and *went to the house*.

snort: (1) what you do through your nose (2) a drink of likker See *swig*

snuck: sneaked, as, "*snuck* up behind him."

snurl: snarl; wrinkle, as to "*snurl up your nose*," when you smelt something bad, or snubbed somebody.

sobby: soggy and heavy. *Doughty* wood gets *sobby* in rainy weather and won't burn.

sofie, sofer: sofa, also called a davenport, couch or settee.

sogrum: sorghum; syrup made from stripped cane; molasses

some body: (some by'-dee) a person who is respected in his/her own right and is of value. See *feel like some body*.

somerce, summerce: somewhere(s)

somerset: (some'-er-set) somersault See *swappin' ends*.

sop: To take a piece of bread and mop up liquid, gravy, or syrup into the bread. When the end of the bread has soaked up all it will hold, you bite that off, then *sop* some more with it. When something is as wet as it can get, it is **soppin'** wet.

sorta, sortie, sorter: sort of, kind of (or, *kindly*)

soup beans: dry beans, usually pinto beans. We cook 'em with enough water to make 'em good and soupy.

souse: This is a word with two definitions and two pronounciations. First, **souse** (rhyme with house) is a gelatin-like meat dish made from the parts of a hog's head, and is also called **souse meat**. Second, **souse** (souze), said with a *z* instead of an *s*, means to plunge something out of sight, like to **souse** it under water or liquid.

spacial, spayshul: special

spar: (rhyme with car) sparrow

sparkin': courting

speak/talk out of turn, or **tell tales out of school:** tell something that shouldn't be told.

specs: (specks) eyeglasses; spectacles. People used to say someone wore **specs**, instead of saying they wore glasses.

'spenders: suspenders

spell: (1) a period of time, like a dry **spell** (2) to relieve somebody of a task for awhile, or take turns with them to let them rest, as to **spell** somebody when they're plowing. (3) a *charm* or curse, as in: If you look a snake in the eyes, it can put a **spell** on you.

spicket: spigot; water tap

spider wibs: spider webs

spile: (1) spoil, as in ruin (*rurn*) (2) spoil, as to *kewter to* and **spile** a youngen, in which case, they'd say that the baby was **spiled** *so rotten that salt woutn't save 'im.*

spin yarns: make up and tell tall tales

spitcan: A tin can used for spitting in. Everyone who used *chawin' tobacker* or snuff had a **spitcan.** One of my chores was to take my gramdma's **spitcan** out to the branch and wash it out each morning.

spitless: The more genteel word to describe how scared somebody was. As: *Scared* **spitless;** *Scared the livin'* **spit** *out of me; So scared I was shakin' like a dog a-spittin' a peach seed.*

sprang: Spring (1) the season betwixt winter and summer (2) The place where water flows up out of the ground (3) **sprangs**—like inunder a mattress (4) clock **sprangs** or other thangs that need **sprangs** to make them work (5) to **sprang** a leak.

sprang sallet: In the early spring when plants start putting out leaves, mountain folks went around the fields and woods and gathered ***sprang sallet.*** It was a mixture of tender young shoots, leaves and buds from plants such as blackberry, dandelion, the curled ends of fiddlehead fern, and other edible plants. These was washed, cooked with a little seasonin' in 'em, and eat, usually with a little vinegar *sprankled* over the sallet.

sprang tonic: There were several, and each family had a favorite, said to *purify the blood.* Some of these were: Sulfur and molasses, castor oil, *poke sallet, sprang sallet,* ramps, garlic.

sprankle: sprinkle

spud: (1) potato (2) a tool used to peel the bark from logs.

squall: (1) to cry or shed tears (2) the noise a cat makes (3) A short period of bad weather

squench, squanch: (skwinch, skwainch) squint; squeeze your eyelids together (***squench up*** your eyes).

squoze, squz: squeezed

sqush, squoish: (skwush, skwo'-ish) (1) squash that you eat (2) what you do when you mash or smush something flat.

stab, stob: both means the same thing, as to shove a knife into somebody or something. But ***stob*** also means like when you hit your toe or finger straight on the end of it and *stove it up.* Example: I ***stobbed*** (stumped) my toe agin' a chair leg. Also, a ***stob*** is a short post in the ground. We drove a ***stob*** up to aim the horse shoe at, when we played horse shoes. See *jab, job, poke*

standard: a post on the side of a sled

stomped: stamped, like you do with your feet, but also means stubbed, as in: I *stomped* my toe on a stob.

stone ache: pain in the testicles

storebought: bought from a store, as opposed to home-made.

storm: (1) in a big way. He was just a-workin' up ***a storm.*** (2) act like you're mad about something, like ***storm*** out of the house.

stout: strong, whether describing a person, a pole, or liquor. A strong person was said to be *as **stout** as a horse* or *strong as a ox.*

stove eye lifter: A metal tool designed to lift an eye from the cookstove top.

strack, stracked: strike, struck. The snake *stracked* at him and missed.

strack (strike) a lick: work. A person who was too lazy to work at anything *woutn't **strack a lick** at nuthin'*, or *woutn't even work as a taster in a pie fact'ry.*

strang: string

straw tick: a homemade mattress stuffed with straw.

stretchin' it, stretchin' the truth: lying, telling a lie

strick, strickly: strict, strictly

strike out, struck out: to head out for somewhere. Dad *struck out* for the mountains to see about his still.

strollop: (1) verb: To git out and loafer around. (2) Noun: A *strollop* is a female that gits out and loafers around a-huntin' fer a man.

struck on: Attracted to—a courtin' term; being "lovesick." When either a girl or boy was in love with a person, they were said to be *struck on 'em, crazy about 'em,* or *took a shine to 'em.*

struddy: sturdy

strop: a strap; you can sharpen a straight razor on a razor *strop.*

stub up: balk; be stubborn; pout. Example: We got ready, an'en he *stubbed up* and woutn't go. Or, to *stub up like a mule a-starin' at a new gate.* See *humped up, mumped up.*

study about it: to keep thinking about the same thing over and over

stumpwater: Poor quality moonshine likker is said to be as weak as *stumpwater.* Also, somebody that *ain't got many smarts* is said to have *a head full of stumpwater fer brains.*

styerr: steer

subscription: a prescription

suey: a hog call; make a hog *suey,* or move over, as when feeding them. When somebody said they'd *"learn you to suey,"* they meant they'd *hurt you bad* if you didn't get away from there and leave them alone, or else they intended to punish you for something you'd done. Another term that meant the same thing was they'd *"break you from suckin' eggs."*

sugar diabetes: (di-beet'-dus) the word "diabetes" was never used alone, it was *sugar diabetes.*

sumbich: SOB

sump'm: something

Sunday shirt: a white shirt

surp: syrup, either *bought surp* or molasses. They were both called **surp,** but generally, when people said **surp,** they meant molasses. If it was bought **surp,** they usually called it *Karo.* There were other brands, like Dixie Dew, but dark Karo was the most common. Kids often heard the threat: *I'll git with you like Karo got with surp,* meaning they were about to *git a good thrashin'.*

sut: soot; *smut*

swaller: Noun or verb. To swallow, or *a* swallow (small drink—just "a taste," or *swaller* of it). See *swig.*

swappin' ends: turning *somersets, end over end; head over heels.* See *somerset.*

swarp: (1) swat at. See *swipe.* (2) brush harshly against something, as, The limbs *swarped* ag'in the ground when the tree fell. Or tell a youngun: I'll *swarp your hind end.*

swear: just about absolutely the worst sin there is, is to *swear* on anything. The Bible says not to do it. *Swearin'* and cussin' are two different things.

sweetbread(s): a hog's pancreas

sweet'nin: (1) sugar or anything such as honey or molasses used to sweeten food or drink (2) Anything sweet, such as cake or candy. *Abody ortn't to eat so much sweetenin'—it'll give you sugar diabetes.*

swelled up: swollen. Her feet and legs were *swelled up.* Or, somebody pouting was said to be *all swelled up* (or humped up) *like a big toad frog.*

swig: either verb or noun. To drink: They were *swiggin'* out of the same bottle. The quantity varies—"just a little swaller," or a *snort*—which is "just a little *swig,*"(a taste), or a "big long *swig,*" or a drink (noun) He took a *swig* (drink) of liquor.

swipe: (1) wipe. She took a dishrag and *swiped off* the tablecloth. (2) have a try, as: *Let him take a swipe (or swarp) at fixin' it.* (3) steal, same as snipe. Some common expressions: He'd *swipe* the butter off a blind man's bread. He'd *swipe* the pennies off a dead man's eyes. He'd steal the Lord's supper and *swipe* his butt on the tablecloth. See *pilfer.*

switchback: a curve in the road so deep that when you round it, you're almost headed back in the same direction you were coming from.

swivel, swiveled up: shrink, shrivel; shriveled up, shrunken

swim, swum or **swimmed:** swam. Said as: He *swim,* he *swum,* or he *swimmed* (all the same).

T

tad: a very small amount. See *smidgin, dab.*

taddick: (1) a certain amount of cornmeal that was held out as a toll (payment for grinding) when the miller ground your corn at the mill. (2) jist a little bit (quantity).

tailor made: (1) a ready-made cigarette. (2) clothing or other article made specifically for a person.

take a fit: (1) have a seizure (2) *bawl and squall and carry on* about something. (3) *take a mad fit,* or *have a hissy* (temper tantrum). See *conniption, raise cane.*

take pity sakes: feel sorry for, have compassion, or *take pity on 'em.* He *took pity sakes* on the pore ol' starvin' dog. Also, to *have pity sakes.*

take things to heart: take everything seriously; easy to *get your feelin's hurt*.

talking machine: a record player; phonograph

talk out of school: (or out of turn) tell something you ortn't to be a-tellin'.

talk out of turn: pretty much like *talkin' out of school*, except *talkin' ugly*.

talk purty, talk nice: Use socially acceptable speech, both in words and content. See *talk ugly*.

talk ugly: to handle (use) foul language, or say words with a sexual connotation. Talk dirty or filthy. Opposite of *talk purty*, or *talk nice*.

taller: (tael'-ler) tallow, *mutton grease*

tar: (1) a tire, also called a *casin'* (casing) (2) thick black sticky stuff used on the roof to stop a leak, or to blacktop a road.

tard: tired

tare: tower

tarment: (tar'-ment) torment; hell

tarnation: A substitute cuss-word but I don't know exactly what it means. As: How in **tarnation** (or *thunderation*) did you manage to do that?

taters: potatoes, spuds.

tattle-tale: a person who can't keep a secret, and *peddles it all over the place*. See *peddler*.

tattlin': (tat'-lin) telling things to people about other people, usually gossip.

tea: (1) not black, pekoe, etc. as is commonly known. In the mountains, **tea** is just about anything put in hot water and drunk. Medicinal herbs, bark or roots are infused, or steeped, and the resulting liquid is called **tea,** usually adding a generous portion of corn likker unless it is for the younguns. Some **teas** are: birch bark, boneset, calamus root (calomel root), ginger, ground ivy, mountain birch, mint, peach bark, sassafras, spignet, spicewood and yaller root. (2) **Birch tea** isn't like the kind of **tea** you drink. A common switch used to give a youngun a whuppin' was a birch limb, so a parent would threaten to *give them a dose of **birch tea*** if they didn't behave.

teached, was teached: (1) taught (2) learned

tearjerker: (tyerr-jer-ker) a song or tale that makes abody cry to hear it.

teejus: tedious

teenincey: (tee'-nine-see) very small, tiny

tenderline: tenderloin

ter'ble, tar'ble: In common English, it means terrible or awful. In Mountainese, it also means in the extreme, as: She's a **ter'ble** good cook (extry good).

terf or **turf:** a method of quilting in which the layers of a quilt are tacked together wiith **terfin'** stitches. The stitches were separated and spaced a few inches apart, with the thread tied off and left a little long. The term probably means tuft, as the threads made a little tuft.

tetch: touch

tetched in the head: A person who acts peculiar or odd; *their mind ain't jist right.* See *addled.*

tetch'ous: easily irritated. (1) a tender place on your body that hurts to touch it is a ***tetch'ous*** spot. (2) a hard-to-get-along-with person is said to be *awful **tetch'ous.***

thang: thing

thank: (1) think (2) Tell somebody you're grateful for something they did for you. *Thank you* was said as, "Thankye." (as one word) (3) blame, as "We got you to ***thank*** for that."

thataway: that way…not thisaway—***thataway!***

theirself, theirselfs: themselves

them'air: those, them (there). ***Them'air*** pigs is a-growin' good.

they: (1) a word used for *there.* as: ***They's*** three of 'em. (2) an exclamation to express surprise or amazement, as: "***They!***", "***They,*** *gosh!*" or "***They,*** *Lordymercy!*"

thisaway: this way. Don't do it *thataway,* do it ***thisaway.***

thoat: (thote) throat

'thout: without. *'**Thout** a doubt,* he's the one that *stoled* it.

thow: throw. When she got his letter out of the mailbox, she ***thowed*** it in the creek.

thow off on: throw off on; villify; talk about someone in a way that is demeaning to them or puts them down. You better not ***thow off on*** nobody's kinfolks. See *low rate.*

thow up: (1) to throw up, vomit (2) to recall past wrongs done to a person. Every time they got into a fuss, she **thowed up** his old sweetheart to him.

thrash: a fungal infection involving the mucous membrane of the mouth and nasopharynx in which there is a painful white patchy coating. Usually affects a newborn or infant.

thrashin': a *wearin' out,* or whipping. *I'll give you a good **thrashin'*** if you don't quit that.

three shakes of a sheep's tail: fast. "I'll be there *in **three shakes*** (or jerks) *of a sheep's tail*" meant they'd be right there. Sometimes they added, "*and two of 'em's done and jerked.*" Or, to be funny, say, "*Three shapes of a sheek's tail.*" See *dreckly, lit a shuck.*

th'u: (thue) through. I'll *stick with ye **th'u** thick and thin.*

thunderation: See *tarnation.*

tickled: very pleased. She was ***tickled** to death* to get some new shoes.

tied up: bandaged. Probably called that because, having no adhesive tape or bandages, we tied cloth strips on a wound for a dressing. She ***tied up*** my sore toe.

tight: (1) very frugal; stingy. Won't turn loose of money. As: *He's so **tight**, he'd skin a flea for its hide and taller.* Or: *He's as **tight** as a hide* (skin). And: *He'd squeeze a nickel til the buffalo bellers.* (2) very strict. As: *They're awful **tight** on their younguns. Parents get **tighter** on girls as they grow up, but easier* (more lenient) on boys.

tilter: a tiller

time a day: time of day—generally said as mornin', evenin' and night. To narrow it down progressively, the ***time a day*** was said as *before daylight* (about 4 in the mornin'), then *daylight,* then *mornin', way up in the mornin'* (10 or 11), then *up towards the middle of the day*—or *clost to dinnertime*—which is at 12 o'clock or high noon. Then right after dinner comes *evenin'* (after 12 noon until about 5). *Suppertime* was about 4 or 5 o'clock in the wintertime, so they'd have time to wash up the dishes, clean up the kitchen, tote in the water, split some kindlin', git in the wood, fill up the lamp, trim the wick, and wipe out the lamp globe before dark. Then it was *late evenin'* (*when the cows come home*) to *dusky dark,* then *dark* (said as *a little before, right around, after,* or *way after dark*). Then it was *a way up in the night* (10 PM), *midnight,* and *after midnight.* After noon is always two words—after noon, meaning that dinner's over with. People used to *go see one another* (visit) after dinner and *stay all evenin',* which meant that they went any time after dinner (noon) and got *back to the house* by supper time.

'tis, 'taint: it is, it ain't

tissic, tizick (tiz'-ik): (? spelling) Must be a catch-all name for various disorders, as I heard it given as a diagnosis of people's sickness from fussy babies to grandpa's stomach ache.

tits, titties: (1) teats, as on a cow, goat, etc. (2) breasts

titty: breast. Babies was *give the **titty*** (breast fed), not bottle-fed.

toe jam: The soft accumulation of malodorous dead skin and sweat between the toes, caused from not keeping the feet clean.

tol'able, tollible: (tahl'-i-bul) (1) tolerable, bearable (2) just so-so; mediocre

took a-holt: caught onto something easily. Example: He ***took a-holt*** jist like he'd allus done it.

took a likin' to: When somebody liked somebody or something, they was said to have ***took a likin' to them*** or it. Lots of times, though it meant that somebody stole something, as: I used to have a good rake, but somebody *musta **took a likin' to it***—it ain't nowhere to be found .

took and: words added in between the person and what they did (reason unknown). As: She **took and** made up some biscuits. See *went and.*

tore, tore into, tore loose, tore out: began, started or did something with vigor, as: She **tore** in the house and **tore into** him with both fists. When she **tore loose** to cussin' and them dogs **tore out** to barkin', he *run like a scalded dog.*

tore up Jack: went at something roughly and wholeheartedly; done some damage. At a wild party, sometimes things got out of hand, and they just **tore up Jack.**

torge, toards: toward(s)

torment: (noun) hell

tote: (1) carry (2) to add or total up; *figger.*

t'other: the other

to the side of: compared to. It was a nice house **to the side of** the one they'd been living in.

tow jew: told you. I done'n **tow jew** oncet to quit that.

triflin': lazy, sorry. *As:* That **triflin** man *ain't worth a dime* for a thang in the world.

tuck: took

tuckered, tuckered out: (1) tired, exhausted. She was plumb **tuckered** when she got done with the washin'. (2) quit. His old car just **tuckered out** on him.

tuck off, tuck out: Took off, took out. Start hurriedly. Example: When them dogs **tuck out** *torge* that bear, it **tuck off** like Lindberg. See *tore loose, lit a shuck.*

turkel: turtle

turnt: turned. When the garden was plowed with a "*turnin' plow*," the dirt was said to be "turned over," or **turnt.**

two rows at a time: as fast as you can; to *git on the ball.* He was takin' it **two rows at a time.** See *lit a shuck.*

tyeres: tears

U

ub'm: oven

'ud: (ood) an abbreviation for would. It **'ud** take *dannymite* to move that stump.

ugly: (1) unattractive in appearance; **ugly** *as a mud fence.* Descriptions of being awful **ugly** to look at: *You could take their pitcher* (picture) *and back Jun'lusky Creek up over the County Corners* (or *back Nantyhaley River up over the dam*). An old sayin': *He's so* **ugly**, *he ort to hafta carry a* **ugly** *license.* (2) **Act ugly:** behave badly; be hateful, mean, or have a **ugly** temper. (3) inappropriate behavior with the opposite sex, such as talk **ugly** in front of them

un, 'n: added to a word, means *one*. That*un*, or that*'n* means "that one."

unbeknownst, unbeknowinst: without anyone knowing, as: ***Unbeknowinst*** to her, he was goin' by to see that *grass widder*.

underpants: women's underwear; bloomers. The word *bloomers* was not said in *mixed comp'ny*, and *panties* was only said in an embarrassed whisper between women, never in public. Even to say them words was *kindly* considered *talking ugly*.

underwear, underdrawers: see *drawers, longhandles, underpants*.

uneasy: worried, nervous. *As **uneasy** as a long-tailed cat in a room full of rockin' chairs.*

ungens: (ung'-ens) onions.

ungen buttons: them little onion sets like you plant in the garden to grow *ungens* from.

union suit: a man's long sleeved, one-piece knit winter underwear. Some of them had a drop seat and some had a split seat. A man was liiable to git *in a bind* if he come down with the *bowel complaint* with a **union suit** on. See *longhandles*.

up and about: out of bed and able to walk around. When asked how they are, an old person might answer, "I'm **up and about**, but that's about it."

up-end: turn over. He just **up-ended** that slop bucket.

up, upped and: took action. She thought about it awhile, then finally **up** *and done it*. He never give no reason, he just **upped** and left. Same meaning as *hauled off*.

uppity: Going around with your nose up in the air, like you think you're better'n everybody else. See *hifalutin, biggety, big-head*.

up to snuff: at your best

use to, useta: (yous-ta) what you habitually did in the past. We **useta** go barefooted all summer.

'us, 'uz: was. It *'uz a* way up in the night before he *come to the house.*

V

varmint: an animal that ain't no use to nobody for nuthin', and goes around destroying or ruining things. The lowest form of critter. A possum or a muskrat is a **varmint** that kills your chickens.

vi'grus: (vie'-grus) (1)vigorous (2) fierce-looking.

vomick: vomit; to throw up. See *puke*.

W

wadermillon: watermelon. We allus had us a big **wadermillon** a-coolin' in the *sprang* for the Fourth of July.

waggin: wagon

wait on: (1) to **do for**, or take care of somebody when they're sick. (2) to **fetch and carry**, a-takin' somebody's orders to bring this or do that. She **waited** *on him,* hand and foot. See *kewter.*

waller: lay, or **waller** *around in the bed* (the *heighth of laziness*). Also, the place where animals bed down is called a **waller.** Where hogs **waller** in the mud is called *a hog* **waller.**

want to: ort to, or suffer the consequences. You **want to** keep your beegums clean or you'll lose your bees. You **want to** get out to work early before the sun gets too hot.

washpan: (woe'-ish-pan) a metal basin used to hold water for bathing.

wash stand: (woe'-ish stand) a small table or stand where the *washpan* set.

wasper, warsper: a wasp

way yon: a lot more than; beyond. He was askin' **way yon** more than I wanted to pay for it. Or: They lived a **way yon** past the forks of the road.

weaked: (week'-ed) wicked.

wear out, wear somebody out: give somebody a good *thrashin'*(or, *whuppin'*).

weasel: (1) a varmint that kills chickens (2) A sly, shifty way of getting out of something or out of trouble is to **weasel** your way out of it.

weed: We was calling a cigarette a **weed** long before we ever heard of marijuana.

well-off: able to afford about anything you want.

well thought of: has a good reputation.

wender: window

wender light: window pane, or the glass in a window. He broke out the **wender light** .

went and, went'n: words added in between the person and what they did. She **went and** told him. They **went'n** sold their place.

whang: a slightly different taste than what you'd expect, as: It had a little sour *whang* to it.

wharp, wharped: warp, warped. Also used the same way as *"swarp, swarped."* He *wharped* his hat against his pants leg.

whistle pig: a groundhog.

whit leather: I don't exactly know what "whit" in **whit leather** means, unless it means a razor strop (used to whet, or sharpen a razor), but when something was so tough that it couldn't be chewed up, or used for anything, it was said to be *"as tough as* **whit leather.** *"* This phrase also describes a person who is tough or has "grit."

whit rock, whet rock: a fine-grained smooth stone used to sharpen a knife or tool.

whole cloth: The only thing it has to do with cloth is the term, "whole cloth." When somebody made up a big *yarn* (story, tale) out of thin air, they *made it up out of* **whole cloth.**

whopperjawed: out of square, uneven, crooked; *catty-cornered.* See *slaunchways.*

whuppin': Noun or verb. A whipping, or the act of whipping. The teacher gave him a **whuppin'** with a paddle.

widder: widow. A **grass widder** is a woman that don't live with her old man.

willer: willow tree

windy: (1) passin' a lot of gas (2) long-winded; a person who *talks more'n he listens;* also called a *blowhard.* See *run off at the mouth.*

wish book: a catalog

wisht: wish, wished

withe: a long, keen *willer* or birch limb used to whip a youngen. As: I'll take a **withe** to your hin'end. See *hickory.*

woish: (woe'-ish) wash

woish board: a rub-board; a wooden framed metal board with ridges used for washing clothes.

woishin': Noun: the washing, or laundry. *Doin' the* **woishin'** is washing the dirty clothes.

woishin' powders: powdered laundry soap or detergent

woman: wife; old lady; ol' woman. Him and his **woman** has been married for forty year.

woods colt: a youngun that nobody knows who its daddy is; a *baisterd.*

wool-gatherin': daydreaming; preoccupied; not keeping your mind on your business, said to be *off a-***wool-gatherin'.**

worded, wordin': The way words are said or written, as: He **worded** his letter good. Or: It's awful hard to read that little **wordin'** in the Bible.

wore out: (1) plumb exhausted (2) got a whuppin' (*got his hide tanned*).

worked off: completed the fermentation process. That blackberry juice has **worked off** and turned to wine. It'll give you the belly-ache if you drink much of it before it's **worked off.**

worked out: A term used to describe finishing a (one time) hoeing of a field or garden. They **worked out** the garden...See *laid by.*

worked up: (1) A term used when they cut firewood, cordwood, etc. to use or sell—they **worked up** the wood. (2) If somebody gets mad or worried (bothered) about something, they're said to be *all* **worked up.** "Don't get *all* **worked up** about it."

woutn't: wouldn't

wrainch: (rainch) (1) wrench (2) how we pronounce rinse—as to rinse clothes.

wrang yore neck: wring your neck—a threat from one person to another, probably derived from the act of wringing a chicken's neck to kill it. I ort to **wrang** *yore neck* fer that!

wrassle: wrestle

writ: wrote. **Handwrit** is handwritten.

wudn't, wutn't/wudn', wutn': (wuh'-d'n) wasn't

wusser: worse. He's **wusser** today than he was yesterday.

W'y: pronounced as "Y". An exclamation I presume to be an abbreviation of *why,* but does not mean the same. Usually, it's the first word of a sentence in response, as if the speaker is taken aback at something he or she has heard. Examples: **W'y,** that old heifer! (referring to the woman she's mad at). **W'y,** I never done *no sich a thang*!

Y

y'all: (yawl) You all. This was a word I never heard until I went to school and heard supposedly educated people saying *"y'all"* instead of *yuns,* like we say. *Ignert people* think all Southerners say **y'all,** but us mountain folks don't.

yaller janders: yellow jaundice—what people call hepatitis.

yander: yonder

yantygogglin': see *slaunchways.*

yarn: a story or tall tale—one you *make up outta whole cloth.* When you're tellin' it, you're *spinnin' a yarn.*

yens/yuns: More than one person. Them Yankees says we say, "you'uns," two syllables with the emphasis on *you,* or "y'all," one, but the way we say it is with one syllable—*yuns,* or *yens,* meaning ever'body, or all of **yuns** in the whole crowd—ever last one of *yens.* To us, the word *you* is one single solitary person.

yenses': your (plural). Git **yenses'** feet washed and git in the bed. See *yornses.*

yer: pronounciation for (1) your (2) year (3) ear

yers: (1) years (2) ears (no, we never said that for *yours*—that would be *yores* or *yorn,* one)

yeself, yerself, yer own self: you, yourself

yeselfs, yerselfs, yer own selfs: yourselves

yisterdy: yesterday

y'ont: (yownt) do you want. *Y'ont* to go with me? *Y'ont* this last piece of pie?

yonways: Not thisaway or thataway—the direction I'm pointin' at. He's gone *yonways.*

yore, yores, yorn: your, yours, your own. Thisun's mine...*that'n over yander* is *yorn.*

yornses': (yorn'-ziz) possessive form of *your* (belonging to *the whole bunch of yuns*). Examples: *Yornses'* clothes is still a-hangin' on the line. *Yornses'* cow is in the cornfield. See *yenses'.*

you: one person—the person I'm a-talkin' to. See *yens, yuns.*

youngens, younguns: young ones, *childern.*

young sprout: young boy

Z

zink: a sink. You know—that's got *spickets* in it.

978-0-595-35682-9
0-595-35682-6